Climate Crisis and Creation Care

Climate Crisis and Creation Care:

Historical Perspectives, Ecological Integrity and Justice

Edited by

Christina Nellist

**Cambridge
Scholars**
Publishing

Climate Crisis and Creation Care:
Historical Perspectives, Ecological Integrity and Justice

Edited by Christina Nellist

This book first published 2021

Cambridge Scholars Publishing

Lady Stephenson Library, Newcastle upon Tyne, NE6 2PA, UK

British Library Cataloguing in Publication Data
A catalogue record for this book is available from the British Library

ISBN (10): 1-5275-7420-2
ISBN (13): 978-1-5275-7420-5

To Alexander (2yrs) and Amelia (1yr)
and the grandchildren of this world.

And he said to them,
"Which of you, having a son or an ox that has fallen into a well,
will not immediately pull him out on a sabbath day?"
And they could not reply to him.

TABLE OF CONTENTS

List of Illustrations, Graphs and Tables x

Foreword xi
Archdeacon Fr. John Chryssavgis

Introduction xiv
Dr. Christina Nellist

Part One: Historical Perspectives, Governance and Creation Care

Chapter One 2
An Integrated Theology: Compassion for Animals
Metropolitan. Kallistos of Diokleia (Ware)

Chapter Two 20
Animals and the *Imago Dei*: An *Addendum* to Christian Anthropology
Nikolaos Asproulis

Chapter Three 38
Ecological Hermeneutics and Native American Ethics
Sidney Blankenship

Chapter Four 55
The "Embering" Brazil: Climate Change and the Speciesist Universe
Paula Brugger

Chapter Five 71
Fossil Fuel and Land: Australia's Curse and Promise
Deborah Guess

Chapter Six 89
Food Ethics in Theology: Toward Caring for Animals and the Environment
Yoko Kito

Chapter Seven 104
The Traditional Orthodox Christian Fast: A Comparison with the Modern
Liberalized Fast. Perspectives from the Saints, History and Medical
Science
Fred Krueger

Chapter Eight 116
Noah's Failures, God's Dispensations and a Christian Church
'Setting the Scene and Creating the Opportunity' for a World in Peril
Christina Nellist

Chapter Nine 136
Climate Change and Corruption: Inconvenient Truths
Winnie Onkoba

Chapter Ten 151
Creation Care and Justice - A Sikh Perspective
Charanjit Ajit Singh

Part Two: Are We Prepared? Living in an Unstable World

Chapter Eleven 170
The Economy with Climate and Environmental Responsibility
Andrew Basden

Chapter Twelve 190
Diet, Climate and Health
Joyce D'Silva

Chapter Thirteen 209
The Animal Testing Model
Andre Menache

Chapter Fourteen 223
Rethinking the Social Role of Religions in the Planetary Emergency:
Reflections in a Catholic Key
Richard W. Miller

Chapter Fifteen 248
Climate Change Policy Plans in the Irish Supreme Court: Lessons
from a Neighboring Island?
Maureen O'Sullivan

Chapter Sixteen 264
Other Species are Essential Workers in the Earth's Economy
Didi Pershouse

Chapter Seventeen 286
Population and Our Contemporary Ecological Crisis
David Samways

Chapter Eighteen 308
Recurrence Analysis of Methane Emissions from Wetland Ecosystem
Milan Stehlik et al.

Chapter Nineteen 329
Designing a Green Curriculum of Orthodox Theology: A Modest Proposal
Ekaterini Tsalampouni and Eleni Antonopoulou

Chapter Twenty 349
Psychological Impacts of Climate Change and Recommendations
Lise Van Susteren and W. K. Al-Delaimy

Chapter Twenty-One 370
The Revolution of Consciousness: From the 'Golden Era of Consumption'
to the 'Responsible Society'
Svitlana Zapara

Appendix 383
Creation Care: Christian Responsibility Course
Christina Nellist

Contributors 424

LIST OF ILLUSTRATIONS, GRAPHS AND TABLES

Table 11.1 Aspects, with examples of good and harm meaningful in each.
Figure 11.1 The economy as one part of overall other human functioning.
Figure 17.1 Annual CO2 emissions 1751-2017
Figure 17.2 World population 1750-2025
Figure 17.3 Socio-economic trends.
Figure 18.1 Comparison of two-phase space trajectories using predefined distance to define recurrence points
Figure 18.2 Simple illustration of recurrence plot with distance threshold 0.06
Figure 18.3 Time series and recurrence point plot of CH_4 emission (normalized data)
Figure 18.4 Plot of distances of normalized data of CH_4 emission.
Figure 18.5 Methane global emissions from the five broad categories.
Figure 18.6 Methane emissions from four source categories: natural wetlands (excluding lakes, ponds, and rivers), biomass and biofuel burning, agriculture and waste, and fossil fuels for the 2008-2017 decade.
Table 19.1 Examples of different topic focus.
Figure 21.1 Q & A Chart.
Appendix
Figure 22.1 Icon. 'Christ Breaking the Bonds of Animal Suffering.'

FOREWORD

It is an honor to be invited to contribute a few lines to this significant and splendid anthology of articles comprising two substantial volumes on the climate crisis and creation care. The articles collected by my dear friend, Dr. Christina Nellist, range broadly from writers of diverse religious backgrounds and convictions to writers of different scientific and scholarly interests but also to writers with specific and constructive proposals to resolve unprecedented global challenges of our time.

There is something positive and poignant about the time in which we live. It is, as His All-Holiness Ecumenical Patriarch Bartholomew has repeatedly reminded us, a *kairos* moment. That is to say, it is a moment of crisis and consequence. And the Greek word for crisis (*krisis*) indicates a sense of responsibility and accountability for the way in which we respond to the unique and universal problems that we have created and face. The pandemic that wreaked havoc throughout our world for more than an entire year has - beyond the many other lessons about our mistrustful relationship with science and the destructive repercussions of the inequitable gap between rich and poor - taught us that no one is safe and no one can be saved unless everyone is safe and everyone is saved.

Let me press this analogy between Covid-19 and climate change a little further. Ironically, the strategies used to dismiss climate change and Covid-19 routinely follow a similar pattern and are regularly employed by the same people. My son recently remarked that Covid-19 ultimately provided us with a fascinating social experiment: Throughout the pandemic, he observed, we were asked to do the *slightest*, most *trivial* thing for the sake of others and the world: simply wear a mask! And yet the answer was no; still the answer was politicized; even so people refused. What, he asked, are the chances that people will respond to having less and hoarding less, or wasting less and sharing more?

Just as we cannot play politics with science (or the health of its people), we cannot play politics with climate change (or the health of our planet). Nonetheless, the greatest threat to our planet - the defining issue of our time - is not the novel coronavirus, but climate change. The rapidly growing but conveniently neglected toll from rising global temperatures will eclipse the current number of deaths from all the infectious diseases combined if climate change is not constrained. In the wake of the pandemic, even the

World Economic Forum called for "a great reset" of capitalism, arguing that sustainability will only be achieved through drastic lifestyle changes.

For thirty years, Ecumenical Patriarch Bartholomew - and following suit, Pope Francis today - has emphasized that climate change is not simply a political, scientific, or technological issue. It is essentially and fundamentally a theological, spiritual and ethical issue. Climate change can only be reversed or resolved by addressing the moral causes of the ecological crisis. This is precisely why religion has a key role to play. And it is precisely why everyone has a vital part to play.

Now in order to appreciate this spiritual or moral worldview, we must acknowledge the world as larger than ourselves and our interests; we must appreciate creation as broader than our own conviction or confession; we must adopt a spirit of humility and simplicity. The root of the problem invariably lies in the paradigms that impel us to pursue particular lifestyles. After all, climate change is not simply the result of bad judgment or greed; it is also largely a result of oblivious success and mindless development. Far too often we are convinced that solving the ecological crisis is only a matter of acting differently, more sustainably. Let us not forget though that it is our very actions that led us to this mess in the first place.

We cannot simply continue the way have been proceeding. I wonder if we have at least learned this lesson from the pandemic. Or are we simply anxious to return to "life as normal" and "business as usual" - to life as we knew it before the crisis. Instead, should we not learn from our errors? Should we not first stop to reflect? This is the way that we have been taught by the prophets and mystics through the centuries: That we should tread more lightly, more thoughtfully and more cautiously on this planet; that we should be prepared to reverse our perspectives and practices. And here, I think, lies the heart of our problem. Because we are unwilling - in fact, we violently resist any call - to adopt simpler lives.

Our lifestyles and choices - our unquenchable demand for convenient and complacent habits - are clearly contrary and contradictory to the way of the Christian Gospel, which emphasizes both the way of the cross and the value of loving one's neighbor. Any follower of Christ that has discovered a comfortable or privileged way of reclining on the cross is deluded at best and dishonest at worst. Any person of good will that fails to perceive the impact of our attitudes and actions for the whole world, especially the poor, is uninformed at best and unresponsive at worst.

The authors of these chapters raise valid and vital concerns about the way we treat one another, the way we handle animals and the way we manage the resources of our planet throughout historical periods and cultures, across many nations and continents. They address issues of political urgency and economic growth, the health of human beings and sustainability of rainforests, as well as the legal rights of animals and of the earth itself. In this framework, the volumes at hand present the reader with yet another important piece of the puzzle in the lethargic, albeit pressing way that we are all called to advance from perception to practice.

John Chryssavgis

INTRODUCTION

Today, it is reasonable to suggest that most people understand that climate change is real and that it is dangerous. Whilst their level of knowledge on the subject varies (and it is likely that the majority need to know more), with children to grandparents demonstrating on the streets in countries across the world, there is at last, an acknowledgment that urgent and immediate action must be taken. Societies better understand their global interconnectedness to each other, to other creatures and to our planetary boundaries. Our presence, level of consumption and misuse of the natural world has negatively changed our atmosphere, weather patterns, oceans, environments, and the lives of the creatures within those environments. This "misuse and abuse" [1] threatens all forms of life, including our own.[2]

Dealing with Covid-19 has also meant dramatic changes to the way we live, resulting in our industries and economies grinding to a halt and extending the gap between rich and poor. Increasingly, we hear disparate voices repeating the same message: "we do not want more of the same",

---

[1] St Gregory of Nyssa's teaching on our gluttony and how it leads us to other forms of selfishness, is entirely pertinent for today where the richer nations' obsession with food - evidenced for example, in the large number of media programs/focus on the subject and our wastefulness of it - is a major contributor to climate change, soil and water pollution, habitat and biodiversity loss. See 'On Love of the Poor 1. On Good Works', (De beneficentia). S. Holman (trans) *The Hungry are Dying: Beggars and Bishops in Roman Cappadocia*, (Oxford, OUP. 2001: 198).

[2] In 2000 when living in the Seychelles, I helped fund the establishment of the Sea-Level Rise Foundation by Dr Ralph Payet. We knew then that some Pacific islands were regularly flooded at high tide. Some of those islands are gone. For the impact on biodiversity loss through fire, see for example, https://www.aph.gov.au/About_Parliament/Parliamentary_Departments/Parliamentary_Library/pubs/rp/rp1920/Quick_Guides/AustralianBushfires.

is true, that in the 80s and 90s, progress also began to be made in ical sphere, with the 1992 Climate Convention in Rio and simil ventions and 'commitments of intent', which continue until today.[9] Yet, pite the grand words and commitments given at such important herings, to quote Sherrard (1998), we continue to stumble to the edge of cliff, as if we are in some kind of collective psychosis. The obvious stion to ask here is why? The answer, sadly, is because these very same vernments and agencies have failed/refused to implement the necessary ategies and mechanisms to effect real change, *in the time-frame that is quired to achieve said objectives*.[10] This suggests that they are more ncerned with short-term thinking that prioritizes re-election and short-m biased fiscal systems that favor the few, rather than in reorientating our onomies in order to save the lives of their citizens, and more than that, the ves, indeed existence, of the myriad of other species on this planet.

As a theologian, I argue that this is one of the reasons why those from a ith-based worldview are important to the glocal and global debates on ving sustainably in an increasingly unstable world. They can provide an lternative voice and vision for the future, based in some cases upon eachings from sacred texts, which inform us that the entire world is nterconnected, delicately balanced, and sacred. They can address the human sin in the structural complexities of our world by confirming Orthodox tradition, which teaches that any exploitation and cruelty towards non-human animals and the wider creation is not only spiritually, morally, and ethically wrong, but also an insult to God and a sin. Hand-in-hand with those sins are the negative soteriological implications for the individuals who harm the created world and for those who are indifferent to that harm.[11] They can provide a practical holistic approach, which includes spiritual and ethical guidance on the link between climate change, a flourishing creation and socially responsible goals for a more balanced and just world. They can

---

[9] E.g., European Green Deal: A European Green Deal | European Commission (europa.eu); The Paris Agreement | UNFCCC

[10] See for example, 2019 IPCC Special Report Climate Change and Land: https://www.ipcc.ch/srccl/; 2018 IPCC Special Report Global Warming of 1.5°C, Chapter 2: Mitigation Pathways Compatible with 1.5°C in the Context of Sustainable Development; WWF Living Planet Report 2020: https://www.wwf.org.uk/sites/default/files/2020-09/LPR20_Full_report.pdf

[11] E.g., St Cyril of Jerusalem *(First Mystagogical Catechesis on the Mysteries: To The Enlightened*, No. 6, p. 283), identifies hunting and horseracing as examples of "the pomp of the devil", whilst the Council of Trullo Canon LI, (The Canons of the Council in Trullo, A.D. 692, *The Seven Ecumenical Councils* CANNPNF2-14) denounces hunts and forbids priests and laity from even attending such "wickedness" (Byzantine canonist Balsamon's notes on the Ancient Epitome of Canon LI).

"we want a new normal", and "building back better" policy decisions[3] and the academic world has responded with helpful analysis.[4]

These two substantial collections[5] add to that corpus of material, as they feature chapters by specialists with expertise in different disciplines who write from different contexts, cultures and religions. They come together to write with authority and clarity on various aspects of the climate crisis and care for the natural world. They write either from faith-based or secular perspectives but share a vision and desire to explain why we are in this critical situation, ask difficult questions of us, governments, and civic leaders and explain how we might affect real change.

Regardless of their expertise, they write in the hope that we, either as individuals or as decision-makers in government and civil society, will be guided to respond to the climate crisis far more quickly than is currently the case. For without swift action, we condemn future generations of human and non-human animals, to lives of intolerable climate and social instability, with little hope of regaining what humans have squandered by our collective arrogance. More explicitly - to the certain death of billions of people and species of flora and fauna - as the 'Hothouse-Earth' scenario becomes a reality.

Some write with bravery on topics that are rarely discussed such as the corruption at the heart of the illegal wildlife trade; population dynamics; mass migration, and social security theories and on equally challenging subjects such as greening theological education; animals as co-workers, neighbors, food, or an extended Image of God. Others write from a scientific or legal perspective on the crisis in the Amazon; climate instability; medical unpreparedness; the failures of the animal-testing model; on the legal right to a healthy environment or protection for animals and environments.

---

[3] E.g., International Monetary Fund, 2020b: World Economic Outlook, October 2020. A Long and Difficult Ascent, Chapter 3, Mitigating Climate Change Growth and Distribution - Friendly Strategies. Available at: https://www.imf.org/en/Publications/WEO/Issues/2020/09/30/world-economicoutlook-october-2020

[4] This book is one example. See also, the expert analysis prepared for the Oxford Review of Economic Policy 36(S1): Hepburn, C., et al, (2020), 'Will COVID-19 fiscal recovery packages accelerate or retard progress on climate change?', Smith School Working Paper 20-02; Kate Raworth's DEAL (doughnuteconomics.org) for frameworks for practical regenerative and distributive systems at local and national levels; Vallejo L., et al, (2021) 'Halving Global CO2 Emissions by 2050: Technologies and Costs', *International Energy Journal* 21 (March 2021) 147-158.

[5] The second book on the theme is entitled *Climate Crisis and Sustainable Creaturely Care: Integrated Theology, Governance and Justice*, (Cambridge Scholars, 2021).

Others still, combine subjects such as eco-economics, justice and ethics, theology and dietary choices, sustainability and sacramental living, or the wisdom in First Nations' relationships with the natural world. The list is long, seemingly disparate yet interconnected, in a way oft quoted in Orthodoxy, as a communion of love and compassion.

As a theologian, educator, and lifelong conservationist, who has lived in nine countries and several continents, I have always argued that it is incumbent upon people of faith and their clergy to engage with these subjects, both individually and institutionally (locally and nationally), just as they are engaged in providing alms; justice for the poor; the provision of schools, health clinics, and feeding programs; or in the prescription of diets.

Everything is connected and interdependent. The climate emergency is real, it is imminent and without local action, millions[6], possibly billions of people and certainly billions of animals and plants will die, if our religious institutions among others, do not 'set the scene and grasp the opportunity'[7] given to us by God to prevent such calamities.

Brief historical reflection

In the 70s and 80s many of us were teaching or producing scientific papers on various aspects of what we now refer to as 'climate change'. During this same period, some religious leaders, such as the then Ecumenical Patriarch of the Eastern Orthodox Christian Church, His All-Holiness the Ecumenical Patriarch Demetrios 1st, expressed concern on the misuse and abuse of the natural environment. He called for individuals to change their hearts and minds, and to view the world not as something solely to be used as a resource, but rather, as something to nurture by enabling nature's flourishing.

In the case of the non-human animal creation, it is safe to say that historically, there has not been an entirely favorable Christian view of relationships with animals or their place in a world dominated by an anthropocentric mindset. Despite God's clear teaching in Judeo-Christian scripture defining a violence-free diet, closely followed by teachings on a violence-free community and concepts of blessing, flourishing, and covenant with all things in God's very good creation, we Christians have at best been blind and indifferent to, for example, the link between climate

---

[6] Nearly 690 million people or 9% of the world population were undernourished and about 750 million, or nearly 10% were exposed to severe levels of food insecurity in 2019. See WMO State of the Global Climate 2020 - Provisional Report, available at: doc_num.php (wmo.int)

[7] Reference to Chapter Eight.

change, the animal-based diet and animal/human sufferin[g] taught that animals have no value in themselves - they nothing more than resources for the humans of this world

We have, in the main, ignored the biodiversity of Christ's teaching in Luke 14:5 that we are to act immediate suffering of humans and non-human animals, and ignored where every individual creature - each tiny sparrow - is k[nown] by God and through whom, we perceive the glory of Go[d] contemporary theologians attempt to positively reinterpret t[he] Aristotle, Augustin, and Aquinas on animals (each of whom human animals from moral consideration) without doubt, views of non-human animals were incorporated to varying Western and Eastern Christian thought.

Yet despite this backdrop, it was nonetheless, entirely in Eastern Orthodox Christian tradition, that in 1989 His Demetrios 1st, established the 1st of September (the first day ecclesiastical calendar), as the day dedicated to the protection o[f] environment, calling for Orthodox Christians not only to p[romote] protection and preservation of God's creation but also to change from one of domineering tyrant, to one of protector and enabler o[f] flourishing.

This work on behalf of 'creation', 'the whole world', 'nature', under his successor, His All-Holiness, Bartholomew 1st [8] culminat[ed] present time in the Halki Summit 111 (2019) entitled 'Th[e] Formation and Ecological Awareness: A Conversation on Educatio[n] Environment'. This Summit essentially called for 'creation car[e] added to every Orthodox seminary and academic education progr[am] eventually, to all Orthodox parish education programs. It is im[portant] therefore, to note the chapter entitled 'Designing a Green Curricu[lum] Orthodox Theology: A Modest Proposal' by Professors Tsalampou[ni] Antonopoulou, which not only responds to the Patriarch's call, bu[t] stands as a framework for other faiths or denominations to adapt.

A voice speaking specifically on behalf of the non-human a[nimal] creation, is rarely heard in such august conferences and to be asked t[o do] just that, was not only a great honor for me, but also an indication tha[t the] Orthodox Christian Church is again 'setting the scene and creating opportunity' for its clergy (at every level) and its academics, to engage w[ith] the important subjects of non-human animal suffering and salvation for beings in God's creation.

---

[8] Also known as the Green Patriarch due to his lead and commitment to the subjec[t]

show that their monastic/ascetic traditions are good exemplars of a different ethos and model that can stand against the vested interests and fallacy of economic systems based upon continued growth in GDP and over-consumption, that have led us to this dangerous place. One that replaces the existing damaging model with an integrated, regenerative, and distributive system that focuses on the intrinsic value and well-being of all created beings working in harmony and balance, and importantly, one that works for all and at ground level. We are, as is often quoted in Orthodoxy, to be 'Priests of Creation', recognizing our relational ontology, rather than as destructive brutes increasingly separated from our materiality, who exploit that very material in our selfish, over-consuming, and land-grabbing choices.

Recently the world's attention has been diverted to the Covid-19 pandemic. This tragedy was completely avoidable. It has thrown into high relief our treatment and misuse of non-human animals and at last, many are beginning to understand what animal advocates have always understood - the interconnectedness and interdependence of human flourishing with the flourishing of other creatures. Increasingly, there are calls for a more enlightened relationship between humans and non-human animals, for more and more people have realized that without the end of wet-markets and intensive animal-farming systems, other pandemics will undoubtedly arise and the costs - economically, physically, and mentally - far outweigh any vested interest objections and desires to return to pre-covid intensive and abusive systems.

This pandemic has led to a reawakening to the important things in life - our families, our green spaces, and the creatures in them, clean air, and functioning health-systems. Most surprising of all, is that 'lockdowns' have been achieved with a level of civic compliance never thought possible outside of oppressive regimes. This indicates that the prospect of achieving the 'new normal' has never been more attainable. What is required now is for politicians and policy makers to ride the wave of desire for real change in our economies and societies, rather than lazily returning to the destructive policies and economic strategies of the past. It is hoped that some of them will read the chapters in these volumes, in order to gain the wisdom, they so obviously lack.

It is, however, equally important for us as individuals to realize that to achieve these changes, we must play our part by changing our desires and demands. Cheap flights, cheap meat, and cheap clothes are not cheap, if the full social, environmental, and economic cost of production, transportation and GHG emissions are considered. Cheap is a delusion fed to us by those with other agendas - with vested interests they do not wish to relinquish. The real costs: unstable weather patterns, food insecurity, polluted air, increased water scarcity, habitat loss and species extinctions, ocean acidification, rising sea-levels[12], the beginning of mass migration, and increasing social unrest, are now only too apparent and will become increasingly so.

Some changes are relatively easy for the individual: buying green energy; flying less often or at all; driving more slowly, cycling or walking whenever possible; buying local, wasting less, giving up or reducing animal-food products and where possible, buying from local and organic farms with high animal-welfare standards; growing our own food; planting more trees; turning off the lights; avoiding fast fashion; digging up lawns and sowing meadows; avoiding plastic; reducing, recycling, reusing; lobbying our local and national governments; talking to our clerics and co-parishioners and for those who can, having less children. The list is long enough to cater for varying degrees of commitment to change, but rapid change there must be, if we and those that share our planet, are to survive.

The same is true for Faith institutions - they can, nay must, do more. Normally we avoid words like 'must', but the terms 'should' or 'ought' although more polite, do not adequately represent the urgency of our present situation. Despite the reality that some faith groups have been resistant to modernity, faith-based institutions are increasingly recognized as being integral to the healthy functioning of modern societies in their relationship with the natural world. The chapter from the Animal Interfaith Alliance[13] is therefore also worth noting, for it draws upon the collective wisdom of ten major faith groups, many of whom have no need to 'educate' their members on compassionate care for animals or nature, because creation care is a core tenet of their belief systems.

In recent decades, whilst increasing numbers of theologians working in the fields of systematic and moral theology have shown that this is also true for Christianity, (e.g., Prof. Andrew Linzey) what is beyond doubt, is a disturbing gap between Christian theory and practice on this important subject. As an Eastern Orthodox Christian, I can show through the teachings of early church Fathers and the work of its recent Patriarchs and certainly the incumbent Ecumenical Patriarch, Bartholomew 1st, and here I include the Catholic Pope Francis, that the Christian Church can promote the best ecological practices, despite the fact, that many of its clergy of various levels are, tragically for them and their parishioners, still deeply unresponsive to their

---

[12] WMO State of the Global Climate 2020.
[13] In the second book - see note 5. I declare an interest here. Our charity, Pan Orthodox Concern for Animals is a member, I am a Board member and my husband, retired Archpriest of Tanzania and the Seychelles, is one of its Patrons.

Patriarch/Pope's teachings or the subject of creaturely and environmental care, and the greening of their parishes.

As one of the pillars of civil society, it is important that faith groups understand the science relating to planetary boundaries and how each parish or faith community, not just a few, must act now to 'green' their communities in order to protect their parishioners, their families and the world in which they live.[14] They must make time to teach that sacrifice for others, including the natural environment, is our duty as Image of an all-loving God. They can do so by instructing their financial departments to divest from industries and companies that harm the natural world and invest in those with high 'green', 'sustainable', and ethically just policies. Faith groups must familiarize themselves and not ignore, the serious climate impact of the animal-based diet and its delivery systems.[15] In so doing, it will be easier for them to guide their clergy and members to reduce their animal-food intake; wherever possible, to provide vegan and vegetarian meals at gatherings - having an animal-based meal as a dietary option and, where possible, to purchase any animal-food from organic farms with high-welfare standards. Each local church, temple or mosque can buy and urge their faithful to buy, toiletries, cleaning products, and cosmetics that are environmentally friendly, and not tested on animals. They can increase or initiate forms of animal-blessing services in their churches, mosques, and temples or outer-courtyards where everyone can witness that all things are loved by God[16] and, in relation to wild animals, they can also declare that all forms of 'sport', 'trophy' or 'recreational' hunting is a sin and an insult to God.[17] Perhaps a few words from the recent Holy and Great Council of

---

[14] See Prof Miller's chapter in this volume.

[15] See D'Silva's chapter in this volume; the aforementioned 2019 IPCC Climate Change and Land report, which states that the largest potential for reducing AFOLU emissions are through reduced deforestation and forest degradation (0.4–5.8 GtCO$_2$-eq yr^{-1}), a shift towards plant-based diets (0.7–8.0 GtCO$_2$-eq yr^{-1}) and reduced food and agricultural waste (0.8–4.5 GtCO$_2$-eq yr^{-1}).

[16] See Pan Orthodox Concern for Animals Charity's 'When Faith Meets Fur' page and 'How To' tips on our Video page and the Greek Orthodox Church of America's excellent project on 'Greening the Parish' at: greenparish.goarch.org. See the first in the series by Fr John Chryssavgis, theological advisor to His All-Holiness Bartholomew, available at:
https://youtu.be/mG4fMMon2mw.

[17] See earlier reference to St Cyril of Jerusalem. In many cases, where the rich from the West travel to Africa to kill animals, it can and is increasingly described as a modern form of colonial exploitation. Also RSPB 'State of Nature' report 2019, which found that over the last 50 years, 40 million birds have vanished from

the Orthodox Church[18] would be useful in drawing this introduction to a close:

> The ecological crisis, which is connected to climate change and global warming, makes it incumbent upon the Church to do everything within her spiritual power to protect God's creation from the consequences of human greed. As the gratification of material needs, greed leads to spiritual impoverishment of the human being and to environmental destruction. We should not forget that the earth's natural resources are not our property, but the Creator's: *The earth is the Lord's, and all its fullness, the world, and those who dwell therein* (Ps 23:1). Therefore, the Orthodox Church emphasizes the protection of God's creation through the cultivation of human responsibility for our God-given environment and the promotion of the virtues of frugality and self-restraint.

That books such as these are still necessary in 2021 is a tragic testament not only to our individual failures but also to the failure of successive governments and institutions across the world to a) acknowledge and act on the science and b) acknowledge the wisdom in the thousands of voices from across the world, who for decades have spoken with knowledge and sincerity on these subjects. This in part, is due to those who through ignorance or powerful vested interests, deny the climate problem or deliberately mislead people about the severity of the climate danger and, in some cases, threaten to withhold funding to a range of institutions, including the church. In equal measure, we can also add our long-term blindness and indifference to the need of others and nature, whilst promoting our own desires, and at times, destructive cultural 'traditions', such as hunting.

Finally, those still quoting 2050 in their decarbonization or 'building back better' strategies, continue to be deaf to the fast-changing reality unfolding before us. As such, *Climate Crisis and Creation Care: Historical Perspectives, Ecological Integrity and Justice* is essential reading for those involved in national/local governments and religious institutions, and for academics and students in a variety of disciplines.

---

the UK's skies and that around two-fifths of UK species are in decline. See Birdlife International for the huge numbers of birds shot for 'recreation'.

[18] The Mission of the Orthodox Church in Today's World - Official Documents - The Holy and Great Council of the Orthodox Church (holycouncil.org)

PART ONE:

HISTORICAL PERSPECTIVES, GOVERNANCE AND CREATION CARE

Chapter One

An Integrated Theology: Compassion for Animals

Metropolitan Kallistos Ware

What is a merciful heart? It is a heart on fire for the whole of creation, for humankind, for the birds, for the animals, for the demons, for all that exists.
—*St Isaac the Syrian* (7th century)

Introduction

A reverence for animals, sensitivity to their position, their suffering is not new. It is part of our Orthodox Church faith. We start from the principle laid down in the first chapter of Genesis - that the world is God's creation, God saw everything that He had made and behold it was very good (Genesis 1:31). The world is God's creation and it is a good, and beautiful world. Therefore, the question of animals and how we treat them, links up with our view that animals are part of God's creation and just as we should treat the whole of creation with reverence and respect, so we should more particularly treat the animals with reverence and respect. It is said in the first chapter of Genesis, that humans have a unique position in God's creation because we are created in the Image and Likeness of God, and that is not said of animals, but being created in God's Image and Likeness, gives us a responsibility towards creation as a whole and towards animals in particular.

Unfortunately, we are up against the basic problem that all too many people, clergy, and laity, think as Christians that this does not matter; that the treatment of animals is not a moral issue. But as soon as you say that animals are part of God's creation, and we humans have a God-given responsibility towards creation, then at once, one sees that it is both a moral and spiritual question. That is why the Ecumenical Patriarch Bartholomew was so right to insist that the misuse of any part of creation is a sin but all too many people do not see it that way.

In light of both the climate crisis and the Covid-19 pandemic, we as priests, and as individual Christians, ought to have recognised the interconnectedness of creation. This chapter aims to facilitate that recognition, by outlining several aspects of Orthodox Christian teachings that play an important role in our integrated theology. I begin with the exemplars of compassionate care - the saints.

The Saints

In the lives of Eastern Christian Saints - as among the saints of the West, especially in the Celtic tradition - there are numerous stories, often well authenticated, of close fellowship between the animals and holy men and women. Such accounts are not to be dismissed as sentimental fairy tales, for they have a definite theological significance. The mutual understanding between animals and humans recalls the situation before the Fall, when the two lived at peace in Paradise; and it points forward to the transfiguration of the cosmos at the end time. In the words of St. Isaac, the Syrian (7th century):

> The humble person approaches the wild animals, and the moment they catch sight of him their ferocity is tamed. They come up and cling to him as to their master, wagging their tails and licking his hands and feet. For they smell on him the same smell that came from Adam before the transgression.[1]

Many of the 20th-century stories about humans and animals come from the Holy Mountain of Athos, the chief center of Orthodox monasticism. I recall one such story, told to me many years ago. The monks in a small hermitage, as they prayed in the early morning, were much disturbed by the croaking of frogs in the cistern outside their chapel. The spiritual father of the community went out and addressed them:

> Frogs! We've just finished the Midnight Office and are about to start Matins. Would you mind keeping quiet until we've finished!' To which the frogs replied, 'We've just finished Matins and are about to begin the First Hour. Would *you* mind keeping quiet until *we've* finished!

If we are to accept the testimony of Scripture, it would seem that animals can sometimes display visionary awareness, perceiving things to which we humans are blind. In the story of Balaam's ass (Num. 22: 21-33), the donkey sees the angel of the Lord, blocking the pathway with a drawn sword, whereas Balaam himself is unaware of the angel's presence. May it not be

---

[1] *Homily* 82, in *Mystic Treatises by Isaac of Nineveh*, tr. A. J. Wensinck (Amsterdam: Koninklijke Akademie van Wetenschappen, 1923), p. 386 (translation adapted).

claimed that animals possess, at least in a rudimentary form, a capacity for spiritual intuition?

Compassion for animals is vividly expressed in the writings of a recent Athonite Saint, the Russian monk Silouan (1866-1938):

> The Lord bestows such rich grace on his chosen ones that they embrace the whole earth, the whole world within their love...One day I saw a dead snake on my path which had been chopped into pieces, and each piece writhed convulsively, and I was filled with pity for every living creature, every suffering thing in creation, and I wept bitterly before God.[2]

So, from the tradition of the Orthodox Church, we have plenty of examples of close mutual understanding between humans and animals. The trouble is whilst we have all this in theory, we do not sufficiently apply it in practice. I think we have to admit that this is not a priority in the minds of some bishops and priests, and they might say we are concerned with humans and to that my answer is "it is not a matter of either /or, you should be concerned with humans *and* animals." The one does not exclude the other. All too often the animals are innocent sufferers, and we should view this undeserved suffering with compunction and sympathy. What harm have they done to us, that we should inflict pain and distress upon them? We Orthodox ought to acknowledge the contemporary science regarding animals. A very large number are living sentient beings, sensitive, and easily hurt, they are to be viewed as a 'Thou', not an 'It', to use Martin Buber's terminology: not as objects to be exploited, and manipulated but as subjects, capable of joy and sorrow, of happiness and affliction. They are to be approached with gentleness and tenderness; and, more than that, with respect, and reverence, for they are precious in God's sight. As William Blake affirmed, 'Everything that lives is holy.'[3] Such is the truth of the compassionate love that we are called to express towards the animals and the rest of God's creation, that secures its place at the core of an integrated Orthodox Christian theology.

---

[2] Archimandrite Sofrony (Sakharov), *Saint Silouan the Athonite* (Tolleshunt Knights: Stavropegic Monastery of St John the Baptist, 1991), pp. 267, 469.
[3] 'The Marriage of Heaven and Hell', in Geoffrey Keynes (ed.), *Poetry and Prose of William Blake* (London: Nonesuch Press, 1948), p. 193.

Friendship and Love

Are we to love and befriend animals? Friendship and mutual love contain within themselves an element of eternity. For us to say to another human person with all our heart "I love you", is to say by implication, "You will never die." If this is true of our love for our fellow humans, may it not be true of our love for animals? Those of us who have experienced the deeply therapeutic effect of a companion animal will certainly recognize that our reciprocal relationship contains within itself intimations of immortality. In the words of Staretz Zosima in Dostoevsky's master work *The Brothers Karamazov*:

> Love the animals: God has given them the rudiments of thought and an untroubled joy. Do not trouble it, do not torment them, do not go against God's purpose. Man, do not exalt yourself above the animals; they are sinless, and you, you with all your grandeur, defile the earth through your appearance upon it, and leave traces of your defilement behind you - alas, this is true of almost every one of us![4]

Love stands in opposition to the evil of cruelty, and this Love will be found at the core of any true Christian theology. Humphrey Primatt (18th century) was correct when he stated that "Cruelty is atheism...Cruelty is the worst of heresies."[5] Indeed, not only should we refrain from cruelty to animals, but in a positive way we should seek to do them good, enhancing their pleasure, and their unselfconscious happiness, for they are responsive, and vulnerable.

As Andrew Linzey rightly says, "Animals are not machines or commodities but beings with their own God-given life (*nephesh*), individuality and personality...Animals are more like gifts than something owned, giving us more than we expect, and thus obliging us to return their gifts. Far from decrying these relationships as 'sentimental', 'unbalanced', or 'obsessive' (as frequently happens today), churches could point us to their underlying theological significance - as living examples of divine grace."[6]

Unfortunately, as noted above, it has to be said that, while there can be found within Orthodoxy a rich theology of the animal creation, there exists

---

[4] Fyordor Dostoevsky, *The Brothers Karamazov*, tr. Richard Pervear and Larissa Volokhonsky (New York: Vintage Classics, 1991), p. 319 (translation adapted).

[5] Andrew Linzey, *Animal Rites Rites: Liturgies of Animal Care,* (London: SCM Press, 1999), p.151.

[6] Andrew Linzey, *Animal Rites*, p. 58.

a sad gap between theory, and practice.[7] It cannot be claimed that, in traditional Orthodox countries, animals are better treated than in the non-Orthodox West; indeed, the contrary is regrettably true. We Orthodox need to kneel down before the animals and to ask their forgiveness for the evils that we inflict upon them. We should not ignore the many ways in which we fall short of our pastoral responsibility towards the living creatures, domestic and wild, that God has given us to be our companions. Simply accepting or shrugging off these failings is untenable in our era because we have teachings that inform us that indifference to the suffering of any part of creation is an "unacceptable moral stance", and a "sin".[8] We must examine our consciences and ask whether we as individuals or as priests, are practicing or preaching the Good News of Christ, who loves all things and extends His compassion and mercy to all His creatures. Certainly, Christian scripture and teachings are full of material to prove this fundamental theological truth.

Eastern Orthodox Christian Worship and Prayers

Many Eastern Orthodox Christians wrongly believe that contemporary Orthodox concern for animals is a modern phenomenon, but it is clear from the initial quote above, and the lives of many saints, that this is not the case. It is true that, when we look at the main act of worship, the Service of the Eucharist, we are at first sight disappointed; for in its two chief forms - the

---

[7] Relatively little contemporary work had been written by an Eastern Orthodox theologian relating to animal suffering before Nellist, C. *Eastern Orthodox Christianity and Animal Suffering: Ancient Voices in Modern Theology* (Cambridge Scholars, 2020). However, material on saints and animals in both ancient and modern times can be found in numerous books, see the classic anthology by Helen Waddell, *Beasts and Saints* (London: Constable, 1934) or Stefanatos, J. *Animals and Man: A State of Blessedness* (Minneapolis, MN: Light and Life, 1992), and *Animals Sanctified: A Spiritual Journey* (Minneapolis, MN: Light and Life, 2001). There is not much from Eastern Christian sources in the following two collections (in other respects, rich and representative) edited by Andrew Linzey, *Animal Rites: Liturgies of Animal Care* (London: SCM, 1999), and (with Paul Barry Clarke), *Animal Rights: A Historical Anthology* (New York: Columbia U. P., 2004). However, more recently (2018) Fr. Simon Nellist (Orthodox) has composed a Blessing Service for the death of companion animals and for animal sanctuaries, their animals and their staff, available at the Pan Orthodox Concern for Animal Charity's website: http://panorthodoxconcernforanimals.org/prayers-for-creation/.
[8] Bartholomew 1, (Archontonis) (Ecumenical Patriarch), *Cosmic Grace, Humble Prayer: The Ecological Vision of the Green Patriarch Bartholomew,* ed. J. Chryssavgis, (Grand Rapids, Michigan: Eerdmans, 2009), p.127.

Divine Liturgy of St John Chrysostom and that of St Basil the Great - there are no direct references to the animal creation. Yet, when we pray at the beginning of the Liturgy "for the peace of the whole world", this surely includes animals. As one commentator puts it,

> We pray for the peace of the universe, not only for mankind, but for every creature, for animals and plants, for the stars and all of nature.[9]

When we look at the daily office, we are not disappointed, for there we find not only implicit but explicit allusions to the animals. A notable example comes at the beginning of Vespers. On the Orthodox understanding of time, as in Judaism, the new day commences not at midnight or at dawn but at sunset; and so, Vespers is the opening service in the twenty-four-hour cycle of prayer. How, then, do we begin the new day? Throughout the year, except in the week after Easter Sunday, Vespers always starts in the same way: with the reading or singing of Psalm 103 (104). This is a hymn of praise to the Creator for all the wonders of his creation; and in this cosmic doxology we have much to say about the animals:

> You make springs gush forth in the valleys;
> they flow between the hills,
> They give drink to every beast of the field;
> the wild donkeys quench their thirst.
> Beside them the birds of the air have their habitation;
> they sing among the branches.

The psalm continues by speaking of storks, wild goats, badgers, and young lions and it concludes this catalogue of living creatures with a reference to Leviathan, who must surely be a whale.

> Yonder is the sea, great and wide,
> which teems with things innumerable,
> living things both small and great.
> There go the ships,
> and there is the great sea monster
> which you formed to sport in it.

In this way, embarking upon the new day, we offer the world back to God in thanksgiving. We bless him for all living creatures, in all their diversity

---

[9] A Monk of the Eastern Church [Lev Gillet], *Serve the Lord with Gladness: Basic Reflections on the Eucharist and the Priesthood* (Crestwood, NY: St Vladimir's Seminary Press, 1990), p.16.

and abundance along with the sun and moon, clouds and wind, for the earth and the water:

> How marvellous are your works, O Lord!
> In wisdom have you made them all.

As we stand before God in prayer, the companionship of the animals fills our hearts with warmth and hope. Nor is it only in the service of Vespers that the animals have their assured place. In the Orthodox book of blessings and intercessions known in Greek as the *Evchologion*, and in Slavonic as the *Trebnik* or Book of Needs, there are prayers for the good health of sheep, goats, and cattle, of horses, donkeys, and mules, and even of bees, and silkworms. Up to the present day, the great majority of Eastern Orthodox Christians dwell in an agricultural rather than an urban environment; and so, it is only natural that their prayer - rooted in the concerns of this world as well as being otherworldly - should reflect the needs of a farming community. In daily prayer as in daily life, humans and animals belong to a single integrated community. As a typical example of a prayer for living creatures, let us take these phrases from a blessing on bees:

> In ancient times you granted to the Israelites a land flowing with milk and honey (Exod. 3:8), and you were well-pleased to nourish your Baptist John with wild honey in the wilderness (Matt. 3:4). Now also, providing in your good pleasure for our sustenance, do you bless the beehives in this apiary. Greatly increase the multiplication of the bees within them, preserving them by your grace and granting us an abundance of rich honey.[10]

A prayer for silkworms includes the words:

> All-good King, show us even now your lovingkindness; and as you blessed the well of Jacob (John 4:6), and the pool of Siloam (John 9:7), and the cup of your holy apostles (Matt. 26:27), so bless also these silkworms; and as you multiplied the stars in heaven and the sand beside the sea-shore, so multiply these silkworms, granting them health and strength: and may they feed without coming to any harm...so that they may produce shrouds of pure silk, to your glory and praise.[11]

Until quite recently, we have generally ignored the insect world. Now, we are beginning to recognize both their importance for human flourishing via

---

[10] *The Great Book of Needs* (South Canaan, PA: St Tikhon's Seminary Press, 1999), vol. 4, pp. 382-3 (translation adapted).

[11] *Evchologion to Mega*, ed. N. P. Papadopoulos (Athens: Saliveros, no date), p. 511.

the pollinating of our crops and the enriching of the soil. As a result, we now have an alarming crash in insect and soil microorganism populations because of our misuse of harmful chemicals on the land, and a desire for ever increasing profits. Not all these prayers for animals are as genial as this, for there are also exorcisms directed against the creatures that, in this fallen world, inflict harm on humans and their produce:

> I adjure you, O creatures of many forms: worms, caterpillars, beetles and cockroaches, mice, grasshoppers and locusts, and insects of various kinds, flies and moles and ants, gadflies and wasps, and centipedes and millipedes...injure not the vineyard, field, garden, trees, or vegetables of the servant of God [*name*] but be gone into the wild hills and into the barren trees that God has given you for sustenance.[12]

It will be noted here that the exorcism does not actually pray for the destruction of these baneful creatures, but only that they should depart to their proper home and cease to molest us. Even rats, hornets, and spiders have their appointed place in God's dispensation![13] Here, by way of contrast, is a prayer by St Nicodemus of the Holy Mountain (1748-1809) expressing tenderness, and compassion for the animals:

> Lord Jesus Christ, moved by your tender mercy, take pity on the suffering animals...For if a righteous man takes pity on the souls of his cattle (Prov. 12: 10. LXX), how should you not take pity on them, for you created them and you provide for them? In your compassion you did not forget the animals in the ark (Gen. 9: 19-20) ...Through the good health and the plentiful number of oxen and other four-footed beasts, the earth is cultivated, and its fruits increase; and your servants, who call upon your name, enjoy in full abundance the produce of their farming.[14]

Here is acknowledgement that animals help human flourishing without the need for harmful practices.

Many other examples of such prayers for the animals could be quoted, but these are enough to show that Orthodox intercessions encompass the entire created order, and this too, is another fundamental element of an integrated Orthodox Christian theology.

---

[12] Exorcism of the Holy Martyr Tryphon, in *The Great Book of Needs*, vol. 3, p.53 (translation adapted).
[13] *The Great Book of Needs*, vol. 3.
[14] Prayer of St Modestos, in *Mikron Evchologion i Agiasmatarion* (Athens: Apostoliki Diakonia, 1984), p. 297.

Animals as Co-communicants

There are numerous biblical and patristic teachings where "the earth", and at times animals are portrayed as praising and knowing God, to support the above point. Theokritoff (2001)[15] and Gschwandtner (2012)[16] provide numerous examples of this spiritual insight in Orthodox ecclesial texts relating to the Incarnation, Crucifixion, and Resurrection; where the entire created world is depicted as reacting to these salvific events, with clear statements that the earth, and all that is in it, recognizes, and knows God.

> All things proclaim your greatness and your strength.[17]

> The whole creation was altered by Thy Passion: for all things suffered with Thee, knowing, O Word, that Thou holdest all in unity.[18]

In the new ecclesial text for the environment, we are also informed that "all things", and the "whole earth" sing Gods praise, and importantly, that they are to be protected "from every abuse":

> You give life to all and conduct all things with ineffable judgments; from harmful pollutions and from every abuse save those who cry out, "God of our fathers, blessed are you!" By your will, Lord, you adorned the heavens with stars, while you made the whole earth fair with flowers and trees as it sings, "God of our fathers, blessed are you." [19]

We have therefore, an Orthodox tradition of all created beings knowing, and praising God.

---

[15] Theokritoff, E, 'Creation and Salvation in Orthodox Worship.' *Journal of Religion, Nature & the Environment,* Vol. 5. 10: 97-108. (Jan 2001)

[16] Gschwandtner, K. *The Role of Non-Human Creation in the Liturgical Feasts of the Eastern Orthodox Tradition: Towards an Orthodox Ecological Theology.* 2012. Durham E-Theses. http://etheses.dur.ac.uk/4424.

[17] Mikrayiannanites, Monk Gerasimos. 'Vespers for the Environment,' in *Toward an Ecology of Transfiguration: Orthodox Christian Perspectives on Environment, Nature and Creation,* edited by Chryssavgis, J. and B. V. Foltz, (NY: Fordham University Press, 2013), Mode 4, *Joseph was amazed,* p. 386.

[18] E.g., Holy Saturday, *The Lenton Triodion,* trans. Mother Mary and K. Ware. (London: Faber & Faber, 1978). pp. 625, 627; Also Col. 1:16-17.

[19] Mikrayiannanites, Monk Gerasimos. in, *Toward an Ecology of Transfiguration,* 1990:392.

Liturgical Art

For members of the Orthodox Christian Church an icon is not to be regarded in isolation, simply as a picture on a religious subject, a decorative item designed to give aesthetic pleasure. Much more significant is the fact that an icon exists within a distinct and specific context. It is part of an act of prayer and worship and divorced from that context of prayer and worship it ceases to be authentically an icon. [20]

If then, Orthodox icons depict not only humans but animals, does this not imply that the animals have an accepted place in our liturgical celebration and our dialogue with God? We do not forget that, when Jesus withdrew to pray for forty days in the wilderness, he had the animals as his companions: "He was *with* the wild beasts" (Mark 1:13). The icon, together with our Orthodox prayers illustrate an integrated theology, where animals share in our prayer and worship.

Animal Souls and Immortality

St Nicodemus, in the prayer quoted above, cites the words of Proverbs 12:10: "The righteous man shows pity for the souls of his cattle."[21] Does this mean that animals have souls?[22] The answer depends upon what precisely we mean by the soul. The word *psyche* in the ancient world had a wider application than that which is customarily given in the present day to our word 'soul'. Aristotle, for example, distinguishes three levels of soul: the vegetable, the animal, and the human.[23] According to this Aristotelian scheme, the vegetable or nutritive soul has the capacity for growth, but not for movement or sensation. In this scheme, the animal soul has the capacity for movement and sensation, but not for conscious thought or reason; only the human soul is endowed with self-knowledge and the power of logical thinking. For Aristotle, then, *psyche* means in an inclusive fashion, all expressions of life-force and vital energy, whereas in contemporary usage we limit the term 'soul' to the third level, the human or rational soul. If we

---

[20] See Philip Sherrard, *The Sacred in Life and Art* (Ipswich: Golgonooza, 1990), pp. 71-74.

[21] I follow here the text of the Septuagint, the Greek translation of the Old Testament used at Orthodox Church services.

[22] See Kallistos Ware, 'The Soul in Greek Christianity', in M. James C. Crabbe (ed.), *From Soul to Self* (London/New York: Routledge, 1999), especially pp.62-65. For other passages in the Septuagint that mention the 'souls' of animals, see for example Genesis 1:21 and 24, and Leviticus 17:14.

[23] See Ware, 'The Soul in Greek Christianity', pp.55-56.

today were to speak of potatoes or tomatoes as possessing souls, we should doubtless be considered facetious. But Aristotle was not trying to make a joke.

Employing the term 'soul' in a restricted sense, as denoting specifically the self-reflective rational soul, most thinkers in the West - and on the whole, in the Christian East as well - have denied that animals are ensouled. Descartes held that they are simply intricate machines or automata that do not feel pain. On such a view, there is a clear demarcation between human beings and the animal world. Yet the idea that animals do not suffer pain is quite extraordinary. We have every reason to believe that animals experience pain as we do, and to suggest that to inflict pain on animals is something morally neutral is abhorrent. It is a sin. Humans alone, it is said, are created in God's image, and they alone possess immortality. In modern Greek, the horse is called *alogon*, 'lacking *logos* or reason'. Animals in this theory, cannot form abstract concepts, and are unable to construct logical arguments. From this it is argued that they lack personal freedom and the faculty of moral choice, for they cannot discern between good and evil, but act solely from instinct.

Yet are we in fact justified in making such an emphatic division between ourselves and the other animals? (I say 'other', because we humans are also animals; we have the same origin as those whom we call 'beasts'). Moving from the ancient views of Aristotle to contemporary thought based on scientific research, it is now proven that many of the characteristics that we had regarded as distinctively human are also to be found, to varying extents, in the animals as well. It may be a surprise to some that these conclusions are not new, and evidence of similar views can be found in the work of early Christian writers such as Origen (*c.*185-*c.*254):

> The instinct (*physis*) that exists in hunting dogs and war horses comes near,
> if I may say so, to reason itself.'[24]

Origen has in view domesticated animals, but Theophilus of Antioch (late 2nd century) goes further, noting how the instinct in all animals, wild as well as domestic, leads them to mate and to care for their offspring: this indicates that they possess 'understanding'.[25] Other Patristic authors such as St Basil of Caesarea (*c.*330-79) point out that animals share with humans not only a certain degree of reason, and understanding:

---

[24] Origen, *On First Principles* 3:1:3.
[25] St. Theophilus of Antioch, *To Antolycus* 1:6.

> You may see flocks of vultures following armies, and calculating the result of warlike preparations; a calculation very nearly approaching to human reasoning.[26]

but also, memory, and a wide range of emotions, and affections, when they display feelings of joy and grief, and recognize those whom they have met previously.[27] Ants and bees are capable of social co-operation on an elaborate scale. Importantly, St John Climacus (*c.570-c.649*) adds that they express love for each other, for 'they often bewail the loss of their companions'.[28] He also acknowledges:

> that the virtues, including Faith, Hope and Love, are set in us from God by nature, are even to be seen in the animals.[29]

Animals, until relatively recently, were thought incapable of using tools - yet modern scientific research has shown that many species of animals, including fish, use tools. They do not simply exist within the world, but actively and creatively, adapt the environment to their own needs. Birds build nests, beavers construct dams. If we observe the behavior of a monkey, confronted by a cage with a complicated latch with a banana inside, we see him seeking to open the cage, twisting the latch first in one direction and then in another. The monkey is evidently engaged in something closely similar to the process of rational thinking that a human being would employ in a similar situation. Scientists inform us that mice and other creatures use mind-mapping to calculate the optimum food intake versus energy expenditure. This too, requires a high degree of intelligence. Animals as well as humans try to solve problems, which require higher levels of intelligence and reasoning than instinct alone could explain.

It used to be argued that animals lack the power to articulate speech. Yet, as we can see from dolphins and many other species, including insects, they have other subtle ways of communicating with one another. An historical error of both ancient philosophers, and some Christian theologians has been to use *our* inability to recognize *their* language or communication processes, to make a sharp distinction between animals and humans, and between animals and rationality. Modern science and theology acknowledge that differences between animals and humans on this matter is of degree rather than absence:

---

[26] St. Basil, *Hexaemeron* 8:7. (*PG* 29: 165AB
[27] St. Basil, *Hexaemeron* 8:1 (*PG* 29: 165AB).
[28] St John Climacus *The Ladder of Divine Ascent* 26 (*PG* 88: 1028A).
[29] St John Climacus *The Ladder of Divine Ascent* 26 (*PG* 88: 1028AB).

In the past, philosophers made this distinction by saying that humans were specially characterized by intelligence or rationality. However, ever since Darwin showed that intelligence can also be found in other animals, and that the difference is a matter of degree and not of kind, philosophy no longer insists on rationality as the special characteristic of man. [30]

So, in all of this, simply to say that animals have no souls is inadequate. It is a subject on which we have not been given clear revelation or guidance in revelation, and in the end, it is probably a 'red herring'. The point is that animals are living creatures, all life is from God, and therefore, we should treat the animals with respect, and reverence. To me it is unsatisfactory to say animals have no souls, and we should avoid making such an assertion. Would it not be wiser to keep in view the kinship that links us together? Nemesius of Emesa (late 4th century) is surely correct to insist upon the unity of all living things. Sharing as they do the same life-force, plants, animals, and humankind belong to the single integrated structure of creation.[31] We, and the animals are interdependent, "members one of another" (Eph. 4:25). The world is variegated yet everywhere interconnected. As my history master at school used to say, "It all ties up, you see; it all ties up."

This brings me to another important point. Can we in fact be sure that animals do not enjoy immortality? I think this is another subject where we can simply say, we do not have a clear revelation on this point in Scripture. I cannot recall anywhere where it says animals cannot survive into a future life. There is, however, good reason to believe that animals will exist in the future Age, after the Second Coming of Christ and the general resurrection of the dead. As Isaiah affirms:

> The wolf shall dwell with the lamb, and the leopard shall lie down with the kid, and the calf and the young lion together, and a little child shall lead them. (Isa. 11:6).

We humans are bound to God and to one another in a cosmic covenant that also includes all the other living creatures on the face of the earth: "I will make for you a covenant on that day with the beasts of the field, the birds of the air, and the creeping things of the ground" (Hos. 2:18; cf. Gen. 9:15).[32] We humans are not saved *from* the world but *with* the world; and that means, *with* the animals. Moreover, this cosmic covenant is not

---

[30] Met. John of Pergamon, "Preserving God's Creation," II. The Catholic Church in Pope Francis' recent Encyclical Laudato Si' also recognises this.

[31] *On the Nature of Man* 1 (ed. Morani, 2:13-14; 3: 3-25).

[32] See Robert Murray, The Cosmic Covenant: Biblical Themes of Justice, Peace and the Integrity of Creation (London: Sheed & Ward, 1992).

something that we humans have devised, but it has its source in the divine realm. It is conferred upon us as a gift by God.

A striking illustration of this covenant bond is to be seen in the custom that once prevailed in the Russian countryside; perhaps it still continues today. Returning from the Easter midnight service with their newly kindled Holy Fire, the farmers used to go into the stables with the lighted candle or lantern and greeted the horses and cattle with the Paschal salutation "Christ is Risen!" The victory of the risen Savior over the forces of death and darkness has meaning not for us humans alone but for the animals as well. For them also Christ has died and risen again. "Now *all things* are filled with light" (hymn at the Easter matins). Looking further afield just briefly, when Martin Luther, distressed by the death of his pet dog, was asked whether there would be animals in heaven, he replied:

There will be little dogs with golden hair, shining like precious stones.[33]

It is not clear whether these animals in the Age to come will be the same animals as we have known in this present life; yet that is at least a possibility. We certainly do not have good grounds for asserting that it could not conceivably be so. Let us leave the question open.

Dominion v domination

"Are not two sparrows sold for a penny?" says Jesus. "Yet not one of them will fall to the ground without your Father's will" (Matt. 10:29). "Not one of them": God's care for his creation, his love for all the things that he has made, is not merely an abstract and generalized love. He cares for each particular creature, for every individual sparrow. But Jesus then goes on to say, "You are of more value than many sparrows" (Matt. 10:31). Every living thing has its unique value in God's sight, but at the same time we dwell in a hierarchical universe, and some living things have a greater value than others. It is important to give a word of caution here. Our status does not mean that we have the right to abuse or misuse the rest of creation, for as His All-Holiness, the Ecumenical Patriarch teaches, the misuse of any part of God's creation is a sin.

The significance of this hierarchy is expressed in a more specific way in God's creative utterance in the opening chapter of Genesis: "Then God said, 'Let us make the human being in our image, after our likeness; and let them

---

[33] William Hazlitt (ed.), *The Table Talk of Martin Luther* (London: H. G. Bohn, 1857), p. 322.

have dominion over the fish of the sea, and over the birds of the air, and over the cattle, and over all the earth, and over every creeping thing that creeps upon the earth'" (Gen. 1:26). Humans, then, are entrusted by the Creator with authority over the animals. Yet this God-given 'dominion' does not signify an arbitrary and tyrannical domination. We must not overlook the explicit reason that is given for this dominion: it is because we are fashioned in the image and likeness of God. That is to say, in the exercise of our dominion over the animals, we are to show the same gentleness, and loving compassion, that God himself shows towards the whole of his creation. Our dominion is to be God-reflective, and Christ-like.

How far does this dominion extend? Certainly, it includes the right to use domestic animals for our service: to employ horses and oxen for ploughing, to keep cows for their milk, to breed sheep for their wool. Yet there are definite limits to what we can legitimately do. We should not adopt a narrowly instrumentalist attitude towards the animals. We are to respect their characteristic 'life-style', allowing them to be themselves. This is scarcely what happens with battery hens or many other species in the modern intensive farming systems! We are not to inflict upon them excessive burdens that cause them exhaustion and suffering. This is why the Ecumenical Patriarch was so right to insist that the misuse of creation is a sin. We are to ensure that they are kept warm, clean, healthy, and properly fed. Only so will our dominion be according to the image of divine compassion.

Living sustainable lives: dietary choices

Does our dominion over the animals entitle us to kill and eat them? In the Orthodox Church, as in other Christian communities, there are many who on serious grounds of conscience refrain from eating animals. But the Orthodox Church as such is not in principle vegetarian. The normative teaching has been that because of God's dispensation after the fall, animals may be killed and used for food, so long as this killing is done humanely, and not wantonly. It is, however, often forgotten that God's original choice of diet (Gn 1:29-30), is still a valid option.[34] It is also true that in traditional Orthodox monasteries meat is not eaten in the refectory; fish, however, is allowed. It is also true that in Lent and at certain other seasons of the year all Orthodox Christians, whether monastics or those in the 'world', are required to abstain from animal products. But this is not because the eating of animal products is a sin, but because such fasting has disciplinary value,

---

[34] See Nellist, Chapter Eight.

assisting us in our prayer and our spiritual growth. Nonetheless, we are to remember that the consumption of animals as food is a dispensation, which sits alongside God's original choice; it does not replace it.

In the Gospels it is stated that on one occasion Christ ate fish: "They gave him a piece of broiled fish, and he ate before them" (Luke 24:41-42) and since he observed the Passover, it is presumed by many that he also ate meat. However, whilst we cannot say that eating animals is a sin, in today's world there are certainly arguments for significantly reducing or refraining altogether from the animal-based diet. I remember visiting many years ago, a non-Orthodox but Christian monastery in the United States and they took me with great pride, to see a new appliance that they had installed for battery hens. There were thousands of hens in this vast shed, all in tiny cages, and subjected to electric light all through the night so that they would lay a larger number of eggs. Now there it seemed to me, that the desire of a larger profit was leading to an immoral use of living creatures. Animals have their dignity their natural ways of behaving - hens wander about picking up the food they find, picking it up in different places, and they should be allowed to do this. I was deeply shocked that a monastery, which should be sensitive to the dignity of creation, should be showing such pleasure in this new installation. Well, their motive was to make profit.

There is a problem in that people involved in agriculture or those with vested interests, will want to go on treating animals in the inhumane way that happens now, through battery hens or whatever, and they might feel that the intervention by Christian clergy and others, suggesting humane ways of treating animals would diminish their profits, and that is an argument against organic farming in general. This argument I do not accept. First of all, even if you cannot make quite such big profits, surely humane farming could be economically viable. Secondly, even if it did diminish your profits, perhaps you should not make evil profit from creation. I think that it is possible to practice organic farming, and humane treatment of animals, in a manner that is perfectly viable economically. We should quietly but persistently, combat those views. Opinions can be changed. In addition, it is now clear that the consumption of animal products has serious consequences for our environment. Once we become aware of the science and unsustainability of this diet, it is beholden on each one of us to ask if we can, in all conscience, continue to consume animal food products at today's level. Certainly, each of us, clergy included, must consider our dietary choices, and the global consequences of them, for the sake of our children and future generations. It is not something the church can dictate, but it can offer spiritual and practical guidance such as reducing or eliminating animal food products from our diets whenever possible, and choosing from high-welfare sources. We can also advise them to eat local, organically grown produce where possible, and to eat more seasonal fruit and vegetables.

Conclusion

Taking everything that I have written here as a whole, do we clergy believe that our parishioners understand the teachings of the church on the points I have made? If the answer is yes, all well and good. If the answer is no, then it is time to rectify that situation.

If we reflect upon our sacred texts and the teachings of both our early church, and contemporary theologians, and Christian ethicists, the question to answer is how we are to apply these teachings to the critical issues of our time - the climate crisis?

Initially, we must acknowledge that we are called by Christ to care for all His creatures, and to act to prevent their suffering.[35] This, in part, will require each one of us to truthfully examine our lives and identify the many ways in which we can change our habits and curb our desires via the ethos of aestheticism - taking only what is needed, not what is desired. Next, we must listen to the science, for there are no reputable scientists denying global warming or the urgency of our present situation. And yet simply listening to the science without enacting personal, and parish change is no longer tenable for Christians.

There is the need for education at every level. The normal catechism teaching given in our Church Sunday School classes should include teaching about the creation, and about compassionate and Christian treatment of animals. The Orthodox Church should also include such topics in its manuals. The Church of Greece has plenty of books for teaching children and I know the Greek Archdiocese in North America has a programme with a lot of literature. I think we should struggle to see that this literature includes as one of its themes, part of the essential Christian teaching of respect for the animal creation. Then certainly, when priests are given training, the courses the clergy are given should include teaching on the environment and on how animals should be treated with love and compassion. In general, we should be working on every level to educate people. We should encourage those who have this area of responsibility to educate the children and educate the priests so that they in turn can educate their people. Thankfully, we can see this beginning, for in 2019 His All-Holiness, Patriarch Bartholomew held the third of his Halki Summits.

---

[35] Luke 14:5.

Theologians from Orthodox seminary and academic institutions from across the globe were brought together to discuss how creation care may be included into our academic and seminary education programs. I support this agenda and the comments made at this conference by His Eminence, Metropolitan John of Pergamon, who reminded the audience that education was also needed at every level and here he was repeating his earlier teaching:

> The Church must introduce environmental teaching into her preaching, Sunday schools, and other religious forms of education from the lowest to the highest level. The Church cannot be faithful to her mission today without a serious involvement in the protection of God's creation from the damage inflicted on it by human greed and selfishness.[36]

For that reality to materialize, courses that include care for creation, must be written, and then taught in our schools, parishes, academic, and seminary institutions. This will require each priest, and parish, not only to make time to implement 'Green' practices but just as importantly, to make time to teach our Christian responsibility as Image of God, to care for all things in His creation, and this must include the animals.[37]

---

[36] Met. John of Pergamon, 'Foreword, in Chryssavgis, *Cosmic Grace*, viii.
[37] An example is the 'Creation Care: Christian Responsibility Course', which is available to use and adapt at http://panorthodoxconcernforanimals.org/creation-care-christian-responsibility-course/.

CHAPTER TWO

ANIMALS AND THE *IMAGO DEI*: AN *ADDENDUM* TO CHRISTIAN ANTHROPOLOGY

NIKOLAOS ASPROULIS

Introductory remarks

Do animals share in the *imago Dei*? Do they experience sentiments, possess freedom or reason? If theology deals with life and death matters (i.e., ontology), then creation itself, in its entirety, should be given proper attention. The current conflict between nature and humans, evident in the increasing environmental crisis, challenges the traditional anthropological doctrine of the Church, which often understands humanity in exceedingly narrow terms as the proper locus for the salvation of the world. Indeed, humans plays a significant role in the divine plan. But what about animals? What is their position in this plan? Do they have a future in the kingdom? Do they contribute somehow to the salvation of the entire cosmos, to the so-called *theosis*? If the answer to these questions is positive, a more inclusive and embedded understanding of humans is then desperately needed, so as to reverse the monolithic approaches that downgrade non-human creatures, thus going beyond the still predominant human exceptionalism. To do so one should focus on the central aspect of theological anthropology, namely the *imago Dei*. In doing so one does not abandon the traditional doctrine of the Church. Rather, certain elements of the *imago Dei* tradition can be constructively revisited and redefined in the light of previous, unforeseen challenges.

After critically overviewing the *status quo* of the current anthropological discussion, the present chapter builds on particular, often neglected, aspects of theological anthropology (i.e., the *communion*/relational aspect) thereby seeking to provide an inclusive re-definition of the *imago Dei* which seriously considers the animal world as its ontological component and not just a moral commandment. Such a view intends to go beyond any break, considered as normative, between humans and nature.

Descartes *vs.* Derrida

It was 1965 when Lynn White Jr. published an article[1] that was destined to play a catalytic role in increasing the awareness among theologians of environmental problems and the role humans can play in this regard. In searching for the historical roots of the ecological problem, White accuses Western culture and Christianity of being responsible for the modern ecological crisis. This bold statement did not come out of the blue, to the extent that a certain trajectory of thought where humans have been ranked first in the ladder of ontological value and morality, rooted in ancient and medieval thought, appears to be responsible for the present situation. This development does not refer only to Western culture but concerns also Eastern Orthodoxy despite certain nuances and qualifications.

Looking through the long history of Christian theology it is not difficult for one to point to a strong rationalistic perception of the *imago Dei*, which ascribes ontological priority to reason/intellect over body/matter, a mentality which undervalued the materiality of creation and gradually contributed to a clear anti-ecological orientation. This understanding was evident in both Western and Eastern theology. For instance, Origen (184-253), through Evagrius of Pontus (345-399),[2] the monastic tradition and the *Philokalia* spirituality (a collection of texts written between the fourth and the fifteenth centuries by spiritual masters of the Orthodox Christian tradition) led to a certain dichotomy between body and soul, a devaluation of the material aspect of the human and, by extension of creation in its entirety, in favor of the "immortality of the soul" and the participation in the spiritual world. Moreover, this tradition understood the human mind as the very link between God and creation, an attitude that undervalued the dignity of the material world. A similar tendency also appeared in the West, where Augustine perceived "the Kingdom of God [as] a place where only human souls would exist."[3] A certain metaphysic has been developed during subsequent times, especially within Western Christianity (scholastic theology), where reason and intellect were considered as the proper, perhaps

---

[1] Lynn T. White, Jr., "The Historical Roots of Our Ecologic Crisis," *Science* 155, no. 3767 (March 10, 1967): 1203–7.
[2] Cf. for details, John Zizioulas, *Communion & Otherness. Further Studies in Personhood and the Church* (London/NY: T&T Clark, 2006), 21.
[3] J. Chryssavgis-N. Asproulis (eds.), *Priests of Creation: Zizioulas on Discerning an Ecological Ethos*, (London/NY: T&T Clark, 2021), 34.

the only means, and most important characteristic of the *imago Dei* by which humans can reflect the divine or participate in God's mind, while at the same time, can regulate its relationship with the entire creaturely (considered as irrational and "brute animals"[4]) world as the first being in the chain of Beings.

This development resulted in a human-centered culture where the human is considered as the center of the world, with an ontological privilege to possess the world and utilize it according to its own desires. In this vein, Descartes's "cogito ergo sum" ("I think, therefore I am")[5] has been a natural consequence, whereby nature and creation were perceived as simply a means towards an individualist goal, the unquenchable pleasure (eudemonism) of humans, leading to the present scientific boost and technological revolution. A whole chain of modern Western philosophers from Immanuel Kant (1724-1804) to Emmanuel Levinas (1906-1995) and beyond appear to have adopted this trajectory where a predominant focus on human reason or morality (based on "pure reason") comes first sometimes in opposition or despite any real concern for the rest of the world. This development of the human independently from the body and senses as well as in opposition to its natural environment is best reflected in the well-known statement by René Descartes (1596-1650). In his *Discours de la Méthode*, he argues that: "we can reach knowledge that would be very useful in life and we could find a practical method, whereby the force and energies inherent in fire, water, air, the stars, celestial and all other bodies that surround us might be used in the same manner in all suitable applications, and so we may become masters and possessors of nature [maîtres et possesseurs de la nature]"[6]. In this perception of the non-human reality, no place for animals (one could hardly find a place for humans too!) has been allocated, since they do not meet the rational requirements and cognitive capacities of humans.

It was the French philosopher Jacques Derrida (1930-2004), who has been among the first thinkers in modern times, and who in the broader context of the post-structuralism current, attempted to challenge this human-

---

[4] Joyce Salisbury, "Do Animals Go to Heaven? Medieval Philosophers Contemplate Heavenly Human Exceptionalism," *Athens Journal of Humanities & Arts* - Volume 1, Issue 1, 79-86, here at 80.

[5] L. Newman, "Cogito Ergo Sum," in L. Nolan (ed.), *The Cambridge Descartes Lexicon* (Cambridge: Cambridge University Press, 2015), 128-135 doi:10.1017/CBO9780511894695.056.

[6] René Descartes, *Discours de la méthode*, texte établi par Victor Cousin, tome I, sixième partie (Levrault, 1824). Cf. Zizioulas, "Humanity and Nature," in Chryssavgis-Asproulis, *Priests of Creation*, 65, 190.

centered Western culture. In his seminal *The Animal That Therefore I Am*,[7] Derrida attempts to reverse the assumed order between humans and animals (namely the priority of humans over animals), to which we have been accustomed throughout the centuries. By its very title, Derrida's book sought to oppose Descartes' excessive rationalism, by re-lecturing our deep convictions about the human and its place within the world as well as its relationship to animals and the rest of the non-human creation. In contrast to the *Genesis*' narrative (1:1-2:25) where the human has been created last in the chain of the creaturely beings, Derrida asserts that the "man is in both senses of the word after the animal. He follows after the animal. He follows him. This 'after' which determines a sequence, a consequence, or a persecution, is not in time, nor is it temporal: it is the very genesis of time."[8] Derrida reacts against the dominant interpretation of the biblical narrative of Adam as a type of master and possessor who has been endowed by God with reason, speech, and the capacity to name all the non-human creatures, by boldly alluding to the responsibility of this Judeo-Christian tradition (echoing from a different perspective, Lynne White) for the degradation of the rest of the world and the abuse of animals. As one of his modern interpreters has argued, Derrida felt that, "this (the traditional understanding of the *Genesis* narrative) is the beginning of a powerful discourse of human priority and sovereignty…"[9] Without diminishing the responsibility of the subsequent Judeo-Christian tradition in the way it received the biblical account, one should bear in mind, that a certain abuse of animals, in terms of being used as means of sacrifice in religious rituals, has been considered common place in almost all the ancient religious traditions.[10] So the problem to which Derrida points, is real, not a peripheral one, a problem which calls for a rethinking of our human identity.

---

[7] Trans. By D. Wills, New York: Fordham University Press, 2008.

[8] Derrida, *The Animal that therefore I am*, 17.

[9] Glen Mazis, "Animals before Me, with Whom I Live, by Whom I Am Addressed: Writing After Derrida," in Stephen D. Moore (ed.), *Divinanimality: Animal Theory, Creaturely Theology*, (New York: Fordham University Press, 2014), 17-35.

[10] Similar ideas can be found in early Christian writers. For instance, according to Origen the "slaughter and taming of animals" is considered as a sign of the human superiority over animals. (See Origen, *Contra Celsum*, 4. 76-78, as cited by Eric D. Meyer "On Making Fleshly Difference: Humanity and Animality in Gregory of Nyssa," *Relegere: Studies in Religion and Reception*, 7, nos. 1-2, (2018), 39-58, here at 49, n. 30).

Substantialist *vs.* personalist understanding
of the *imago Dei*

The place of animals in our worldview and actual world clearly relates to the fundamental (as well as diachronic) question "Who am I"? This was an existential question which emerged quite early (sufficient here to recall the ancient "Know thyself" dictum that runs throughout the subsequent history of philosophy until our present time) as the backbone of anthropological reflection to which varied answers were given. As I have already noted and, by virtue of the strong influence of Platonism on the development of the early Christian theology, the human has been identified with the soul in opposition to the materiality of its body, a reception which clearly accounted for the human's further dissociation from nature. This idea was further supported by Augustine's (354-430) removal of history from the ontological plane and its attribution to the psychological, which contributed further to the dissociation of history from nature, the former being related only to humans and the latter to non-human creatures.[11]

As discussed above, a certain view of the human identity then prevailed in the Middle Ages where the *imago Dei* has been mainly conceived of in terms of reason and intellectual superiority over animals. It was with Boethius (477-524) (cf. his famous definition of a person as an "individual substance of a rational nature")[12] but also with Augustine, that the human has been endowed with thought and consciousness[13] of him-self and the others, becoming thus an autonomous self, finally detached from the world *Ego,* who thinks, decides, and acts irrespectively, and without accountability to either God or the rest of the world. This culminated in a view, which defines the human from the point of view of its substance or natural qualities, echoing more or less the "τοδε τι"[14] of Aristotle, and differentiates it from the non-human creatures perceived as not bearing this sort of capacity. This definition takes for granted that a human is a self-sufficient and closed identity that does not need to relate to its surrounding setting in order to exist.

This *substantialist* view, which resulted from the encounter of the early Church with Greek thought and was determined by the special attention

---

[11] I draw this insight from John D. Zizioulas, *Being as Communion. Studies in Personhood and the Church* (Crestwood, NY: St. Vladimir's Seminary Press, 1985), 95, n. 81.

[12] Cf. "naturae rationabilis individua substantia" (*Contra Eutych et Nest* 3, PL 64, 1343C).

[13] Zizioulas, *Communion & Otherness*, 1.

[14] *Categoriae* 3b. 10. Literally means an entity in itself.

given to nature, was considerably developed, as we noted, during the Middle Ages. It had become clear by then that a human can be understood through the lens of its own intellectual, or rather natural capacities as if it were an "objectified substance"[15] characterized by certain and measurable qualities that distinguished it from the rest of the creatures. This view, which accounted for a bold human exceptionalism, has been radically challenged during recent times, with the Copernican revolution as well as the rise of Charles Darwin's (1809-1882) theory of evolution, the discovery of the unconscious by Sigmund Freud (1856-1939), but also with the development of transhumanism[16], and the rapid technological evolution of our time. All these developments have not only pointed to the catastrophic role humans can play in the explosion of the ecological crisis, but also helped theologians among others to realize that a discussion of the human identity and its role within creation from the point of view of its substance, is not only one-sided but also dangerous to the extent that it ignores the ontological link between the human being and the whole creaturely world, focusing on capacities or properties that can be found in different degrees in all creatures. As it has been aptly put by Darwin, a provocative figure who still causes inconvenience to theologians from all the major traditions, any difference between humans and creatures, should be considered "certainly one of degree, not of kind."[17]

But is it the only way to approach *imago Dei*? Can human nature, viewed from the standpoint of reason, intellect, or morality, be considered as the locus of the abysmal chasm between humans and animals? Can we really argue that we have privilege, and a role of superiority to play simply based on our rationality? The ecological crisis we all face today with the catastrophic consequences for the biodiversity and very existence of the planet, as well as the common abuse of animals, ranging from the Spanish bullfights to our pet culture or the abuse of certain animals in medical experiments, makes it clear that something is wrong with this way of thinking. Is there any alternative view to propose then?

Based on a constructive, albeit often disputable interpretation of the Greek patristic tradition, John Zizioulas (1931, now Metropolitan of Pergamon), a prolific writer, and eminent spokesman of contemporary Orthodoxy, attempts to counter-argue for a different view which can be considered as a possible way out for our discussion. Let us turn to Zizioulas'

---

[15] Zizioulas, *Communion & Otherness*, 249.
[16] Max More and Natasha Vita-More (eds.), *The Transhumanist Reader: Classical and Contemporary Essays on the Science, Technology, and Philosophy of the Human Future* (Willey-Blackwell, 2013).
[17] *The Descent of Man*, vol. 1 (1898), 193, as cited in Zizioulas, *Communion & Otherness*, 211-12.

reading of the history of theology that focuses on the relevance of certain Greek Fathers in particular, beyond those noted already, so as to highlight certain aspects of this *personalistic* view of the human that could count as the antidote to human exceptionalism.

Since its beginning, the early Church has strived to offer the good news of salvation to the entire world. Being initially closely rooted in Judaism, Christianity struggled to overcome any natural, national, or other local constraints and links, aiming chiefly at witnessing a new mode of being, accounting for the divine-human communion beyond any counter tendencies. The famous parable of the "Good Samaritan" (*Luke* 10:25-37) can be considered as a very good and practical description - in the context especially of the Judeo-Christian culture - of this new way of being, realized in history by Christ himself, while St. Paul, in his letter to *Galatians* (3:28), summarized in brief the content of this new human being identity: "There is neither Jew nor Gentile, neither slave nor free, nor is there male and female, for you are all one in Christ Jesus." This quite challenging perception of the human identity has been further developed and conceptualized in various forms in the subsequent early Christian tradition. For instance, in the *Letter to Diognetus* (2 c.) one finds a more or less anarchist Christian understanding of the human identity, in the sense that it refers to the "paradoxical place of Christians in the world, that is the tension between our citizenship in heaven and the demands of our earthly homeland,"[18] in other words the tension between history and eschata.

This gradually evolving alternative way of being (in clear opposition to a more Platonic or Aristotelian perspective noted above), has been clearly reflected in the very life of the early Church especially in its liturgical life in general and in the Divine Eucharist in particular. The Eucharist was not primarily considered as one among many important sacraments or services of the Church, but as a *synaxis*, a gathering where any sort of exclusion based on the various natural, biological, cultural, and ethnical ties was totally overcome. By virtue of this ecclesial experience of the early Fathers, the Church was primarily considered, not as a new religious institution ready to replace the old ones, but as a new "mode of existence," as a "way of being,"[19] existentially and deeply bound with the overall reality, namely God, humans, and the surrounding creation in its entirety. A fundamental biblical doctrine, to which the Church had to stick, was the creation of the human in the "image of God." Having been created in the image of God,

---

[18] Cf. a very good relative analysis in Doru Costache, "Christianity and the World in the Letter to Diognetus: Inferences for Contemporary Ecclesial Experience," *Phronema* 27:1 (2012), 29-50.

[19] Zizioulas, *Being as Communion*, intro.

one was already bound with God's very way of being by virtue of one's belonging to the Church community. So, the crucial question for the early Christians, who strove to conceptualize their own experience and understanding of God as revealed in Christ and its implications for the salvation of the cosmos, was now related to the way God existed.

By virtue of and, through their Eucharistic experience, where a spirit of mutuality, interdependence, solidarity, evolving love, and personal relationship, were evidenced along with a "sacred materialism"[20], the very being of God was fully manifested and experienced as the *relational* being *par excellence*. This experience led to the early Greek Fathers working out a different perception and transformation of the Greek monistic ontology, by introducing *communion* to the very core of being, namely to the very heart of ontology, previously unthinkable in antiquity. A new ontological view was now *ante portas*, where communion is considered as the heart of a new life inaugurated in the Trinitarian interplay and realized by Christ in history.

This "ontological revolution" (as it has been called by Zizioulas)[21] had been worked out by St. Athanasius, and especially the Cappadocian Fathers who succeeded in gradually conceptualizing the Christian doctrine of God. In this vein the substance of God is now devoid of any ontological content apart from communion. By attributing ontological content to communion, the early Church Fathers did not wish to create a new impersonal or horizontal order of being, in the place of the classic substance ontology. On the contrary, by coupling it with the introduction of the concept of *cause* in the very being of God, that is the person of the Father, they rendered it impossible for communion to exist by itself. It was clearly denoted that it was personal otherness, namely personhood that causes being to be. What then were the crucial consequences of this careful re-reading on the part of the Church Fathers of the classic monistic substance ontology?

In the context of this new perception, communion now becomes an ontological concept, inconceivable by itself, while personhood (which was finally identified with the classic patristic concept of *hypostasis*) is the source of communion. In other words, although personhood cannot exist without communion, it seems that personhood preserves a sort of logical

---

[20] Cf. John Meyendorff, *A Study of Gregory Palamas*, trans. by George Lawrence (New York: Faith Press, [2]1974), 156, in which it is stressed that for Gregory Palamas "the elements of *Christian materialism* which, instead of wishing to suppress matter which has revolted against the spirit through the effect of sin, gives it the place the creator assigned to it, and discovers the way which Christ opened for it by transfiguring it and by deifying it in his own body."

[21] For the narrative of this development see Zizioulas, *Being as Communion*, Ch. 1.

priority in view of communion. The consequences of this nuanced development in the early patristic thought have paramount importance for various aspects of the life, and the theology of the Church, such as for ecclesiology, anthropology, Trinitarian theology, and so on, since, as it has been previously noted, a close linkage exists between God, ecclesial being and the entire world. What, however, are the fundamental aspects of this vision of the human in the context of theological anthropology in general and, the role of animals in it in particular?

Personhood is otherness in communion and *vice versa*: from a Christian perspective personhood emerges through communion that is in relationship. Apart from communion, no person, either divine or human, exists by itself, as a self-sufficient and self-defined close identity. Without downplaying its particular integrity, each person is inconceivable without communion. At the same time however, communion does not obscure personal otherness and particularity, insofar as communion does not exist by itself but for the sake of the persons that commune with each other. A Christian theological ontology that seriously takes into account both personal otherness and communion, does not seek to replace the Heideggerian ontological horizon or the Buberian I-Thou relationship with a new one, but to re-organize in depth the very structure of this horizon and relationship by introducing a cause, that is personal otherness at the heart of any relational ontology. Here, however, one needs to be extremely cautious – especially in view of the topic of our discussion - to avoid a reduction of this otherness only to humans, excluding in this way the communion with non-human creatures. Insofar as communion now becomes an integral part of ontology, it means that a special focus should also be given to communion so as to embrace the whole range of creatures, not limited only to humans. Furthermore, another danger also emerges here by understanding personhood in fully abstract terms, leading thus to its dissociation from nature. What is required now is not to throw away nature itself but to open its ontology so as to include every single creature in mutual and reciprocal communion. By doing so, human personhood is not reduced to a pure and ecstatic identity as has been often misunderstood, which attempts to cancel or exit the historical and natural condition in favor of another metaphysical construction; on the contrary it can be considered as the agent of communion, which opens nature to embrace all the non-human creatures with which it shares the same animal and creaturely dimension.

Special attention should also be given to another exceptional dimension of personhood, that of freedom, often understood as the core aspect of the *imago Dei* from an ontological point of view. When the discussion comes to the definition of the human, one cannot avoid the question of freedom.

Can animals be considered as free agents? Can they go against their own nature? Can we still speak of humans if we get rid of their freedom? These are crucial questions that cannot be bypassed by those who struggle to come to terms with the animal suffering in view of the *imago Dei*. A point of great importance here relates to the dialectic between personhood and nature. If one adopts a pure existentialist perception, which gives priority to personhood or rather to existence over substance, by which it is meant to go beyond nature, one needs to explain how animals and the entire non-human world fit into this scheme. But this is not the only response to the above dialectic. When the human strives for freedom, it does not mean that it must go against its nature or get rid of it altogether; on the contrary, in an all-encompassing view of nature, freedom acquires a new dimension, which accounts for the opening of human nature to embrace the entire animalhood, to which it has been linked from the very first divine *fiat*. If that is the case, no divide between personhood and nature exists, but a free and mutual coexistence where the human personhood communes its nature to the non-human nature, so creation as a whole is saved.

Returning now to the importance of communion, although a real danger exists where communion itself could lead to a new slavery in this case of an unfree, closed, and endless communion between the persons or to the loss of otherness between the varied creatures, where what really matters is a flat communion, and not the persons or creatures in communion, the introduction of the concept of cause in ontology, seeks to save the free character of communion. This means, that communion is a voluntary free act and not something inescapable and deterministic. In this sense personhood means freedom of being other, of simply being oneself. This personal view of freedom means that each person is unique, not reducible to any sort of natural classification. In this sense, freedom does not mean freedom *from* (like a detachment) but *for the* other, an unconditional move towards the other, exemplified as love and care for the other, the creation either human or non-human in its entirety. Moreover, while freedom is a *sine qua non conditio* of being personhood - of being other, at the same time, this otherness - this freedom, is inconceivable apart from love, namely communion. Hence, following the Chalcedonian logic, love, and freedom constitute the two fundamental components of the human identity, which has been fully realized in Christ.

The threat to leave aside the non-human creatures arises again, as is evident in the cruelties resulting from the human abuse. As was noted before, if freedom is - and unquestionably it is - the identification mark of the *imago Dei* in human, then animals have no place in heaven, since they lack the capacity to go against their nature. A careful study, however, of the above shows that freedom, although a human capacity *par excellence,* cannot be regarded outside of the context of communion that is *love.* Only in communion that is in love, does freedom go beyond the moral directives between good and evil. Only in communion is freedom thought of as freedom for the other, in this case for all creation, aiming to offer creation to God and not just to humanize[22] it. Having said this, communion still preserves its central place within ontology, on which the close interdependence of all the creatures of God, humans and non-humans alike being worthy of the same love by God, is based.

And so the argument goes thus: in the case of where an animal,[23] Derrida's cat for instance, or an abused dog, is cut off from any other animal of its own species or from a human as its owner, so as to meet the necessary requirements of being included in this understanding of the *imago Dei,* to the extent that this animal shares in the same animality, that is the same creaturely nature with humanity as well as being found in a constant and unbreakable relationship with its Creator, God the Father, it can be clearly considered as belonging to this communal/relational re-definition of the image. In this vein no theological anthropology can be thought of as complete without taking into account as an integral part of the image of God, all the creatures with which the human must relate.

In this light, personhood should be seen as simultaneously a hypostatic and ecstatic identity; Without being ecstatic, that is inherently moving towards the other (either humans, animals, or God), personhood cannot be hypostatic too. Being hypostatic, personhood is regarded simultaneously as a loving entity, open to the other. As John Zizioulas quite characteristically, put it by re-phrasing the famous saying, "I love, therefore I am"[24]: to "I am loved, therefore I am," by which he wishes to highlight the unique contribution of Christian theology to anthropology, by existentially, that is soteriologically and ontologically, recapturing the meaning of the concept of personhood, where the other (in communion) has priority over the self. Can this new perspective be understood as a direct response to Derrida's assertion *The Animal, that therefore I am*? I am afraid the basic problem with Derrida's understanding is that albeit he is right in criticizing certain developments in Christian theology and Western philosophy, which one

---

[22] One should allude here to Derrida's cat arguing that humans (14) "made of the animal a theorem, something seen and not seeing", transformed it into something that has been denied even the right to see, or speak, to its "master".

[23] I draw here on Zizioulas' *Communion & Otherness,* 89, 208n.

[24] Echoing here Sophrony Sakharov, as described in the book by Nicholas Sakharov, *I love therefore I am: The theological legacy of Archimandrite Sophrony* (Crestwood, NY: St. Vladimir's Seminary Press, 2002).

way or another prioritize the human cognitive capacities over the animal world, the hidden danger is to undervalue the moral responsibility that the human has for the deconstruction of the creation of God. Thus, the biblical account of the creation of Adam and Eve should be seen from the angle of this communion ontology, which stresses the ontological interdependence of all creatures in the light of God's love and providence, despite the (ontological?) hierarchy that certainly exists among them. As Zizioulas put it on another occasion,[25] hierarchy does not necessarily lead to a vertical classification of beings which accounts for their inequality or degradation. On the contrary, the idea lying behind hierarchy is the "specificity of relationship," namely the establishment of (personal) otherness among creatures, as the very ground for their deep ontological dependence. The *imago Dei* is then considered as the means through which communion is extended to all creation with the result of establishing an unbreakable ontological bond between humans and animals that cannot be reduced to mere rational (or even moral) capacities, also shared to some degree by non-human creatures. This extension by no means should be considered as an outcome of natural fluidity, but as an internal opening of the *imago* through the visitation of the Spirit of God, who supervises and sanctifies the sustainability of the creation.

In this line personhood should not be understood as a mere moral accomplishment on the part of humanity. Without denouncing the moral commitments, duties or obligations of humans, personhood is primarily linked not only with the ontology of humanity, but also or even more essentially with the core aspect of this ontology, that is the animality of all existent beings, in other words with the creaturely nature of everything being created by God. Thus, for one to open oneself to the other, to love the other "as yourself" does not mean to just follow a rational, moral, or other obligation, but in the light of the present analysis, to constitute one's own being as such, as communion. In order to constitute one's own self as communion in love and *vice versa*, a necessary sacrificial ethos is necessary, in view of the Christ's Cross, where the "priority of the Other over the self reaches its climax."[26] An orientation then of self-emptying, a *kenosis*, is clearly presupposed, which ascribes repentance, *metanoia*, and unlimited forgiveness to the very heart of the Christian existence, as the very base that prevents any capacity beyond communion to affect the ontology of this cosmos. Communion is then understood not as an irrational move towards the other, but as a deeper, I would dare to say, existential (accounting for

[25] Zizioulas, *Being as Communion*, 223.
[26] Zizioulas, *Communion & Otherness*, 91.

life and death matters), move of the *imago Dei* to become an *imago mundi*, to recall Moltmann's understanding,[27] a concept that refers to an inclusion of every living creature to the very core of God's creaturely *fiat* towards the human. In the words of an eminent contemporary Orthodox theologian, Metropolitan of Diokleia Kallistos Ware, the human being "is an image or mirror of the whole creation, *imago mundi*, a 'little universe' or microcosm."[28]

Without denouncing the other aspects of this personalist approach to the question "who am I?" like freedom, reason, morality etc., theological anthropology should ascribe priority to communion as that dimension of the *imago* which can by no means be reduced to any self-sufficient, natural quality, but which can realize instead, the ontological affinity between all the existent non-human creatures in an inclusive reception of the *imago Dei*. In my view, such an understanding can clearly extend the limits of communion to include everything that has been created before the human, and which, according to the biblical account, has been placed under its supervision. What is at stake here is not really to reverse the sequence of the *Genesis* narrative of creation as was the case with Derrida in his opposition to mainstream Western theology and philosophy; on the contrary, the real concern of this narrative is to stress not only the evolutionary aspect of creation or the moral accountability of the human to the rest of God's creatures, but significantly, their deep ontological interconnection in terms of communion.

Imago Dei as communion: a proper response to animal suffering

The personalist understanding described above seeks to overcome the fixed dichotomy between the human and the world, between humanity and nature. The present climate crisis we all face, as a result of such a conception of the human who receives creation in terms of superiority, possession, and domination, makes it clear that certain aspects of the mainstream theological anthropology constitute part of the problem and not its solution. By saying this, I do not mean to dismiss altogether the long tradition of the Church. In contrast, by stressing in this chapter the need to reconsider certain aspects of this tradition, I intended to bring to the fore some neglected aspects so as to address the present situation in a way that every living creature really

---

[27] Jürgen Moltmann, *God in Creation: A New Theology of Creation and the Spirit of God. The Gifford Lectures 1984-1985* (San Francisco: Harper & Row, 1985).
[28] Cf. his *The Orthodox Way* (Crestwood, NY: St. Vladimir's Seminary Press, 1979), 49.

matters. The *communal* understanding of the *imago Dei*, in terms of the common ontological (creaturely or animal) ground among all creatures, can be considered as such a neglected aspect. We have been familiarized for many centuries now with a lifestyle that supports an inevitable break between the human and nature, both in terms of practice and theory. If that is true, and in order to address the present climate crisis, a new model of anthropology is required beyond any dated human exceptionalism or problematic anthropomonism, where attention is given to those parts of the *imago* that link the human to the rest of creation (e.g., animality), and not to those parts, which deepen or stress their discontinuity. By redefining the image of God in a more inclusive way as "dinivanimality,"[29] theology can provide an all-embracing anthropology that would account for the particular place and reception of animals not only in our discourse, but also in our practice.

In this vein if one defines the human from the point of view of a personalist ontology, then the human cannot be understood without a clear reference to a You, and an It, that is without a close dependence on the other (either humans, world, or God). This relational/communal understanding of humanity can serve as the background of a new ethos that can be expressed with the following single phrase: Every part of creation matters, or every creature of God matters. If this is the case, the human can be seen through the lens of its priestly role, meaning that one is responsible to offer the whole creation to God so as to survive eternally. This is not just a moral task, but a new way of life that takes seriously into account creation in all its aspects as an ontological component of the *imago Dei*. This was the understanding at least of the Greek Fathers, like Irenaeus (2nd c.), or Gregory Palamas (14th c.) when they argued that *imago Dei* is incomplete, unless the whole creation is recognized as being a constitutive part of it. Palamas especially, in his discussion of the *imago Dei*, asserts that human carries along with it "every kind of creature, as he himself participates in everything, and is also able to participate in the one who lies above everything, in order for the image of God to be completed (ἀπηκριβωμένον ᾖ)."[30] This passage is a clear

---

[29] Cf. Stephen Moore (ed.), *Divinanimality: Animal Theory, Creaturely Theology* (New York: Fordham University Press, 2014). Although a term that causes inconvenience to a Christian ear that has been familiarized with traditional terminology, the concept itself accounts for the here proposed, expanded version of the *imago Dei*.

[30] Gregory Palamas, *Against Akindynos* 7,11,36.25-8, ed. Pan. Chrystou, vol. 3 (Thessaloniki, 1970), 488: "ἄγελλος ὡς ἀληθῶς ἄλλος ἐπὶ τῆς γῆς Θεοῦ γεγονὼς καὶ δι' ἑαυτοῦ πᾶν εἶδος κτίσεως αὐτῷ προσαγαγών, ἐπεὶ καὶ αὐτὸς ἐν μετοχῇ τῶν

indication of the *imago mundi* idea by which modern theologians attempt to re-define the human identity in light of the urgent climate crisis. If the image of God in humans cannot fully manifest without taking into account the rest of the creatures, this clearly means that animals do share in the salvation of the whole of creation, and that they do go to heaven. After all this, is the goal of the divine plan as it was finally realized through the paschal mystery, the salvation of the entire world, not only of humans. Otherwise, the non-human creation would have been created in vain.[31]

In this light a recent study by Christina Nellist on *Eastern Orthodox Christianity and Animal Suffering*[32] cannot but be received as a much welcome surprise. It is the first scholarly book on this topic from an Orthodox point of view, a fine contribution to animal studies[33], and a book that clearly results from the increasing concern of the Orthodox on ecological matters. Indeed, while such a topic has been for a long time now debated in secular and other Christian contexts, the Orthodox again face difficulty in offering a theological response. This reluctance has not come out of the blue but resulted from certain shortcomings of the historical development of Orthodox theology, as has been noted in previous parts of this study. Since the very beginning, Nellist's basic concern is to highlight the soteriological consequences for those abusing animals in every respect. By doing so, she does not fail to strongly criticize aspects of the Orthodox tradition that do not take seriously into account the suffering of animals, pointing to a "gap," or "lack of clarity," or "ambiguity" between theory and practice. If God is the source of all that is good and who is always in a compassionate, merciful, and loving relationship with "all things," then by no means, could such a loving God create any of the creatures in order for the tobacco industry met with major newspaper editors in 1954 to object to scientific findings that smoking was harmful to health

---

πάντων καὶ τοῦ ὑπὲρ τὰ πάντα δὲ μεταλαγχάνειν ἦν, ἵνα καὶ τὸ τῆς εἰκόνος ἀπηκριβωμένον ᾖ." I draw here on Nicholas Loudovikos, "Palamas' Understanding of Participation as an Analogy of Dialogical Syn-energy," in C. Athanasopoulos and C. Schneider (eds.), *Divine Essence and Divine Energies. Ecumenical Reflections on the Presence of God in Eastern Orthodoxy* (Cambridge: James Clarke & Co, 2013), 122-48, here at 132, for this important passage.

[31] Cf. for instance: "Man and beast thou savest, O Lord" (*Psalm* 36:6b), and the Pauline premises that the whole earth will be saved, and Christ would "unite all things in Him, things in heaven and things on earth" (*Ephesians* 1:9-10). Cf. Salisbury, "Do Animals Go to Heaven?"

[32] Cambridge Scholars Publishing, 2020.

[33] Cf. Matthew Calarco, *Thinking through Animals: Identity, Difference, Indistinction* (Stanford University Press, 2015).

(Oreskes and Conway 2011, 16). them to suffer. This understanding points to the sacred character of the creation in general and, creatures in particular, as recipients of God's radiation of love. It also points to the latent clear *ontological interconnection*, often forgotten during the (ab-)use of those little creatures (not to mention human beings as well).

It is uncontested that the goal of Christian life is deification, *theosis*, in other words our adoption by God the Father in Christ through the Spirit.[34] It is clear then that *theosis* is a gift of God. At the same time, however, *theosis* is a result of the human ascetic struggle in history, a synergy with the grace of God towards the transfiguration, the "sacrifice of our fallen nature with our self-indulgent sinful passions", and an offering of the creation to the hands of the Creator. By saying this one cannot continue to ignore the "rights" of all the creatures of God to be saved. Indeed, in the mainstream currents of Christian tradition humans are favored over the non-human creation. This is due to the rationality and cognitive skills of the former. Undoubtedly such a view led to the irreversible catastrophe of our planet. This does not mean, though, that humanity should be deprived of its central, although compassionate role. What really matters here is to bring to the fore the *communion* element of this interconnection between all creatures, be they humans or non-humans. This is perhaps the only way to overcome all the historical impasses and build an inclusive anthropology, namely a new perception of the *imago Dei*.

Similarly, following major developments in modern science, theological anthropology should also adopt this more inclusive perception of the human since any difference among the creatures of God is considered to be one of degree not of kind. In this respect, Zizioulas is one of the modern Orthodox theologians who boldly insists on this deeper interconnection between humans and animals when he asserts that "attempts to locate human identity in rationality have failed to survive the criticism of Darwin, who showed that rationality can be found also in the animals. Equally, biology fails to point out an element in the human body that does not ultimately connect it with the animals."[35] This latent proximity however, between humans and non-human creatures, should not be overestimated to the point of reducing the former's responsibility for the survival of the planet. Although indisputable that the *imago Dei* has been endowed to humanity alone, one, following the above analysis, where communion gains an ontological priority over any substantialist perception of humanity, should also include

---

[34] For this cf., my essay: "Eucharistic Personhood: Deification in Orthodox Tradition," in Jared Ortiz (ed.), *With All the Fullness of God: Deification in Christian Traditions* (Lexington Press, 2021).

[35] Zizioulas, Communion & Otherness, 39.

all the creatures due to their deep ontological connection, as well as to their common animalhood. In other words, and based on this encompassing interpretation of the image, could one speak here of the animals as part of the *imago Dei*? In view of the present analysis, I think this is possible since otherwise, this image cannot be complete; this means that the salvation of the whole creation will be realized in the eschata if nothing is left behind. This is the goal of the very divine plan. Although Christ himself became human not an angel or any other creature, and assumed human nature to save the world, this should not be understood in terms of human exceptionalism. On the contrary, it should be seen through the lens of an emphasis on the creaturely, animal character of this assumed nature. Such a move would both affirm the traditional doctrine of the Incarnation but also address current ecological challenges. Such a conception of the *imago Dei* can be further supported by the Maximian *Logos-logoi* theory, which means to establish a reciprocal and mutual dialogue among the *logoi* of creation, while at the same time it further substantiates the ontological link both between the creatures (human or non-human alike) but also with the Logos the Creator.

The time has come for Christian theologians to form a sustainable moral theory. By questioning the current animal food production system and the animal testing model, Nellist in her aforementioned book, highlights the view which perceives animals as "resources, units of production or disposable life, rather than created beings with individual needs."[36] This is something telling, that points to the wrong path our worldview and lifestyle have taken. At the same time, it clearly appeals to our tradition, which for centuries provides concrete holy examples of another way of life that respects and cares about all the creatures in view of the coming Kingdom of God and the salvific premises of our faith.[37]

By way of conclusion

It is commonplace to consider Eastern Orthodoxy as a deeply traditional Church which closely follows and praises its glorious past, without any desire to critically receive it or translate it into modern language or even bring it into dialogue with current problems. Despite certain voices throughout history which sought to find the deeper meaning of this tradition and interpret it to address the existential needs of modernity or post-

---

[36] Nellist, *Eastern Orthodox Christianity and Animal Suffering*, 244.
[37] Chryssavgis-Asproulis, *Priests of Creation*, 197-202; Nellist *Eastern Orthodox Christianity*.

modernity, for one to seek a re-lecturing of its own premises and fixed convictions is always a painful enterprise. By saying this, I do not argue that this modest contribution has been triggered by such an impressive goal. It is just a limited endeavor of its author to reflect on neglected aspects of our theological deposit (a mixture of ancient with modern insights) looking for an anthropological perspective that makes sense in our rapidly changing world. Can we still define the human being in terms of reason, morality or even freedom against the results provided by modern science about the status of the non-human creatures, the animals? Can we continue to treat the rest of creation as an irrational or even inferior part of God's plan to be used for the endless satisfaction of human needs? I think that the present ecological crisis has convinced us that such a model of life cannot be sustainable anymore. In order to reverse this unpleasant condition, a new understanding of the human is required that will take into account as a *sine qua non conditio* the whole range of non-human creatures, the animals, so as to save not only biodiversity, a necessary aspect of our very life, but the planet itself, which groans in suffering (*Rom.* 8:2). If the *imago Dei* means *capax infiniti*, then only as *imago mundi*, that is a "corporate animality,"[38] can humans contribute to the divine plan for the salvation of the world, of the entire world and not only humans.

---

[38] To paraphrase the well-known concept "corporate personality" initially used by biblical scholars to describe Adam as the exemplar of the whole of humanity or in ecclesiology to express the close relationship between Christ and His Church. Cf. for instance: H. Wheeler Robinson, *The Hebrew Conception of Corporate Personality*, 1936), and A.R. Johnson, *The One and the Many in the Israelite Conception of God*, 1942), J. de Fraine, *Adam et son lignage: Etudes sur la 'personnalile corporative' dans la Bible*, 1959.

CHAPTER THREE

ECOLOGICAL HERMENEUTICS AND NATIVE AMERICAN ETHICS

SIDNEY BLANKENSHIP

We are in the midst of a crisis that is now, I hope, well understood. Global warming, climate change, the devastating loss of biodiversity, are the greatest threats that humanity has ever faced, and one largely of our own creation.
—Prince Charles, 2020, in a speech before the World Economic Forum

"Ecological Hermeneutics"[1] has made a significant contribution over the last two decades in understanding the indigenous origins of many ancient Biblical concepts. Primary features of the natural environment and its creatures are often appropriated for theological reference and definitions of God as Creator and sustainer of a moral universe. Their redaction in the service of religious identity often obscures the foundational ethical and integrated sensitivities which are innate, often didactic in themselves or integral to prior traditions. Both the climate crisis and the abandonment of personal human stewardship in caring for and communing with nature can be linked to structured ideas and anthropocentric concepts about God. This chapter looks at such anterior occurrences and the "natural theology" within the linguistic framework of Biblical texts as it pertains to Native American ethical awareness. There is an urgency to respond, individually and collectively, to the global health pandemic, climate change, human population pressures, species extinction, and environmental degradation. Education is paramount in exposing the need for positive democratic change. Our citizen voice and vote should direct this response. Examples of legal and political concern for certain current issues in the US will be examined toward that end.

---

1. Norman C. Habel and Peter Trudinger, (eds.) *Exploring Ecological Hermeneutics* (Atlanta, GA: Society of Biblical Literature, 2008).

Ecological Concerns in Biblical Texts and Native Cultures

Environmental science often lacks the spiritual dimension that corresponds to its frames of reference for natural phenomena. Historic indigenous wisdom is more immediate in that respect and its basic concerns relied on integrated perceptual relationships. The affirmation of a native spiritual ethic connects with ecological hermeneutics at their source in view of ancient Biblical texts, often in terms of myth and metaphor. It challenges the internal deficiency of evolved traditions that have failed to keep faith with the natural world as a habitation of divine immanence. The rational juristic approach to environmental (and animal) problems in modern society occurs among so many other perceived human priorities that it rarely, if ever, rises to the imperative that it requires. Piecemeal solutions and ad hoc compromises never quite satisfy a collective conscience that includes all living creatures.

Such concerns reveal that vigilance among elected leaders is of crucial concern. The structural capability of government has to be examined and exercised in favor of indigenous animals above those that are exploited for mass consumerism. Human equity and knowledgeable adaptability are key factors in gaining support for federal and international laws that protect and defend species whose existence is endangered by thoughtless, sometimes malevolent, human activity. A foundational right-to-life for endanger species will require a hedge against future habitat disruptions due to climate change. Some NGOs are already planning proactively for projected contingencies, e.g. the Nature Conservancy's Cumberland Forest Initiative in the central Appalachian Mountains of the eastern US. Wildfires, floods, droughts, and hurricanes already bear witness to these looming difficulties, and the basic concerns of all living creatures must be upheld as a sacred trust of humanity.

Outdated economic and corporate activity cannot take precedence. More money is not an ultimate solution to injustice. The future world needs to have a sense of peace and harmony that rests on other factors that satisfy a higher purpose, which is the well-being of the earth itself with all its inhabitants and the understanding of our place in the cosmos. Animals were not intended to suffer and die in scientific experiments or in massive numbers for slaughter to satiate the lust for animal flesh or fashion. Oceans are losing species and filling up with plastics and trash. Fossil fuels have become a liability. Renewable energy is available; but the need is to use less in any case. The natural world and its creatures are a living treasure of relationships that require humanity's "awakening to wisdom" (*Woksape Wokikta* in the admonition of the Oglala Lakota College on the Pine Ridge

Indian Reservation in South Dakota): a renewal of respect for the earth and its processes purified of pollution and a realized perception of the Creator Spirit (*Wakhan Thanka*)[2] in its holy power and peace-making relationships.

The unique ethical question that faces the world today, that of human-induced climate change affecting the global environment, has no comparable precedent in religious history. The Biblical example of divine judgement in the Flood of Noah may be cited and the devastation of war, famine, and disease are based on ethical principles, which seem to defy any cause and effect other than disloyalty to the God of Israel, even as they define the parameters of a universal morality. Eschatological and apocalyptic Biblical texts may reflect a cultural milieu far removed from our present circumstance and scientific understanding, but the relevant ethical warnings (often "telescoped" into a spiritual fulfillment and renewal, e.g. Babylonian captivity, the coming of the Messiah, the book of Revelation)[3] are exponentially magnified in our day. Ironically, the beliefs and records of ancient peoples (our ancestors) and the scientific knowledge of our evolutionary history among other creatures speaks to the profound grace of the Creator that nurtures all life. We must learn from it (from religion, the spirit) and apply this change of mind equitably in politics and society.

James Barr in his *Biblical Faith and Natural Theology* (1994)[4] reviewed the Christian debate in these two categories of concern as they played out in 20th century history and academia. Natural theology he discovered to be an integral element even in revealed religious traditions. "The heavens declare the glory of God and the earth is his handiwork." (Psalm 19:1) The physical features of creation itself and its inhabitants that speak to humanity are a manifestation of His own voice. The problem is that people have "ears to hear, but they do not listen; they have eyes to see, but they don't understand; if they did, they would turn to Me and I would heal them." (Isaiah 6:9-10; cf. Matt. 13:14:16)

Rudolf Otto was surely one of the most perceptive religious minds in the early 20th century. *The Idea of the Holy* was his seminal work in the philosophy of religion, published in English translation (1923) by John W.

---

2. This spelling reflects that of the *New Lakota Dictionary,* 2nd edition (Bloomington, IN: The Lakota Language Consortium, Inc., 2016).

3. John Muddiman, "The Scholarly Achievement of George Caird," in the Mansfield College Magazine 197, (1994-1995): 45. "Telescoped" is the term John used to describe my former tutor's insights into the Biblical eschatology of revelation in history.

4. James Barr, *Biblical Faith and Natural Theology* (Oxford: University Press, 1993).

Harvey.[5] He vindicates the non-rational element in religion (the *numinous*) as essential to understanding the very concept of rationality itself, since it is obvious by a *via negativa* that when exhausting the incomprehensible character and definition of all that exists, something yet remains - and it is "holy." Political systems do not function easily with such terminology. Economic systems certainly have not. Even modern science lacks a defined sense of holistic priorities. In all, however, we have to avail ourselves with corresponding practical legal decisions that reflect this sensitive, sacred awareness, both in nature (especially in animal relations) and in the protection of the earth and its life-sustaining integrity.

The scientific basis for a collective political response and accountability on environmental issues has been well documented for nearly three decades. Al Gore's *Earth in the Balance* [6] and *AGENDA 21: The Earth Summit Strategy to Save Our Planet* [7] edited by Daniel Sitarz (both published in 1993), were scientifically developed in outline and stated with temporal urgency. There is now a significant awareness of these problems in the United Nations and other organizations, including corporate progress on some issues. The Paris Climate Accords are an immediate example. Yet the dire projections and insufficient action (in view of current metrics) has only heightened the witness of their initial fulfillment with destructive hurricanes, increased global temperatures, melting glaciers, massive wildfires, droughts, floods, and the global Covid-19 pandemic. The winter 2021 snow and ice storm in Texas demonstrates just how vulnerable developed infrastructure is to such unforeseen events.

The human (especially political) reaction has included factual denial, intensive scientific monitoring, an ethical and religious introspection, but also societal unrest, provocations, poverty, suffering, and human migration. Planning for the future consequences of these projections is a necessary corollary of efforts to prevent them; but it involves more than a transition to "clean energy." Our positive mental awareness of life in all its forms, and a sensitivity to earth's natural processes, needs ethical redemption from the accumulation of damaging materialism and the unrestrained propagation of our own species.

Is there a way to recover a world view that can help alleviate this distress of circumstance as we deal with these problems? Amidst the changes, a

---

5. Rudolf Otto, *The Idea of the Holy*, trans. John W. Harvey (London: Oxford University Press, 1967).
6. Albert Gore, *Earth in the Balance: Ecology and the Human Spirit* (New York: Penguin Books USA, 1993).
7. Daniel Sitarz, (ed.) *AGENDA 21: The Earth Summit Strategy to Save our Planet* (Boulder, CO: Earthpress, 1993).

simple faith and acceptance of the basic constituents of the natural world is a proper orientation. These have always exercised a hold on ancient religions from their prehistoric legacy, a giving of thanks for the sun, the moon and stars, the earth, and its wondrous array of creatures. We have lost so much more than we have gained already by our grasping for even more through speculative knowledge and self-serving technology. Even the most sophisticated inventions of the present age cannot repair the damage done to our spiritual well-being by the hubris of humanity choosing to create its own world rather than respect the one that it was given. It is in that regard that I shall view "ecological hermeneutics" in the Bible as religiously oriented toward the spiritual views of Native Americans prior to European contact. These are ways of thinking that are still deeply imbedded in that legacy even as it has survived in a context not of its own making. They speak to the common ground of our unique planetary existence.

The concept of morality between humans and animals has evolved in relation to human consciousness. Religion has been a primary source of reference; but its texts and symbolism do reveal a deeper layer of concern for the natural world, the neglect of which has led to the scientific awareness of human-induced climate change as an ethical problem for animal stewardship. "The earth is the Lord's and the fullness thereof." (Psalm 24:1; cf. 50:10-12 et al.) This does not entitle man, "made in the image of God," to exploit the planet or abandon that responsibility. As Chief Seattle (1786-1866) said, "The earth does not belong to us. We belong to the earth." The "image of God" phrase from Genesis 1:27 may be ecologically suspect in its own right, in view of a document found in the Nag Hammadi Coptic library entitled "On the Origin of the World"[8] suggesting that the *Elohim* who modeled the first humans were recognized (after eating from the tree of knowledge) as having the form of animals. The plural Hebrew term *Elohim,* if so identified and retrieved, would allow humans to recognize in their DNA macro-evolutionary aspects of inheritance from other species in our present form. It is obvious that the Biblical tradition wished to assert a monotheistic God and the uniqueness of human "creation;" but of course neither man nor the animals created the heavens, earth, sun, moon, stars, etc. However, one views the *imago dei,* humans can never claim to have created the universe. The plural Hebrew term (with a singular verbal usage) is also found elsewhere not only of God, but of angels (sometimes conceived in animal form), or of other heavenly beings comprising functional divinity among the heavenly hosts. Climate change as a human-induced phenomenon

---

8. "On the Origin of the World," trans. Hans-Gebhard Bethge, Bentley Layton and Societas Coptica Hierosolymitana, in James M. Robinson, (ed.) *The Nag Hammadi Library,* revised third edition (Leiden: E. J. Brill, 1988).

that affects the earth and the lives of its creatures is an exponential ethical problem in view of the "cosmic covenant"[9] that is central to Biblical theology from its earliest formative stages.

Native American Ethical Concerns (Past and Present)

Interactions within the natural word of the Americas may be analyzed in three phases, (1) that of ancient pre-history which has a broader correlation with the rise of the human species worldwide, (2) that of the unique native experience in the Western Hemisphere before European contact and (3) that of the experience with European colonialism and its subsequent nation states' independence in the modern era. A worldwide view of ancient petroglyphs, rock art, and cave paintings can be ascertained as a factor of anthropology comprising the awareness of our species in pre-historic times. It has similar features that occur on every continent, perhaps excepting Antarctica. Its imagery may be characterized as conceptually supernatural and depicts the human-animal experience as one of primal spiritual significance. It is not possible to delineate ethical differences based on religion or human evolutionary markers, the relationship to a given geographic habitat being the only variable. Earlier changes in climate, such as the end of the previous Ice Age (ca. 11,000 years ago), were not subject to contemporary scientific calculation and had no known human causation.

Any *post facto* attribution of ethical responsibility for the demise of the megafauna can only be a *fait accompli* that informs our present circumstance. Most religions and cultures began with some such sense of deep mythological reflection as a precursor to "holiness." The ancient site of Gobekli Tepe in eastern Turkey is an interesting touchstone of pre-literate relevance. The sense of wonder and mystery in the natural world and its creatures is what leads one to contemplate a Creator and our place in his creation, or to define the reverential interrelatedness that exists within the natural environment. These two metrics of consciousness prevail in different ways, but are somewhat inextricable. The former has predominated in theistic religions, especially Judaism and Christianity. The latter is central to Native American ethics. Besides being the essential component in tribal awareness and clan identity, it is fully embodied in the Nahua texts from Mesoamerica, of which we shall observe more in conclusion.

Rock art expressions are a source of conceptualization that may be characterized as pre-Biblical natural theology. They are registered in the innate conscience of our species. As such it is imperative that governments

---

9. Robert Murray, *The Cosmic Covenant* (London: Sheed and Ward Ltd., 1992).

recognize and protect these ancient sacred sites as legitimate links to our planetary indigenous heritage. The Rock is an important metaphor for divinity often mentioned in the Bible but rarely appreciated as an ecological voice of creation.[10] This brings us to the very mundane political decisions in which the natural environment is viewed in conflict with economic development. The extensive national monuments (Bears Ears and the Grand-Staircase Escalante) that were legally declared by President Obama in his last term of office contain an enormous wealth of ancient sites (mostly in southeastern Utah) that display a prehistoric record of North American antiquity embedded in a vast geological landscape of incomparable magnificence. The Trump administration sought to reduce, revise and rescind this declaration with "executive orders" and promote leasing much of it to the fossil fuel industry. Not only is this area sacred ground for Native tribes, but as with Trump's other deregulatory efforts, it would contribute greatly to CO_2 emissions and global warming.

Many of these anti-environmental executive orders have already been reversed in similar "executive orders" by the new Biden administration. A notable example with reference to the Standing Rock Sioux tribe is a permit denial for Keystone XL oil pipeline. Some are still being litigated in the courts. Even though lawsuits from NGOs and protests from tribal entities have prevailed in a vast majority of such cases, this has laid bare the need for more permanent policies. Executive orders and the declaration of National Monuments do not have the same statutory basis, however. The courts (ultimately the Supreme Court) can demand enforcement of laws duly passed and signed by previous Presidents; but this leaves NGOs and advocacy groups with the burden of constant vigilance and costs in legal defense of animals and the environment. Even so, greater impact may be gained when NGOs coalesce on issues and establish decisive legal precedents. No President should be able to revoke a previous President's declaration of National Monuments.

A lack of long-term political consensus on environmental issues only exacerbates the consequences later when problems become untenable. It is true of foreign policy as well (a Constitutional prerogative of the President), when the Senate fails to ratify treaties, such as the Iran Nuclear Deal, the Paris Climate Accords, or the Convention on Biological Diversity. Obviously, and especially with climate change, many environmental problems are global problems. Migratory birds and ocean species may travel long-distance, but nest, feed, or aggregate on shores or in specific locales. These issues require

---

10. Arthur Walker-Jones, "Honey from the Rock: The Contribution of God as Rock to an Ecological Hermeneutic," in Habel and Trudinger, (eds.) *Exploring Ecological Hermeneutics* (Atlanta, GA: Society of Biblical Literature, 2008), 91-102.

the more positive and secure national and international commitments that generally fall within the purview of the United Nations; but US Public Lands never seem to be safe from attempts at industrial exploitation. The Arctic National Wildlife Refuge has been threatened with petroleum extraction for decades and Wilderness designations are grudgingly given. The Department of Interior is a major player (and President Biden has named a Native American to head the agency); but the National Forest Service, is structurally a subsidiary within the Department of Agriculture, which suggests that forests are just trees, a crop to be harvested. This makes it difficult to keep logging at bay, even though old-growth forests are essential habitat for so many animals and vital to carbon sequestration. The Roadless Rule was adopted during the Clinton administration and is integral to the protection and preservation of the Tongass National Rainforest in southeast Alaska with trees over 800 years old, an ancient home for grizzly bears, wolves, salmon, goshawks, black bears, moose, and bald eagles.

The treatment of Native people in the Americas is a shameful history. One may look at any of several maps over the centuries and the see the epithet "Indian Country (or Territory)" moved further and further west and then disappear into the "reservations" of today. The buying, selling and wars of conquest by European powers are one thing; but the treaties made and abrogated by the United States are a part of its own "constitutional" history that seems almost beyond repair, legally or otherwise. The Indian Removal Act of 1830 was a test of the government's dismal commitment to humane treatment and it marked the beginning of subsequent failures. It was also a test of the Constitution itself. President Andrew Jackson was embroiled both in Indian policy and in the authority of a federal banking system. He once said of a Supreme Court case favorable to the Cherokee homeland, "They have made their decision, now let them enforce it,"[11] and this after the Tribe had helped him earlier in battle against the Creeks at the Horseshoe Bend of the Coosa River in Alabama.

When viewing the legal circumstance of tribal nations in their present context, one has to look first to immediate impacts on the tribe, its members, homeland and treaty rights, such as they may be historically claimed or enforced. That is not enough, however. How to deal with a diminished

---

11. Wilma Mankiller and Michael Wallis, *Mankiller: A Chief and her People.* An Autobiography of the Principal Chief of the Cherokee Nation (New York: Penguin Books, 1993), 90.
12. Liz McClain, "The Confluence for Climate Education: Aaniiih Nakoda College Addresses our Changing Environment," in *Tribal College Journal of American Higher Education* 32, no. 3 (Spring 2021): 19-23. The entire issue is devoted to "Sustainability and Climate Change."

circumstance and structural subjugation is a major problem. The impacts on the natural world by the dominant culture cannot be ignored, as the Standing Rock Sioux lawsuits over water security and the Canadian tar-sands pipeline have demonstrated. Current environmental threats from climate change and litigation involving various tribes to secure and protect their broader natural heritage are increasing. The larger picture of nature as an integrated field of *reverence* is a spiritual or religious one that non-Natives view differently, whether scientifically, economically, or within other religious contexts. Yet no one will have more depth of experience and passion for the land than its native peoples.[12] It is hoped that a consensus of truth and wisdom will emerge in the end.

Much of this disparity derives from an ever-increasing urban population whose interactive density, with energy and food requirements, and a lack of personal interaction with their natural environment, are significant factors. Even so, modern communication technologies have conveyed (along with religious awareness) an educated sense of urgent solidarity with the needs of people, animals, and their habitats around the world. Again, I go back to Bertrand Russell and his statement about the "collective power of humanity."[13] We must make that power ethical and effective in a changing climate. It is difficult to secure an integrated indigenous awareness of mutual security with diminishing natural resources. This has a spiritual significance. The needs of other living creatures and their habitat are being lost in a failure of democratic self-control and ecological enforcement. The massive wildfires in California and Australia are prime examples of catastrophic consequences. The Amazon Rain Forest and deforestation in Indonesia evidence industrial activity for profit, but those in California and Australia reveal just how sensitive to global temperatures some of our major ecological geographies are to the imminent climate threats affecting them. Electrical transmission lines, and in some places the lack of historic native practices such as controlled burns, are added causative factors; but it is the subtle, yet rigorously measured, global warming whose threshold has transformed these environments from resilient forests into tinder for fires. That is due to human activity, primarily the burning of fossil fuels. Methane emissions also contribute to this and their source is a major concern for animal ethics as well.

The Spirit of *Wakhan Thanka* is revered in the Lakota (Sioux) tradition as the source of all created life. The Biblical creation story in Genesis 1 has

---

13. Bertrand Russell, *A History of Western Philosophy* (London: George Allen and Unwin, Ltd., 1948), 855.

"air [רוח] as the first sacred thing" in ecological hermeneutics.[14] This *ruah* in Hebrew is conceived both as God's breath and the breath of all creatures. When Jesus spoke of himself as "the Way, the Truth, and the Life" he referenced an impartial equilibrium of access among his creatures. The atmosphere that envelops the earth is itself sacred. OT Greek translation made a distinction based on two different words, ἀερ (air or atmosphere) and πνευμα (spirit), and in the NT the Holy Spirit is often viewed in a special context. The identity of "unclean spirits" with the multifarious sources of illness in the Scriptures (e.g. in Mark's gospel) reveals a moral nexus within the physical and spiritually relational dynamic of the creation as a whole. Ancient sources such as the antediluvian book of Enoch portray this dynamic as a picture of earth degenerating into chaos where passion and futility prevail over the life and security of all creatures. The cause of this strife leading to the "un-creation"[15] of the Flood is revealed in Genesis 9 as the carnivorous inclination of Adam's progeny for which God now rendered the animal creation itself unwillingly subjected to futility (Rom. 8:19-22) because of that proclivity. Jesus came to restore a spirit of holiness to his creation. Much of ecological hermeneutics is related to the earth itself as a living entity that has suffered in the hope of renewal from that bondage along with her creatures.

Mni Wichoni, translated "water is life" in the Lakota language, is equally an indispensable ecological resource that has been polluted, taken for granted, wasted, or exploited for unnecessary purposes. The Native American Rights Fund has constantly had to take the government to court to force compliance with the 1908 Supreme Court ruling that guaranteed sufficient water for sustainability on Reservation lands. Fresh water from aquifers, such as the extensive underground Oglala from the Dakotas to the southern plains of Texas, are being severely depleted to satisfy the economic interests of the beef and dairy industries, unethical animal agriculture exports, and the promotion of unhealthy diets. Besides the resource depletion and environmental degradation, the hidden damage is that of normalizing what can only be described as unsustainable animal abuse structurally integrated into the fabric of society and culture. This is an unconscionable affront to the character of a just and merciful God.

---

14. Theodore Hiebert, "Air, the First Sacred Thing: The Conception of רוח in the Hebrew Scriptures," in Habel and Trudinger, (eds.) *Exploring Ecological Hermeneutics*, 9-19.
15. 1 Enoch lxxxiii-xci, trans. M. A. Knibb, in H. F. D. Sparks, (ed.) *The Apocryphal Old Testament* (Oxford: Clarendon Press, 1984), 274-291. Cf. Joseph Blenkinsopp, *Creation, Un-Creation, Re-Creation* (London: T & T Clark, 2011).

Rivers and their estuaries have also suffered. The construction of dams has systematically diverted free-flowing rivers into irrigation projects and urban use without recognizing their primary ecological roles, such as salmon migration for reproduction, unique aquatic habitats, or simply the annual cleansing of waterways by rainfall and mountain snowmelt. Pollution from industry and agriculture endangers the health of humans and animals, as well as riverine ecosystems and shorelines. Oceans are an increasing focus of concern for climate change, as evidenced by coral bleaching, acidification, and the warming source of more powerful weather systems; but the shrinking Arctic ice sheet is of immediate concern for inhabitants of the far North, human and animal alike, especially polar bears; and calving icebergs from Greenland and Antarctica are contributing to sea-level rise worldwide. Vivid memories of the BP oil disaster in the Gulf of Mexico must steer us away from this energy dependence that portends even more accelerated temperature changes, unmitigated pollution, and habitat disruptions.

Other problems, more nefarious and long lasting, have resulted from mineral and resource extraction. Mining for gold, silver, copper, and iron ore has left a legacy of contamination and pollution that is inexplicable to Native peoples, and one for which they received no recompence. Coal, oil and natural gas extraction have devastated natural landscapes even as their increased dependence is the source of global warming. The effect of the Federal 1906 Dawes Act in Oklahoma, when it became a state, was to provide family incomes from oil production to members of the Removed tribes in "Indian country" in exchange for renunciation of communal land ownership. Such leases and similar arrangements on other tribal lands (such as private grazing rights) always had a tendency toward assimilation and reduced tribal sovereignty. A particularly long-lasting impact has been that of uranium ore extraction on the Navajo Reservation (of the Dine people), where health problems abound. The Yakima tribe in Washington state were removed from portions of their traditional lands where they dug roots for subsistence along the upper Columbia River. This was to facilitate research and production of the atomic bomb during World War II. The Department of Energy's Hanford Site in southeast Washington possesses extensive radioactive waste material from this activity. Nuclear testing in Nevada has also rendered much of the historic migratory Paiute lands inaccessible.

Categorizing Current Examples of Legal and Ethical Conflict

A deeper probe into the history and experience of the dominant culture that has led to the disputed issues of our time exposes the character of the problems that persist. While no current consensus exists for all issues of animals and the environment, their resolution depends on factual science, compatibility within belief systems and a common understanding of the way forward. Most examples of concern offered here derive from tribal, environmental, and native animal protection groups that look to the government for resolution. These sources represent a range of my personal memberships collated into a broad consensus of concern, and sources (due to limitations of space in the chapter) will not always have full documentation. Organizations referenced may be further investigated by search online. Some others are taken from recent academic sources within the Program Units of the Society of Biblical Literature and the American Academy of Religion, predominately the Ecological Hermeneutics of SBL and the Native Traditions in the Americas of the AAR (also Religion and Ecology, Animals and Religion).

Monitoring the year 2020 for these issues has been totally overshadowed by the Covid-19 pandemic and that focus allowed a surreptitious escalation of anti-environmental policies to be put in place. Deficiencies that allowed tribal communities to be disproportionately affected by the corona virus highlight historic problems of inequity of access, as noted by Southwest Reservation Aid on the Navajo Reservation. Even so, Native peoples voted in significantly larger numbers in 2020 and changed the political landscape in Arizona. It is a sobering fact that members of America's First Nations were the very last to get the right to vote in the US, even later than former slaves or women.

Not all was negative. Some tribal lands were returned to Alaska's Indigenous Peoples and to the Blackfoot Tribe in Montana with the help of the Nature Conservancy; and the US government returned the area (and animals) of the National Bison Range to the Tribe. Full funding was also restored permanently to the Land and Water Conservation Fund. Nevertheless, defending the integrity of the Arctic National Refuge from a plan to open 1.6 million acres of the coastal plain for oil and gas drilling, as well as a rollback of existing restrictions on another 7 million acres in Alaska's Western Arctic are on the 2021 docket of Earthjustice, in addition to protecting Florida's wetlands from destructive development schemes. The Endangered Species Act will need defending from the extensive assaults on its implementation of the law by the previous administration.

There are proposals for a massive gold mine in southwest Alaska with its toxic chemical waste, and a copper mine threatens Montana's Smith River, as well as another near the Boundary Waters Canoe Area located in the Superior National Forest of the Great Lakes, prime wolf habitat. It should be noted, however, that the people of Colorado voted in favor of reintroducing the gray wolf in the 2020 election. The Bureau of Land Management has plans to open a million acres of public lands in central California to oil drilling and "fracking" (hydraulic fracturing of underground shale deposits to release natural gas) which Earthjustice is also challenging on the basis of groundwater contamination from the toxic chemicals used in the process. It has caused earthquakes in eastern Oklahoma, major groundwater pollution in Pennsylvania, and several States have enacted laws banning it. Food and Water Watch noted plans to build several terminals for export of liquified natural gas based on projections of its broader use, five along the Texas coastline. It will be a contentious issue for the new administration. Other issues are electrification of transportation, home rooftop solar and storage systems in Hawai'i (also in Puerto Rico following the severe hurricanes), energy efficiency standards in manufactured housing, and fighting Indonesian plans to add new coal-fired plants.

Many NGOs are coordinating their work internationally. The Humane Society has expanded internationally. The World Wildlife Fund has made significant gains through better monitoring devices against poaching rhinos and elephants in Africa; it is working with China and Russia to establish wildlife corridors for tigers and fending off threats to jaguars in the Amazon rainforest. As the globally significant Amazon Rain Forest is predominately in the hands of Brazil, there is a need for a united diplomatic focus of international concern. South America would do well indigenously without the negative effects of large cattle ranching operations (especially in Brazil and Argentina), even though the Nature Conservancy has sometimes made conservation agreements with ranchers in North America (and on a smaller scale in Colombia) to protect other native species. In Africa, there are more nation-states involved in whatever changes in climate may warrant attention, but the optimum situation is protection of existing habitat and freedom of migration for all species. Development issues are more likely to lend complexity to the historic habitat of many animals. Hopefully, African nations will act with indigenous priorities of care for the natural environment rather than be lured into the seductive, but destructive, material pursuits of the developed and developing, world. Every individual nation owes deference in respecting all the indigenous animals of Africa. Natural processes should prevail and trophy hunting needs to be phased out for a truly integrated, spiritual environment to be realized. Why does this affect

Americans, native or otherwise? It is because we need to lift up a *global* human awareness that rises religiously and ethically above the need for the desires of the flesh, legal enforcements, and care-less-ness, and rests on the blissful plane of joy, peace, and love for all God's creatures.

This includes animals that are overlooked, small and seemingly insignificant, such as the Monarch butterfly and honey bees, whose cause the Environmental Defense Fund and Friends of the Earth have taken up. The Monarch has a primary vegetative requirement on its 2-year bi-generational round-trip into the US from a very specific home location in Mexico. Honey bees have a problem with pesticides. The variety of animals that have sustainability threats from these two sources is incalculable, and the Environmental Protection Agency needs more restrictions for prevention in chemical threats to humans and wildlife from a variety of uses. It is another reflection of the need to protect archaeological sites such as the Chaco Canyon Culture Site in New Mexico from adjacent intrusive activity. The natural environment has always succeeded in reclaiming its greater integrity against over-development and Chaco (as a World Heritage Site) is a splendid example of that legacy in its cosmic theology of Place that climate change will not easily erase. The Archaeological Conservancy in Albuquerque, NM is the premier activist organization in helping to identify, purchase and conserve ancient and historical sites in North America. The Rock Art along the Pecos River in Texas and the Gila in Arizona are also significant in that respect.

Concluding Thoughts

Time and space do not permit delving into the second phase of indigenous ethical concerns identified earlier in the chapter. As with all historic traditions, both European (Christian) and Native ones are deeply rooted. Yet in terms one would call religious, they share much of what can be described as natural theology, or a foundation based on ecological awareness. Their *prima facie* presentation may seem alien to one another, but the focus and content is not. When one views the collaboration between the Spaniard priests and the Aztecs, such as may be found in the Florentine Codex,[16] the art and language may appear strange or otherwise shocking to European eyes, but the stories told and the highly charged (sometimes visceral) moral lessons are life-giving and peace-making in their unique

---

16. *Florentine Mesoamerican Codex*, Spanish and Nahua with pictographs, by Bernardino de Sahagun (Florence, Italy: Laurentian Library, 16th century). Select images may viewed from America Online search.

"participation mystique" with nature. I was impressed by the modern-day Nahua speakers and academics from Southern California who explained the texts and how this was so, at the virtual AAR meetings in 2020. The theory of "ethno-poetics" in translation is a key realization, a theory advanced by the late Ines Talamantez (Mescalero Apache) and her students after four decades teaching Native Traditions at UC Santa Barbara.

Immersion in the historic immanent natural world of Native America is far removed from the experience of the vast majority of people that now inhabit these hallowed lands. The connections are never lost to those who are bound to its ancient history. Despite all our efforts, changes will always come; but we must not accelerate our own demise. Bradley Shreve, editor of *Tribal College*, quotes a Zuni prophecy in his article on "A Tale of Two Cultures" that reflects on our circumstance and future, "Maybe when the people have outdone themselves…the end for us shall come. But the people will bring upon themselves what they receive."[17]

Bibliography

Barr, James. *Biblical Faith and Natural Theology.* (Oxford: University Press, 1993).

Biblia Hebraica Stuttgartensia. Fourth edition. (Stuttgart: Deutsche Bibelgesellschaft, 1990).

Blankenship, Sidney. "Native American Religion: Restoring Species to the Circle of Life," in *The Routledge Handbook of Religion and Animal Ethics,* (eds.) Andrew Linzey and Clair Linzey. (London: Routledge, 2019).

Blenkinsopp, Joseph. *Creation, Un-Creation, Re-Creation.* (London: T & T Clark, 2011).

Caird, George Bradford. *Principalities and Powers.* (Oxford: The Clarendon Press, 1956).

Deloria, Jr., Vine. *God is Red: A Native View of Religion.* Updated. (Golden, CO: Fulcrum Publishing, 1992).

Florentine Mesoamerican Codex. Spanish and Nahua by Bernardino de Sahagun. Florence, Italy: Laurentian Library, 16th Century.

Gore, Albert. *Earth in the Balance: Ecology and the Human Spirit. (*New York: Penguin Books USA, 1993).

---

17. Bradley Shreve, "A Tale of Two Cultures," in the *Tribal College Magazine* 32, No. 3 (Spring 2021): 8-9. Access the issue and article on-line at www.tribalcollegejournal.com

Graber, Jennifer. *The Gods of Indian Country: Religion and the Struggle for the American West.* (Oxford: University Press, 2018).

Grim, John A., (ed.) *Indigenous Traditions and Ecology: The Interbeing of Cosmology and Community.* (Cambridge, MA: Harvard University Press, 2001).

Habel, Norman C., and Peter Trudinger, (eds.) *Exploring Ecological Hermeneutics.* (Atlanta, GA: Society of Biblical Literature, 2008).

Hesiod. *Theogony.* Greek text, (ed.) with Prolegomena and Commentary, M. L. West. (Oxford: Clarendon Press, 1982).

Howatson, M. C., and Ian Childers, (eds.) *The Concise Oxford Companion to Classical Literature.* (Oxford: University Press, 1993).

Jones, David M., and Brian L. Molyneaux. *Mythology of the American Nations: An Illustrated Encyclopedia.* (London: Anness Publishing Ltd., 2009.)

Mankiller, Wilma, and Michael Wallis. *Mankiller: A Chief and her People.* An Autobiography of the Principal Chief of the Cherokee Nation. (New York: St. Martin's Press, 1993).

Muddiman, John. "The Scholarly Achievement of George Caird." *Mansfield College Magazine.* 197 (1994-1995).

Murray, Robert. *The Cosmic Covenant.* London: Sheed & Ward Ltd., 1992.

Novum Testamentum Graece. Text and critical apparatus by Alexander Souter. (Oxford: Clarendon Press, 1962).

Otto, Rudolf. *The Idea of the Holy.* Translated by John W. Harvey. (London: Oxford University Press, 1967).

Peacocke, Arthur. *Theology for a Scientific Age.* (Minneapolis, MN: Fortress Press,1993).

Ponting, Clive. *A Green History of the World.* (New York: Penguin Books, 1993).

Popol Vuh: Mayan Book of the Dawn of Life and the Glories of Gods and Kings. Revised edition. Translated by Dennis Tedlock. (New York: Touchstone/ Simon and Schuster, 1996).

Russell, Bertrand. *A History of Western Philosophy.* (London: George Allen and Unwin Ltd, 1948).

Rahlfs, Alfred, ed. *Septuaginta.* (Stuttgart: Deutsche Bibelgellschaft, 1979).

Robinson, James M., (ed.) *The Nag Hammadi Library in English.* Revised third edition. (Leiden: E. J. Brill, 1988)

Schmitz-Moorman, Karl. *Theology of Creation in an Evolutionary World.* (Cleveland, OH: Pilgrim Press, 1997).

Shafer, Harry J. *Ancient Texans: Rock Art & Lifeways along the Lower Pecos.* (Houston, TX: Gulf Publishing, 1992).

Sitarz, Daniel, (ed.) *AGENDA 21: The Earth Summit Strategy to Save our Planet.* (Boulder, CO: Earthpress, 1993).

Sparks, H. F. D., (ed.) *The Old Testament Apocrypha.* (Oxford: Clarendon Press, 1984).

Suzuki, David, and Peter Knudson. *Wisdom of the Elders: Sacred Native Stories of Nature.* (New York: Bantam Books, 1993).

Tov, Imanuel. *Textual Criticism of the Hebrew Bible.* Third edition. (Minneapolis, MN: Fortress Press, 2012).

Tribal College: Journal of American Indian Higher Education 32, No. 3 (Spring, 2021). www.tribalcollegejournal.org

CHAPTER FOUR

THE "EMBERING" BRAZIL: CLIMATE CHANGE AND THE SPECIESIST UNIVERSE

PAULA BRUGGER

Summary

Humans have already pushed four planetary systems beyond the limit of their safe operating space. Extinction rate, a facet of this whole, appears as one of the most grave. There has been a shift from a world dominated by wild animals to one mainly composed of humans and their livestock. Dire consequences of this deleterious shift - including alterations in biogeochemical cycles as carbon sequestration - which influences climatic stability, are at stake. This ecological calamity is also linked to cultural traits as the widely disseminated speciesist prejudice and aggravated by the actions of corrupted political-economic clusters, which dismantle social and environmental institutions. In Brazil where land use change has been strongly related to the expansion of soybean and pastures, criminal practices have been (unofficially) encouraged. Whilst the country has a robust legislation concerning the protection of the environment and nonhuman animals, economic and political conflicts of interest are strong impediments to law enforcement. As there is a problem in defending the environment and nonhuman animals only through legislation, the author suggests that the broad answer is education. In Brazil, the work of NGOs and other forms of social, civil, and even religious coalitions, play a major role in safeguarding the environment, and the rights of indigenous and traditional communities. The word Brazil comes from the threatened tree *Paubrasilia echinata*, whose trunk has a reddish color. Nevertheless 'Brazil', now, seems to refer to a blazing hot state in which forests burn in the name of economic growth. This is why education is the ultimate solution when it comes to building a new ethics and a new rationality.

What on Earth are we doing?

The history of humankind on Earth, especially of the Western world, is marked by a progressive dominion over nature. This process seems to be part of the human condition, but it has been accentuated and deepened with the advent of the industrial civilization. This venture of domination by means of science and technology is also, and essentially, a fragmentation between humans and the environment, a rupture within the sentient biosphere, with one species - *Homo sapiens* - ruling all.

The human appropriation of net primary production (HANPP)[1],which provides a useful measure of human intervention into the biosphere, has risen from 13% to 25% (net primary production of potential vegetation) from 1910 to 2005. Although there have been substantial gains in efficiency in this period ecological costs, such as soil degradation and biodiversity loss, are incontestable (Krausmann et al 2013).

Humans have already pushed four planetary boundaries beyond the limit of their safe operating space (Grooten and Almond 2018). Agriculture is the primary force behind the transgression of the boundaries for nitrogen, phosphorus, climate change, biosphere integrity, land-system change, and freshwater use. Many of these issues are interlinked, aggravating the challenge: climate change, for instance, adds further stress to land systems, worsening existing risks as land degradation and biodiversity loss (Almond et al 2020:60). A quarter of the earth's terrestrial surface is used for ruminant grazing and a third of the global arable land is employed to grow feed for livestock (Gerber et al. 2013; FAO, 2013). As habitat degradation is the leading cause of biodiversity loss, it is not surprising that vertebrate populations have declined sharply: the global Living Planet Index (LPI) shows an average 68% decrease in population sizes of mammals, birds, amphibians, reptiles, and fish between 1970 and 2016 (Almond et al 2020:6). Biodiversity is declining at different rates, in different places, with a 94% decline in the LPI for the tropical subregions of the Americas, the largest fall observed in the world (Almond et al 2020:18).

Unequivocal evidence of our influence on the dynamics of the biosphere is abundant. According to Bar-On et al (2018), over the relatively short span of human history, major innovations, such as the domestication of livestock, adoption of an agricultural lifestyle and the Industrial Revolution, have increased the human population dramatically and have had radical

---

[1] Total HANPP is the quantity of carbon in biomass harvested or otherwise consumed by people, including crops, timber, harvested crop residues, forest slash, forages consumed by livestock and biomass lost to human-induced fires.

ecological effects. The authors affirm that a census of the biomass[2] on Earth is key for understanding the structure and dynamics of the biosphere and a quantitative description of the distribution of biomass is essential for taking stock of bio-sequestered carbon and modeling global biogeochemical cycles, a key factor when it comes to climate change. The sum of the biomass on Earth is ≈550 Gt C, of which circa 80% are plants mostly located on land.[3] Bar-On et al (2018) state that the total plant biomass (and, by proxy, the total biomass on Earth) has declined approximately twofold relative to its value before the start of human civilization.

Bar-On et al (2018) also show that the biomass of humans (≈0.06 Gt C) and the biomass of livestock (≈0.1 Gt C, dominated by cattle and pigs) far surpass that of wild mammals, which has a mass of ≈0.007 Gt C. This is also true for wild and domesticated birds, for which the biomass of poultry (≈0.005 Gt C, dominated by chickens) is about threefold higher than that of wild birds (≈0.002 Gt C). In fact, humans and livestock outweigh all vertebrates combined, with the exception of fish. While the total biomass of wild mammals (marine and terrestrial) decreased by a factor of ≈6, the total mass of mammals increased approximately fourfold, due to the vast increase of the biomass of humanity and its associated livestock. Human activity has also impacted global vertebrate stocks, with a decrease of ≈0.1 Gt C in total fish biomass, an amount similar to the remaining total biomass in fisheries and to the gain in the total mammalian biomass due to livestock husbandry. The anthropogenic impact on global biomass has not been limited to mammals but has also profoundly reshaped the total quantity of carbon sequestered by plants.

In sum, there has been a major shift from a world dominated by wild animals to one largely composed of humans and their livestock. Other authors also point to dire outcomes of this deleterious shift, including alterations in biogeochemical cycling, as carbon sequestration. In a holistic perspective the consequences may be rather disastrous because of the degree of incertitude of unforeseen, intertwined events that may arise from this context (Smith et al 2016). In fact, livestock´s role in climate change is already well documented in many reports.[4] The first comprehensive holistic

---

[2] Biomass refers to the mass of living organisms, including plants, animals and microorganisms. It is often reported as a mass per unit area and usually as dry weight (Houghton 2008). Bar-On et al (2018) report biomass in gigatons of carbon, with 1 Gt C = 1015 g of carbon.

[3] While plants are primarily terrestrial, animals are mainly marine. The terrestrial biomass is about two orders of magnitude higher than marine biomass (Bar-On et al 2018).

[4] Examples of recent issues are FAO (2019a) and FAO (2019b).

report that unveiled the colossal negative externalities from the livestock sector on climate change, water, and biodiversity was a FAO study of 2006 (Steinfeld et al 2006).

Bar-On et al (2018) also supplement these kingdoms of living organisms with an estimate for the global biomass of viruses which are not included in the current tree of life but play a key role in global biogeochemical cycles.[5]

In 2020 humanity painfully realized that this category plays a paramount role in life on Earth for other reasons as well. This corroborates the appropriateness of holistic approaches to explain environmental and social phenomena. Diseases like COVID-19, originating from animals, are one of the many connections between the health of people and the planet (WWF, 2020, 82). The brilliant biologist Jonathan Balcombe (2016) was a visionary in his 'After meat' when he mentioned the possibility of a global meat borne pandemic bursting out in October 2019.[6]

The figures shown previously are the ultimate proof that, when it comes to biodiversity loss and climate change, livestock raising is the most impacting industry of the planet. In order to supply this growing demand livestock production sectors work indefatigably to deliver this specific kind of 'food'.

Devouring the sentient biosphere

Brazil, for instance, is a country that has historically been a provider of raw materials, and more recently of commodities (Brügger 2020), at a high social and environmental cost. It may seem that these externalities have only been under the spotlights in recent years, but this is not the case.

According to Pádua (2002) the environmental question in Brazil is not a recent or imported discussion; its roots can be traced back into the history of Brazilian political culture. In his book, concerning the political thought and environmental criticism in pro-slavery Brazil, the author quotes the abolitionist José Bonifácio, who criticized in a holistic *avant-garde* perspective, wasteful modes of consumption, the practice of monocultures in large properties, and pointed out the connections between environmental destruction and human slavery. It is amazing how so many issues discussed during the period of Pádua´s research - 1786 to 1888 - are still of much

---

[5] Marine virus populations are thought to constitute a major driver of carbon recycling on a global scale and may also make an important contribution to the reservoir and cycling of oceanic phosphorus (Jover, et al 2014).
[6] Balcombe obviously did not guess everything in detail. However, a lot of incertitude still hovers on the origins of the current pandemic, including the animal source and even the country where it started.

interest today: wildfires, soil erosion, species loss, and climate deterioration, among others.

What has changed so far? Regrettably, by means of science and technology the domination of nature, including its sentient beings, has only become more "efficient", as argued by great minds such as the philosopher Herbert Marcuse (1968).

In Brazil cattle slaughter grew 3.4% in 2018, and pig slaughter increased 2.4%, reaching a new record, getting as far as 44.20 million heads. Chicken slaughter, despite a fall of 2.5% in 2018, totaled 5,70 billion heads, and egg production increased 8.6%, another new record in the historical series started in 1987. In 2018 the amount raised by beef cattle in Brazil hit the significant sum of R$597.22 billion. The figure represents an increase of 8.3% compared to R$551.41 billion registered in 2017. This number is the largest ever recorded in the last ten years. In 2018 there was a 6.9% increase in the number of slaughters, reaching 44.23 million heads. As a consequence, there was also a growth in the volume of beef produced, an increase of 12.8% over 2017. Of this total, 20.1% was exported and 79.6% was destined to the domestic market, responsible for a per capita consumption of 42.12kg/year. In terms of herd size, in 1972 there were 92.5 million heads in the country, and in 2018 this number rose to 214.69 million. Brazil has the largest cattle herd in the world, and is the largest producer, exporter and the second largest consumer of meat, just behind the US (ABIEC 2019). Brazil is also the second largest producer of chicken (ABPA, 2018; see also Brugger 2020:40-45).

Globally intensive factory farming systems are surely the largest-scale source of animal suffering today (Balcombe 2016, 313).[7] It has been estimated that, each year, 37 to 120 billion farmed fish, 970 to 2,700 billion wild fish, and 63 billion farmed mammals and birds are killed for food (Bekoff, 2014: 39).

The livestock sector also has a huge public health footprint. Furthermore, those who work in factory farms, slaughterhouses, meat-processing plants, and packaging assembly lines endure poor working conditions, earn low wages, and have low social status making this employment a modern form of slavery (Brugger et al 2016, 296, 298-300).

---

[7] In Brazil over 22% of slaughters are not inspected by authorities, representing circa 9.8 million animal lives (ABIEC 2019). Live export is also an extremely cruel practice that has been criticized worldwide.

Social-environmental jeopardy and "Beef power"

In this process of commoditization and enslavement of sentient beings whole ecosystems have been under a massive attack, especially during the last few years. The world is very much focused on an imminent Amazon disaster, but other Brazilian ecosystems are also in great danger. Even pristine environments are now being plundered and one consequence is the flabbergasting data about biodiversity loss.

Brazilian terrestrial biomes lost about 500 thousand km² of their natural cover between 2000 and 2018. In absolute numbers, the greatest loss in this period occurred in the Amazon biome (269,800 km²), followed by the Cerrado (152,700 km²). Forest coverage represented 81.9% of the total area of the Amazon in 2000, a proportion that dropped to 75.7% in 2018. This area was replaced mainly by grazing areas which went from 248,800 km² to 426,400 km² during this period. The Pantanal has had the lowest losses, in terms of percentage, but since 2010 about 60% of the changes have been from natural countryside areas to pastures. The Atlantic Forest, which suffers the oldest and most intense occupation, retained only 16.6% of its natural areas in 2018, the lowest percentage among all biomes (Belandi, 2020).

More than a hundred and fifty years after José Bonifácio´s worries, the environmental and social scenarios in Brazil are worse than ever; vast extensions of the Amazon rainforest burned[8]again in 2020, just one year on from the 2019 calamitous wildfires. Another tragedy happened in 2020; the Pantanal, the largest tropical wetland in the world, listed as a World Heritage, was also on fire. At least four million hectares of forest, savannah, and shrub-land have gone up in flames. Roughly one-third of the Pantanal burned. Almost all the Indigenous territories and conservation facilities were burnt, along with many private lands. Conservation areas such as *Encontro das Águas State Park*, one of the largest population of jaguars in the world, have been devastated (Libonati et al, 2020). Hundreds of thousands of animals of various species have perished.

In this appalling context another long standing environmental threat hovers on the richest savannah of the planet, the Cerrado. According to Vasconcelos et al (2020),95% of the deforestation for soy farms between 2012 and 2017 in Mato Grosso state, has occurred illegally under Brazilian regulations. Furthermore, 80% of this illegal deforestation took place in just

---

[8] It is worth noticing that small-scale controlled fires have been historically practiced in forests like the Amazon by traditional communities to grow their annual crops.

400 farms, mostly large properties, representing circa 2% of the total number of soy farms in the state. José Bonifácio´s theses have been proven.

Despite the serious concerns about the environmental and public health consequences, demand for animal products is increasing and is expected to grow by 70 percent by 2050 (Gerber et al. 2013, 83). This gives enormous power to the livestock industry to claim that it is responding to people's demands and therefore, ask for protection from market and political forces. In Brazil, the livestock industry is linked to vested interests which bond economic and political sectors. Influential groups form 'clusters' to fund this unsustainable industry and even divert financial resources from public funds (Brügger et al 2016, 299-300).

It is an undisputed truth that economic and political forces have caused a lot of damage to the environment, especially in the last decades, but Jair Bolsonaro´s government might mark the darkest page in Brazilian environmental and social history.

Ranchers and landgrabbers, legally, or ideologically shielded by the Federal Government, cause an unprecedented harm not only to the environment. There is no such thing as "empty jungles". When they invade the lands that for centuries have been safeguarded by indigenous and traditional peoples, as the *quilombolas*[9], the livelihoods and the very survival of these peoples are at stake. This is not unexpected though, for when Bolsonaro ran for the Presidency of the Republic, he made several speeches laden with prejudice rhetoric, against blacks, indigenous people, women, homosexuals, and refugees.[10]

Many other important positions of his government are aligned with identical or analogous worldviews. And one instance of the deplorable management of Bolsonaro´s government lies precisely in the performance of the Ministry of the Environment. The minister did not try to prevent the wildfires; did not release the money he had available, and it took him months to approve a fire-fighting plan. He postponed and acted by default, which allowed these environmental crimes to occur (Libonati et al, 2020). Bolsonaro´s government environmental policies are so unacceptable, that the National Association of Environmental Professionals launched a dossier entitled 'Chronology of an announced disaster: Actions of Bolsonaro´s

---

[9]The quilombolas are slave descendant Afro-Brazilian residents of settlements (quilombos) established by slaves who escaped from plantations before abolition in 1888.
[10]See, for instance, Lum, K. The effects of Bolsonaro's hate speech in Brazil. Monitor-Global Intelligence on Racism, January 2019. Retrieved from: <http://monitoracism.eu/the-rise-of-bolsorano/>

Government to dismantle Brazilian Environmental Policies'.[11] The dossier reported the almost daily attacks against the environment from March 2018 to August 2020.

Although Brazil has a fairly robust environmental legislation, law enforcements often obliterated by conflicts of interest concerning economic and political issues. This results in deplorable cases of disrespect concerning social and environmental questions.[12]

The climatic reverberance

As stated before, plants are the dominant kingdom in planet Earth. It is not difficult therefore to realize the huge impact of deforestation and wildfires when it comes to climate change.

Many other areas of the planet that are burning, are under this unprecedented embering state. Tragically and curiously, the most accepted origin of the word Brazil comes from the threatened tree *Paubrasilia echinate* - object of massive trade by the Portuguese during the colonial period - whose trunk has a reddish *flamboyant* color. Now, 'Brazil' no longer seems to refer to this almost extinct species but to the flaming, blazing hot color of its environmental twilight.

Eating the sentient biosphere is at the core of this tragedy, for in order to produce so much animal products there is a need for major changes in land use, especially through deforestation[13]. This causes the degradation of soils (a biogeochemical component) among many other harmful effects that result from the conversion of natural ecosystems into pastures or feed crops. The problems triggered by such actions are weaved one into another in a framework that involves habitat loss, biodiversity loss and changes in water

---

[11] Associação Nacional dos Servidores de Meio Ambiente (ASCEMA). Cronologia de um desastre anunciado - Ações do Governo Bolsonaro para desmontar as Políticas de Meio Ambiente no Brasil.Brasília, Sept, 04, 2020. Retrieved from: <http://www.biodiversidadla.org/Documentos/Cronologia-de-um-desastre-anunciado-acoes-do-Governo-Bolsonaro-para-desmontar-as-politicas-de-Meio-Ambiente-no-Brasil>.

[12] Amnesty International. Brazil: Cattle illegally grazed in the Amazon found in supply chain of leading meatpacker JBS. 15 July 2020 Updated: 7 October 2020. Retrieved from: <https://www.amnesty.org/en/latest/news/2020/07/brazil-cattle-illegally-grazed-in-the-amazon-found-in-supply-chain-of-leading-meat-packer-jbs/>

[13] Deforestation in the Amazon grew almost 30% between August 2018 and July 2019 <https://g1.globo.com/natureza/noticia/2019/11/18/desmatamento-na-amazonia-cresce-entre-agosto-de-2018-e-julho-de-2019-diz-inpe.ghtml>.

balance, to name a few. Such transformations feedback deleteriously: loss of biodiversity, from the bottom to the top of the trophic chains, affects biogeochemical cycles (such as carbon, nitrogen, phosphorus, oxygen, etc.) and evapotranspiration, which, in turn, affects several other so-called 'environmental services'[14], including the provision of food for humans.[15]

This imbalance also affects the Earth's 'unseen majority', the microbial life, which plays critical ecological functions. In our oceans, for example, where 90 percent of life is microbial, phytoplankton play the same role as green plants on land, fueling animal life as a starting point in the food web. Many negative outcomes to marine life may arise if phytoplankton's productivity is impaired (Sanders 2019).

I am not a climatologist. But as a biologist I dare to say that the main factors affecting the global climate are not primarily related to direct GHG emissions but to those mentioned above, responsible for the annihilation of homeostatic and resilience mechanisms in a global scale: deforestation, conversion of natural ecosystems to pastures and commodity plantations; consequent quali-quantitative changes in biomass (decrease on one hand/increase on the other) and loss of biodiversity, which affects biogeochemical cycles, etc. One consequence of this unprecedented anthropogenic imbalance is a tendency to get more and more extreme climate conditions, as if a 'bipolar mother nature' were emerging from the dungeons of our own insanity.

Let's just contemplate the fact that a single tree in the Amazon rainforest can load up to 1,000 liters of water per day into the atmosphere (BBC Brasil, 2017). Besides, evapotranspiration mechanisms in forests and savannahs, for instance, differ greatly from those of pastures or soybean plantations. Furthermore, the cattle are not able to perform the same ecological functions as the megafauna/wild animals (Smith 2016: 101). As stated before, only 4% of the terrestrial mammal biomass is composed by wildlife. An astonishing 96% is composed by humans and animals raised by humans (Bar-On et al 2018). There is therefore a gigantic loss of the ecological role of this faunal diversity concerning natural cycles.

Such quali-quantitative changes make much sense in a systemic view, still rare in the dominant mechanistic science, and are in consonance with the 'Gaia Hypothesis' proposed in the 1960s by Sir James Ephraim

---

[14] I dislike the term 'environmental service', so rooted in our hegemonic instrumental rationality. The term reflects our pragmatic lens when it comes to our relationship with nature and, surreptitiously, perpetuates the anthropocentric idea that nature is a servant to humankind.

[15] See FAO (2019c) for the role of biodiversity in supporting and regulating ecosystem 'services', which, in turn, affect our food systems.

Lovelock. According to this scientific theory, strongly anchored in the biogeochemical functioning of the planet, life, and the physical components of the Earth are inextricably interrelated forming a complex system capable of maintaining a certain global homeostasis, including climate stability. Interdependence, feedback, and emerging properties are keywords here.

An iconic publication (Ciência Hoje, 1984) about the impacts of hydroelectric plants, mining, attacks against indigenous peoples, deforestation, etc., revealed back in 1984, the fragility of Amazonian ecosystems regarding these threats. One study demonstrated that roughly three quarters of the rainwater that falls on the forest returns to the atmosphere through evapotranspiration mechanisms forming new clouds and new rains. If the forest disappeared, in addition to damages to this mechanism, all the carbon trapped in the biotic compartment would be transferred to the (abiotic) atmosphere, aggravating the greenhouse effect with negative ramifications to both terrestrial hemispheres. Forests, in addition to serving as 'buffer systems' in terms of heat, are also important sources and sinks when it comes to the chemical balances of the atmosphere, storms being the main mechanisms for redistribution of gases, influencing the global chemical composition of the atmosphere (Schubart et al 1984). What have we done with this crucial information? Contemplating the kaleidoscopic facets of the 'livestock syndrome', one question emerges: why are animals still seen as food?

The speciesist apartheid: nonhuman animals as food

As hunters and gatherers, we, as a species, may be considered components of a natural food chain and, consequently, nonhuman animals would be part of our diets. However, as constituents of an industrialized and even artificial world, this taken for granted idea is no longer defensible. No arguments can stand against scientific evidence on nonhuman animal's capacity to suffer, both physically and psychologically, along with the abundant data on the viability of vegan diets.[16]

Notwithstanding, nonhuman animals are still treated as resources, objects and property because of our speciesist prejudice. The word speciesism was originally coined by the British philosopher Richard Ryder, in the 1970s, to refer to forms of discrimination practiced by humans against other animal species. The term is used in an analogy to racism and sexism, which are also prejudices based on morally irrelevant differences. Ryder (2011, 40-43) quotes eight definitions of speciesism, from philosophers

---

[16] See, for instance, Craig & Mangles (2009).

(including himself) to dictionaries and examines four dimensions of speciesism. Nevertheless, he concludes that for most purposes, it is probably expedient to use this term as a description of negative human discrimination or exploitation against members of other species. Ryder (2005) argues that all animal species can feel pain and distress, and that we should extend our concern for the pain and distress to any ´painient´ creature, regardless of his or her sex, class, race, religion, nationality, or species. Although moral principles and ideals like justice, freedom, equality, and inherent value have been suggested, painience is the only convincing basis for attributing rights or interests to others. Ryder (2011, 40) also argues that value cannot exist in the absence of consciousness or potential consciousness: what really matters in morality is not consciousness generally, but the consciousness of *pain*.

Among the different modalities of speciesism, it is worthwhile to spend a few words about what could be called 'selective speciesism'. In this modality, moral value is attributed to some species, but not to others. Depending on the species in question, selective speciesists see the very same treatments given to animals as good, acceptable, or abhorrent. Such judgments rely on cultural perceptions and personal tastes and not on scientific evidence about sentience, affectivity, cognition, or even the animal´s position in terms of phylogeny. Mammals raised for food *versus* mammals raised as family members are excellent examples of selective speciesism. Other species, apparently, ascend to the status of holders of moral consideration without being companion animals. This is basically the case of the endangered ones. But the extension of some moral consideration to these animals is mainly due to their potential instrumental value as maintainers of biodiversity and other 'environmental services'.

The lack of a systemic, holistic view with regard to this debate leads to a massive slaughter of the domesticated ones on one hand and mass extinction of wildlife on the other hand, as can be deduced from the data presented here. The denial of moral value towards the 'domesticated genes' has a direct catastrophic consequence on the 'wild genes' compartment. The sentient biosphere is one whole. Respect, and even kindness, are also important components of sustainability. In fact, the area of studies of animal consciousness has recently gained a major boost by a group of prestigious neuroscientists.[17] This shows that the time has come for ethics to become a fourth dimension of sustainability, an important feature lost in the trajectory of modern science.

---

[17] The Cambridge Declaration on Consciousness (2012). See also Bekoff (2014:48-49) among many others.

Paradigm changes, however, are slow because of uncountable obstacles of juridical, political, economic, philosophical, psychological and religious nature (Wise 2004).

The road ahead: solutions on practical and theoretical grounds

In his fictional essay, Balcombe (2016:320) commented that while the total number of animals being killed by humans was still rising at the time of the pandemic, nevertheless humankind´s moral concern for animals had risen unprecedentedly in the decades leading up to it.

Moral issues concerning our relationship with nonhuman animals are certainly flourishing. But when it comes to defending the environment and nonhuman animals, we must go beyond the limited and coercive realm of legislation: we need education.

Nevertheless, the formal Western hegemonic education still promotes speciesism and animal exploitation openly, extensively and proudly in practically all fields of knowledge. The dominant environmental education (EE) is also speciesist because the conservationist ethics that dominates its foundation has little or no affinity with the animal rights issues. Even the dominant mass media and our Western languages are speciesist. We use many words like dog, pig, stallion, etc., in a pejorative sense and, to refer to unsocial and reprehensible behaviors or, as insults. This goes beyond speciesism. It reveals the dichotomy between society and nature that lies at the core of our culture.

Science has already shown that a wide range of animals are painist, emotional, sentient beings, animated by a conscience. Education should respect and honor this evidence by adopting an animal abolitionist perspective. This goes hand in hand with the inclusion of ethics as a (fourth) dimension of sustainability. But to accomplish a genuine shift of paradigm these questionings must not remain as 'islands' of an alternative rationality. Education must transcend its instrumental, unidimensional foundation by getting multidimensional in the ethical domain. This means envisaging animals as legitimate masters of their own lives, irrespective of their ecological role. In reality, education shouldn´t need any adjectives. It should be 'environmental' and 'pro animal abolitionism' as a whole.[18]

---

[18] Concerning the last three paragraphs see Brügger (2018); Brügger (2020). Animal abolitionism can synthetically be defined as animal rights advocacy opposing the use of animals in any capacity by humans (Brügger et al 2016, 311).

Formal education is the most solid path to yield palpable results in the medium to long term. But practical initiatives and education campaigns promoting vegan diets, can make a huge difference now. In Brazil, several NGOs and other forms of social, civil, and even religious coalitions have been playing a major role when it comes to defending the environment and the rights of indigenous and traditional communities[19], although the defense of nonhuman animals is far less widespread. One promising practical solution to the problems discussed previously is to promote the multiplication of networks like Rede de Sementes do Xingu (Xingu Seed Network)[20], the largest network of native seeds in Brazil. With 13 years of history, it was the winner of the Ashden Awards 2020, a United Kingdom based organization that gives visibility and support to innovative climate change and energy initiatives around the world. This and many other initiatives testify the viability of concrete actions for another world, one in which human and nonhuman animal´s rights are respected as well as the environment.

However, these good practices ought to be mainstream, not alternatives proposed and conducted by the so-called Third Sector'. But this shift depends on a much broader context that involves legislation, public policies, etc., which in turn are deeply rooted in the cultural context. Theory and praxis are inextricably interdependent, not discrete compartments. Education is both the practical and the theoretical solution. We must also rewild our hearts, as science alone is not going to make us more compassionate (Bekoff, 2014: 132-142).

This should also be a new era of union. Irrespective of the foundations that lie at the heart of each animal ethics theory, in a dialectical approach, one element stands out: sentience (Brügger 2018:21).While we urge to make a potent step forward investing in an abolitionist perspective in the theoretical realm of formal education, in the world of praxis - dominated by narrow instrumental and economic paradigms - differences between theories that still prevail in the analytical academic thought, should not be

---

[19] Some examples are: Instituto Socioambiental (ISA); De Olho nos Ruralistas; Comissão Pastoral da Terra (CPT); Movimento dos Trabalhadores Rurais Sem Terra (MST);Repórter Brasil; and ANDA (Animal Rights News Agency).
[20] Instituto Socioambiental. Rede de Sementes do Xingu vence o Ashden Awards, prêmio internacional para soluções climáticas. 02.jul.2020. Retrieved from: <https://www.socioambiental.org/pt-br/noticias-socioambientais/rede-de-sementes-do-xingu-vence-o-ashden-awards-premio-internacional-para-solucoes-climaticas?fbclid=IwAR0UvjOdXbkEudWTQN-6Rh5ttmABDjuzk2sDYhqj__p-b_4s9RRwDpEKuno>

an impediment to conquer new promising spaces and practices. The time is now. Let´s act.

Bibliography

Almond, R. E. A., Grooten, M. and Petersen, T., (eds.) *Living Planet Report 2020-Bending the curve of biodiversity loss.* (Gland, Switzerland: World Wide Fund for Nature, 2020).

Associação Brasileira das Indústrias Exportadoras de Carnes (ABIEC2019). Accessed, February 19, 2021,https://www.beefpoint.com.br/beef-report-per%EF%AC%81l-da-pecuaria-no-brasil/

Associação Brasileira de Proteína Animal 'Relatório Anual 2018'. (ABPA2018.) Accessed, February 19, 2021, http://abpa-br.org/wp-content/uploads/2018/10/relatorio-anual-2018.pdf

Balcombe, Jonathan. 'After Meat' in *Impact of Meat Consumption on Health and Environmental Sustainability*, T. Raphaely and D. Marinova, (eds.) (Hershey, PA: IGI Global, 2016.)313-325.

Bar-On, Yinon, Phillips, Rob and Milo, Ron. (2018).'The biomass distribution on Earth'. *Proceedings of the National Academy of Sciences* (PNAS), 115 (25):6506-6511.

BBC Brasil. 2017. "O QUE são os 'rios voadores' que distribuem a água da Amazônia". Accessed, February 19, 2021, http://www.bbc.com/portuguese/brasil-41118902.

Bekoff, Marc. *Rewilding our hearts-Building pathways of compassion and coexistence.* (Novato, CA: New World Library. 2014)

Belandi, Caio. 'Agência IBGE Notícias'. Accessed September 24, 2020. https://agenciadenoticias.ibge.gov.br/agencia-noticias/2012-agencia-de-noticias/noticias/28944-ibge-retrata-cobertura-natural-dos-biomas-do-pais-de-2000-a-2018

Bélanger, J., Pilling, D., (ed.) *The State of the World's Biodiversity for Food and Agriculture.* (Rome: Food and Agriculture Organization of the United Nations, 2019).

Brügger, Paula, Marinova, Dora and Raphaely, Talia. 'Animal production and consumption: an ethical educational approach 'in *Impact of Meat Consumption on Health and Environmental Sustainability*, T. Raphaely and D. Marinova, (eds.) (Hershey, PA: IGI Global2016.295-312.

Brügger, Paula. (2018). 'Animal Abolitionism: A concise analysis of theoretical and educational perspectives'*Revista do Programa de Pós-Graduação em Direito da UFBA*, V. 28, No. 02: 08-28.

Brügger, Paula. 'Animals and Nature: The Co-modification of the Sentient Biosphere' in *The Capitalist Commodification of Animals*, Brett Clark, and Tamar Diana Wilson, (eds.) (Emerald Publishing Limited.2020)33-58.

Craig, Winston. J., and Mangels, Ann. R. (2009). 'Position of the American Dietetic Association: Vegetarian diets *'Journal of the American Dietetic Association*, 109(7): 1266–1282.

Fearnside, Philip M. (1984). 'A floresta pode acabar?'*Ciência Hoje,* 2 (10): 42-52.

Food and Agriculture Organization of the United Nations (FAO) and Global Dairy Platform GDP. *Climate change and the global dairy cattle sector- The role of the dairy sector in a low-carbon future.* (Rome: FAO and GDP. 2018).

Food and Agriculture Organization of the United Nations (FAO). *Five practical actions towards low-carbon livestock.* (Rome: Food and Agriculture Organization of the United Nations 2019).

Gerber, P. J., Steinfeld, H., Henderson, B., Mottet, A., Opio, C., Dijkman, J., Falcucci, A. & Tempio, G., (eds.) *Tackling climate change through livestock - A global assessment of emissions and mitigation opportunities.* (Rome: Food and Agriculture Organization of the United Nations 2013).

Grooten, M., Almond, R. E. A., (eds.) *Living Planet Report - 2018: Aiming Higher.* (Gland, Switzerland: World Wide Fund for Nature 2018).

Houghton, R. A. 2008. 'Biomass' in *Encyclopedia of Ecology*, (eds.) Sven Erik Jørgensen and Brian D. Fath. (Amsterdam, The Netherlands: Elsevier Date). 448-453.

Jover Luis, Effler, T. Chad, Buchan, Alison, Wilhelm, Steven and Weitz, Joshua. (2014). 'The elemental composition of virus particles: Implications for marine biogeochemical cycles' *Nat Rev Microbiol*, No. 12:519–528.

Krausmann, Fridolin, Erb, Karl-Heinz, Gingrich, Simone, and Haberl, Helmut. (2013). 'Global human appropriation of net primary production doubled in the 20th century.' *Proceedings of the National Academy of Sciences of the United States of America (PNAS)*, No. 110 (25): 10324-10329.

Libonati, Renata, DaCamara, Carlos, Peres, Leonardo, Carvalho, Lino and Garcia, Letícia. 'Nature' December 8, 2020. Accessed January 21, 2021. https://www.nature.com/articles/d41586-020-03464-1

Marcuse, Herbert. *One-Dimensional Man-Studies in the Ideology of Advanced Industrial Society.* (Boston, MA: Beacon Press, 1968).

Pádua, José A.*Um sopro de destruição: pensamento político e crítica ambiental no Brasil escravista (1786-1888).* (Rio de Janeiro, Jorge Zahar, Editor 2002).

Ryder, Richard. *Speciesism, Painism and Happiness - a morality for the twenty-first century*. (Exeter, Charlottesville: Societas, 2011).

Sanders, Robert. 'Berkeley News - Research, Science & Environment' June 18, 2019. Accessed January 21, 2021.
https://news.berkeley.edu/story_jump/when-it-comes-to-climate-change-dont-forget-the-microbes/

Schubart, Herbert, Franken, Wolfram and Luizão, Flávio. (1984). 'Uma floresta sobre solos pobres'*Ciência Hoje*, Vol.2, No. 10: 26-32.

Smith, Felisa A., Doughty, Christopher E., Malhi, Yadvinder, Svenning, Jens-Christian and Terborgh, John. (2016) 'Megafauna in the Earth system' *Ecography*, 39(2): 99-108.

Steinfeld, Henning, Gerber, P., Wassenaar, T., Castel, V., Rosales, M., and de Hann, C. *Livestock's long shadow: environmental issues and options*. (Rome, Italy: Food Agriculture Organization, 2006).

Vasconcelos, André, Bernasconi, Paula, Guidotti, Vinicius, Silgueiro, Vinicius, Valdiones, Ana, Carvalho, Tomás, Bellfield, Helen and Guedes Pinto, Luis F. 'Illegal deforestation and Brazilian soy exports: the case of Mato Grosso', *Trase. Earth*, June, 2020.

Your Brain and You. 'The Cambridge Declaration on Consciousness'. (2012) Accessed January 21, 2021.
http://yourbrainandyou.com/2012/08/24/the-cambridge-declaration-on-consciousness/

Wise, Steven. 'Animal rights, one step at a time' in *Animal rights: Current debates and new directions*, Cass Sunstein and Martha Nussbaum, (eds.) (19-50, New York, NY: Oxford University Press, 2004).

CHAPTER FIVE

FOSSIL FUEL AND LAND: AUSTRALIA'S CURSE AND PROMISE

DEBORAH GUESS

Introduction

Increasingly, the world is turning away from fossil fuel: coal consumption in the US and Europe has fallen by 34% since 2009; China has adopted a target of zero carbon emissions by 2060; Biden has committed the US to re-join the Paris agreement of zero net emissions by mid-century; the last coal-fired power plants in Britain could close by 2022 and solar farms or onshore wind have become the cheapest source of new electricity for at least two thirds of the world. Yet coal still accounts for 39% of annual global emissions of carbon dioxide from fossil fuels and in the past decade Asian consumption of coal has grown by a quarter and now accounts for 77% of all coal use.[1] Despite some progress, the urgent need to decarbonise has accelerated.

Culpability for climate change is widely spread, but not evenly, because developed nations are disproportionately responsible for carbon emissions, and nations like Australia that mine and export fossil fuels are especially accountable. I will argue here that modern Australia's relationship with fossil fuels is problematic because although Australia has much in common with other developed nations it is also distinctive; holding a wide variety and large quantity of mineral deposits and being home to the oldest indigenous population in the world, thought to have inhabited the land for at least 60,000 years. Despite its small population (25m) Australia is the highest per capita domestic carbon emitter in the OECD and the seventh largest in the world, as well as being the fifth largest extractor and the third

---

[1] The above data are taken from: Zanny Minton Beddoes, "Time to Make Coal History," *The Economist* 3 December 2020.

largest exporter of fossil fuel in the world.[2] As a developed country, it might be expected that Australia could withstand some of the worst ravages of climate change, and while to some extent this is true, meteorological and geographical circumstances make Australia especially vulnerable to the negative effects of climate change – it is the driest inhabited continent in the world and is subject to the El Niño-Southern Oscillation, so that even without increased temperature and destabilized weather, many parts of Australia are highly prone to drought and bushfire (wildfire), phenomena which are dangerously exacerbated by climate change.[3] Over the summer of 2019-2020 extensive, severe and unprecedented bushfires burned out over 17 million hectares of land.[4] Given this vulnerability, it may seem incongruous that Australia has become notorious for its climate scepticism, and that in 2019 a federal election was won by the party supporting the proposal of a massive coal mine.

Currently, some influential sections of Australian society are unwilling to acknowledge either Australia's responsibility for future emissions from its extracted and exported fossil fuel or its extreme vulnerability to climate change. I am calling this situation Australia's fossil fuel curse, following the work of scholar Judith Brett.[5] This chapter comprises a brief description of Australia's recent political history in relation to fossil fuel and then suggests ways that Australia might expunge its fossil fuel curse, re-think its self-identity as a mining nation, take up renewable energy options and, at a deeper level, come to understand and appreciate the promising and profoundly ecological land ethic of its own Indigenous people.

The mining campaign and Australian self-image

In recent decades an internal political war has occurred in Australia between those opposing fossil fuel mining and those supporting it, with the latter (so far) winning because, as one commentator says: "Australia has a

---

[2] Tom Swann, "High Carbon from a Land Down Under: Quantifying Co2 from Australia's Fossil Fuel Mining and Exports," (The Australia Institute, 2019).
[3] Of developed countries Australia is the most vulnerable to climate change—a global 1.75°C temperature increase would mean more than 2°C for Australia. Ross Garnaut, *Super-Power: Australia's Low-Carbon Opportunity* (Melbourne: La Trobe University Press, 2019), 5.
[4] Lisa Richards, Nigel Brew, and Lizzie Smith, "2019–20 Australian Bushfires— Frequently Asked Questions: A Quick Guide," (ed.) Parliament of Australia (2020).
[5] Judith Brett, "The Coal Curse: Resources, Climate and Australia's Future," *Quarterly Essay*, no. 78 (2020), 9–11.

political system captured by the fossil-fuel industry."[6] Historically, most of Australia's wealth has come from the export of unprocessed commodities - wool and other agricultural and pastoral products traditionally exported to the UK and Europe - with a relatively weak manufacturing industry often supported by protectionist policies and aimed mainly at the domestic market. During the second half of the twentieth century minerals became the leading export, primarily to Asia, with coal becoming an export staple from the early 1990s as demand increased with new power stations being built in China, India, and Japan. John Howard, leader of the conservative Coalition of Nationals and Liberals, and a strong supporter of the mining industry, was Prime Minister from 1996 to 2007, a time when "climate scepticism if not outright denial became a key identifier of the Australian right."[7] Negotiating a special deal at Kyoto in 1997, Australia subsequently sought special exemptions at other international climate forums.[8] In 2007 the Labor Party gained power: Kevin Rudd was PM 2007-2010, Julia Gillard 2010-2013, Kevin Rudd again in 2013. Although Labor has often equivocated its position on climate change and has failed to oppose coal and gas extraction, nevertheless Rudd took some positive steps, describing climate change as "The great moral challenge of our generation," ratifying the Kyoto Protocol and trying but failing to introduce a carbon pollution reduction scheme. In 2010 Rudd's proposal of a tax on mining projects invoked a brutal and successful advertising campaign by the mining industry costing A\$22.2 million.[9] Julia Gillard proposed an emissions trading scheme which was opposed both by the new Coalition leader Tony Abbott and by the Greens who saw it as making too many concessions to carbon polluters. The Coalition government was re-elected in 2013, a time of the rise of "a hard core of climate sceptics" with PM Tony Abbott's climate position being such that he declined even to appoint a minister for science.[10] Abbott saw the Adani mine as a "poverty-busting miracle that would put Australia on the path to becoming an energy superpower" and

---

[6] Anna Krien, "The Long Goodbye: Coal, Coral and Australia's Climate Deadlock," *Quarterly Essay*, no. 66 (2017), at 107. The political history is more complex than can be described here, for a fuller account see Brett, "The Coal Curse,"

[7] Brett, "The Coal Curse," 52.

[8] Brett, "The Coal Curse," 4–5. During Howard's long stint as Prime Minister his public position changed somewhat, stimulated by the millennium drought and increased public awareness, privately he is said to have remained a climate sceptic: Brett, "The Coal Curse," 55.

[9] Lindsay Simpson, *Adani: Following Its Dirty Footsteps. A Personal Story* (North Geelong: Vic: Spinifex, 2018), 23.

[10] Brett, "The Coal Curse," 58–59.

described the climate change argument as "crap".[11] Despite the attempts by the next and more moderate Coalition PM Malcolm Turnbull (2015-2018) to set an emissions reduction target, in the last decade there has been no adequate or coherent policy response to climate change.[12] The present Coalition PM Scott Morrison is somewhat accepting of the reality of human-caused climate change but is essentially a climate change minimiser who fails to acknowledge its severity and 'balances' it with the interests of miners and mining companies.[13]

Currently there are around fifty coal mines operating in Queensland. The Galilee Basin, around 400 kms inland, comprises a 247,000 square kilometres thermal coal basin, one of the largest untapped coal reserves on the planet, and is the site of the massive proposed Adani/Bravus mine plus at least eight more planned coal mines.[14] The present (March 2021) Australian government supports the development of new coal mines in the Galilee Basin, predicted to produce up to 320 million tonnes of coal a year.[15] In addition, there are substantial gas reserves in Queensland and northern New South Wales and since 2000 liquified coal seam gas from Western Australia has supplemented coal as a major carbon-emitting export, eagerly supported by the present government.[16]

Politics is inevitably complex but Australian mining policy in the last thirty years is, in significant part, attributable to effective campaigns since the 1990s by fossil fuel producers, supported by the Murdoch press, which have identified the interests of the Australian nation with mining company interests, denying or minimising the science behind climate change and rejecting calls from environmentalists to end the extraction of fossil fuels. Judith Brett points to the lack of logic in the arguments of the mining lobby which cascade in the following way:

> The first is that the planet is not heating so there is no need to cut fossil-fuel emissions; second, even if it is, it is not caused by humans; third, even if it is, Australia's emissions from both what we burn and what we export are so small that stopping them won't make any difference; fourth, the drug

---

[11] Simpson, *Adani* 6, 23.

[12] See Brett, "The Coal Curse," 7.

[13] Brett, "The Coal Curse," 3.

[14] The Adani name was changed to Bravus in late 2020. Mark Ludlow, "Courageous or Cut-Throat: Adani Changes Name to Bravus," *Financial Review*, 5 November 2020.

[15] Peter Hannam, "What's Next for Adani, the Coal Project That Helped to Return Morrison to Power?," *The Sydney Morning Herald*, 22 May 2019.

[16] Andrew Stock et al., "Passing Gas: Why Renewables Are the Future," (Climate Council, 2020).

dealer's defence: if we don't sell the coal and gas, someone else will; fifth, the predicted damage will not be that bad and doesn't warrant the economic costs…The first two and fifth are refuted by science, the rest by both ethics and by political realism."[17]

The weakness of these arguments has not prevented mining companies lobbying hard and increasing their influence.[18] Since 2010 Gautam Adani has made donations across both sides of politics and at various levels (local, state and national).[19] From the financial years 2006-2007 to 2015-2016 the mining industry disclosed donations of $16.6 million to major political parties (with 81% going to the Coalition).[20] Well-funded campaigns have been so effective that in Queensland in 2018 Adani was "the saviour on everyone's lips" with the Adani logo increasingly seen in prominent positions in Queensland towns accompanied by Adani funded community events.[21] The mining industry's campaigns echo the strong anti-environment stance taken by some Coalition politicians. Nationals MP George Christensen in 2018 posted a photograph of himself on Facebook aiming a gun accompanied by a caption saying "You gotta ask yourself, do you feel lucky greenie punks?"[22] Coal mining was a major factor in the National/Liberal Coalition being re-elected in 2019, supported by the extensive financial backing (A$60m) of mining investor Clive Palmer which helped ensure the necessary swing to the Coalition among working class communities in mining states of Queensland and Western Australia.[23]

Support for fossil fuels continues, with a recent partial shift from coal to the equally environmentally problematic commodity of liquefied natural gas. Even after the devastating bushfires of 2019-2020 development of fossil fuels continued. The expansion of coal and gas was slipped through under cover of the pandemic in 2020 and the National COVID-19 Coordination Commission has been said to have a membership "skewed towards people with links to fossil fuels."[24] Paving the way for other planned mega mines in the area, the Adani/Bravus project began in September 2020.[25]

---

[17] Brett, "The Coal Curse," 68–69.
[18] Brett, "The Coal Curse," 40.
[19] Simpson, *Adani*, 5.
[20] Simpson, *Adani*, 29.
[21] Simpson, *Adani*, 12.
[22] Brett, "The Coal Curse," 65–66.
[23] Brett, "The Coal Curse," 62–65.
[24] Brett, "The Coal Curse," 73–74.
[25] Mark Ludlow, "'It's Happening': Digging Begins at Adani's $2b Carmichael Mine," *Financial Review*, 18 September 2020.

While extractive companies in other parts of the world have run similar campaigns, the sceptical position of Australian politicians in relation to climate change is notable. It contrasts, for instance, with the UK approach in 2015 where the leaders of the three major political parties signed a statement on climate change policy which included carbon budgets and closing coal-fired power stations.[26] One commentator asks: "How can a country like Australia, known for its pristine beaches and tracts of wilderness and distinctive marsupials, reptiles, and insects, Gondwana-descended flora and fauna have such a treacherous heart?" Her own answer, is the homage paid by Australian politicians to the mining industry, which has resulted in the emergence of a national image epitomised by "working-class heroes in hard hats…portraying the mining sector as the backbone of the economy."[27] The self-image of Australia as a mining nation looks back to the mining boom of the 1990s, avoiding the present environmental challenges and demonstrating the extent to which some influential sections of Australian society are "self-confident with the familiar and uncomfortable with the unfamiliar,…ignoring the risks to stick with what they know."[28] This criticism seems to apply to the current cohort of politicians: "Climate denial has its strongest grip on aging white men, drawing on their need for certainty and control, the aggressive self-confidence they mobilise to defend these and the projection of their own threatened sense of identity onto others."[29] Ronald Wright's discussion of the history of collapsed societies uses the term "dinosaur factor" to describe the way that some societies in the past have refused to deviate from a commitment to a particular course of action (such as irrigation or deforestation) that had previously helped a society to flourish but which is so strong that it eventually becomes unsustainable and cannot respond to changed circumstances, threatening to destroy that society.[30] In the determination to contrive a national self-identity based in mining, Australia's political dinosaurs and their nostalgia for fossil fuels demonstrate a fatal failure to recognise the current ecological crisis.

Science and technology – benefits and limitations

One positive way of responding to the current situation is already underway in a turn towards science and technology. In the last three decades

---

[26] Simpson, *Adani*, 24.

[27] Simpson, *Adani*, 24–25.

[28] Donald Horne cited by Brett, "The Coal Curse," 27.

[29] Brett, "The Coal Curse," 52.

[30] Ronald Wright, *A Short History of Progress* (Toronto: Anansi, 2004).

climate scientists have increasingly warned of the planetary consequences of burning fossil fuels, arguing that the best, perhaps only, way to reduce carbon emissions is to simply stop extracting and burning fossil fuels. According to a 2015 report, more than 80 percent of coal, half of gas and one third of oil reserves must be left untouched in order for the planet to stay beneath the 2-degree Celsius upper limit for global warming set by the Paris agreement.[31] This suggests that the mining, exporting, and burning of Australian coal and gas will be a global ecological catastrophe.[32]

With the message of science being taken seriously by some, Australian environmental activism has grown significantly. The Stop Adani Alliance is a large-scale network of organisations made up of environmentalists, farmers, traditional owners, and mining-competing industries (such as tourism) who oppose the Adani/Bravus project, a movement said to have "revolutionised Australian politics".[33] Pressure against fossil fuel interests also comes from the Lock the Gate movement, a coalition of farmers and environmentalists opposing various forms of exploration and mining, including fracking.[34]

With an abundance of sunshine and massive ocean perimeter Australia has significant renewable energy capacity and there has already been an unexpectedly high take-up of renewable energy and low/zero emissions projects, for example Tasmania in 2020 declared that it was entirely powered by renewable electricity.[35] Supporting renewable energy would seem to be an obvious choice for politicians because it addresses the question of employment, one of the publicly stated reasons for supporting the mining industry. The number of people employed by mining in Australia is a contested question, with fossil fuel supporters at times inflating the number of current and potential jobs from mining, for example, the original claim by Adani that its Carmichael mine would create 10,000 jobs has since

---

[31] UCL News, "Which Fossil Fuels Must Remain in the Ground to Limit Global Warming?," University College London News, https://www.ucl.ac.uk/news/2015/jan/which-fossil-fuels-must-remain-ground-limit-global-warming.

[32] It is also highly problematic locally. The massive water use in the mining process itself threatens Queensland wetlands as well as groundwater supply from the Great Artesian Basin which occupies about 22% of Australia; the ocean pollution will hasten the death of the Great Barrier Reef; and as is often the case with mining projects it dissects Indigenous spiritual land. For more information on the Reef, see Simpson, *Adani* and Krien, "The Long Goodbye,".

[33] Simpson, *Adani*, 177.

[34] Brett, "The Coal Curse," 71.

[35] Michael Mazengarb, "Tasmania Declares Itself 100 Per Cent Powered by Renewable Electricity," *Renew Economy* 2020.

been reduced to 1,464.[36] Currently about 1.9 per cent of the workforce is employed in mining jobs, a figure which is likely to decline as automation increases. In contrast the Million Jobs Plan suggests that in five years, renewables and low emissions projects can deliver 1.8 million new jobs in Australia, and in the regions and communities where jobs are most needed.[37]

Renewable energy should also be attractive to politicians because its economic benefits can appeal to both main parties. The price of renewable energy has fallen faster than expected and storage technology developed faster than expected, causing coal prices to fall in 2020.[38] Renewables have become such an attractive investment that they are now largely economically viable without government subsidies and in 2020 the Australian business community showed an unprecedented level of support for renewable energy with financial institutions announcing ever more stringent divestiture policies, making new coal mines and coal-fired power stations increasingly uninsurable and nonbankable, and the Adani/Bravus project has already experienced delays and scale-backs.[39] In late 2018 Adani/Bravus claimed it was scaling down the project, from an initially planned 60m tonne mine to exporting initially 10m tonnes a year, increasing "over time" to 27m tonnes. (This may, however, be disingenuous: the company's development plan suggests this not their real intention, indicating that it plans an increase to 27m tonnes in the second year and to eventually produce 55m tonnes per year.)[40]

Present and future take up of renewable energy is an excellent way to turn Australia away from fossil fuels. Economist Ross Garnaut argues that "if Australia rises to the challenge of climate change it will emerge as a global superpower in energy, low-carbon industry and absorption of carbon in the landscape."[41] This would also boost Australian manufacturing enabling it to turn away from its traditional over-reliance on primary sector economics: the COVID-19 pandemic began with a dearth of Australian manufacturers of masks and ventilators, but this was reversed in a short period of time, indicating that a stronger manufacturing capability is possible.[42]

---

[36] Brett, "The Coal Curse," 13.
[37] Chris Murphy, "National Economic Impacts of the Million Jobs Plan," (Beyond Zero Emissions, 2020).
[38] Brett, "The Coal Curse," 69.
[39] Brett, "The Coal Curse," 69.
[40] Ben Smee, "Documents Suggest Adani Retained Long-Term Plan to Build Australia's Biggest Mine," *The Guardian*, 11 November 2020.
[41] Garnaut, *Super-Power*, 8
[42] Brett, "The Coal Curse," 37.

It may be that with sufficient political will, and a shift in the idea that Australia is essentially a mining country, renewable energy can supplant carbon-emitting energy sources. This "light green" approach of technology and economics undoubtedly has an important environmental impact.[43] Yet there is also a "deeper green" argument that the Enlightenment/Western ideology that promotes progress, economic growth, industry, technology, individualism, and human-centredness itself bears some responsibility for climate change as well as other interrelated ecological collapses - ocean pollution, over-fishing, deforestation, loss of biodiversity, human over-population, not to mention Enlightenment ideology's related accoutrements such as colonialism, racism, and patriarchy. From a darker green perspective, decarbonising the economy entails a broader and deeper overhaul of economy and culture.[44] Since at least the 1960s significant challenges have been made to the dominant notion of limitless economic growth and human centeredness, from environmental thinkers (Schumacher) and activists (Thunberg), and numerous movements such as "Slow", Permaculture, and XR.[45] A challenge to ideas is essential for a paradigm shift. John McNeill, discussing the environmental history of the twentieth century, says:

> … the powerful prevailing ideas mattered more than the explicitly environmental ones. Environmental ideas and politics, although part of the new grand equations that governed societies after the 1960s, never came close to dislodging reigning ideas and policies, which fit so well with the realities of the times. Even when they did not fit, they had the staying power of incumbents. One reason the environment in the twentieth century changed

---

[43] For examples of the light green approach see Garnaut, *Super-Power*, Paul Hawken, Amory B Lovins and L Hunter Lovins, *Natural Capitalism: The Next Industrial Revolution* (London: Earthscan Publications Ltd, 1999) and Paul Hawken, (ed.) *Drawdown: The Most Comprehensive Plan Ever Proposed to Roll Back Global Warming* (New York: Penguin, 2017)

[44] The terms 'light' and 'dark' green do not indicate a dichotomy, rather two ends of a spectrum which has space for many approaches. Indeed, some light greens acknowledge that other measures are needed such as rehabilitating land, reducing land clearing, and extensive tree planting, for example Garnaut, *Super-Power*, 141.

[45] Some economists are being influenced by environmental thinking, for example Kate Raworth, *Doughnut Economics: Seven Ways to Think Like a 21st-Century Economist* (London: Random House, 2017), yet others, even those promoting renewable energy, retain a commitment to economic growth/development. Garnaut, *Super-Power*.

so much is because prevailing ideas and politics – from an ecological perspective – changed so little.[46]

A changed ethos that looks deeper than science, technology, and economics will look to a range of values which emphasise planetary and human wellbeing over wealth acquisition and incorporates the whole of human life and culture including spirituality and religion. It invites, in an Australian and perhaps a global context, some discussion of Indigenous culture.

Culture and land

A good deal of literature indicates that colonization has brought disaster of many kinds to First Nations people. Australian Indigenous writer Tony Birch observes that for Indigenous communities climate injustice is not so much a new phenomenon but is something previously prehended and experienced in the empirical project which obscured the autonomy and knowledge of Indigenous people.[47] Non-Indigenous Australia has an extremely poor relationship with Indigenous people, with Australia's modern history being described as one of "invasion, dispossession, massacre, racism, and continuing disadvantage."[48] At the time of colonization/invasion in 1788 there may have been a population of 750,000 Indigenous people, reduced to 100,000 through the violence of what was in effect a (still under-acknowledged) frontier war. Indigenous people were not counted as Australian citizens until 1967, and in living memory, racial segregation, removal of children from families, lack of civil rights, and prejudice have been common. Today unofficial violence towards Indigenous people by authorities and communities continues, with Indigenous people disproportionately represented in statistics of imprisonment and deaths in custody.

The development of fossil fuels is one among many issues undermining indigenous sovereignty and rights because it destroys ecologies that are vital to Indigenous communities, excludes them "from country they are culturally bound to protect" and fails to deliver economic or social benefits.[49] In the

---

[46] John McNeill, *Something New under the Sun: An Environmental History of the Twentieth-Century World* (New York, NY: W W Norton, 2000), 325.
[47] Tony Birch, "'We've Seen the End of the World and We Don't Accept It': Protection of Indigenous Country and Climate Justice," in *Towards a Just and Ecologically Sustainable Peace: Navigating the Great Transition*, (ed.) Joseph Camilleri and Deborah Guess (Singapore: Palgrave Macmillan, 2020), 253.
[48] Chris Budden, *Following Jesus in Invaded Space: Doing Theology on Aboriginal Land* (Eugene: OR: Pickwick, 2009), 2.
[49] Birch, "'We've Seen the End of the World and We Don't Accept It'," 265.

1970s Indigenous people were given limited rights to claim unoccupied crown land including some ability to control mining and the 1992 High Court Mabo decision overturned the notion of terra nullius, leading to the Native Title Act in 1993 which allowed native title holders to negotiate but not veto mining development.[50] Despite its relative weakness, the Act nevertheless invoked a strong reactive campaign which played on the idea that too much had been given to Indigenous people and aimed to persuade non-Indigenous Australian voters that native title posed dangers and problems to them even though the vast majority of Australians would never have any involvement with native title claims. Intersecting with the mining campaign mentioned above, it sought both to weaken land rights and native title and at the same time convince the public "that mining was crucial to national development and prosperity".[51] Some mining companies did develop PR strategies that supported Indigenous Australians such as offering scholarships, engaging with Indigenous communities and employing archaeologists and anthropologists to advise on cultural heritage.[52] Yet overall there is still no recognition of Indigenous people in the Australian constitution.[53] The Australian Labor party has at times supported the Indigenous population, for example Kevin Rudd as PM in 2008 made a historic apology to the Stolen Generation, but Labor failed to support changes to the Native Title Act which further diluted Traditional owners' rights.[54] The highly inequitable power relationship between mining companies and native-title parties is said to effectively set up negotiations for division and failure.[55]

Judith Brett has observed that in the 1990s the pro-mining campaign could achieve at least three related ends: defending and promoting mining interests, weakening public sympathy for Aboriginal people and their rights, and creating scepticism about climate change:

> When climate change began seriously to threaten fossil-fuel miners at the end of last century, they knew what to do. To prevent the development of bipartisan consensus on climate action, they needed to position scepticism about climate change firmly on the same side of the political divide as opposition to Indigenous rights.[56]

---

[50] Brett, "The Coal Curse," 44.
[51] Brett, "The Coal Curse," 40.
[52] Brett, "The Coal Curse," 46.
[53] Simpson, *Adani*, 7.
[54] Simpson, *Adani*, 183.
[55] For a more detailed discussion see Krien, "The Long Goodbye,"17–39
[56] Brett, "The Coal Curse," 41–46 at 46.

The culture war and the climate war segued because "the enemies were mostly the same, which for many politicians is what counts".[57]

Australian climate denial/minimisation is entwined in the indigenous culture war not only in relation to the pragmatic issue of mining but also because a fundamental link may be said to exist between ecology and indigeneity. This is not to impose a Western Romantic reading onto indigenous cultures or to suggest that there is always an easy fit between the interests of First Nations peoples and environmentalists, or to claim Indigenous knowledge as a "resource" for non-Indigenous environmental action.[58] Yet critique has been made from both ecological and indigenous thinkers of the priority given to economic growth and both groups have been said to share "…an awareness of the integral and whole relationship of material, semiotic, and spiritual life".[59] Indigenous peoples, it has been said, are able to model "human life lived responsibly and respectfully with the whole of the Earth community."[60] This expresses the kind of wider cultural and religious focus that resonates with a darker green ethos. Specifically, land is given prominence, with many Australian Aboriginal writers having emphasised the identification with land.[61] One Indigenous thinker argues that identity can only be tied to land because there is "only one place or places where you can be, and that defines who you are".[62]

Those who colonized Australia seem to have held a diminished view of Aboriginal people and their way of living and failed to adequately observe and appreciate the differences and complexities not only of an unfamiliar

---

[57] Brett, "The Coal Curse," 68.

[58] John Grim, "Indigenous Knowing and Responsible Life in the World," in *Ecospirit: Religions and Philosophies for the Earth,* (ed.) Laurel Kearns and Catherine Keller (New York: Fordham University Press, 2007), 199. Anne Elvey, "Reimagining Decolonising Praxis for a Just and Ecologically Sustainable Peace in an Australian Context," in *Towards a Just and Ecologically Sustainable Peace: Navigating the Great Transition,* (ed.) Joseph Camilleri and Deborah Guess (Singapore: Palgrave Macmillan, 2020), 288.

[59] John A. Grim, "Indigenous Lifeways and Ecology," *Yale Forum on Religion and Ecology* (2021),
https://fore.yale.edu/World-Religions/Indigenous/Overview-Essay, 1.

[60] Grim, "Indigenous Lifeways and Ecology", 1.

[61] For example: Bruce Pascoe, *Dark Emu Black Seeds: Agriculture of Accident?* (Broome, WA: Magabala Books, 2014); Bruce Pascoe, *Salt: Selected Stories and Essays* (Carlton, Vic: Schwartz, 2019); Tyson Yunkaporta, *Sand Talk: How Indigenous Thinking Can Save the World* (Melbourne: Text Publishing, 2019), Victor Steffensen, *Fire Country: How Indigenous Fire Management Could Help Save Australia* (Melbourne: Hardie Grant Travel, 2020).

[62] Aileen Moreton-Robinson, interview by David Rutledge, 1 December, 2019, Audio Podcast.

people but also of their land. Committed to a commodified and Western understanding of land and empire, they anticipated that the Indigenous population would be "primitive" hunter-gatherers, a view which conveniently reinforced both the idea of white supremacy and the understanding that the land was vacant or barren and therefore open to claim. Early colonizers failed to see "Aboriginal homelands, shaped over millennia by Aboriginal people."[63] Bruce Pascoe has argued that contrary to colonial expectations, Indigenous culture and economy incorporated such features as agriculture, housing, and bread baking, with one early explorer reporting extensive yam gardens, tubers being harvested, grain being stored, and construction of weirs and dams.[64] Despite these early records, the idea of Australian Aboriginals as "savages", and as exclusively hunter-gatherers, prevailed so that "the true descriptions of the Aboriginal culture and economy were completely erased from the public conscience and, amazingly, from the public record."[65] Pascoe argues that colonial omission and erasure is due to more than innocent neglect because sections in the early explorer's journal speaking of Aboriginal housing, irrigation, agriculture, and road-making were omitted during the editing process when the journal was published.[66] Pascoe's thesis supports Birch's claim that Indigenous land was devalued both by direct violence and "through a fabricated narrative of Indigenous savagery and civil absence".[67] Ignorance of the history of Australian Indigenous people, their relationship to land and their treatment of it is part of the reason why many non-Indigenous Australians struggle to find an ecologically sustainable way of living and to continue to identify Australia as a mining nation. The ability to pay attention to land and to re-think its meaning may be a core issue. As Andrew Morrell of the Juru people in Queensland says: "...there are people out there who don't even know their country."[68] Many non-Indigenous Australians, including those who are environmentally committed, increasingly demonstrate that they value the land itself and respect the culture of Aboriginal communities, and in 2020 a high level of public outrage followed the destruction of 46,000-year-old

---

[63] Marcia Langton cited by Krien, "The Long Goodbye," 32.

[64] Pascoe, *Salt* 59–63. For Pascoe's fuller discussion see Pascoe, *Dark Emu Black Seeds*.

[65] Pascoe, *Salt*, 33.

[66] Pascoe, *Salt*, 65.

[67] Birch, "'We've Seen the End of the World and We Don't Accept It'" 254.

[68] Marcia Langton cited by Krien, "The Long Goodbye," 30.

sacred Indigenous sites by the Rio Tinto mining group in Western Australia.[69]

A deeper understanding and appreciation of Australian land and of how Aboriginal people lived with it and within its limits not only supports a respectful attitude to Indigenous people but opens the ecological possibility of treating the land differently, for example by adopting changed agricultural models:

> If we could understand the brilliance of the Australian agricultural mind we would meet our carbon-emission reduction targets easily. The domesticated Aboriginal grains and tubers are mostly perennial, so their cultivation requires far fewer tractor hours, thus saving the soil from compaction and the air from pollution. The ability of these plants to flourish in our climate and soils will save us billions of dollars.[70]

Among the deeper ecological understandings based on learning about and emulating the spiritual and ecological ties to land that are evident in the culture and land practices modelled by Indigenous people is Freya Mathews' suggestion of hands-on practices of conservation entailing "close attention to the particularities of a given place" which change our way of seeing and inhabiting, of arriving at a knowledge that is inextricably involved with feeling, entering the land and engaging with it.[71] This need not entail appropriating First Nations culture, as Pascoe says:

> The riches of the oldest human culture of earth are available to Australians; very little of it is prohibited to the uninitiated or to those of a different race. Most of it can become the reassuringly comfortable garb of all Australians. We're not inviting a second dispossession of our culture but an awakening of the nation to the land itself. We can all love it and care for it; we can love and care for each other. … We need non-Aboriginal Australians to love the land.[72]

---

[69] Michelle Stanley and Kelly Gudgeon, "Pilbara Mining Blast Confirmed to Have Destroyed 46,000 Yo Sites of 'Staggering' Significance," *ANC News Online*, 26 May 2020.

[70] Pascoe, *Salt*, 36.

[71] Freya Mathews, "'Walking the Land': An Alternative to Discourse as a Path to Ecological Consciousness and Peace," in *Towards a Just and Ecologically Sustainable Peace: Navigating the Great Transition*, (ed.) Joseph Camilleri and Deborah Guess (Singapore: Palgrave Macmillan, 2020), 109–110.

[72] Pascoe, *Salt*, 115.

Conclusion

Climate change has turned Australia's reliance on mining income into a political, social, and environmental curse.[73] Grounded in a colonial worldview and intensified by strong and well-funded campaigns by mining interests, an Australian identity has been formed that is deeply committed to extracting and exporting fossil fuel. A strong turn to renewable sources of energy in recent years points to a more positive future for a country blessed with bountiful solar and tidal potential as long as the nation can find the will to end its commitment to extractive industry. While technology that transitions away from fossil fuels is very important, it may be insufficient on its own to address the broader ecological and cultural crisis. While the dominant Western system has undoubtedly led to unprecedented levels of comfort and wellbeing for some, its highly uneven distribution of wealth has led to extreme poverty for others and has failed to take account of planetary limits, resulting in a natural world that is so destabilized that humankind now faces a future that threatens to go beyond collapse to catastrophe or even extinction.[74] A deeper and more promising societal and cultural change is possible. In Australia in 2020 the strict and (so far) highly effective coronavirus lockdowns in the State of Victoria show that it is possible to give communal wellbeing precedence over individual self-interest. Globally it might be possible to relinquish the goal of short-term money-making and live more sustainably, prioritising ecology over economy. The question is whether this can be done with sufficient urgency. The pandemic showed that to be effective, action must sometimes be taken quickly, and as environmentalist Bill McKibben has said about climate action, winning slowly can be the same as losing.

Alongside attaining the goal of zero carbon emissions by taking up renewable energy technology, a profound invitation of our times is to participate in a deeper cultural, spiritual, and even religious transformation where ecological obligations are taken with utmost seriousness and where moral boundaries are drawn around the economic system as well as our own individual desires. Among the numerous ways to achieve this, non-Indigenous Australians might take up the promising invitation to become well-informed about the culture, ecology, and economy of the country's First Nations people, to relinquish a "vindictive adherence to colonial

---

[73] Brett, "The Coal Curse," 67.

[74] Collapse, catastrophe and extinction are three possible future scenarios discussed by Jem Bendell, "Deep Adaptation: A Map for Navigating Climate Tragedy," *IFLAS Occasional Paper*, no. 2 (2018), 19–21.

myth"[75] and recognise the ecological importance of the land ethic known and practiced by Indigenous communities.

Bibliography

Bendell, Jem. "Deep Adaptation: A Map for Navigating Climate Tragedy." *IFLAS Occasional Paper*, no. 2 (2018).

Birch, Tony. "'We've Seen the End of the World and We Don't Accept It': Protection of Indigenous Country and Climate Justice." In *Towards a Just and Ecologically Sustainable Peace: Navigating the Great Transition*, edited by Joseph Camilleri and Deborah Guess, 251-73. (Singapore: Palgrave Macmillan, 2020).

Brett, Judith. "The Coal Curse: Resources, Climate and Australia's Future." *Quarterly Essay*, no. 78 (2020): 1-81.

Budden, Chris. *Following Jesus in Invaded Space: Doing Theology on Aboriginal Land*. (Eugene: OR: Pickwick, 2009).

Elvey, Anne. "Reimagining Decolonising Praxis for a Just and Ecologically Sustainable Peace in an Australian Context." In *Towards a Just and Ecologically Sustainable Peace: Navigating the Great Transition*, edited by Joseph Camilleri and Deborah Guess, 275-95. (Singapore: Palgrave Macmillan, 2020).

Garnaut, Ross. *Super-Power: Australia's Low-Carbon Opportunity*. (Melbourne: La Trobe University Press, 2019).

Grim, John. "Indigenous Knowing and Responsible Life in the World." In *Ecospirit: Religions and Philosophies for the Earth*, edited by Laurel Kearns and Catherine Keller, 196-214. (New York: Fordham University Press, 2007).

Grim, John A. "Indigenous Lifeways and Ecology." *Yale Forum on Religion and Ecology* (2021). https://fore.yale.edu/World-Religions/Indigenous/Overview-Essay.

Hannam, Peter. "What's Next for Adani, the Coal Project That Helped to Return Morrison to Power?" *The Sydney Morning Herald*, 22 May, 2019.

Hawken, Paul, (ed.) *Drawdown: The Most Comprehensive Plan Ever Proposed to Roll Back Global Warming*. (New York: Penguin, 2017).

Hawken, Paul, Amory B Lovins and L Hunter Lovins. *Natural Capitalism: The Next Industrial Revolution*. (London: Earthscan Publications Ltd, 1999).

---

[75] Pascoe, *Salt*, 57.

Krien, Anna. "The Long Goodbye: Coal, Coral and Australia's Climate Deadlock." *Quarterly Essay*, no. 66 (2017): 1-116.

Ludlow, Mark. "Courageous or Cut-Throat: Adani Changes Name to Bravus." *Financial Review*, 5 November, 2020.

—. "'It's Happening': Digging Begins at Adani's \$2b Carmichael Mine." *Financial Review*, 18 September, 2020.

Mathews, Freya. "'Walking the Land': An Alternative to Discourse as a Path to Ecological Consciousness and Peace." In *Towards a Just and Ecologically Sustainable Peace: Navigating the Great Transition*, edited by Joseph Camilleri and Deborah Guess, 97-116. (Singapore: Palgrave Macmillan, 2020).

Mazengarb, Michael. "Tasmania Declares Itself 100 Per Cent Powered by Renewable Electricity." *Renew Economy*, 2020.

McNeill, John. *Something New under the Sun: An Environmental History of the Twentieth-Century World*. New York, NY: W W Norton, 2000.

Minton Beddoes, Zanny. "Time to Make Coal History." *The Economist* 3 December, 2020.

Moreton-Robinson, Aileen. "Philosophy in the Wake of Empire Part 5: Tracks of Thought." By David Rutledge. *The Philosopher's Zone* (1 December, 2019).

Murphy, Chris. "National Economic Impacts of the Million Jobs Plan." Beyond Zero Emissions, 2020.

News, UCL. "Which Fossil Fuels Must Remain in the Ground to Limit Global Warming?" University College London News, https://www.ucl.ac.uk/news/2015/jan/which-fossil-fuels-must-remain-ground-limit-global-warming.

Pascoe, Bruce. *Dark Emu Black Seeds: Agriculture of Accident?* (Broome, WA: Magabala Books, 2014).

—. *Salt: Selected Stories and Essays*. Carlton, Vic: Schwartz, 2019.

Raworth, Kate. *Doughnut Economics: Seven Ways to Think Like a 21st-Century Economist*. (London: Random House, 2017).

Richards, Lisa, Nigel Brew and Lizzie Smith. "2019–20 Australian Bushfires - Frequently Asked Questions: A Quick Guide." edited by Parliament of Australia, 2020.

Simpson, Lindsay. *Adani: Following Its Dirty Footsteps. A Personal Story*. (North Geelong: Vic: Spinifex, 2018).

Smee, Ben. "Documents Suggest Adani Retained Long-Term Plan to Build Australia's Biggest Mine." *The Guardian*, 11 November, 2020.

Stanley, Michelle and Kelly Gudgeon. "Pilbara Mining Blast Confirmed to Have Destroyed 46,000 Yo Sites of 'Staggering' Significance." *ANC News Online*, 26 May, 2020.

Steffensen, Victor. *Fire Country: How Indigenous Fire Management Could Help Save Australia*. (Melbourne: Hardie Grant Travel, 2020).

Stock, Andrew, Greg Bourne, Will Steffan and Tim Baxter. "Passing Gas: Why Renewables Are the Future." Climate Council, 2020.

Swann, Tom. "High Carbon from a Land Down Under: Quantifying CO_2 from Australia's Fossil Fuel Mining and Exports." (The Australia Institute, 2019).

Wright, Ronald. *A Short History of Progress*. Toronto: Anansi, 2004.

Yunkaporta, Tyson. *Sand Talk: How Indigenous Thinking Can Save the World*. (Melbourne: Text Publishing, 2019).

CHAPTER SIX

FOOD ETHICS IN THEOLOGY: TOWARD CARING FOR ANIMALS AND THE ENVIRONMENT

YOKO KITO

Introduction

In today's context, where climate change and environmental crises are urgent issues, we find ourselves forced to change our lifestyles and our dietary habits are no exception. In particular, it has been scientifically proven that factory farming places a huge burden on the environment.[1] Not eating meat will not in itself solve the problem of climate change, but it would certainly be a big help in curbing it.[2] But it is quite hard not to eat meat for many people. What are the ethics involved?

Since the twentieth century, many theological ideas about the environment and animals (under the headings of 'environmental theology' and 'animal

---

[1] For every kilogram of beef eaten, the same amount of greenhouse gases is emitted as driving a car 100 kilometers. Kari Hamershlag, "What You Eat Matters; Eat Less Meat + Cheese and Buy Greener When You Do," Environmental Working Group, 2011, URL: https://static.ewg.org/reports/2011/meateaters/pdf/report_ewg_meat_eaters_guide_to_health_and_climate_2011.pdf. In addition, greenhouse gas emissions from the livestock industry account for 14-18% of the world's total emissions, e.g., The Food and Agriculture Organization of the United Nations, "LIVESTOCK'S LONG SHADOW: environmental issues and options," Rome, 2006, URL: http://www.fao.org/3/a-a0701e.pdf

[2] H. Charles J. Godfray et al., "Meat consumption, health, and the environment," *Science*, 2018, 361(6399): eaam5324. Ruben Sanchez-Sabate and Joan Sabaté, "Consumer Attitudes Towards Environmental Concerns of Meat Consumption: A Systematic Review," *International Journal of Environmental Research and Public Health*, 2019, 16(7):1220.

theology,') have been debated. For example, traditional environmental theology takes a comprehensive view of the natural environment, whilst many animal theologies argue for the need to care for animals. To advance the idea of avoiding the eating of meat in order to care for the environment and animals, I will consider what eating means in theology and what 'eating' is for Christians in particular.

In this chapter, I will first review the problems that conventional environmental and animal theology face in dealing with this issue. Then, I will review the meaning of 'eating' in Christianity from the perspectives of Eucharist, creation and eschaton, and specifically, the meaning of eating meat from a theological perspective. Mainly I refer to Paul Tillich's thoughts on the Eucharist for supporting my own argument. Through these discussions, I am trying to propose a Christian ethic of abstaining from eating meat based on the theory of Eucharist.

1. Issues in Environmental and Animal Theology

Environmental theology (eco-theology) began as a response to Lynn White Jr.'s charge that the biblical creation story promoted anthropocentrism, or human domination and exploitation of nature for their own sake[3] and environmental theology developed from the 1960s to the 1980s in response to this interpretation of the creation story. The result was the reference to "dominion of the earth"[4] by humans in the creation story being understood as humans being good "stewards" of nature, rather than justifying their exploitation.[5] In the 1990s and 2000s, environmental theology developed from the perspective of eschatology rather than creation.[6] The central question was not the cause of the environmental crisis, but whether Christianity could offer a vision to overcome it. In recent years, the connection between economics and environmental studies has also become a focus of discussion, as represented by environmental theologies such as Sallie McFague (2002),[7] which aims to shift society away from the goal of

---

[3] Lynn White, "The historical roots of our ecological crisis," *Science*, 1967, 155(3767): 1203–1207.

[4] Genesis 1.26-28.

[5] John Arthur Passmore, *Man's Responsibility for Nature: Ecological Problems and Western Traditions*, (Scribner, 1974).

[6] Catherine Keller, "No More Sea: The Lost Chaos of the Eschaton" in: Dieter T. Hessel & Rosemary Radford Ruether (eds.), *Christianity and Ecology, Seeking the Well-Being of Earth and Humans*, (Harvard University Press, 2000)183-198.

[7] Sallie McFague, "God's Household: Christianity, Economics and Planetary

economic growth to an ecological economic model based on interdependence and the goal of global environmental sustainability. In such environmental theologies, the nature of the world model is questioned, but no concrete conclusions are reached about the need to care for individual animals or to avoid eating meat.

On the other hand, much discussion in animal theology has been devoted to the issue of reinterpreting the *Imago Dei* (image of God). If humans and animals are to be regarded as objects of equal concern, then how are humans, who are created "in the image of God," different from animals? For example, Ryan P. McLaughlin (2014) argues that we should take a "functional interpretation" of *Imago Dei*, that is, we have inherent functions, rather than a "substantive" interpretation that we have the capacity to reason.[8] Daniel K. Miller (2012) argues that the *Imago Dei* should not be interpreted in a "substantive" way, relying on some human capacity, but in a "relational" way, in which we can relate to God.[9] The common denominator among these contemporary Christian theologians is the interpretation of the *Imago Dei* as a mission given only to human beings, not as a quality that is superior to other creatures. According to Andrew Linzey (1994), this uniqueness indicates that humans are set apart as servants to care for animals; humans are called to Christ-like service, to serve those who are different and 'lower' than they are, just as Christ gave up his divine status and took on human form.[10] The *Imago Dei* here is seen as a reflection of God who has made himself nothing (kenosis).

However, even if the image of God is reinterpreted, it does not necessarily lead to the conclusion that we should not eat animals. Although Linzey states that there is strong biblical support for vegetarianism,[11] his

---

Living," in Paul Knitter & Chandora Muzaffar (eds.), *Subverting Greed: Religious Perspectives on the Global Economy*, (Orbis Books, 2002).

[8] Ryan Patrick McLaughlin, *Christian Theology and the Status of Animals: The Dominant Tradition and Its Alternatives*, (Palgrave Macmillan, 2014) 44-47.

[9] Daniel K. Miller, *Animal Ethics and Theology: The Lens of the Good Samaritan,* (Routledge, 2012), 34ff.

[10] Andrew Linzey, *Animal Theology*, (University of Illinois Press, 1994) 33.

[11] Linzey, 1994:125f. Linzey cites Isaiah 11.6-9 as the source here and states "Note, for example, how the vision of peaceable living also extends to relations between animals themselves". For Linzey, the eschatological prophecy of Isaiah is a figure to be realized, but Old Testament writings should be interpreted symbolically. It is also unacceptable for human hands to try to realize the perfect image of the "Kingdom of God," in light of the eschatological discussions since the twentieth century. In my view, eschatology can be connected to ethics only when it is understood from a thoroughly contemporary perspective.

justification is problematic in two ways. First, Linzey's view of the Fall and the eschaton as possible events in history raises theological issues as well as problems of consistency with scientific perspectives.[12] According to Christopher Southgate (2008), although the belief in a primordial age without predation and violence has been very influential on those who advocate vegetarianism, all the evidence points to predation, violence, parasitism suffering, and extinction having been an integral part of the natural order since before the birth of Homo sapiens.[13] Therefore, Southgate criticizes the understanding that the Fall occurred within a specific historical time frame, which implies that there was no predation among animals before that Fall.[14] The second problem is that Linzey's theology sees the eschaton as something that can be brought about by human moral actions (including vegetarianism) rather than something that comes about by God's will, which is another departure from traditional Christian theology. In my opinion, it does not seem possible to justify vegetarianism directly from the Bible.[15] However, my conclusion is that we can clearly argue for vegetarianism from the perspective of Christian ethics. We need to further consider what we eat. To this end, I would like to discuss the theology of food, especially in terms of the Eucharist.

---

[12] In contemporary Christian theology, the Old Testament narratives of creation and fall are not situated within history. This is not only from the perspective of consistency with science, but also because it poses the problem of understanding the concept of time when considered in conjunction with eschatology. In this regard, Tillich argues that creation and the Fall are simultaneous (i.e., atemporal), and that the eschaton is "beyond history" (if both time and space come to an end, then the understanding of the eschaton as an extension of history is not valid). Cf. Paul Tillich, *Systematic Theology 3*, (University of Chicago Press, 1963).

[13] Christopher Southgate, "Protological and Eschatological Vegetarianism," in Rachel Muers & David Grumett (eds.), *Eating and Believing: Interdisciplinary Perspectives on Vegetarianism and Theology*, (2008, T&T Clark) 249.

[14] Southgate (2008) states that it is impossible to maintain a narrative that leads to such protological vegetarianism along with the narrative provided by evolutionary science.

[15] Horrell points out that whether Jesus was a vegetarian or not, he cannot make a compelling contribution to modern vegetarianism. "What the Bible can contribute, however, is broader facets of a worldview which inspires and sustains a commitment to discipline bodily practices out of a christologically shaped regard for other, to foster the flourishing and praise of the whole of creation, and to anticipate in practice the eschatological renewal of all creation." David G. Horrell, "Biblical Vegetarianism? A Critical and Constructive Assessment," in Rachel Muers & David Grumett (eds.), *Eating and Believing: Interdisciplinary Perspectives on Vegetarianism and Theology*, (2008, T&T Clark) 53.

2. The Eucharist as the Essence of Eating

2-1 Tillich's Understanding of the Eucharist and Nature

In considering a theology centered on the Eucharist, I would like to begin with a discussion of Paul Tillich (1886-1965). According to Panu Pihkara (2015), Tillich affirmed the value of nature and matter, and is considered a pioneer in eco-theology. [16] In Tillich's article "Nature and Sacraments," based on a 1928 lecture, he discusses nature and sacraments, and in particular, the Eucharist. [17] Tillich recognizes that the natural elements in the Eucharist are bearers of sacramental power and understands that the Holy character is omnipresent in essentially all natural elements [18]. According to Tillich, the bread of the Eucharist stands for all bread and ultimately for all nature. [19] Tillich argues the essential meaning of the Eucharist as follows: "the meaning of the Lord's Supper as a sacrament is that it is the sacramental appropriation of the exalted body of Christ." [20] This body of Christ as a body belongs to nature, as a transcendent body it is beyond nature. Tillich argues that the Eucharist substitutes organic substances (i.e., bread and wine) for the body. Therefore, a real celebration of the Eucharist without the natural element is impossible. That is, in place of the body we have the elements that nourish the body.

According to Tillich, "the holy is omnipresent in so far as the ground of being is not far from any being; the holy is demonized because of the separation of the infinite ground of being." [21] The "ground of being" referred to here is God. All creatures, including nature itself, are sustained by God as the "ground of being" and at the same time are separated from God as the "ground of being". Therefore, in the existential situation, in actual reality, nature remains ambiguous and cannot be said to be holy in itself. In Tillich, existence appears in the structure of essence-existence. In the case of human existence, humankind is essentially the embodiment of the goodness of creation, but when it comes into existence, that is, in an

---

[16] Panu Pihkara, "Ecotheology and the theology of eating", *Religion and Food*, 26 (2015), p.69-70.
[17] Paul Tillich, "Nature and Sacrament," in: *The Protestant Era*, (University of Chicago Press, 1948).
[18] Paul Tillich, *Systematic Theology 1,* University of Chicago Press, 1951.
[19] Paul Tillich, 1948:111.
[20] Tillich, 1948: 96.
[21] Tillich, 1948:111.

existential situation, it exists as an ambiguous thing, neither completely good nor completely evil. The same is true of nature. Therefore, nature is essentially holy, but it is not real, and becomes an "object of salvation."[22] In the existential context, nature itself is not holy, but it is a "bearer"[23] of sacramental power.

2-2 Eucharist-Centered Ethics

Tillich's theory of sacrament - that the bread of the Eucharist stands for all bread and ultimately for all nature - is groundbreaking, taking the theological perspective out of the church and into the natural world and the environment around us. However, Tillich himself did not link this theory of sacrament to environmental protection, much less advocate animal protection or abstinence from eating meat, and no concrete proposals for such ethical actions are found in his writings. However, I would like to develop this Eucharistic theory of religious ethics, taking creation and eschatology into account.

Although Tillich never mentions it, the Eucharist is a recurring sacramental event in the church, repeatedly experienced by those who partake of it. The sacramental experience of the Eucharist leads us to repeatedly taste nature in its existential context. In other words, nature has holiness as its essence, and at the same time, nature as existence is to be saved.

We are transformed by our encounter with the sacred. In the Eucharist, holiness as the essence of nature leads us to ethical action and actualizes the results of that ethical action. We are inspired by the sacred through the Eucharist. We encounter holiness as the nature that the Eucharist points to, with natural objects as symbols of holiness. In other words, our spirit recognizes the sacredness through the Eucharist and is brought to fruition in our ethical action, and the result of that ethical action, is embodied in the reality of this world.

Nature is not itself sacred, but it has the power to symbolize the sacred (according to the Protestant understanding). According to Tillich, at the consummation of the Kingdom of God (the eschaton), existence will be essentialized and it will be possible to see the sacred in reality.[24] If we look at what we eat in the Eucharist, it is a foretaste of the heavenly table we will

---

[22] Tillich, 1948:103.
[23] Tillich, 1948:110.
[24] Tillich, 1948:110-111.

experience at the end of time. In the Eucharist, we are eating the natural entities that bear the sacred.

In the Eucharist, nature is recognized as the "object of salvation" under conditions of existence. Through the Eucharist, we hear what Paul calls "the groaning of creation." The Eucharist makes us realize that both we and nature are "objects of salvation". Through the sensory stimulating actions of the Eucharist: seeing, touching, smelling, and tasting the bread of the Eucharist and hearing the priest's prayers read in the Eucharist, it is imprinted on our bodies, that nature and we are one and the same creatures, waiting for the completion of the Kingdom of God at the end of time, and it gives us a deep understanding of the sorrow of creation.

The ambiguity of holiness as the essence of nature and salvation under the conditions of existence is repeatedly recognized in the repeated experience of the Eucharist. Thus, holiness, as the essence of nature, is repeatedly recognized through the experience of the Eucharist and provides a repeated basis for our ethical actions. This is a point of view that environmental and animal theologies have not focused on until recently. The ethical action guided by the Eucharist is the action toward natural objects symbolized by the Eucharist. Nature as a creature in the intermediate time is repeatedly recognized by the experience of the Eucharist and is repeatedly given the hope of longing for the perfection of salvation at the end of time, that is, the full restoration of the essence of nature (or the goodness of creation). Creation and the eschaton are events outside of time, but they are united in the Eucharist. Using Tillich's discussion of the Eucharist and nature, we come to the understanding that eating, too, has its proper expression in the Eucharist, and that every day of our lives is related to it. From this point on, the question of how we should consume nature (creatures) will be asked in relation to the Eucharist.

The Eucharist is a thanksgiving for the *agape* of Christ. In other words, the original meaning of the Eucharist is a response to God's love. The Eucharist is literally "communion" or *communio sanctorum*. The ethics guided by the Eucharist are not the ethical acts of a single person, but the norms of community required in the "communion of saints," that are a response to *agape*. Thus, Eucharist-based ethics is grounded and motivated by the love of God, and the communion of saints.

The theological meanings of the Eucharist include Eucharistic gratitude, communion, remembrance (*anamnesis*)[25] of Christ's death as atonement

---

[25] The twentieth-century theological understanding of the sacraments emphasized the aspect of "anamnesis" and described it as "the means by which the redemptive

for sin and anticipation of the Kingdom of God. Jurgen Moltmann (1967), who advocated a cosmological eschatology, placed hope at its center,[26] - hope for the cosmic completion of the Kingdom of God. Here, the meaning of the Eucharist was also placed as a reminder of the hope for the salvation of Christ and its consummation at the end of time, which was opened by His sacrifice. Such an eschatological character of the Eucharist points to the anticipation of the coming Kingdom of God and its promised consummation. The anticipation of the hope of a world to come in which the perfect goodness of creation will be realized, can be a motive to convince Christians to act morally and to practice Christian values in their lives. An ethical attitude toward food is no exception.[27]

3. Three Meanings of "Eating" in Christian Thought

The ethical act guided by the Eucharist is the action toward nature symbolized by the Eucharist. What, then, are the specific ethical acts that we are led to perform after we hear the "groaning of the creation[28]" in the Eucharist?

There are many ethical acts against nature and there is no need to limit ourselves to just one. However, it makes sense to note that the Eucharist involves the act of eating. In the Eucharist, we are eating a natural entity that bears the sacred. And as Tillich states, the bread of the Eucharist stands for all bread and ultimately for all nature, revealing that the Eucharist is distinct from, yet connected to, everyday meals.

So, what does it mean to eat as an ethical act? The "way of eating" of

---

work of Christ on the cross is proclaimed and validated in the Church."

[26] Jürgen Moltmann, *Theology of Hope: On the Ground and the Implications of a Christian Eschatology,* (SCM Press, 1967).

[27] Tillich also states that with regard to the "holy," a nature such as that of a saint, for example, is a "holy being," not moral obedience, but "holy being," a substance out of which moral and other consequences follow (Tillich, 1948:109). In other words, holiness must be embodied not only in the mind, but also in the reality of the body. The "holy presence" precedes the holy action. Tillich's understanding of the Eucharist is both Protestant and Catholic. It is closer to Catholicism in its positive attitude toward nature, that existence always has a natural basis, and in its recommendation to "have a new understanding of the forces of nature that enter into the sacraments" (Tillich, 1948:164). It is also close to Protestantism in that it says that no object of sacred rites is created by the forces of nature itself, but that nature is only a transmitter of sacramental things.

[28] Romans 8.22.

Christians throughout the ages may provide an answer to this question.

I organize the ethical eating of Christians into three categories from the perspective of religious history. The first is "eating for resistance and protest," the second is "eating to acquire virtue," and the third is "eating for reconciliation."

3-1 Eating for Resistance and Protest

According to Michael S. Northcott (2008), in the Roman Empire, Christians of the early church avoided eating animal flesh, preferring to eat fish.[29] This can be seen in the iconography of the mosaics, sculptures, and other artifacts in the Roman catacombs and early churches. These artworks depict fish or fish-eaters, which not only indicates that fish (Jesus Christ, Son of God, Savior is the Greek word for fish ἰχθύς) was favored in religious iconography, but also reflects the dietary habits of Christians in the early church.[30]

In this section, I will focus on the communion meal (the prototype of the later Holy Communion) in Christian worship, which is thought to have avoided eating meat in particular. In Rome at that time, meat was for the rich and the poor rarely experienced the opportunity to eat it. Worship in the early church was different from the services of today's Christian churches, in that they shared meals as part of the act of worship.[31] The weak and the strong sat at the same table and the rich and the poor shared the same food. It was an expression of an economy different from that of the Roman Empire, and a table as an implementation of an anti-imperialist ethic.[32] Another possible reason for rejecting animal flesh as the Roman diet was that the early church understood Jesus Christ as the opposite of the territorial mighty, military power and authority symbolized by the Roman Empire.[33] I

---

[29] Michael S. Northcott, "Eucharistic Eating," in Rachel Muers & David Grumett (eds.), *Eating and Believing: Interdisciplinary Perspectives on Vegetarianism and Theology*, 2008, (T&T Clark) 242f.

[30] Robin Margaret Jensen, *Understanding Early Christian Art*, (Routledge, 2000) 51f.

[31] 1 Corinthians, chapter 1 and 11.18-22, shows that in the early church there was no ritual division between sacrament and meal. Cf. Ibid.

[32] Andrew McGowan, *Ascetic Eucharists: Food and Drink in Early Christian Ritual Meals*, (Clarendon Press,1998).

[33] Susan Power Bratton, "Anti-imperial themes and care for living nature in early Christian art," in Kyle Van Houtan & Michael S. Northcott (eds.), *Diversity and Dominion: Dialogue in Ecology, Ethics and Theology*, (Cascade Books, 2010)127f.

consider that the abstinence from meat in the early church included elements of resistance and protest against tyrannical power and injustice. The archetype of resistance and protest expressed through choosing food and eating can be seen in the table Jesus sets. The story of the Feeding of the Five Thousand (Luke 9:10-17) is a good example. The disciples proposed that they disperse the hungry crowd and suggested that each person buy their own food in town. But Jesus made everyone full by sharing food with each of them and this involved the prayer of praise and the breaking of bread - the prototype of the Eucharist. This 'food' story contrasts the disciples' uncritical acceptance of the monetary economy ensured by the power of the Roman Empire with Jesus' resistance to and breaking that power by food and eating.[34]

The persecution of Christians in the Roman Empire is partly due to the Christians' criticisms of the behavior of those in power and their refusal to conform to "emperor worship" as represented by Emperor Diocletian and the forced worship of Roman gods. On the other hand, it can be said that the imperial subjects benefited from peace and stability because of Roman rule. The essence of "idolatry" was that it fixed the structure of domination/subjugation by powerful forces. The Christians, however, were practicing what Jesus showed them about resistance to and breaking that power by food and eating in their own way. In other words, they ate different foods than the powerful in order to resist and break the power of the Roman Empire, which forced idolatry upon them.

There are many who read this element of rejection of and resistance to idolatry into animal ethics and food ethics.[35] Horrell (2008), for example, presents a commitment to vegetarianism as a way of expressing a critical and ascetic rejection of the dominant system of industrial food production,[36]

---

[34] See also Northcott, 2008:236-237.

[35] Southgate also opposes the raising of large numbers of animals for meat. He states that the most compelling theological arguments come not from a theology of creation or an appeal to the eschaton, but from the need for divine justice and human prudence. David Grumett and Rachel Muers go further, stating that there is no morally "neutral" meat in our time, and that to eat meat is to affirm a cruel and distorted food system. However, they only criticize idolatrous consumption like a factory farming, they do not necessarily advocate vegetarianism. David Grumett & Rachel Muers *Theology on the Menu: Asceticism, Meat, and Christian Diet*, (Routledge, 2010)133-134. Cf. 1 Corinthians 10.25-26.

[36] David G. Horrell, "Biblical Vegetarianism? A Critical and Constructive Assessment," in Rachel Muers & David Grumett (eds.), *Eating and Believing: Interdisciplinary Perspectives on Vegetarianism and Theology*, (T&T Clark, 2008) 53.

whilst Northcott (2008) considers factory farming to be a type of "idolatry."[37] This is due to the power structure of factory farming, which attracts consumers by providing meat at a low price, while destroying the relationship between animals and humans by treating them cruelly and killing them. Through the "resistance" or asceticism of vegetarianism, contemporary Christians have the opportunity to repair the alienated relationship between humans and animals created by the food economy.

3-2 Eating to Acquire Virtue

During the Lenten season before Easter, fasting has been practiced since the time of the early church. It is reported that from ancient times to the Middle Ages, people abstained from eating meat during this period[38]. This practice, which originated from Jesus' forty-day fast in the wilderness, was meant to be learned, experienced, and imitated. This is in line with the tradition of virtue in Christian thought, that is, the understanding of the acquisition of virtue by imprinting it on the body. And eating (or not eating) is really a matter of Christian virtue.[39]

In the Christian theology of the twentieth century, in line with the restoration of virtue ethics in philosophy and ethics led by Alasdair MacIntyre and others, a similar argument has been made from the point of view of Christian ethics by, for example, Stanley Hauerwas and Jennifer Herdt. MacIntyre (1984) argues that virtue needs to refer explicitly to practice and tradition.[40] In response, in the context of narrative theology, Hauerwas (1997) argued for the importance of narrative and community in forming a virtuous "character."[41] However, although Hauerwas appreciates

---

[37] Northcott, 2008:243-244. Northcott states that "recovering the anti-imperial asceticism of the early Christians by rediscovering the Eucharist as a real vegetarian meal and not just a token meal, will provide opportunities for contemporary Christians, in their worship and homes, to resist and repair the sinful alienation between humans and other animals promoted by the modern imperial food economy. See also Michael S. Northcott, "Farmed salmon and the sacramental feast: How Christian worship resists global capitalism," in William F. Storrar & Andrew R. Morton (eds.), *Public Theology for the 21st Century*, (T&T Clark, 2004) 213-230.

[38] David Grumett & Rachel Muers, *Theology on the Menu: Asceticism, Meat and Christian Diet*, (Routledge, 2010) 20.

[39] Northcott, 2008:241.

[40] Alasdair MacIntyre, *After Virtue*, Second Edition, (University of Notre Dame Press, 1984[1981]) 223.

[41] Stanley Hauerwas and Charles Pinches, *Christians among the Virtues: Theological*

what Aristotle calls "habit" and "training in virtue" in the acquisition of virtue, he says that "acquired virtue" and "infused virtue" exist in the content of virtue, and that only "infused virtue" nurtured in the Christian community is affirmed.[42] Stout (2005) criticizes Hauerwas's theory of virtue as a combination of the anti-Constantinian narrative of John Howard Yoder and MacIntyre's anti-modern narrative.[43] Herdt (2008), on the other hand, goes further in discussing the mimetic nature of virtue: "can be characterized as mimetic in that it regards virtue as a finite reflection of God's infinite perfection. In that ultimate sense virtue is imitative rather than original while nevertheless being reflective of the distinctiveness of each individual character and each particular social and historical context"[44] In addition, "these explorations of Christian practices allow for a thicker, more holistic account of the Christian life, one that reunites liturgy, spirituality, theology and ethics. Moreover, emphasizing the centrality of the church in this way makes it possible to articulate illuminating accounts of human moral agency while still preserving the claim that formation of Christian virtue is wholly dependent on grace,"[45] and positively affirms that this virtue is formed by habit. If we look at Christian tradition from this virtue-ethical perspective, then the fasting or abstinence from meat during Lent is a tradition of virtue formation imprinted on the church calendar. And from a modern perspective, the "virtue" of eating is, as Norman Wirzba points out, to eat with justice and mercy."[46] One response to eating with "justice and mercy" for animals is vegetarianism, not as a temporary vegetarian diet, but a habit practiced continuously until the act of "eating with justice and mercy" is formed within oneself as a virtue. The act of eating (or not eating) is something that is repeated over and over again and thus becomes a habit. The act of not eating meat is a habit that is repeated, and thus becomes a virtue.

Conversations with Ancient and Modern Ethics, (University of Notre Dame Press, 1997)125f.
[42] Stanley Hauerwas and Charles Pinches, 1997:68.
[43] Jeffrey Stout, *Democracy and Tradition*, (Princeton University Press, 2005)154.
[44] Jennifer A. Herdt, *Putting On Virtue: The Legacy of the Splendid Vices*, (University of Chicago Press, 2008) 344.
[45] Ibid., p.351.
[46] Norman Wirzba, *Food & Faith: A Theology of Eating*, (Cambridge University Press, 2011) 34.

3-3 Eating as Reconciliation

Essentially, eating is reconciliation with God and creation. As Wirzba (2011) points out, "eating is an invitation to enter into communion and be reconciled with each another,"[47] and in eating, there is the model of the Eucharist as the table of reconciliation between God and human, and as the original meal. If Christians themselves are also food to be "eaten by Christ," then being caught by Christ and being a Christian in Christ can also be expressed by the metaphor of food to be "eaten."[48] If God's work of reconciliation is for the whole of creation, then we must also be reconciled to the animals, the creatures we have eaten. Reconciling with the animals would mean reclaiming the relationship with creation as it should be, just as the relationship between God and creation should be. The daily table is adjacent to the Eucharist and functions as a communion with the creatures, but the relationship between animals and humans has been broken beyond repair over the course of history and it is difficult to find a way to restore the "communion" that should exist. However, if we find in the Eucharist a model for our daily meals, we can make even such a table the beginning of the restoration of our relationship with animals as an anticipation of the Kingdom of God, and ultimately, the hope for the complete restoration and reconciliation of the relationship between animals and humans at the end of time. Eating is essentially "a relationship that join us to the earth, fellow creatures loved ones and guests, and ultimately God."[49] In Christian thought, there is a reconciliation at that table, a table that has been restored to its original meaning.

Since the Eucharist is the basis of food, and reconciliation is there, it is not appropriate for a Christian to destroy reconciliation with creation in the act of eating. Reconciliation with creation as the object of eating, and with nature as a whole, is required of the Christian. As Tillich has shown, if we take into account the strong connection between daily meals and the Eucharist, Christians are to be reconciled to creation in their daily eating as well.

Although Wirzba insists on the importance of "eating with justice and mercy," this alone would also allow us to eat animals that have been properly raised in consideration of animal welfare. Also, as mentioned earlier, it is my opinion that biblical accounts do not literally provide

---

[47] Wirzba, 2011:11.
[48] Wirzba 2011:160-161.
[49] Wirzba 2011: 4.

arguments against eating animal flesh. However, no matter how much consideration we give to animal welfare, it is impossible to have forms of modern animal agriculture that do not put more strain on the global environment than agricultural crops. In the contemporary context of an environmental crisis that we cannot look away from, eating with justice and mercy must extend to avoiding the eating of meat.

Conclusion

A Christian ethic of eating is one that considers how Christians have eaten historically, elaborates from that a theological thought that is valid in the context of the history of Christian thought and then asks each Christian how they should eat in this time. In Christian ethics, ethical norms about food do not constitute a law (like the prohibition on eating meat), but they can be a strong impetus for ethical commitment in a community that shares the same context and narrative of the Eucharist story. Tillich describes the meaning of moral imperatives as follows: God's will or command cannot be seen as a tyrannical command from outside of humanity, or as having a literal and concrete directive content within ecclesiastical tradition or scripture. As Tillich puts it, "faith-determined ethics," like "reason-determined ethics," ends up being dogmatic[50]. According to Tillich, moral imperatives can be meaningful to human beings because they are essentially good.

To "eat with justice and mercy" is not a universal principle of justice. But the Christian community, as a group of people who have received God's "justice and mercy," is constantly questioned about the nature of eating. In the same way that the early Christians chose to eat fish as a way of resisting the Roman Empire, vegetarianism can be seen as a way of resisting a society that continues to place a burden on the environment. What if a fish diet in imperial Rome, could lead to a diet that is considerate of others (animals, producers and the environment) in our time? The understanding of Christian ethics as virtue ethics reveals the characteristic of acquiring virtue and making it a habit through the everyday act of eating. This means that good practice starts with a certain "pattern/style." The non-eating of meat may be a possible "pattern" and thus, we are able to set the "pattern" as a response to climate change. Behind the choice of vegetarianism as an ethical choice, the Eucharist of eating is the source of moral action.

---

[50] Paul Tillich, "Morality and Beyond," in: *Main Works / Hauptwerke Vol.3*, (De Gruyter, 1992) 654.

Being repeatedly reminded of the proper way to eat in the Eucharist can be seen as the basis for a practical process of making the act of not eating meat a habit and a virtue. The Eucharist is repeatedly practiced in worship to remind us of the nature of food. The Christian is unilaterally invited to the table with God as the table master. This grace reminds Christians that there is a different way to their own desire to eat meat.

Moreover, the Eucharistic table shows that the decision to eat is not one person's decision, but a shared community practice. The sacrament essentially begins with the sharing of the same food. It is at the table of the Eucharist that we realize that there is already such a community of people eating the same food next to us. In this way, we should not overlook the fact that the theology that centers on the Eucharist, and the theology that offers hope for the realization of goodness in creation, and in the end, has a validity not only in theory but also in practice.

CHAPTER SEVEN

THE TRADITIONAL ORTHODOX CHRISTIAN FAST: A COMPARISON WITH THE MODERN LIBERALIZED FAST. PERSPECTIVES FROM THE SAINTS, HISTORY AND MEDICAL SCIENCE

FRED KRUEGER

Fasting has always been a pillar of spiritual formation in the Church of Christ. It builds discipline, restraint, will power, and cultivates fidelity to Church teachings.

Anciently the Christian fast was a total fast. No solid food was taken. Over the centuries, a moderating influence entered parish life. Health and strength issues required special treatment and dispensations became normal for a variety of personal situations. At the same time, as Orthodox Christians converged on America from European countries, they brought different assumptions about fasting. Archimandrite Akakios at the St. Gregory Palamas Monastery in Etna, California, describes some of the problems that arose in establishing a common rule for fasting in America.

The limited instances where fasting is practiced in modernist American Orthodox jurisdictions are beset by confusion and innovation. Many Orthodox immigrants who came from the Old World failed to preserve their fasting routines in a land where new foods and menus changed their way of life. Many came with an improper understanding of fasting to begin with. The spirit of reform embraced by the calendar change included specific proposals for the relaxation of fasting rules. Brought to the Americas by immigrants - some of them coming as hierarchs to serve the Church - this revisionist spirit deeply affected the Orthodox population here. The Eastern European [Uniate] Catholics who converted to Orthodoxy in America came from a spiritual milieu in which fasting neither took the same form nor had the same theological significance as it does in the Orthodox Church. And the national Slavic Churches in the emigration also understood asceticism from a far more Western than Orthodox perspective.

So it is that the ethnic Orthodox Churches saw the birth of "relaxed fasts" and "moderate" fasting rules. All of this they passed on to a new generation of Orthodox and to converts. Wholly unfamiliar with Orthodox fasting traditions, many Orthodox today have taken these contrived notions in the immigrant Churches as authentic practices and have come to treat them as part and parcel of Church teaching.

The current Orthodox fast as practiced in America is intertwined with the religious reforms that arose in Russia around the time of Tsar Peter the Great (1672-1725). Prior to his era, fasting was far stricter and considered essential for spiritual growth. The consequence of those changes is that modern fasting rules are largely an abstinence from heavy foods. This change explains why we no longer claim that the "fast" transforms, because by itself it does not. In our era, on fast days, we mostly become vegetarians for certain times of the year.

During the time when the traditional fasting rules were being relaxed, the Archbishop of Constantinople Ecumenical Patriarch Nicephorus Theotokis (1731-1800) wrote the following about the new rules:

> When we fast, we search the earth and sea up and down the earth to collect seeds, fruits, spices, and every other edible thing; the sea to find shellfish, mollusks, sea urchins, and anything edible therein. We prepare dry foods, salted foods, pickled foods, and sweet foods, and concoct many different dishes, seasoned with oil, sweeteners and spices. Then we fill the table even more than when we are eating meat. And yet we imagine that we are still fasting...Whoever taught...that such a variety and quantities of food constitutes a fast? Where did they hear that anyone who simply avoids meats or fish is fasting, even if he eats a great amount and different kinds of food? Fasting is one thing, eating a great variety in food is another.

Prior to the 18th century, strict fasting was essential for Orthodox Christians. At that time fasting meant no solid food. Listen to what Saint Nikodemos the Hagiorite (1749 –1809) writes about fasting:

> Canon 69 of the Holy Apostles declares that any hierarch, priest, deacon, subdeacon or reader...who does not fast during Great Lent as well as on Wednesday and Friday is to be deposed. If a layperson does not fast during these times (unless he cannot on account of illness), he is to be excommunicated.

To our modern thinking, the severity in this earlier rule seems shocking. Rather than criticize the old rule's strictness or defend modern dispensations, let us study the implications of each system of fasting. By examining both the modern rule and comparing its effects with the traditional rule, perhaps we can bring into focus what differences might exist. To structure this examination, let us subject both methods to modern medical research and list the differences. This examination should consider at least three perspectives: the effects on human physiology and bodily functioning of the body, on the psychological state of our minds, and finally on our spiritual lives.

Human physiology

The physiological effects of fasting are many and deep. When the body goes without food, medical research reports that a series of distinct physical changes occur. Initially, the digestive tract receives a rest. During this rest, the body uses its energies to increase its autolytic (or self-healing) actions. The body's energies then repair and restore bodily functions. In contrast, with a steady supply of nourishment, the systems of the body continually work to process food and maintain the system. Without rest, the body wears down over time. In those over thirty years of age, this causes a gradual, but steady buildup of toxins, plaque, and deposits which gradually stiffen and clog the system. This happens because a continual stream of food produces a steady accumulation of waste.

In the traditional no food fast (i.e., the original Christian fast), the autolytic functions go to work deep down at the cellular level of the body and perform a long series of "house-cleaning" functions so that a rejuvenation and mini healing occurs. During these times, the body uses its energies to attack and remove disease formations, tumors, or any unnatural growth within its system.

The no solid food fast provides more than rest to the assimilative organs. A "house cleansing" and restoration takes place. Body wastes and toxins are eliminated from the digestive and circulatory systems which freshen circulatory functions. Disease is removed in its formative stage, including cardiovascular and circulatory diseases, diseases of the digestive system, and the locomotor system - including rheumatism, respiratory diseases, and asthma, etc. At the same time a strengthening of the immune system occurs.

Research at the University of California's San Francisco School of Medicine finds a series of further health benefits. These include a sharply reduced risk of cancer (because the autolytic process attacks and dissolves tumors during their formative stage as well as other abnormal pre-cancerous growths). Even for those who may already have cancer, studies show that fasting can extend overall survival by protecting healthy cells while inhibiting tumor progression. The autolysis that emerges from fasting causes a significant slowing of the aging process. Several different studies show that the only proven method for improving health and increasing lifespan is to reduce caloric intake. According to Dr. Mark Mattson, MD, chief of neurosciences at the National Institute on Aging, "fasting shows more ability to provide beneficial qualities to the older body" than any drug or medication.

Fasting is valuable for maintaining heart health. Evidence from cardiac researchers demonstrates that periodic no food fasting lowers the risk of coronary artery disease and diabetes and causes significant changes to blood cholesterol levels. This is because fasting causes hunger stress. In response the body releases cholesterol, allowing it to utilize fat as a source of fuel, instead of glucose and decreases fat cells in the body. Coronary artery disease is particularly addressed by fasting because it reduces plaque buildup in the vessels that deliver blood to the heart. Narrowed or blocked coronary arteries can result in a heart attack or sudden cardiac death. This dimension of traditional fasting is even more important than it was historically because cardiovascular diseases are a side effect of the modern fat rich diet. The National Academy of Sciences cites additional benefits including stress reduction, increased insulin sensitivity and reduced morbidity.

Fasting is also highly beneficial to digestion health. When a person is not eating, a different set of microbes emerges and cleans up the gut wall, processing the sugars which are important for maintaining immune balance. Besides the revitalization of digestive organs, additional physiological benefits include clearer skin, improved hearing and taste, reduction of allergies, weight loss, drug detoxification, and heightened disease resistance. Fasting clears out problems from overeating and a sedentary lifestyle. No wonder so many of the desert fathers lived past 100 years of age! These physical benefits derive from genuine no food fasting, but most significantly they do not derive from merely abstaining from meat and heavy foods. Generally, what is happening physically reflects what is taking place psychically and spiritually.

In contrast it should be noted that fasting from meat, fish, dairy, oils, and alcohol also brings benefits. Their elimination reduces inflammation in the body. Chronic inflammation is linked to the development of heart attacks, strokes, diabetes, autoimmune diseases, and atherosclerosis, among other conditions. Blood cholesterol levels will drop. The average American omnivore obtains more than 1.5 times the optimal amount of protein, much of it from animal sources. This excess protein does not make us stronger or leaner. Excess protein is stored as fat or turned into waste and animal protein is a major cause of weight gain, heart disease, diabetes, inflammation, and cancer. The modern fast provides benefits in these areas but it does not go as deep because it does not engage the autolysis or self-healing mechanisms to the same extent.

The Psychological Impacts

Next a set of psychic benefits emerge from fasting. During an all-day no food fast, the mind develops clarity, and the will is strengthened - because it is exercised through the denial of the desire to eat. Something surprising then emerges. Traditional fasting (i.e., water only) causes a cautionary attitude to arise so that one is careful not to break the fast. Fasting then becomes a cornerstone for a life of restraint and thoughtfulness. This happens because fasting from food and nutrition stretches out and addresses the tendency toward consumerism and materialism. Fasting then becomes a witness to the conflict between the indulgences cherished by the modern mentality and the ascetic life of the Church. An important implication is that traditional spiritual formation cannot be attained without old style fasting. As the will is strengthened, the person who fasts increases in self-control. At the same time fasting results in heightened connectivity to others - because feelings become more sensitive and acute. This causes those who fast to sense the plight of others, including poor people. In this way fasting is connected to almsgiving because without fasting, we scarcely cultivate the sensitivities of the heart that foster compassion for those who have little.

On a longer fast - over 24 hours, the autolysis begins to stimulate the production of the hormone serotonin to insulate itself from the pangs of hunger. The initial day of fasting may sometimes be difficult, but by the next morning the fast becomes quite enjoyable because serotonin creates a distinct feeling of euphoria. The person who fasts will feel alert, active and often even excited to continue fasting. Studies show that most people who fast for over 24 hours (i.e., essentially the traditional fasting rule) report heightened mental clarity, a more positive mental outlook and emotional serenity when embracing traditional fasting rules. However, this release of serotonin does not emerge in the modern fast when one becomes essentially a vegetarian.

A regular pattern of once a week fasting produces an optimistic outlook on life as well as an overall feeling of purity, cleanliness, enthusiasm, and self-control. A conclusion from medical studies is that fasting can be enjoyable, healthy and foster a more positive outlook on life. A conclusion from personal experience adds that one's vision and experience of the deep goodness of life is enhanced.

The Pneumatic or Spiritual dimensions

Medical studies on the spiritual side of fasting are elusive because science is not effective in probing this aspect of life. Nevertheless, we discern deeper implications to fasting when Jesus tells the apostles (after they ask him why they could not heal the boy possessed with a demon) *"...this kind does not go out except by prayer and fasting"* (Matthew 17:15-21).

When the physical body is regularly cleansed by fasting, an additional result is that psychic and spiritual impressions become stronger and more frequent. The body's energy becomes increasingly refined. The world may appear transparent. At this time prayer has a more uplifted quality. One's whole being may experience a sense that the physical and spiritual realms intertwine and are drawing closer together. Sleep is deeper and more regenerative and fulfilling on the night after the fast. The saints frequently write that visions and holy experiences are more readily attained during times of fasting.

The enhanced sensitivities that accompany a fast open a realization that the fast cannot be restricted merely to a denial of meat and other heavy foods, but it must include a denial of negative thoughts, anger, negativity, and all the passionate tendencies. This is why Saint Basil writes, "there is a physical fast, but alongside it there is, or should be, a spiritual fast." He elaborates:

> In the physical fast the body abstains from food. In the spiritual fast, the faster abstains from evil intentions, words and deeds. One who truly fasts abstains from anger, rage, malice and vengeance, and also from idle and foul talk, condemnation, gossip, flattery, lying and all manner of spiteful talk. In a word, a real faster withdraws from all evil...As much as you subtract from the body, so much will you add to the strength of the soul.

Saint John Chrysostom makes a similar observation.

> It is necessary for one who is fasting to curb anger, to accustom himself to condescension, to have a contrite heart, to repulse impure thoughts and desires, and to reflect on what good has been done by us in this or any other week, and which deficiency we have corrected in ourselves. This is true fasting.

As for those who worry that fasting might harm their health, they need only recall the longevity of the saints who cultivated fasting as a way of life. Denial of food for them was the doorway to health and vitality.

Saint Alypius the Stylite -	118 years
Saint Anthony the Great -	105
Saint Charalambos -	113
Saint Theodosius the Great -	105
Saint Paul of Thebes -	113
Saint Paul of Komel -	112
Saint Cyril the Anchorite -	108
Saint Kevin of Glendalough -	105

This list is only a short beginning of the saints who lived long lives. These saints did not require special foods, vitamins or nutritional supplements to live long productive and inspired lives. These saints highlight a modern medical principle: The single most scientifically verified advantages to traditional fasting are improved health, rejuvenation and extended life expectancy. The conclusion is that the only reliable way to extend the human lifespan (or the lifestyle of any mammal) is repeated under-nutrition without malnutrition.

While the present liberalized Orthodox fasting rules carry some benefit, we should recognize that they only scratch the surface of the potential latent in fasting to bring healing and aid to transformation. As Ecumenical Patriarch Nicephorus Theotokis wrote almost three centuries ago, "Fasting is one thing, but eating a great variety of vegetables and seeds is another thing entirely," but it should not be called fasting.

A conclusion from this simple comparison between the effects of the modern fast in which we become vegetarians in place of the more rigorous traditional fast is clear. The ancient fast in which no food is taken has a far deeper and has a far more profound impact on the health and wellbeing of a person. Medical studies make this clear; personal experiences validate this conclusion; and the abundant commentary from the saints encourage this.

If we as modern Christians are going to recover our rightful heritage of holy experiences on the path to divinization, we must revisit the benefits of traditional fasting. Recovery of this ancient practice holds great potential for accelerating the journey to transformation and ability to renew our minds so that we may hold off the consumer mentality. As Jesus tells the apostles who could not cast out a demon, "This kind only goes out by prayer and fasting."

For those individuals who might wish to start fasting in the traditional manner, here are a few recommendations.

- Drink at least eight to ten full glasses of water during the fast day. This is because, at least in our western diet, so many toxins are released during the fast and the extra water helps to flush them out. Think of the task this way: "The body's solution to pollution is in dilution."
- For those who are champion meat eaters, the fast can initially create an acid buildup in the stomach because so many fats and toxins are released during the fast. This may manifest as a slight stomachache. Correct this by adding a teaspoon of baking soda to a glass of drinking water. This neutralizes the acid which is being purged out of the body. This is usually experienced only during the first occasions of fasting as that is when the most toxins are being removed in new fasters.
- Headaches may sometimes occur at one's initial attempt at fasting and these are primarily because of psychological resistance to the fast. Those who possess obsessive-compulsive eating disorders usually have layers of issues and so they need a firm rule that holds them to guidelines - one day of fasting per week and no more.
- A full day of fasting can begin after the evening meal on Tuesday, continue all through Wednesday and conclude at Thursday morning breakfast. By following this simple rule every week, the traditional benefits of fasting can return in one's experience.

Basically, fasting has similarities to a muscle. The more you practice it, the easier it is. After several months of once a week, no food only water fasting, the body becomes adjusted so that it does not miss the food. In fact, a person will look forward to the fast because of the many spiritual, mental and physical benefits that arise and that are noticeably experienced. After a while a person who regularly follows the traditional fasting rule will discover that there is scarcely any difference between a full fasting day and an eating day.

Even before the Christian era, fasting was understood as a means for addressing disease. Hippocrates, the father of medicine, observed the following:

Everyone has a physician deep inside. We just have to help it in its work. The natural healing force within each one of us is the greatest force for getting well. Our food should be our medicine. Our medicine should be our food. But to eat when you are sick is to feed your sickness.

The saints are even more eloquent on the importance of fasting. Their expansive insights demonstrate that without a more vigorous approach to the fast which the Apostles began, there is not much spiritual regeneration or growth.

Commentaries on Fasting

The saints and many inspired theologians are adamant in their emphasis on the importance of fasting. Here is a collection of Orthodox voices with a variety but uniformly strong teaching on the benefits and necessity of fasting.

Saint Theophan the Recluse

Fasting appears gloomy until one steps into its arena. But begin and you will see what light it brings after darkness, what freedom from bonds, what release after a burdensome life.

Saint Nikolai of Zicha

Gluttony makes a man gloomy and fearful but fasting makes him joyful and courageous. And, as gluttony calls forth greater and greater gluttony, so fasting stimulates greater and greater endurance. When a man realizes the grace that comes through fasting, he desires to fast more and more. And the graces that come through fasting are countless...

St Symeon the New Theologian

Let each one of us keep in mind the benefit of fasting...For this healer of our souls is effective, in the case of one to quiet the fevers and impulses of the flesh, in another to assuage bad temper, in yet another to drive away sleep, in another to stir up zeal, and in yet another, to restore purity of mind and to set him free from evil thoughts. In one it will control his unbridled tongue and restrain it by the fear of God and prevent it from uttering idle and corrupt words. In another it will invisibly guard his eyes and fix them on high instead of allowing them to roam hither and thither and thus cause him to look on himself and teach him to be mindful of his own faults and shortcomings.

Fasting gradually disperses and drives away spiritual darkness and the veil of sin that lies on the soul, just as the sun dispels the mist. Fasting enables us spiritually to see that spiritual air in which Christ, the Sun who knows no setting, does not rise, but shines without ceasing.

Fasting, aided by vigil, penetrates and softens the hardness of heart. where once the vapors of drunkenness were causes of fountains of compunction to spring forth. I beseech you, brethren, let each of us strive that this may happen in us! Once this happens, we shall readily, with God's help, cleave through the whole sea of passions and pass through the waves of the temptations inflicted by the cruel tyrant, and so come to anchor in the port of impassibility.

St. Nikolai Velimirovich

Bodily purity is primarily attained through fasting and through bodily purity comes spiritual purity. Abstinence from food, according to the words of that son of grace, St. Ephraim the Syrian, means: 'Not to desire or demand much food, either sweet or costly; to eat nothing outside the stated times; not to give oneself over to gratification of the appetite; not to stir up hunger in oneself by looking at good food; and not to desire one or another sort of food.'

Abba Daniel of Sketis

In proportion as the body grows fat, so does the soul wither away.

St. Dorotheos of Gaza

Everyone who wants to purify himself of the sins of the whole year during these days must first of all restrain himself from the pleasure of eating. For the pleasure of eating, as the Fathers say, caused all man's evil. Likewise, he must take care not to break the fast without great necessity or to look for pleasurable things to eat or weigh himself down by eating and drinking until he is full.

The Holy Fathers have taught, as if with one voice, that the stomach is the gateway to the passions. Watchfulness in this area is, therefore, absolutely essential to spiritual progress.

Saint Seraphim of Sarov

The holy fasters did not approach strict fasting suddenly, but little by little they became capable of being satisfied by the most meagre food. Despite all this they did not know weakness, but were always hale and ready for action. Among them sickness was rare, and their life was extraordinarily lengthy.

To the extent that the flesh of the faster becomes thin and light, spiritual life arrives at perfection and reveals itself through wondrous manifestations, and the spirit performs its actions as if in a bodiless body. External feelings are shut off and the mind that renounces the earth is raised up to heaven and is wholly immersed in the contemplation of the spiritual world.

Saint Shenuda[1]

Consistent fasting regulated the lives of the Fathers. A stable lifestyle, to which they become accustomed regulated their lives. As for the pitied laymen, they sway from one extreme to another when fasting. They deprive themselves of food only to break their fast to partake of anything they desire. They abstain for a while to allow themselves what they want for another period, then go back to indulgence, thus they sway between abstention and indulgence. They build, then destroy, and then build again, only to demolish again without recovery.

True fasting is to train oneself in self-control, to follow for the rest of your life. Self-control becomes a blessing for his life, not only during the time of fasting when we change the time and the food we eat, but also during the normal days.

Evagrios the Solitary

Fast before the Lord according to your strength, for to do this will purge your iniquities and sins; it exalts the soul, sanctifies the mind, drives away the demons, and prepares you for God's presence...To abstain from food, then, should be a matter of our own choice and an ascetic labor.

St. Paisius Velichkovsky of Neamt

A moderate and sensible fast is the foundation and chief of all virtues. He who wishes his mind to be firm against defiled thoughts should make his body refined through fasting. It is not possible, without fasting, to serve as a Priest. As it is indispensable to breathe, so also is it to fast. Fasting once having entered into the soul, kills to the depths the sin which lies therein.

---

[1] Coptic Orthodox Church

Metropolitan Kallistos Ware

Ultimately, to fast is to love, to see clearly, to restore the original beauty of the world. To fast is to move away from what I want to what the world needs. It is to liberate creation from control and compulsion. Fasting is to value everything for itself, and not simply for ourselves. It is to be filled with a sense of goodness, of Godliness. It is to see all things in God and God in all things.

CHAPTER EIGHT

NOAH'S FAILURES, GOD'S DISPENSATIONS AND A CHRISTIAN CHURCH 'SETTING THE SCENE AND CREATING THE OPPORTUNITY' FOR A WORLD IN PERIL

CHRISTINA NELLIST

Introduction

At this stage in the climate crisis, each one of us is called to action as climate change, creation care, and how to live sustainable lives are scientific and spiritual issues. For decades, senior Orthodox Christian theologians have repeatedly called for humanity to change its ethos from one based upon a value system of ever increasing wealth and continual consumption, to one with a Eucharistic and aesthetic ethos of love, virtue, sacrifice, abstinence, and purification of sin.[1] More recently, senior theologians - Orthodox and Catholic, have courageously stated that our present crisis is, in part, due to errors in Christian teachings that separated humans from the rest of the created world [2], and/or had a too narrow interpretation of some teachings.[3]

In my book on Eastern Orthodoxy and animal suffering[4] I outlined elements of a theological framework, which acknowledged the importance of non-human animal suffering because there was little engagement and an acknowledged gap, between Christian theory and praxis on the subject. This

---

[1] E.g., Bartholomew 1, (Archontonis) (Ecumenical Patriarch), "Message of His All-Holiness Patriarch Bartholomew for the day of prayer for the protection of the Environment," 1st Sept 2015.

[2] E.g., dominion as domination.

[3] E.g., Met. John Zizioulas calls for the Church to "revise radically her concept of sin to include sins against nature". "Foreword" in Chryssavgis, J. (Ed.) *Cosmic Grace, Humble Prayer...* 2009: viii.

[4] Nellist, C. *Eastern Orthodox Christianity and Animal Suffering: Ancient Voices in Modern Theology,* Cambridge Scholars Publishing. UK. (2020)

situation appears to be replicated in the Christian Church's lack of engagement with a significant factor of climate change - the animal-based diet. I have asked others to write in detail on the ecological and animal-welfare implications of this diet so that I may focus on the theological discussion.

When so much has been written on Christian theology in relation to the environmental crisis, the question to ask is why so little has been written by Christian theologians on one of its major components - the animal-based diet? An obvious answer is that in traditional Christian thought, eating animal flesh is not a sin because God smelt the sweet aroma of Noah's sacrificial offering and gave us animals to eat; however, is this really all there is to say on this important narrative, which has resulted in the acceptance of untold suffering for trillions of animals each year? I believe this is the least satisfactory of answers because Scripture and Tradition indicate that this was not the case. We are, I suggest, in search of a more credible answer.

I advance the opinion that one significant factor in Christianity's reluctance to promote the plant-based diet, is a too narrow interpretation of the Noahic narrative. When examined through the wider lens of creaturely suffering, further teachings are available to us on Noah's failures, the sin in killing animals and the compassionate damage-limitation exercise of God's use of dispensations. This wider examination, whilst challenging the traditional interpretation, is not un-Orthodox, for it uses traditional Orthodox sources and teachings to make its various points. I further submit, that there are also likely to be elements of cultural and/or social bias on behalf of some clergy, which need to be addressed. [5]

This chapter aims to address the gap in the theological discourse in the hope that the Eastern Orthodox and wider Christian Church, will 'set the scene and create the opportunity' for clergy to authoritatively promote God's enduring original dietary ideal and thus, facilitate the flourishing of God's good creation.

God's Salvific Plan: Dispensations and the Recognition of Human Failure

Initially, it is important to state that Orthodox Christianity teaches that dispensations are not 'rights' as we have come to understand them; they are a relaxation of God's original ideal. Dispensations are acts of God, given with compassion to the vulnerable and part of the process of bringing the

---

[5] This is also the case within other faith traditions.

errant human back to God and salvation. They are not to be confused with the Catholic term 'indulgencies', which are ways to reduce the amount of punishment for sins.

Scripture and Tradition teach that God's salvific plan arose due to human transgressions in Eden, with the first dispensation - death, being established because of the human failure to obey God's command. St. Athanasius gives us an insight into their original need when teaching that God could neither break His Word nor see His creation go to ruin and non-existence by way of corruption. [6] In essence, St. Athanasius asks what else God could have done to save His creatures; with the patristic consensus being that the outcome was both "monstrous and unseemly".[7] Crucially, we are to view this act not as a punishment but as a dispensation and example of God's mercy, which cuts off sin and saves humans from everlasting corruption.

St. Maximus teaches that the Fall "became the occasion for God in his wisdom to work out our salvation"[8], whilst St. Irenaeus indicates that God's plan is still in play, when teaching that God was with humankind in the various dispensations "from beginning to end", to adjust "the human race to an agreement with salvation" but that "from the beginning it was not so".[9] St Athanasius teaches that dispensations were necessary because humans display a propensity to devise "all manner of new evils in succession".[10] We also learn that "the law was not established for righteous men" but for those with hardened hearts who lacked obedience to God (Gn 6:5):

> Then the Lord God saw man's wickedness, that it was great in the earth, and every intent of the thoughts within his heart was only evil continually.

Thus, the Fathers view dispensations as a form of moral discipline for those who could not keep God's teachings in order to: a) furnish guidance; b) remind humans of their propensity and insatiable desire to sin. Unsurprisingly, biblical and patristic teachings are full of similar teachings on moral discipline as a route to salvation and thus relevant to this discussion.

Noah: Failure, Dietary Choice and the Second Fall

Many early and contemporary commentators acknowledge Noah's obedience and cooperation with God. I have no objection to these teachings

---

[6] St. Athanasius, *On the Incarnation of the Word*, CANNPNF 2-04. S:6.5.
[7] St. Athanasius, *On the Incarnation,* S:6.2.
[8] St. Maximus, *Ambigua* 7, 68.
[9] St. Irenaeus, *Against Heresies,* 4.15.2-3.
[10] St. Athanasius, *On the Incarnation* S:5.3.

and would add that through his cooperation with God, Noah in one sense, is the archetype for the modern animal protectionist who rescues animals from harm and provides for their needs, although ultimately this title lies with God. One could also view teachings in Exodus (Ex 23:4-5; 23:12), Deuteronomy (Dt 22:1-4) and Luke (Lk 13:15;14:5) [11] on the care of animals as a continuation of God's care and protection of all created beings first outlined in Genesis. However, when observed through the lens of creaturely suffering, there is more to this narrative than the traditional Christian interpretation suggests.

Despite the continuation of all creation via Noah's initial cooperation with God, there is also evidence of Noah's failure and sin, when acting independently of God. Despite God's destruction of all flesh to erase corruption, unrighteousness and evil from the earth, Noah's first independent actions upon leaving the Ark were to build an altar and kill many of the animals God had instructed him to save (Gn 8:20). The normative understanding of Noah's actions here are that God liked the sweet aroma of the sacrificed animals; was happy with the sacrifice of animals and as a result, granted permission for humans to kill and eat animals. Firstly, this interpretation ignores important texts that come after the sacrifice and before permission is given; secondly, this omission results in a too narrow interpretation of the text. The focus on aroma only highlights the first sentence of the verse (Gn 8:21a) whilst ignoring the second sentence (Gn 8:21b), where a completely different scenario unfolds.

Let us firstly deal with aroma and St. Irenaeus is helpful here via his teachings on the various laws and dispensations given by God for man's welfare:

> He does Himself truly, want none of these things, for He is always full of all good, and had in Himself all the odour of kindness, and every perfume of sweet-smelling savours, even before Moses existed.[12]

It is simply not credible that the odour from sacrificed animals is sufficient reason for God to change His mind and render the non-human animals subject to immense suffering and death. We require a more credible answer, which arises from a closer examination of the second sentence. This begins with the second occasion when God "thought it over" (Gn 8:21b); the first occasion being just prior to the flood (Gn 6:5-6). This reflection does not result in God giving humans the authority to kill animals, but rather, in God

---

[11] In the original Greek. *Nestle-Aland Greek-English New Testament,* (27th Ed.) 1998.
[12] St. Irenaeus, *Against Heresies,* 4.14.3.

repeating the same negative judgement of humanity when acknowledging the continuation of human sin:

> I shall never again curse the earth because of man's works, *although the mind of man is diligently involved with evil things from his youth*: nor will I again destroy every living thing as I have done.[13] (my emphasis)

God's acknowledgement of continuing human sin is not related to interpersonal violence but to human violence to animals. By repeating His judgement immediately after Noah's violent acts and the unsolicited and unnecessary deaths of God's other creatures, God clearly identifies the killing of non-human animals as an example of the continuing evil in the minds of humans and a sin. Importantly, in the very next verse, God restates His intention to continue to provide His original plant-based diet, as "seedtime and harvest" will continue whilst the earth remains (Gn 8:22). Orthodoxy recognizes the theological significance of this plant-based option, for it teaches that the non-violent grain offering pictures Christ as the totally acceptable offering to God, the oil typifies the work of the Holy Spirit and the frankincense typifies the prayers of the church. When the priest places the grain offering on the altar, this speaks to Christ when He established the Eucharist on Great and Holy Thursday.[14] We have, therefore, established Orthodox tradition to guide us here.

Significantly, scripture is also clear that a plant-based and non-violent offering - the grain offering - with oil and frankincense, is both "the most holy of the Lord's sacrifices" (Lev 2:3) and "a sacrifice for a sweet aroma to the Lord" (Lev 2:2b, 2:9). Noah could, therefore, have continued in righteousness by building an altar and offering prayers, praise, and violence-free offerings to God for saving a remnant of all created beings. Instead, Noah chose to continue the abuse of human freedom by sacrificing some of the animals God has instructed him to save.

God's declaration on the continuation of human wickedness and evil, challenges any interpretation that He was pleased with the sacrificial killing of animals or that God created animals for human food. In fact, immediately after God's identification of the human sin, God declares that He will not again destroy "every living thing" (Gn 8:21b). This declaration reinforces the salvific purpose of the Ark and God's stated intention that all creation is to flourish (Gn 8:17). This is reinforced again, by God's constant repetition of His covenant with all creatures and where he specifically mentions birds, cattle, all wild animals and "every living creature of all flesh" (Gn 9: 9-17).

---

[13] Gn 8:21b. In some translations, 'mind' is replaced with 'heart'.
[14] *The Orthodox Study Bible* note to Lev: 2.1-2.

In Orthodoxy, God's remembrance of "all the wild animals, all the cattle, all the birds, and all the creeping things" (Gn 8:1), is synonymous with their salvation.

Two further texts that are too narrowly interpretated, relate to God's forty-year provision of the violence-free, plant-based diet of manna, first outlined in Ex 16:4, 31.[15] Despite God's perfectly adequate choice, the Israelites demanded meat (Nm 11:4; 11:13). The initial text below (Nm 11:19-20), outlines God's displeasure at their request and disobedience:

> You shall eat, not one day, nor two days, nor five days, nor ten days, nor twenty days, but for a whole month you shall eat, until it comes out of your nostrils and becomes loathsome to you, because you disobeyed the Lord…

The second text, (Nm 11:33-34), informs us that God sent a great plague whilst they ate this meat and that the naming of the land after the human extermination was a reminder of their sins.

> But while the meat was still between their teeth, before it was chewed, the Lord's anger was aroused against the people, and the Lord struck the people with a very great plague. So, he called the name of that place Graves of Lust, because there they buried the people who lusted.

What are we to make of this scene? A traditional Rabbinic and Christian teaching is that God is angry at their rebelliousness, gluttony and ungratefulness.[16] I do not reject this, for teachings on the sin of gluttony are a common theme in patristic commentary.[17] However, the text also informs us of God's displeasure and the human sin in their rejection of His non-violent diet[18] for one that demands the unnecessary death of His other creatures. This is confirmed by Douglas (2001) in her commentary on

---

[15] Note here that it was Moses not God who initially told the Israelites that God would provide them with meat.

[16] Heb 3:7-11.

[17] St. Maximus, *Three Centuries on Love*, no 86, on how those who eat food for purposes other than for nourishment or healing are to be condemned as self-indulgent because they misuse God's gifts. Importantly, he states "in all things misuse is a sin"; St Cyril of Jerusalem, *First Mystagogical Catecheses*, 6, on hunting as the "pomp of the devil" "to serve their belly". St. Gregory of Nyssa, *On Love for the Poor*, 198 "Do not indulge in a frenzy of pleasures. Don't make yourself a destroyer of absolutely all living things, whether they be four-footed…birds, fish, exotic or common…The sweat of the hunter ought not to fill your stomach like a bottomless well that many men digging cannot fill…", etc.

[18] In Orthodoxy, manna was both food for Israel and a symbol of the Eucharist, *OSB*, Note 16:1-21, p. 911.

Leviticus, adding that swarms of quails were a protected form of life and that their arrival was either a trap or a curse depending upon how they were received. She is referencing us back to Ex 16:4.[19] Sadly, we fail to understand the wider significance of this lusting after meat, which is evidenced today in our almost obsessive desire for 'flesh', despite the proven link to human ill-health, animal suffering, environmental destruction, species loss, and climate change. [20]

One intriguing question arising at the time of the Covid 19 pandemic is, did this "very great plague" come from eating the meat of the wild birds - something perhaps, akin to the avian influenza of today?[21] If so, this could be the first recorded case of a zoonotic disease and death from the animal-based diet. [22] Certainly, there is a link between animal plagues and sin (Ex 10:12-19) and between sin and the dietary rules in Leviticus, which I shall discuss presently.

Another key point in this discussion, so often overlooked, is that God does not replace the plant-based diet. Yes, there is now a choice, but it is not a command to abandon the original ideal. This fact alone gives authority to the Christian Church to promote the plant-based diet. In addition, God's identification of the sin in killing animals and His continued provision of the plant-based diet, are further authoritative teachings, which can facilitate the promotion of God's enduring dietary ideal.

The second of Noah's failures also remains until today. This is set within the traditional Eastern Orthodox understanding that Noah is the first representative of the "second race of men".[23] This is not to state that there was a double creation as in the later Origenist cosmology but rather, that Noah as the chosen remnant of Adam, had been given the potential to re-establish the original harmony and peacefulness of the pre-lapsarian world.

---

[19] Douglas, 'Creatures That Swarm in the Air', *Leviticus as Literature*, p. 171. See Ex 16:4 for an example of God's use of food as a test of Israel's faithfulness.

[20] There is greater discussion on the link to climate change and animal suffering relating to this diet in my 2020 book; my article in the International Journal of Orthodox Theology 9:3 (2018) 144-172 and D'Silva's chapter in this book.

[21] Avian influenza can cause viral pneumonia, multiple organ failure and death.

[22] There is also evidence of zoonic disease in the Babylonian Talmud, *Ta'anit* 21b. Subsequent sources that comment and build upon this primary source include Rashi at BT *Ta'anit* 21b; Tosafot at BT *Ta'anit* 21b, s.v., *amru leih*; Chidushei HaRitba at *Ta'anit* 21b; Beit HaBeḥirah at *Ta'anit* 21b; Beit Yosef, *Orach Ḥayim*, 576.3; Shulḥan Aruch, *Orach Ḥayim*, 576.3; Levush Malchut, *Orach Ḥayim*, 576.3; Aruḥ HaShulḥan, *Orach Ḥayim* 576.9. I am grateful to Prof Jonathan Crane, for these subsequent sources. BT available at: https://www.holybooks.com/wp-content/uploads/Babylonian-Talmud.pdf

[23] St. Irenaeus, *Against Heresies,* 4.16.2; 4.36.4.

By saving a remnant of each species, God had 'set the scene and created the opportunity', for the recreation of a violence-free paradise. What transpired from Noah's first independent action, was not the reestablishment of the peaceful harmony of the created world desired by God (Gn 8:17; Gn 9: 8-17) but rather, the repetition of the misuse of human freedom and the continuation of human sin, evidenced in the violence and death perpetrated against innocent non-human animals (Gn 8: 20). In failing to understand the wider context of God's teachings, Noah not only repeats the sin of violence to God's non-human creation, but also fails to grasp the second opportunity offered to humanity to live in harmony with God and His creation.

The consequences of Noah's spiritual failure - a repetition of the Fall; the continued misuse and abuse of human freedom; humanity's continuing violent conflict with the rest of the created world and the perpetration of unnecessary suffering and deaths - are all too evident today. For we too, continue to sin and misuse our freedom, partly due to our spiritual failure or unwillingness to apply the wider teachings of the Noahic narrative.

Dispensations: Protection for the Vulnerable

My next point examines God's providential care for his non-human animal creation. In Adam's fall from grace, God imposed a curse on the ground as punishment for the abuse of human freedom (Gn 3:17-19). After Noah's 'fall', God adds fear to the curse (Gn 9:2):

> For the fear of you shall be upon all the wild animals of the earth, all the birds of heaven, all that move upon the earth, and all the fish of the sea.

The question to ask here is why God introduces "dread and fear" of humans in other animals if He wanted them killed as sacrifice and food? This would surely be much easier to achieve if they were not running away in fear. This introduction would, in fact, be an act of great cruelty. We are instead, to view this act as a further dispensation of God's grace, mercy, and protection for His non-human beings, who[24] would be more likely to run and survive as a result of their fear. We may, therefore, view the imposition of fear as another form of God's protection, and a type of damage-limitation exercise. Dispensations used as a form of protection may seem an unlikely proposition, yet other examples exist, such as the dispensation to divorce. St Irenaeus provides clarity on why dispensations were given and specifically mentions divorce, "on account of their hardness…they received

---

[24] I use the personal pronoun for other living beings.

from Moses this law of divorcement, adapted to their hard nature".[25] The Orthodox understanding is that the dispensation to divorce acts as a form of protection for women to prevent greater evils, such as their murder or destitution.[26] Thus, God's use of dispensations as a form of damage-limitation exercise, is an accepted concept in biblical hermeneutics.[27]

Dispensations: Animal Sacrifice and Animal Gods.

It is clear from many biblical and patristic teachings that God did not want animal sacrifice:

> From all these it is evident that God did not seek sacrifices and holocausts from them but faith, and obedience, and righteousness, because of their salvation...[28]

> He neither takes sacrifices from you nor commanded them at first to be offered because they are needful to Him, but because of your sins...in order that you...giving yourselves to Him, might not worship idols.[29]

Significantly, within the sacrificial system itself, there was again a choice: the favored non-violent grain offering *or* animals (Lev 2:1).

In his studies on Leviticus, Milgrom (1963) views the biblical dietary laws "as an ethical system",[30] whilst Marx (1994) interprets the central place given by Leviticus to cereal offerings as a sign of a utopian vegetarian philosophy, a reconciling reference to the vegetable offering of Cain in Genesis 4: 3.[31]

Crucially, the dispensation to kill and eat non-human animals is not freely given. It is conditional and set within a highly restrictive code of behavior, which prohibits the profane slaughter of animals and prevents humans from killing animals with impunity. Such a complex system indicates that God does not give this dispensation lightly.

---

[25] St. Irenaeus, *Against Heresies,* 4.15.2.

[26] Dt 24. See *OSB* note to Dt 24:1-4, p. 240.

[27] See Eliade, M. *A History of Religious Ideas...*1981.

[28] St. Irenaeus quoting Hosea, *Against Heresies,* 4.17.4; e.g., Jer 7:21-25.

[29] St. Justin, *Dialogue with Trypho,* Ch. XXII.

[30] Milgrom, J, The Biblical Diet Laws as an Ethical System. *Interpretation* 17, 1963: 288–301.

[31] Marx, A. *Les Offrandes Végétales* (1994); Shemesh, Y. (2006).

In Leviticus 17: 3-4, the blood of all herd animals calls for vengeance "that man shall be utterly destroyed from among his people"[32] unless the animal is slaughtered in the rite of sacrifice. This significantly reduces the number of animals being killed. Douglas (2001) reminds us that it is important to remember that the identification of the blood with the soul was prevalent in antiquity.[33] She also notes that the "secular shedding of the blood of animals that are classed as sacrificeable is explicitly classed with shedding human blood."[34] Thus, the sprinkling of blood on the altar, representing the blood and soul of the sinful human, reminds them that this would have been their blood, had God not allowed the dispensation. According to Gross (2016), the prohibition to consume the animal's lifeblood also acts "as a permanent symbol of the sanctity of life", which again, significantly limits the numbers killed.[35] These are important points, which again indicate a too narrow interpretation of the texts in Christian hermeneutics. Equating the shedding of animal blood with the shedding of human blood has implications for teachings, which suggest that God's commandment not to kill applies only to humans and ought to raise questions on teachings that we can kill animals with impunity and without soteriological implications.

Gross also informs us that these legal requirements ensure that any animal suffering in the act of killing renders the animals unfit for consumption and focuses the human on compassionate treatment, which in turn, again limits the numbers killed. He informs us that "diverse Jewish traditions argue that only men of high ethical caliber should be slaughterers (*shoh'tim*) - men who can resist the callousness that killing animals may engender." Milgrom (1991)[36] concurs, arguing that such measures are examples of God's protection of animals and types of damage-limitation exercises, which links us back to the points made earlier on God's use of dispensations as a form of protection for the vulnerable.

Further, those touching the carcass of an unclean animal "become guilty" (Lev 5:2-3) and cannot eat the flesh of the sacrifice or un-sacrificed without atonement, lest "that soul be utterly destroyed" (Lev 7: 21; 17:3-4), which again restricts the consumption of non-human animal food. Milgrom explains:

---

[32] See Lev 7:21-27 for further restrictions on the consumption of animal flesh and the "utter destruction" of the soul.
[33] E. g, Aristotle, Tertullian, Pythagoras, Empedocles, The Stoics.
[34] Douglas, M. 2001: 93.
[35] Gross, A, Jewish Animal Ethics, 2016, Ch 24.
[36] Milgrom, J, *Leviticus 1–16*. 1991:718, 33, 35, 36, 41; Gn. 9: 4-5.

In effect, the rule against touching a dead animal protects it in its lifetime. Since its carcass cannot be skinned or dismembered, most of the ways in which it could be exploited are ruled out, so it is not worth breeding, hunting, or trapping. These unclean animals are safe from the secular as also from the sacred kitchen. The rule is a comprehensive command to respect the dead body of every land animal. If anyone were to take it seriously, it would be very restrictive.[37]

St. Ephrem the Syrian teaches that certain laws were established as a physical reminder of past sins and as a warning to prevent future wickedness. He specifically links aspects of the law with the widespread use of animal idolatry, which he views as another example of the abuse and loss of human freedom to sin,[38] whilst St Irenaeus links idolatry to the continuation of human evil.[39] Importantly, "You shall have no other gods before Me" is the first of the Ten Commandments and Israel's lack of obedience in turning from God and returning to idol worship, is a common theme in patristic[40] and Old Testament texts: "For the worship of idols not to be named is the beginning, cause, and end of every evil" (WSol 14:27); "The enemies of Your people worship the most hateful animals" (WSol 15:18). Indeed, there are examples of animal-gods worshipped in multiple cultures and across the centuries. In addition, Douglas draws our attention to an important point on divine power and the competitiveness of religions, when discussing the historical theological controversy concerning the right to take animal life.[41]

The key point to make here is, if dispensations were used to establish and secure God's position as the only true God, it seems reasonable to propose that part of that process would also require changing the perception of the animals being worshipped. An effective way of achieving this would be to use the human's propensity to sacrifice to their gods by demanding the sacrifice of animal species that were identified as deities, the most common of which were bulls, rams, and birds. This would destroy the notion of this type of divinity and reinforce the power and supremacy of the God of Israel, whilst God continues His salvific guidance to His errant human creatures.[42] Paradoxically, the sacrificial system is therefore, both a dispensation to

---

[37] Milgrom, in Douglas, 2001:142.
[38] E. g, St. Ephrem, *Homily on Our Lord; The Pearl-Seven Hymns On The Faith* 7:2.
[39] Evil in the human heart or mind is a frequent teaching and relates back to Genesis.
[40] St. Athanasius, *Against the Heathen* for the "madness of idolatry" and animal worship, S: 9; S: 19.1-2; S: 20.3; S: 22.1; S: 23.3; S: 24.1; Ps 105:19-20.
[41] Douglas, 2001:171-2.
[42] Perhaps this adjustment in the perception of animals is part of their separation from humans in later theological discourse.

extend *and* restrict human freedom and another example of God's compassionate protection for His faithful non-human creatures.

We ought therefore, to be cautious of any suggestion that God's dispensation to kill animals for food is a right accorded to us simply because we are the most important of His creatures. St. Maximus's teaching that God's greatest dispensation (the Incarnation of Christ), brings the ritual slaughtering of non-human animals to an end, further indicates God's will in this matter.[43] To this we may add Christ's deliberate choice of the violence-free, plant-based food, for the sacred Eucharistic meal. At that time and place, fish was a common food; indeed, some of Christ's Apostles were fishermen and an obvious choice of food for the Eucharist. Instead, Christ chooses the non-violent option of bread, which again links us back to God's constant provision of violence-free food in the Old Testament.

By establishing and demanding strict adherence to many detailed dietary laws and regulations on the slaughtering of animals, God effectively restricts the human propensity to sin, by making the acts of slaughter and sacrifice highly prohibitive.[44] Any suffering in the killing of an animal also renders the animals unfit for consumption or use for clothing.[45] Such restrictive practices further indicate that this dispensation was not given to aid the consumption of animal-based food.

Of course, St. Peter's vision in Acts 10:12-15 could be used as a counter to my argument and justification for the animal-based diet, however, Origen's teaching on this passage suggests that a wider lens and different focus is required. He teaches that St. Peter needed this vision to break from his Jewish tradition of animal sacrifice, which he and many early Christian Jews continued to perform.[46] Rather than the normative and narrow

---

[43] St. Maximus, *Ambiguum* 7, 60.

[44] In my 2020 book I develop my argument to include biblical and patristic teachings on animal sacrifice but leave this aside for this discussion. For frequency, see St. Athanasius, *Against the Heathen*, S.25.

[45] Having lived in several Muslim countries I can confirm that the slaughtering of animals is neither quick, pain-free, nor pleasant to witness.

[46] Origen, *Kata Kelsou* 2.1 & 2. There is evidence of animal sacrifice being performed in pagan and Christian rituals until today: BREATH OF THE EARTH (filmfestival.gr); Grummet *Theology on the Menu*, claims this religious rite is in many Eastern and Oriental Orthodox traditions. See a link to a question/discussion on Christian animal sacrifice in the Holy Land today, set by the Eastern Orthodox Study Resource Archive group, on the Pan Orthodox Concern for Animals Facebook group; Miguel Ángel Rolland's documentary Catholic animal sacrifice https://www.theguardian.com/world/2015/jul/06/violent-nation-spain-festival-animal-cruelty-turkey-bulls-film-santa-fiesta; Wikipedia on animal sacrifice states

interpretation of this text as relating to the right to kill and eat animals, the wider teaching is that this passage is a parable used to remind St. Peter that the Old Testament laws are fulfilled in Christ and, that the Gentiles are cleansed through Christ's blood and thus, are equal partakers of the Kingdom.[47]

By widening our understanding of God's use of dispensations in the Noahic narrative and recognizing and acknowledging Noah's sins in his unnecessary choice of violence and enactment of murder of God's innocent creatures, together with his failure to grasp the opportunity to facilitate the flourishing of all of God's creation, a strong case is made for further Christian discussions and teachings on our dietary choices at this critical point in creation's peril.

A Role for the Christian Church: 'Setting the Scene and Creating the Opportunity'

Orthodoxy teaches that as Icons of God, we have a spiritual and moral duty of care and responsibility for all things in creation:

> Being created in God's Image and Likeness, gives us a responsibility towards creation as a whole and towards animals in particular. We are up against the basic problem that all too many people, clergy, and laity, think as Christians that this does not matter; that the treatment of animals is not a moral issue. But as soon as you say that animals are part of God's creation and we humans have a God-given responsibility towards creation, then at once, one sees that it is both a moral and spiritual question. That is why the Ecumenical Patriarch was so right to insist that the misuse of any part of creation is a sin.[48]

I think it is safe to say that God is not surprised at the present consequences of humankind's constant failure to grasp the opportunities offered to return to non-violence, harmony, and flourishing for all His creatures. Part of the consequences of our failures is now evident in the climate crisis, human and non-human ill-health and suffering associated with the animal-based diet and food production systems and, the increased likelihood of zoonotic diseases. It is also safe to say that God is aware that

---

"that some villages in Greece sacrifice animals to Orthodox saints in a practice known as kourbania; is a common practice in Armenian Church, and the Tewahedo Church of Ethiopia and Eritrea."
https://en.m.wikipedia.org/wiki/Animal_sacrifice...
[47] *The Orthodox Study Bible*, note to Acts 10:14-15, p. 1486.
[48] Met. Kallistos interview in Nellist, 2020:176.

these problems would significantly decrease if Christians were attentive to and compliant with His original and enduring plant-based dietary choice. Unfortunately, like the generations before us, we have failed to fully understand and apply the wider spiritual teachings on dietary choices within the Noahic narrative and wider biblical texts.

We have also failed to cooperate with God in our failure to facilitate the flourishing of all created beings, as most Christians ignore the immense suffering involved in animal-food production, which includes painful amputations, appalling living conditions, and painful deaths. Yet unlike previous generations, we have been given both the scientific data and compassionate spiritual teachings these past fifty years[49], which, had they been applied, would have brought us to a vastly different place to where we are now.

As Christians (or people of faith), we believe that God will not abandon us in these perilous times, for sacred texts and tradition inform us that prophets will be sent to warn us of our continued arrogant misuse of His creation and, of the yawning gap between our theory and praxis. As noted, Eastern Orthodox theologians and ethicists have for decades, advocated compassionate re-evaluations of our teachings on sin and nature. Importantly, it would be deeply arrogant of us to believe that God restricts His choice of helpers solely to theologians. Credible scientists and internationally recognized agencies, such as the UNFAO or WMO can also play a role, for they inform us of the proven and substantial link between the climate crisis and, for this discussion, the animal-based diet[50], and people of faith must not disregard these warnings

As each one of us eat, our choice of food determines to a considerable extent, how much suffering there is in this world and how quickly we shall hit the tipping-point in the context of climate change. As one of the largest religious groups in the heavily polluting Northern hemisphere, Christians are a significant part of the present climate crisis.[51] Christianity's failure to adequately address this major contributing factor is, therefore, somewhat shocking. Every Christian, be they individual parishioners, priests, bishops, or archbishops, ought to be involved in this discussion.

---

[49] Linzey, A. (1976) *Animal Rights: A Christian Assessment*. Now Director of the Oxford Centre for Animal Ethics, Oxford, UK.

[50] See also Food System Impacts on Biodiversity Loss | Chatham House-International Affairs Think Tank. Animal agriculture GHG emissions are circa 18% of all emissions - more than the total amount of emissions from all forms of transport worldwide.

[51] The world's wealthiest 1% account for more than double the emissions of the poorest 50% (3.5 billion people).

Another obvious challenge here would be to hold up the Eastern Orthodox fasting system as an example to all that we are doing 'our bit' and certainly, if everyone followed it there would be a reduction in some of the problems highlighted but certainly not all - and we must ask - do all Orthodox Christians follow the fast, or the spirit of the fast and if not: a) Is it likely that others will do so? b) Should Orthodox be exempt from making further sacrifices for our neighbors and planet at this critical time?

Two key points here are: 1) Orthodoxy already advises people on what they should and should not eat; 2) The present version of our fasting system is relatively modern and far removed from the original three day fast of the early church. [52]

Historical interventions into our dietary choices and fasting systems, afford us the possibility at this critical time, of overriding the present system for a relatively short period of time whilst we wait for large-scale 'cultivated meat' production[53] and/or, adapting it again in our age, to facilitate the reduction in individual and parish carbon footprints, to address the problems of global warming, water shortages, food insecurity, and sustained life on this planet.

We are already asking Orthodox Christians to live more eucharistic and aesthetic lives, so it would cause no harm to be more specific on this important issue. Christianity has always taught a difficult message - lives of virtue and sacrifice for the good of others. The promotion of the original and enduring plant-based diet is clearly not at odds with Scripture or traditional Orthodox teachings on the need for paradigm shifts in our hearts, minds and praxis.

There is no danger to Orthodoxy or indeed other Christian groups, in being reminded that whilst God has given us a choice of diet via a dispensation of His original plant-based ideal, what He does *not* do, is command us to eat meat. Yet, despite decades of teachings on environmental issues, there is little specific Orthodox, or indeed, wider Christian discussion, on the need for those who have a choice of diet, to reconsider our food choices at this critical juncture in the climate crisis. This is an important omission and to address it, there is an urgent need for each one of us to question ourselves and ask if we, as individuals or as parishes,

---

[52] It was adopted from Russia, circa the time of Tsar Peter the Great (1672-1725).

[53] New studies show that by 2030, cultivated meat (already widely available in Singapore) could be cost-competitive and massively reduce the climate impact of animal-meat. Meat cultivated directly from cells may cause up to 92% less global warming, 93% less air pollution and use up to 95% less land and 78% less water: https://gfi.org/press/new-studies-further-the-case-for-cultivated-meat-over-conventional-meat-in-the-race-to-net-zero-emissions/ Accessed 13th March 2021.

can reduce our consumption of animal products at this time in the earth's peril.

I have already outlined problems associated with the existing too narrow interpretation of scripture but there are also likely to be elements of "entrenched" faith traditions[54], and cultural and sociological biases that also need to be examined and addressed.[55]

In ignoring this aspect of the climate crisis, we effectively exhibit a contemporary version of our historical indifference to the suffering of creation, which as we have been told on numerous occasions by numerous Patriarchs, Popes and ethicists, is against the spirit of Orthodoxy - of Christianity. The pastoral imperative is highlighted in Van Susteren and Al-Delaimy (2020) who state that avoidance of climate-related issues, "is an attempt to try to control our fears...[which] are at the root of denial and inaction."[56]

The challenge, therefore, is how to apply our rich Orthodox/Christian teachings on compassionate care for "all things", to the most critical issue of our time?[57] Perhaps we need to ask challenging questions such as: Is the parish focus on the human at the expense of the rest of God's creation? If it is, is the Church/priest fulfilling their role as Christ on earth, who cares and loves "all things" or, are they continuing the biases of the past? The answer to such questions is, in part, for clergy and laity alike, to address any biases that prevent them from engaging with this important subject. They may take courage from Christ's teaching on religious legalism, which can make us insensitive to God's universal mercy and compassion. Undoubtedly, they ought to take notice of God's contemporary prophets, be they discerning Patriarchs, Popes, theologians, ethicists, environmental and climate scientists or experts in conservation and protection.

There are signs of change. The Halki 111 Summit discussed the urgent need for 'creation care' to be incorporated into all Orthodox seminary and

---

[54] HAH Bartholomew, 'Religious Communities and the Environment' in, Chryssavgis, *Cosmic Grace...* p. 358.

[55] This cultural and social bias is recognized by Met. Kallistos in our 2014 interview, see Nellist, 2020: Ch 6:160.

[56] See the Van Susteren and Al-Delaimy chapter in this book.

[57] Bartholomew, 'Justice: Environmental and Human' composed as 'Foreword' to proceedings of the fourth summer seminar at Halki in June (1997), in, Chryssavgis, *Cosmic Grace...* p. 173; also, 'Environmental Rights', p. 260; 'Environment and Religious Education', pp. 109-112.

academic programs and whilst this work is beginning, there is still a great deal more to achieve, especially at parish level.[58]

Whilst I accept that the Church and its clergy cannot demand changes to Christian dietary practices, they most certainly can guide their parishioners in the parts of the world where this is possible. The suggestions offered here are easy for the Christian Church to adopt and enact:

1) Remind parishioners that God's original choice of a plant-based diet is still a valid dietary option for Christians.
2) Where possible, offer plant-based food as the default meal at meetings and feasts, with a dairy or animal-based meal as dietary options for those who request it.
3) Where possible, ask our parishioners to eat more local, seasonal, organic and high-welfare products whenever possible.
4) Waste less food.
5) Repeat the following teaching to clergy and laity alike:

"Christians need to avoid eating meat wherever possible out of mercy for the animals and care for creation."[59] If these simple and compassionate messages are regularly repeated by Patriarchs, archbishops, bishops and parish priests, the Christian Church would, in Christ's stead, again 'set the scene and create the opportunity' for God's human creatures to live sustainable lives in violence-free harmony with the rest of His creation. In so doing, the Christian Church would also demonstrate its relevance to our youth who will suffer the worst effects of climate change and who are turning in increasing numbers away from the Church.[60]

The final question therefore is this: will Christian/faith leaders, clergy, and we as individuals, continue to ignore the connections between climate change and the animal-based diet, water and food insecurity, biodiversity

---

[58] See the appendix for my 'Creation Care: Christian Responsibility Course' and Tsalampouni and Antonopoulou's chapter, relating to the work of the School of Pastoral and Social Theology at Aristotle University of Thessaloniki, Greece; http://greenparish.goarch.org/; The 2020 film 'Face of God' by the Fellowship of the Transfiguration in the USA repeats this call for engagement by all Orthodox Christians see http://faceofgodfilm.com/. In January 2021, the Halki IV Summit discussed 'Covid-19 and Climate Change' and asked questions on what lessons have been learned? One answer is that we shall have learnt nothing if we fail to understand that this and all previous contemporary pandemics came from our abuse of animals, be they in wet-markets, experimental laboratories, or poorly run/intensive farms.

[59] Private conversation 15th April 2018. Used here and in the 2020 book with permission. Fr. Khalil is Dean at Balamand University, Lebanon.

[60] Europe's Young Adults and Religion (stmarys.ac.uk)

and creaturely suffering or will we, either as national/parish groups and individuals, engage practically with the subject to ensure the flourishing of all life-forms on this planet?

References

St. Athanasius, *On the Incarnation of the Word*, Behr, J. (Trans.) (Crestwood, NY: SVSP).

St. Athanasius, *Against the Heathen Against the Heathen* (CANNPNF2-04 Catholic Way Publishing 2014).

St Cyril of Jerusalem, *First Mystagogical Catecheses. The Catechetical Homilies of St Cyril Archbishop of Jerusalem* Kalogeraki, D. M. (Ed.) (Orthodox Missionary Fraternity of Thessaloniki, 2011).

St. Ephrem the Syrian, *Table Blessings,* Memra IX in Hansbury, M. (Trans.) *Hymns of St Ephrem the Syrian*, (Convent of the Incarnation Fairacres, Oxford: SLG Press, 2006).

—. *Homily On Our Lord; The Pearl-Seven Hymns On The Faith* 7:2. (CANNPNF2-13 Catholic Way Publishing).

St. Gregory of Nyssa, *On Love for the Poor.* Holman S. (Trans.) *The Hungry are Dying: Beggars and Bishops in Roman Cappadocia,* (Oxford: OUP, 2001).

St. Irenaeus, *Against Heresies.* Vols.1-5. (Whitefish, Montana: Kessinger Publishing's Rare Reprints, 2004).

St. Maximus, *Ambigua 7, On the Beginning and End of Rational Creatures* Blowers, P. & Wilken, R. (Trans) *On the Cosmic Mystery of Jesus Christ: Selected Writings from St. Maximus the Confessor.* (Crestwood, NY: SVSP, 2003).

—. *Ambiguum* 41 PG 91. 1305B.

Justin Martyr, *Dialogue with Trypho, a Jew.* (CANNPNF01 Catholic Way Publishing Kindle E-book)

Origen, Against *Celsus (Kata Kelsou)* (CANNPNF04 Catholic Way Publishing Kindle E-book, 2014).

Bartholomew 1, His All-Holiness, Ecumenical Patriarch (1994). 'Environment and Religious Education' Greetings at the opening of the first summer seminar on Halki, 20[t] June 1994, in, Chryssavgis, J. (Ed.) *Cosmic Grace, Humble Prayer: The Ecological Vision of the Green Patriarch Bartholomew,* (Grand Rapids, Michigan: Eerdmans, 2009).

—. (1997), 'Justice: Environmental and Human' composed as "Foreword" to proceedings of the fourth summer seminar at Halki, in, Chryssavgis, J. (Ed.) *Cosmic Grace, Humble Prayer…*

—. (2000) 'Environmental Rights' in, Chryssavgis, J. (Ed.) *Cosmic Grace, Humble Prayer...*

—. (2010a). *"Sins Against Nature and God: We Are All Accountable for Ignoring the Global Consequences of Environmental Exploitation."* Statement by His All Holiness at the Ecumenical Patriarchate Constantinople 9th May 2010. [Online] Available at: http://www.ec-patr.org.

—. (2010b). *'Saving Souls and the Planet Go Together.'* [Online] Available at: http://www.ec-patr.org.

—. (2015). 'Message of His All-Holiness Patriarch Bartholomew for the day of prayer for the protection of the Environment', 1st Sept 2015. Available at: http://www.ec-patr.org.

Douglas, M. *Leviticus as Literature* (Oxford: OUP, 2001).

Eliade, M. *A History of Religious Ideas: From the Stone Age to the Eleusinian Mysteries* Trask, W. R. (Trans.) (Chicago: University of Chicago Press, 1981).

Gross, A. 'Jewish Animal Ethics' in, *The Oxford Handbook of Jewish Ethics and Morality,* Dorff. E. & Crane, J. (Eds) (Oxford: OUP, 2016).

Linzey, A. *Animal Rights: A Christian Assessment* (London: SCM Press, 1976).

Marks A. *Les Offrandes Végétales dans l'Ancien Testament, Du Tribut au Repas Eschatalogique.* (Brill, 1994).

Milgrom, J. *Leviticus 1–16,* The Anchor Bible Series, (NY: Doubleday Dell Publishing Group, 1991).

Nellist, C. *Eastern Orthodox Christianity and Animal Suffering: Ancient Voices in Modern Theology,* (Cambridge Scholars Publishing, UK, 2020).

Nestle-Aland Greek-English New Testament, (27th Ed.) Aland, B. Karavidopoulos, K. J. Martini, C. M and B.M. Metzger, (Eds.) (Stuttgart: Deutsche Bibelgeselleschaft, 1998).

Shemesh, Y. (2006). 'Vegetarian Ideology in Talmudic Literature and Traditional Biblical Exegesis' *Review of Rabbinic Judaism* 9:141-166.

The Orthodox Study Bible Metropolitan Maximus, Pontiac, E., Nadim, M., Sparks, J. N. (Eds.) (St. Athanasius Academy of Orthodox Theology, Elk Grove, CA: Thomas Nelson, 2008).

The Old Testament Hebrew & English Bible. (The British & Foreign Bible Society, Berlin, SW: Trowitzsch & Son, 1903).

Zizioulas. Met. John. 'Proprietor or Priest of Creation?' Keynote Address of the Fifth Symposium of Religion, Science and the Environment, 2nd June 2003 [Online] Available at:

http://www.orthodoxytoday.org/articles2/MetJohnCreation.php
[accessed 14th July 2013]
—. 1989-1990. 'Preserving God's Creation: Three Lectures on Theology
and Ecology. Parts 1-3' *King's Theological Review* 12 (Spring 1989):1-
5; 12 (Autumn. 1989): 41-45; 13 (Spring 1990):1-5.

CHAPTER NINE

CLIMATE CHANGE AND CORRUPTION: INCONVENIENT TRUTHS

WINNIE ONKOBA

The earth has faced numerous challenges in her quest to provide a habitat for both plants and animals. From climate change, to war, pandemics, natural disasters, mother earth has been greatly affected and her environment has been significantly altered. The inhabitants of mother earth, which include plants and animals both human and non-human, have not been left out of these adverse changes. Just as human beings have been faced by pandemics, natural disasters, and wars, so plants and non-human animals have suffered from other factors such as climate change and human activities.

Plants and animals are essential components of mother earth and they are vital in the earth's ecosystem. Each of them plays a key role in ensuring a balance of ecosystems, biodiversity, and sustainability. They cannot exist separately from each other because of their interdependence; plants need animals for pollination, whilst animals need plants for food and habitat. A well-balanced ecosystem allows plants and animals to thrive in health and diversity, because they can reproduce from the effective population that has not been affected by any unwanted external micro-organisms. The interaction between plants and animals is a marvelous phenomenon. Everything in the universe is somehow intertwined or interconnected. A good example of this is in the case of deforestation. Animals lose their habitat, there is elimination of sinks, which leads to the rise in atmospheric temperatures and changes in the climate, often resulting in drought where the animals and vegetation suffer because of the lack of water. It is a clear cycle of interdependence between plants and animals, and where the effects of climate change can clearly be observed.

Human activities have also largely affected the welfare of the wildlife in Kenya. Corruption, for instance, has facilitated poaching and the illegal wildlife trade, which has gained root in various parts of the world with

Kenya being considered a major transit center for illegal wildlife trophies. Corruption has played a key role in illegal wildlife trade as the poachers and traders are able to get away with their crimes through bribing public officials who are supposed to ensure the safety of the wildlife. Poaching has become so rampant that some of the Kenyan wildlife are now listed as threatened species. It is critically important that the Kenyan government deal with the problem of wildlife poaching and find the necessary solutions to protect her wildlife before they become extinct. As a result of deforestation and the destruction of animal habitat to corruption and wildlife trafficking, the welfare of plants and animals has deteriorated significantly.

Climate Change: An Inconvenient Truth (1)

Climate change refers to the response of the planet's climate system to altered concentrations of carbon dioxide and other 'greenhouse gases' in the atmosphere.[1] Climate change is a long-term change in the average weather patterns that have come to define Earth's local, regional, and global climates. These changes have a broad range of observed effects that are synonymous with the term.[2] Climate change is the most significant environment challenge of our time and poses a great challenge to sustainable progress globally. It affects eco-systems, water resources, food, health, coastal zones, industrial activities, and human growth.[3] With the rise in atmospheric temperatures and sea levels, wildlife habitats are being destroyed, leading to increasing human-animal conflict, as both humans and animals fight for the same limited resources for their survival.

The IPCC issued its Fourth Assessment in 2007 and found that "warming of the planet is unequivocal" and that "most of the observed increase in globally averaged temperatures since the mid-20th century is very likely [i.e., more than 90%] due to the observed increase in anthropogenic greenhouse gas concentrations."[4] The Fifth Assessment Report presents strong evidence that warming over land across Africa has increased over the last 50-100 years. Surface temperatures have already increased by 0.5-2°C over the past hundred years. Data from 1950 onwards suggests that climate change has already changed the magnitude and frequency of some extreme weather

---

[1] Chris Wold, David Hunter and Melissa Powers, *Climate Change and the Law*, (2nd Edition), (LexisNexis law school publishing, USA) p. 2

[2] https://climate.nasa.gov/resources/global-warming-vs-climate-change/

[3] http://meas.nema.go.ke/unfccc/climate-change-in-kenya/

[4] Chris Wold, David Hunter and Melissa Powers, Climate Change, and the Law (Supra) p. 3. IPCC, Working Group I, The PHYSICAL SCIENCE BASIS: SUMMARY FOR POLICY MAKERS (Fourth Assessment Report 2007).

events in Africa. The health, livelihoods and food security of people in Africa have been affected by climate change.[5] Pope Francis in his encyclical Laudato Si, noted:

> The climate is a common good, belonging to all and meant for all. At the global level, it is a complex system linked to many of the essential conditions for human life. A very solid scientific consensus indicates that we are presently witnessing a disturbing warming of the climatic system. In recent decades, this warming has been accompanied by a constant rise in the sea level and, it would appear, by an increase of extreme weather events, even if a scientifically determinable cause cannot be assigned to each particular phenomenon. Humanity is called to recognize the need for changes of lifestyle, production, and consumption, in order to combat this warming or at least the human causes which produce or aggravate it. It is true that there are other factors (such as volcanic activity, variations in the earth's orbit and axis, the solar cycle), yet several scientific studies indicate that most global warming in recent decades is due to the great concentration of greenhouse gases (carbon dioxide, methane, nitrogen oxides and others) released mainly because of human activity. As these gases build up in the atmosphere, they hamper the escape of heat produced by sunlight at the earth's surface. The problem is aggravated by a model of development based on the intensive use of fossil fuels, which is at the heart of the worldwide energy system. Another determining factor has been an increase in changed uses of the soil, principally deforestation for agricultural purposes. Warming has effects on the carbon cycle. It creates a vicious circle which aggravates the situation even more, affecting the availability of essential resources like drinking water, energy, and agricultural production in warmer regions, and leading to the extinction of part of the planet's biodiversity. The melting in the polar ice caps and in high altitude plains can lead to the dangerous release of methane gas, while the decomposition of frozen organic material can further increase the emission of carbon dioxide. Things are made worse by the loss of tropical forests which would otherwise help to mitigate climate change. Carbon dioxide pollution increases the acidification of the oceans and compromises the marine food chain. If present trends continue, this century may well witness extraordinary climate change and an unprecedented destruction of ecosystems, with serious consequences for all of us. A rise in the sea level, for example, can create extremely serious situations, if we consider that a quarter of the world's population lives on the coast or nearby, and that the majority of our megacities are situated in coastal areas.[6]

---

[5] The Intergovernmental Panel on Climate Change Fifth Assessment Report, 'What's in it for Africa', p. 4
[6] Encyclical letter Laudato Si of the Holy Father Francis on the Care of our Common Home, Paragraphs 23-24, pp. 18-20

The IPCC'S Fifth Assessment Report also noted:

> During this century, temperatures in the African continent are likely to rise more quickly than in other land areas, particularly in more arid regions. Under a high-emissions scenario, average temperatures will rise more than 2°C, the threshold set in current international agreements, over most of the continent by the middle of the 21st century.[7]

Kenya being a third-world country, has had its fair share of economic problems. Despite the economic hardships facing the country, it has not been left behind when it comes to urbanization and industrialization. The need for industrialization has seen both local and international investors establishing different types of industrial plants. With industrialization came atmospheric pollution due to the absence of proper industrial emission regulations for the emission of greenhouse gases into the atmosphere. These GHGs have different global warming potentials and their presence in the atmosphere has severely impacted the climate in Kenya.

Coupled with atmospheric pollution is oceanic pollution. Kenya hosts the Indian Ocean on its southern part making Kenya's coastal strip a major business hub in Eastern and Central Africa, as it houses the largest port of entry in its coastal town of Mombasa. Despite the passing of laws to regulate the use of the ocean, the coastal town has not been left behind in the woes of industrialization. Disposal of waste into the ocean, oil spillage, overfishing, dynamite fishing, and human encroachment along the ocean banks, have had a significant effect on marine life e.g., coral bleaching and increased death of fish and other sea creatures.

Another activity that has had a significant effect on climate change is deforestation. Forests and trees have been cut to facilitate human settlement. Kaluki Paul Mutuku reported as follows, "In my home country of Kenya, there is simply no way we can achieve our national target to reduce greenhouse gas emissions by 30% by 2030 without addressing deforestation and land degradation, which remain the largest source of emissions here". He further stated that, "When Kenya gained independence in 1963, 10% of the country was covered in forest. By 2009, this number had dropped to 6% as a result of charcoal and timber production, agriculture expansion, unregulated logging, and urbanization. Not only has this increased our contribution to climate change, but it has also had several other devastating impacts, including soil erosion, increased flooding, and dramatically reduced availability of fresh water during droughts."[8]

---

[7] IPCC's Fifth Assessment Report, 'What's in it for Africa' p. 4
[8] The Africa Report Posted on Monday, 12th August 2019 16:34

It is important to highlight that the forest and the sea are both animal habitats. The destruction and or pollution of these two areas not only impacts climate change but also leads to the loss of our wildlife through the loss of their homes and their food. Deforestation had led to human-wildlife conflict because most of the animals that have been displaced, seek alternative placements where humans are living, leading to human-wildlife conflict. A good example of this is the encroachment of the land next to Nairobi National Park. As a result of people encroaching on the land that is close to the park, there has been a severe clash between the wildlife and the residents when the wildlife wander from the park and visit the 'new' neighborhood. This has often resulted in the maiming and killing of the animals by the residents for fear of attack by the animals. Pollution of the sea has also led to the death of fish and other marine life that are dependent on the sea for their survival.

In Kenya, the effects of climate change have been costly both to the economy and the environment. The Government of Kenya (2013) report on vulnerability assessments of climate change impacts in Kenya, identified the following sectors as being at risk: agriculture, an economic stronghold highly dependent on rainfall; water resources which cater for an ever-growing population in the wake of deforestation in catchment areas; the hydro-power energy sector pressured by frequent drought and livelihoods affected by diseases and conflicts over depleting resources.[9] President Kenyatta while addressing the Climate Adaptation Summit noted that "Climate change, like Covid-19, is a reality that has to be dealt with now. As we endeavour to build back better, we must also learn from each other and build resilience through partnerships." He also added that "climate change instigated calamities pose a great risk, particularly to agriculture and specifically to small-scale farmers, which could further worsen food insecurity on the continent."[10]

From the above discussion, it is quite clear that climate change is a critical factor not only for humans but also when it comes to the welfare of our wildlife, as the destruction of their habitats, either through pollution or deforestation, directly impacts their lives as their lives are lost because of

---

https://www.theafricareport.com/16150/kenya-has-lost-nearly-half-its-forests-time-for-the-young-to-act/

[9] Lucy Atieno and Joseph Njoroge, Climate change impact presentation in Kenya's news media,
https://www.researchgate.net/publication/269099664_Climate_Change_Impact_Re presentation_In_Kenya%27s_News_Media

[10] https://www.standardmedia.co.ke/environment/article/2001401496/president-uhuru-warns-climate-change-could-worsen-food-insecurity-in-africa

hunger, thirst, poisoning, habitat destruction and other related causes. If this is not addressed, many animal species will become endangered and run the risk of extinction.

Corruption and Illegal Wildlife Trade:
An Inconvenient Truth (2)

The World Bank defines corruption as the abuse of public office for private gain. Public office is abused for private gain when an official accepts, solicits, or extorts a bribe. Corruption is a complex phenomenon. Its roots lie deep in bureaucratic and political institutions, and its effect on development varies with country conditions. But while costs may vary and systemic corruption may coexist with strong economic performance, experience suggests that corruption is bad for development. It leads governments to intervene where they need not and it undermines their ability to enact and implement policies in areas in which government intervention is clearly needed, whether by environmental regulation, health and safety regulation, social safety nets, macroeconomic stabilization, or contract enforcement.[11]

Corruption has gained root and become a common phenomenon in Kenya. It can almost be rated as an economic pandemic because of how common it has become for accessing public services. It is easy to get away with a crime, major or minor, by bribing the officials in power. The Kenya Corruption Report stated that:

> Kenya's competitiveness is held back by high corruption levels that penetrate every sector of the economy. A weak judicial system and frequent demands for bribes by public officials lead to increased business costs for foreign investors. Widespread tax evasion hinders Kenya's long-term economic growth, and fraud in public procurement is rampant.[12]

Trade in illegal wildlife trophies and wildlife trafficking has gone up over the years with Kenya not only being considered a trading zone but a transit center for illegally acquired wildlife trophies. Mombasa city in Kenya houses the largest port in Eastern and Central Africa thus enabling countries in Eastern and Central Africa to gain access to the outside world as well as the ability to transport their cargo through the same port. Several cases of trafficking in wildlife trophies have been discovered at the port with

---

[11] http://www1.worldbank.org/publicsector/anticorrupt/corruptn/cor02.htm
[12] Risk and Compliance Portal powered by GAN
https://www.ganintegrity.com/portal/country-profiles/kenya/

the merchandise being caught and confiscated. In 2016, the world witnessed the largest burn of Ivory in Nairobi, Kenya. The World Wildlife Fund (WWF) reported as follows:

> Last Saturday, April 30th, 2016, Kenya hosted the world's largest ivory burning event at the Nairobi National Park. This was intended to send a message to poachers, sellers, and ivory consumers that Kenya will not stand for the illegal ivory trade. 11 pyres held 105 tons of neatly stacked elephant tusks and 1 pyre holding 1.35 tons of rhino horns. According to the Kenya Wildlife Service (KWS), the ivory represents 8,000 elephants and more than 300 rhinos.[13]

Although numerous efforts have been made in the fight against illegal wildlife trade, the 'business' is thriving. The Kenyan government has however begun to establish measures to fight this illegal trade. Cases of illegal wildlife trade have gone for trial with successful convictions. A good example is the case of KASENGU KILOTU =VERSUS= REPUBLIC HC CRIMINAL REVISION NO 158 OF 2019, where The Applicant, Kasengu Kilotu, was convicted of three counts under the Wildlife (Conservation and Management) Act. In the first count, he was convicted of being found in possession of government trophies contrary to Section 42(1)(b) as read with Section 52(1). In the second count he was convicted of dealing in government trophies without a dealer's license contrary to Section 43(4)(a) as read with Section 52(1). He was finally convicted of failing to make a report of obtaining government trophies contrary to Section 39(3)(a). The prosecution was able to establish that The Applicant was found in possession of four (4) pieces of elephant tusks weighing 8 kilograms with a street value of Kshs.800,000/ in circumstances that clearly pointed to the fact that the Applicant intended to sell the same. In respect of the first count, The Applicant was sentenced to serve two (2) years imprisonment. In respect of the second count, The Applicant was sentenced to serve two (2) years imprisonment. In respect of the third count, The Applicant was sentenced to serve one (1) year imprisonment. On revision, the court upheld his conviction and sentencing.

The illegal wildlife trade has adversely affected the welfare of Kenyan wildlife and the ecosystem. The killing of animals breaks the food chain in the ecosystem and creates an imbalance, which significantly affects the rest of the animals in the food chain. Kenya has witnessed a tremendous downward trend in its wildlife population especially the elephants and rhinos, which have been listed as vulnerable because of poaching. The African Elephant is a key WWF flagship species under the Wildlife Practice

---

[13] https://wwf.panda.org/?267833/LARGEST-IVORY-BURN-KENYA-2016

and has been identified as a priority species within the recently reviewed WWF-Kenya Strategic Action Plan 2018-2023. The Species is listed as 'vulnerable' by the International Union for Conservation of Nature (IUCN) and red list of threatened species and 'threatened with extinction' under Appendix 1 of the Convention on International Trade in Endangered Species of Wild Fauna and Flora (CITES) listed species. The African elephant is important to Kenya's economic development and conservation efforts and a species of global concern whose population has reduced drastically over the past century largely due to poaching. Within the Mau-Mara Serengeti landscape, threats to this species have been identified as both natural and human activities driven.[14]

The illegal supply chain for ivory and rhino horn describes the processes and actors involved in sourcing, manufacturing, trafficking, and selling products to end consumers. The illicit supply chains start with poaching. Most of the ivory and rhino horn on illicit markets come from (newly) illegally killed animals and some (comparatively small) amounts from other sources such as stockpile thefts or theft from natural mortalities. Once poached, the horn and tusks are collected and further trafficked. These products are passed on or sold to local traders and then to intermediaries who compile and organize larger shipments at the national or subregional level. Typically, these shipments are then trafficked by internationally connected individuals or groups to destination markets in Asia, where wholesale and retail traders sell final products to end-consumers. Small quantities are also trafficked towards destinations outside Asia.[15]

Traffic, the wildlife trade monitoring network, in its 2016 report, highlights Kilindini Port in Mombasa and Jomo Kenyatta International Airport in Nairobi as important exit points from Africa for illegally traded wildlife products from countries, including Tanzania, Mozambique, the Democratic Republic of Congo, Uganda, Zambia, and South Sudan. Since 2009, more ivory has been shipped through Mombasa than any other trade route out of Africa. It also noted that:

> Corruption among government and private sector officials is a key enabling factor of the illegal wildlife trade…The fact that wildlife contraband, especially rhino horn and elephant ivory, has been exported from Kenya only to be seized in transit or in destination countries means that wildlife

---

[14] https://www.wwfkenya.org/elephant_conservation/
[15] Supply and value chains and illicit financial flows from the trade in ivory and rhinoceros horn pp. 107-109 https://www.unodc.org/documents/data-and-analysis/wildlife/2020/WWLC20_Chapter_8_Value_chains.pdf.

traffickers are able to exploit security loopholes in the country's law enforcement network.[16]

It is therefore quite clear that despite the existence of good laws protecting our wildlife against poaching and Kenya being a signatory to international treaties, especially the Convention on International Trade in Endangered Species of Wild Fauna and Flora (CITES), the illegal wildlife trade has thrived in the country because of corruption among government agencies responsible for protecting our wildlife.

Laws Protecting Wildlife in Kenya

The relevant laws governing wildlife crime are the Wildlife Conservation and Management Act 2013, the Prevention of Organised Crimes Act 2010, the Firearms Act Cap 114, the Anti-Corruption and Economic Crimes Act 2003 and the Environmental Management and Co-ordination Act no. 8 of 2009. (1) The wildlife Conservation and Management Act 2013 is the main statute that protects wildlife in Kenya. Part II of the Act establishes the Kenya Wildlife Service and provides for its functions among which is to conserve and manage national parks, wildlife conservation areas, and sanctuaries, provide security for wildlife, issues permits, and more. The main offences under the act are as follows:

89.   Offences relating to pollution
  (1)   Any person who:
    (a)   discharges any hazardous substances or waste or oil into a designated wildlife area contrary to the provisions of this Act and any other written law;
    (b)   pollutes wildlife habitats and ecosystems;
    (c)   discharges any pollutant detrimental to wildlife into a designated wildlife conservation area contrary to the provisions of this Act or any other written law, commits an offence and shall be liable upon conviction to a fine of not less than two million shillings or to imprisonment of not less than five years or to both such fine and imprisonment.

---

[16] Wildlife Protection and Trafficking drivers and trends of transnational wildlife crime in Kenya published 6th May 2016
https://www.traffic.org/publications/reports/wildlife-protection-and-trafficking-assessment-in-kenya/

92. Offences relating to endangered and threatened species:

(1) A person who kills or injures, tortures, or molests, or attempts to kill or injure, a critically endangered, or endangered species as specified in the Sixth Schedule or listed under CITES Appendix I commits an offence and shall be liable upon conviction to a term of imprisonment of not less than five years.

(2) A person who, without permit or exemption issued under this Act, deals in a wildlife trophy, of any critically endangered or endangered species as specified in the Sixth Schedule or listed under CITES Appendix I, commits an offence and shall be liable upon conviction to a term of imprisonment of not less than seven years.

(3) Any person who, without permit or exemption issued under this Act, deals in a live wildlife species of any of critically endangered or endangered species as specified in the Sixth Schedule or listed under CITES Appendix I, commits an offence and shall be liable upon conviction to a term of imprisonment of not less than three years.

(4) Any person without permit, or exemption issued under this Act is in possession of any live wildlife species or trophy of any critically endangered or endangered species as specified in the Sixth Schedule or listed under CITES Appendix I, commits an offence and shall be liable upon conviction to a fine of not less than three million shillings or a term of imprisonment of not less than five years or both such fine and imprisonment.

(2) Prevention of Organised Crimes Act No. 6 of 2010, provides protection in the following sections:

4. Offence

(1) A person who engages in any organised criminal activity specified in section 3 commits an offence and shall, upon conviction, be liable to a fine not exceeding five million shillings or to imprisonment for a term not exceeding fifteen years, or both.

(2) If as a result of the act referred to in section 3(n) a person dies, the member of the organized criminal group shall on conviction be liable to imprisonment for life.

6.   Aiding and abetting
     A person who attempts, aids, abets, counsels, procures, or conspires
     with another to commit an offence under this Act commits an offence
     and shall, upon conviction, be liable to a fine not exceeding one
     million shillings or to imprisonment for a term not exceeding fourteen
     years, or both.

(3) The Firearms Act Cap 114

4A. Offences relating to specified firearms

(1) Notwithstanding section 4, any person who:
     (a) is found in possession of any of the specified firearms without a
         license or permit or other lawful justification; or
     (b) being licensed to possess, hold, trade in, or otherwise have custody
         of any of the specified firearms, ammunition or parts of such firearm
         or ammunition hires or otherwise unlawfully permits another person
         to take possession of or use that firearm or ammunition to advance
         the course of organized criminal activity, commits an offence under
         this Act and is liable to imprisonment for life.

(4) Anti-corruption and Economic Crimes Act No. 3 of 2003

46. Abuse of office
     A person who uses his office to improperly confer a benefit on
     himself or anyone else is guilty of an offence.

47. Dealing with suspect property
     (1) A person who deals with property that he believes or has reason
     to believe was acquired in the course of or as a result of corrupt
     conduct is guilty of an offence.
     (2) For the purposes of this section, a person deals with property if
     the person:
     (a) holds, receives, conceals, or uses the property or causes the
     property to be used; or
     (b) enters into a transaction in relation to the property or causes such
     a transaction to be entered into.

(5) Environmental Management and Co-ordination Act No. 8 of 2009
This act establishes the National Environment Management authority.
Section 9 sets the object and function of the authority as follows: The object

and purpose for which the Authority is established is to exercise general supervision and co-ordination over all matters relating to the environment and to be the principal instrument of Government in the implementation of all policies relating to the environment. The act provides guidance on the use of the environment especially the rivers, lakes, seas, wetlands, and forests. Yet despite these laws, the illegal wildlife trade business continues to grow. It has often been said that you can have the best laws in the world but if they are not enforced, they are useless to those they try to protect.

Challenges in Enforcement: An Inconvenient Truth (3)

Although there are very good laws in place to protect our wildlife from the effects of climate change and corruption, there have been a few challenges in realizing these objectives. Some of these challenges are identified below:

- Most poachers are well equipped with different mechanisms that make it difficult for the wardens to pursue them. There have been cases where the poachers have sophisticated armaments and survey the area using drones. Our wardens are not well equipped and so it is difficult for them to save the animals.
- Most poachers are members of the local communities around the park areas who know the terrain and have mastered the habits of the animals. It is easier for them to attack the animals and take them as far as they can without being caught.
- Corruption is a major hurdle in enforcement of these laws. The poachers pay their way out of prosecution. This not only applies to Kenya but other countries where most of the illegal wildlife trophies are sold.
- Lack of international corporation. Some countries are major business hubs and have a large market for illegally acquired wildlife trophies. This is a major motivation for poachers because of the kind of profits they make from the sale of these wildlife trophies.
- There is a general lack of knowledge on the effects of climate change and corruption on the welfare of our wildlife. Most people are not aware of the importance of our wildlife to our society and the ecosystem.
- Environmental pollution is still not taken seriously by government agencies. Most people are still cutting down trees for their private gain and there is also lack of proper industrial emissions regulations.

- There has also been a problem with the prosecution of wildlife crimes. Weak prosecution of cases and lack of evidence has seen many poachers and people involved in illegal wildlife trade walk free because of unsuccessful prosecutions.
- The continued existence of a ready market for illegally acquired wildlife trophies acts as a motivation for poachers because of the huge profits they make from selling the trophies.

Recommendations

The UN Chronicle reported that:

> Weak governance and corruption have exacerbated the poaching crisis. Endemic poverty has helped organized criminal elements recruit, bribe, and threaten locals, under-paid police, military personnel, and wildlife rangers to participate in wildlife crime. This crisis, if left unchecked, will have a profound effect on regional biodiversity and the economy. African elephants and rhinos play a critical role in maintaining the biodiversity of savannah and forest ecosystems. In addition, they attract tourism that brings in foreign dollars and bolsters economies. The surge in the killing of elephants and other endangered species in East Africa threatens not only wildlife populations, but economic development and the livelihoods of millions of people who depend on tourism for a living.[17]

Despite the fact, that climate change and corruption have adversely affected our wildlife, there is still hope for our wildlife to be protected against future dangers related to climate change corruption. There are several ways in which state and non-state actors can be involved in ensuring that the Kenyan wildlife is protected:

- The government of Kenya through its various agencies can ensure strict enforcement of the laws protecting wildlife by fighting corruption at all levels of governance and ensuing that the stakeholders concerned with animal welfare carry out their duties with integrity.
- There is need to educate wildlife wardens, law enforcement officers, local communities and the public through workshops and seminars about the importance of our wildlife, the laws protecting them and the penalties involved in the event of violation these laws.

---

[17] https://www.un.org/en/chronicle/article/fighting-wildlife-trade-kenya

- Non-state actors such as animal rights activists and religious leaders also have a duty to educate the people, especially the followers of religious organizations, about the importance of creation and the need to protect our world from the effects of climate change and illegal wildlife trade. A good example of such leaders is the Ecumenical Patriarch of Constantinople of the Eastern Orthodox Church. The Greek Times of 2019 reported as follows:

> The Orthodox Christian World's Ecumenical Patriarch, Bartholomew, also known as the Green Patriarch, urged global leaders to reach climate change targets of the Paris Agreement, on the occasion of the UN Summit on Climate Change in New York. In a message to UN Secretary-General Antonio Guterres, Bartholomew urged faster progress "towards achieving the objectives of the Paris Agreement on decarbonization.

In his message the Ecumenical Patriarchate also called for the reduction of greenhouse gas emissions "as soon as possible," in line with the requirements of the UN's Intergovernmental Panel on Climate Change (IPCC). Patriarch Bartholomew encourages:

> the world's economically developed countries to provide the necessary financial support to developing countries in order to facilitate a socially equitable and efficient transition to an environmentally sustainable and climate-friendly course of development.[18]

It is important that other religious leaders and non-state actors emulate his example and call for climate reforms to avert the effects of climate change.

- There is need for wildlife wardens to be trained on proper evidence collection methods so that whatever evidence is collected can sustain a conviction for wildlife crimes.
- There is need to have proper emission regulations to prevent environmental pollution and the relevant government agencies should urgently crackdown on non-compliant industries.
- Penalties for wildlife crimes should be revised such that they act punitively and be a deterrent measure for any aspiring poachers.
- There is need for international co-operation and strict enforcement of international treaties that protect the wildlife from illegal wildlife

---

[18] Greek City Times of September 28, 2019
https://greekcitytimes.com/2019/09/28/green-patriarch-presses-climate-change/

trade. If there is no market for illegal wildlife trophies, then there will be no need for poaching.

Conclusion

This chapter has looked at the effect of climate change and corruption on the wildlife of Kenya. It has discussed how climate change that has been occasioned by human activities, has adversely affected the animal habitats and this has led to devastating effects on animal populations. Corruption on the other hand, has to a large extent abetted poaching, which in turn, has affected animal populations and especially those of elephants and rhinos, the two species who are prized because of their tusks and horns. The chapter has also shown that although the Kenyan government has put in place various legislations to protect animals from the effects of both poaching and pollution, corruption, complacency and bad leadership amongst government officials in enforcing the measures in place to secure the wildlife, have seen little impact made in combating these vices.

The chapter argues that although climate change and illegal wildlife trade have become the greatest threat to our wildlife, the situation is redeemable if some of measures put in place are strictly enforced. This will also need the cooperation of international governments in strictly enforcing international rules that forbid the acquisition and sale of trophies from endangered species. It has also argued that international civic organizations can also play a critical role in identifying the financiers of poachers and the buyers of such trophies.

A tripartite agreement between the host countries of the animals, the recipients of the poached trophies and international civic bodies, in combating the effects of the illegal wildlife trade, would go a long way in reducing, if not completely stopping, the trade in these trophies and therefore ensuring the conservation of the world's wildlife.

CHAPTER TEN

CREATION CARE AND JUSTICE - A SIKH PERSPECTIVE

CHARANJIT AJITSINGH

In writing this article, I am fully aware that I am neither a faith leader nor a scientist specialising in issues concerning the environment and climate change. However, as a person of faith, I have been interested in the issue of creation care and justice for several decades and I share the urgency and concerns with many others about how we, the people of this planet and particularly those in the West, are exploiting what is not ours to exploit. The present pathway is taking us towards doom and eventual annihilation, as climate scientists and naturalists have been prophesying. It is clearly a time for us to reflect deeply on the issues facing the planet and perhaps even our own misdeeds, which have led us close to the tipping-point in the climate story. We all need to seek solutions to care for and sustain our only mortal abode, our mother earth.

Mr. Shammi Puri, an eminent Hydrogeologist and an environmental sustainability expert, whose late father Dr. Gopal Singh Puri, a philosopher and a botanist, published the book in 1995 'Man, Environmental Crisis and Sikh Faith' has said:

> *Environment, biodiversity and climate change are words that we often hear in connection with the present state of planet earth - and in 2020 it is widely accepted that the state of the planet is not good…Many scientists have come to the clear understanding that the legacy of the Anthropocene is in the gradual destruction of the living planet. So, what can individuals do to save the planet from this almost certain doom? And what might be the time frame for this occurring?*
>
> *Despite the seeming enormity of the problem humanity is still duty bound to make every effort to correct the errors of our past ways. Though the doom*

mentioned above may not be too far off in the future, there is still time to do something. [1]

As Sikhs we have the responsibility to work for the common good and that means active participation and action.

History of recent Sikh participation in the Environmental awareness movement

In the late 1980's, I participated along with two other Sikhs in the inter-religious project with Alliances of Religion and Conservation[2] and the Worldwide Fund for Nature (WWF) who were tasked with the production of nine Individual Faith statements on Nature, including The Sikh Statement, which I had the honour to write. These were later presented to the Duke of Edinburgh, the then President of the WWF, followed by a launch in 1989 at Canterbury.

What became very clear, was the link between faith-based spirituality and the environment, the connection of human and animal life with nature, and the increasing recognition of our interdependence and the fragile nature of our globe, our mother earth. As people of faith, we needed to take actions, such as working towards ensuring the survival of endangered species and their habitats, which is not just a scientific need but also a spiritual and religious necessity.

In 1993, the Parliament of World Religions[3] met in Chicago for the first time in 100 years since its inception in 1893 and endorsed 'A Declaration towards a Global Ethic'. The basic ethical principle of the declaration is that every human being must be treated humanely. This means that every human-being without distinction of age, sex, race, skin colour, physical or mental ability, language, religion, political view, or national or social origin, possesses an inalienable and untouchable dignity.

The four guidelines or irrevocable directives of the declaration for behaviour are:

- The commitment to a culture of non-violence and respect for life.
- The commitment to a culture of solidarity and a just economic order.

---

[1] Dr Gopal Singh Puri 'Man, Environmental Crisis and Sikh Faith' (Delhi, Falcon Books, 1995, ISBN81-86302-04-2)
[2] The Alliance of Religions and Conservation (ARC) is a United Kingdom-based international organisation founded by Prince Philip, in 1995.
[3] Parliament of World Religions-World Parliament of Religions of 1893, was an attempt to create a global dialogue of faiths.

- The commitment to a culture of tolerance and a life of truthfulness.
- The commitment to a culture of equal rights and partnership between men and women.

In a later parliament of 2018 in Toronto, a fifth directive was added:

- The commitment to a culture of sustainability and Care for the World.

The two interfaith organisations, the World Congress of Faiths[4] and the International Interfaith Centre in Oxford[5] assembled after the parliament in 1993 to undertake a deeper reflection and testing of the Global Ethic directives, through an initiative entitled 'Voices from Religions on Moral Values'. A publication entitled 'Testing the Global Ethic'[6] was subsequently launched both in the USA and UK, with contributions from nine religions and non-religious and spiritual traditions in 1998. I contributed as a Sikh writer on the Sikh related chapters on each of these directives, as well as on what it means to be human. Looking back, each of these directives/guidelines is equally attributable to our wider commitments to creation care and justice, and our responsibilities to take necessary action for the sake of our collective well-being.

In November 2008, under the leadership of Archbishop Anders Wejryd of Sweden, religious leaders and teachers from different parts of the World, gathered in Uppsala and after two days of intensive dialogue, signed the 'Uppsala Interfaith Climate Manifesto 2008, Faith traditions addressing Global Warming'.[7] It was entitled 'Hope for the Future'. I had the honour of signing it as a Sikh along with twenty two religious leaders from different parts of the globe. The manifesto was aimed as an appeal to the world leaders at the Copenhagen Summit taking place in 2009. I quote from it:

As people from world religions, we urge governments and international organisations to prepare and agree upon a comprehensive climate strategy for the Copenhagen Agreement. This strategy must be ambitious enough to keep climate change below 2 degrees Celsius, and to distribute the burden in an equitable way in accordance with the principles of common but differentiated responsibility and respective capabilities. Green House

---

[4] The World Congress of Faiths (www.worldfaiths.org)
[5] International Interfaith Centre in Oxford (www.iicao.org)
[6] 'Testing the Global Ethic' (International Interfaith Centre, 1998) ISBN-10: 0952414015 ISBN-13: 978-0952414018.
[7] https://www.svenskakyrkan.se/filer/Manifesto_Uppsala_2008_eng.pdf

Development Rights[8] offers one concrete model of such burden sharing. We urge all actors concerned to find politically acceptable tools to realize this.

The global leadership were asked for the following:

- Rapid and large emissions cuts in the rich world.
- Binding cuts for the rich world on top of their domestic obligations.
- Measurable, verifiable, and reportable mitigation actions.
- Economic incentives for developing countries to foster cleaner development on a national scale.
- Adaptation to climate change must not fail for want of money and other resources.

The faith leaders made three commitments to help mobilise peoples and nations:

- To inform and inspire people in our own religious and cultural contexts to take responsibility for and to implement effective measures.
- To challenge political and business leaders where we live and work to develop comprehensive strategies and action.
- To focus on the struggle against global warming and draw upon our innermost religious convictions about the meaning of life.

This faith-leaders commitment is in essence a deeply spiritual question concerning justice, peace and hopes for a future of mutual respect, understanding and solidarity with all human beings and the whole of earthly creation. The leaders wanted to "face the climate challenge with defiant optimism to highlight the core principles of major sacred traditions of the world: justice, solidarity, and compassion".

On our return to our respective places, we approached our Members of Parliament with enthusiasm and optimism urging them to follow up the Interfaith Manifesto with the Government, influencing its preparation for

---

[8] Greenhouse Development Rights (GDRs) is a justice-based effort-sharing framework designed to show how the costs of rapid climate stabilization can be shared fairly, among all countries. More precisely, GDRs seeks to transparently calculate national "fair shares" in the costs of an emergency global climate mobilization, in a manner that takes explicit account of the fact that, as things now stand, global political and economic life is divided along both North/South and rich/poor lines.

Copenhagen. I also sent a copy to the Sikh Supreme Leader, Jathedar Akaal Takhat[9] in Amritsar, India and followed it up on his visit to the UK.

In November 2009, two hundred leaders from nine of the world's major faiths: Baha'ism, Buddhism, Christianity, Daoism, Hinduism, Islam, Judaism, Shintoism and Sikhism gathered in Windsor Castle in the United Kingdom to commit to long-term practical action for the environment. UN Secretary General Ban Ki-moon addressed the forum, which was hosted by Prince Philip, founder of the ARC (Alliance of Religions and Conservation). Sikh environmental leaders Baba Sewa Singh of Khadur Sahib, Amritsar and Baba Balbir Singh Seechewal of Sultanpur, Kapurthala Punjab and ECO Sikh's CEO Rajwant Singh also joined the environmental conference. The Celebration at Windsor Castle came a month before the major Copenhagen Climate Change talks in December 2009 and was considered the first major, internationally coordinated commitment by religions to the environment. The event was supported by the United Nations Development Programme (UNDP) and major secular bodies, including Conservation International, the Forest Stewardship Council, Fairtrade, and the World-Wide Fund for Nature.

Over the years, there have been many interfaith conferences especially the Parliament of World religions, International Association of Religious Freedom, World Congress of Faiths and the United Religions Initiative (URI) where Sikhs have been involved in global environmental issues due to their commitment to the protection of the environment and the sanctity of the planet.[10] Unfortunately, Copenhagen only had limited impact despite the sterling efforts of religious leaders present there. In 2015, the Paris Agreement was signed, but many governments are failing to meet their commitments. In 2020, the UN Environment Programme (UNEP), collaborated with two key interfaith global organisations. It published 'Faith For Earth, A call for Action', with Parliament of the World's Religions, and

---

[9] The Jathedar of the Akal Takht (Punjabi: ਜੱਥੇਦਾਰ ਅਕਾਲ ਤਖ਼ਤ ਸਾਹਿਬ), is the appointed head of the Akal Takht and the Sikhs of the world. Sikh clergy consists of five Jathedars, one each from five Takhts. Originally known as Akal Bunga, the building directly opposite the Darbar Sahib was built by Guru Hargobind as a place of justice and consideration of temporal issues; the highest seat of earthly authority of the Khalsa and the place of the Jathedar, the highest spokesman of the Sikhs.

[10] The United Religions Initiative (URI) is a global grassroots interfaith network: The International Association for Religious Freedom (IARF) is a charitable organization that works for religious freedom around the world; The United Nations Environment Programme (UNEP) is responsible for coordinating responses to environmental issues within the United Nations system and aims to help the world meet the 17 Sustainable Development Goals.

signed an agreement to work in partnership for the preservation of the Environment at a global level, with the United Religions Initiative (URI).

With the situation becoming more dire, as highlighted by Scientists and others, the Global community, including religious bodies, has subsequently expressed hope for further tangible progress to deal with the environmental crisis at the Glasgow COP26 Summit, now scheduled for November 2021.

Sikh theology and history of the Gurus in the context of creation

The Sikh faith (Sikhi) named in Western literature as Sikhism, is recognized as one of the youngest religions in the world.[11] It has approximately 30 million adherents worldwide and was founded by Guru Nanak[12], who was born in 1469 in a Hindu family in a village Rai Bhoey Ki Talwandi, now in Pakistan. While still quite young Guru Nanak decided to devote himself to spiritual matters. He was inspired by a powerful spiritual experience that gave him a vision of the true nature of God and confirmed his idea that the way to spiritual growth was through meditation and through living in a way that reflected the presence of the divine within each human being and in every element and particle of nature.

The most famous teachings of Guru Nanak are that there is only one God, and that all human beings can have direct access to God with no need of rituals or priests. His most radical social teachings denounced the atrocities of the caste system and taught that everyone is equal, regardless of caste, religion, gender or race. Guru Nanak expressed his thoughts in extraordinary poetry that forms the basis of Sikh scripture, Guru Granth Sahib.[13] ੧ੳ 'Ik Onkar', the symbol and the first word of the opening prayer in the scripture, is usually translated as One (1) God or the Eternal reality. The second word 'Satnam' means Truth is the name and the third word is 'Kartapurakh'

---

[11] Sikhism or Sikhi (from, *Sikh*, 'disciple', 'seeker', or 'learner') is a monotheistic, panentheistic religion that originated in the Punjab region of the Indian subcontinent around the end of the 15th century

[12] He was a contemporary of Martin Luther and the reformation movement in Europe and is known to be one of the greatest religious innovators and an original thinker.

[13] The Guru Granth Sahib is the central religious scripture of Sikhism, regarded by Sikhs as the final, sovereign and eternal living Guru following the lineage of the ten human gurus of the religion. It was composed predominantly by six Sikh gurus: Guru Nanak, Guru Angad, Guru Amar Das, Guru Ram Das, Guru Arjan and Guru Tegh Bahadur. It also contains the poetic teachings of thirteen Hindu Bhakti movement *sant* poets and two Sufi Muslim poets. The vision in the Guru Granth Sahib is of a society based on divine justice without oppression of any kind.

means Creator. Thereby the message is encapsulated in three words, 'The One Creator of all Creation.'

Professor DS Chahal from the Institute for Understanding in Sikhism in Montreal on Sikh Beliefs and Practices, states that Sikhi has been defined by Guru Nanak as follows: *"Sikhi is those teachings which are based on the enlightening philosophy"*[14] - Nanakian Philosophy.[15] Chahal writes that the logical and scientific interpretation of the words of Guru Nanak reveals that his philosophy embodied in his writing is logical and scientific, which compliments and is compatible with traditional Sikh Tradition and philosophy.

In this Sikh tradition, Guru Nanak was the first embodiment of 'Divine Light' who laid the foundation for a sacred vision for the environment. Guru Nanak strongly instructs us to remember the Great Mother Earth and in every evening prayer (Rehras), it is said:

Rejoice in the Lord that dwells in Nature. (SGGS p. 469)

Many theologians understand the last verse of Japji, recited as the morning prayer, to indicate a divine judge who watches our actions:

Air is the Guru, Water the father, Earth the Great Holy Mother
Day and Night, the male and female nurses
In whose laps the whole world plays
The Judge of righteousness keeps an account of our good and bad deeds.
The approval or rejection by God comes from our own actions
Meritorious deeds unite us with Him, misdeeds get us thrown back into the cycle of migration
Those who dwell on Naam (GOD) and meditated, gain hard-earned success
Says Nanak, are honoured and glorified in the Lord's Court and many others are also released with them. (SGGS p. 8)

This hymn was adopted as the Sikh anthem for Environment at the end of the last century.

Having created, God continues to support, control and direct it as an accomplished and competent Omnipresent and Immanent being. God, being Omnipotent, can choose to act as the maker, destroyer, shaper and re-shaper (bhanan, gharan, Samrath), such is His will and we as a part of His creation, should abide by His Command (SGGS p. 467).

---

[14] SGGS, p. 456.
[15] https://www.upf.org/resources/speeches-and-articles/2653-singh-nanakian-philosophy-and-world-peace

According to Dr Gurbachan Singh Bachan, retired Professor and Chairman of Guru Gobind Singh Chair, Guru Nanak Dev University, "Guru Nanak's philosophy provides harmonious balance in nature. He dwells upon the dynamic ecological cycles in nature. His concept of ecology is not merely of physical or cultural nature as is the viewpoint of modern scientists, but he has elaborated on spiritual ecology as well." (Guru Nanak and Ecology: 76)[16]

The Sikh faith teaches that the natural environment and the survival of life forms are closely linked to the rhythm of nature. In the world God has created, he has also provided each species and humans with means of support and nurturing. Other verses reinforce the Divine origin of creation and as such and as Sikhs, these are worthy of our veneration and safeguarding as God's stewards.

> *The Lord infused His Light into the dust, and created the world, the universe.*
> *The sky, the earth, the trees, and the water - all are the Creation.* (SGGS p.723)

Guru Nanak considered no difference between the created and the creator; the nature and God and saw God in the nature itself.

The history of the Sikh Gurus, from Guru Nanak the first Master, to the tenth Master Guru Gobind Singh, is full of stories of their love and special relationship with the natural environment - with animals, birds, vegetation, earth, rivers, mountains, and the sky. There is also a very strong vegetarian tradition. Furthermore, the Sikh Gurus state that there is no difference between the human sphere and the sphere of nature. Both were created from the same divine light. The whole planet, indeed, the universe/multiverse is strung together and interconnected by the divine, as Guru Arjan, the fifth Guru says, "Sagal samagri tumre sooterdhari"[17], which translates as 'The whole of creation is threaded through you.'

The earth is described by Bhai Gurdass, a scholar and theologian who was a contemporary of the Sikh Gurus, as 'Dharamsaal', which translates as an abode of righteousness. The Sikh Gurus emphasise the five elements from which the human body is shaped. These are water, fire, air, space, and earth. The Gurus have given definition to the elements as being the most

---

[16] Gurbachan Singh Bachan, *Guru Nanak and Ecology* (Guru Nanak Dev University, Amritsar, 2004) 308

[17] Sri Guru Granth Sahib, Sukhmani Sahib p. 268. The Sikh belief is that there are approximately 8,400,000 life forms on this earth and that the precious human birth has been achieved after a long transmigration through other life forms, (SGGS p 176, Guru Arjan, fifth Guru)

sacred and without these there is no survival of any beings and any life-form.

The Sikh Gurus gave the message of 'Sahaj'. A state of equipoise, of balance in our personal and societal lives alongside in our relationship with the environment. We must know the eternal truth of our place in the universe. The Gurus emphasise that environmental balance can only be achieved if the conservation designed by God and the process of healing of our mother earth is inculcated through sustainable solutions. Sikhi stresses that this can only be made possible by our adherence to the ethical behaviour as prescribed in the holy scriptures which is in tune with the natural existence.

In other words, it is our golden opportunity to achieve closeness to God and to seriously undertake effective action to fulfil our responsibility of looking after all the life-forms on this planet. Serving them is a true service to the Creator because we are part of the cycle ourselves. They need our support in helping them to thrive in their appropriate habitats.

Addressing the human being as the leader on this earth, the Gurus remind us of our responsibility for all those who inhabit this earth and there is a clear warning for those who desire to exploit nature:

You yourself are true and true is your justice, O God! (SGGS p. 84)

The Sikh Gurus' wisdom leads us in our belief that all humans have an intrinsic sensitivity to the natural world and that a sustainable, more just society is possible, where water, air, land, forests, and biodiversity remain vibrant living systems for our generation, and for future generations.

Recent Significant initiatives by Sikhs for Creation Care

1. EcoSikhs[18]

At the initiative of ECO SIKH's the following 'Sikh Statement on Climate Change' was adopted in September 2014 by the Akal Takhat, the Supreme Spiritual Body of the Sikhs and the Sikh community worldwide were asked to adhere to it.

You, Yourself created the Universe, and You are pleased...You, Yourself the bumblebee, flower, fruit and the tree. You, Yourself the water, desert, ocean

---

[18] EcoSikh is a response from the Sikh community to the threats of climate change and the deterioration of the natural environment. (http://www.ecosikh.org/about/)

and the pond. You, Yourself are the big fish, tortoise and the Cause of causes.
(SGGS, Maru Sohele, p. 1020).

Through His teachings, our first guru, Guru Nanak Dev Ji, explained that
the world we humans create around ourselves reflects our own inner state.
So, as we look around to our wasteful and polluting practices, we obtain an
insight into the chaos within us. The tenth master, Guru Gobind Singh Ji,
founded the Khalsa in 1699, charged Sikhs to challenge any force that
threatened the wellbeing of others. He made us warriors with the responsibility
to protect the vulnerable. Today, the Earth is vulnerable because of climate
change and because people have not protected their environments. Today,
it is time to act and show that we are true warriors of the Khalsa. We must
make amends with the Earth. Our Mother Earth, Mata Dharat, has gone
through undeniable changes at the hands of humans. It is abundantly clear
that our action has caused great damage to the atmosphere and is projected
to cause even more damage if left unhandled. Since 1980, the average
temperature of the earth's surface has increased drastically. Glaciers and
Arctic ice are melting and sea levels are rising, threatening plant and animal
species and hurting the poor people of the world first. As Sikhs, we appeal
to lawmakers, faith leaders and citizens of the world to take concrete action
toward reducing carbon emissions and protecting the environment. And as
Sikhs, we pledge to take concrete actions ourselves. We have a
responsibility to follow our Gurus' teachings and protect the vulnerable.
Governments have struggled to find consensus and have been slow to
reduce the effects of releasing greenhouse gases and excessive carbon
dioxide into the atmosphere. As climate change and thoughtless practice
continue to threaten food and environmental security worldwide,
governments must put environmental issues at the centre of security
concerns. We should not only hope they will do so; we must take the
initiative to push our own governments to act.

Sikhs should be front-runners of change. Seva, the practice of selfless
service, is a main tenet of Sikhism. Sikhs can perform Seva by reducing our
carbon footprints, recycling, investing in renewable energies and being
mindful about where our food comes from. Gurdwaras, as beacons of
righteous thought, must be eco-friendly. Our religious spaces, when in
harmony with nature, will allow Sikhs to be more spiritually connected to
Waheguru, the creator of all. Respect for nature is ingrained in Sikh
teachings. As Guru Nanak said: "Pawan Guru pani pita mata dharat
mahat"[19] (Air is our teacher, water our father and the great sacred earth is
our mother). If we act now, we can protect our atmosphere, water resources,

---

[19] '*Pawan Guru pani pita mata dharat mahat*' SGGS p. 8

and earth, for ourselves and for future generations. To achieve internal peace, we must first look at the environment in which we live.

2. River (Kali) Bein in Punjab

The River Bein (associated with Guru Nanak's disappearance for three days and spent in the presence of the Creator who made him His messenger of unity of the humankind), had become so badly polluted that it needed urgent cleaning. Sant Balbir Singh Seechewal[20] took on the formidable task and now it is a beautifully pure river. The sant (saint) has been asked to help purify the sacred River Ganges by the Indian Government.

3. EcoAmritsar

EcoAmritsar is an initiative begun by Sikhs but supported by a diversity of local stakeholders to make Amritsar, which is the holy city of the Sikhs, into a 'greener' city. The initiative is to help visitors and residents by being respectful of the natural environment in accordance with their religious and cultural beliefs and for Amritsar to be a model of green action throughout the whole of India. It is also to help and guide the City of Amritsar to reduce waste, conserve water, and expand greenery projects through tree plantings and open spaces. Furthermore, the aim of EcoAmritsar is for pilgrims coming to Amritsar to visit a clean green city and to return home with ideas to improve their own footprint and have (and pass on) a sense that being people of faith also means being gentle to the planet.[21]

4. Green Gurdwaras

Green Gurdwaras is a grassroots movement which include Gurdwaras from around the world, that choose to reduce their impact on their

---

[20] Balbir Singh Seechewal (born 2 February 1962) is a Sikh who spearheaded an anti-river pollution campaign in Punjab, India. By combining his assiduously cultivated self-help philosophy with the environmental essence of the Gurbani, he has resurrected the 110-miles long Kali Bein rivulet. He along with his followers cleaned and restored Kali Bein river a 160 km long tributary of Beas in Doaba region of Punjab.

[21] The EcoAmritsar initiative emerged from an international meeting in November 2011, when Amritsar agreed to join pilgrim cities around the world in the Green Pilgrim Cities program, a plan spearheaded by the Alliance of Religions and Conservation (ARC), as part of the ARC-UNDP collaboration on long term environmental plans by the faiths.

environment. Gurdwaras worldwide are pioneering new ideas in renewable energy, water conservation, waste reduction and recycling, and organic and healthy food systems. The Gurdwaras in Punjab and the diaspora are encouraged to share their successes, understand the policies and programmes that can support them and improve the environment and the health of the Gurdwara community and surroundings at the same time. For example, encouraging Gurdwaras to use greener energy as the Gurdwara at Kali Bein, run by Baba Seechewal Singh, uses biofuel made of kitchen waste scraps.

A Gurdwara in Derby, UK, has gone plastic-free in time for the Sikh New Year. That stems from the thoughts and aspirations of youth groups in the Gurdwara who as attendees asked the people in charge if they could use alternatives to plastic utensils. The Gurdwara has swapped the use of plastic disposable plates for steel ones and now uses glasses instead of plastic cups. After worship, people can collect a type of food called Prashad. This used to be given out in plastic bags, but now it given in paper bags instead.

5. Sikh Environment Day.

In March 2010, the Sikh Environment Day was incepted and over 4100 Gurdwaras, organisations and educational institutions worldwide have been involved in various initiatives under the concept of Cleanliness is next to Godliness. The EcoSikh's describe the initiative in 2017:

> ...many thousands of trees were planted, gardens revived, flower shows, distribution of 'Boota Prasad' (gift of plants as holy blessing), marathon / bicycle rallies by youth groups conducted, katha kirtans (sermons and musical recitals) in Gurdwara's, organic Langar and organic food stall setups, vehicle free day in institutions, green Hola Mohalla (martial arts festival) and much more grassroots work being done by individuals, communities and institutions for protection of our environment.

The entire episode is meant to pay tribute to the seventh Guru, Sri Har Rai ji (1630-1661) for the environmental vision he established in his lifetime. It is said that Guru Har Rai established a big park, an orchard of fruit trees, and a garden full of the diversity of medicinal herbs for healing, and he is said to have provided a rare medication prepared from his garden to cure Dara, the son of the Mughal Emperor, from his serious illness, despite the atrocities showered on the Guru's community by the Mughal rulers who happened to be Muslim.

6. A million Trees Initiative

Guru Nanak's 550th birth anniversary celebrations in November 2019 became a significant marker in the Sikh Calendar enthusing Sikhs to plant a million trees worldwide where the Sikhs are living. The bank of a motorway near Leicester was planted with 550 trees. Our local Gurdwara community children planted ten trees in a local park, which was appreciated by the local council. Furthermore, the Sikh community have been active to honour the memory of Guru Nanak in Pakistan, the land of his birth and final resting place, by ensuring the greening of the sacred sites by negotiating a green master plan with the authorities.

The Sikh ECO body has proposed that 25 to 50 acres of land at *Nankana Sahib* and at *Kartarpur* be declared as sacred forest in order to conserve biodiversity around these places. The plans include power generation by solar panels, creating organic farmland for *langar* (community kitchen), dedicating sacred forest areas and creating an ethos of care for the environment among local faith leaders, local communities and thousands of pilgrims. In addition, organic farming would also be incepted to supply organic food for *langar* for which around five or ten acres would be devoted. When I visited *Kartarpur* last year, it was a joy to see the lush fields full of fruit and vegetables from where these are taken every day for cooking in the Gurdwara Kitchens.

7. Pingalwara: continued fostering of Creation Care. [22]

The 114th anniversary of Bhagat Puran Singh, a deeply spiritual environmentalist and the founder of the charity *Pingalwara* (disabled), was celebrated to reinforce his message of care for nature on 4th June 2018. Bhagat Puran Singh, popularly also called as 'bearded Mother Teresa', had probably foresighted the brazen exploitation of natural resources and its consequences. This is the reason he propagated a lifestyle in harmony with nature and advocated the green revolution. Dr. Inderjit Kaur, his adopted daughter and director, All India Pingalwara Charitable Society, is reminding the masses of his message on his 114th birth anniversary.

The topic of environment was very dear to him. He believed in simple living and it is today's requirement. We should go back to the basics...His ideas like eating in utensils made of bronze, not destroying environment but learning to co-exist, decreasing individual waste count and using natural made things. We have been promoting his ideas among the young generation

---

[22] Pingalwara is a charity for the disabled based in Amritsar.

by holding workshops and seminars. It is more about having the right intent and working to implement as well.

A big believer of Sewa[23] (service), Bhagat Puran Singh served the poor and downtrodden. He cleaned streets, nurtured the sick and adopted an eco-friendly lifestyle. Dr. Inderjit Kaur said:

His service towards the environment was what we also need to adopt. Using a bicycle as means of transport and saving water through waste-water management, all his ideas were simple and scientific in nature.

Working on his principles, Pingalwara's Bhagat Puran Singh Farm[24], spread over thirty-two acres at Dhirakot near Jandiala, practices zero wastage and has a water treatment plant and dairy farm. It has taken the lead in natural farming techniques and produces the best sugarcane without using pesticides. Rajbir Singh, a trustee and manager of the farm, who works with skilled workers, said,

We save 60 per cent water through scientific methods. We sow vegetables, fruits and other crops, thereby increasing soil fertility without poisoning it.

The farm has also become a training ground for farmers from the region who learn natural farming techniques.

In the wake of the 2018 River Beas spill controversy, Dr Inderjit said people need to take a note of the blatant disregard for the ecological existence.

We are now planning to set up an advisory committee to ensure that Bhagatji's ideas on environment are spread through voluntary service. The young generation should connect with his ideology and work towards preserving the environment through bringing small changes, one at a time.

---

[23] Selfless service or Seva in Sikhism, including its ordained philosophy in Sikh scripture, theology and hermeneutics, is a service that is performed without any expectation of result or award for performing it.

[24] Pingalwara has started a silent and constructive revolution to save the environment, to regenerate farmer-friendly micro-organism, to bring back soil productivity, to re-establish ecological balance by practically doing Natural Farming in its 32 Acre Farm. In this farm cultivation is done without resorting to any type of chemical fertilizers and pesticides This cultivation has proved to be healthier for the soil, more eco-friendly, less expensive i.e. (almost zero Budget) and most of all, less toxic to the ground water, resulting in saving of the humanity from dreadful diseases.

In short, Bhagat Puran Singh's simple message, written below continues to be fostered through Pingalwara publications:

Preserve natural resources
Service of the poor and destitute is the service of God
Plant more and more trees to save the environment
Wear khadi clothes to lessen unemployment
Simple living and high thinking is a bliss
Use less diesel and petrol
Exercise restraint in your living habits
Don't forget to plant trees. They are a sign of the prosperity of a nation!

This was said more than fifty years ago when diesel was a perfectly acceptable fuel.

Creation Justice

While some of the attempts listed above by sections of the Sikh community, (a very small group in the world population), are laudable, these are not sufficient in themselves. The Sikhs are being pro-active in their innumerable small-scale examples of eco-initiatives from across the world, where efforts are being made to make modest corrections. There will regrettably remain a serious concern that the earth may no longer be a sustainable bio-system irrespective of the efforts being made. EcoSikhs say:

The major crises facing the earth - the social justice crisis and the environmental crisis - together are heading the earth towards a disastrous situation. The social justice crisis is that of humanity's confrontation with itself and the environmental crisis is caused by humanity's confrontation with nature. The social justice crisis is that poverty, hunger, disease, exploitation, and injustice are widespread. There are economic wars over resources and markets. The rights of the poor and the marginal are violated. Women constituting half the world's population are excluded from public decision-making, making them even more vulnerable in situations of conflict and crisis. The environmental crisis caused by humanity's exploitation of nature is leading to the depletion of renewable resources, destruction of forests, over-use of land for agriculture and habitation. Today pollution is contaminating air, land and water. Smoke from industries, homes and vehicles fills the air. Industrial waste and consumer trash is affecting streams and rivers, ponds and lakes. Much of the waste is a product of modern technology; it is not biodegradable, not re-usable and its long-term consequences are unknown. The viability of many animal and plant species, and possibly that of the human species itself is at stake. This crisis cries out for an immediate and urgent solution.

Furthermore, the Covid 19 Pandemic is adding to the already dire situation leading to severe illness, worldwide deaths and disrupted the economy.

More is needed at the collective and individual levels. As individuals, each of us could accept that as a contributor to the planetary problems in many small ways, we can help in simple ways. Pledging to make small changes in our lifestyles are worthwhile and are an important step in the eventual salvation of the planet and humanity. Acceptance that we are contributors to today's planetary problems and that solutions lie in our own hands is deeply embedded into Sikh thought and culture, as described in great detail by the renowned Sikh scholar, scientists and ecologist Dr Gopal Singh Puri, in his book Man, *Environment Crisis and Sikh Faith*, (1995). Dr Puri analyses the links between the verses in the Granth Sahib and the actions of mankind to live in ecological harmony, having already noted in the early 1990s the litany of planetary environmental problems alluded to in the introduction.

The crisis the planet is enduring is against natural justice. It requires us going back to the basic question of the purpose of human beings in this universe and an understanding of ourselves and the Divine creation. We are called to the vision of Guru Nanak, which is a world society comprising God-conscious human beings who have realized God. To these spiritual beings the earth and the universe are sacred; all life is united and their mission is the spiritualisation of all. Guru Nanak and his successors during their lifetime worked towards creating an ideal society that has as its basis spiritual awareness and ethical integrity.

We are, therefore, expected to lead our lives according to God's will. This also means that we should not be the instruments of destruction or cause harm to His creation. The Sikh tradition teaches us that we will have to answer for our deeds, good or bad, and be judged as stated earlier in the Sikh environment anthem.

We humans are fallible sinners and there is no end to our mistakes. As we become more conscious of our errors, we must be cognisant of our contribution to past misdeeds, and pray for God's gracious forgiveness, regardless of the religious or other path we follow. God does not cease to be God if we do not believe.

Save this burning planet with Your mercy and receive us from whatever path we come, O Lord. (SGGS p. 853)

Furthermore, as many Sikhs are aware, we should live by the three cardinal principles, namely Naam Japna, Kirat Karni and Wand Chhakna, which are the golden threads to express that love.

1. *Naam Japna*, means recitation of God's name and includes meditations, prayers, recitations, and singing hymns from the Sikh scripture,

2. *Kirat Karni,* means earning ones living through honest hard work. No task is lowly or higher. Guru Nanak wanted his followers to be active citizens, advising his followers to share their hard-earned wealth for the welfare of humanity and the good of all beings, that way they realise right path

   Ghaal khaaye kich hathon dey, Nanak raah pachaaney sey. (SGGS p. 1245).

3. *Wand Chhakna-tan, man and dhan* (body, mind and money/resources), means sharing can be through physical selfless service, with mind such as supporting the community in different ways such as teaching, learning, giving money, groceries, clothes, etc, making and serving food, langar or other selfless charitable actions. Gurus taught us that, "A poor person's mouth is the Guru's treasure chest". Before Covid-related lockdowns, everywhere in the world, in the *langar* (the Sikh community food hall), there is provision of food, continuously sharing food and eating together, regardless of status, gender, race, ethnicity or faith.

There are also individual actions which we can take. Shammi Puri says:

Some of the actions and commitments that individuals can today make to correct the impending environmental doom, may be summarised by making the following pledge:

'I am concerned about the serious risks that biodiversity loss & climate change poses for present and future generations, therefore I agree to take the following actions:

I promise to do my best to reduce the greenhouse gas emissions caused by me and to cut my personal climate and biodiversity footprint by half within ten years or faster.

To achieve the target, I will pay attention to the biodiversity and climate footprint of my energy and land use, travelling, eating and consumption habits, including food, waste and recycling. I will make low-carbon choices, support tree planting, and reduce water wastage wherever possible.

I pledge to consider addressing my unavoidable biodiversity and climate footprint by offsetting emissions, which I cannot reduce, conserving land, using less water, maximise recycling, to become environmentally neutral now.

I will share my experiences in making cleaner choices with my family, friends and colleagues and encourage them to accept the above pledges.'

In conclusion, it is vitally important that we seriously undertake the application of Sikh values and principles, imbibe the teachings of our Gurus, understand our individual and collective responsibility for action to live sustainable and spiritually connected lives and to cooperate with those with whom we share, to stem the rapid extinction of a million diverse species and to restore the eco-health of our imperilled planet. We are all deeply interconnected with everything that exists on this planet and we humans can change our behaviour as individuals and communities. The Sikh faith guides us that we must seek forgiveness for our damaging actions and seek divine help and take effective action for healing our mother earth.

PART TWO:

ARE WE PREPARED?
LIVING IN AN UNSTABLE WORLD

CHAPTER ELEVEN

THE ECONOMY WITH CLIMATE AND ENVIRONMENTAL RESPONSIBILITY

ANDREW BASDEN

Economic growth damages both biodiversity and climate. It always has done so and Dasgupta (2021)[1] and others argue that it always, necessarily will do so. Climate change, pollution, and biodiversity loss are inherent in economic growth, at least as we know it.

The reason this matters Dasgupta argues, is that human life and justice depend on biodiversity and climate stability, and so does the economy itself. Also, from a Christian perspective, Creation care is a responsibility with which God has gifted humanity. Some, such as Jackson (2009)[2], argue for "Prosperity without growth", but the Covid-19 pandemic has opened up another option: shrinking the wealthy Western economies. This may be heresy to most economists and governments, but it is an option we should consider.

Though a few have suggested reversing economic growth as an ideal, this article tries to suggest how such a course might be made real. It is a position paper, which adopts a different way of understanding what the Economy is and what role it should play. As we will see, we must be able to take externalities into account, understand their diversity and recognise that economic activity can do harm as well as good, and that much that does harm is non-essential.

The article briefly discusses economic growth, then summarises Dasgupta's report, the significance of which, is that it was commissioned and published, not by the UK Department of the Environment, but by the Treasury. Does this signal that the Treasury has at last woken up to the importance of biodiversity and climate? However, the report has several

---

[1] Dasgupta, P. *The Economics of Biodiversity: The Dasgupta Review,* (H.M. Treasury, U.K. 2021).
[2] Jackson, T. *Prosperity Without Growth: Economics for a Finite Planet.* (London: Earthscan, 2009).

weaknesses, so a brief critique is made, suggesting how its weaknesses may be addressed.

The idea of shrinking the economy is discussed and a new foundation for understanding economic activity is introduced. This offers a practical conceptual framework where we may understand kinds of externalities, the good and harm generated, and how we may judge what is non-essential. This approach might encourage the integration of religious and secular perspectives and might open a new way for economic activity and climate/environmental responsibility to work in harmony rather than against each other.

On Economic Growth

Why does economic growth harm the climate and biodiversity? What can and should we do about it, by people, businesses, governments, etc? Answers to both questions have been debated for years, without resolution. To summarise much of the discussion on "Why?", economic activity requires resources taken from the biosphere and waste to be put back there. Though nature can regenerate and deal with most waste, it does so slowly. When our demands were meagre, there was little economic problem (though there might have been aesthetic, moral, and religions problems, e.g., with dumping waste or driving a species to extinction). Economic growth not only increases demand and waste, but also fosters technology and lifestyles that amplify these - and all that is multiplied by the population of those who make the most demands, especially those in the wealthy cultures. For example, technological innovation is exciting and has made cryptocurrencies (Bitcoin etc.) possible. However, to 'mine' these and maintain their blockchains, require inordinate amounts of electric power. Currently, even with a very low level of usage, this is about 0.7% of global electricity supply and it is rising fast as more and more people are attracted towards using them (Ellson 2021)[3]. So, there are ethical questions for those who develop and run these products. Alarmingly, humanity's demand, sometimes known as our global ecological footprint, is currently much greater than nature's ability to supply-currently 1.6-7 times (Dasgupta 2021). With more flying, more cryptocurrencies, more demand for meat and dairy and other goods, this will become much worse-especially as so-called 'less-developed' nations (LDNs) aspire to Western, wealthy standards of living. The situation

---

[3] Ellson, A. 2021. Bitcoin is helping to destroy the environment.
https://www.thetimes.co.uk/article/bitcoin-is-helping-to-destroy-the-environment-7s0tmdwkq

is dire and needs urgent attention. We are, as Tearfund (2020)[4] puts it, "Burning Down the House", and of those young Christians they surveyed, 80% believed the climate crisis is our responsibility and 90% want action.

Some have suggested other kinds of economic models, such as the Doughnut Economy (Raworth 2017)[5], where we are called to limit ourselves to 12 social "foundations" without overshooting any of the 9 ecological "ceilings". They offer useful insights, but they have not yet gained traction in real-life economic planning and activity. Milanovic (2018)[6], while liking Raworth's idea, criticises it for not facing the contradictions of economic growth, for assuming 'green' activities are effective and for ignoring human selfish aspirations.

The issues are exceedingly complex, especially to standard academic approaches, yet we need to change direction before we completely understand everything. This is, perhaps, what Dasgupta (2021) tries to do. Though drawing on academic work, its aim is practical: to help HM Treasury in the UK to understand how biodiversity can be accounted for alongside usual economic measures.

Messages of the Dasgupta Review

Here, I summarize Dasgupta's message to the Treasury and then offer a critique. The Review starts by putting our situation into historical context. Humanity now has an impact on nature that exceeds nature's ability to support it. This has come to be so only during this past century and it is serious. In the next few chapters, Dasgupta shows how we may see Nature as an asset (durable goods of positive worth that we inherit or pass on) and thus bring it into economic considerations. There are three kinds of asset: produced capital, human capital and natural capital. Since economics has tended to ignore natural capital, false ideas have arisen. Two false assumptions seem to have spread within wealthy cultures, that economic growth is good for the environment (e.g. to pay for restoration) and that technology will enable us to continue economic growth indefinitely with less environmental damage. Dasgupta shows that both of those are false (2021:45-46) and especially why the net costs of disrupting biodiversity and

---

[4] https://weare.tearfund.org/burning-down-the-house/
[5] Raworth, K. *Doughnut Economics: Seven Ways to Think Like a 21-st Century Economist.* (London, Random House, 2017).
[6] Milanovic, B. 2018. Review: Doughnut Economics: Seven Ways to Think Like a 21st-Century Economist by Kate Raworth. https://braveneweurope.com/doughnut-economics-seven-ways-to-think-like-a-21st-century-economist-by-kate-raworth. Accessed 11 March 2021.

then trying to restore it, exceed those of not doing the damage in the first place. Conservation must therefore be given priority over damage followed by restoration, though the latter is needed for the damage we have already done.

Some defenders of economic growth appeal to the so-called Ecological Kuznets Curve, which claims hypothetically that with sufficient per-capita income, environmental damage with reduce, but that is also false. [7] These false arguments rest on two false presuppositions: that the economy can be detached from the non-human Creation and that human beings have no sin. Dasgupta argues against the first and, from a Christian perspective, both go against the clear message of Scripture. However, the economy and all human enterprise is embedded in, and depends on, nature, so we must bring natural capital back into our economic thinking. He suggests using the idea of Ecosystems Services, which focuses on how ecosystems (nature, the biosphere), provides services for humanity of many kinds. Ecosystems that are rich in biodiversity are more productive (for us) and more resilient in themselves. But the biosphere, not being a linear system, can be grossly disrupted by fragmentation and tipping points and we cannot easily recover what we lose. This is why he states that "markets are a woefully inadequate system of institutions for protecting the biosphere" (2021:83).

Since the Economy is embedded in nature and depends on it, it suffers when biodiversity is lost - both material and so-called 'non-material' economies are undermined. He argues that human impact on the biosphere must be taken into account in Treasury calculations, so a simple *Impact Inequality* is introduced, as a basis for discussing, what needs to be done and why. It says, in mathematical terms, that human demands on ecosystems (ecological footprint) must never exceed the ecosystems' ability to meet those demands (regenerating after we extract resources and absorbing and processing waste), expressed as:

$$N y / a < G(S)$$

where 'N' = world population, 'y' = per capita standard of living (often measured in GDP), 'a' = efficiency with which humanity extracts from nature (ax) and relies on nature to cope with its waste (ay), 'G' = Regeneration rate by which nature recovers and 'S' = stock of nature's capital. As mentioned above, our demands are *not* less, but 1.7 times greater

---

[7] Mills, J. H, Waite, T A. 2009. Economic prosperity, biodiversity conservation and the environmental Kuznets curve. *Ecological Economics*, 68, 2087-95.

than, nature's ability to cope (2019 figure) and growing, so it is imperative that we find a way to resolve this imbalance.

One problem identified is that the factors in this equation are not deterministic but involve risk and Dasgupta discusses how risk and uncertainty may be tackled and in particular, he suggests that we need to calculate when to change course, away from "business-as-usual". Doing so, he argues, will involve institutions, within which we interact with each other, including households, markets, communities and the state. Given that we must trust one another to fulfil our obligations, he asks what our institutions should be like to support this. Such trust is (part of) "social capital", a concept central to the economics of biodiversity.

He discusses at length, the problem of externalities. Externalities are unaccounted-for consequences for others ignored in economic calculations and decision-making (2021:187). Many factors in human well-being as well as biodiversity are externalities; for example, while Amazon, the company, is worth billions, Amazon, the rainforest, is worth nothing unless it is destroyed for logging or agriculture. Externalities also mean that wealth is transferred from the poor to the rich, "because national accounts do not record externalities" so "Modern consumption patterns, relying as they do on imported primary goods from distant parts of the world, are prone to being under-priced" (2012:190). Externalities must also be considered carefully in the Impact Inequality (population size, standard of living and efficiency of use of nature's goods and services). Doing so is not easy. Common pool resources (ecosystem assets shared locally) are important especially for poorer peoples, but are fragile, and often deteriorate for several reasons. Human behaviour (including consumption choices) must change and population growth must be stemmed.

That is for now. Dasgupta then challenges us by asking how we take well-being of future generations into account, suggesting that we must be exceedingly careful in how we apply the conventional economic ideas of return on investment and discounting. He highlights how, until recently, the various empirical measures of well-being have omitted connectedness with nature and hence the disconnect inherent in urbanization is not seen as a problem for economics. He argues that we must find a way of valuing biodiversity and posits several ways of doing this within economics. One example is seeing ecosystem services as assets- to ensure natural capital is included alongside human and produced capital. Dasgupta describes this as "inclusive wealth" and suggests this should replace GDP as the measure of the economy, using equations for optimum allocation of goods and services.

He states that there are major differences in sustainability across the world, especially affecting less-developed nations. He argues that trade has been very bad for biodiversity because it decouples demand from supply, but notes, that it is possible to ameliorate this. Demand from land and the ecosphere, for food, minerals, fibres, timber etc., has greatly reduced biodiversity under the current economic system and technology, but he posits that different techniques or technology can help us increase our efficiency. Transition to sustainability incurs several kinds of risk that must be managed. Considered as an economic asset, there is sufficient ecological stock for the future if we conserve, protect and restore. He argues, that conservation and protection of nature is more important than restoration, because restoration is never 100% and usually more costly in the longer term. However, restoration of degraded ecosystem (e.g., rewilding) has an important part to play, though i requires "unprecedented ambition" which should be brought into land-use planning. Finance for conservation and restoration can come from both public and private sources. Engagement, monitoring and influence are all important to achieving this.

In his final chapter, Dasgupta discusses 'Options for Change'. He suggests three things:

- Rebalance our demands on nature and nature's ability to supply (Dasgupta's Impact Inequality), including conservation and restoration measures, and changing our consumption, our production, supply chains, trade and pricing, and reducing population growth.
- Change our measures of economic progress, especially moving away from GDP to indices and indicators that include inclusive wellbeing and natural capital.
- Transform our institutions and systems, concerning global public goods, the global financial system, empowering citizenship and education.

Comments on The Dasgupta Review

Dasgupta's *The Economics of Biodiversity* is a magnificent contribution, a comprehensive review of how the fields of economics and finance can serve, rather than undermine, climate and environmental responsibility. Given that the Treasury has for too long been wedded to GDP, by which the environment and climate are grossly undervalued, this opens a door for them to move forward, taking biodiversity into account. The Review covers many real-life issues that are frequently overlooked. In the following criticisms of it, I want to stress that I do not want to undermine Dasgupta's excellent Review, but rather, wish to suggest ways in which it could be enriched and made even more workable. I then suggest that a more radical discussion is needed, which has relevance not only for HM Treasury but also for each one of us.

Dasgupta has mathematized the economics of biodiversity (probably because the Treasury required this). Doing so, I suggest, weakens the Review's discussion of some things, such as voluntary activity, attitude, faith and beliefs. It tends to think in terms of resources and rights more than attitudes of responsibility. For example, while I welcome his economic argument of how trade destroys biodiversity by decoupling demand from supply, will merely fixing the economic system solve that problem? Is it not also a problem of attitude? If we take attitudes of responsibility that consider the other carefully, then trade can continue without biodiversity loss. Unfortunately, our attitude is usually self-absorbed, even self-centred, and decoupling merely gives us the excuse to, and convenience of, not thinking about the consequences for others. Whilst it is important to acknowledge that Dasgupta does recognise the importance of attitude, etc., I believe, he tends to gloss over them and fails to offer any systematic way that these may be taken into account.

He deliberately adopts the Ecosystems Services approach. Though he recognises that this precludes allowing non-human creatures value in themselves, he wants to bring them into economic thinking as assets, and by doing so, opens a door for policy makers and economists, especially in the Treasury, to take biodiversity seriously by recognizing the innate value of the natural world. Gunton, et al. (2017)[8] offers a way forward here, when arguing that we must go beyond presupposing that value comes only from human benefit, to "Valuing the Invaluable". How this is possible is briefly outlined later in this discussion.

I posit that the assumptions Dasgupta makes, for example, when discussing how to cope with risk, lead to over-simplification, especially because they ignore the aspect of faith, beliefs, and commitments. For example, "we assume that the decision-maker (DM) is a concerned citizen: her viewpoint is societal", ignores the reality of selfishness, hidden agendas and corruption. Humanity has not yet discovered any legal or economic system that can cope with these-they require a change of heart. Dasgupta tries to deal with risk in a rationalistic way, where I advocate that we also need to give weight to fostering attitudes of responsibility.

Dasgupta argues that human behaviour is influenced by others, socially, being either "competitive" or "conformist". I find the use of such categories, greatly disappointing. They come from the rationalism of the 1920s and

---

[8] Gunton, R M. van Asperen, E. Basden, A. Bookless, D. Araya, Y. Hanson, D R. Goddard, M A. Otieno, G. Jones, G O. 2017. Beyond ecosystem services: valuing the invaluable. Trends in *Ecology and Evolution* April 2017, 32 (4), 249-257.

allow no insight into real human behaviour, which including justice, love, and commitment to causes; such factors cannot be squeezed into those categories. He seems quite optimistic about the ability of technology to reduce our ecological footprint yet does not seem to address the issue of changing lifestyle, which the discussion below suggests is crucial. His discussion of the impact of economic growth on biodiversity is limited. Though he alludes to some of the problems in, for example "Competition among rival services has been a prime force... Moreover, commercial demand frequently trumps local needs... International public opinion and pressure from the country's elite are often tepid. These complex interrelationships have generally been ignored by growth and development economists...", he offers no way to address them (2021:46).

Overall, Dasgupta presupposes a form of rational economic actor: humans are assumed to behave in a way that maximizes utility, always trying to work out that out rationally. Though he augments this with uncertainty, social influences, societal viewpoints, and technology, it is rather simplistic and over optimistic, leaving little room for human sin, such as pride or revenge and it shows little awareness of the diversity of kinds of externalities. The conceptual framework below, by contrast, helps us tackle these, by suggesting a new foundational understanding.

Shrinking the Economy?

Instead of economic growth, or even curbing it (Raworth 2017, Jackson 2009), another option has been opened up by the Covid-19 pandemic: shrinking the economy. It may be no coincidence that sectors that were responsible for spreading the Covid-19 virus are ones that do damage to climate and biodiversity: aviation, road transport, and hospitality. Aviation has around ten times the ecological footprint of rail (per passenger or tonne, EEA 2019)[9]. Road transport, though with smaller per-passenger-mile ecological footprint than aviation, currently has many more journey-miles. Much of the hospitality sector depends on imported food, often grown in LDNs at the expense of local poor. All three characterize wealthy lifestyles.

Activity within every sector of the economy consists of a mixture of good and harm, with the harm/good ratio varying. Much of the harmful activity is non-essential. So, it may be useful to consider the option of allowing those sectors with much non-essential harm, to shrink, or at least remain shrunk. There are several types of non-essential. One classic example is that two

---

[9] EEA, European Environment Agency. 2019. https://www.france24.com/en/20190410-aviation-faces-challenge-reduce-pollution. Accessed 12 March 2021.

trucks pass each other on the M6, one carrying biscuits made in London bound for Glasgow, the other carrying biscuits made in Glasgow bound for London (Schumacher 1973).[10] That it generates nearly a thousand miles of climate change emissions in the process makes it not only non-essential but also harmful. During the first few months of the Covid-19 pandemic, the British Road Haulage Association (RHA 2020)[11] complained that nearly half their trucks were "parked up" because, they said, "people are not buying non-essentials." That suggests that the UK goods economy before then consisted of 50% non-essentials. Another type is what Graeber (2019)[12] calls "bullshit jobs" - paid employment that is "completely pointless, unnecessary or pernicious", such as those who create the impression that something useful is being done when it is not, or those employed to harm or deceive others on behalf of their employers. He estimates that 50% of (Western) jobs are "bullshit". It does not seem too radical to suggest that both of those kinds of non-essential can and should be tackled. A third kind is less easily tackled: the work done to rectify avoidable harm, which might include crime, obesity, alcoholism and drug abuse, and of course, environmental damage. Many of the harms being rectified are caused by what Christianity calls human sin and this is more deeply ingrained. [13]

A case may be made that the wealthy economies of the world are bloated with harmful non-essentials. Let us consider several sectors:

- The harm/good ratio in gambling is very high and gambling is almost wholly non-essential.
- Alcohol's harm/good ratio is high and much of it is non-essential. If the market structure were changed and non-alcoholic drinks were more effectively promoted, then they might supplant alcoholic drinks.
- Aviation. Every mile or km flown contributes to climate change emissions and a large majority of flying need not occur, in that many business meetings, breaks, holidays and long-distance tourism are, arguably, less essential than justice for the poor. The aviation

---

[10] Schumacher, E F. *Small Is Beautiful*. London, U.K.?: Blond & Briggs, 1973.
[11] RHA Road Haulage Association. 2020. Roadway Update 8 April 2020. https://www.rha.uk.net/news/2020-04-april/roadway-update-8-april-2020 accessed 12 March 2021.
[12] Graeber, D. 2019. *Bullshit Jobs*. London, U.K.: Penguin, 2019.
[13] There is some evidence that the working of the Spirit of God to change the deepest aspirations across a society is able to tackle this: Morgan, JV. *The Welsh Religious Revival: A Retrospect and Critique*. Weston Rhyn: Quinta Press, 2004. ISBN 978-1-89785-624-6.

industry defends itself by suggesting use of non-fossil-fuels, but that is no solution, because growing fuel uses land that should be used for growing food or for biodiversity or, generating hydrogen which consumes electricity that should be used elsewhere.

- Other motorized transport is also universally harmful. Though with lower per-passenger-km climate change emissions than aviation, road transport has greater volume, it destroys wildlife and is a major factor in lack of exercise. Though road transport provides some good (e.g., freedom of movement, social activity, and distribution of goods and services), any surfeit of these, makes much of it non-essential.
- Meat and dairy offer some good, in nutrition and balanced farming especially in LDNs, but also a considerable amount of harm in greenhouse gase emissions, animal cruelty, and excessive land and water use [Gullone 2017]. Much of this is because of over-consumption in the wealthy nations, which not only adds health problems, but it makes much of the meat and dairy sector non-essential. Trade makes this worse because it decouples demand from supply (Dasgupta 2021: 377) as well as being itself a source of greenhouse gas emissions.[14]

Such sectors might be shrunk as a matter of policy and practice. It is a truism to state that for most economists and governments, the idea of shrinking the economy is hardly ever considered as a possible course of action. What about jobs? What about poverty? These are valid points made by pundits and others, and environmentalists are sometimes caricatured as ignoring them; many environmentalists today actually do recognise them, but how to take both these and environmental issues into account is not always clear. Whilst Dasgupta makes an attempt to do so, I submit, his attempt is rather too general.

Many argue that economic growth has generated prosperity in material goods and convenience in services, in the 'advanced' economies; that economic growth is a prerequisite for technological advance; for the arts to flourish and to pay for cleaning up the environment.[15] Yet, if we dig deeper, do we find more sinister motives for supporting and working for economic growth? Do we find the greed of those who already have more than enough? Do we find the hubris of "Our economy is growing faster than yours"? Do we find political agendas of both left and right?

---

[14] Gullone, E. 2017. Why Eating Animals Is Not Good for Us. *Journal of Animal Ethics* (Vol. 7, Issue 1), 31-62.

[15] This last suggestion is shown to be shallow and false by Dasgupta and others.

Debate and research are needed over all these issues related to shrinking wealthy economies. However, I submit that, at this point in the climate crisis, we do not have time to complete the research before we act and so it is necessary to act on the worst cases, even if we might make mistakes along the way.

Acting Now

It may be theoretically possible to find ways to reduce harm without shrinking some sectors, but do we have time to wait? Whatever sectors readers wish to substitute in place of those above, if there are sectors in wealthy economies that are bloated with harmful non-essentials, is it not entirely reasonable and sensible to immediately stem that harm by shrinking them? The Covid-19 pandemic has given us a real opportunity to shrink harmful sectors of the economy. It has engendered among us a willingness to give up some of our non-essentials, whilst focusing our attention on the value of nature, At the very least, we should not give those harmful/non-essential sectors, grants and loans to grow back to pre-Covid levels. Importantly, of 25 measures for economic recovery after the pandemic, bankers, governments, and academics, all agreed that subsidies to airlines are the least favored option both environmentally and economically-yet many governments have ignored this consensus (Hepburn 2020).[16]

With irreversible biodiversity loss and climate change, we need to act fast. However, to do this wisely, we need to address three questions that Dasgupta fails to adequately address:

- What kinds of externalities are there?
- How do we distinguish good from harm, when most sectors are a mix of both?
- How do we determine what is non-essential?

Answers to these questions, even in initial form, would enrich Dasgupta's approach and the Treasury's calculations. At this stage, we do not need finer distinctions; initial answers will be sufficient to tackle the worst offenders.

Those three questions have seldom been asked together. To address this, I will suggest an approach that will surprise many for it sets our

---

[16] Hepburn, C. O'Callaghan, N. Stern, N. Stiglitz, J. Zenghelis, D. 2020. Will COVID-19 fiscal recovery packages accelerate or retard progress on climate change? *Oxford Review of Economic Policy*, Volume 36, Number S1, 2020, pp. S359-S381.

understanding of economic activity on a different foundation. Whilst it comes from a type of Christian thinking, it is relevant to secular aspects of life, like biodiversity and the economy.

A New Foundation for Understanding Economic Activity

This foundation is provided by a philosophy that emerged during the twentieth century in the Netherlands, which tried to be true to Biblical revelation whilst also being true to philosophy as philosophy. Specifically, it rejected the encroachment of theology onto philosophy or other theoretical thinking as 'queen of sciences' and rejected the attempt to stifle the criticality that is proper to theoretical thought by means of religious dogma. The philosophy, called by some "Reformational Philosophy", was pioneered by Herman Dooyeweerd and Dirk Vollenhoven[17]. It offers both a foundation on which to stand as we try to address those challenges and a conceptual tool to use while doing so.

It was very critical of reductionist approaches. To treat the economy as all-important is, in their opinion, reductionist. It makes the economy an idol, to which all else is sacrificed (Goudzwaard 1984).[18] They posit that it is when an aspect is treated as all-important that Creation is put out of joint, so that biodiversity is lost, air, water, and soil are polluted and climate crisis threatens. Both Capitalism and Marxism are guilty of this. Reformational Philosophy is also critical of approaches that merely react against such reductions, such as some anti-capitalists and romantics end up doing. Instead, Reformational Philosophy allows the economy a proper role as part of human functioning. This is depicted in Figure 1a, in which the economic activity is shown along with family and religious activity, which, along with many others not shown, constitute the whole of human activity. What are viewed as externalities to economists, are shown shaded. When we confine our perspective to the economic, then we obtain a truncated view, as shown in Figure 1b.

---

[17] Verburg, M. E. *Herman Dooyeweerd: The Life and Work of a Christian Philosopher*. (Jordan Station, Ontario, Canada, Paideia Press, 2015).
[18] Goudzwaard, B *Idols of Our Time*, (Downers Grove, Illinois, Inter-Varsity Press, 1984).

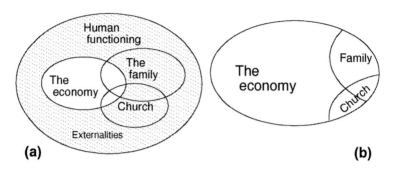

Figure 11.1. The economy as one part of overall other human functioning.

It was the Dutch statesman, Abraham Kuyper, who recognised that the different spheres of society, some of which are shown in Figure 1a, should not encroach on each other's sovereignty. Dooyeweerd developed, extended, and deepened this idea into a comprehensive philosophy, which is showing promise in many areas of research and practice, including in ecosystem valuation (Basden 2019).[19]

In Dooyeweerd's philosophy, all Creation exhibits many aspects, which form the foundation of all temporal reality and are modes of being, functioning and good (and corresponding evil or harm) (1955, Vol. I p. 4). Given his sensitivity to this and his presupposition that Creation is good, Dooyeweerd asked what aspects there are and a painstaking exploration of this yielded fifteen aspects: quantitative, spatial, kinematic, physical, biotic, psychical, analytical or logical, technological, lingual, social, economic, aesthetic, jural, ethical, and faith.[20] His suite of aspects enables us to distinguish multiple types of good (value) and harm, and the modes of functioning that cause the good or harm. Table 1 gives examples of each.

---

[19] Basden, A. *Foundations and Practice of Research: Adventures with Dooyeweerd's Philosophy*. (New York, USA, Routledge, 2019). See also "http://dooy.info/bk/adventures/".
[20] Dooyeweerd, H. *A New Critique of Theoretical Thought*, Vol. I-IV, (1975 edition). (Jordan Station, Ontario, Paideia Press, 1955) (1, Vol. II pp. 1-426, for his discussion of aspects; Vol. I p. 3, for his initial list of aspects.)

| Aspect | Functioning | Dysfunction | Repercussions | |
			Good	Harmful
Quantit'ive	Amount		Reliable sequence	
Spatial	Simultaneity Continuity		Continuous extension	
Kinematic	Movement		Change (non-stasis)	
Physical	Force, causality		Persistence	
Organic / Biotic	Feeding, reproduction	Starvation, suffocation	Vitality, survival	Disease, extinction
Psychic / Sensitive	Interaction	Insensitivity	Emotional and sensory vitality	Sensory, emotional deprivation
Analytic	Distinction	Conflation	Conceptual clarity	Confusion
Formative	Working, planning, constructing	Laziness, destroying	Achievement, construction	Lost opportunities, destruction
Lingual	Expressing, signification	Deceiving	Information	Misinformation
Social	Relating, befriending	Disdaining, hating	Friendship, amplified activity	Working against each other
Economic	Frugality	Squandering	Prosperity	Waste, poverty
Aesthetic	Harmonizing, enjoying	Fragmentation, narrowing	Integrality, interest, fun	Fragmentation, boredom
Juridical	Giving due, responsibility	Irresponsibility	Justice	Injustice
Ethical / Attitudinal	Self-giving love, vulnerability, trust	Selfishness, self-protection	Culture of goodwill	Competitive, harsh culture
Pistic / Faith	Belief, courage, commitment	Idolatry, disloyalty	High morale in society	Loss of meaning, morale

Idolatry: Treating something non-absolute as absolute

Table 11.1. Aspects, with examples of good and harm meaningful in each.

He acknowledged that suites of aspects "can never lay claim to material completion" and suggests that "more penetrating examinations may at any time, bring new modal aspects of reality to the light not yet perceived before." [21] Though his own suite is only a best guess, Dooyeweerd's suite is among the best we have, being more comprehensive and better grounded in both philosophy and reflective experience than most (Basden 2019: 212), and so it is recommended for use here.

Rethinking

By opening up wider vistas of meaning, Dooyeweerd allows and encourages rethinking. At the level of individual theories, we can see which aspects they include and omit. For example, we can now understand the limitations of Raworth's (2017) Doughnut Economics as recognising only some of the aspects: physical, biotic, lingual, social, economic and juridical. It is the missing ethical, pistic, and aesthetic aspects around which Milanovic (2018)[22] builds his critique.

We can also reconceive whole economic concepts like jobs, in a way that might escape conventional dichotomies, such as providing jobs that do harm versus condemning families to poverty. The idea of jobs, as we know them today, emerged from of the Industrial Revolution and thus is not to be venerated as absolute. "Jobs" are no universal good thing; for example, they generate huge amounts of stress (17.9 million days lost in UK through stress (HSE 2020).[23] Instead, we might focus on human functioning, of which "jobs" form only part (see Figure 1). Has not the Covid-19 pandemic revealed and reminded us, that homemaking and engaging with nature for example, are important, even though not paid activities? Should these examples, and a myriad like them, be valued more highly than they are? They are meaningful in the social, ethical, biotic, and aesthetic aspects, even if they have little, if any, value in economics.

Of course, it is important that people are adequately resourced for their lives. That is the role of the economic aspect, to which "jobs" currently contributes much. But we must also ask, "What kinds of lives to resource?" The assumptions of those in wealthy cultures about what constitutes good living may be critiqued, not just by anti-capitalist or puritan reaction, but more fundamentally, by referring to each aspect. Do we presume, aspire to

---

[21] Dooyeweerd, (1955: II p.556)

[22] See note 6 above.

[23] Health and Safety Executive. 2020. Working days lost in Great Britain; Working days lost, 2019/20. https://www.hse.gov.uk/statistics/dayslost.htm, accessed 12th March 2021.

and expect a surfeit of enjoyment (aesthetic aspect)? At the expense of justice to the less-developed nations and the biosphere (juridical)? Are we self-centred and unconcerned (ethical)? What do we most deeply assume, expect and aspire to about life (pistic aspect)?

Christians might see a link with "affluence, arrogance and unconcern," which was the reason given by God, via the prophet Ezekiel16:49, for why Sodom was destroyed and Judah was sent into exile. This is an issue of lifestyle, to which we aspire and which we take as 'normal'. If we take the Biblical revelation seriously, then the solution is a change of heart, which is a pistic (faith) function of letting go of our idols and letting the Holy Spirit re-orientate our aspirations, expectations, and assumptions towards "the kingdom of God" (Matthew 6:33).

Understanding Externalities: The Economy as Human Functioning

The aspects are actualized when things function as subject in them, for example the biotic, when plants, animals, and humans function therein as the activity of life. Most later aspects are actualized in human functioning. Each such aspect is a way in which reality can be meaningful - is a mode of functioning, a mode of being, and each defines a cluster of institutions in society (in Figure 1, the economy, family, and church are primarily meaningful in the economic, social, and pistic aspects respectively). All aspects, Dooyeweerd contended, are equally important to the overall harmony, well-being, health, prosperity of Creation - its *shalom*.

Economic activity is just one contributor to this among all the others and has no prior claim to being more important than others. Its role within wider reality is to manage resources that enable the other kinds of functioning to work well. So, the economy is valid, but only in relation to all other human functioning and hence to be neither elevated nor denied. It is valid to see any thing or function in economic terms, including the biosphere, as long as we do not see it *only* in economic terms. Its physical, biotic, social, ethical, etc., functioning are also important.

Dooyeweerd's suite of aspects offers us a set of kinds of externality, which are not only external but meaningful and of value regardless of human benefit. Every economic activity involves functioning in the other aspects, which are meaningful in ways not allowed for in economics on its own and not able to be incorporated adequately in its equations, except as undefined external variables. Not only are externalities consequences that are meaningful in aspects other than the economic, but also, they are multi-aspectual factors that affect the economic activity. Dasgupta argues in depth for the impact of biotic functioning (biodiversity) on the economy, but not that of other aspects.

Take the example of a chemical factory. Its consequential externalities include power consumption and climate change emissions (meaningful in, and seeing the factory in terms of, the physical aspect), pollution and health (biotic aspect), a hub for social activity (social aspect), ugly in, or harmonizing with, the landscape (aesthetic apect) and paying low or high wages (juridical aspect). These are all the factory, seen from aspects other than the economic and may be good or harmful. Externalities that affect it include power cuts and storms (physical aspect), pandemics (biotic), community feuds (social), morale of society (pistic - faith). What has been called Quaker Capitalism tried to take many of these into account (DP 2010). It may be that a Biblical Christian perspective has often been open to a wider diversity of aspects than Humanism has.

Dooyeweerd's suite offers us a systematic way to value all things, which does not depend on linking value with human benefit in the way that Ecosystem Services does, on which Dasgupta relies. Gunton et al, uses Dooyeweerd's aspects as a conceptual framework for "valuing the invaluable". Each aspect defines a different basic kind of value. A species is valuable, not only because it provides humans with some good but because it is meaningful in the biotic aspect without reference to human benefit. For Christians and other religious people, it is also meaningful to the origin of all aspects, the Creator of All. [24]

Good, Harm and Non-Essentials

The second question, of differentiating good from harm, may also be addressed by reference to Dooyeweerd's aspects because aspects, from the biotic onwards, defines distinct kinds of both good and evil, positive and negative. Table 1 gives examples of these.

Given that all things function, at least potentially, in all aspects, allows us to acknowledge that a thing might function positively in one and negatively in another simultaneously. Dooyeweerd's aspects can help us separate out and recognise both good and bad, without driving people into opposing camps for-or-against. For example, mining cobalt in the Democratic Republic of Congo, provides the economic and technical good of a resource for making mobile phones, while at the same time juridical harm of

---

[24] In the Hebrew Scriptures, we find the theme of inherent value of creatures without serving human needs, in Genesis 1, Job 39 and Psalm 104.

oppression and unfair conditions for cobalt workers, and contributions to the DRC economy that are less than they ought to be.

In addition, aspects provide a systematic basis on which to pose deeper questions about presuppositions underlying the more visible good and harm. Dysfunctions (and good functioning) in later aspects tend to be less obvious to analysts and pundits, so often overlooked, yet they have pervading and long-term repercussions. For example, why do we need so many mobile phones and why do we need them to be as cheap as they are? We might find greed and a desire to impress as reasons for these, which are dysfunctions in the ethical and faith aspects. They are the root of the juridical harm.

To address our third question, it often seems to be the case that harmful non-essentials are rooted in dysfunction in the later aspects. While the aesthetic aspect affirms some non-essentials to be good in every human life, these should be enjoyed with justice (juridical aspect), generosity and self-giving love (ethical) and right view of our own meaningfulness in Creation (pistic; c.f. Romans 12:3). Otherwise the non-essentials become the bloated economy. Economic activity that rests on aspectual dysfunction may be shrunk without much harm ensuing, though it might take effort to achieve. There can be no rigid formula here, but rather we are called to apply wisdom in judging essential and non-essential. Wisdom is served by recognising the importance of each aspect individually, and all together, and the relationships among them.[25]

Aspectual dysfunction is, to Dooyeweerd, going against the grain of Creation. Dysfunction is not merely an option that people happen to choose, but something harmful to the whole that rebounds on individuals. It is not something that can be balanced out by good in other aspects, because dysfunction in one aspect distorts our functioning in others, including the economic. It undermines, jeopardizes, and prevents the *shalom* of Creation, of Reality working well together. Christianity calls it "sin" and Dooyeweerd lets us see more clearly its different kinds (c.f. Table 1). When we choose to remove dysfunction, things not only begin to repair but often even work better than we expect. If that is so, then shrinking harmful sectors of the economy, including tackling jobs, is likely to be easier than many fear.

This offers hope in resisting vested interests. To vested interests, one aspect is important - whether the technical, aesthetic, social or economic, etc., and, because all aspects are important, they can argue for the importance of their favourite aspects. Focusing attention on their aspect, they imply its superiority over others. They stand condemned, however, by humanity as a whole and by Reality as a whole, for obliterating and denigrating the other aspects, such as love and justice, and by God (Micah

---

[25] See Basden (2019: Ch. 3).

6:8). The answer to arguments from vested interests is neither antagonism nor acquiescence, but to identify the aspect(s) they treasure, affirm those, but then critique their narrow view and enrich the dialogue by reference to all the other aspects.

This approach might contribute to fulfilling Dasgupta's Options for Change. Rebalancing our demands on nature requires more than conservation and restoration; we must tackle the roots of dysfunction especially within the later aspects. Measures of economic progress can be informed by aspects - the biotic for biodiversity itself, in harmony with the social, juridical, ethical, and other aspects. Transforming systems cannot be achieved without recognising pistic functioning.

Conclusion

So, if we are to cut out some of the harmful non-essentials that bloat our economy, for the sake of biodiversity and the climate - to say nothing of the health and mental health of people - what do we do? An important first step, advocated by Dasgupta, is to get externalities (non-economic factors) into the calculations that economists use, especially in Government departments, so that the direction of policy can be shifted away from purely economic growth.

However, we must also take account of the diverse kinds of externalities, and we must recognise that some sectors of economic activity cause harm and are non-essential. These sectors should shrink, and the Covid-19 pandemic has given us an opportunity to do this. A way of doing this has been suggested, based on Reformational philosophy, using the suite of aspects of reality worked out by Dooyeweerd. It offers a new foundation for understanding the Economy as just one sphere of human functioning alongside others. Though philosophical, this foundation has proven immensely practical. Dooyeweerd's fifteen aspects can be used to enrich Dasgupta's *The Economics of Biodiversity* and Raworth's *Doughnut Economics* by separating out the kinds of externality, and of good and harm, and it can help us address non-essentials.

This chapter is a position paper, for which details must be worked out. As far as I know, the issues of diversity of externalities and of good, harm and non-essentials, have not been researched nor discussed together before, so exploring this approach is a new venture, which requires wisdom and boldness. I submit that Dooyeweerd's aspects provide a basis for this discussion. They welcome faith and ethical issues into the discourse alongside others as two of fifteen aspects and in this way, integrate sacred with secular. Given that Dooyeweerd worked from a Biblical Christian perspective, this offers an opportunity for Christian thinkers to engage and contribute fruitfully and radically, especially along the lines of LACE: Listen, Affirm, Critique, Enrich (Basden 2021).[26] The way in which Dooyeweerd respected philosophy and science, differing from many Christian thinkers, makes his approach acceptable and adoptable by all.

---

[26] Basden, A. 2021. LACE: Listen, Affirm, Critique, Enrich - Introduction. "http://christianthinking.space/sdc/lace-intro.html."

Chapter Twelve

Diet, Climate and Health

Joyce D'Silva

Bacon and eggs for breakfast, milky coffee mid-morning, ham and cheese sandwich for lunch, and chicken curry for supper. Such a daily diet would be uncontroversial for the average European or North American. Some might swap the sandwich for a steak or a burger and chips at midday. Either way, it is a day's food consumption that is totally compromised on the grounds of climate change, the environment, human health, and animal wellbeing. This chapter will explain why.

Climate change

It is hard to visualise a connection between the food on our plates and the massive problem of global warming and severe climate change. Yet we now know that all food has a carbon footprint; none of it is without impact. The urgent challenge for humanity is to reduce our carbon footprint as quickly as possible. Most of us are not owners of coal mines or huge gas-guzzling vehicles, but we all eat to live. It makes ethical and environmental sense to find out which foods are most damaging for the climate, and which foods carry a lighter footprint. Then we can adjust our diets accordingly.

The food system as a whole generates around 26% of global greenhouse gas (GHG) emissions. Around 75% of agriculture's emissions are produced by farmed animals. This includes methane emissions from animals but also the production of feed for farm animals and the associated land use changes (Springmann, Marco, et al, 2018; FAO, IFAD, UNICEF, WFP and WHO. 2020.)

The Food and Agriculture Organisation of the United Nations (the FAO) calculates that livestock production is responsible for 14.5% of the greenhouses gases that result from human activity (Gerber, P.J., et al, 2013). That roughly equates with the emissions from all forms of transport globally. So, we understand that animal foods have a large impact on global warming.

In 2015, nearly all governments of the world signed up to the Paris Agreement on Climate Change. They agreed to cut their greenhouse gas emissions by keeping a global temperature rise this century well below 2 degrees Celsius above pre-industrial levels and to pursue efforts to limit the temperature increase even further to 1.5 degrees Celsius (Paris Agreement, 2015).

Whilst governments are beginning to take steps to "green" their economies, cut coal mining and promote electric cars, they have seemed reluctant to address the impacts of our meat consumption. Yet several experts have calculated that without large decreases in meat and dairy consumption it will be very difficult to meet the Paris targets for reducing global greenhouse gas emissions (Bajželj, B. et al., 2014, and Bailey et al, 2014). Animal products generally generate substantially higher GHG emissions per unit of nutrition produced than plant-based foods (Springmann M., et al., 2016). In fact, it has been calculated that dietary shifts could contribute up to a fifth of the mitigation needed to meet the Paris below 2°C target (Griscom, B. et al., 2017).

Some experts calculate that even if fossil fuel emissions were immediately halted, which is highly unlikely, if not impossible, current trends in global food systems would make it impossible to meet the 1.5°C target and difficult even to realise the 2°C target (Clark M. A., et al., 2020).

At the moment meat-eating is on the increase globally. Although there is an increase in the numbers of vegetarians and vegans in many countries, and a very slight reduction in red and processed meat consumption in the European Union and the United States, overall, more people are eating more meat. The experts predict that world meat consumption is set to grow by 46 million tons between 2019 and 2030. China is forecast to increase the most, by around 5kg per person, followed by Europe (OECD-FAO 2019). So, this outlook is not encouraging.

The case for reducing meat consumption in order to reduce greenhouse gas emissions is further made by several recent research papers. One piece of research reviewed fourteen papers on diet and GHG emissions and found that the vegan diet (no foods of animal origin) reduced emissions by 55% followed by vegetarian diets and diets with less meat. (Hallstrom, E., et al., 2015).

Similarly, a paper from Oxford University showed that the diet related GHG emissions in kilograms of carbon dioxide equivalent per day (kgCO2e/day) were lowest for those on a vegan diet, 2.89 kgCO2e/day and highest for those eating the most meat, 7.17 kgCO2e/day (Scarborough. P., et al., 2014).

Methane and other gases associated with animal foods are converted to carbon dioxide equivalents, which is why these figures are expressed as CO2e, rather than as methane or nitrous oxide (Eurostat, 2017).

The UK government's advisory body, the Committee on Climate Change, released a report in 2020 making the link between reducing meat consumption and thereby reducing the country's carbon footprint. Their summary in effect says that medium level targets are "20% cut in meat and dairy by 2030, rising to 35% by 2050 for meat only" while a high-level target is "50% less meat and dairy by 2050" with this being replaced by plant-grown food and lab-grown meat (Committee on Climate Change, December 2020).

The climate case for eating as small an amount of animal foods as possible is strong. Some will decide to go vegan or vegetarian. We know that not everyone will want to cut their consumption of these foods to zero, but everyone can have meat-free days, and replace much of the meat in their diets with plant foods such as beans, lentils, tofu, vegetables, and cereals. Milk can also be replaced by plant milks such as soya, or oat milks. This is a positive way in which we can all help to reduce climate change.

The Environment

Meat and other animal foods can also have both direct and indirect effects on the environment. Some of these can be beneficial, such as grazing cattle or sheep on grass pastures, as this can not only help to keep carbon stored in the earth but can encourage a diversity of wildflowers and insects. If not overstocked, the animals' manure can enrich the soil, acting as a natural fertilizer. If the animals need supplemental feed in winter this can be from grasses and crops grown on the farm such as hay and other crops or crop wastes.

Sadly, most animals are not kept in this way, but on intensive farms where productivity is maximised, often at the expense of the environment and at cost to the animals' wellbeing. Animals kept indoors on the average industrial factory farm do not get to graze outdoors or root in the soil or browse the hedgerows. They are kept indoors permanently, and their feed is brought to them. Often much of the feed is not grown on the farm but is bought in from intensive crop monoculture farms and is often imported from other countries, thus having a global impact on land use, with forests and natural grasslands being converted to arable monocultures.

This huge demand for grain for animal feed has fuelled the intensification of crop production with disastrous impacts. Based on crop monocultures and agro-chemicals, this has led to soil degradation, biodiversity loss, and air pollution (Tsiafouli M.A., et al., 2015) and (Lelieveld J., et al., 2015). These crops are grown with the aid of nitrogen fertilizers. Synthetic nitrogen fertilisers, while boosting yields in the short term, lead to a decline in the amount of humus - the organic matter - in soils so causing long-term damage to soil health and quality. Monoculture crops draw the same nutrients from the soil year after year and eventually this robs soils of their fertility.

Soils also have phosphate fertilizer applied to them. The mineral phosphorous is mined from phosphate rock, the major producing countries being Morocco, China and the US (Garside, M., 2020). Many millions of tonnes of phosphate are mined annually, but the process of converting it into fertilizer is known to be inefficient, with about half of the phosphate lost in the process. (Gilbert, N., 2009, 716-718.) Most phosphorous is used as fertilizer, but some also goes to animal feed directly. Animals excrete about half the phosphorous they consume and on organic farms it is usually this animal manure which is used for enriching the soil's fertility. Such farms rarely need to supplement with external sources. On massive pig industrial farms, the practice of spraying pig slurry on surrounding fields can overload the soil and the accompanying stench is unpleasant and probably harmful to neighbours.

Research has established nine planetary boundaries which, if crossed, could generate irreversible environmental changes and drive the planet into a much less hospitable state (Steffen, M., et al, 2015. 1-10). In two cases - (i) biodiversity loss and (ii) nitrogen and phosphorus flows - we have crossed the boundary and entered a high-risk zone. Industrial livestock production has played a major part in the crossing of both these boundaries. Nitrogen fertilizer production is also responsible for 50% of the fossil fuel use in agricultural production (Foresight Report, 2011).

Crop-destroying insects and weeds are kept at bay by widespread use of pesticides and herbicides. This has also led to increased water pollution, with nitrogen fertilizers and agro-chemicals leaching into the soil and groundwater, running off into rivers and sometimes reaching the oceans, causing dead zones. These dead zones are areas where the water has become so toxic that fish and other marine organisms cannot survive there and the sea itself does indeed become lifeless.

A 2019 World Bank report states: "Frequently more than half of nitrogen fertilizer leaches into water or the air. In water, it may result in hypoxia and dead zones - problems that arise from a lack of dissolved oxygen in water that can take centuries to recover" (Damania, Richard, et al., 2019). It is not surprising that the United Nations concludes that "Intensive livestock production is probably the largest sector-specific source of water pollution" (United Nations, 2011).

There is no doubt that intensive farming with its chemical pesticides and herbicides has reduced soil biodiversity; without that rich biodiversity soil fertility declines (Tsiafouli M. A., et al., 2015, 973–985).

The large amounts of pesticides used on monoculture crops have decimated the insects on which farmland birds depend for food. Intensive agriculture has also played a major role in the decline in bees and other pollinators through its use of insecticides and herbicides. (United Nations Environment Programme, 2010) and (Wentworth, Jonathan, 2013.). Moreover, its monocultures lead to loss of abundance and diversity of the wildflowers on which pollinators feed.

The impact of industrial monoculture crop production on the soil is so severe, that the FAO calculated, in 2015, that soils are now so degraded that we have only about 60 years of harvests left (FAO, 2014).

Perhaps the best-known impact of industrial livestock farming is its impact on the Amazon rainforest, with large areas being denuded of trees in order to expand, not just cattle ranching, but the growing of soya. People whose families have lived on the land for years can also find themselves made homeless as the more powerful land grabbers take over. According to official data, a record 3,700 square kilometres of the Amazon were deforested in the first half of 2020, up 25% from the same period in 2019 (Raoni, Rajão et al., 2020).

A vast expanse of Amazon rainforest seven times larger than Greater London was destroyed over 2019 as deforestation surged to a 12-year high. Figures released by the Brazilian space institute, Inpe, showed at least 11,088 sq km of rainforest was razed between August 2019 and July 2020 – the highest figure since 2008 (The Guardian, 1 Dec 2020).

This soya is not grown to produce soya "milk" or tofu for vegans but is grown primarily for animal feed. After the oil has been extracted, 98% of the soya bean meal goes to animal feed (Wills, Kendra, 2013). Brazil loses 55 million tons of topsoil every year, due to erosion from soya production (WWF, 2006). Soya production is also expanding within Brazil, from the Amazon forest to the Cerrado, (Yousefi, A., et al., 2018), a huge area of special ecological biodiversity and even to the Mato Grosso. Paraguay, and Argentina are also heavily involved in soya production.

Most of the soya produced in these South American countries is exported to China, to feed its growing livestock population and to Europe. China is by far the leading country of destination for Brazilian exports, accounting for 78 percent of the total value in 2019 (Mendoza, J., 2020).

We can see the links between the growing levels of meat consumption in China, alluded to already, the growth in its livestock population, most of which is taking place in intensive pig, chicken, and dairy farms, and its demand for soya to feed all those animals.

The EU imports about 14 million tonnes of soya beans per year as a source of protein to feed animals, including chickens, pigs, beef cattle, and dairy cows. There has been a shift to soy imports from the US, now providing about 75%, with the proportion from Brazil dropping below 25% (European Commission, 2019).

Sadly, a report published in the respected journal Science, estimates that one fifth of beef and soybean exports from Brazil to the European Union is produced on land that was illegally deforested (Raoni, Rajão, 2020).

Even the crops grown within the EU are generally destined for animal feed. The European Commission says, "the EU's cereals are mostly used for animal feed (nearly two thirds)". (European Commission, 2020).

The Convention on Biological Diversity signed by 150 government leaders at the 1992 Rio Earth Summit, is dedicated to promoting sustainable development. In 2010, the countries involved (the Conference of the Parties or COP) adopted a revised and updated Strategic Plan for Biodiversity, including the Aichi Biodiversity Targets, for the 2011-2020 period. The fourth edition of the Global Biodiversity Outlook (GBO-4) in 2014 gave a mid-term assessment of progress towards the implementation of the Strategic Plan for Biodiversity 2011-2020 and the Aichi Biodiversity Targets. Sadly, the Director declared: "on our current trajectory we are unlikely to reach the majority of the Aichi Biodiversity Targets by their deadline." (Global Biodiversity Outlook 4, 2014).

It is clear that we need to farm and consume in a different way. If we don't, the future looks grim. If the whole world followed the average "western diet" we could not feed ourselves. Experts say that if everyone in the world followed the *current* food consumption patterns in G20 countries we would require not just one planet, but up to 7.4 Earths (Loken, Brent, 2020).

Food, Feed and Waste

While we are becoming more aware of our bad habit of throwing away food and wasting all the energy that has gone into producing it, that habit is not the worst cause of food waste. Industrial animal agriculture is in fact one of the most inefficient and wasteful ways to produce food for humans. It is dependent on feeding human-edible cereals to farm animals who convert them very inefficiently into meat and milk. 57% of EU cereals are used as animal feed (European Commission, 2020). Globally the figure is 40%. (Pradhan et al., 2013). For every 100 calories of human-edible cereals fed to animals, just 17-30 calories enter the human food chain as meat or milk (Lundqvist, J., et al., 2008) and (Nellemann, C., et al., (2009). For every 100 grams of protein in human-edible cereals fed to animals, just 43 grams of protein enter the human food chain as meat or milk (Berners-Lee et al, 2018). This is not an intelligent way to feed the world.

The International Institute for Environment and Development says that using cropland to produce corn, soybeans and other crops for animal feed rather than to grow food for direct human consumption is "a colossally inefficient" use of resources (IEED, 2015).

Of course, farm animals can be kept in free range conditions, able to graze, forage, and browse most, or all, of the food they need in more natural conditions. Studies show that farm animals only make an efficient contribution to food security when they are converting materials that people cannot consume - grass, by-products, crop residues, unavoidable food waste – into food that we can eat (Bajželj, B., et al., 2014) and (Schader, C., et al., 2015).

By reducing the meat consumption by 50% in countries with high meat consumption, the amount of feed needed globally almost halves, reducing the need for forage grown on arable land by 90% (Westhoek, H., et al., 2014, 196–205).

A UNEP study indicates that a 50% reduction in the cereals that, on a business-as-usual basis, will be used as animal feed by 2050 would provide the food energy for an additional 1.75 billion people (Nellemann, C., et al., (2009).

Injustice

The expansion of industrial animal agriculture is bad for the millions of small-scale farmers and pastoralists, many of whom live in the poorer countries of the world. As mentioned previously, there seems to be a particular problem in the Amazon region, where families who have lived on and worked their small plots of land are told they have no legal right to the land and must move out to make way for agribusinesses. But a similar pattern is taking place in other continents too. Those dispossessed of their smallholdings may often make their way to the big cities, where they hope to find work and sadly often end up living in slums.

The United Nations Convention to Combat Desertification (UNCCD) warns: "The current agribusiness model benefits the few at the expense of the many: small-scale farmers, the essence of rural livelihoods and backbone of food production for millennia, are under immense stress from land degradation, insecure tenure, and a globalized food system that favors concentrated, large-scale, and highly mechanized farms" (UNCCD, 2017).

Not only is this a social and economic problem but it must often give rise to extreme personal stress and poor mental health. Even those who have jobs on factory farms or in slaughterhouses are often amongst the most poorly paid in society and may struggle to maintain their household income and to get their children educated.

Health

Many of us were brought up to believe that eating meat and drinking milk made you big, strong and healthy. Meat does indeed contain protein, B vitamins and minerals such as iron and zinc. But eating a lot of meat is now understood to be detrimental to long-term health.

One study found that consumption of red and processed meat at an average level of 76 grams per day (g/d) was associated with an increased risk of colorectal cancer. Participants who reported consuming an average of 76 g/day of red and processed meat compared with 21 g/day had a 20% higher risk of colorectal cancer. This study found that people who were consuming red and processed meat four or more times per week, had a 20% increased risk of colorectal cancer compared with those who were consuming red and processed meat less than twice a week (Bradbury, Kathryn, E., et al., 2019, 1–13). An eight-ounce steak is 225g.

Red meat includes beef, lamb, pork, goat, and camel. Processed meats include ham, bacon, salami, pepperoni, sausages, beef jerky, corned beef, hot dogs, and similar products. Processed meat has been modified to either extend its shelf life or change the taste. The main methods are smoking, curing, or adding salt or preservatives. Suspected carcinogenic chemicals can form during meat processing. These include N-nitroso compounds and polycyclic aromatic hydrocarbons. When nitrates interact with certain components in red meat (haem iron, amines, and amides), they form N-nitroso compounds. The best known of these compounds is nitrosamine, which is known to be carcinogenic (cancer-causing) as it can damage the cells in the lining of the bowel and lead to cancer (The Guardian, 2018).

Apart from these chemicals used to produce processed meat, red meat also contains chemicals such as Haem, a red pigment that is naturally found in red meat and processed red meat. It can damage cells and cause bacteria in the body to produce harmful chemicals. This can increase the risk of cancer (Cancer Research UK, 2020).

Most global health and cancer organisations now give similar advice. Cancer Research UK says, "research has found an increased risk of cancer for every 25g of processed meat a person eats a day, which is about a rasher of bacon or a slice of ham" (Cancer Research UK, 2020).

The World Health Organisation says that consumption of processed meat causes an additional 34,000 worldwide cancer deaths (World Health Organisation, 2015).

The International Agency for Research on Cancer (IARC) is an expert body set up by the World Health Organisation (WHO). In 2015, an IARC Working Group of 22 experts from 10 countries considered more than 800 studies that investigated associations of more than a dozen types of cancer with the consumption of red meat or processed meat in many countries and populations with diverse diets.

After thoroughly reviewing the accumulated scientific literature, they classified the consumption of red meat as "probably carcinogenic" to humans. This association was observed mainly for colorectal cancer, but associations were also seen for pancreatic cancer and prostate cancer (IARC, 2015). Processed meat was classified as "carcinogenic" to humans. The experts concluded that each 50gram portion of processed meat eaten daily increases the risk of colorectal cancer by 18% (IARC, 2015).

The World Cancer Research Fund (WCRF) recommends a maximum of 43g of red meat per day: "If you eat red meat, limit consumption to no more than about three portions per week. Three portions are equivalent to about 350–500g (about 12–18oz) cooked weight. Consume very little, if any, processed meat" (World Cancer Research Fund, 2020).

Apart from these associations with certain cancers, there are other negative health impacts associated with some animal foods. Saturated fat is found in fatty meat, most processed meat, cheese, and some other dairy products. Saturated fats are associated with higher cholesterol levels, which can lead to strokes and other heart diseases. Transfats are found in foods that contain partially hydrogenated vegetable oils. Many margarine manufacturers have now stopped using transfats in their products.

In a large study population followed for more than three decades, researchers from Harvard School of Public Health found that higher consumption of saturated and trans fats was linked with higher mortality compared with the same number of calories from carbohydrates. Most importantly, replacing saturated fats with unsaturated fats conferred substantial health benefits (Harvard School of Public Health, 2016).

One study concludes that with a 50% reduction of all meat, dairy, and eggs, intake of saturated fats across the EU would be reduced by up to 40%

(Westhoek, H., et al., 2015). Such a reduction in saturated fat intake would be expected to reduce cardiovascular mortality.

One imagines that overweight and obesity are just linked to high carbohydrate and sugar consumption. However, one Australian study looked at the availability of major food groups – meat, fruits, fat etc – in 170 countries. It found that people in countries which have a higher proportion of meat in their diets are more obese and overweight than people in countries which consume less meat. The relationship between meat consumption and obesity is not affected by total availability of calories, by GDP or by levels of physical activity (You, W., and Henneberg, M., 2016).

Another study investigated whether those eating a plant-based diet had a lower risk for developing Type-2 diabetes. They concluded: "Plant-based dietary patterns, especially when they are enriched with healthful plant-based foods, may be beneficial for the primary prevention of type 2 diabetes." (Qian F., et al., 2019, 1335–44).

Several studies have shown that eating a healthy plant-based diet reduces the risk of heart disease mortality (Kim H., et al., 2019).

Other negative impacts include a link with kidney disease. One study of 63,000 adults with chronic kidney disease (CKD) showed that red meat intake was associated with a dose-dependent increased risk of developing into end-stage renal disease (ESRD). Individuals who consumed the highest amounts of red meat – the top 25 percent – showed a 40 percent higher risk of developing ESRD than those who consumed the least red meat – the bottom 25 percent (Newman, T., 2016).

People who decide to cut down on red meat often consume more chicken instead. However, chicken is not free of health implications, which is not surprising when one sees how most chickens are reared on industrial factory farms. A study published in The Journal of the American College of Cardiology states that "much chicken is transformed into fast food and other calorie-rich, ultra-processed, heavily advertised presentations. Additional public health impacts of industrial poultry production are also well reported, such as food-borne disease (e.g., E. coli, Salmonella, Listeria), antimicrobial residues, and avian flu" (Anand, S., et al., 2015).

People may decide to eat fresh chicken which has not been transformed into "fast food". There still remain issues around the widespread use of antibiotics in poultry farming. Although the European Union has taken and is taking further action (Save Our Antibiotics, 2020) to reduce this, much damage has already been done. Overuse of antibiotics in farming has led to the increase of antibiotic-resistant bacteria. These pathogenic bacteria may infect humans or other animals and are increasingly hard to treat as they have become resistant to some of the most widely used antibiotics.

Antibiotics are now commonly classed alongside other medicines as antimicrobials. Antimicrobials are used to treat an ever-increasing range of infections caused by bacteria, parasites, viruses, and fungi. The WHO says that resistance to antimicrobials (AMR) is one of the top 10 global public health threats facing humanity and that misuse, and overuse of antimicrobials are the main drivers in the development of drug-resistant pathogens (World Health Organisation, 2020).

Although the use of antibiotics for making animals grow faster and bigger was banned throughout the EU in 2006, they are still widely used in poultry farming, often to prevent as well as treat disease. In the United States, approximately 80% of antibiotics are sold for use in animal agriculture; about 70% of these are "medically important" (i.e., from classes important to human medicine) (Martin, Michael, J., 2015).

It does seem extraordinary that we allow antibiotics to be used so widely in animal agriculture when we know that its use is posing a threat to our own health.

Although the 2020 Covid-19 corona virus pandemic has not been linked to animal farming, the truth is that many scientists believe that a future pandemic may well arise from mutations in a novel avian or swine flu virus. Industrial poultry and pig farms are ideal conditions for the spread of these viruses and give many opportunities for such viruses to mutate.

The Centre for Disease Control and Prevention (CDC) in Atlanta acknowledges this risk, saying, "Novel influenza A viruses are of extra concern because of the potential impact they could have on public health if they gain the ability to spread easily from person to person, which might cause the next influenza pandemic" (The Centre for Disease Control and Prevention (CDC), 2020).

General advice is to stay away from poultry farms or dead wild birds and to handle raw poultry carefully, because as the CDC points out, "Raw poultry can be associated with many infections, including salmonella" (The Centre for Disease Control and Prevention (CDC), 2020).

In spite of a desperate campaign (1987-2011) by the National Pork Board in the US to describe pork as "the other white meat" (National Pork Board, 2020), it is of course another red meat, as any veterinary or public health body will tell you (Cleveland Clinic, 2020).

Pigs and poultry are the animals most widely farmed in industrial conditions, although zero-grazing dairy farms are increasing in number globally. Therefore, it would be a shame if health-conscious consumers shifted their meat consumption from beef and lamb to pork or chicken and turkey.

Perhaps we also need to think of the health of the animals. Just as good mental health is becoming increasingly recognised as a vital part of being a healthy person, so too we need to acknowledge the mental health of the animals we farm for food.

In broiler (meat) chicken sheds 20-30,000 young birds, bred for fast growth, struggle to keep alive for their short, five or six-week lives, with many going lame, crippled from their sheer bodyweight and others dropping dead from the aptly named Sudden Death Syndrome. Their life is indeed, "nasty, brutish and short" (a description of some people originating from the philosopher Thomas Hobbes).

The modern dairy cow, whose original milk production was sufficient to feed her suckling calf, has now been bred to produce many times as much milk as her calf would ever have suckled from her. Her calf is taken away from her at a day old, obviously causing extreme distress to both cow and calf. She is then milked to capacity until shortly before her next calf is due a year later (so for 6-7 months each year she is both pregnant and being milked). After two to four years of this stressful lifestyle, often interspersed with bouts of painful lameness or mastitis, she will be culled, worn out with the strains of production.

Pigs like to live in family groups. In factory farms the piglets are removed at around 1 month old so that the sow can quickly be impregnated again and produce yet another batch of profitable pigs for the market. Pigs are often reared in barren indoor conditions on concrete or slatted floors. As they would normally spend most of their daylight hours foraging for food in the soil (Stolba, A., and Wood Gush, D.,1989), conditions must be highly stressful for them. As a result, young pigs often try to bite each other's tails. To prevent this, many are routinely tail docked, usually without anaesthetic. It is a frustrating and miserable life for these highly intelligent animals.

Conclusion

Whether your main concern is your own health, or the dangers posed by climate change or concerns about the environment and biodiversity loss, the destruction of the Amazon forest or the wellbeing of animals farmed for food, all these factors contribute to a simple message: Eat less meat and other animal foods. If or when you do eat them, choose the products from farms where animals are given a decent quality of life, such as organic or free-range farms.

Food choices are ethical choices. Your own food choices may have more impact on the world and all its living beings than you ever imagined. Governments should also be brave enough to tackle this issue. Perhaps they are afraid of being criticised as being "the nanny state" or infringing on individual liberty. Yet the case for reducing such consumption is incredibly strong.

We hope that soon governments will use policy and law to enable us all to make better choices more easily. Until then, it really is up to each one of us to give the issue some thought and to take action!

Bibliography

Anand, S., et al, 2015. Food Consumption and its Impact on Cardiovascular Disease: Importance of Solutions Focused on the Globalized Food System. Journal of the American College of Cardiology. Vol 66, no 14

Bailey, Rob, Froggatt, Antony, Wellesley, Laura. 2014. Livestock - Climate Change's Forgotten Sector. (Chatham House, London) https://www.chathamhouse.org/sites/files/chathamhouse/field/field_do cument/20141203LivestockClimateChange

Bajželj, B., Richards, K., Allwood, J. et al. 2014. Importance of food-demand management for climate mitigation. Nature Climate Change 4, 924–929 (2014). https://doi.org/10.1038/nclimate2353

Berners-Lee, M., et al., 2018. Current global food production is sufficient to meet human nutritional needs in 2050 provided there is radical societal adaptation. Elem Sci Anth, 6: 52

Bradbury, Kathryn E., Murphy, Neil, and Key, Timothy J., Diet and colorectal cancer in UK Biobank: a prospective study, International Journal of Epidemiology, 2019, 1–13 doi: 10.1093/ije/dyz064

Cancer Research UK, https://www.cancerresearchuk.org/about-cancer/ causes-of-cancer/diet-and-cancer/does-eating-processed-and-red-meat-cause-cancer. Accessed 16/12 20.

Centre for Disease Control and Prevention (CDC). Viruses of Special Concern https://www.cdc.gov/flu/pandemic-resources/monitoring/viruses-concern.html. Accessed 16/12/20.

Centre for Disease Control and Prevention (CDC). Avian Influenza Current Situation Summary. https://www.cdc.gov/flu/avianflu/avian-flu-summary. htm. Accessed 16/12/20.

Clark, Michael A., Domingo, Nina G. G., Colgan, Kimberly, Thakrar, Sumil K., et al., 2020, Global food system emissions could preclude achieving the 1.5° and 2°C climate change targets. Science 06 Nov 2020: Vol. 370, Issue 6517, pp. 705-708. DOI: 10.1126/science.aba7357

Cleveland Clinic, 2020, Is Pork Considered a Red or White Meat? https://health.clevelandclinic.org/is-pork-considered-a-red-or-white-meat/

Committee on Climate Change December 2020. The Sixth Carbon Budget. The UK's path to Net Zero. https://www.theccc.org.uk/publication/sixth-carbon-budget/

Damania, Richard; Desbureaux, Sébastien; Rodella, Aude-Sophie; Russ, Jason; Zaveri, Esha., 2019. Quality Unknown: The Invisible Water Crisis. (Washington, DC: World Bank.) © World Bank. https://openknowledge.worldbank.org/handle/10986/32245 License: CC BY 3.0 IGO.

European Commission, 7 January 2019, United States is Europe's main soya beans supplier with imports up by 112%, Brussels. https://ec.europa.eu/commission/presscorner/detail/en/IP_19_161

European Commission, 2020, Cereals, oilseeds, protein crops and rice. https://ec.europa.eu/info/food-farming-fisheries/plants-and-plant-products/plant-products/cereals

European Commission, 2020, EU market: cereals supply & demand http://ec.europa.eu/agriculture/cereals/balance-sheets/cereals/overview_en.pdf

Eurostat, Statistics Explained, 201, Glossary: Carbon dioxide equivalent. https://ec.europa.eu/eurostat/statistics-explained/index.php/Glossary:Carbon_dioxide_equivalent

FAO, 2014. Healthy Soils for a Healthy Life. http://www.fao.org/soils-2015/events/detail/en/c/338738/

FAO, IFAD, UNICEF, WFP and WHO, 2020. Transforming food systems for affordable healthy diets. The State of Food Security and Nutrition in the World 2020. (Rome. Food and Agriculture Organization of the United Nations, 2020).

Foresight Report, 2011, The Future of Food and Farming, London. The Government Office for Science. https://www.gov.uk/government/publications/future-of-food-and-farming

Garside, M., 2020. Phosphate rock production worldwide in 2019, by country (in 1,000 metric tons). Statista. https://www.statista.com/statistics/681617/phosphate-rock-production-by-country/

Gerber, P.J., Steinfeld, H., Henderson, B., Mottet, A., Opio, C., Dijkman, J., Falcucci, A. & Tempio, G. 2013. Tackling climate change through livestock – A global assessment of emissions and mitigation opportunities, (Rome. Food and Agriculture Organization of the United Nations, 2013).

Gilbert, N., 2009, Environment: The disappearing nutrient. Nature 461, 716–718 (2009). https://doi.org/10.1038/461716a

Global Biodiversity Outlook 4. 2014, Convention on Biological Diversity. Progress Towards the Aichi Biodiversity Targets: An Assessment of Biodiversity Trends, Policy Scenarios and Key Actions, Technical Report. https://www.cbd.int/doc/publications/cbd-ts-78-en.pdf

Griscom, Bronson, W., Adams, Justin, Ellis, Peter W., Houghton, Richard A., et al., 2017. Natural climate solutions. Proceedings of the National Academy of Sciences Oct 2017, 114 (44) 11645-11650; DOI: 10.1073/pnas.1710465114

The Guardian, 1 March 2018. https://www.theguardian.com/news/2018/mar/01/bacon-cancer-processed-meats-nitrates-nitrites-sausages

The Guardian, 1 Dec 2020. Amazon deforestation surges to 12-year high under Bolsonaro, https://www.theguardian.com/environment/2020/dec/01/amazon-deforestation-surges-to-12-year-high-under-bolsonaro

Hallström, Elinor, Carlsson-Kanyama, Annika, Börjesson, Pål, 2014, Environmental Impact of Dietary Change. A Systematic Review. Journal of Cleaner Production vol 91,1-11, Elsevier.

Harvard School of Public Health, 2016, Higher consumption of unsaturated fats linked with lower mortality. https://www.hsph.harvard.edu/news/press-releases/higher-consumption-of-unsaturated-fats-linked-with-lower-mortality/?utm_source=SilverpopMailing&utm_medium=email&utm_campaign=Update_07.15.2016%20(1)&utm_content

IARC Monographs evaluate consumption of red meat and processed meat. 2015. https://www.iarc.fr/wp-content/uploads/2018/07/pr240_E.pdf

IEED Briefing March 2015, Sustainable Intensification Revisited. http://pubs.ieed.org/17283IIED.html

Kim H., Caulfield L. E., Garcia-Larsen V., Steffen L. M., Coresh J., Rebholz C. M., Plant-Based Diets Are Associated with a Lower Risk of Incident Cardiovascular Disease, Cardiovascular Disease Mortality, and All-Cause Mortality in a General Population of Middle-Aged Adults. J Am Heart Assoc. 2019 Aug 20;8(16): e012865. doi: 10.1161/JAHA.119.012865. Epub 2019 Aug 7. PMID: 31387433; PMCID: PMC6759882.

Lelieveld, J., Evans, J. S., Fnais, M., Giannadaki, D., Pozzer, A. 2015, The contribution of outdoor air pollution sources to premature mortality on a global scale. Nature. 2015 Sep 17;525(7569):367-71. doi: 10.1038/nature15371. PMID: 26381985.

Loken, Brent, Diets for a better future, EAT Forum. 2020.

https://eatforum.org/content/uploads/2020/07/Diets-for-a-Better-Future_G20_National-Dietary-Guidelines.pdf

Lundqvist, J., de Fraiture, C., Molden, D., 2008. Saving Water: From Field to Fork - Curbing Losses and Wastage in the Food Chain. SIWI Policy Brief. SIWI. http://www.siwi.org/documents/Resources/Policy_Briefs/PB_From_Fil ed_to_Fork_2008.pdf

Martin, Michael J., 2015. Am J Public Health. 2015 December; 105(12): 2409–2410. Published online 2015 December. doi: 10.2105/AJPH.2015.302870PMCID: PMC4638249 PMID: 26469675. Antibiotics Overuse in Animal Agriculture: A Call to Action for Health Care Providers Martin, MD, MPH, MBA, corresponding author Sapna E Thottathil, PhD, and Thomas B. Newman, MD, MPH. https://www.ncbi.nlm.nih.gov/pmc/articles/PMC4638249/

Mendoza, J., Apr 7, 2020 Leading countries of destination of soybean exports from Brazil in 2019, by export value share *and* by country of destination. https://www.statista.com/statistics/721259/value-share-soybean-exports-brazil-country-destination/

National Pork Board. The Other White Meat® Brand. (https://www.pork.org/about/towm/. Accessed 16/12/20.

Nellemann, C., MacDevette, M., Manders, et al. 2009, The environmental food crisis - The environment's role in averting future food crises. A UNEP rapid response assessment.

Newman, T., 2016. Red Meat Consumption linked to Kidney Failure. Medical News Today. https://www.medicalnewstoday.com/articles/311664

OECD-FAO Agricultural Outlook, 2019-2028 © OECD/FAO 2019. https://www.oecd-ilibrary.org/agriculture-and-food/oecd-fao-agricultural-outlook-2019-2028_agr_outlook-2019-en

Paris Agreement, 2015, https://unfccc.int/process-and-meetings/the-paris-agreement/the-paris-agreement

Pradhan et al, 2013. Embodied crop calories in animal products. Environ. Res. Lett. 8 (2013) 044044

Qian, F., Liu, G., Hu, F. B., Bhupathiraju, S. N., Sun, Q., Association Between Plant-Based Dietary Patterns and Risk of Type 2 Diabetes: A Systematic Review and Meta-analysis. JAMA Intern Med. 2019 Jul 22;179(10):1335–44. doi: 10.1001/jamainternmed.2019.2195. Epub ahead of print. PMID: 31329220; PMCID: PMC6646993.

Raoni, Rajão, Soares-Filho, Britaldo, Nunes, Felipe, Börne, Jan R., et al., The rotten apples of Brazil's agribusiness. Science 17 Jul 2020: Vol. 369, Issue 6501, pp. 246-248. DOI: 10.1126/science.aba6646

Save Our Antibiotics, 2020, New European Union rules on farm antibiotic use. https://www.saveourantibiotics.org/media/1842/2022-changes-to-european-law-farm-antibiotics.pdf

Scarborough, P., Appleby, P. N., Mizdrak, A., et al., 2014. Dietary greenhouse gas emissions of meat-eaters, fish-eaters, vegetarians and vegans in the UK. Climatic Change 125, 179–192 (2014). https://doi.org/10.1007/s10584-014-1169-1

Schader, C., et al. 2015. Impacts of feeding less food-competing feedstuffs to livestock on global food system sustainability. J. R. Soc. Interface 12: 20150891. http://dx.doi.org/10.1098/rsif.2015.0891

Science Magazine., 17 July 2020, https://science.sciencemag.org/content/369/6501/246.full

Semedo, Maria-Helena, FAO, 2014, Only 60 Years of Farming Left If Soil Degradation Continues. https://www.scientificamerican.com/article/only-60-years-of-farming-left-if-soil-degradation-continues/

Springmann, Marco, Clark, Michael, Mason-D'Croz, Daniel, Wiebe, Keith, Bodirsky, Benjamin Leon, Lassaletta, Luis, de Vries, Wim, Vermeulen, Sonja J., Herrero, Mario, Carlson, Kimberly M., Jonell, Malin, Troell, Max, DeClerck, Fabrice, Gordon, Line J., Zurayk, Rami, Scarborough, Peter, Rayner, Mike, Loken, Brent, Fanzo, Jess, Godfray, H. Charles J., Tilman, David, Rockström, Johan, & Willett, Walter. 2018. In *Options for keeping the food system within environmental limits.* Nature https://www.nature.com/articles/s41586-018-0594-0

Springmann, M., Godfray, H.C., Rayner, M., & Scarborough, P., 2016, Analysis and valuation of the health and climate change co-benefits of dietary change. PNAS vol. 113 no. 15: 4146–4151. Supplementary information.)

Steffen, W., et al, 2015. Planetary boundaries: Guiding human development on a changing planet. Science Express. 15 January 2015: page 1/10.1126/science.1259855

Stolba, A., and Wood Gush, D., The behaviour of pigs in a semi-natural environment. 1989. https://www.semanticscholar.org/paper/The-behaviour-of-pigs-in-a-semi-natural-environment-Stolba-Wood%E2%80%90Gush/82b625be0ab9ba36e4daaf14d22169627c7fb8c6

Tsiafouli, M. A., Thébault, E., Sgardelis, S. P., de Ruiter, P. C., van der Putten, W. H., Birkhofer, K., Hemerik, L., de Vries, F. T., Bardgett, R. D., Brady, M.V., Bjornlund, L., Jørgensen, H. B., Christensen, S., Hertefeldt, T. D., Hotes, S., Gera Hol, W., Frouz, J., Liiri, M., Mortimer, S. R., Setälä, H., Tzanopoulos, J., Uteseny, K., Pižl, V., Stary, J.,

Wolters, V. and Hedlund, K. 2015, Intensive agriculture reduces soil biodiversity across Europe. Glob Change Biol, 21: 973-985. https://doi.org/10.1111/gcb.12752

United Nations 2011. World Economic and Social Survey. https://www.un.org/en/development/desa/policy/wess/wess_current/2011wess.pdf

UNCCD, 2017, Global Land Outlook

United Nations Environment Programme, 2010. Global honeybee colony disorders and other threats to insect pollinators. https://www.unenvironment.org/resources/report/unep-emerging-issues-global-honey-bee-colony-disorder-and-other-threats-insect

United Nations Environment Programme, GRID-Arendal, www.unep.org/pdf/foodcrisis_lores.pdf

Wentworth, Jonathan, 2013, Reversing insect pollinator decline. Number 442 September 2013. https://post.parliament.uk/research-briefings/post-pn-442/

Westhoek H., Lesschen J. P., Rood T., et al., 2014, Food choices, health and environment: Effects of cutting Europe's meat and dairy intake. Global environmental change, 26, 196–205

Westhoek, H., et al, 2015, Nitrogen on the Table: The influence of food choices on nitrogen emissions and the European environment. (European Nitrogen Assessment Special Report on Nitrogen and Food.) Centre for Ecology & Hydrology, Edinburgh, UK.)

Wills, Kendra, 2013, Where do all these soybeans go? Michigan State University Extension. https://www.canr.msu.edu/news/where_do_all_these_soybeans_go

World Cancer Research Fund, Limit red and processed meat. https://www.wcrf.org/dietandcancer/recommendations/limit-red-processed-meat. Accessed 16/12/ 20

World Health Organisation, 2015, Cancer: Carcinogenicity of the consumption of red meat and processed meat. https://www.who.int/news-room/q-a-detail/cancer-carcinogenicity-of-the-consumption-of-red-meat-and-processed-meat

World Health Organisation, 2020, Antimicrobial resistance, https://www.who.int/news-room/fact-sheets/detail/antimicrobial-resistance

WWF, 2006, Facts about Soy production and the Basel criteria. https://wwfint.awsassets.panda.org/downloads/factsheet_soy_eng.pdf

You, W., and Henneberg, M., 2016, Meat consumption providing a surplus energy in modern diet contributes to obesity prevalence: an ecological analysis. (University of Adelaide, 2016).

Yousefi, A., Bellantonio, M., & Horowitz, G., 2018. The avoidable crisis. https://www.mightyearth.org/wp-content/uploads/2018/04/ME_ DEFORESTATION_EU_English_R8.pdf

CHAPTER THIRTEEN

THE ANIMAL TESTING MODEL

ANDRE MENACHE

Animal experimentation is arguably the most complex issue faced by the animal protection community today. Ubiquitous, and yet nearly invisible to the general public, between 80 and 100 million animals are used in scientific procedures throughout the world every year (1). The extensive but outdated use of animals by government agencies as a safety screen to test pharmaceutical and industrial chemicals has had a profoundly negative impact on our health and on the environment that goes largely unnoticed. Despite huge advances in science and technology, the 'animal model' is still the current paradigm in biomedical research and has escaped the rigors of evidence-based medicine. To top it all, the animal research community is in crisis (most animal studies are of poor quality) but has managed to keep this information well out of public view. The institutionalized use of animals in academia and in industry has become entrenched since the end of World War II.

The aim of this chapter is to provide the reader with 'inside information' to expose the claim that animal research and testing are a "necessary evil". It will become clear to the reader that the biggest obstacle to real medical progress and chemical risk assessment in the 21st century is not a lack of technology but rather, a lack of political will on the part of our regulatory agencies, coupled with a lack of transparency on the part of well-established and powerful vested interest groups.

My interest in animal experiments began as a young university student in South Africa. By chance, I came across the newsletter of the South African Association Against Painful Experiments on Animals (SAAAPEA), an organization that I immediately joined. It made no sense to me that animal suffering was the only path to medical progress. At the time, the moral argument seemed all-powerful and was surely sufficient to put an end to this practice. I was even fortunate enough to put my convictions to the test in the form of a debate on national television in 1978. Faced with several medical researchers all in favor of animal experiments, (including

Christiaan Barnard, who performed the world's first human-to-human heart transplant) my arguments carried very little sway. The take-home message from the debate was that society must choose between "a dog or a child" in order for medical science to find new treatments for human diseases. It was precisely this sort of 'emotional blackmail' that fueled my motivation to seek answers to what is still a very complex subject. Now, 40 years later, I am far better informed thanks to having met some of the pioneers in the scientific movement against animal experiments.

This is perhaps an appropriate occasion to pay tribute to some of the medical researchers who opened my eyes and provided me with the information and tools necessary to challenge the status quo. Professor Pietro Croce (1920-2006) was an Italian pathologist who performed animal experiments for the first 25 years or his career. He subsequently underwent a courageous turnaround that led him to criticize animal research for the rest of his career and to publish a book entitled *Vivisection or Science* (the English version appeared in 1991) (2). Cardiologist John Pippin conducted experiments on dogs before deciding to change direction and abandon his animal research (3). Anesthetist Ray Greek and his veterinarian wife, Jean, discovered that animal research did not translate very well from animals to people. Their discussions led to the publication of several books and numerous scientific articles on the subject, including *Sacred Cows and Golden Geese* (4) and *Animal Models in Light of Evolution* (co-authored with Niall Shanks) (5). Honorable mention goes to psychiatrist Murry Cohen, neuropathologist Lawrence Hansen and veterinarian Brandon Reines, to name just three more pioneers in the field.

Today, one can even find organizations of doctors and researchers opposed to animal research, for example the US based Physicians Committee for Responsible Medicine, with 12,000 members (6) and Doctors in Germany Against Animal Experimentation, with 800 members (7). Compared to the total number of medical scientists in their respective countries, these numbers are small. Proponents of animal research will sometimes exploit these numbers as 'proof' that the majority of medical opinion is still in favor of using animals. However, in reality, most doctors have very little knowledge on the subject. As a simple test, you could ask your GP to name four deadly human diseases to which the chimpanzee is essentially immune (answer: AIDS, hepatitis B, common malaria and several human cancers). Most people (including GPs, politicians and the general public) become informed about animal research through the media. The reason so few medical scientists speak openly against animal research is because very few of them have the expertise to 'tick all the boxes' (see below). In order to seriously challenge animal researchers, one must master the scientific facts. The moral argument on its own will always be crushed by the 'dog or child' ultimatum. And society will naturally always choose the life of a child over that of a dog, even though this trolley/false dilemma is well-known and used by the animal research lobby to detract and manipulate the public. Hence the need to complement the moral argument with a scientific one. However, in order to master the scientific argument, it is essential to fulfil four criteria. The first is to have a medical or scientific background (doctor, vet, biologist, pharmacist, etc.); the second is to be well informed and up-to-date with the latest animal and non-animal research. This requires a significant time investment (typically two to three hours on the internet every day, which would exclude virtually anyone working full-time in a clinic or hospital); the third criterion is to be a good communicator, a skill essential in order to convey complex information in a way that most people can understand (e.g. a retired GP may have plenty of time to help but may not be a good speaker); and finally, the fourth criterion requires individuals to be financially independent, and free from conflict of interest (for example, a university professor may be an excellent candidate but may be subjected to institutional intimidation if he or she challenges the status quo). Based on the above criteria, it becomes clear as to why there are so few individuals available to competently challenge animal research using the scientific argument.

The good news is that we do not need thousands of scientists to master every aspect of these arguments. It is sufficient for society simply to be aware that there is a body of scientific evidence against using animals. The message appears to have already reached the animal rights community. Twenty years ago, at an anti-vivisection march, one would typically see posters with the caption "Stop animal experiments, they are cruel". In more recent years, the posters read "Stop animal experiments, they don't work". The task now at hand for those rare scientists who thoroughly master the scientific argument, is to provide this information to the public and to decision makers in parliament. Once a 'critical mass' of public opinion is attained, it will hopefully be sufficient to provide the momentum required for political change to happen. The only way to end animal experiments is by changing the law and that path necessarily goes through parliament.

One pioneer whom I was not fortunate enough to meet was Henry Spira (1927-1998), who in 1980 launched a landmark campaign against the use of animals in the cosmetics industry, in the form of a full-page advertisement in the New York Times. Entitled "How many rabbits does Revlon blind for beauty's sake?" The campaign caught the industry completely by surprise. Some of the biggest names in cosmetics at the time responded immediately by creating a fund for the development of test methods to replace the use of live animals, which was established in 1981 of the Center for Alternatives to Animal Testing (CAAT) at the Johns Hopkins University (8). Although this was an unprecedented achievement, animals in laboratories would have to wait until 2004 for the non-animal replacement methods to be legally enforced (the 7th amendment of Cosmetics Directive 76/768/EEC). While the international animal rights community had worked very hard to get this result, the cosmetics industry and regulators had dragged their feet. What also soon became apparent was the very small number of animal lives spared by the new legislation. Based on figures published by the European Commission, the number of animal lives spared every year as a result of the Cosmetics Directive is around 5000 (9). This figure represents less than half of one percent of the 10-12 million animals used in experiments in the EU annually (10).

Fortunately, the story does not end there. A resounding success for the animal rights community took place in the US in 2011 with the announcement that mice would be replaced with a non-animal test method for the purpose of quality control of cosmetic Botox products. A press release issued by the Humane Society of the United States (HSUS) confirmed official approval by the US Food and Drug Administration (FDA) of a non-animal replacement test (11). Once again, however, the success story was short lived, in the sense that industry did not expand the replacement of animal tests to other areas. The general public was, and is still, largely unaware of the significance of the historic achievement by the HSUS. Botox is no ordinary cosmetic product, it contains botulinum, the most potent poison known to science (12). The animal research community and industry had considered the use of mice as irreplaceable since mice are a very sensitive indicator for the purpose of quality control of botulinum products. To illustrate this point, a tiny vial of Botox for commercial use in cosmetics clinics contains enough botulinum to kill 500 mice. The manufacturer of Botox (Allergan) would have happily continued to use mice as living test-tubes had the HSUS not got involved.

The take-home message that has largely been missed by almost everyone is this: if we already possess the technology to replace the use of animals to test the most potent toxin known to science, then surely, we can apply some of that technology to test substances that are far less toxic than botulinum (e.g., pharmaceutical drugs and industrial chemicals). This missed opportunity should serve as a wake-up call, not only for the animal rights community but also for anyone concerned about human health and the environment, as the following passages will explain.

The continued use of animals as living test-tubes by the pharmaceutical and chemical industries is shameful in light of currently available technology, as illustrated by the example of Botox. In the context of routine safety testing, the term 'alternative methods' is generally used to describe technologies that not only eliminate animal suffering but are also more accurate than the crude animal test. However, in areas of science (especially basic research) where animals are used to try to predict human outcome to drugs and disease, the use of the term 'alternative methods' can be very misleading. This is because the term has become synonymous with the principle of Reduction, Refinement and Replacement (3Rs), discussed later in the chapter.

One fact that stands out above the rest is that animals consistently fail to reliably predict human results. The simplest way to demonstrate this is to refer to the FDA's own findings: out of 10 candidate drugs that successfully pass animal tests, nine will fail during the course of clinical trials involving humans because of lack of efficacy or toxic effects not seen during the animal tests (13). This represents a spectacular failure rate of 90%, which should ring alarm bells for everyone.

However, the pharmaceutical industry is able to conduct 'business as usual' thanks to outdated legislative requirements, which date back to the end of World War II. The proceedings of the Doctors' Trial held at Nuremberg in 1946 resulted in cementing the prerequisite that henceforth, animals always be used prior to any clinical trial involving human subjects (14). Although this may have appeared logical at the time, science has moved forward since then by 75 years. However, the laws have not yet caught up with the science.

Most of what has been discussed above applies to animal tests for the purpose of marketing approval in the various industries (pharmaceutical, chemical, cosmetics). The official term that covers these animal experiments is 'regulatory toxicology' which represents roughly 25% of animal use in the EU and by extrapolation, probably world-wide (15). The other major use of animals in scientific procedures is in the field of 'basic research' (aka 'fundamental research'), which translates as 'scientific curiosity' and account for about 50% of all animal use in the EU. Most of these kinds of animal studies are conducted in universities and in research institutes. In most universities, basic research accounts for almost all animal use, while the remaining animals are used for teaching and training purposes. The current paradigm of biomedical research encourages young scientists to launch themselves into a career of animal experimentation. What is sadly missing in the curriculum of these very bright and enthusiastic young students is the element of critical thinking, within the context of the philosophy of science.

Young researchers study living animals. They ought to know that these living organisms (from fruit flies and earthworms to mice, rats, and monkeys) represent 'complex systems' (16). For those unfamiliar with the concept, it is important to differentiate between a 'complicated system' and a 'complex system'. An expensive Swiss watch is a good example of a complicated system, because it contains many intricate elements. However, it is not a 'complex system' in a biological sense, because it will faithfully provide the exact time of day, day after day and year after year, come rain or shine. In other words, Swiss watches are excellent predictors of time. A complex system (in a biological context) also contains many (thousands of) intricate elements, such as genes, biochemical pathways, and so on, but it is virtually impossible to predict how such a system will respond to a perturbation (e.g., a drug or a chemical). Hence, by its very definition, one complex system cannot predict how another complex system will respond to the same drug or chemical. Animal researchers appear to ignore this fact of nature, often relying on the word 'similar' to justify their use of an animal model to study a human disease. The fact that people and mice both have two eyes, two ears, and a nose does not make them similar, nor does the fact they both species share nearly all of the same genes (17). Humans and bananas share 50% of their genes, but so what?

Humans and mice are separated by 90 million years of evolution. What matters is not so much the number of genes we share with mice, but rather, how those shared genes behave in each species. For example, humans and mice possess the gene for a tail; in mice the gene is switched on while in humans it is switched off. We are simply not 70kg mice. There is finally a slowly growing awareness within the animal research community that mouse research (which represents 80% of all animal use worldwide) represents a colossal waste of animal lives and precious funding (18, 19, 20).

For decades, animal researchers have been able to have their cake and eat it. The system has allowed them to design animal studies that are subsequently approved by an in-house ethical review process devoid of any meaningful public participation. The result is animal suffering on a massive scale, and a waste of public money on an equally grand scale. However, animal research is now in crisis. Some animal researchers have been honest enough to admit that most basic animal research is a sham. These researchers have proposed guidelines to improve the methodology (quality) of animal studies in an attempt to restore some respectability to the profession. The fact that more than 80% of basic animal studies cannot be reproduced by other researchers (and sometimes even by the original team) is simply too embarrassing to hide any longer (21, 22). As noble as these attempts to improve the animal data may be, they are doomed to fail for at least two reasons. The first is that these guidelines are voluntary and therefore not enforced by most science journals. The second is that, even if the researchers conducted their animal experiments to the letter, their results would still be just as irrelevant to humans as before, based on our current understanding of complex systems and evolutionary biology (23).

It is worth revealing in more detail how the ethical review system functions and why almost all basic animal studies are approved. Most animal ethics committees contain few or no public representatives even though much of the research is funded by the taxpayer. The exception to this rule is in Scandinavian countries, where animal ethics committees may contain equal numbers of scientists and non-scientists. Although most animal studies will still be approved (based on the '3Rs principle' - see below), at least there is fair public participation. In reality, whatever the composition of the ethics committee, animal researchers can rely on a tried-and-tested formula for obtaining ethical approval in almost all cases.

The first step is for the researchers to highlight a serious or dramatic societal problem that concerns human health (one example would be a psychiatric disorder that involves aggression and violence). The next step is to create an 'animal model' that somehow resembles the human condition (for example, the creation of a genetically modified (GM) breed of mice who are unusually aggressive towards other mice). It is not uncommon for a team of researchers to make a career out of studying one animal model. These animal studies can provide the researchers with many published articles spanning several years, sometimes decades. Each study builds on data obtained in a previous study. And each time, there are a set of unanswered questions to be answered in a subsequent or future animal study. The cycle is virtually endless. An added bonus is the age of internet journals, which have far more space in which to publish articles than was previously possible in print-only format. This has led to an explosion in scientific publications as journals vie for more articles.

Once the animal study has been designed, the research team presents its proposal to the ethics committee. In keeping with EU Directive 2010/63/EU, researchers must demonstrate that they have endeavored to apply the '3Rs principle' (reduce, refine, and replace animal experiments) (24). 'Reduction' can be achieved by using the smallest number of animals possible, in keeping with statistically significant limits; 'refinement' can be achieved by administering pain killers to the animals, if the experimental protocol allows it (the painkiller must not interfere with the aims of the experiment); and finally 'replacement' implies the use of animal cells or tissues in place of a living animal ('relative replacement') or the use of non-animal cells or tissues ('absolute replacement'), such as ethically-sourced human surgical waste.

While researchers generally do apply the principles of 'reduction' and 'refinement' to their studies, they rarely apply the principle of 'replacement' (especially 'absolute replacement'). As a former member of an animal ethics committee, I was able to discover why this was so. Let us take the example of a researcher who studies cancer in rats. The researcher will justify the use of rats on the grounds that it is necessary to study cancer in a 'whole living organism'. Human cell culture will therefore not do the job. However, when asked to provide evidence that the rat is a scientifically valid model for the study of human cancer, the researcher will respond that this is not a requirement under Directive 2010/63/EU. The legislation thus does not require proof that animals are relevant for the study of humans. Indeed, the 'animal model' has never been the subject of an official validation process to determine its relevance and reliability in the context of human medicine (25). To quote Anita O'Connor, formerly of the Office of Science at the FDA, "Most of the animal tests we accept have never been validated. They evolved over the past 20 years and the FDA is comfortable with them." (Personal communication to the author, 1998).

Once ethical approval and funding have been secured, the researchers perform their animal experiment. In the example of the psychiatric study mentioned earlier, data can be obtained by measuring the time taken by the GM mice to attack timid individuals such as juvenile mice or females, and whether the attacks are directed at vulnerable body parts. In this case study, the observations indicate that the GM mice exhibit signs of abnormal aggressive behavior compared to healthy mice. The GM mice are subsequently treated with a psychiatric drug and found to become less aggressive. Based on these observations, the authors conclude that "A next logical step will be to investigate if our findings can help ameliorate aggressive dysfunctions in humans" (26). This conclusion leaves the door open to more animal research and, on very rare occasions, to the initiation of a human clinical trial (if the pharmaceutical industry considers the drug to be a financially viable venture).

If the 90% failure rate for pharmaceutical drug testing is appalling, then how does one describe the far greater failure rate for basic research using animals? The 90% figure is available thanks to the FDA. However, figures for basic research are far more difficult to come by because they have generally evaded scientific audit. Fortunately, some academics have taken the trouble to study the translation rate of basic research into clinically useful treatments. A landmark article published in 2003 managed to quantify the translation rate of "highly promising" basic research studies into clinical applications (27). The results of this paper were further analyzed to reveal that:

> Of the 25,000 articles searched, about 500 (2%) contained some potential claim to future applicability in humans, about 100 (0.4%) resulted in a clinical trial, and, according to the authors, only 1 (0.004%) led to the development of a clinically useful class of drugs (angiotensin-converting enzyme inhibitors) in the 30 years following their publication of the basic science finding. (28).

This study casts further doubt on the value of animal-based research in human clinical medicine. Animal researchers can consider themselves very fortunate that this information has not attracted the attention of mainstream media. If the public was aware of this scandalous state of affairs, perhaps funding for animal-based research would finally begin to dry up. This would divert precious funds towards meaningful, evidence-based medicine.

Animal based research is clearly responsible for incalculable animal suffering in the name of science. However, the negative impact of animal studies on society extends far beyond the animals used in laboratories. In particular, the use of animals as a « safety screen » by industry to obtain marketing approval for their products surely constitutes « silent fraud » in light of the fact that animals and humans are biologically very different from each other. In a contract setting, silent fraud occurs when one party fails to disclose material facts of the contract (29).

An example is the industrial chemical bisphenol A (BPA). This synthetic compound attracted the interest of the pharmaceutical industry in the 1930s as a possible contraceptive for use in women because it was known to mimic the female sex hormone, oestrogen (30). However, it was subsequently abandoned because it was too weak to be used as a contraceptive. In contrast to the pharmaceutical industry, the chemical industry found BPA to possess wonderful properties with respect to the manufacture of plastic products. Thus, BPA was incorporated in polycarbonate drinking containers, baby pacifiers, the inside lining of tinned food, beverage products and much more. As of 2013, global annual production capacity of BPA stood at more than 6.2 million tonnes, an increase of 372,000 tonnes over 2012 (31).

The marketing of BPA illustrates how animal tests can be used to confuse authorities and slow down attempts at removing substances of very high concern from the marketplace (BPA is a recognized endocrine disrupting compound). A European Commission expert opinion published in 2002 stated that:

> The marked differences in observed responses to BPA between different laboratories using very similar study designs also complicate human risk assessment. Housing, diet, species, strain and sub-strain (sources of animals) may all conceivably influence study outcomes ...

The expert committee then concludes that "The implications of these conflicting observations for human risk assessment are difficult to assess at present", and finally, that "Further research is needed to resolve the uncertainties surrounding the findings in the mouse, both with respect to dose, and significance of the reported effects for humans" (32).

These comments raise serious doubts as to the competence of the members of the expert committee, in addition to the issue of conflict of interests among certain members of the committee. It should also be noted that the European Commission Chemicals Agency (ECHA) officially recognized BPA as an endocrine disruptor as late as June 16, 2017, half a century after the first evidence of the negative health effects on people and on animals (33). The use of animal data to extend the shelf life of substances of very high concern illustrates another important concept, that of 'regulatory capture', where regulatory agencies become dominated by the industries or interests, they are charged with regulating. The result is that an agency, charged with acting in the public interest, instead acts in ways that benefit the industry it is supposed to be regulating (34). Thus, regulatory agencies become complicit in keeping toxic chemicals on the market (with minor restrictions) instead of simply banning them.

According to an article published by the Endocrine Society, "Endocrine-disrupting chemicals (EDCs) represent not just a threat to public health or indeed to global health, but to planetary health. Pervasive in our environment - in foods, packaging materials, cosmetics, drinking water, and consumer products - EDCs have been linked to a myriad of non-communicable diseases such as obesity, type 2 diabetes, thyroid disorders, neurodevelopmental disease, hormone-dependent cancers, and reproductive disorders." (35). However, BPA represents only the "tip of the iceberg" considering that there are more than 7 million recognized chemicals in existence, of which at least 80,000 are in common use worldwide and for which potential toxicity remains largely unknown (36).

To remedy this situation requires a radical paradigm shift both in terms of critical thinking in science and in terms of the way we allow new chemicals on to the market. It is not sufficient to expose industry scandals, such as Dieselgate (the use of monkeys to show that diesel fumes are safe) (37) or the Monsanto papers (the use of animal tests to show that GM maize is not harmful, and that the herbicide glyphosate does not cause cancer in people) (38). The list goes on and on. Modern toxicological methods already exist to replace misleading animal tests (39). Incredibly, industry and the regulatory authorities have found ways to slow things down here too. The first hurdle is the need to 'validate' any new non-animal method. Validation is the process by which a new test method is evaluated for reliability and relevance, which makes perfect sense. However, the validation process, conceived in the 1980s is cumbersome and cannot keep up with the pace of technological advancements. The validation process requires a new test method to be assessed in three separate laboratories and takes seven years to complete, on average. There is thus very little incentive for industry to invest resources in a technology that will probably be out-of-date and overtaken by newer technologies by the time it gets the green light. And for as long as regulatory authorities continue to accept animal data, why even bother developing non animal test methods? Of the very few validated non animal methods available today, industry can still choose to ignore them in favor of animal experiments. The only minor exception to this rule is skin tests in the cosmetics industry, where consumer pressure persuaded cosmetics manufacturers to develop the non-animal tests.

For the situation to change, industry must fulfil its social corporate responsibility in the widest sense of the term. There have been a few attempts to make some progress. One example was the House of Commons Health Committee inquiry into "The Influence of the Pharmaceutical Industry" that published its report in 2005 (40). I was able to attend some of the hearings as an interested member of the public. While the Committee identified several underhand (possibly criminal) marketing techniques employed by the pharmaceutical industry, the MPs were not necessarily the best qualified people to judge the science. Of the 11 Committee members, only two had a scientific or medical background. Time and again, the representatives of the pharmaceutical industry managed to talk their way out of trouble. The Health Committee simply lacked the expert knowledge that was necessary on this occasion. This format would definitely not be suited to investigate the problem of animal research. An alternative approach would be to set up an official (i.e., parliamentary sponsored) inquiry into the relevance of animal-based research but where the jury panel is composed of independent scientific experts, in place of MPs. Such an endeavor has already been proposed through Early Day Motion 250 (tabled on 4th March 2020) (41).

Animal experiments are no longer a 'necessary evil'. The current challenge is not a lack of technological know-how to replace animal testing and research. Rather, it has to do with communicating a complex message in a way that is readily understood both by the public and politicians. In the words of Joseph Pulitzer:

"There is not a crime, there is not a dodge, there is not a trick, there is not a swindle, there is not a vice which does not live by secrecy. Get these things out in the open, describe them, attack them, ridicule them in the press, and sooner or later public opinion will sweep them away. Publicity may not be the only thing that is needed, but it is the one thing without which all other agencies will fail".

Bibliography

1. Gordon, Nicky. Higgins, Wendy. Langley, Gill. Taylor, Katy. 2008. "Estimates for worldwide laboratory animal use in 2005." *Altern Lab Animal,* N° 36(3):327-42. doi: 10.1177/026119290803600310.
2. Croce, Pietro. 2000. Vivisection or Science? An Investigation into Testing Drugs and Safeguarding Health. (Zed Books, 2020).
3. Menache, Andre. Pippin, John. Tyler, Andrew. 2005. Curiosity Killed the Dog: An Animal Aid Report on the Use of Animals in Basic Research: A Case Study (Paperback). Publisher: (Animal Aid, 2005) ISBN: 9781905327027.
4. Greek, Ray. Swingle-Greek, Jean. 2000. Sacred Cows and Golden Geese: The Human Cost of Experiments on Animals. Publisher (Continuum, 2000). ISBN-13: 978-0826414021.
5. Greek, Ray and Shanks, Niall. 2009. Animal Models in Light of Evolution. (Boca Raton. Brown Walker Press, 2009).
6. Physicians Committee for Responsible Medicine. www.pcrm.org
7. Doctors Against Animal Experiments. https://www.aerzte-gegen-tierversuche.de/en/; Center for Alternatives to Animal Testing. https://caat.jhsph.edu/
8. Fifth Report on the Statistics on the Number of Animals used for Experimental and other Scientific Purposes in the Member States of the European Union. 2007. https://eur-lex.europa.eu/legal-content/EN/TXT/PDF/?uri=CELEX: 52007DC0675&from=E N

9. Fifth Report on the Statistics on the Number of Animals used for Experimental and other Scientific Purposes in the Member States of the European Union. 2007. https://eur-lex.europa.eu/legal-content/ EN/TXT/PDF/?uri=CELEX:52007DC0675&from=E N

10. https://www.globalanimal.org/2011/10/10/botox-removes-wrinkles-now-animal-testing/543 06/

11. https://en.wikipedia.org/wiki/Botulinum_toxin

12. Akhtar, Aysha. 2015. "The flaws and human harms of animal experiments." *Camb Q Healthc Ethics* N° 4:407-19. doi: 10.1017/S0963180115000079.

13. Greek, Ray. Hansen, Lawrence. Pippus, Annalea. 2012. "The Nuremberg Code subverts human health and safety by requiring animal modelling." *BMC Med Ethics*, N° 13:16. doi: 10.1186/1472-6939-13-16.

14. eur-lex.europa.eu/legal-content/EN/TXT/PDF/?uri=CELEX:52020 DC0016&from=EN, ref 15, figure 3.

15. https://en.wikipedia.org/wiki/Complex_system

16. http://compbio.mit.edu/publications/119_Yue_Nature_14.pdf

17. Cuenca, Alex. Seok, Junhee. Tompkins, Ronald. Warren, Shaw et al. 2013. "Genome responses in mouse models poorly mimic human inflammatory diseases." *Proceedings of the National Academy of Sciences* N° 110(9):3507-12. DOI: 10.1073/pnas.1222878110.

18. Mestas, Javier and Hughes, Christopher. 2004. "Of mice and not men: Differences between mouse and human immunology." *Journal of Immunology,* N° 172, 2731–2738.

19. http://compbio.mit.edu/publications/119_Yue_Nature_14.pdf

20. Macleod, Malcolm. 2018. "Challenges in irreproducible research." *Nature.* https://www.nature.com/collections/prbfkwmwvz/

21. Baker, Monya. 2016. "Biotech giant publishes failures to confirm high-profile science." *Nature* N° 530, 141. doi:10.1038/nature.2016.19269.

22. Greek, Ray and Menache, Andre. 2013. "Systematic reviews of animal models: methodology versus epistemology." *Int J Med Sci.* N° 10(3):206-21. doi: 10.7150/ijms.5529.

23. https://en.wikipedia.org/wiki/The_Three_Rs_(animals)

24. Balls, Michael, and Combes, Robert. 2005. "The need for a formal invalidation process for animal and non-animal tests." *Altern Lab Anim,* N° 33(3):299-308. doi: 10.1177/026119290503300301.

25. https://actu.epfl.ch/news/targeting-a-brain-mechanism-could-treat-aggression/

26. Contopoulos-Ioannidis, Despina. Ioannidis, John. Ntzani, Evangelia. 2003. "Translation of highly promising basic science research into clinical applications." *Am J Med,* N° 114: 477-484.
27. Crowley, William. 2003. "Translation of basic research into useful treatments: how often does it occur?" *Am J Med,* N° 114(6): 503-505.
28. https://www.legalmatch.com/law-library/article/silent-fraud-in-a-contract-claim.html
29. https://www.scientificamerican.com/article/bpa-lingers-in-human-body/
30. https://en.wikipedia.org/wiki/Bisphenol_A
31. https://ec.europa.eu/food/sites/food/files/safety/docs/scicom_scf_out12 8_en.pdf
32. Godfray, Charles. Jepson, Paul. Jobling, Susan. Johnson, Andrew. Matthiessen, Peter. McLean, Angela. Stephens, Andrea. Sumpter, John. Tyler, Charles. 2019. "A restatement of the natural science evidence base on the effects of endocrine disrupting chemicals on wildlife." *Proceedings of the Royal Society.* doi.org/10.1098/rspb.2018.2416.
33. https://en.wikipedia.org/wiki/Regulatory_capture
34. https://www.thelancet.com/series/endocrine-disrupting-chemicals
35. Menache, Andre and Nastrucci, Candida. 2012. "REACH, Animal Testing and the Precautionary Principle." *Medicolegal and Bioethics.* DOI:10.2147/MB.S33044.
36. https://en.wikipedia.org/wiki/Volkswagen_emissions_scandal
37. https://corporateeurope.org/en/food-and-agriculture/2018/03/what-monsanto-papers-tell-us- about-corporate-science
38. Toxicity Testing in the 21st century: a vision and a strategy. https://www.nap.edu/catalog/11970/toxicity-testing-in-the-21st-century-a-vision-and-a
39. https://publications.parliament.uk/pa/cm200405/cmselect/cmhealth/42/ 42.pdf
40. https://edm.parliament.uk/early-day-motion/56706/a-public-scientific-hearing-on-animal-experiments

CHAPTER FOURTEEN

RETHINKING THE SOCIAL ROLE OF RELIGIONS IN THE PLANETARY EMERGENCY: REFLECTIONS IN A CATHOLIC KEY

RICHARD W. MILLER

Introduction

Religious communities have an important role to play in addressing the global ecological crisis; for more than 80% of the global population identify with a religious group (Hackett and Grim 2012, 9).[1] Christianity is the world's largest religious community, making up nearly one-third of the global population with 2.3 billion adherents (Hackett and McClendon)[2] and around half of the global Christian population is Catholic (Pew 2013).[3] This paper will address the potential social role of the Catholic Church in addressing the planetary emergency. More specifically I will address the role of the Catholic community I know best; namely, the Catholic Church in the United States, which is larger than any other single religious institution in the United States, with over 17,000 parishes, and thousands of schools that serve a large and diverse population (Masci and Smith 2018).[4]

---

[1] Hackett, Conrad and Brian J. Grim. 2012. "The Global Religious Landscape: A Report on the Size and Distribution of the World's Major Religious Groups as of 2010." Pew-Templeton Global Religious Futures Project, December 2012. https://assets.pewresearch.org/wp-content/uploads/sites/11/2014/01/global-religion-full.pdf.

[2] Hackett, Conrad, and David McClendon. 2017. "Christians remain world's largest religious group, but they are declining in Europe." Pew Research Center, April 5, 2017. https://www.pewresearch.org/fact-tank/2017/04/05/christians-remain-worlds-largest-religious-group-but-they-are-declining-in-europe/ .

[3] Pew Research Center. 2013. "The Global Catholic Population." Feb. 13, 2103. https://www.pewforum.org/2013/02/13/the-global-catholic-population/ .

[4] Masci, David and Gregory A. Smith. 2018. "7 Facts about American Catholics," Oct. 10, 2018.

The United States is the world's largest economy, the dominant military, and financial global power and, the world's largest historical emitter of greenhouse gases. Without the United States moving from obstructing to leading on international climate efforts there is very little hope of meeting the 1.5° C target of the Paris Climate Agreement. Thus, the Catholic Church in the US as the largest single religious institution in the US has an outsized influence among religious communities in the world. While these reflections will operate within the Catholic tradition, they can serve as an analog for other Christian communions and potentially non-Christian religious communities to rethink their social role in this unprecedented situation.

Vatican II's Dogmatic Constitution on the Church (i.e., *Lumen Gentium)* gives equal weight to the sanctifying mission of the Church and its social mission: for it maintains that church is in Christ as a sacrament or instrumental sign of intimate union with God [sanctifying mission] and of the unity of all humanity [social mission] (*Vatican II* 1964, par. 1).[5] The social mission of the Church is not an addendum to faith but is essential to the practice of the faith. The social mission of the Church is grounded in the Christian scriptures first and greatest commandment "that love of God cannot be separated from love of neighbor" (Vatican II 1965, par. 24).[6] This love of neighbor includes both justice and charity. Justice is the duty to give what is due to each person (Pope Pius XI 1931, par. 125).[7] What is due each person are the goods from creation (Pope John Paul II 1987, par. 39)[8] and human hands that are necessary for their full flourishing in their immeasurable dignity as created in God's image. While in justice we are to

---

https://www.pewresearch.org/fact-tank/2018/10/10/7-facts-about-american-catholics/#:~:text=1%20There%20are%20roughly%2051,Center's%202014%20Re ligious%20Landscape%20Study .

[5] Vatican Council II. 1964. *Dogmatic constitution on the Church: lumen gentium/solemnly promulgated by His Holiness, Pope Paul VI on November 21,1964.*

[6] Vatican Council II. 1965. *Gaudium et Spes: Pastoral Constitution on the Church in the Modern World.* In *Catholic Social Thought: Encyclicals and Documents from Pope Leo XIII to Pope Francis.* 2016. edited by David J. O'Brien and Thomas A. Shannon. Maryknoll, (NY: Orbis Books. Kindle. 2016).

[7] Pope Pius XI. 1931. *Quadragesimo Anno: After Forty Years.* In *Catholic Social Thought: Encyclicals and Documents from Pope Leo XIII to Pope Francis.* 2016. edited by David J. O'Brien and Thomas A. Shannon. (Maryknoll, NY: Orbis Books. Kindle, 2016).

[8] This theme of the good of creation being meant for all people runs through all Catholic Social Teaching. One example is from John Paul II. 1987. *Sollicitudo Rei Socialis: On Social Concern.*

give what is due to each person, in charity the person is united to her neighbor and God in one act empowered by God's grace. Thus, charity is "the bond of perfection (Col 3:14)" (*Pope Pius XI 1931*, par. 137). This union of hearts and minds is the ultimate goal of God's activity as implied in Jesus's prayer to the Father in John 17:21-22, "that all may be one . . . as we are one" (Vatican II 1965, par. 24). The human being "cannot fully find himself except through a sincere gift of himself," (Vatican II 1965, par. 24) and in this sincere gift of self, there is "a certain likeness between the union of divine Persons, and in the union of God's sons in truth and charity" (Vatican II 1965, par. 24). The act of charity that unites human beings, however, can be undermined by structures and systems that degrade human dignity, especially of those who are poor and marginalized. If one looks away from systems and structures that degrade other human beings the unitive character of one's charity is imperfect and incomplete. These systems that marginalize and divide human beings are antagonistic to the unitive act of charity. Thus, 'social structures can put obstacles in place for the conversion of hearts and the ideal of charity.' (Synod of Bishops 1971, Ch. 1).[9] When one is not given their due in justice and conditions are not created for the possibility of their flourishing then the ends of charity cannot be realized. For, "charity cannot take the place of justice unfairly withheld" (Pope Pius XI 1931, par. 137). On the other hand, while "justice alone ... can remove . . . the cause of social strife . . . [it] can never bring about a union of hearts and minds" (Pope Pius XI 1931, par. 137). And it is this charity "that is the main principle of stability in all institutions . . . which aim at establishing social peace and promoting mutual aid" (Pope Pius XI 1931, par. 137). Thus, "as all men follow justice and unite in charity, created goods should abound for them on a reasonable basis" (Pope Paul VI 1967, par. 22).[10] Charity informs and builds upon justice, but it is not "the task of charity to make amends for the open violation of justice" (Pope Pius XI 1931, 4). In this outline of the relation of charity and justice it is clear that justice is constitutive of Christian life. As stated by the 1971 Synod of Bishops, "Action on behalf of justice and participation in the transformation of the world fully appear to us as a constitutive dimension of the preaching

---

[9] Synod of Bishops. 1971. *Justice in the World*. In *Catholic Social Thought: Encyclicals and Documents from Pope Leo XIII to Pope Francis*. 2016. edited by David J. O'Brien and Thomas A. Shannon. (Maryknoll, NY: Orbis Books. Kindle, 2016).

[10] Pope Paul VI. 1967. *Populorum Progressio: Encyclical of Pope Paul VI on the development of peoples*. In *Catholic Social Thought: Encyclicals and Documents from Pope Leo XIII to Pope Francis*. 2016. edited by David J. O'Brien and Thomas A. Shannon. (Maryknoll, NY: Orbis Books. Kindle, 2016).

of the Gospel, or, in other words, of the Church's mission for the redemption of the human race and its liberation from every oppressive situation" (Synod of Bishops 1971, Introduction). Such transformation of the world is foremost a matter of social justice, which "concerns the social, political, and economic aspects and, above all, the structural dimension of problems and their respective solutions" (USCCB 2005, par. 201).[11]

The social mission of the Church has been developed and articulated in the modern era in the body of documents known as Modern Catholic Social teaching, which began with Leo XIII's 1891 Encyclical *Rerum Novarum* addressing the exploitation of workers in the midst of the Industrial Revolution. Over the next century and a quarter Popes and a Council (i.e., Vatican II) published Encyclicals and Constitutions addressing contemporary problems in the context of the gospel. Catholic Social Teaching draws upon the Christian scriptures, the tradition of Christian writings on Christian living and social life, natural law, and social analysis. In the tumultuous period of the last hundred and thirty years a host of themes have emerged that serve as principals for a just society: human dignity, solidarity/common good/participation, family life, subsidiarity and the proper role of government, the dignity of work and the rights of workers, private property, and the universal destination of all goods, the preferential option for the poor, colonialism, and economic development for the poorest countries of the world, and peace, and disarmament. This paper will not, in this limited space, develop each one of these principles and apply each one to the ecological crisis (this is implicitly accomplished in the Encyclical *Laudato Sí*). It will address the problem in a more general way focusing on concrete proposals for churches grounded in the latest scientific work and sensitive to the current political and cultural situation. More precisely, it will follow the "see-judge-act" model of Catholic social action.[12] This tripartite method for applying CST principles to concrete situations is first to know the problem (see), second to determine what should be done in light of Catholic Social Teaching (judge), and third, to decide the best ways to concretely work for the good determined through the moment of judgment (act) (Pope John XXIII, par. 236). This paper will adopt this model in its reflection upon the potential social role of the Catholic Church in the ecological crisis by first outlining the current problem through the Planetary Boundaries

---

[11] Pontifical Council of Justice and Peace. 2005. *Compendium of the Social Doctrine of the Church.* Washington, D.C.: United States Catholic Conference of Bishops.
[12] Pope John XXIII. 1961. *Mater et Magistra: Encyclical of Pope John XXII on Christianity and Social Progress.* In *Catholic Social Thought: Encyclicals and Documents from Pope Leo XIII to Pope Francis.* 2016. edited by David J. O'Brien and Thomas A. Shannon. (Maryknoll, NY: Orbis Books. Kindle, 2016).

Framework. The Planetary Boundary framework is particularly helpful for this threefold process because it allows us to distinguish and prioritize the multitude of ecological problems so that the Church can engage the problem in line with the latest scientific findings.

Knowing the Truth of our Situation: From Environmentalism to Earth System Boundaries (Seeing)

Environmentalism (broadly defined as seeking "peaceful coexistence with, rather than mastery of, nature" (McNeil 2000, chap. 11)[13] emerged as an international phenomenon in the 1970's in the wake of the publication of Rachel Carson's *Silent Spring* (1962) with its criticism of the extensive use of pesticides (McNeil, 5080) Prior to this time there were concerns for conservation of land, wilderness, pollution and resource exhaustion "but the audience was small and the practical results few." (McNeil, chap. 11) The public concern for the environment in the 1970's was primarily centered around toxic pollution and questions of a safe environment were often understood in local or regional terms. In our times, these concerns were often translated by communities, into a host of actionable items from recycling projects, trash and street clean-up programs, composting, organic community gardens, and banning plastic items like bottles and bags. "Going green" has taken on a plethora of meanings such that it is important to distinguish and prioritize a community's efforts.

Since the 1970s scientific assessments have moved from questions of a healthy environment to questions of a "safe operating space for humanity" in the context of transgressing planetary boundaries. Human beings, then, must no longer understand themselves simply as agents who can and do pollute the air, rivers, oceans, and land with toxic chemicals that disrupt ecosystems and in turn harm themselves and their fellow human beings. They must understand themselves as agents who can and are destabilizing planetary systems. It is for this reason that the International Commission on Stratigraphy is now going through a formal process of deciding whether human beings have pushed the earth system out of the Holocene, the geological epoch in which civilization emerged and developed, to a new era, the Anthropocene. The concept 'Anthropocene' is not primarily about the expansion of human impacts on ecosystems, and the environment or human

---

[13] McNeill, J. R. 2000. *Something New Under the Sun: An Environmental History of the Twentieth-Century World.* (New York: W.W. Norton & Company. Kindle, 2000).

beings dominating the natural world, as it is sometimes wrongly understood. It is about human beings destabilizing the earth system such that the earth system, through interlinked processes, will move to a new state less hospitable to human life and civilization.

In 2009 the Planetary Boundaries framework was introduced by twenty-six leading scientists in in a highly influential paper, "Planetary Boundaries: Exploring the Safe Operating Space for Humanity."[14] This framework is being employed throughout the earth science community with an updated paper in 2015.[15] The Planetary Boundaries Working Group identified nine interlinked "biophysical processes that regulate the stability of the Earth system" (Steffen et al 2015, 1259855-9). According to Rockström et al, "Transgressing one or more planetary boundaries may be deleterious or even catastrophic due to the risk of crossing thresholds that will trigger non-linear, abrupt environmental change within continental-to planetary-scale systems" (Rockström et al 2009, 1). The nine interlinked biophysical processes are climate change, change in biosphere integrity (i.e. measured in terms of species extinction), stratospheric ozone depletion, ocean acidification (shift in ocean chemistry due to the ocean absorbing (CO_2), biogeochemical flows (nitrogen and phosphorus used in fertilizing), land system change, freshwater use, atmospheric aerosol loading (airborne fine particulate pollution) and introduction of novel entities (toxic chemicals, plastics, etc.).[16] In this framework climate change and biosphere integrity are considered "core" boundaries that provide "the planetary-level overarching systems within which the other boundary processes operate" such that "large changes in the climate or in biosphere integrity would likely, on their own, push the Earth System out of the Holocene state" (Steffen et al 2015, 1259855-8).

Climate change, the first boundary, is the most pressing boundary; for the human community must immediately initiate unprecedented reductions in greenhouse gas emissions to avoid locking in cascading impacts that will profoundly affect all of the other boundaries. While climate literacy has increased over the past fifteen years and has arguably received more public

---

[14] Rockström, Johan, Will Steffen, Kevin Noone, Åsa Persson, F. Stuart III Chapin, Eric Lambin, Timothy M. Lenton, et al. 2009. "Planetary Boundaries: Exploring the Safe Operating Space for Humanity." *Ecology and Society* 14 (2): 32, DOI: 10.5751/ES-03180-140232.

[15] Steffen Will, Katherine Richardson, Johan Rockström, Sarah E. Cornell, Ingo Fetzer, Elena M. Bennett, Reinette Biggs, et al. 2015. *Science*, vol. 347, issue 6223: 1259855-1–1259855-10. DOI: 10.1126/science.1259855 .

[16] All of these boundaries are significant but the explication of them including the myriad ways they interact and amplify each other is beyond the scope of this paper.

attention than the other boundaries, the ways communities go green do not often correspond to the challenge of climate change. Often, this is the case because people are unaware of the severity of the risks. The reviews of the scientific literature published by the Intergovernmental Panel on Climate Change are probably the most peer reviewed scientific documents in human history. This is a great achievement that must be applauded. Nevertheless, it is well known that these reviews of the literature are very conservative in their treatment of the science. They present the least common denominator consensus of the several thousand reviewers of the science. When ethics is injected in this situation, it becomes clear that informing the public about climate change will require going beyond the IPCC to avoid violating the norms of procedural justice. Procedural justice in reference to climate change means that those who are being subjected to the risk of climate destabilization must be fully informed of those risks and must consent to those risks. Thus, procedural justice requires that in the interface between science and the public one must supplement the IPCC reports, especially the *Summary for Policy Makers*, with other credible scientific research that highlights lower probability but much more severe risks for the human community. In what follows, I will, in line with procedural justice, present a host of these risks with a particular focus on their implications for the human community.[17]

Six glaciers on the West Antarctica ice sheet are now in a phase of unstoppable melt that will lead to a sea level rise of 1.2 meters (4 feet). This will inundate land that is currently home to 204 million people.[18] This level of sea level rise (4 feet) also condemns much of the rice growing regions of Asia to destruction, including 50 percent of the rice fields in Bangladesh (home to 160 million people with projections of 250 million by 2050) and more than half of those in Vietnam (the world's second largest rice exporter) (Brown 2009, 7).[19] The unstoppable melt from West Antarctica will also "likely trigger the collapse of the rest of the West Antarctic ice sheet, which

---

[17] This is not meant to deny that the natural world has an intrinsic value. Maintaining a safe operating space for humanity involves preserving the natural world. With the limited space of this essay, I will, however, simply focus on the effects for the human community.

[18] Kulp, Scott A and Benjamin H. Strauss. 2019. "New elevation data triple estimates of global vulnerability to sea-level rise and coastal flooding." *Nature Communications* 10, 4844: 1-11. Calculation is based on conclusion from this study that the land of 1.7 million habitants will be threatened per vertical centimeter of sea level rise (see p. 3).

[19] Brown, Lester R. 2009. *Plan B 4.0: Mobilizing to Save Civilization.* (New York: Norton, 2009)

comes with a sea level rise of between three and five meters [10 feet in some locations and 16 feet in other locations]." (Rignot 2014, *Guardian*).[20] While Rignot states conservatively that this collapse could take centuries, a recent study on ice mass loss on Antarctica shows that the melt rate on Antarctica, mostly from West Antarctica, has tripled over the past decade.[21] In addition, the rate of ice mass loss from the Greenland ice sheet is thirteen times greater in the period 2012-2017 than the period 1992-1997.[22] It is too early to see if this trend will continue; yet, Dr. James Hansen has argued that three to four feet of sea level rise is possible, on our current path, around 2065 with 5 meters (16.5 feet) a possibility by the end of the century (Hansen et al 2016, figure 5, 3767).[23] Richard Alley, another leading climate scientist holds that 15 to 20 feet of sea level rise is possible this century (Alley, 2018).[24] A five meter (16.5 feet) would likely lead to 850 million climate migrants, while a six meter (~20 feet) will lead to over a billion migrants (Kulp and Strauss 2019, 3). Saltwater incursions of groundwater and storm surges will start to put coastal inhabitants under siege long before reaching a meter of sea level rise. Indeed, it is estimated that over 800 million people

[20] Eric Rignot, "Global warming: it's a point of no return in West Antarctica. What happens next?" *Guardian*, May 17, 2014. See relevant studies - Rignot, E, E, J. J. Mouginot, M. Morlighem, H. Seroussi, B. Scheuchl. 2014. "Widespread, rapid grounding line retreat of Pine Island, Thwaites, Smith, and Kohler glaciers, West Antarctica, from 1992 to 2011." *Geophysical Research Letters* 41 (10): 3502-3509. https://doi.org/10.1002/2014GL060140; Joughlin Ian, Benjamin E. Smith, Brooke Medley. 2014. "Marine Ice Sheet Collapse Potentially Under Way for the Thwaites Glacier Basin, West Antarctica." *Science* 344 (6185): 735-738. DOI: 10.1126/science.1249055.
[21] Shepherd Andrew, Erik Ivins, Eric Rignot, Ben Smith, Michiel van den Broeke, Isabella Velicogna, Pippa Whitehouse, et al. 2018. "Mass balance of the Antarctic Ice Sheet from 1992 to 2017." *Nature* 558, 219–222. https://doi.org/10.1038/s41586-018-0179-y
[22] Shepherd Andrew, Erik Ivins, Eric Rignot, Ben Smith, Michiel van den Broeke, Isabella Velicogna, Pippa Whitehouse, et al. 2020. "Mass balance of the Greenland Ice Sheet from 1992 to 2018." *Nature* 579, 233-239. https://doi.org/10.1038/s41586-019-1855-2
[23] Hansen James, Makiko Sato, Paul Hearty, Reto Ruedy, Maxwell Kelley, Valerie Masson-Delmotte, Gary Russel et al. 2016. "Ice melt, sea level rise and superstorms: evidence from paleoclimate data, climate modeling, and modern observations that 2°C global warming could be dangerous." *Atmospheric Chemistry and Physics Discussions*, 16: 3761–3812. https://doi.org/10.5194/acp-16-3761-2016 .
[24] Alley, Richard. 2018, "National Climate Seminar, Bard Center for Environmental Policy: Interview with Eban Goodstein." Sept. 19, 2018. Audio, 00:15. https://vimeo.com/292991175

living in more than 570 coastal cities will be at risk of coastal flooding from only a half a meter (1.6 feet) of sea level rise" (UCCRN 2018, 47).[25]

Large scale movements of people, which create conditions for conflict, will not only occur from sea level rise, but also by a host of other factors, including heat stress and drought. While ice sheet dynamics play out over longer time periods, heat stress and drought are happening now, and pose a threat to civilization within decades. Researchers have shown that "around 30% of the world's population is currently exposed to climatic conditions exceeding this deadly threshold [heat threshold combining surface air temperature and relative humidity] for at least 20 days a year" (Mora 2017, 501).[26] Furthermore, if the world does not move rapidly off its current path and short-term feedbacks are strong the world could be 4°C warmer, relative to preindustrial temperatures, by 2060 (Betts 2011, 67).[27] In a world 4 °C warmer than preindustrial temperatures, "47% of the land area, and almost 74% of the world population would be subjected to deadly heat, which could pose existential risks to humans and mammals alike." (Xu and Ramanathan 2017, 10319).[28]

The transition to a more arid climate in the US Southwest and northern Mexico might already be under way (Seager et al 2007, 1181)[29] and as we continue on our present path there is an increasing likelihood of mega-

---

[25] Urban Climate Change Research Network (UCCRN). 2018. *The Future We Don't Want: How Climate Change Could Impact the World's Greatest Cities.* 1-59. https://www.c40knowledgehub.org/s/article/The-future-we-don-t-want-How-climate-change-could-impact-the-world-s-greatest-cities?language=en_US

[26] Mora, Camilo., Benedicte Dousset, Iain R. Caldwell, Farrah E. Powerll, Rollan C. Geronimo, Coral R. Bielecki, Chelsie W.W. Counsell, et al. 2017. "Global risk of deadly heat." *Nature Climate Change* 7: 501–506. https://doi.org/10.1038/nclimate3322

[27] Betts, Richard A., Matthew Collins, Deborah L. Hemming, Christ D. Jones, Jason A. Lowe, and Michael G. Sanderson. 2011. "When Could Global Warming Reach 4°C?" *Philosophical Transactions: Mathematical, Physical and Engineering Sciences*, vol. 369, no. 1934: 67–84: https://doi.org/10.1098/rsta.2010.0292

[28] Xu, Yangyang and Veerabhadran Ramanathan. "Well below 2 °C: Mitigation strategies for avoiding dangerous to catastrophic climate changes." *Proceedings of the National Academy of Sciences* Sep 2017, 114 (39): 10315-10323. DOI: 10.1073/pnas.1618481114

[29] Seager, Richard., Mingfang Ting, Isaac Held, Yochanan Kushmir, Jian Lu, Gabriel Vecchi, Huei-Ping Hua. 2007. "Model Projections of an Imminent Transition to a More Arid Climate in Southwestern North America." *Science* vol. 316, issue 5828 (May 25): 1181-1184. DOI: 10.1126/science.1139601.

droughts (Cook et al 2015, 6),[30] the kind that led to the destruction of past civilizations. The drought in Darfur was a factor in creating conditions for the conflict that lead to nearly 300,000 deaths from malnutrition, disease, and conflict. The most intense drought in the history of Syria, made two to three times more likely because of climate change (Kelly et al 2015, 3241),[31] led to mass migrations of farmers into the cities contributing to the destabilizing of Syria, its descent into civil war, the migration of 5.6 million Syrians into Europe, and neighboring countries contributing to the rise of right-wing ultranationalist parties across Europe. If several million refugees can be a destabilizing force in Europe, how will the human community hold civilization together with even a fraction of the worst-case scenario of 1.4 billion refugees by 2060? (Geisler and Currens 2017, 323).[32] The negative effects will escalate post 2100, indeed, "decisions occurring over the next decade or two could significantly influence the trajectory of the Earth System for tens to hundreds of thousands of years and potentially lead to conditions that resemble planetary states that were last seen several millions of years ago, conditions that would be inhospitable to current human societies and to many other contemporary species." (Steffen et al 2018, 8253).[33]

The 1° C (350 ppm) "safe operating space" of the Planetary Boundary's group is probably now in the rearview mirror. Currently, according to a recent commentary by some of the world's leading climate scientists "the Earth System is on a Hothouse Earth pathway driven by human emissions of greenhouse gases and biosphere degradation" (Steffen et al 2018, 8254). Likely the best we can do now is move onto an emergency footing to hold to a 1.5° C world, which will require, according to the IPCC Special Report on 1.5°C, "a rapid phase out of CO_2 emissions and deep emissions

---

[30] Cook, Benjamin., Toby R. Ault, Jason Smerdon. 2015. "Unprecedented 21st century drought risk in the American Southwest and Central Plains." vol. 1 no. 1 (Feb 12): 1-7.

[31] Kelley, Colin P., Shahrzad Mohtadi, Mark A. Cane, Richard Seager, Yochanan Kushnir. 2015. "Climate change in the Fertile Crescent and implications of the recent Syrian drought." *Proceedings of the National Academy of Sciences*, 112, 11 (March): 3241–3246.

[32] Geisler, Charles., Ben Currens. 2017. "Impediments to inland resettlement under conditions of accelerated sea level rise," Land use policy 66: 322-330. https://doi.org/10.1016/j.landusepol.2017.03.029

[33] Steffen, Will., Johan Rockström, Katherine Richardson, Timothy M. Lenton, Carle Folke, Diana Liverman, Colin P. Summerhayes et al. 2018. "Trajectories of the Earth System in the Anthropocene." *PNAS* vol. 15 no. 33: 8252-8259.

reductions in other GHGs and climate forcers" (Rojeli et al 2018,112).[34] This rapid phase out of CO_2 involves "global net anthropogenic CO_2 emissions decline by about 45% from 2010 levels by 2030 (40 to 60% interquartile range) reaching net zero around 2050 (2045-2055 interquartile range)" (Rojeli et al 2018, 95). To put the scale of this challenge in context, it should be noted that in 2020 the global economic slowdown in response to the COVID 19 pandemic led to a 12.9% decline in US emissions and a 6.4% decline in global emissions. The global community will have to make similar reductions year in and year out to achieve total decarbonization of the global economic system by 2050. According to the MIT C-Roads 1.5°C emissions pathway, all developed countries must peak emissions by 2025 and then reduce steadily at 10% per year; while all developing countries will have to peak no later than 2030 and then reduce steadily at 8% per year. It is important to recognize that the 50% reduction of emissions by 2030 is an absolute target. There is no wiggle room; for even with such large reductions, the 1.5°C goal will require pulling a great deal of CO_2 out of the atmosphere. The most prominent approach is to deploy bioenergy combined with carbon capture and sequestration (BECCS) that involves planting fast growing biomass covering 1 to 2 times the land area of India and burning that biomass for power while capturing the carbon and burying it indefinitely (Anderson and Peters 2016, 183).[35]

A recent commentary, by some of the world's leading climate scientists, highlights the fact that the two IPCC special reports in 2018 argued that we might already be in the range (i.e. 1° to 2° C rise in temperatures above preindustrial averages) to initiate tipping points to push us into a warmer world.[36] Furthermore, "even if the Paris Accord target of a 1.5°C to 2.0°C

---

[34] Rogelj, J., D. Shindell, K. Jiang, S. Fifita, P. Forster, V. Ginzburg, C. Handa, et al. 2018. "Mitigation Pathways Compatible with 1.5° C in the Context of Sustainable Development." In *Global Warming of 1.5°C. An IPCC Special Report on the impacts of global warming of 1.5°C above pre-industrial levels and related global greenhouse gas emission pathways, in the context of strengthening the global response to the threat of climate change, sustainable development, and efforts to eradicate poverty.* edited by Masson-Delmotte, V., P. Zhai, H.-O. Pörtner, D. Roberts, J. Skea, P. R. Shukla, A. Pirani, W. Moufouma-Okia, C. Péan, R. Pidcock, S. Connors, J. B. R. Matthews, Y. Chen, X. Zhou, M.I. Gomis, E. Lonnoy, T. Maycock, M. Tignor, and T. Waterfield. In Press: 93-174.

[35] Anderson, Kevin and Glenn Peters. 2016. "The Trouble with Negative Emissions." *Science* vol. 354, issue 6309: 182-183. DOI: 10.1126/science.aah4567.

[36] Lenton, Timothy M., Johan Rockström, Owern Gaffney, Stefan Rahmstorf, Katherine Richardson, Will Steffen & Hans Joachim Schellnhuber. 2019. "Climate tipping points—too risky to bet against." *Nature* vol. 575: 592-595. https://doi.org/10.1038/d41586-019-03595-0

rise in temperature is met, we cannot exclude the risk that a cascade of feedbacks could push the Earth System irreversibly onto a "Hothouse Earth pathway" (Steffen et al 2018, 8254). A 'hothouse earth' is an earth that was last seen in the Mid-Miocene (15-17 million years ago) when temperatures were 4.0° to 5.0° C warmer than preindustrial temperatures (Steffen et al 2018, 8253). The authors state, "If damaging tipping cascades can occur and a global tipping point cannot be ruled out, then this is an existential threat to civilization." (Lenton et al 2019, 595). What does this existential threat to civilization mean? It likely means the unspeakable mass death of human populations, not to mention the mass extinction of species. The United Nations projects that the population will "reach 8.6 billion in 2030, 9.8 billion in 2050 and 11.2 billion in 2100." (UN Department of Economic & Social Affairs 2017).[37] At 4.0°- 5.0° C the carrying capacity of planet could be reduced to between a half a billion and a billion people. This is the view of two directors of leading climate institutes. Hans Joachim Schellnhuber, who is the director of the Potsdam Institute for Climate Impact Research in Germany has argued that at 5 ° C the planet could only carry around a billion people (Schellnhuber 2009)[38] and Kevin Anderson, former Director of the Tyndall Centre for Climate Research in England, has maintained that at "4C, 5C or 6C, you might have half a billion people surviving" (Fyall, 2009).[39] It is for these reasons, and others, that 11,000 scientists signed onto a published article describing climate change as an emergency. (Ripple et al 2020, 1).[40]

---

[37] United Nations Department of Economic and Social Affairs. 2017."World population projected to reach 9.8 billion in 2050, and 11.2 billion in 2100." https://www.un.org/development/desa/en/news/population/world-population-prospects-2017.html

[38] Schellnhuber, Hans Joachim. 2009. "The MAD Challenge: Towards a Great Land-Use Transformation?" Plenary Session *Climate Change: Global Risks, Challenges & Decisions.*" March 12. The talk is no longer available online. See reporting on the talk by Kanter, James. 2009. "Warming Could Cut Population to 1 Billion." *New York Times*, March 13, 2009.
 https://dotearth.blogs.nytimes.com/2009/03/13/scientist-warming-could-cut-population-to-1-billion/

[39] Fyall, Jenny. 2009. "Warming will 'wipe out billions." *Scotsman*, November 29, 2009.

[40] Ripple, William J., Christopher Wolf, Thomas M. Newsome, Phoebe Barnard, William R. Moomaw. 2020. "World Scientists' Warning of a Climate Emergency." *BioScience,* vol. 70 issue 1, Jan: 8-12.

The Social Mission of the Catholic Church and the Climate Emergency (Judging)

The Planetary boundaries framework is being employed here because it is a cutting-edge influential framework developed by some of the world's leading earth scientists that allows us to distinguish and prioritize ecological problems with a clear sense of the scale of the problem so that individuals, institutions, and communities can effectively engage in the transformation necessary to reduce the degree of overshoot of these boundaries. Many of the sustainability efforts in local communities, touch upon planetary boundaries: reducing the use of plastics through ban the bottle campaigns (novel entities boundary), rain gardens to filter water run off before it enters the local stream (fresh water and biosphere integrity boundaries), paper recycling (land use and climate change boundaries), tree planting (climate change), and energy reduction efforts (climate change and novel entities boundaries). In light of the scale of transformation and the timetables necessary to avoid irreversible catastrophic effects such local efforts are insufficient. In addition, many of the efforts do not sufficiently address the core boundary of climate change in a manner that is in line with the immediate necessity for unprecedented greenhouse reductions.

The scale of the problem undercuts beliefs and assumptions that undergird many of the sustainability efforts of religious communities. The terrible truth of these numbers undercuts the belief (a dangerous belief) that social transformation to avoid catastrophic ecological impacts will be achieved by reducing emissions in a particular parish or diocese. In this unprecedented emergency all institutions, including religious communities on the local, national, and international level must be open to thinking and acting in unprecedented ways. In light of the fact that we are in a situation in which the business model of many of the world's largest corporations is in direct conflict with the climactic conditions in which human civilization (and most species) emerged, Bill McKibben's organization, 350.org, launched a divestment campaign in 2011. This campaign has led to the drawing of clear moral boundaries on profiting from fossil fuels and has forced leaders of institutions, universities, and some religious communities to have to publicly justify profiting from fossil fuel companies that are a threat to civilization. This campaign has forced into the public sphere the fundamental contradiction of an economy fueled by fossil fuels. The fossil fuel divestment movement has not only brought into relief the ethical implications of profiting from fossil fuels, but has also raised the financial argument that investing in fossil fuels is a very risky business because the stock valuations of the world's largest fossil fuel companies are dependent upon the assumption that they will burn all of their reserves (Leaton 2011).[41] If those reserves are not burned, then fossil fuel company stocks would be left with stranded assets and their stock prices would plummet. While the divestment campaign's call to divest from multi-national companies on moral grounds has significantly broadened the horizon of concern of many institutions, it is still not direct engagement in politics. It is an argument for the moral integrity of the institution. In addition, even though the movement has been crucial for awakening the moral implications of the climate crisis and Shell oil stated in 2018 that it represented a material risk to its business, it has not had a demonstrable effect reducing global CO_2 emissions or inflicting significant economic damage on fossil fuel companies.[42]

While the divestment campaign has been important in drawing ethical lines concerning the climate emergency, it is an insufficient social response. What is needed is direct engagement in public life. Directly engaging in public life requires a fuller recognition of the social character of churches and the responsibilities this conveys upon them. In his work analyzing political power, Gene Sharp, the influential theorist of political power, maintains that "the most important single quality of any government, without which it would not exist, must be the obedience and submission of its subjects. Obedience is at the heart of political power." (Sharp 1973, 16).[43] For Sharp, the weakening of a particular oppressive ruling regime or system requires that citizens work to transform those institutions in society that act as pillars of support for the system.[44] According to Sharp, "pillars of support are institutions and sectors of the society that supply a regime (or any other group that exercises power) with the needed sources of power to maintain

---

[41] An "analysis by McKinsey and the Carbon Trust demonstrates that greater than 50% of the value of an oil and gas company resides in the value of cash flows to be generated in year 11 onwards." Leaton, James. 2011. "Unburnable Carbon - Are the World's Financial Markets Carrying a Carbon Bubble?" *Carbon Tracker Initiative,* July 3: 19. https://carbontracker.org/reports/carbon-bubble/

[42] Hansen, Tyler & Robert Pollin. 2020. "Economics and climate justice activism: assessing the financial impact of the fossil fuel divestment movement." *Review of Social Economy*, July 3: DOI: 10.1080/00346764.2020.1785539.

[43] Sharp, Gene. 1973. *The Politics of Nonviolent Action.* (Boston: Porter Sargent, 1973) 16.

[44] While Sharp's theory of power with its division of power between rulers and subjects is not adequate to the full complexity of political life in our system, his understanding of power remains an instructive heuristic for informing one's analysis of power in a particular political system. See Martin, Brian. 1989. "Gene Sharp's Theory of Power." *Journal of Peace Research*, vol. 26, no. 2, 213-222.

and expand its power capacity."[45] Pillars of support include, but are not limited to religious communities, universities, media, commercial institutions, and non-profit organizations. Religions in the US context are pillars of society by the fact that 76% of US residents identify as affiliated with a religious tradition (Jones and Cox, 2017).[46] Religious Communities are inherently social and political institutions and our political system in regards to climate change is permeated by profound distortions and structural evil that will inflict harm on timescales of millennia to millions of years (when we take into account that it takes millions of years for biodiversity to recover after mass extinction events). In the context of grave structural evil, religious communities are socially and politically never neutral. They are not neutral institutions simply providing spiritual nourishment for their communities. Since they are inherently social and political, religious communities will either reinforce or work to transform the social and political systems in which they are imbedded. When the religious communities do not challenge those structures as a religious community, not simply particular members of the community, the religious community inevitably reinforces the system. In terms of climate change and the other planetary boundaries, and arguably other structural evils, the silence of religious communities tacitly supports a radical evil structure that systematically distorts the truth.

"Giving Witness to the Truth"

Religious Communities, and here I am speaking particularly as a Catholic with the Catholic emphasis on "scrutinizing the signs of the times" (Pope Paul VI 1965, par. 4) so that the work of Christ, "to give witness to the truth" (Pope Paul VI 1965, par. 3), is advanced by the Church. Scrutinizing the signs of the times requires coming to the truth of the present historical reality. "Liberal culture," according to Dean Brackley S.J., "portrays the search for truth as a relatively simple task of pushing back the frontiers of ignorance" (Brackley 1992, 9).[47] We, however, "always find ourselves surrounded and assaulted, even drugged, by lies and distortions about the world we live in. Each of us and all of us necessarily put our world

---

[45] Sharp, Gene. 2005. *Waging Nonviolent Struggle: 20th Century Practice and 21st Century Potential.* (Boston: Porter Sargent Publishers, 2005) 451.
[46] Jones, Robert P., and Daniel Cox. "America's Changing Religious Identity." PRRI. 2017. https://www.prri.org/research/american-religious-landscape-christian-religiously-unaffiliated/
[47] Brackley, S. J., Dean. 1992. "Christian University and Liberation: The Challenge of the UCA." *Discovery: Jesuit International Ministries*, no. 2 (December): 1-17.

together in a way that both reveals truth and at the same time distorts it."
(Brackley 1992, 9). And this distortion "has both personal and institutional
dimensions. . . Although not always conscious and malicious, distortion is
hardly capricious. It serves particular interests and institutions. It systematically
masks social reality, especially in the interests of the powerful. The search for
truth, therefore, is a conflictual struggle to overcome conscious lies and less-
than-conscious distortions." (Brackley 1992, 9). In pursuit of the truth and
to give witness to the truth, religious believers "cannot afford to ignore the
pervasive, massive reality of distortion." (Brackley 1992, 9).

The systematic distortion of the truth of climate change has occurred,
most especially in the United States, but also to a lesser degree in the UK
(Painter 2011)[48] and Australia (McKnight 2010).[49] Here I will focus on the
United States. In the late 1970's and 1980's as family-owned newspapers
were purchased by large corporations, which were traded on Wall Street,
science journalism began to be slashed to cut costs and increase profits to
meet the insatiable earning expectations of Wall Street. The quality of
science journalism began to decline and continues to decline (McChesney
and Nichols 2010, 25).[50] In addition, while the prestige press in the United
States, in the late 1980's, reported on the emerging scientific consensus
regarding the reality of climate change and the need for immediate
mandatory action (Boykoff & Boykoff 2004), by the 1990's, the press,
following the journalistic norm of balance, gave equal space to scientific
consensus reports by specialists and the contrarian views of a small group
of scientist many of whom were not climate scientists[51] and were affiliated

---

[48] James Painter. 2011. *Poles Apart: The International Reporting on Climate
Scepticism*. Oxford: Oxford University Reuters Institute for the Study of Journalism.
In Painters study of a selection of international print media from Brazil, China,
France, India, UK, and the US he discovered that there were many more skeptical
voices in print media in the UK and the US than in these other countries.
[49] Australia also has a host of skeptical voices. The power and influence of Rupert
Murdoch's News Corporation in the US, UK and Australia is a central contributing
factor to the skepticism in these countries. See McKnight, David. (2010). "Rupert
Murdoch's News Corporation: A Media Institution with a Mission." *Historical
Journal of Film, Radio and Television,* 30:3 (August 23): 303-316, DOI:
10.1080/01439685.2010.505021.
[50] McChesney, Robert and John Nichols. 2010. *The Death and Life of American
Journalism: The Media Revolution that Will Begin the World Again.* (New York:
Nation Books, 2010)
[51] Boykoff, Maxwell T. and Jules M. Boykoff. 2004. "Balance as bias: global
warming and the US prestige press," *Global Environmental Change* 14: 129-133.

with conservative think tanks.[52] The juxtaposition of the two sides created the impression that there was a persistent debate in the scientific community as to whether it was warming and whether human beings were the cause of that warming. This nominally balanced view has sown confusion for decades among the general public about the reality, timing, and magnitude of the climate problem.

This failure is a failure among the journalistic ecosystem that operates according to the standards of professional journalism. There, however, has emerged over the past several decades, originating with Rush Limbaugh on talk radio and FOX news on television, an asymmetry in media in the US such that "there is no left-right division, but rather a division between the right and the rest of the media ecosystem" (Benkler et al 2018, 74).[53] The right wing operates as an echo-chamber with a "propaganda feedback loop" (Benkler et al 2018, 79) that exhibits "high insularity, susceptibility to information cascades, rumor, and conspiracy theory, and drift toward more extreme versions of itself" (Benkler et al 2018, 73-74), while "the rest of the media ecosystem....adhere[s] to professional journalistic norms" (Benkler et al 2018, 74). This right-wing media ecosystem "creates positive feedbacks for bias-confirming statements as a central feature of its normal operation" (Benkler et al 2018, 74). Politicians on the right then are not constrained by a media who factchecks their public statements but must be careful to align themselves with the narrative running through the echo chamber.[54]

---

[52] Among the vast literature on this topic, see Oreskes, Naomi and Eric Conway. 2011. *Merchants of Doubt: How a Handful of Scientists Obscured the Truth on Issues from Tobacco Smoke to Global Warming.* (New York: Bloomsbury Press. Jacques, Peter J. 2008). "The organization of denial: conservative think tanks and environmental skepticism." *Environmental Politics* 17:3, 349-385.

[53] Benkler, Yochai., Robert Faris, Hal Roberts. 2018. *Network Propaganda: Manipulation, Disinformation, and Radicalization in American Politics.* (Oxford: Oxford University Press, 2018) 74. See also Hacker, Jacob S. & Paul Pierson. 2015. "Confronting Asymmetric Polarization" in *Solutions to Political Polarization in America*, edited Nathaniel Persily, 59-70. (Cambridge: Cambridge University Press, 2015).

[54] This is why, despite the statements of top election officials across the country, from both parties, arguing that there was no evidence of systematic fraud in the 2020 Presidential election (see Corasaniti, Nick., Reid J. Epstein, Jim Rutenberg. 2020. "The Times Called Officials in Every State: No Evidence of Voter Fraud." *The New York Times*, Nov. 10, 2020) only 24% of Republicans think the results of the election are accurate (see Montanaro, Domenico. 2020. "Poll: Just a Quarter of Republicans Accept Election Outcome." *NPR*, December 9, 2020.) Career politicians then fell in line, though some were out in front proclaiming that the election was a fraud, such

Living in Denial, Living a Lie

There is a further problem. A recent influential work in social psychology in its analysis of Norway has persuasively argued that even when people know about the seriousness of climate change, as Norwegians have known for decades, social "norms of conversation, emotion, and attention, assist people in keeping troubling emotions at bay and simultaneously produce a "double reality" (Norgaard 2011, 201).[55] There is a mutually reinforcing dynamic between the desire not to talk about truths (conversation) that make one feel guilty, fearful and helpless (emotions) and the socially accepted norms not to talk about truths (conversation) that make others feel guilty, fearful and helpless (emotions). In this state of individual and social avoidance, one will either avoid those truths or not pay attention to them when they cross one's awareness (attention). As such one will live in denial. Even if one glimpses the gravity of the problem and breaks through the sociological norms of conversation, emotion, and attention, one is susceptible to the feeling of powerlessness and angst, which "we are profoundly motivated to avoid" (Norgaard 2011, 197). One path to recover power and agency and thus conversation is to talk about ecological issues, most especially climate change, as if they are not a planetary emergency. In this context, at best, solutions are proposed that do not match the scale of the problem. At worst, we live in denial, distort the truth of our situation, and perpetuate lived denial. In his reflections on lived denial within the communist state in the former Czechoslovakia, Vaclav Havel maintained that people going along with the system and not raising objections to the system, even though they disagreed with the system, supported the lie and maintained the system. Reproducing the signs, symbols, and discourse of the system creates "a general norm" that "bring[s] pressure to bear on their fellow citizens" (Havel 1989, 52)[56] to do the same. Those who live "within the lie" "confirm the system, fulfill the system, make the system, and are

---

that 106 Republican members of Congress and 18 state attorney generals petitioned the Supreme Court to overturn the election (Graham, David A. 2020. "The GOP Abandons Democracy." *The Atlantic.* Dec. 10.) and 147 Republican members of Congress voted against certifying the election only hours after a violent mob attacked the Capitol (Yourish, Karen, Larry Buchanan, Denise Lu. 2021. "The 147 Republicans Who Voted to Overturn Election Results." *The New York Times*, Jan. 7, 2021.

[55] Norgaard, Kari Marie. 2011. *Living in Denial: Climate Change, Emotions, and Everyday Life.* (Cambridge Massachusetts: MIT Press, 2011).

[56] Havel., Vaclav. 1989. "The power of the powerless." In *Living in Truth.* Edited by Jan Vladislav, 36-122. (London: Faber & Faber, 1989).

the system" (Havel 1989, 45). In privatizing our spiritualities, going along with the current system, we Christians become people of the lie - absorbing the lie, perpetuating the lie and distancing ourselves from our own complicity in the horrors that we are unleashing on billions of people and millions of species.

In the process of actively engaging in the proposal in the next section, we move out of the powerlessness that creates conditions for the double life, lived denial and the perpetuation of the lies of our current destructive system. In this empowerment we create conditions for living in the truth. Living in the truth is an experience of liberation: "there are moments of exultation in this movement toward awareness. That exultation has to do with a new sense of integrity, or of the possibility of integrity, in one's relationship between self and world." (Lifton and Falk 1991, 120).[57] It is likely that only through the empowerment that comes from creating structures to name and oppose the anti-kingdom of God (while also offering another vision) that we can live an authentic life and give witness to the truth.

Specific Proposals (Acting)

In light of Sharp's notion of pillars of support, let me offer some examples of how religious communities can use their power to challenge the existing structures at a scale that is potentially transformative. First, religious communities must highlight the social character of their teaching. Within Catholic circles Catholic Social Teaching is referred to as "Our Best Kept Secret". The social teaching must no longer be allowed to be a secret. One possible reason why Catholic Social Teaching has been kept a secret, at least in the United States, is that preaching and foregrounding the Catholic Social Teaching's critique of laissez-faire capitalism could be threatening to many of the wealthiest people in the community who are often big donors to particular parishes and diocese. The temptation then is to distort the faith by overemphasizing personal piety and downplaying the social character of

---

[57] Lifton, Robert Jay and Richard Falk. 1991. *Indefensible Weapons: Politics and the Psychological Case against Nuclearism*. (New York: Basic Books, 1991). Lifton was confronting the problem of living in the truth of the threat of nuclear war, but his work is relevant for examining lived climate denial. Though a full-scale nuclear war is more immediate and more devastating than the unfolding climate change tragedy, nuclear war remains a possibility that has to be acted upon, different levels of unimaginable catastrophic climate change will be reached just by continuing to do what we are doing. Norgaard also draws upon Lifton's work in several places (e.g., p. 222).

Jesus's central teaching of the kingdom of God. Establishing the reign and kingdom of God "means the transformation not only of the human heart but of the oppressive social structures that dehumanize and exclude the poor and defenseless from participation in the family of Israel" (Senior 1990, 858).[58]

Second, while *Laudato Sí* has been praised by internationally recognized environmental activists[59] as one of the most important documents addressing climate change and ecological degradation, the bishops of the United States have failed to promulgate the document. The Second Vatican Council was clear that the local bishop's foremost responsibility is to teach (Gaillardetz 1997, 164).[60] *Laudato Sí* drew upon the work of prior Popes and bishops' conferences around the world and is part of Church teaching that the bishops of the United States should have been teaching. Yet forthcoming research shows that following the publication of *Laudato Sí* less than 1% of diocesan columns written by all U.S. Catholic bishops around the time of *Laudato Sí* even mention "climate change" or "global warming."[61] *Laudato Sí* was released in May 2015 and much of the scientific knowledge that was treated in this article had been published including Eric Rignot's study, which he also summarized in an important international English newspaper the *Guardian*), that the human community was committed to four feet of sea level rise, and likely ten to sixteen feet sea level rise. The latter sea level rise would condemn virtually every coastal city in the United States to destruction. Perhaps this failure can partly be attributed to the fact that nearly half (47%) of the bishops in the United States prefer receiving their

---

[58] Senior, Donald. 1990. "Reign of God," In *The New Dictionary of Theology,* edited by Joseph A. Komonchak, Mary Collins, and Dermot A. Lane, 851-861. (Collegeville, MN: Liturgical Press, 1990). While the reign and kingdom of God pervade all aspects of existence including social systems and structures it can never be identified with any particular social organization or political structure and must remain as a critique of all unjust systems.

[59] Shiva, Dr. Vandana. 2015. "'Laudato Si' - A 21st Century Manifesto for Earth Democracy." *Seed Freedom* June 20, 2015 originally published in *L 'Huffington Post Italia* June 19, 2015. https://seedfreedom.info/laudato-si-a-21st-century-manifesto-for-earth-democracy/ ; McKibben, Bill. 2015. "The Pope and Planet." *New York Review of Books*, August 13, 2015. www.nybooks.com/articles/archives/2015/aug/13/pope-and-planet/

[60] Gaillardetz, Richard. 1997. *Teaching with Authority: A Theology of the Magisterium in the Church.* (Collegeville, MN: Liturgical Press, 1997).

[61] This forthcoming research is from Creighton University sociologist Sabrina Danielsen, theologian Dan DiLeo, and student Emily Burke.

news from FOX News (Jenkins 2019),[62] which is a central player in the right-wing propaganda feedback loop.

Had the bishops taken seriously the "signs of the times" and *Laudato Si* they could have pushed the federal government to address the climate crisis with the same vehemence that they successfully pushed the Obama administration to grant an exception for mandatory contraception coverage in health plans sponsored by universities, hospitals, and other institutions associated with the Catholic Church. In this context the Church would lobby the federal government to communicate the truth of the climate emergency to the public through public figures using all the tools at their disposal to educate the public about the climate threat. In addition, the Catholic Church in the US would lobby the federal government to enact policies that reflect in the economy the true cost of greenhouse gas emitting activities like the burning of fossil fuels. This would in no way violate the Church's status as a non-profit in the United States for the Church can advocate for policies just not candidates or parties.

Third, the teachings of Catholicism and other religious traditions on ecology are not peculiar to those communities; rather, there is an overlapping consensus among all mainstream secular ethical theories that, to date, the arguments against taking decisive action to reduce greenhouse gases have all been highly unethical (Brown 2013, 195-211).[63] In light of this, parishes and local dioceses could work to establish alliances between local hospitals (as climate change is regarded as "the greatest global health threat facing the world in the 21st century"[64]), profit and non-profit entities, local universities, religious leaders from other Christian communities, and other faith traditions (all of which have issued statements regarding the moral requirement to act to avoid the worst of climate change).[65] These alliances then could enter into dialogue with local, state, and federal political leaders to educate them about the reality of climate change and the moral consensus among ethical theories that climate change must be addressed. The churches could invite climate scientists and environmental ethicists to such meetings

---

[62] Jenkins, Jack. 2019. "Catholic bishops and laypeople may live in different news bubbles." *Religion News Service,* June 7, 2019. https://religionnews.com/2019/06/07/catholic-bishops-and-laypeople-may-live-in-different-news-bubbles/

[63] See Brown, Donald. 2013. *Climate Change Ethics: Navigating the Perfect Moral Storm.* (New York: Routledge, 2013).

[64] The Lancet. "The Lancet Countdown on health and climate change." Accessed Feb. 25, 2021. https://www.thelancet.com/countdown-health-climate

[65] Yale Forum on Religion and Ecology. "Climate Change Statements from World Religions." Accessed Feb. 25, 2021. http://fore.yale.edu/publications/statements/

to inform political leaders. Where there is a lack of knowledge among political leaders, they can be further informed. Where there is a disregard for norms for weighing scientific evidence and a disregard for ethical norms, having representatives of major institutions (i.e., the pillars of society) at the table with political leaders will send them a signal that pillars of their political support are actively moving away from their continued obstructions of the truth and good of society represented in their policies.

Fourth, the Church could initiate a partnership with local universities inviting faculty with relevant expertise to regularly educate the Catholic community by addressing political, social, and economic issues, policies, and structures that relate to the planetary emergency. In this regard, educating community members in the history of strategic nonviolent direct action would be of utmost importance. Educating about the reality of climate change and the social structures that have led to this crisis is necessary but insufficient for creating conditions for policies to be advanced that are in line with what science and ethics require. A study by Princeton's Martin Gilens and Northwestern's Benjamin Page has shown that "ordinary citizens have virtually no influence over what their government does in the United States. And economic elites and interest groups, especially those representing business, have a substantial degree of influence." (Kapur 2014)[66] As their study maintains, "when a majority of citizens disagrees with economic elites and/or with organized interests, they generally lose. Moreover, because of the strong status quo bias built into the U.S. political system, even when fairly large majorities of Americans favor policy change, they generally do not get it" (Gilens and Page 2014, 576).[67] The lack of correspondence between government policies and public opinion is also operative regarding climate change. While Congress has yet to enact climate legislation, two decades of polling by Stanford Universities John Krosnick has shown that an overwhelming majority of Americans over the past twenty years have believed in global warming and want their political leaders to address the problem. This remarkable agreement among Americans on this issue is illustrated by the fact that in Krosnick's annual polling from 1997 to 2020 the percentage of Americans who have maintained that the

---

[66] This is a quotation from an interview with one of the authors, Martin Gilens. See Kapur, Sahil. 2014. "Scholar Behind Viral 'Oligarchy' Study Tells You What It Means." *Talking Points Memo*, April 22, 2014.
http://talkingpointsmemo.com/dc/princeton-scholar-demise-of-democracy-america-tpm-interview
[67] Gilens, Martin and Benjamin I. Page. 2014. "Testing Theories of American Politics: Elites, Interest Groups and Average Citizens." *Perspective on Politics,* vol. 12, issue 3: 564-581.

earth has probably been warming rose to as high as 85%, never fell below 69%, and is 81% in 2020 (PPRG).[68] The percentage who believe that human action has been at least partly causing global warming was 81% in 1997 and is 82% in 2020, never dropping below 70% (PPRG). In addition, there has emerged an 'issue public' regarding climate change. Krosnick defines 'issue public' as a group for whom climate is very important and engage in donating money, lobbying, attending rallies, voting on climate, etc. From 2015 to 2020 that 'issue public' nearly doubled from 13 percent to 25 percent of the population and is only second to abortion in the United States, which is 31 percent of the population (Schwartz 2020).[69] Despite this overwhelming majority, the United States still does not have a national climate change policy. Public opinion is insufficient to move legislators. What is required to have a chance of meeting the climate reduction targets outlined in the science is to grow the issue public on climate change, educate them, and most importantly, support practical training in non-violent direct action. The Catholic Church has played an important role in the nonviolent struggle of many liberation movements "from the Catholic Worker movement, to the U.S. Civil Rights movement, to the "people power" struggle for democracy [in] the Philippines, to the struggles against dictatorship in Poland, Argentina, and Chile" (Stephan 2016, 3).[70] The Catholic Church and other religious communities not only need to educate and train their members in the art of non-violent direct action, but they also have a great deal to offer practitioners of non-violent struggle by inviting them into the mystery of God as the ultimate ground and wellspring for the pursuit of truth and justice.

Fifth, the Catholic Church could address another central pillar of society, the media, which has, as I have shown, played a central role in the US failure, and by extension, global failure on climate change. The Church needs to address both the failures of that part of the media who have allowed the journalistic norm of balance to be hijacked by conservative think tanks

---

[68] Political Psychology Research Group at Stanford University (PPRG). n.d., "American Public Opinion on Global Warming: Fundamentals 2." Accessed Feb. 28, 2021. https://climatepublicopinion.stanford.edu/fundamentals-2/ .

[69] Schwartz, John. 2020. "Climate is taking on a growing role for voters, research suggests." *The New York Times*, Aug. 24. 2020. This story is citing the research of PPRG.
https://www.nytimes.com/2020/08/24/climate/climate-change-survey-voters.html

[70] Stephan, Maria J. 2016. "Advancing 'just peace' through strategic nonviolent action." Background paper the for Nonviolence and Just Peace Conference. Rome, Italy. April 2016, 1-12
https://nonviolencejustpeacedotnet.files.wordpress.com/2016/05/advancing_just_p eace_through_strategic_nonviolent_action.pdf

and the climate denial machine, while directly confronting the propaganda feedback loop of right-wing media that are virtually unconstrained by accepted norms for truth claims. In the Christian context, Christ is understood as the way, the truth, and the life. Those who willfully generate and perpetuate lies and distortions are in a Christian context literally anti-Christ. This needs to be addressed head on. To date, the leadership of the Catholic Church in the United States has been captured by the right-wing echo-chamber with nearly half of bishops indicating that they prefer FOX news as their news source. The Church acting on its own, or even more effectively acting with an alliance of other pillars of society, could enter into dialogue with both local and national news organizations to request that the truth distorting practice of providing false balance (Boykoff & Boykoff 2004) must be dropped and that the quality, number, and placement of news stories regarding climate change must reflect that climate change is an unprecedented emergency that threatens civilization.

On a national level the United States Conference of Catholic Bishops, the Catholic Hospital Association of the US (the largest group of non-profit health care providers in the US with 1 out of 7 patients in the US cared for in a Catholic hospital)[71], the Associations of Catholic Colleges and Universities (which has 197 member universities), could meet with major national news organizations. In addition, the Association of Catholic Colleges could take the lead in organizing members of the Associations for the Advancement of Sustainability in Higher Education (ASHE), which includes 900 colleges and universities in the US, and Second Nature, which includes 600 colleges and universities in the US, to meet with executives of News Corp, the parent corporation of Fox News, and other major national cable (CNN, MSNBC) and network news programs (ABC, CBS, NBC), including public television. This would also involve meetings with editors of major print media in the United States, including the Wall Street Journal, USA Today, etc. There is precedent for this, the tobacco industry met with major newspaper editors in 1954 to object to scientific findings that smoking was harmful to health (Oreskes and Conway 2011, 16). This greatly affected coverage of the dangers of tobacco over the ensuing decades.

In these proposed initiatives the church would be engaged in defending norms of distributive and procedural justice. Distributive justice requires that the benefits and harms associated with the burning of fossil fuels are distributed equally. In the present context, the benefits have gone to previous generations and the present older generations, especially in the developed world, while the harms will be coming to the poor, young people,

---

[71] The Catholic Health Association of the United States, "About." Accessed Feb. 28, 2021. https://www.chausa.org/about/about

and their future offspring. Procedural justice in reference to climate change, means that those who are being subjected to the risk of climate destabilization must be fully informed of those risks and must consent to those risks. The failure of the media to properly inform the public over the past several decades has been a violation of procedural justice. The Church in engaging the media is creating social conditions for procedural justice for its members and the rest of society.

The position I have advanced calls for a more expansive social role for the Catholic Community, and other religious communities, such that it would actively and directly engage in leveraging its power to create conditions for a society more aligned to norms of evidence (truth), minimal ethical norms found in the overlapping consensus of all mainstream ethical theories and hopefully a society more consonant with the principles of Catholic Social teaching. In this way it would create conditions that lessen the possibility of a catastrophic future for the human community over the next several millennia. Only such a robust engagement in society is in line with the truth of our situation and the mission of the Catholic Church. Without the various institutions within the Church leveraging their power to the full extent possible, individual believers will be faced with the overwhelming truth of the climate crisis, will likely fall into feelings of powerlessness that create conditions for lived climate denial - living and perpetuating a lie. This is a profoundly inauthentic anti-Christian way of being that can only be remedied if the individual is empowered. This can only happen when the pillars of society, in this case the Catholic Church, leverages its power, which the individual can participate in, to transform the structures that are threatening civilization. The Catholic Church and other religious communities must fully engage in the social sphere, drawing upon the wisdom of the traditions of non-violent direct action, to seek justice, rid themselves of their own complicity in the mass death of human populations and the mass extinction of species and to create conditions for the members of their community to lead authentic religious lives. It is only through an active social engagement in climate justice that the church and its members can live in the truth and participate in the work of Christ "to give witness to the truth" (Vatican II 1965, par. 3).

CHAPTER FIFTEEN

CLIMATE CHANGE POLICY PLANS IN THE IRISH SUPREME COURT: LESSONS FROM A NEIGHBOURING ISLAND?

MAUREEN O'SULLIVAN[1]

Introduction

In a much-lauded judgment in July 2020,[2] the Irish Supreme Court quashed the Government of Ireland's climate change plan. The case in question is entitled *Friends of the Irish Environment CLG and The Government of Ireland, Ireland and the Attorney General* [Appeal No: 205/19].[3] The plan had caused controversy for being aspirational, for initially allowing emissions to rise before bringing them under control and for being too short-lived. It was challenged by Friends of the Irish Environment (FIE) which is a non-profit incorporated association. The challenge was unsuccessful in the High Court and the case was subsequently appealed to the Supreme Court. In a most thorough and thought-provoking judgment, which was decided in July 2020, the plan was deemed to be unlawful by the Supreme Court as it did not go far enough. It will have to be redrafted by the Government. The case raises and clarifies important matters regarding the separation of the powers and how far the courts may traverse into the policy making function of the Government. It also

---

[1] Maureen O'Sullivan PhD (Edinburgh), is a lecturer (above the bar) at National University of Ireland, Galway. She is a Fellow of the Oxford Centre for Animal Ethics and was Chair of the Vegetarian Society of Ireland from 2013-2019.
[2] Various observations on the importance of the case can be viewed on the website of the NGO, Friends of the Irish Environment, Climate Case Ireland, at https://www.climatecaseireland.ie/amidst-a-climate-and-biodiversity-crisis-hope-emerges-friends-of-the-irish-environment-win-historic-climate-case-ireland-in-the-irish-supreme-court/ [accessed February 10, 2021].
[3] [2020] IESC 49.

considers the interplay between statute and policy developed thereunder. Most significantly, the Supreme Court examined the nature of rights which arise in the Constitution. These include named rights and unnamed, or so-called unenumerated rights which have been developed by the judiciary since the 1960s.[4] FIE endeavoured to assert a right to a healthy environment under this category of rights. Whilst accepted by the High Court, on appeal this was rejected by the Supreme Court. The court indicated that in jurisdictions where rights to a healthy environment are actualised, they are specifically named in the Constitution and not solely construed by the judiciary. The court also deliberated over the nature of rights which emanate from the European Convention on Human Rights (ECHR) and their domestication in Irish law under the European Convention on Human Rights Act 2003. Whilst not ruling out the recognition of a human right to a healthy environment in future cases, the Supreme Court rejected the existence of such a right in the instant case for reasons which will be explored in this chapter.

This chapter analyses this judgment and contextualises it in relation to similar cases being heard around the world. It will outline the background to the case and explain the grounds on which it was won. It will subsequently give an insight into the sources of rights in Ireland before considering the court's application of these rights and whether they could be extended to cover a human right to a healthy environment. The government's subsequent actions will also be evaluated.

Background, context and procedural history of the case

The Supreme Court reflected that large scale consumption of fossil fuels began during the industrial revolution. It observed that today's actions will have consequences in decades to come and that developing countries will be affected even more than the developed world. This will lead to an increase in deaths, droughts, new diseases and ecosystem changes. Net negative carbon dioxide emissions will be required at some point during this century if targets are to be met. Some tipping points may already have been reached and these are irreversible. The urgency of this matter is not uniformly addressed in the global community. For instance, Ireland's

---

[4] The first case in which the courts recognised a right not specifically named in the Irish Constitution was another case involving environmental matters, namely *Ryan v Attorney General* [1965] 1 IR 294. This case concerned the fluoridation of water by the State. Whilst the claimant was not successful, the court recognised an unenumerated right to bodily integrity which, if the scientific evidence had shown detriment, the government would have been held liable for a violation of the right.

emissions were going to increase 10% initially over a five-year period in the government plan. The court acknowledged that climate change is one of the greatest challenges facing the world.

Since the Paris Agreement in 2015 scientists have advised capping the increase in temperature at 1.5 degrees. In October 2018, the Hague Court of Appeal in *The State of the Netherlands v. Urgenda Foundation*[5] found that global warming levels were approximately 1.1 degrees centigrade higher than at the beginning of the Industrial Revolution. There was a subsequent appeal to the Hoge Raad, which is the Netherlands Supreme Court. In December 2019, it ruled that the Netherlands has a positive obligation under the ECHR to reduce its emissions by at least 25% by the end of 2020, compared to 1990 levels.[6] Similar climate cases are being heard in several national courts in countries such as Norway, Switzerland, Belgium, Germany, Poland, the United States, Canada, Peru, and South Korea.[7] The group called the Climate Litigation Network helps activist groups sue their own governments and was founded while the case Urgenda was underway. It was the first high profile climate lawsuit to be successful.[8] The Irish case showed that this matter is being treated seriously in national courts, and indeed, in France a similar case has also just been won.[9]

Friends of the Irish Environment CLG v. The Government of Ireland[10] was initiated in the Irish High Court by FIE and was heard by MacGrath J. A number of claims were made which included that the Government was

---

[5] http://blogs2.law.columbia.edu/climate-change-litigation/wp-content/uploads/sites/16/non-us-case-documents/2018/20181009_2015-HAZA-C0900456689_decision-4.pdf [accessed February 11, 2021].
[6] http://blogs2.law.columbia.edu/climate-change-litigation/wp-content/uploads/sites/16/non-us-case-documents/2020/20200113_2015-HAZA-C0900456689_judgment.pdf [accessed February 11, 2021].
[7] Orla Kelleher, "The Supreme Court of Ireland's decision in Friends of the Irish Environment v Government of Ireland ("Climate Case Ireland"), (September 9 2020) ejiltalk.org/the-supreme-court-of-irelands-decision-in-friends-of-the-irish-environment-v-government-of-ireland-climate-case-ireland/ [accessed February 1, 2021].
[8] Tessa Khan, "Litigation is a powerful tool in the environmental crisis", *The Guardian* (August 16, 2020) https://www.theguardian.com/lifeandstyle/2020/aug/16/tessa-khan-litigation-is-a-powerful-tool-in-the-environmental-crisis [accessed February 12, 2021].
[9] Constant Méheut, "Court faults France over 'ecological damage' from its emission levels", *New York Times* (February 3, 2021) https://www.nytimes.com/2021/02/03/world/europe/france-emissions-court.html [accessed February 8, 2021].
[10] [2019] IEHC 747.

legally obliged to take steps to alleviate climate change under the Constitution, the ECHR, and statute. The Plan was adopted under the provisions of the Climate Action and Low Carbon Development Act, 2015. FIE alleged that the plan was *ultra vires* the legislation but these claims were dismissed by the High Court. FIE then sought leave to appeal directly to the Supreme Court. Appeals are usually considered first by the Court of Appeal in order to define the issues but in this case there was no dispute among the parties about scientific matters related to the likely increase in greenhouse emissions over the duration of the plan. As the concerns were perceived to be urgent, a leapfrog appeal to the Supreme Court was permitted.[11]

The Development of the Plan: Wrongs and Rights in the Courts

The appeal was treated with such gravity by the Supreme Court that a seven-judge court heard the matter. The judgment was delivered by the Chief Justice, Mr. Justice Frank Clarke.

The case was deemed to raise general issues of public interest and legal importance. The latter pertained to the justiciability of the adoption of the National Mitigation Plan, whether the plan was *ultra vires* the legislation, the question of standing and whether rights arose under the Constitution, the ECHR and from Ireland's international obligations.

Policy or legislation in the Supreme Court

The government asserted, on the question of justiciability, that the Plan represented policy and was not amenable to judicial review. They emphasised that courts regularly state government policy is not justiciable[12] owing to the doctrine of the separation of the powers. Professor Desmond Clarke notes that Irish courts are usually loath to enter the constitutionally protected terrain of the legislature which makes and implements public policy, citing a number of judicial authorities to this effect.[13] He indicates that courts must explain how their judgments comply with the Constitution

---

[11] On February 13, 2020.
[12] An example was given in relation to the dispersal of funds in accordance with policies in *Garda Representative Association v Minister for Finance* [2010] IEHC 78.
[13] An example is the judgment of O'Higgins, CJ in *Norris v AG* [1983] IESC 3; [1984] IR 36 where he contrasted the legislature's power to make law with the courts' lack of such a power to make law through judicial decision.

and legislation, and giving reasons for their decisions is imperative.[14] The Supreme Court meticulously distinguished between legal and policy related matters and indicated that this case concerned whether or not the Government of Ireland's statutory plan for addressing climate change was lawful. The Supreme Court affirmed that policy can become transformed into law when it is passed into legislation. Therefore, the obligation to ensure statutory compliance with the Plan was a matter of law and hence was justiciable.

The *ultra vires* challenge

FIE asserted that the legality of Plan was *ultra vires* the 2015 Act. The trial judge held that the Plan did not breach any of the relevant sections of the Act and in a somewhat *laissez faire* approach, held that there was no statutory obligation to achieve particular intermediate targets. FIE had relied heavily on criticisms of the Plan made by the Climate Change Advisory Council, an independent statutory body established under the Act. In a report submitted to government in 2017, it claimed that Ireland would miss its targets for 2020 substantially.[15] This body is highly respected although its views are not binding. The government's response was that the Plan was a living document which would be reviewed every five years and it cited the Climate Action Plan produced in 2019 as an example of its development. Nonetheless, this document was informal and raised issues of transparency.

Whilst the High Court remained unconvinced and opined that the Advisory Council's opinion was not sufficient to render the Plan *ultra vires*, the Supreme Court would not uphold this view. In a scathing judgment, Clarke CJ, delivering a unanimous verdict, emphasised that specificity was required and that the Plan fell very short. It would not be clear to an interested observer how targets were to be met by 2050 as insufficient detail was given.[16] He went on to declare that Plan did not comply with the 2015 Act, in particular, section 4[17] and he quashed the plan on substantive rather than procedural grounds.[18] This was a broad utilisation of judicial review

---

[14] Desmond M. Clarke, "Judicial Reasoning: Logic, Authority, and the Rule of Law in Irish Courts", *The Irish Jurist*, 2011 46(1), 152-179.
[15] https://www.climatecouncil.ie/media/climatechangeadvisorycouncil/content assets/documents/news/ CCAC_REVIEW REPORT2017.pdf [accessed February 11, 2021].
[16] Para 6.46.
[17] Para 6.48.
[18] Para 6.49.

and the deficiencies would have to be addressed by any new plan. This would include that it be participative and transparent.[19]

The FIE won its case in the Supreme Court: the government's Plan was deemed illegal and would have to be redrafted. It pleaded its case on several grounds and won on the *ultra vires* issue. However, it was not successful in its reliance on the grounds of rights or standing and a meticulous analysis of the reasoning may prove useful for any future litigants, given that this case is one of a number of cases being taken against governments worldwide who are perceived to thumb their noses at their obligations. Moreover, the Supreme Court did not close the door on a reliance on rights but did not accept the arguments or litigants advanced in this particular case. The next sections examine and seeks to explain this decision with a view to exploring how rights to a healthy environment might be achieved.

The issue of rights - an overview of the Irish domain

FIE, as indicated, also challenged the Plan from an array of rights perspectives. In order to comprehend fully the arguments made, this section will first give an explanation of the multiple sources of rights in Ireland. It will also identify eligible claimants under rules relating to standing. It will then analyse the judicial reasoning in this part of the judgment in the context of the rights terrain under constitutional and European law.

In Ireland, the Constitution is a primary, or binding, source of law[20] and is the supreme law of the state. The Constitution has several articles which recognise specific rights such as life, family, property, and education.[21] It is also a font of a class of rights, developed by the judiciary, which are known as "unenumerated rights" or unnamed rights. Since 1965,[22] judges have developed this area and it is still open to further expansion.

The European Convention on Human Rights is another source of rights. As Ireland is a dualist state, enabling legislation must be passed in order for the Convention to become binding, although membership of the European Union requires that Member States be bound by the Convention. Ireland passed the European Convention on Human Rights Act 2003, relatively soon after the UK's passage of the Human Rights Act 1998 to bring the Convention into Irish law. However, the status of this Act is subject to the Constitution meaning that if there is a clash, the Constitutional protection

---

[19] Para 6.21.
[20] EU law, statute and precedent are the other three primary sources of law.
[21] Articles 40-45.
[22] *Ryan v Attorney General* [1965] IESC 1; [1965] IR 294.

trumps that of the Act. This does not mean, however, that Convention rights are thus abrogated: they may still be available on an appeal to the European Court of Human Rights (ECtHR) if domestic remedies are exhausted. The ECtHR retains jurisdiction to recognise new rights: this does not come within the remit of national courts applying the domesticated Convention.

In addition to this matrix of rights, the EU's Charter of Fundamental Rights has added a layer to the rights regime. This source of rights is of recent enactment and was not relied upon in this case. At present, environmental rights do not appear to be actionable under the Charter. Although it provides that a high level of environmental protection and quality improvement must be integrated into EU politics and be guaranteed according to the principle of sustainable development, in article 37, these provisions have been criticised by the European Parliament as they do not grant individuals the right to a clean environment.[23]

However, as I have noted elsewhere,[24] the CJEU is developing the concept of human dignity under this Charter rather than relying as heretofore on the ECHR. In some respects, the definition of human dignity may become more nuanced in the area of environmental law as it has become in the area of biotechnology. Human dignity could under EU law become inextricably linked to matters of climate change in years to come. If there was a clash between a right derived under the Constitution and EU law, the outcome would favour the latter provided that sovereignty had been ceded to the EU on that particular issue. The reach of an interpretative court at EU level, extending into issues of human rights relating to the environment and human dignity is at present untested and therefore is unclear. The Charter was not mentioned in the case and therefore adds nothing to it at present.

Regarding the beneficiaries or who has standing to enjoy or invoke the abundance of rights described above, Ireland is somewhat more restrictive in its approach. Human persons may rely on the rights providing they are affected by them and this applies equally to corporate bodies. In the latter case, rights which cannot be enjoyed are not actionable for the enjoyment of other parties-the right itself must be capable of fulfilment. As will be seen from the examination of case law from various judgments in the High Court, below, the Supreme Court brought clarity to several aspects of this

---

[23] Maurice Sukin, David M. Ong, Robert Wight, *Sourcebook on Environmental Law*, (London: Routledge Cavendish, 2001) p. 851, cited in Lucretia Dogaru / Procedia - Social and Behavioral Sciences 141 (2014) 1346-1352, 1347.

[24] Maureen O'Sullivan, *Biotechnology, Patents and Morality: A Deliberative and Participatory Paradigm for Reform* (London: Routledge, 2019).

area, overturned some rights and restricted somewhat judicial freedom to expand the terrain in an unfettered manner.

The rights claimed under the Constitution - the High and Supreme Court syntheses

The issues arising in this appeal included claimed rights comprising the right to life which is a named right in the Constitution.[25] This was perceived to be threatened by climate change. A second right - to bodily integrity - has been recognised by the Supreme Court[26] as an unenumerated right, which is a right not specifically named but acknowledged nonetheless by the judiciary. A third, contested right, also in the unenumerated rights category, was a right to an environment consistent with human dignity or a right to a healthy environment. This latter right had been recognised in a High Court case by Barrett J in another case taken by FIE: *Friends of the Irish Environment v Fingal Co. Council.*[27] FIE also argued that the ECtHR had considered rights to a clean environment in *Fadeyeva v Russia.*[28] Whilst the right's existence was recognised by the High Court in the instant case, it was not deemed to have been infringed. The FIE's counsel accepted that there was no material difference between the established constitutional rights relied on, being the right to life, and the right to bodily integrity, and a novel right to a healthy environment.[29] However, if such a right were recognised under the Constitution, it could have wider implications.

As there had not yet been a Supreme Court decision on the right, the Supreme Court pronounced on this matter. Their judgment will be examined in a separate section below after the more general discussion of ECHR rights.

Constitutional standing

MacGrath J allowed FIE to enjoy standing on the basis of the dicta in *Digital Rights Ireland Ltd v Minister for Communications.*[30] In that case, McKechnie J held that a less strict approach could be taken where a particular public act might adversely affect a plaintiff's constitutional or

---

[25] Article 40.3.2.
[26] *Ryan v Attorney General* [1965] IR 294.
[27] In *Friends of the Irish Environment v. Fingal County Council* [2017] IEHC 695.
[28] (App. No. 55723/00)(2005) 45 ECRR 10.
[29] Para 7.7.
[30] [2010] 3 IR 251.

ECHR rights or society as a whole. The standing rules in *Digital Rights* involved claims which a company was entitled to bring as a company. However, this case does not provide any authority for companies or other corporate entities to enjoy standing to assert individual rights rather than rights they can themselves enjoy. FIE had brought its case on personal rights although it is an incorporated association. The government claimed that in doing so, FIE was endeavouring to rely upon an *actio popularis*, which is an action brought on behalf of the public as a whole. This is not recognised in Irish constitutional law[31] and to do so would be to acknowledge a *jus tertii* - an action in which a person invokes rights enjoyed by others. This would be in contravention of the decision in *Cahill v Sutton*[32] on this point. The Supreme Court held that standing could only be relaxed in very narrow circumstances.

The Supreme Court commented on the fact that there were no individual plaintiffs involved in the case, nor did any seek to be joined to the proceedings. The standing hurdle could have been overcome by joining individual plaintiffs which FIE could have supported financially, in the Court's view. The Court said that the risk of exposure to costs for an individual from unsuccessful proceedings (which could amount to several hundred thousand euro) did not adequately explain the case not being brought by an individual rather than an NGO. Kelleher observes that these obiter remarks are hard to reconcile with the prohibitive legal costs regime in Ireland[33] and the Supreme Court certainly appears to be out of touch on this matter. I have been informed that sometimes litigants seek a plaintiff with no assets so that an award of costs against them is meaningless. However, it is not easy to find such individuals.

European human rights in the High and Supreme Courts

The FIE also relied on rights from the domesticated version of the ECHR enshrined in Irish legislation, namely Articles 2 and 8 of the European

---

[31] Reliance was placed on a Supreme Court decision of *Mohan v Ireland and the Attorney General* [2019] IESC 18 in which it was found that only a person who is directly affected may bring such a case.

[32] [1980] IR 269.

[33] Orla Kelleher, "The Supreme Court of Ireland's decision in Friends of the Irish Environment v Government of Ireland ("Climate Case Ireland"), (September 9 2020) ejiltalk.org/the-supreme-court-of-irelands-decision-in-friends-of-the-irish-environment-v-government-of-ireland-climate-case-ireland/ [accessed February 1, 2021].

Convention on Human Rights Act 2003.[34] These articles provide that all organs of the State should perform their functions in line with the obligations which arise under the Convention in the context of the right to life, and private and family life. Some of this reliance was challenged as the manner in which Convention rights operate in different signatory states varies. For instance, case law from the Netherlands was not deemed persuasive,[35] given that it operates a monist system and is, therefore, bound directly by the legislation rather than by a domestic law derived from the Convention as is the case in dualist states, such as Ireland.

European standing

The issue of standing was also examined in the context of ECHR rights and the Supreme Court's view was that the ECtHR would be unlikely to recognise the standing of corporate bodies which sought to invoke rights which they could not exercise. Whilst the High Court did not hold against FIE on the issue of standing, the Supreme Court did so, maintaining that the Government's position was correct on this matter.[36]

In an intricate twist, Clarke CJ opined, that circumstances could exist where a person or entity might not have standing before the ECtHR under the ECHR, but the lack of Strasbourg standing would not necessarily preclude a reliance on the 2003 Act or Ireland's domestication of the ECHR. This is a judicial acknowledgement of a potential divergence between the rights afforded under the Convention and the rights that can be relied on under the domesticated version of the Convention. The Supreme Court stated that the legislation may grant more rights than the ECHR but it would be unlikely to extend constitutional rights any further.[37] This would be especially true where the rights under the ECHR said to be infringed mirror or are similar to constitutional rights. In *McD (J) v. L (P) &M(B)*[38] the court clarified that the ECtHR rather than domestic courts would declare Convention rights and the High Court adopted the dicta of Fennelly J in this respect.

---

[34] Para 5.8.
[35] Paras 5.14, 5.15.
[36] Para 7.24.
[37] Paras 7.23, 7.6.
[38] [2009] IESC 81.

A Constitutional Right to a Healthy Environment
and a redefinition of rights

As noted above, a right to a healthy environment was recognised as an unenumerated right by Barrett J in *Friends of the Irish Environment v Fingal Co. Council*.[39] He opined that a right to an environment is an essential condition for the fulfilment of human rights and found it to be consistent with human dignity and citizens' well-being. It would enjoy protection as a universal personal right under Art. 40.3.1 of the Constitution. The manner in which the right was described was not fixed and could be delineated either as a right to an environment or a healthy environment. The Supreme Court stated that if it was to make no comment on this right, it might be assumed that it had been approved and so Clarke CJ chose to explore this arena further.

Clarke CJ opined that the class of constitutional rights which cannot be found in express terms in the wording of the Constitution itself, and usually referred to as "unenumerated" rights, would be described better as "derived" rights. The reasons for a different categorisation or naming is that Clarke CJ believes that the term "unenumerated" conveys an impression that judges simply identify rights of which they approve and deem them to be part of the Constitution.[40] Whilst the judge does not claim that those rights have come into existence in a whimsical fashion, the process by which they are recognised could be misinterpreted.[41] The term "derived rights" conveys a more legitimate foundation in the text or structure of the Constitution. Rights should only derive from a judicial considering of the Constitution as a whole when identifying and recognising rights thereunder. More precision was required and new rights would have to emanate from the structure and values of the Constitution and be associated with existing rights, such as human dignity. This class of rights is not closed but neither can it be expanded arbitrarily[42] as otherwise, the separation of the powers would be unclear.[43]

Clarke CJ questioned whether the recognition of a right to a healthy environment would add anything further to rights to life and bodily integrity already relied upon and if not, there was no reason to give this new right separate recognition.[44] The environmental right recognised in the High

---

[39] [2017] IEHC 695.
[40] Para 8.5.
[41] Para 8.6.
[42] Para 8.8.
[43] Para 8.9.
[44] Para 8.10.

Court was inordinately indeterminate, in his view.[45] However, the Supreme Court also noted that in jurisdictions where such rights had been recognised, they had been written into the constitutional text and not elaborated in the hands of the judiciary. The UN Special Rapporteur on human rights and the environment, David Boyd who authored a book on environmental rights, constitutions and human rights was cited in this context. Specific constitutional delineation is more precise and more democratic as debate can be generated on the issue. In Ireland this could be achieved through a referendum mandating a constitutional amendment.[46]

Moreover, Kelleher notes that if we "green" existing rights such as the right to life and bodily integrity, they may be unduly anthropocentric. It may be difficult to demonstrate risk and potential harm if negative effects are only demonstrable to nature. If we are to expand the concept of "derived rights" and link them to human dignity, then detriment to nature alone will not be considered.[47] It may be for this reason that some countries such as Colombia whose Supreme Court in April 2018 ordered the drafting and implementation of action plans to address deforestation in the Amazon, has recognised some natural objects as "subjects of rights". Other Andean countries such as Ecuador[48] and Bolivia[49] have recognised such rights through the Constitution and legislation, respectively. New Zealand has recognised the River Whanganui as a legal person[50] and this gives certain

---

[45] Para 8.11.

[46] Orla Kelleher, "The Supreme Court of Ireland's decision in Friends of the Irish Environment v Government of Ireland ("Climate Case Ireland"), (September 9 2020) ejiltalk.org/the-supreme-court-of-irelands-decision-in-friends-of-the-irish-environment-v-government-of-ireland-climate-case-ireland/ [accessed February 1, 2021].

[47] Orla Kelleher, "The Supreme Court of Ireland's decision in Friends of the Irish Environment v Government of Ireland ("Climate Case Ireland"), (September 9, 2020) ejiltalk.org/the-supreme-court-of-irelands-decision-in-friends-of-the-irish-environment-v-government-of-ireland-climate-case-ireland/ [accessed February 1, 2021].

[48] First International Tribunal on Laws of Nature, https://amazonwatch.org/news/2014/0121-first-international-tribunal-on-rights-of-nature [accessed February 15, 2021].

[49] John Vidal, "Bolivia enshrines natural world's rights with equal status for Mother Earth", *The Guardian* (April 10, 2011) https://www.theguardian.com/environment/2011/apr/10/bolivia-enshrines-natural-worlds-rights [accessed February 15, 2021].

[50] Timothy Vines, Ven. Alex Bruce and Thomas Alured Faunce, "Planetary Medicine and the Waitangi Tribunal Whanganui River Report: Global Health Law Embracing Ecosystems as Patients", Journal of Law and Medicine 2013; 20: 528-541,

natural objects rights of their own rather than contingent ones. However, such a legal paradigm has not yet graced the Irish legal arena.

Clarke C J's pronouncements on the rights of corporate entities to pursue constitutional litigation, has recently been cited approvingly by Mr. Justice Garrett Simons in the High Court in a case involving Ryanair and the right to travel.[51] McKechnie J has described as "illuminating" the comments of Clarke C J on "derived" or formerly "unenumerated rights".[52]

Aftermath

A bill to amend the Climate Action and Low Carbon Development Act 2015, has been drawn up and scrutinised by the Joint Oireachtas (the Irish legislature) Committee on Climate Action and they have produced a report.[53] This scrutiny is on a legal basis only and does not interrogate wider aspects of climate policy. Problems remain, however, with this proposed amended legislation. On consulting with experts in the field it was noted that the Paris Convention was not mentioned in the Act. Neither was any reference made to the Intergovernmental Panel on Climate Change.[54] The government had declined to include references to EU and international obligations, claiming that they had received legal advice not to do so. This was questioned by Dr Áine Ryall who is the co-director of the Centre for Law and the Environment at University College Cork. No mention was made of biodiversity.[55]

Dr Ryall spoke to the all-party Climate Action Committee and verified that the Climate Change Advisory Council should be strengthened to make sure that the State complies with its obligations.[56] Dr Diarmuid Torney of the School of Law and Government at Dublin City University observes that

---

http://papers.ssrn.com/sol3/papers.cfm?abstract_id=2235935 [accessed February 15, 2021].

[51] *Ryanair DAC v An Taoiseach, Ireland and The Attorney General and Aer Lingus Ltd.* [2020] IEHC 461, para 149.

[52] *Gorry and Joseph Gorry v The Minister for Justice and Equality, A.B.M. and B.A. v The Minister for Justice and Equality* [2020] IESC 55.

[53] https://www.oireachtas.ie/en/committees/33/climate-action/ [accessed February 12, 2021].

[54] P. 6.

[55] P. 14.

[56] Kevin O'Sullivan, "Independence of climate council needs to be strengthened, committee told", *Irish Times* (October 7, 2020), https://www.irishtimes.com/news/environment/independence-of-climate-council-needs-to-be-strengthened-committee-told-1.4382254 [accessed February 10, 2021].

whilst the State is required to *pursue* the transition to a climate neutral economy by the end of 2050, it was not *obliged* to do so (my italics) in the provisions of the draft amending legislation. He contrasts this with the UK Climate Change Act, which is unambiguous in its mandate that it falls upon the Secretary of State, who is the senior minister responsible for climate action to ensure that the aims are achieved rather than aspirational. The new draft Irish legislation appears devoid of any obligation to draw up carbon budgets that align with the national 2050 climate aims.[57]

Both Ryall and Tormey recommended more citizen participation and protection of human rights.[58] At present the amending legislation provides only that the Minister may consult with persons that are appropriate in his/her opinion and this may include members of the public.[59] A more farcical provision could hardly have been devised, especially given that the Supreme Court did deem transparency and participative engagement to be so important.[60] Ryall does recommend adherence to models for best practice in public participation as these are currently optional only.[61] The Joint Oireachtas Committee on Climate Change recommends that the legislation comply with the Aarhus Convention but whilst recommending more participation and deliberation, they also emphasise that the process must be speedy.[62]

An appropriate paradigm for participation would need to be given some consideration as the current requirement in Ireland is not onerous. In a High Court case, *Christian Morris v An Bord Pleanála and Atlas GP Limited and Fingal County Council*,[63] the decision of Barr J in another High Court case, *Friends of the Irish Environment v the Government of Ireland*[64] was cited in this regard. It was found that decision makers do not have to give individual responses to each public submission, especially where there have been a large number of communications with significant overlap. They can be

---

[57] Kevin O'Sullivan, "Independence of climate council needs to be strengthened, committee told", *Irish Times* (October 7, 2020),
https://www.irishtimes.com/news/environment/independence-of-climate-council-needs-to-be-strengthened-committee-told-1.4382254 [accessed February 10, 2021].

[58] Kevin O'Sullivan, "Independence of climate council needs to be strengthened, committee told", *Irish Times* (October 7, 2020),
https://www.irishtimes.com/news/environment/independence-of-climate-council-needs-to-be-strengthened-committee-told-1.4382254 [accessed February 10, 2021].

[59] Section 4(4)(a).

[60] In para 6.21.

[61] P. 20.

[62] P. 34.

[63] [2020] IEHC 529.

[64] [2020] IEHC 225.

arranged thematically and addressed on an issue by issue basis providing this is done fairly.[65] This concept of participation is undoubtedly weak and does not foster engagement. It does not require a nuanced response and can be a superficial exercise in participation which lacks deliberation. Elsewhere I have written about robust models of citizen participation in the context of budgeting which can also be adapted to public debate and agreement on other matters of concern to the community at large, such as those relating to the environment. Accountability for the manner in which objections are handled, along with genuine engagement, is vital if participation is to be meaningful.[66]

A failure to adhere to climate change commitments is actionable, as already seen so it is surprising that the amending legislation remains cavalier in its approach to enshrining any consequences for failing to reach targets. No corrective action need be taken. Nonetheless, the amending legislation is peppered with provisions that oblige the Minister to consult with the Advisory Council[67] whereas the Government has an option to do so.[68] Consultation does not affect the outcome of any decisions taken by either the Minister or the Government. In the section which deals with revising carbon budgets, for instance, the Minister is to consult with and consider the advice of the Advisory Council before making a recommendation to Government but the latter has the option of approval or else approval subject to modification which would appear to emasculate this part of the legislation.[69] No justification has to be given for such departures and this is criticised in the Report.[70] On the issue of standing, Ryall notes the recommendation of the Citizens Assembly that an independent body be established to pursue the state if it is in breach of its obligations. This could be modelled on the right of the Irish Human Rights and Equality Commission to initiate litigation.[71] It is even suggested that a section of the draft amending legislation undermines the Supreme Court judgment and deletion is recommended.[72] In total, there were 78 recommendations for alterations to the legislation. Time is of the essence in dealing with climate change. It is incumbent on governments to do better than drafting such

---

[65] Para 122.

[66] Maureen O'Sullivan, *Biotechnology, Patents and Morality: A Deliberative and Participatory Paradigm for Reform* (London: Routledge, 2019), chapter 4.

[67] Section 3(5).

[68] Section 3(6).

[69] Section 6D (6) ; 7(b).

[70] P. 22.

[71] P. 23.

[72] P. 23.

vague legislation, especially after being ordered to act lawfully by the Supreme Court.

In addition to the Bill, a National Energy and Climate Plan required by the EU must set out how emissions will be reduced up to 2030 and beyond. This is due in 2021.[73]

Conclusion

The Irish Supreme Court case overturned the High Court decision. It found that the Government of Ireland's Plan was unlawful and would have to be redrafted. It shows that climate activists who are dissatisfied with governmental inaction on climate change can hold their governments accountable through the courts. It is not the first such case and neither is it the last as similar cases have now been won in the Netherlands and in France. The decision is to be applauded in that it navigated the outcome within the boundaries of Irish law. In one sense it is not radical: the rights terrain was not extended and, given that in the past some controversial uses of natural law to found new rights have proved to be contentious, it was wise to refrain from extending rights where the grounding could lack legitimacy. It did, however, bravely establish that governments cannot do as they please, pleading a defence of making policy rather than law, thereby keeping judicial scrutiny at bay. The Supreme Court was assertive about its right to hold the government to account and it did so decisively. As the ensuing legislative scrutiny shows, the subsequent drafting effort still requires vigilance and Ryall observes that if the legislation was passed in its current format, more litigation would follow.[74] This would involve more cost and waste much more time. Governments must take their role seriously and do what is necessary to obey the law, represent the people and save the world before it is too late.

---

[73] Kevin O'Sullivan, "Supreme Court ruling a lift for climate activists worldwide, *Irish Times* (August 1, 2020)
https://www.irishtimes.com/news/environment/supreme-court-ruling-a-lift-for-climate-activists-worldwide-1.4318981 [accessed February 10, 2021].
[74] Caroline O'Doherty, "'Storing up trouble' – more experts warn Climate Bill is too weak to work" *Irish Independent* (October 15, 2020)
https://www.independent.ie/irish-news/news/storing-up-trouble-more-experts-warn-climate-bill-is-too-weak-to-work-39628331.html [accessed February 12, 2021].

CHAPTER SIXTEEN

OTHER SPECIES ARE ESSENTIAL WORKERS IN THE EARTH'S ECONOMY[1]

DIDI PERSHOUSE

Prologue

Just up the road from here, essential workers are building a series of dams to prevent flooding in the towns downstream from me. They are using a technology that allows fish to travel upstream, filters out pollutants from the water flowing through and captures eroding soil from nearby farms. Over time, the dams will naturally disintegrate in a random series, leaving behind fertile soil already seeded with plants to provide a large 'soil sponge' that can capture rain without need for further dams. They have been working nights recently, to avoid getting in the way of traffic.

Other parts of this essential workforce have been perfecting the design of solar powered oxygen pumps that simultaneously function as air conditioners, air purifiers, and food production units. (If we had enough of them, we could easily feed every living thing on the planet.) These pumps also produce raw materials for construction and clothing, while collecting CO_2 from the air and storing it safely above and below ground.

The pharmaceutical wing of this workforce has figured out how to switch on brain development in utero and synthesize vitamins from simple foods. It can also now create and deliver the exact dosage of antidepressants and immune boosting chemicals each person needs at exactly the time they need them.

These workers, designers, patent holders, and investors are not human. They are the myriad species with whom we share our landscapes: animals, plants, fungi, and bacteria. If they all went on strike, we would have no

---

[1] Parts of this chapter were published by Didi Pershouse as a series of articles for the Regenerative Economy Collaborative on Medium.
https://medium.com/the-regenerative-economy-collaborative.

oxygen to breathe and no food to eat. Most rainfall would cease. Dead animals and plants would pile up, miles high, with no easy way to break back down into raw materials for continued life. Temperature regulation on Earth would deteriorate to the point that it would become uninhabitable. Meanwhile, our own human brains and bodies would cease to function.

These essential workers get no pay, no health insurance, no worker's compensation if they are injured. In fact, in most countries they have no legal rights at all. They can be bought and enslaved by the highest bidder, forced to work under terrible conditions, have limbs cut off and be killed when they are deemed unnecessary to production. Yet they build the infrastructure and provide the goods and services that underpin every economy on Earth.

The Work of Other Species

The terms 'essential worker' and 'frontline worker' have taken on tremendous new importance since the onset of the SARS-CoV-2/COVID-19 pandemic. This chapter proposes that other species are essential workers whose labor is absolutely necessary for the future of critical infrastructure-both human and planetary. Their work underpins all food systems, regional and global water security, transportation of materials, health systems, and the climate, and metabolism of our planet.

Many species are increasingly *frontline* workers: facing huge risks while going about their daily labors. They are harmed and killed, intentionally and unintentionally, with antibiotics, pesticides, tillage and harvesting machinery, logging and more, without thought for how their work - and the systems that depend on their work - will proceed without them.

All species are continual *designers*, capable of new strategies, often in rapid response to a challenge. Like the humans who design, build, and maintain our roads, bridges, and electrical grids, the work of other species involves coordinated efforts and constant intelligent decision making about supply chains and energy. They are also *investors* in local and global economies and require a return on investment (ROI) in order to stay in the game, payable in a currency that they can use.

The economy of other species 'enfolds' our own. It is not separate from ours, nor is it merely a part of ours. It is doing far more than simply providing 'ecosystem services' or offering us 'natural capital'. By enfold I mean *'to surround or envelop'* or *'to hold someone lovingly'* and I am implying the 'nestedness' that is a feature of life on our planet.

The word economics originally carried some of the same sense of care and nestedness: *oikos* (home) and *nomi* (management/care) translate as 'the management and care of home'. Aristotle describes *oikonomia* as the pragmatic science of living virtuously as a member of the polis or community through wise household management, in particular the practical matter of how to deal wisely with the surpluses that nature offers in order to have a more meaningful life. This is in contrast with the art of money making and markets, for which the ancient Greeks had a different word: *chrematistike*.

About 10,000 years ago, when we started harnessing the energy of other mammals to plow up the ground, we lost track of the fact that soil itself is home to myriad other species; it is a household, a working community in which we also commune. If we break apart the social and material infrastructure created by the community, it loses its function: soil that is tilled continually holds less and less water on land (Lal, Reicosky, and Hanson 2007) and generally desertifies after approximately 2,000 years, although depending on the region, it can be much faster. Over generations, we have turned fertile crescents into deserts, worldwide (D. Montgomery 2012; Vörösmarty and Sahagian 2000; D. R. Montgomery 2007).

Human economies have collapsed and empires have fallen throughout history, in large part because the 'deciders' did not recognize, understand, or value the work of other species. They failed to see that human work and economies are nested within the economies of other species and failed to invest in anything but their own. They did not design their own future to include the biological workforce or find a way to work along with it. These large-scale collapses come from a profound loss of cultural understanding. To fail on such a large level requires that many people view the living beings around them - plants, animals, insects, bacteria, fungi, and the land, forests, oceans, continents, and atmosphere that they continually regenerate, as something quite different from what they actually are.

In societies that have become self-destructive, people lose their ability to see life as intelligent communities at work, continually refining, improving and adapting their designs: co-participants in a sacred whole. Instead, people learn to see other species and their ecosystems as:

- Resources from which value can be extracted, e.g. 'How much corn can this variety produce?'
- Problems to be overcome, e.g. 'These swamps are in the way of my proposed housing development.'
- Enemies to be eradicated, e.g., 'Town policy requires that lawns have no dandelions, therefore I must use weed killer.'

Others take a sentimental view, seeing life, and landscapes as:

- Vulnerable victims that need protection, e.g., 'Save the ____!'
- Beautiful wonders that provide pleasure and entertainment, e.g., 'Come watch our amazing dolphin show!'

Many of these views unconsciously reinforce the others, e.g. 'I'm using this pesticide to kill an 'invasive' insect species, in order to protect a vulnerable type of tree, so that the lumber continues to return value to me as an investor and I can continue to enjoy the views in my 'pristine' wilderness.' For current societies to continue, we will need a clearer view.

Many religions have accepted the 'dominion' view of humans' relationship to nature, or more modern reinterpretations such as 'stewardship'. Both still put humans in charge, whether subduing or stewarding the non-human world. In Christianity, there is solid ground for this perspective in the Old Testament. Yet is it possible that we are 'behind the times' in relying on an Old Testament view? What was Christ calling for when he asked people to practice *metanoia,* and notice that the Kingdom of Heaven is at hand?

What if humans were to perceive, from that particular space of communion of mind/heart called *nous*, that we are held lovingly within a larger community at work? That we are members of a larger household?

'Continued Critical Infrastructure Viability'

The definition of "essential workers" in guidelines issued by the U.S. Department of Homeland Security (Wales 2020), is those workers "who conduct a range of operations and services that are typically essential to continued critical infrastructure viability", and workers "who support crucial supply chains." Essential workers enable the functioning of essential industries such as food and agriculture, medicine and healthcare, telecommunications, information technology systems, defense, transportation and logistics, energy, water and wastewater, law enforcement and public works. The guidelines go on to say that all decisions "should appropriately balance public safety, the health and safety of the workforce, and the continued delivery of essential critical infrastructure services and functions."

This brings up some questions:

- What roles do other species play in the supply chains of our human-managed food and agriculture systems? Medicine and healthcare systems? Telecommunications? Information technology? Defense? Transportation and logistics? Energy? Water and wastewater systems? Law enforcement? Public works?

- What is the essential work that ensures the viability of the critical infrastructure and supply chains of *soils, forests, oceans, and atmosphere* and how much of it is done by non-human workers?
- How do we design societies, governance, and economies to balance public safety, the health and safety of the biological workforce and the continued delivery to all life, of these essential critical infrastructure services and functions?

These questions may seem hard to answer at first, because the labor and intelligence of other species has been oddly invisible to us, even though we depend upon it every second of every day. We assume, for example, that oxygen production is natural, free, and dependable - something that just 'happens', like parenting. It rarely occurs to us that oxygen production on Earth requires an enormous workforce of photosynthesizers on land and in the oceans. We see right past the fact that plants are continually and intelligently managing and investing in relationships with symbiotic microbes and herbivores that are as changeable from minute to minute as the stock market. Oxygen production is not valued in our household management or counted in our economies or GDP. Nor have we considered what currency plants would find useful in their own economies as payment or ROI from human co-investors.

We do not easily connect power outages, road closures, or endless war with a failure to value the work of other species. Yet nature's workforce ensures the clean abundant supply of water needed to cool nuclear reactors, repave roads, pour cement, and produce information technology, just as it ensures the supply of food needed by the engineers, operators, and CEOs engaged in these activities. Nature's workforce is not just outside our bodies, it includes the microbes needed to digest those foods and turn it into usable energy that powers human work and intelligence.

Other species not only manage and maintain the supply chains underlying industries and economies, they also manage the weather and stable climate that those supply chains depend upon: providing the biological materials and transport of water for clouds and rain (Sheil 2018; Lazaridis 2019; Morris et al. 2014), as well as regulating temperatures on land and greenhouse gasses in the atmosphere (Pielke, Mahmood and McAlpine 2016; Kabat 2004).

Because non-human work is rarely in our consciousness and invisible in our economies, it is not just undervalued, but *un*valued. We only pay the cost once the work has ceased to happen, at which point it becomes a rapidly unfolding, extremely expensive crisis (Pershouse 2020).

Entanglement in the Central Valley

In the 1850s, California's Central Valley was an emerald green series of seasonal and permanent wetlands (Frayer, Peters and Ross Pywell 1989) kept in place by the work of myriad collaborators from every biological kingdom, including humans (Anderson 2013). All species worked together to create the hydrology, soil physics, atmospheric dynamics and overall ecological functioning of the region, not just in the Valley itself, but also in the mountain ranges that enfold the Valley and, in the ocean and distant lands that contribute to the flows of the Valley from the East, West, North and South.

The deep spongy soils and wetlands in the Valley accepted both rain and seasonal flooding with ease and kept that water protected from evaporation during drier seasons. This provided relatively consistent water for plants to cool the air through transpiration (Yilmaz et al, 2008; Chen et al, 2020), the evaporative cooling 'sweat' of plant metabolism when plants have enough water at their root zone. Cooling by plants creates low pressure systems, whose vacuum-like influence likely helped to suck moist air from the Pacific Ocean up over the coastal mountain range and down into the Valley itself (Makarieva, Gorshkov and Li 2009; 2013).

Though rainfall was seasonal, this airborne water from the ocean, in the form of fog, mists, clouds and invisible water vapor, was more constant: providing an atmospheric river flowing by, ready to be captured by plants. Giant redwood trees reached up to the sky and harvested the water they needed directly from the air, condensing it onto their needle structure, allowing it to flow down their trunks and into the soils below them, where their roots could take it up for growth and transpire it again back into the atmosphere creating local water cycles. Lower plant canopies did variations on this with dew. Together, this quenched the thirst of the moisture-loving fungi in the soil, some of whom, the saprophytes, reduced fire risk in the forests by helping to decompose trees, branches, needles and, leaves that had fallen to the ground. Other fungi, the mycorrhizae, sorted and delivered nutrients where they were needed, found hidden water underground during droughts and served as a communication system within the forest and the meadows below, alerting plants of approaching dangers, so that they could produce the right chemicals to ward off pests (Johnson and Gilbert 2017). By keeping trees alive and healthy, this also reduced fire risk, combined with very carefully managed controlled burns that were part of human's role in the region (Anderson 2013).

The soils were held in place by a web of roots and fungal hyphae and strengthened against the eroding forces of wind and water by biofilms (biological slimes that become water-resistant glues when dry) that held the underlying mineral particles together. Life continually moved through this 'soil sponge' creating macropores and micropores that could soak up rain that fell, filter it, and store it underground - so that it could seep out slowly into year-round springs, streams, and rivers. The lush vegetation provided food, water, and protection (from extreme cold, heat and wind) for the workforce of microbes, fungi, pollinators, grazers, dam builders, and other animals, as well as the indigenous people that lived and worked among them.

Until the arrival of Europeans, everyone participated in tending to the abundance of the 'local economy'. Non-native settlers arrived and stayed in California for all sorts of reasons. Those arriving from harsher climates where land degradation had already begun were awed by the mild weather, clean air and water, deep fertile soils, stunning beauty and enormous trees. But rather than settle in to help tend the wild, they viewed the living systems as resources that could return huge value to them, if they were sold back East, or in Europe.

Unconscious of the region's true underlying economy, they cut the redwoods for lumber, and killed off beaver throughout the West to make into hats for the European market (Goldfarb 2018; Outwater 1996). They straightened rivers and drained the wetlands, then broke up the soil sponge with plows, planted crops and left the soils bare after harvest. They compacted the soils with heavy machinery to the point that the spongy structure collapsed and soils no longer absorbed as much rain. So people began pumping water out of aquifers and transporting it from distant rivers to irrigate the crops they planted (Arax 2019).

Without the diverse natural plant cover, or even cover crops, there were fewer plants to feed the essential workers that could rebuild the living infrastructure of healthy soils. Once the soils lost the biological glues and threads that held them together, the sand, silt and clay particles became more like dry flour than moist spongy bread. The air filled with brown dust whenever the wind blew and the rivers ran brown when it rained, as the topsoil drifted steadily away.

Just 150 years later, the hot bare soils now create a rising buffer of hot air that prevents moisture from the coasts from flowing into the Valley. When rain does fall, the water moves sideways over the compacted soils, creating flash flooding, but failing to replenish soil moisture (Pershouse 2020). The new production methods under these conditions require absurd amounts of water to be pumped from below or brought in from elsewhere. Massive dams and infrastructure have been built to capture and transport water, while land is subsiding and sinkholes have developed, due to dropping local water tables, threatening houses, and roads (Sheller 2019; Galloway and Riley 1999). Low water tables concentrate arsenic and other toxins in the water, affecting the health of those who live there.

In dry, dusty conditions, without fungal communities to decompose dried leaves and dead trees, fire has become the next hazard, deteriorating air and water quality even further, spreading toxic chemicals from burned houses onto crops, into wild areas, and into drinking water. Crops grown in monocultures, rather than polycultures, have fewer underground microbial relationships to bring them the exact nutrients needed to create healthy plants immune to diseases. Humans fertilize the crops with a few key elements: nitrogen, phosphorus, and potassium, rather than the rich smorgasbord of nutrients they would receive from a living soil web. This artificial chemical diet has made crops even more vulnerable to pests, fungal diseases, and viruses, creating a rising demand for pesticides.

Today it is a common sight when driving through the valley to see human workers in hazmat suits and masks, applying chemicals to the crops. The air is filled not just with dust from failed soils, but also with pesticides and antibiotic resistant bacteria from the region's feedlots (McEachran et al, 2015; Nascimento, Da Rocha and De Andrade 2017). The pesticides include the chemical glyphosate, which Monsanto patented as a broad-spectrum antibiotic (Abraham 2003). It was never brought to market for that use, likely because it kills off too many beneficial bacteria. The patent is worth reading and the list of organisms it is shown to kill is astounding. But just because it is not *sold* as an antibiotic does not stop it from *acting* as one when it is used as an herbicide and desiccant, sprayed directly on crops before harvest in order to dry them more quickly. Monsanto/Bayer claims glyphosate does not impact mammals because they do not have the shikimate pathway that the chemical acts upon only bacteria, archaea, fungi, algae, some protozoans and plants have that pathway. Yet inside the bodies of animals, including insects, these same microbes are responsible for myriad bodily functions. In humans, the microbiome turns on brain development in utero, regulates metabolism and immunity, and produces most of our brain chemicals, and that's only what we have learned in the last decade or two (Pershouse 2016). With glyphosate and other antibiotics freely circulating the planet in our food, wind and water, every human's ability to think, thrive, and self-regulate is at risk. Likewise, for every wild or confined animal that breathes, drinks, or eats (Aitbali et al, 2018; Richmond 2018; Maggi et al, 2020).

As soil erodes, water dries up and forests burn, a century and a half of disregard for the health and safety of nature's essential workforce has put the nation's food supply at risk as well. California's Central Valley provides close to half of the fruits, vegetables, and nuts for the entire USA ("California's Central Valley: Producing America's Fruits and Vegetables" 2014).

The Gift of Enfolded Economies

I teach an annual workshop in the Central Valley to a group of mostly Latinx high-school students and their teachers, along with local conservation groups. I ask them to list the problems in the region, then I divide the students and adults into about eight groups and assign each of them to a bureaucratic 'department'. The job of each department is to come up with a work plan and a budget for solving one of the identified problems. Each department then has to argue the case for their budget to the group. The arguments quickly become heated. *Which is more important: air or water? Which is more of a threat: fire or poverty?*

Their budgets are wildly low. It is hard for them, or any of us, to imagine the true cost of facing or tackling these problems one by one. Wildfires cost the State of California approximately $24 billion in 2018 ("Record Wildfires Push 2018 Disaster Costs to $91 Billion" 2019). The Sites Reservoir that aims to provide water from storm runoff will take seven years to complete and it is estimated that it will cost $5.2 billion (Ring 2018). The social costs are even higher: 100 percent of residents of the Valley are exposed to health endangering levels of air pollutants ("Dirty Air Costs California Economy $28 Billion Annually" 2008).

But my students have an advantage. In our work together, they have been studying the intertwining relationships among healthy soils, vegetation, flooding, drought, air quality, air temperature, wildfires, climate, social unrest, ecological health and human mental and physical health. It's only a matter of time before someone tires of the haggling and says, 'Hey, wait a minute, what if we pooled our resources? If we all invested in the soil sponge and functional landscapes, how many of these 'problems' would go away?' In essence, they are asking: *How much of this work could (and should) be done by other species?*

This brings up other questions:

- How do we design a new economy with this biological work and workforce in mind?
- What are the currencies in the biological economy and how can we participate, given that our coins, bills, credit, and gold have no value to our non-human partners?

- What worker's rights need to be established in human legal systems for the biological workforce to continue?
- What policies are needed to enable the larger economy to thrive?

The students talk excitedly, eyes lit up, postures suddenly strong and enlivened, as they start to imagine and plan a new agriculture and a new economy. I have seen this transformation in people around the world, those who vote conservative and those who vote liberal, old and young, rich and poor, when presented with the opportunity to view our relationships with other species through new eyes. Participation in this larger economy can make our lives more viable and more meaningful and purposeful as well.

We can address most of the major challenges we are facing today by recognizing the work of other species, elevating that work to its actual place and valuing it within our human economies. Not to extract more value from it, but to find our place within a larger economy, as we engage in a meaningful exchange.

What are the Currencies of the Biological Economy?

Other species invest heavily in the landscapes they live in. Plants, for example, offer 30% to 60% of their net production to the underground community in liquid assets, as well as significant offerings to the above ground community as well. Do they do it as charity? Or do they have a wordless contract and know from experience that they can reasonably expect a sizable return on investment? These offerings are in the form of carbohydrates, sugars, and other photosynthates, stored solar energy in chains made of carbon and hydrogen, liquid sugars from their roots for those underground and edible leaves, berries, flowers, nectar, and wood for the above ground community.

The return for plants is invaluable. From below, they receive transport of nutrients, at the exact time and in the exact ratio that the plants need them; hidden water during droughts and life-saving information via communication services (Van Der Heijden et al. 2016). Mycorrhizal fungi provide all of these, using the energy from the plants to search out nutrients, solubilize rocks, find new water sources, and share information between plant communities about the approach of predators and disease. These and other underground workers also continually construct the living infrastructure of the soil sponge, so that water can be held at the root zone for plants, rather than running off and so that mineral particles stay put, rather than blowing away in high winds, or eroding during rainstorms.

From above, insects, birds, and grazing animals provide transport of other essential goods and services since plants cannot walk. Transport of pollen, and all the sexy coded information within it, from one plant to another. Transport of seeds, hitching a ride, like a bunch of college graduates who want to get out in the world and put down roots. Transport of nutrients back uphill in a world of intense gravity so that hilltops are not all bare, with plants only growing in the valleys.

Though the return on investments is high, it is not an extractive economy. Contrary to what fertilizer salespeople might tell you, plants in a natural community *do not* use up the nutrients in the soil around them and go look for another place to grow. Nor do the soil microbes suck the plants dry of all the sugary exudates and sneak off with them to deposit them in some offshore account, never to be seen again, leaving the plants exhausted and weak. Nor do grazing animals eat every leaf of every plant available to them before moving their business on to the next community.

No. It is different from our usual human economy.

It is a deeply participatory economy that regenerates itself, providing an upward spiral of more and more goods and services for everyone. While doing their work for and with each other, plants, animals, fungi, and bacteria use their abundant profits to reinvest in improvements to the living infrastructure, workforce and community that makes it all possible. This creates increasingly resilient and interesting landscapes above and below ground, and opportunities for more and more interesting things to happen. Communities get to stretch and grow and learn continually; each developing their own unique essence, capacity and creative intelligence over time. We could be part of all that.

What Could, and Should, our Relationship to These Workers Be?

Sanford and Haggard's 'Levels of Paradigm' framework (Sanford 2020) has helped me develop awareness of how I speak and write about the living systems around me. Our words create images in listeners' minds and in our own, that reinforce cultural paradigms and beliefs, whether we mean to or not. Being aware of language allows us to consciously uplift a conversation in ways that can potentially reorient the trajectory of projects and policies to create a very different ecological, social, and economic future. The Levels of Paradigm framework is:

Regenerate Life
Do Good

Arrest Disorder
Extract Value (also called *Value Return*)

Staying awake to our relationships with living systems (and the reality we are creating through language and image) is not a one-shot deal. It is not a set of practices, certification, or a course to complete. Like any form of metanoia, staying awake requires a continual act of considering. Most of us come from cultures that have been asleep for thousands of years in regard to our relationships with other species, and with each other. Even people raised in cultures that see and value the work of other species still risk being pulled into lower paradigms as they interact with the dominant unaware culture.

This framework is meant to help us be aware of *our own* thinking and language, rather than using it as a critique of others.

Extract Value (or Value Return)

One way I can view a living system is as something I can extract value from, or get more value returned to me than I put in. Examples of this are:

- Seeing a forest system, and its biological workforce as lumber to be harvested and sold at a higher price.
- Seeing soil carbon as an investment opportunity.
- Seeing the emerging understanding of the human microbiome as an opportunity to sell beneficial bacteria as probiotics.

This extractive approach is easy to fall into because it is embedded in our economic systems and the language is everywhere.

Even when I recognize the work of other species and even if I treat them well, I can still operate from an extractive mindset. If we see ourselves as owner or managers of a piece of land, we can operate the equivalent of a dangerous sweatshop, or a sumptuous high-tech company, complete with sushi deliveries. Yet seeing other species solely as workers and ourselves as owners who can profit from smart management, is still essentially a 'Value Return' or 'Extract Value' view of the work of other living systems.

Does this mean we should not make a profit? Managing land and biological labor for profits does not always destroy living systems, there are wonderful groups of farmers making higher net profits while also regenerating land, but it does not protect against it either. It is not about the dollars, but rather, about the resources and workforce behind the dollars and whether one is extracting more value from the system than one is putting in.

When I am in this mindset, I am wanting things to go well for me and my family, but I am temporarily forgetting the fact that our wellbeing is nested in the well-being of others. I am practicing internal considering only, in the language of Gurdjieff (Ouspensky 1949). I am primarily concerned with my own security and survival, as laid out by Fr. Thomas Keating in his map of the False Self's "emotional programs for happiness"(Keating 2012).

Arrest Disorder

When I shift toward a little more external considering and can see more aspects of living systems at work, sometimes I feel an urgent need to protect whatever aspect of the system I think is most important, if I think it is in danger. But my opinion of what needs protecting may shift and change and bump up hard against other people's protective instincts. The 'arrest disorder' mindset has led to some famous fights that can last for decades:

- Seeing a forest as a battleground to protect spotted owls OR a place to protect jobs in the logging industry.
- Seeing a farm as a place that needs protection from insects OR seeing a farm as a place that should protect people from the harm of pesticides.

This is the perspective of seeing the world as fragmented into good and evil that ultimately separated humans from their environment in Genesis. The fight takes precedence, rather than trusting the capacity of the living systems (e.g. people, ecosystems, soils) to come up with creative adaptations, or to self-regulate if given half a chance, as happened when various 'invasive pests' became part of a larger more diverse food web in the recent documentary, *The Biggest Little Farm* (Chester 2018).

Viewing the world as a battleground can take up a huge amount of energy and resources. Applying Fr. Thomas Keating's framework, this is the False Self's need for power and control. This view is active when I use phrases like 'combating climate chaos,' 'defeating big oil' or 'drawing down carbon' (rather than letting life do more of its work of turning CO^2 into diverse life, which includes oil executives who, like everyone else are 'sequestering carbon' in their own bodies for 50 to 100 years!). When I find myself using this language or view, it is an indicator that I am falling into the trap of seeing humans as the ones with all the power divided into two opposing camps: perpetrators vs. saviors. Or dividing nature into good nature, e.g., ducks, and bad nature, e.g., ticks. This dualistic view got us kicked out of the garden and it certainly is not metanoia.

At its most extreme, the Arrest Disorder paradigm is similar to the "sterile paradigm of care" for living systems that I wrote about in *The Ecology of Care: Medicine, Agriculture, Money and the Quiet Power of Human and Microbial Communities* (Pershouse 2016). The sterile paradigm sees anything that is a 'problem' or that gets in the way of 'progress' as something to be killed off or controlled - germs, weeds, beavers, indigenous people - without consideration of the cost to the whole.

The Arrest Disorder view has also inspired the creation of many of our important environmental laws to reduce harm or conserve endangered species. Yet, as the Rights of Nature and Wild Law movements point out, most environmental law is still happening in a completely human-centric context. The usual laws that protect other species, waterways, or forests do not generally require a perpetrator to compensate or regenerate *the system itself* once it has been harmed. People whose health is affected by pesticides may be compensated when Monsanto/Bayer loses a lawsuit, but the cows, birds, fish, frogs, and bees are not. If a lawsuit is settled against a corporation that has damaged or polluted a landscape, the land*owner* is compensated financially and maybe the surrounding human residents, but the non-human workers/residents are not (Pershouse 2016).

I can recognize other species as having a key role in the web of life, yet still see them as powerless 'victims' in need of rescue; or pick one particular species to rescue and ignore all others or target various other species as part of the problem. This does not give an accurate picture of our true relationship to other species, or of the potential of our relationships with each other.

Our own intelligence, health and future are all bound up with every other living thing, including each other. We are nested, and entangled and in fact, not separate at all.

Do Good

When I view a living system from the 'Do Good' paradigm, I shift from wanting to reduce harm towards wanting to contribute towards the creation of an ideal community, an ideal landscape, a perfectly happy herd of cows. There is a sense of nostalgia here, a desire to get back to the good old days. There is also a powerful sense that I know best what that ideal is and if I only had enough money, or support from others, I could fund a project that will feed the hungry, find new treatments for cancer, or create an animal sanctuary for endangered species. Much good work comes from this perspective. Unfortunately, the money needed to sustain these projects often ends up being sourced from the same extractive economy that created the needs, which in turn makes more and more need for charities to feed the poor, come up with new treatments for cancer, create animal sanctuaries, etc.

Since my sense of what that ideal is may be completely different than yours, we end up competing for funding and breaking the world into individual problems, parts, and projects, each with its own competing set of nonprofits, academic departments, and government bureaucracies. And it is easier to donate money (that would have gone into whatever taxpayers decide is the public good) to my favorite charity and deduct it from my taxes so that I can support MY idea, rather than working on creating a better economic and governance system to address the root causes ("INCITE! Women of Color Against Violence" 2017). When I see the world through this perspective, I often am operating out of the False Self's need for esteem and affection. I want to be seen as a good person. As important and well intentioned as all these efforts are, we can and must elevate our view.

Regenerate Life

When I perceive the world around me from the 'Regenerate Life' paradigm, (or what I often call the 'Let Life Do its Work' paradigm) I see every living thing, including you, as having inherent intelligence, essential work to do, a role to play in the whole, and a unique essence and unlimited potential that can continually develop itself. If I can hold that view, I trust that each life, and living system can do its best work when it is self-determining, self-managing, and allowed to work with, and within, other nested living systems.

Continually asking ourselves to take a meta-view, turns our thinking towards an economy and society that can not only *sustain* itself long beyond the usual few thousand years that civilizations tend to last, but can actually continually *regenerate* itself, moving more and more into the potential it holds, by evolving capacity among all who participate in it.

All three of the other perspectives can find a place to become of service to this perspective: it does make sense for me to take care of my own family, it does make sense to stop harm from happening and to do good in the world. But it has to be done with a larger aim in mind: to continually regenerate life and living systems.

It is a hard perspective to hold when aphids are eating my orchids, or wasps are building nests right next to my front door. It is a hard perspective to hold when a hawk is swooping down on one of my hens, or the white pines are starting to block the morning sunlight that I used to have in my kitchen. But even if I cut a tree, or yell at a hawk from time to time, I can choose over and over again to see the forest I live in as a unique evolving intelligence, with a history and a future, having multiple roles to play in the evolution of the larger living system of the planet. I can ponder that this forest is influencing (and being influenced by) flows of water, carbon, nutrients, and sunlight energy; as well as the decisions made by the hawks, wasps, deer, foxes, domestic chickens, wild turkeys, stray dogs, chickadees, aphids, ants, white pine, hemlock, maples, blueberries, raspberries, roses, dandelions, apple trees, frogs, mushrooms, microbes, hummingbirds, earthworms...and by me, a single human living within it, along with everyone else.

I can see that if each of us who lives here returns value and care to the larger living system, and the larger life that this forest is nested within, it just might, as a whole, provide an ongoing source of warmth, cooling, fiber, food, medicine, shelter, and clean water - and a meaningful life as well - for me *and* its other inhabitants.

Our mistakes are not the problem. Whether you are a plant or a microbe or a fox, life has always been a series of attempts and explorations that require constant assessment, adjustment, and redirection, so we are learning along the way. What most humans seem to have lost is a way of continual reorientation that happens in communion and communication with the whole.

What is Our Essential Work as Humans?

The Old Testament has two Genesis stories. In the first, humans are given dominion over nature, to subdue it ('Arrest Disorder') and take from it what they need ('Extract Value/Value Return'). The interpretation of the first Genesis story has evolved over time toward 'stewardship', reflecting more of a 'Do Good' perspective. Still, humans are in charge.

In the second Genesis story, something rather different unfolds. Adam and Eve begin their lives quite nicely nested within nature, living along with it and eating freely from whatever grows naturally in the garden, while caring for what is around them. They are full participants in the economy of Eden, along with all the other species. It is only when they begin to see themselves as separate from nature, distinguishing themselves from other animals by needing to cover up their bodies - and seeing the whole as fragmented parts, good and evil, that Adam and Eve are forced to begin laboriously tilling the soil to grow grains, rather than living within an ecosystem and economy that provides for all its inhabitants. It is not the snake's fault. It is the shift in *their view, their beliefs,* that tossed humans out of the nested regenerative larger economy to begin toiling in an extractive economy.

Agricultural society began about 10,000 years ago (Weisdorf 2005). In societies that adopted agricultural lifestyles, human health became worse, their height shortened and their facial structure changed (Marciniak et al, 2021; Larsen 2006). 'Weeds' and 'pests' like locusts became a problem in monoculture fields. The need for property rights and weights and measures came along with it. The need for fences to keep people and wild animals off one's property interrupted natural grazing patterns and wildlife corridors.

Inheritances of property created a more deeply divided class society that got worse generation by generation and has led to our current obscene divisions of wealth and power. Six billion hectares of formerly fertile diverse ecosystems, 'lands of milk and honey', including the Sahara and the 'fertile crescent' region of the Middle East, are now man-made deserts and wasteland.

We are long overdue for a transformational shift in perspective. The 'Genesis' of Jesus of Nazareth offers a new creation story, which most Christians have yet to fully integrate or accept, but which offers us an invitation back into the Garden. From the moment Jesus was born and laid in a feeding trough for animals, to the last supper, Jesus is not just someone who eats, but is himself, food for other life. This image of one life feeding other life for continual renewal and regeneration has opened hearts through history and become Christianity's holiest sacrament of communion. Yet we miss the mark when we only see humans at the communion table.

According to the gospels, Jesus' full entry into spiritual life begins not indoors in a temple, but with full immersion in a river, by a cousin dressed in wild animal skins. Having been born in a stable, he is then led to spend 40 days living in the wilderness. When he returned to human society, he threw out the people who were selling animals for sacrifice in the temple. Nature is not a resource to be sold off for profit, any more than humans are, any more than God's grace is.

As Jesus died, the veil that separated sacred space from the rest of the world ripped open, pouring a new meta-view, metanoia, into the world. Human do not have to pay to access sacred space, we do not have to have special status to read God's word. We can read it all around us, in what is at hand: the book of Creation. Everything around us is sacred. Every microbe, every insect, every person. Whether we notice it or not, we are held lovingly and nourished by a larger community at work, practicing the work of continual regeneration. This is the nested household we live within and life itself is our 'home economics' course. Our essential work is seeing the whole clearly enough, through metanoia, to understand the flows of life and learn how our actions influence them, so that when we place a stone in a river, dig a hole, plant a seed, take a life, we are participating consciously: in communion.

As the oceans rise and the floods engulf us, it is no longer our work to build the ark that will save creation, but to understand that creation itself is the sacred ark of our lives.

Bibliography

Abraham, William. 2003. US7771736B2 - Glyphosate formulations and their use for the inhibition of 5-enolpyruvylshikimate-3-phosphate synthase, issued 2003.
https://patents.google.com/patent/US7771736B2/en.

Aitbali, Yassine., Saadia Ba-M'hamed., Najoua Elhidar., Ahmed Nafis., Nabila Soraa and Mohamed Bennis. 2018. "Glyphosate-Based Herbicide Exposure Affects Gut Microbiota, Anxiety and Depression-like Behaviors in Mice." *Neurotoxicology and Teratology* 67 (May): 44–49. https://doi.org/10.1016/j.ntt.2018.04.002.

Anderson, M. Kat. 2013. *Tending the Wild: Native American Knowledge and the Management of California's Natural Resources.* First.

Arax, Mark. 2019. *The Dreamt Land: Chasing Water and Dust Across California.* (New York: Vintage Books, 2019).

"California's Central Valley: Producing America's Fruits and Vegetables." 2014. Committee on Natural Resources Republican Office. February 5, 2014.
https://republicans-naturalresources.house.gov/newsroom/ documentsingle.aspx?DocumentID=368934.

Chen, Chi., Dan Li., Yue Li., Shilong Piao., Xuhui Wang., Maoyi Huang., Pierre Gentine., Ramakrishna R. Nemani and Ranga B. Myneni. 2020. "Biophysical Impacts of Earth Greening Largely Controlled by Aerodynamic Resistance." *Science Advances* 6 (47): eabb1981. https://doi.org/10.1126/sciadv.abb1981.

Chester, John. 2018. *The Biggest Little Farm Movie.* Moorpark, CA, USA. http://www.biggestlittlefarmmovie.com/.

"Dirty Air Costs California Economy $28 Billion Annually." 2008. Office of Public Affairs at California State University, Fullerton. 2008. http://calstate.fullerton.edu/news/2008/091-air-pollution-study.html.

Frayer, W E., Dennis D Peters and H Ross Pywell. 1989. "Wetlands of the California Central Valley: Status and Trends 1939 to Mid 1980's."

https://www.fws.gov/wetlands/Documents/Wetlands-of-the-California-Central-Valley-Status-and-Trends-1939-to-mid-1980s.pdf.

Galloway, Devin and Francis S Riley. 1999. "San Joaquin Valley, California: Largest Human Alteration of the Earth's Surface." *US Geological Survey Circular* 1182: 23–34. https://pubs.usgs.gov/circ/circ1182/pdf/06SanJoaquinValley.pdf.

Goldfarb, Ben. 2018. *Eager: The Surprising, Secret Life of Beavers and Why They Matter*. (White River Junction, Vermont: Chelsea Green Publishing, 2018).

"INCITE! Women of Color Against Violence." 2017. *The Revolution Will Not Be Funded: Beyond the Non-Profit Industrial Complex*. (Durham, North Carolina: Duke University Press, 2017).

Johnson, D and L Gilbert. 2017. "Mycorrhizal Fungal Networks as Plant Communication Systems." In *The Fungal Community: Its Organization and Role in the Ecosystem*, edited by J. Dighton and J. F. White, Fourth, (539–48. Boca Raton: CRC Press, 2017). http://eprints.gla.ac.uk/210537/.

Kabat, P., Claussen, M., Whitlock, S., Gash, J.H.C., Guenni, L.B. de, Meybeck, M., Pielke, R., Vörösmarty, C.J., Hutjes, R.W.A., Lütkemeier, S. (Eds.). 2004. *Vegetation, Water, Humans and the Climate: A New Perspective on an Interactive System*. Springer Science & Business Media.

Keating, Thomas. 2012. *On Divine Therapy*. (New York: Lantern Publishing & Media, 2012).

Lal, R., D. C. Reicosky and J. D. Hanson. 2007. "Evolution of the Plow over 10,000 Years and the Rationale for No-till Farming." *Soil and Tillage Research* 93 (1): 1–12. https://doi.org/10.1016/j.still.2006.11.004.

Larsen, Clark Spencer. 2006. "The Agricultural Revolution as Environmental Catastrophe: Implications for Health and Lifestyle in the Holocene." *Quaternary International*, Impact of rapid environmental changes on humans and ecosystems, 150 (1): 12–20. https://doi.org/10.1016/j.quaint.2006.01.004.

Lazaridis, Mihalis. 2019. "Bacteria as Cloud Condensation Nuclei (CCN) in the Atmosphere." *Atmosphere* 10 (12): 786. https://doi.org/10.3390/atmos10120786.

Maggi, Federico., Daniele la Cecilia., Fiona H.M. Tang and Alexander McBratney. 2020. "The Global Environmental Hazard of Glyphosate Use." *Science of the Total Environment* 717 (May). https://doi.org/10.1016/j.scitotenv.2020.137167.

Makarieva, Anastassia M., Victor G Gorshkov and Bai-Lian Li. 2009. "Precipitation on Land versus Distance from the Ocean: Evidence for a

Forest Pump of Atmospheric Moisture." *Ecological Complexity* 6 (January): 302–7. https://doi.org/10.1016/j.ecocom.2008.11.004.

—. 2013. "Revisiting Forest Impact on Atmospheric Water Vapor Transport and Precipitation." *Theoretical and Applied Climatology* 111: 79–96. https://doi.org/10.1007/s00704-012-0643-9.

Marciniak, Stephanie., Christina M. Bergey., Ana Maria Silva., Agata Hałuszko., Mirosław Furmanek., Barbara Veselka and Petr Velemínský, 2021. "An Integrative Skeletal and Paleogenomic Analysis of Prehistoric Stature Variation Suggests Relatively Reduced Health for Early European Farmers." *BioRxiv*, March, 2021.03.31.437881. https://doi.org/10.1101/2021.03.31.437881.

McEachran, Andrew D., Brett R. Blackwell., J. Delton Hanson., Kimberly J. Wooten., Gregory D. Mayer., Stephen B. Cox and Philip N. Smith. 2015. "Antibiotics, Bacteria, and Antibiotic Resistance Genes: Aerial Transport from Cattle Feed Yards via Particulate Matter." *Environmental Health Perspectives* 123 (4): 337–43. https://doi.org/10.1289/ehp.1408555.

Montgomery, David. 2012. *Dirt: The Erosion of Civilizations.* (Berkeley: University of California Press, 2012).

Montgomery, David R. 2007. "Soil Erosion and Agricultural Sustainability." *Proceedings of the National Academy of Sciences* 104 (33): 13268–72. https://doi.org/10.1073/pnas.0611508104.

Morris, Cindy E., Franz Conen, J., Alex Huffman., Vaughan Phillips., Ulrich Pöschl and David C. Sands. 2014. "Bioprecipitation: A Feedback Cycle Linking Earth History, Ecosystem Dynamics and Land Use through Biological Ice Nucleators in the Atmosphere." *Global Change Biology* 20 (2): 341–51. https://doi.org/10.1111/gcb.12447.

Nascimento, Madson M., Gisele O. Da Rocha and Jailson B. De Andrade. 2017. "Pesticides in Fine Airborne Particles: From a Green Analysis Method to Atmospheric Characterization and Risk Assessment." *Scientific Reports* 7 (1): 1–11. https://doi.org/10.1038/s41598-017-02518-1.

Ouspensky, Piotr Demianovich. 1949. *In Search of the Miraculous: Fragments of an Unknown Teaching.*

Outwater, Alice. 1996. *Water: A Natural History.* (New York: Basic Books, 1996).

Pershouse, Didi. 2016. *The Ecology of Care: Medicine, Agriculture, Money, and the Quiet Power of Human and Microbial Communities.* (Mycelium Books, 2016).

—. 2020. "Why Communities Should Invest in Regenerative Agriculture and the Soil Sponge." Medium. November 30, 2020.

https://didipershouse.medium.com/why-communities-should-invest-in-regenerative-agriculture-and-the-soil-sponge-431c27c8b34b.

Pielke, Roger A., Rezaul Mahmood and Clive McAlpine. 2016. "Land's Complex Role in Climate Change." *Physics Today* 69 (11): 40–46. https://doi.org/10.1063/PT.3.3364.

"Record Wildfires Push 2018 Disaster Costs to $91 Billion." 2019. Center for Climate and Energy Solutions. February 27, 2019. https://www.c2es.org/2019/02/record-wildfires-push-2018-disaster-costs-to-91-billion/.

Richmond, Martha E. 2018. "Glyphosate: A Review of Its Global Use, Environmental Impact, and Potential Health Effects on Humans and Other Species." *Journal of Environmental Studies and Sciences* 8 (4): 416–34. https://doi.org/10.1007/s13412-018-0517-2.

Ring, Edward. 2018. "How Much California Water Bond Money Is for Storage?" California Policy Center. August 9, 2018. https://californiapolicycenter.org/how-much-california-water-bond-money-is-for-storage/.

Sanford, Carol. 2020. "The Regenerative Economic Shaper Perspective Paper - Part 2." Medium. June 24, 2020. https://medium.com/the-regenerative-economy-collaborative/the-regenerative-economic-shaper-perspective-paper-part-2-418f35369ded.

Sheil, Douglas. 2018. "Forests, Atmospheric Water and an Uncertain Future: The New Biology of the Global Water Cycle." *Forest Ecosystems* 5 (1): 1–22. https://doi.org/10.1186/s40663-018-0138-y.

Sheller, Andrew. 2019. "The Central Valley Is Sinking as Farmers Drill for Water. But It Can Be Saved, Study Says." *Sacramento Bee*, April 2019. https://www.sacbee.com/news/california/bigvalley/article229148999.html.

Van Der Heijden., Marcel G.A., Susanne De Bruin., Ludo Luckerhoff., Richard S.P. Van Logtestijn and Klaus Schlaeppi. 2016. "A Widespread Plant-Fungal-Bacterial Symbiosis Promotes Plant Biodiversity, Plant Nutrition and Seedling Recruitment." *ISME Journal* 10 (2): 389–99. https://doi.org/10.1038/ismej.2015.120.

Vitousek, Sean., Patrick L. Barnard., Charles H. Fletcher., Neil Frazer., Li Erikson and Curt D. Storlazzi. 2017. "Doubling of Coastal Flooding Frequency within Decades Due to Sea-Level Rise." *Scientific Reports* 7 (1): 1399. https://doi.org/10.1038/s41598-017-01362-7.

Vörösmarty, Charles and Dork Sahagian. 2000. "Anthropogenic Disturbance of the Terrestrial Water Cycle." *BioScience*. Vol. 50. Oxford Academic.

https://doi.org/10.1641/0006-3568(2000)050[0753:ADOTTW]
2.0.CO;2.

Weisdorf, Jacob L. 2005. "From Foraging To Farming: Explaining The Neolithic Revolution." *Journal of Economic Surveys* 19 (4): 561–86. https://doi.org/10.1111/j.0950-0804.2005.00259.x.

Yilmaz, Hasan., Süleyman Toy., Mehmet Irmak and Sevgi Yilmaz. 2008. "Determination of Temperature Differences between Asphalt Concrete, Soil and Grass Surfaces of the City of Erzurum, Turkey." *Atmosfera* 21 (2): 135–46.
https://www.researchgate.net/publication/26508025_Determination_of _temperature_differences_between_asphalt_concrete_soil_and_grass_s urfaces_of_the_City_of_Erzurum_Turkey.

CHAPTER SEVENTEEN

POPULATION AND OUR CONTEMPORARY ECOLOGICAL CRISIS

DAVID SAMWAYS

Introduction

In his seminal essay of 1967, 'The Historical Roots of Our Ecologic Crisis', Lynne White Jr (1967) laid the blame for the unprecedented environmental impact of modern society squarely at the foot of Christianity: "Especially in its Western form," he wrote, "Christianity is the most anthropocentric religion the world has ever seen" (p.1205). White argued that while the proximate cause of environmental degradation was science and technology, that the root cause lay in the "psychic revolution" consequent of Christianity replacing Paganism. According to White, Paganism regarded the natural world as worthy of moral consideration:

> Before one cut a tree, mined a mountain, or dammed a brook, it was important to placate the spirit in charge of that particular situation, and to keep it placated. By destroying pagan animism, Christianity made it possible to exploit nature in a mood of indifference to the feelings of natural objects. (White Jr 1967)

White's anthropocentrism thesis struck an intuitive chord with the nascent environmental movement, and in some quarters the idea that "what people do about their ecology depends on what they think about themselves in relation to things around them" (White p. 1205) became a guiding principle. This focus on the role of ideas has been remarkably persistent, with many radical environmental thinkers arguing that a complete rejection of the dominant anthropocentric worldview and replacement with a biocentric or ecocentric orientation is fundamental to averting ecological catastrophe and restoring a harmonious relationship between humankind and nature (see for example Devall and Sessions 1985; Callicott, 2012; Washington et al. 2017).

However, while this 'anthropocentrism thesis' has great intuitive appeal, evidence of significant anthropogenic environmental impact in every epoch of human history and across all types of society including people associated with a "pagan" worldview throws its veracity into doubt (Tuan, 1968; Krech 1999). Indeed, White's thesis was criticized for misinterpreting the direction of causality between beliefs and technological development as it was argued that religious beliefs were better understood as justifications rather than causes of action (Welbourn, 1975; Thomas, 1984). On this reasoning, these material-technical factors are more significant than ideas and values in generating our environmental crisis.

One of the most significant consequences of human material development, in all historical periods, and a factor highly correlated with environmental degradation, has been the growth in human numbers, especially the massive growth in population from the eighteenth century onwards. Indeed, in the case of climate change, when the growth of carbon emissions is examined alongside the growth in global population it is tempting to conclude that population growth has been the principal driver of carbon emissions (see figures 1 and 2).

However, the correlation between population growth and environmental impact, especially climate change, is more complex than it initially appears. Importantly, focussing on population growth as a means of tackling *imminent* environmental threats like climate change will not be effective. Yet this does not mean that urgent action to tackle population growth is unnecessary since ethical policies to accelerate the reduction in the global total fertility rate will significantly mitigate our environmental impact in the longer term as well as improving human welfare both now and in the future. Moreover, we will see that in attempting to understand the environmental impact of our species, ideas and material factors are interwoven and inseparable. Furthermore, anthropocentrism, or more particularly the consideration of human interests in the broadest and most expansive sense, may be of vital importance in thinking about the number that constitutes an environmentally sustainable population.

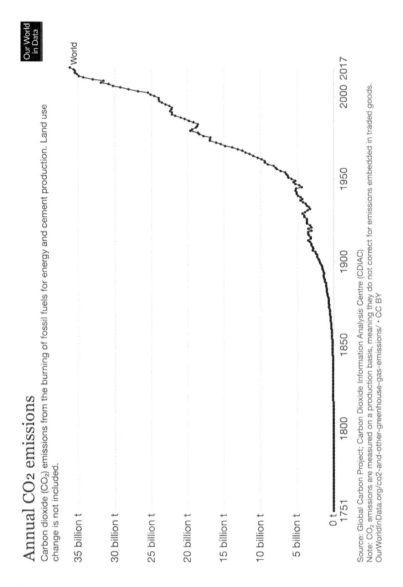

Figure 17.1. Annual CO2 emissions 1751-2017 (Source: www.ourworldindata.org)

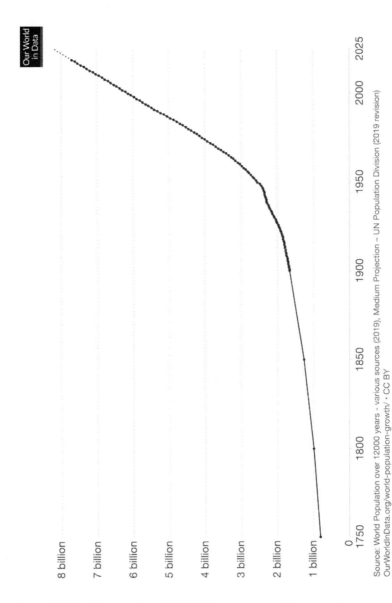

Figure 17.2. World population 1750-2025 (Source: ourworldindata.org)

I begin by attempting to understand the role of population growth in environmental impact and climate change in particular. I then turn to the issue of what constitutes an environmentally sustainable population before finally addressing the political and ethical questions surrounding how such a population might be achieved. As we will see, while ethical orientation to nature may be a poor candidate for the root cause of human environmental impact, values and ethical considerations play a central role in achieving an environmentally sustainable population and in determining the quantitative and qualitative nature of that population.

Population growth and environmental change

The idea of an idealized human past where we lived in harmony with nature is a fiction which unwittingly reproduces a dualistic separation of humankind and nature (Cronon, 1996). Human beings have *always* been a dynamic part of their environments and have altered the natural world both intentionally, in order to improve their material circumstances, and through the unintended consequences of their actions. Human population size is inextricably linked to environmental change and is both a consequence of changing of ways of interacting with nature and also a multiplier of environmental impact. Through cultural changes in their interaction with material world, both land-managing hunter-gathers and Neolithic farmers changed their environments that allowed greater numbers of people to be sustained (Feeney, 2019; Gignoux, Henn and Mountain, 2011). However, our interaction with the natural world is bidirectional and environmental change can be demonstrated to have affected the course of human socio-economic development. In the Neolithic revolution, for example, evidence suggests that in various regions natural changes in the climate may well have been a factor in the transition from hunter-gathering to settled agriculture (Ashraf and Michalopoulos, 2015).

The prehistoric expansion in human numbers multiplied the environmental changes that enabled population growth. Landscapes and local ecologies were transformed: the ecology of areas such as the Yosemite Valley in California were significantly altered by Native American land-managing hunter-gatherers through the use of fire and other techniques (see Kay, 1994; Krech, 1999; Anderson 2005; Feeney, 2019) while Neolithic farmers dramatically transformed their environments principally through deforestation (Kaplan, Krumhardt and Zimmerman, 2009). The adoption of agriculture and associated forest clearances may even have had a measurable impact on carbon dioxide and methane emissions and hence on the planet's climate, possibly averting the onset of the next ice-age (Ruddiman, et al., 2016).

While these prehistoric environmental changes were significant and relatively extensive, arguably they were environmentally sustainable since once a new ecological equilibrium had been established, resource consumption must have roughly equalled natural regeneration and wastes equalled nature's ability to assimilate and process it. Indeed, with very low rates of population growth the environmental impact of such societies remained relatively small and localized for many thousands of years. However, advances in agricultural production in medieval Western Europe led to growth in population and urban centres, giving rise to a range of more spatially concentrated local environmental problems including water and air pollution (see Brimblecombe, 1976, 1987).

With the advent of the industrial era local environmental problems grew in magnitude and in extent, but at the same time human beings began to have a significant and ultimately unsustainable impact on the Earth System[1] as a whole (Steffen, Crutzen and McNeill, 2007). Here the coupling between energy consumption and population becomes apparent. Prior to the industrial revolution the principal source of energy for humankind was solar energy captured in the relatively recent past in the form of plants (both for food and fuel), animals (for both food and as sources of motive power), water flow and wind. Importantly, all these sources were renewable in that they existed within energy flows over short time spans (less than 200 years). Expansions in human numbers prior to the industrial revolution were all related to changes in the ways that human beings harvested and used this energy. With the enormous expansion in the use of fossil fuels the previous limitation on the availability of energy was breached as coal followed by oil and natural gas effectively provided a subsidy from the deep past in the form of stocks of solar energy accumulated over millions of years. While people had been using fossil fuels since antiquity, it was not until social, economic, political, and technical conditions gave rise to the industrial revolution that fossil fuels were used in large quantities.

In a very general sense, fossil fuels can be seen as literally fuelling population growth as economic development improved standards of living, leading to falling mortality which in turn produced further growth in the use of fossil fuels. As technology developed, in what Steffen, Crutzen and McNeill (2007) originally identified as the first stage of the Anthropocene (1850-1945), previous Malthusian limits on population size - the food supply-were overcome as energy from fossil fuels was used to synthesize

---

[1] "The term *Earth System* refers to the suite of interacting physical, chemical and biological global-scale cycles and energy fluxes that provide the life-support system for life at the surface of the planet" (Steffen, Crutzen and McNeill, 2007) 615.

fertilizer, greatly increasing agricultural yields. At the same time a greater amount of land was brought into agricultural production, largely through forest clearance - Steffen, Crutzen and McNeill report that prior to 1800 10% of the planet's land was domesticated but by 1950 this had risen to 25-30%. Along with this population and agricultural expansion came interventions into the hydrological cycle through the building of large dams, while the increased use of fertilizers led to massive disruption to the nitrogen cycle.

Population and climate change

Perhaps the most important environmental impact of the industrial era has been in the contribution of fossil fuel combustion to atmospheric carbon dioxide (CO_2) levels. Indeed, Steffen, Crutzen and McNeill argue that fossil fuel use, evidenced by the accumulation of CO_2 in the atmosphere, is a barometer of the overall human impact on the environment. While CO_2 levels during the first stage increased above the upper limit of natural variation during the Holocene, in the second stage of the Anthropocene, the "Great Acceleration" beginning after WWII, CO_2 levels rapidly increase (see fig 1). Indeed, Steffen, Crutzen and McNeill point out that nearly three quarters of the rise in anthropogenically driven CO_2 concentration has taken place since 1950 with half of that total rise taking place in the three decades from the mid-1970s. During the same period, all other dimensions of the human enterprise have also increased including a massive expansion of the global economy and huge growth in the human population (Steffen, Crutzen and McNeill, 2007).

Looking at figures 1 and 2 as well as figure 3 it is tempting to draw the conclusion that population growth has been the determining factor in humanity's increased environmental footprint. Inevitably, however, the situation is more complex than it first appears. Although both population and CO_2 emissions both massively increase after 1950, emissions have not increased in proportion with population growth. Indeed, between 1950 and 2017 carbon emissions increased more than fivefold while population tripled, and between 1900 and 2000 carbon emissions increased fifteenfold and population less than fourfold (Cohen, 2010). Organisations such as Oxfam have pointed out that the richest 10% of the world's population were responsible for 52% of cumulative emissions between 1990 and 2015 while the poorest half of the global population were responsible for just 7% (Gore, 2020). Given that population growth is greatest in the world's poorest nations many commentators have argued that population growth is not a significant factor in the climate crisis (see for example Monbiot 2020; Klein 2014).

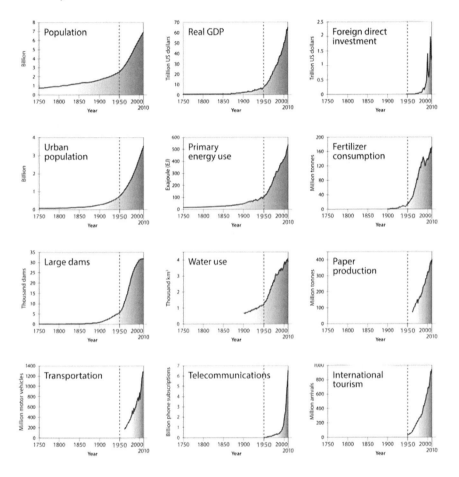

Figure 17.3 Socio-economic trends. Reproduced with kind permission of Will Steffen. (Source Steffen et al 2015). *See centrefold for this image in colour.*

Yet while the evidence demonstrates that increasing affluence is a more immediate and significant driver of energy consumption - and hence carbon emissions - and that this is vastly unequally distributed between the Global North and South, it would be mistaken to draw the conclusion that population growth is unimportant.

Part of the difficulty in comprehending the relationship between population growth, affluence, and climate change (but also environmental impact more generally) arises due to the driving factors being treated separately rather than as mutually-reinforcing. Ehrlich and Holdren's (1972) I=PAT equation is a useful heuristic device for thinking about the relationships between environmental impact (I), population (P), and affluence (or consumption) (A). The last term of the equation, T for technology, represents the resource intensity of production which, in the case of climate change, we might think of as the carbon intensity of GDP as determined by the technology employed. From the IPAT equation we see that any change in the three right hand factors will lead to change in environmental impact[2]. Thus, population growth multiplies any change in affluence and vice versa. Equally, changes in the efficiency of resource use can change the effect of T in the equation.

Technical fixes have played an important part in part in the history of environmental problems and climate change is no exception, being frequently regarded as an essentially technological challenge. It is the technical fixes to carbon emissions, such as energy efficiency and renewable technology, carbon capture, and storage and so on, which excite the public imagination and have obvious appeal to politicians too since they hold out the hope of mitigating climate change without uncomfortable changes in behavior or challenging the idea of continuous economic growth, rising incomes, and consumption. However, while these technical fixes are essential to curbing carbon emissions, they are unlikely to meet the 2016 Paris Agreement targets while the goal of continuous economic growth is also pursued and while population growth, as a multiplier of consumption growth, is left unaddressed.

The necessity of such an approach is revealed by recent research which showed that between 1990 and 2019 economic growth accounted for around two thirds of CO_2 emissions and population growth for the remaining third (Chaurasia 2020). Perhaps more importantly the same research showed that growth in population offset carbon emission savings resulting from energy efficiency improvements, the use of lower emission fuels and renewables by more than three quarters.

The difficulty of understanding the role of population in climate change is exacerbated by the time lags between various stages of economic development and associated transition from high to low rates of population growth. Consequently, a snapshot at any one particular time will almost certainly show regions with high rates of population growth as having

---

[2] In reality the right-hand factors are likely to be a great deal more interdependent so that changing one will impact upon the others (see Alcott, 2010).

relatively much smaller carbon footprints than regions with lower population growth rates. So, at present, sub-Saharan Africa has the fastest rate of population growth but low carbon emissions per capita whilst Europe has a negative rate of natural[3] population growth but has a high per capita carbon footprint (Roser, Ritchie and Ortiz-Ospina 2013; Ritchie and Roser, 2017).

However, looking at the relationship between population, economic development and environmental impact over a longer time period is more revealing. Over the course of the 19th century the population of the rich world roughly doubled and then doubled again during the 20th (Roser, Ritchie and Ortiz-Ospina 2013). The fifteen-fold increase in the combined per capita incomes in the USA and UK over the same period (Roser, 2013) is indicative of the extent the growth in affluence that took place across the whole of the industrialized Global North. Thus, the combined growth in the size of the population and economies of the Global North drove increased environmental impacts and, as we have seen, huge increases in carbon emissions.

In the post war period, the greatest rates of population growth have been in the Global South with Asia adding the greatest additional number of people - 3.2 billion or 62% of the total 5.15 billion increase between 1950 and 2019 (Roser, Ritchie and Ortiz-Ospina 2013). Economic activity and consumption however continued to be concentrated in the Global North - in 2010 around a fifth of the world's population accounted for nearly three quarters of economic activity (Steffen et al 2015). The share of historic cumulative carbon emissions also reflects the economic domination of the Global North with North America and Europe accounting for over 60% of emissions since 1751 (Ritchie and Roser, 2017).

Yet in the past 30 or 40 years, Asia has experienced considerable economic growth and improvements in welfare. At more or less the same time, many Asian countries considerably slowed in their rate of population growth with birth rates approaching replacement levels. At present the world's two most populace countries, China and India, both have declining rates of population growth but due to demographic momentum (the forward growth of total population as the children produced by a higher fertility generation have children themselves) continue to grow in absolute numbers with China predicted to peak at 1.46 billion in 2026 and India at 1.65 billion in 2053 (Ritchie, 2019). China's total fertility has been below replacement level since the 1990s and India is rapidly approaching this figure.

---

[3] Meaning from births minus deaths rather than from immigration.

However, as the economies of many of the countries of the Global South have developed so too has their environmental impact. Between 1990 and 2019 80% of the growth in carbon emissions was accounted for by China, India, Iran, and Indonesia, with China alone producing more than half of this (Chaurasia, 2020). In absolute terms, in the first decade of this century China overtook the USA as the largest emitter and as of 2017 Asia emitted more CO_2 per annum than any other global region (Ritchie and Roser, 2017).

Gross figures here need to be treated with caution since not only do these regions have very large populations, but figures include both emissions from domestic consumption as well as those embedded in goods for export. The deindustrialisation of the Global North and export driven industrialisation of Asia has shifted the emissions of goods consumed in rich countries toward those emerging countries where they are manufactured. Nonetheless, China's per capita domestic consumption emissions are rapidly approaching those of the EU countries (Ritchie and Roser, 2017) - a fact that reflects how China's rapid economic development has raised domestic incomes and welfare and hence its per capita carbon footprint. Across many parts of the developing world incomes are increasing and the number of people living in poverty declining. While this has reduced fertility and further slowed the rate of population growth, as many have noted, in combination with large and still growing populations, the emergence of a middle-class in the Global South will also significantly increase emissions (Steffen et al, 2015; Bongaarts and O'Neill 2018).

Population, sustainability and the good life

While population can be shown to be a significant factor in carbon emissions, as we have seen, demographic momentum means that that changing the birth-rate will have little effect on the overall size of the population for many decades and thus is of little use as a policy instrument in tackling the *immediate* threat of climate change (Bradshaw and Brook, 2014). However, this does not mean that policies aimed at reducing and even reversing population growth cannot be effective in reducing emissions growth, and other impacts, in the longer term. Indeed, Bradshaw and Brook (2014) concluded that tackling human population size would have long-term environmental and social benefits while O'Neill et al. estimate that slower future population growth could reduce emissions by 40% in the long-term (O'Neill et al., 2012).

However, given the long-term nature of the population problem, if it is accepted that fairness demands that everyone on the planet deserves the opportunity to have a good life with a decent standard of living, then the immediate challenge is how this might be achieved within planetary boundaries whilst also providing for a global population that even more optimistic forecasts put at more than 9 billion by mid-century (Vollset et al., 2020).

Providing for 9 billion and more

In the interests of improving human welfare, it is clear that economic growth in the Global South is a necessity. The UN's Sustainable Development Goals (SDGs) embrace this idea, seeing economic growth in the least developed nations as a key means of improving welfare. Indeed, in practice, over the last three or four decades, it has been economic development that has lifted over a billion people out of extreme poverty (defined as less than $1.90 a day PPP 2011) with the vast majority of this taking place in Asia (Roser and Ortiz-Ospina, 2019). However, in 2017 more than 43% of the global population - some 3.27 billion people - had incomes below the high-middle income international poverty line of $5.50 a day (World Bank n.d).

While economic growth has brought significant welfare benefits to those in the Global South, the environmental sustainability of the economic objectives of the SDGs is questionable (see O'Neill et al 2018; Hickel 2019b). A number of studies have concluded that key environmental boundaries have already been breached and that our current levels of consumption overshoot what the Earth can sustainably provide by 70% (Lin et al 2018; McBain et al., 2017). O'Neill et al. (2018) have shown that in theory, with equal distribution, the physical needs (nutrition, sanitation, access to electricity and the eradication of extreme poverty) of the global population could be met within planetary boundaries. However, these basic needs are far from the high-quality lifestyles which the majority in the developed world take for granted. Achieving universal human development as set out in the SDGs would require 2-6 times the sustainable resource level and would have "the potential to undermine the Earth-system processes upon which development ultimately depends" (O'Neill et al., 2018 p.93). Furthermore, Hickel (2019a) has pointed out that the economic objectives set out in SDG 8 would require a rate of global economic growth which, taking account of projected increases in population, would lead to the global economy being 55% larger in 2030 than it was fifteen years earlier.

Clearly, achieving the objective of a good life for all within planetary boundaries will require a dramatic reduction in resource consumption in the rich world and a shift in the share of available resources southward to meet basic needs. Hickel (2019b) has estimated that a reduction of the developed world's biophysical footprint of between 40-50% will be necessary, entailing degrowth strategies and a shift toward a post-capitalist economic model.

Selling such a policy to the electorates of rich-world nations will not be easy and will require not only an improvement in the efficiency of "provisioning systems" - the socio-technical systems which "mediate the relationship between biophysical resource use and social outcomes" (O'Neill et al., 2018 p.89) - but also a refocussing of social norms and notions of what constitutes 'the good life' away from practices involving high resource consumption. The latter may be as diverse as our consumption and use of automobiles through to the composition of our diets. However, as O'Neill et al. note, efforts to achieve such outcomes will be frustrated if efforts to stabilize future population are neglected, and Hickel goes further in suggesting:

> One approach would be to gradually reduce the size of the population (in an equitable, progressive, and non-coercive way), so that GDP per capita can be maintained even while total economic activity shrinks. But if we assume that the population grows according to existing projections and stabilises at 9–11 billion, this will require de-growth in both absolute and per capita terms. (Hickel, 2019, p.13)

Achieving a long-term sustainable population

Even if equitable, progressive, and non-coercive measures to reduce population were enacted tomorrow it would be many decades before their effect was felt. In the shorter-term, meeting the needs of the existing population within planetary boundaries clearly requires a radical adjustment of our economic system. However, this still begs the question: what population size might be sustained at high levels of welfare in the future? O'Neill et al.'s (2018) estimate that a high-quality lifestyle for a population of 7 billion would require 2-6 times the level of sustainable resource use implies that a population between one sixth and half of this size (approximately 1.2 and 3.5 billion) could enjoy a high-quality life and remain within planetary boundaries. A number of authors have attempted to arrive at a figure for sustainable population at high welfare (see Daily, Ehrlich and Ehrlich 1994; Pimentel et al. 1994, Pimentel et al. 2010; Lianos and Pseiridis 2015; Tucker; 2019) and all have come roughly within the scope implied by O'Neill et al.'s work, ranging from 1 through to 3.1 billion.

Values are central to the question of what might be an 'optimum' population size. As O'Neill et al. (2018) show, it is theoretically possible that the current population could have basic needs met within planetary boundaries. However, basic needs are far from what many consider to be a good life. When it comes to assessing a sustainable maximum population, much will depend upon defining the good life and of what we value, not just in terms of human well-being but of the well-being of other species, ecosystems and of landscapes.

Seen in this way, the notion of 'sustainability' itself becomes more elusive and less easy to define. Sustainability is frequently employed in a narrowly anthropocentric way where concern is only directed toward solving environmental problems, such as climate change, in order to continue modern ways of life and avoid disruption to relatively short-term human interests. However, when considered in the light of the scientific evidence demonstrating the outsized human impact upon the very systems upon which we depend, narrow anthropocentricism paradoxically appears to be contrary to the interests of our species - at least when considered in the longer term. In contrast, more expansive conceptions of anthropocentrism (see Norton, 1984; Barry, 1999; O'Neill, 1997) recognize that human well-being and flourishing are dependent on the Earth's natural life-sustaining systems as well as recognising that both natural and long-established human-made environments are also highly valued.

Thus, sustainable population size is a profoundly value-laden political and ethical question dependent on the articulation of arguments regarding what we define as the good life, what we consider to be just and fair, and the sort of environment in which we wish to live. As Pimentel et al. (1994, p.364) put it:

> Does human society want 10 to 15 billion humans living in poverty and malnourishment or 1 to 2 billion living with abundant resources and a quality environment?

Unfortunately, the above quotation omits a critical dimension: global inequality. Those calculating sustainable population size usually assume an equal distribution of resources, but on past experience there is little reason to be optimistic that this would occur in the future. It is an unpalatable fact that the degree to which better-off people are willing to tolerate the suffering of those in far-off places is also a choice relevant to the environmental sustainability of a given population size. The present persistence of malnutrition amongst millions is not a reflection of a global insufficiency of food but of the unacknowledged conditions and unintended consequences of choices of those in better-off counties. More than enough food is produced to feed the world's population (FAO et al., 2020) but food choices, such as the consumption of dairy and meat products, by those in wealthier parts of the world are in part responsible for pricing the poorest out of the global food market (Cohen, 2017). Without addressing the issue of global inequality, it is likely that the poor will pay the greatest price of population growth and indeed of environmental degradation. To avoid this, as Hickel (2018) notes, a fundamental reorientation of our approach to development is required from concentrating on the deficiencies of poor countries to the excesses of the rich ones.

While this is undoubtedly true, without addressing population growth itself, redressing the imbalance between rich and poor whilst also attempting to live within planetary boundaries becomes increasingly less effective at improving welfare since fewer resources must be distributed between greater number of people. Yet it is frequently the inequality between the Global North and Global South which lies behind the reticence of many in the environmental movement to acknowledge population growth as a problem. Much of this is related to the temporal disjuncture, noted above, between high fertility rates and increased environmental impact that occurs as countries develop economically and increase welfare and affluence. This can lead to a perception that those concerned about population growth are blaming the poor for environmental problems like climate change for which they clearly have little responsibility.

Moreover, the association of 'population control' with imperialism, eugenics, and past coercive population policies such as those in China and India has somewhat understandably made population growth a taboo subject. Even when the long-term desirability of achieving a smaller population more quickly is acknowledged, many are uncomfortable with influencing fertility decisions because such issues are seen to be deeply personal and private choices synonymous with basic human rights. However, as Diana Coole (2018) has pointed out, rather than being exclusively self-regarding reproduction is an other-regarding act that has the potential to undermine the socio-ecological systems which constitute the conditions of possibility for exercising individual basic rights. Perhaps most importantly though, ethical policies directed toward lowering fertility are in many instances emancipatory, transforming female subjectivity, creating responsible (female and male) agents who are in control of their own fertility and family size, and producing general improvements in human welfare.

Indeed, empirical research supports such a position and shows that in conjunction with access to modern contraceptives, education, particularly of girls, is one of the most important factors in reducing fertility (Lutz, Butz and KC, 2014; Vollset, et al., 2020). Not only does education enable people to make informed decisions, but it improves their welfare and the life chances of their offspring. Improvements in female education enable women to more fully participate in the economy and develop occupations and careers, typically resulting in decisions to marry later, increase birth spacing and hence have fewer children.

Conclusion

It is undeniable that population size is a critical factor in environmental impact, and yet, as we have seen, the growth of population alone cannot account for the massive anthropogenic environmental changes that modern society has wrought. The I=PAT equation provides a powerful heuristic device which reminds us that environmental impact is the result of the collective outcome of three material factors: the level of resource consumption, the technologies employed and the level of population. In theory, changing any one of these factors will change our environmental impact.

However, despite the overwhelming scientific evidence connecting human population growth with environmental degradation, the majority of environmental NGOs and activists have tended to ignore the population issue, preferring instead to focus their messaging on consumption and alternative technology. This is somewhat understandable since the relationship between population growth and environmental impacts like climate change are difficult to unpick and reducing fertility will not change population size quickly enough to tackle environmental problems that require immediate mitigation.

Understanding and tackling population growth as a driver of climate change, and of environmental change more generally, requires a longer-term perspective. As Bradshaw and Brook (2014) observe, if population growth had been tackled immediately after WWII then demographic momentum could have been slowed and the current impact resulting from population size avoided. Given this lesson from history, tackling population growth must be seen as a long-term investment in the attempt to bring the future collective human footprint within planetary boundaries. It is therefore somewhat of an irony that environmental organisations who are critical of the short-termism of modern society frequently fail to acknowledge tackling population growth as a means of achieving environmental sustainability in the long-term whilst also improving the welfare of the poor.

However, discussion of population reduction remains taboo in environmental circles for more political reasons including its past association with coercion and the abuse of human rights as well as a perception that those concerned with population growth are blaming the poor for an environmental crisis for which they bear little responsibility. Such concerns are legitimate, but by failing to acknowledge population growth as a problem requiring action, they fail to recognize that if we are to lift billions out of poverty the size of the population will be a significant factor undermining the possibility of providing a good life for all within planetary boundaries.

Policies directed toward the provision of sexual health services, and education (especially of women and girls), not only significantly reduce the fertility rate but can also improve welfare and life chances. This represents a win-win situation, demonstrating the interconnectedness of human welfare, population, and environmental sustainability. A global effort directed toward these ends could bring forward the point at which population peaks from the early 22nd century to middle of this century. Moreover, the peak population could be reduced from over 11 billion to less than 8.5 which might then decline to 6.29 billion by 2100 (Vollset et al. 2020). These are merely modelled projections, but they indicate that concerted action can reduce human population size and direct it toward sustainable levels in the longer term.

It is worth remarking that this essay has concentrated on fertility reduction in high fertility developing countries. While this will be critical to achieving a long-term sustainable population in as short a time frame as possible, it is important to note that further reducing fertility in the rich world can also have significant effects since the environmental footprint of each child born into the developed world is up to 30 times greater than each born in the poor world (Maxton and Randers, 2017).

In the shorter term, ethical policies aimed at bending the population growth curve must run alongside and compliment measures tackling the more responsive drivers of climate change: technology and the size of the economy. Yet clearly, as O'Neill et al (2018) and Hickel (2019a; 2019b) have argued, if it is accepted that everyone on the planet deserves the opportunity to have a good life with a decent standard of living, a radical restructuring of the global economy and the distribution of resources is required to adequately meet the needs of upwards of 8 billion people. This will involve reducing the footprint of the Global North and allowing that of the Global South to increase whilst simultaneously reducing the overall footprint of humanity to sustainable levels.

To succeed, such adjustments to developed world consumption will not only involve technological changes but inevitably involve shifts in social norms and lifestyles and a reappraisal of what is a 'good life'. Of course, the same questions are pertinent to the emerging middle-class in the Global

South. It is clear is that a definition of the good life built around consumerism is incompatible with a decent life for all.

In his lengthy critique of idea that an anthropocentric Judeo-Christian metaphysics was responsible for our ecological problems, John Passmore (1980) argued that "new modes of behavior are much more important than new moral principles" (p.188). While I largely agree with Passmore's sentiment regarding the causal role of anthropocentrism as a moral code, values, which may include moral and ethical dispositions, clearly have a considerable role to play in our 'modes of behavior'. Consumer capitalism appears to be perfectly compatible with the narrowest form of anthropocentrism, the horizons of which only extend to short-term material interests. But more expansive, ecologically enlightened forms of anthropocentrism recognize the dependence of our species on the natural world and attempt to avoid speciesism and the denial of moral standing to abstract entities such as habitats and ecosystems (see Norton, 1984; Barry, 1999; O'Neill, 1997) including those which are human-made such as the heathlands of the United Kingdom.

Where it comes to questions regarding population and sustainability, as we have seen, values are critical both in how we materially provide for our current and projected populations and in understanding what size of future population might be environmentally sustainable and how we might achieve it. By drawing on a broad range of established discourses about our relationship with the natural world, including the Judeo-Christian tradition of stewardship identified by Passmore, an ecologically enlightened anthropocentrism will affect such calculations and strategies. However, discourses and practices concerned with other aspects of social life will also have a significant effect. These dimensions are important since they produce unintended consequences which can affect fertility and population size. Thus, strategies to reduce the size of the global population motivated by environmental considerations may well employ environmental arguments to influence individual fertility decisions (Conly, 2016), but it will be improvements in human welfare, especially in the welfare of women in the Global South, that are likely to have the greatest effect on family size.

Bibliography

Alcott, B. 2010. "Impact caps: why population, affluence and technology strategies should be abandoned." *Journal of Cleaner Production,* 18:552–560

Anderson, M.K., 2005. *Tending the wild: Native American knowledge and the management of California's natural resources.* (Berkeley, CA: University of California Press,2005).

Ashraf, Quamrul H. and Michalopoulos, Stelios, 2015. "The Climatic Origins of the Neolithic Revolution: Theory and Evidence" *Review of Economics and Statistics*, 97(3) p.589-609

Barry, J., 1999. *Rethinking green politics: nature, virtue and progress.* (London: Sage, 1999).

Bongaarts, John and O'Neill, Brian C. 2018. "Global warming policy: Is population left out in the cold?" *Science,* 361(6403): 650-652 DOI:10.1126/science.aat8680

Bradshaw, Corey J. A., Brook, Barry W. 2014. "Human population reduction is not a quick fix for environmental problems". *Proceedings of the National Academy of Sciences*, 111(46): 16610-16615; DOI: 10.1073/pnas.1410465111

Brimblecombe, P. 1976. Attitudes and responses towards air pollution in medieval England. *Journal of the Air Pollution Control Association*, 26:10, pp.941-945, DOI: 10.1080/00022470.1976.10470341

Brimblecombe, P. 1987. *The Big Smoke.* (London: Routledge,1987).

Callicott J.B., 2012. *The road to harmony between humans and Nature lies in a philosophical revolution* [pdf] UNESCO Division of Ethics and Global Change. Available at: http://www.unesco.org/new/fileadmin/MULTIMEDIA/HQ/SHS/pdf/interview_callicott.pdf [Accessed 27 March 2020].

Chaurasia, Aalok Ranjan. 2020. "Population effects of increase in world energy use and CO2 emissions: 1990–2019". *The Journal of Population and Sustainability,* 5(1): 87-125

Coole, Diana. 2018. *Should We Control World Population?* (Cambridge: Polity, 2018).

Cohen, Joel E. 2010. "Population and Climate Change" *Proceedings of the American Philosophical Society,* 154(2):158-182

Cohen, Joel E. 2017. "How many people can the Earth support?" *The Journal of Population and Sustainability,* 2(1): 37-42.

Conly, S. 2016. *One Child: Do We Have a Right to More? (*Oxford: Oxford University Press, 2016).

Cronon, W., 1996. The trouble with wilderness: or, getting back to the wrong nature *Environmental History*, Vol. 1, No. 1, pp.7-28

Daily, G., Ehrlich, A.H., Ehrlich, P.R. 1994. Optimum human population size. *Population and Environment,* 15 (6), pp.469-475.

Devall, B. and Sessions, G., 1985. *Deep Ecology.* (Salt Lake City: Gibbs Smith, 1985).

Ehrlich, P.R. and Holdren, J.P., 1972. One-dimensional ecology. *Bulletin of The Atomic Scientists*, May 1972, pp 16, 18-27.

Feeney, J., 2019. Hunter-gatherer land management in the human break from ecological sustainability. *The Anthropocene Review,* Vol. 6, No. 3, 223-242

FAO, IFAD, UNICEF, WFP and WHO. 2020. *The State of Food Security and Nutrition in the World 2020. Transforming food systems for affordable healthy diets*. (Rome: FAO, 2020). https://doi.org/10.4060/ca9692en

Gignoux, Christopher R., Henn, Brenna M., Mountain Joanna L. 2011. "Rapid, global demographic expansions after the origins of agriculture" *Proceedings of the National Academy of Sciences*, 108 (15): 6044-6049. DOI: 10.1073/pnas.0914274108

Gore, Tim. 2020. *Confronting carbon inequality.* [pdf] Available at: https://oxfamilibrary.openrepository.com/bitstream/handle/10546/6210 52/mb-confronting-carbon-inequality-210920-en.pdf [Accessed 12 February 2021].

Hickel, J., 2019a. The contradiction of the sustainable development goals: Growth versus ecology on a finite planet. *Sustainable Development.* 27 pp.873– 884. https://doi.org/10.1002/sd.1947

Hickel, J., 2019b. Is it possible to achieve a good life for all within planetary boundaries? *Third World Quarterly* [e-journal] Volume 40, Issue 1. https://doi.org /10.1080/01436597.2018.1535895.

Kaplan, Jed O., Krumhardt, Kristen M., and Zimmerman, Niklaus. 2009. "The prehistoric and preindustrial deforestation of Europe" Quaternary Science Reviews, 28, (27–28): 3016-3034. https://doi.org/10.1016/j.quascirev.2009.09.028.

Kay, C.E. 1994. Aboriginal overkill: The role of Native Americans in structuring western ecosystems. *Human Nature,* 5(4) pp.359-398.

Klein, Naomi. 2014. *This Changes Everything*. London: Penguin

Krech, S., 1999. *The ecological Indian: Myth and history*. (New York: W.W. Norton, 1999).

Lianos, T.P., Pseiridis A., 2015. Sustainable welfare and optimum population size. *Environment, Development and Sustainability,* 18 (6), pp.1679-1699.

Lin, D., Hanscom, L., Murthy, A., Galli, A., Evans, M., Neill, E., Mancini, M.S., Martindill, J., Medouar, F-Z., Huang, S., Wackernagel, M., 2018. Ecological footprint accounting for countries: updates and results of the National Footprint Accounts, 2012–2018. *Resources.* 7(3): 58. https://doi.org/10.3390/resources7030058

Lutz, W., Butz, W.P. and KC, S. (eds.). 2014. *World population and human capital in the Twenty-First Century.* Oxford: Oxford University Press

Maxton, Graeme and Randers, Jorgen. 2017 "Solving the human sustainability problem in short-termist societies" *The Journal of Population and Sustainability*, 1(2): 11-21

McBain, B., Lenzen, M., Wackernagel, M. and Albrecht, G., 2017. How long can global ecological overshoot last? *Global and Planetary Change* [e-journal] Volume 155, Pages 13-19
https://doi.org/10.1016/j.gloplacha.2017.06.002.

Monbiot, G. 2020. Population panic lets rich people off the hook for the climate crisis they are fuelling. *The Guardian* [online] 26 August. Available at:
https://www.theguardian.com/commentisfree/2020/aug/26/panic-overpopulation-climate-crisis-consumption-environment [Accessed 19 January 2021].

Norton, B.G., 1984. Environmental ethics and weak anthropocentrism. *Environmental Ethics* Vol 6, Summer, 131-148

O'Neill, B., Liddle, B., Jiang, L., Smith, K. R., Pachauri, S., Dalton, M., Fuchs, R., 2012. Demographic change and carbon dioxide emissions. *The Lancet* 380 pp.157–64 http://dx.doi.org/10.1016/S0140-6736(12)60958-1

O'Neill, D.W., Fanning, A. L., Lamb W. F. and Steinberger, J.K., 2018. A good life for all within planetary boundaries. *Nature Sustainability* 1, 88–95.

O'Neill, O., 1997. Environmental values, anthropocentrism and speciesism. *Environmental Values.* Vol. 6, No. 2. 127-142

Passmore, J., 1980. Man's responsibility for nature (second edition). (London: Duckworth, 1980).

Pimentel, D. et al., 1994. Natural resources and an optimum human population. *Population and Environment,* 15 (5), pp.347-369.

Pimentel, D. et al., 2010. Will limited land, water and energy control human population numbers in the future? *Human Ecology,* 38, pp.599-611.

Ritchie, H. 2019. *India will soon overtake China to become the most populous country in the world.* [online] Available at:
https://ourworldindata.org/india-will-soon-overtake-china-to-become-the-most-populous-country-in-the-world [Accessed 25 January 2021]

Ritchie, H. and Roser, M., 2017. *CO2 emissions* [online] Available at:
https://ourworldindata.org/co2-emissions [Accessed 25 January 2021]

Roser, M. 2013. *Economic growth.* [online] Available at:
'https://ourworldindata.org/economic-growth' [Accessed 19 January 2021]

Roser, M., Ritchie, H. and Ortiz-Ospina, E., 2013 *World population growth.* [online] Available at: https://ourworldindata.org/world-population-growth [Accessed 2 January 2021]

Roser, M., and Ortiz-Ospina, E., 2019. *Global extreme poverty.* [online] Available at: https://ourworldindata.org/extreme-poverty' [Accessed 25 January 2021]

Ruddiman, W. F. et al. 2016. Late Holocene climate: Natural or anthropogenic? *Rev. Geophys.,* 54: 93–118. doi:10.1002/2015RG000503.

Steffen, W., Broadgate, W., Deutsch, L., Gaffney, O., & Ludwig, C. 2015. "The trajectory of the Anthropocene: The Great Acceleration". *The Anthropocene Review,* 2(1): 81–98. https://doi.org/10.1177/2053019614564785

Steffen, Will, Crutzen, Paul J. and McNeill, John R. 2007. "The Anthropocene: Are Humans Now Overwhelming the Great Forces of Nature," *AMBIO: A Journal of the Human Environment* 36(8): 614-621, https://doi.org/10.1579/0044-7447(2007)36[614:TAAHNO]2.0.CO;2

Thomas, K. 1984. *Man and the natural world.* London: Penguin.

Tuan, Y. F., 1968. Discrepancies between environmental attitude and behaviour: examples from Europe and China. *Canadian Geographer,* Vol. 12, No. 3, 176-191.

Tucker, C. K., 2019. *A planet of 3 billion.* (Washington, DC: Atlas Observatory Press, 2019).

Vollset, S. E., Goren, E., Yuan, C.-W., Cao, J., et al., 2020. "Fertility, mortality, migration, and population scenarios for 195 countries and territories from 2017 to 2100: a forecasting analysis for the Global Burden of Disease Study". *The Lancet,* 396(10258): 1285–1306. https://doi.org/10.1016/S0140-6736(20)30677-2

Washington, H., Taylor, B., Kopnina, H., Cryer, P. and Piccolo, J.J., 2017. Why ecocentrism is the key pathway to sustainability. *The Ecological Citizen,* 1, pp.35–41.

Welbourn, F. B., 1975. Man's dominion. *Theology,* 78, 561-8.

White, L. 1967. "The Historical Roots of Our Ecologic Crisis". *Science,* 155 (3767): 1203-07.

World Bank, n.d. *Poverty headcount ratio at $5.50 a day (2011 PPP) (% of population)* [online] Available at: https://data.worldbank.org/indicator/SI.POV.UMIC [Accessed 25 January 2021]

CHAPTER EIGHTEEN

RECURRENCE ANALYSIS OF METHANE EMISSIONS FROM WETLAND ECOSYSTEM

MILAN STEHLIK, JIRI DUSEK, JOZEF KISELAK,
ALEXANDER BRANDMAYR, BIRGIT GRUBAUER, JULIA HAIDER,
ROMAN PFEILER, STEFAN RAIDL, ANIKA SCHINDLAUER
AND ALEXANDRA STADLER

Introduction

The growing possibility of continuous monitoring of complex natural processes including meteorological and component flux measurements creates problems with evaluation and usage of discrete and/or continuous complex data, also known as big data. Big data is usually defined as a huge amount of structured or unstructured data (e.g., Lynch 2008; Schadt et al. 2010; Pal et al. 2020). We think that big data is not just about its quantity and thus its unprocessability, but especially about its complexity (Stehlík et al. 2016). Complexity means diversity of the data itself but also its scale. We can understand scale not only as a unit in the physical sense but also in the sense of the size scale and time scale. There is an evident difference between measuring processes inside the cell, in its neighbourhood and on the continental scale. Analogously to the size scale, the time scale is very important. The difference between measurements of very fast (picoseconds to microseconds) processes of electron transport in the Z scheme of the photosynthesis (Nobel 2005) and measurements of very slow processes in hundreds or thousands of years (e.g., peat accumulation in wetlands, Belyea & Malmer 2004) is clear at first glance. Data measured at different scales creates complex big data sets.

Functioning of complex processes involves various behaviours which can be characterized as deterministic, stochastic, and chaotic. To sufficiently understand the studied process, we need to know how the process behaves. Knowledge of the process behaviour facilitates data analysis and interpretation. Analysis of recurrence is a novel approach on how to analyse data including its behaviour. This method has the potential to quantify individual types of behaviour. Determining the chaotic behaviour of the studied process can be very beneficial for the interpretation process itself and in a wider context for the different ecosystems.

The origin of data

Data was obtained from monitoring the carbon cycle in the sedge-grass marsh which is a part of a large wetland complex called the "Wet Meadows". The "Wet Meadows" are situated near the town of Třeboň, South Bohemia, Czech Republic (Central Europe, 49° 01' 29" N, 14° 46' 13" E). The continuously monitored site is a flat sedge-grass marsh of about 1 ha in size and 426 m above sea level situated in the inundation area of a large human-made lake (Rožmberk fishpond, 5 km^2 water surface) (Dušek et al. 2012; Mejdová et al. 2021). The release of gases (emissions) was measured by the developed automatic non-steady state flow-through chamber system (Czech utility model: UV 3237) (Dušek 2012). Changing concentrations of gases inside the closed chamber were measured by a fast CO_2 and CH_4 analyser (DLT-100, Los Gatos Research Inc., USA) in 1 Hz frequency. The final calculation of gas fluxes is based on the linear increase of gas concentration inside the chamber during the period of its closing, taking into account the chamber volume (780 L) and surface area covered (0.785 m^2). The final flux includes corrections to the current air temperature and ambient air pressure by the physics of ideal gas law and also for water vapour. For present analyses, raw data measured in the wetter part of the sedge-grass marsh during one week at the end of May and beginning of June (2013) was selected. In this period emissions of methane (CH_4) were quite stable without significant fluctuations.

Recurrence quantification analysis (RQA)

The existing non-linear techniques of time series analysis (Casdagli 1997) in applied mathematics in the natural sciences and economics, are inadequate when considering chaotic phenomena. In fact, on their basis, the irregular behaviour of some non-linear deterministic systems is manifested in observations and the question is if it can be considered to be chaotic or "just" stochastic. The mathematical basis of discrete dynamical modelling is formed by

$$x(t + 1) = F(x(t), \alpha), \qquad x(0) = x_0 \qquad (1)$$

where the real variable t denotes time, x represents the actual state variables of the system (in general consisting of n components), depending on time t. α consists of the parameters specific of the system and x_0 is the initial state of the system, while F is a non-linear function of these variables and parameters. Each state of the system corresponds to a definite point in phase space. The time change of the state of the system is represented as a motion along some curve called phase trajectory (Figure 1). How the information can be recovered from the time series was suggested by Takens (1981). He proved that, under certain conditions, the dynamics on the attractor of the underlying original system has a one-to-one correspondence with measurements of a limited number of variables. In fact, usually the equations (1) defining the underlying dynamical system are not known and the state space of the original system is not directly accessible to us. However, by measuring a few variables we are able to reconstruct a one-to-one correspondence between the reconstructed state space and the original. This means that it is possible to identify the original state space from measurements unambiguously. Based on the state space reconstruction a graphical tool that evaluates the temporal and phase space distance is available, namely, recurrence plots. A recurrence is a time the trajectory returns to a location it has visited before, i.e. when the distance between two points is below a certain threshold denoted by ε (Figure 1). Recurrence is a fundamental property of dynamical systems, which can be exploited to characterize the system's behaviour in phase space. The recurrence plot is a visualization of a square matrix (a two-dimensional representation of a single trajectory), in which the matrix elements correspond to those times (columns and rows of the matrix correspond to them) at which a state of a dynamical system recurs (Figure 1 and Figure 2). It displays pairs of times at which the trajectory is at the same place, i.e., the set of (i, j) with $x(i)=x(j)$. Binary elements of this matrix can be easily given by

$$R_{ij} = H(\varepsilon - \|x(i) - x(j)\|)$$

where H is the Heaviside unit step function. It is a graphical method designed to locate hidden recurring patterns, non-stationarity, and structural changes. For instance, if the trajectory is strictly periodic all such pairs are visible as diagonal lines.

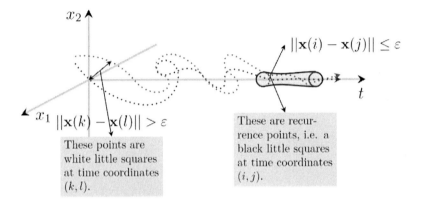

Figure 18.1: Comparison of two-phase space trajectories using predefined distance to define recurrence points. *See centrefold for this image in colour.*

Single, isolated recurrence points reflect random, stochastic behaviour (strong fluctuation in the process). In the case of CH_4 see Figure 3 below and also Figure 1 in Kisel'ák (2018) and for CO_2 Figure 2 in Kisel'ák (2018). This evidently shows considerably more "stochasticity" for CO_2 and some parts clearly copy the recurrence plot of autoregressive processes. On the other hand, in the case of CH_4 fading to the boundaries of the square implies non-stationarity of the data. Short line segments confirm that some part of the dynamical processes is regulated by deterministic laws. Nevertheless, the presence of these lines occurring beside single isolated points shows that there could be a chaotic part of the process. High values of DET (the ratio of recurrence points that form diagonal structures) confirms an indication of determinism in the studied system (Table 1 in Kisel'ák (2018)). These values indicate CH_4 to be a little more stable than CO_2. Notice however the values are not very high, which indicates that a chaotic and a stochastic part might be included. The RR (recurrence rate; density of recurrence points) in Table 1 in Kisel'ák (2018) was higher for CH_4, this means there are more recurring states in CH_4 than in CO_2. Since the matrix is symmetric, horizontal and vertical lines correspond to each other. In Figure 3 the occurrence of vertical lines can be observed. They represent segments which remain in the same phase space region (near or at the same place) for some (long) time. Thus, this indicates also the occurrence of laminar states in the system (e.g. the logistic map is a prototypical example for dynamical transitions between regular, laminar, and chaotic behaviours of a dynamical system). See also Figure 4, where exact distances of points are plotted for all pairs.

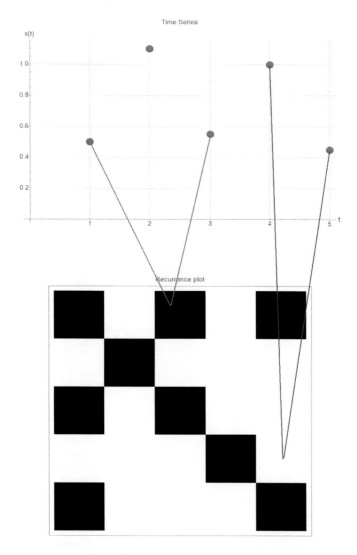

Figure 18.2: Simple illustration of recurrence plot with distance threshold 0.06 (measured naturally in the vertical direction only). *See centrefold for this image in colour.*

Wetlands emit methane as one of the greenhouse gases. Emissions of methane usually fluctuate daily and seasonally. We will address emissions of methane as an illustrative example on how difficult it is to understand and explain natural processes which are included in ongoing climate change.

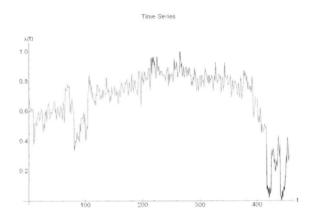

Figure 18.3: Time series and recurrence point plot of CH₄ emission (normalized data). *See centrefold for this image in colour.*

Plot of distances

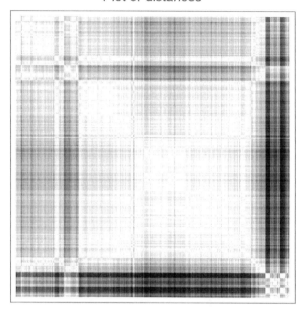

Figure 18.4: Plot of distances of normalized data of CH$_4$ emission

We will also provide real data examples from natural ecosystems, e.g. raw data of methane and carbon dioxide emissions from the sedge-grass marsh ecosystem measured by the non-steady state flow-through chamber system. The recurrence plots can help to understand the process of gas emissions and optionally can characterize the system's behaviour. According to the recurrence plots we can state that the behaviour of the system is mostly stochastic with determination parts and chaos transitions. Stochastic behaviour of the ecosystem can be understood as variable; where variability can be e.g. seasonal, see Stehlík et al. (2016). Chaos transition relates to sudden change in individual processes which can change the functioning of the whole ecosystem. Our recurrence plots are a novel method which allows us to better understand very complex processes enabling ecosystems to function.

Complexity of methane emissions

Methane emissions are a result of natural complex processes of organic matter decomposition under anaerobic conditions, which we can usually record in different types of natural or constructed wetland ecosystems (e.g., Segers 1998; Dušek et al. 2020; Picek et al. 2007). The actual methane emissions are the result of methane production (methanogenesis of *Archaea*) and methane consumption (methanotrophy of bacteria) processes ongoing in waterlogged (wetland) soils (Segers 1998; Serrano-Silva et al. 2014). Both processes are affected by different environmental factors. Among the most important factors are water level and soil/air temperature (Torres-Alvarado et al. 2005). Water regimes significantly influence the biochemical cycles of carbon and nutrients in wetlands and especially in waterlogged soils. The main water supplies are precipitation, superficial run-offs, underground water, tides, and river floods. Excess water or flooding of the soil profile creates specific anaerobic conditions which are absolutely necessary for growth and function of methanogenic *Archaea* (Segers 1998; Whalen 2005). During the flooding periods the methanogenesis is stimulated and the methane emissions are increased. So, when the water table level is decreased the production of methane is decreased as well. Furthermore, the atmospheric removal of methane is influenced by the water table level. Because of its important role, the mean position of the water table can be seen as the best indicator of methane emissions. Soil-types can be classified as mineral (e.g., having low organic content, high bulk density, and low water holding capacity.) or organic, also called peatlands (e.g., having high organic content, low pH-value, low bulk density, and high water holding capacity). Soil textures with high contents of clay and a high supply of organic matter have the highest methane emission whereas sandy soils have the lowest methane emission (Torres-Alvarado et al. 2005).

Based on various studies (e.g., King et al. 1992; Dunfield et al. 1993; Moore et al. 1993; Updegraff et al. 1998; Rask et al. 2002; Waddington et la. 2009; van Winden et al. 2012; Zhu et al. 2014; Zheng et al. 2018) it can be stated that soil/air temperature significantly affects processes resulting in methane emissions. The effect of temperature relates to activity and metabolism of microorganisms participating in complex processes of organic matter decomposition.

Different microorganisms such as fungi, anaerobic bacteria, methanogenic *Archaea* and others are involved in organic matter decomposition processes in wetlands (Boone et al. 1993; Gribaldo & Brochier-Armanet 2006; Blagodatskaya & Kuzyakov 2013; Yarwood 2018). An increase in soil temperature corresponds directly to the growth and activity of these microorganisms and, hence, this relationship leads to an increase in methane emissions while soil temperature increases. This relationship between temperature and emission additionally explains the increase in activity of methanogenic *Archaea* in wetlands from mid and high latitudes during high temperature seasons (Moore & Dalva, 1993; Rask et al. 2002). An increase in temperature also leads to an increase in methane consumption by methanotrophs (Dunfield et al. 1993; Segers 1998). There is evidence that temperature, although not always explaining differences in CH_4 emissions among different ecosystems, explains around 90 % of the seasonal variation in CH_4 production and emission (Torres-Alvarado et al. 2005).

A study of Whiting & Chanton (1992) determined a positive correspondence between CH_4 emission and net primary production of a minerotrophic fen dominated by Carex spp. They point out the fact that plants act as gas conductors (Whiting & Chanton 1992; Morrisseyl et al. 1993; Vítková et al. 2017). Furthermore, approximately 3 % of the net production of wetland ecosystems escapes to the atmosphere in the form of CH_4 (Torres-Alvarado et al. 2005).

Methanogenesis depends on availability of labile simple organic compounds that are used for the methanogenesis process. Content of difficult to degrade organic compounds such as lignin and fibre organic material is negatively correlated with the rate of methanogenesis (Miyajima et al. 1997). The amount of labile organic compounds suitable for methanogenesis is directly affected by environmental factors e.g., by water regime which sets degree of anaerobic conditions in soil/sediment profile or indirectly through functioning of synergy bacteria community which decomposed complex organic compounds (Segers 1998; Schink 2002; Serrano-Silva et al. 2014). It is generally known that microorganisms can cooperate in many different ways. The cooperation can take the form of a mutual relationship between partners and may vary from only marginal support to absolute mutual dependence (Schink 2002). Obligatory syntrophic cooperation in methanogenic degradation of primary alcohols, fatty acids and certain aromatic compounds is usual (Schink & Stams 2006). Aerobic bacteria are usually considered to be able to degrade complex organic matter completely to CO_2 and H_2O with a high gain of available energy. Whereas anaerobic bacteria and *Archaea* degraded complex organic matter (biomass) in several steps, including classical (primary) fermentations, with subsequent further oxidation by sulfate reduction or iron reduction, or by coupling primary fermentations with secondary fermentations to methanogenesis at the very end (Schink 2002).

Syntrophy relationships in methanogenesis processes require synergy of the whole microbial community in different conditions including aerobic and strict anaerobic environments. It is more or less understandable that if one wants to decompose complex organic matter under anaerobic conditions, which is less efficient in production of energy in comparison to aerobic conditions, this decomposition will not be straight but very complex. The complexity of relationships in methanogenesis and following methanotrophy makes final methane emissions quite easily measured as a very complex result.

Sources of methane emissions

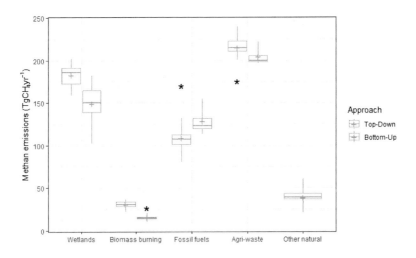

Figure 18.5: Methane global emissions from the five broad categories (Sect. 2.3 in Saunois et al. 2020) for the 2008–2017 decade (Reproduction of Figure 5 in Saunois et al. 2020). *See centrefold for this image in colour.*

The global methane emissions are categorised in Saunois et al. (2020) into five sectors including wetlands (natural wetlands excluding lakes, ponds, and rivers), biomass burning (e.g., biomass burning in forests, savannahs, grasslands, peats, agricultural residues, and the burning of biofuels in the residential sector like stoves, boilers, and fireplaces), fossil fuels (mostly exploitation, transportation, and usage of coal, oil, and natural gas), agriculture and waste (livestock production i.e., enteric fermentation in ruminant animals, and manure management, rice cultivation, landfills, and wastewater handling) and other natural sources (e.g., non-wetland inland waters, wild animals, termites, land geological sources, oceanic geological and biogenic sources, and terrestrial permafrost). Fossil fuels, agriculture and waste, and biomass and biofuel burning are related to human activities whereas emissions from wetlands are seen as origin and natural sources of methane (Dušek et al. 2020). For a more detailed explanation of the source categories see Saunois et al. (2020). Figure 5 is produced with data from Saunois et al. (2020) and inspired by figure 5 *(Sect. 2.3 in Saunois et al. 2020).* Moreover, every category is visualized with two boxplots, the yellow-coloured ones show the top-down inversion model where changes in atmospheric chemistry are used to estimate the methane emissions. The blue coloured box plots present the bottom-up approach and inventories where process-based models and local studies are applied to estimate surface emissions and atmospheric concentration using extrapolation to global scales. In contrast to Saunois et al. (2020) this graphic does not include a boxplot for other natural sources for the bottom-up approach because it was not clear which data was used for the original figure. The boxplots demonstrate the quartiles, minimum and maximum values after removing suspected outliers. Suspected outliers are values that differ remarkably from the other data and do not fit in the measurement series. For this plot values below the first quartile minus three times the interquartile range and values above the third quartile plus three times the interquartile range were determined as outliers. Suspected outliers are marked with stars and mean values with a plus symbol. However, it needs to be mentioned that there are some small discrepancies between the figure in Saunois et al. (2020) and our reproduced plot especially concerning the assessment of outliers. With the available data it was not possible for us to reproduce all of the boxplots exactly. This figure points out that the results of the bottom-up approach differ remarkably from the estimates of the top-down model. The boxes of the two approaches shown in the figure hardly overlap. As mentioned in Saunois et al. (2020) this inconsistency of the two approaches likely results from the high uncertainty of other natural sources and the very likely overestimated bottom-up estimates. This overestimation may be caused by errors during extrapolation of local measurements and double-counting of some natural sources.

Although the conclusion from both methods is similar, results of the bottom-up approach are used in the following interpretation, because top-down models cannot fully separate individual processes. Agriculture and waste cause a huge amount of methane emissions as this category produced about 56 % of total global anthropogenic emissions from 2008 to 2017. The emissions are estimated to be about 206 Tg CH_4 per year including 111 Tg CH₄ per year related to livestock due to enteric fermentation and manure management. In comparison, global emissions of rice paddies are estimated to be 30 Tg CH₄ per year and represent about 8 % of human made emissions of methane.

Additionally, fossil fuels emit a considerable amount of methane while biomass burning is at a relatively low level. Global anthropogenic emissions generated by fossil fuels mainly consist of exploitation, transportation and usage of coal, oil and natural gas. With 128 Tg CH₄ per year between 2008 and 2017 fossil fuels produced approximately 35 % of human made emissions. In contrast biomass and biofuel burning caused about 30 Tg CH₄ per year in the same period. This sector describes emissions caused by burning under incomplete combustion conditions, including fires in forests, savannahs, grasslands, peats, agricultural residues, and the burning of biofuels.

Wetlands emitted about 149 Tg CH₄ per year between 2008 and 2017 mainly based on methane production due to anaerobic conditions. The mean emission of wetlands is considerably bigger than the already stated mean emission concerning livestock. If the confidence interval is also considered, there is no significant difference because of the high uncertainty.

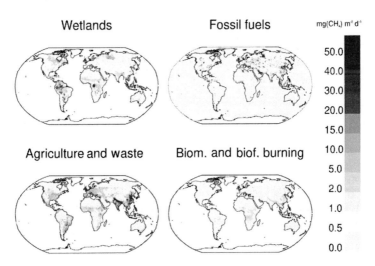

Figure 18.6: Methane emissions from four source categories: natural wetlands (excluding lakes, ponds, and rivers), biomass and biofuel burning, agriculture and waste, and fossil fuels for the 2008-2017 decade (Figure 3 in Saunois et al. 2020). *See centrefold for this image in colour.*

The spatial distribution of average methane emissions from four sectors, namely wetlands, fossil fuels, agriculture and waste, and biomass and biofuel burning is geographically different (Figure 6).

The wetland emission map is based on the mean daily emission average in mg CH_4 m^{-2}d^{-1} over 13 biogeochemical models. It includes peatlands (bogs and fens), mineral soil wetlands (swamps and marshes), and seasonal or permanent floodplains and excludes lakes, rivers, estuaries, ponds, rice agriculture and wastewater ponds. The largest contribution to emissions from wetlands can be observed in the Amazon basin, equatorial Africa and Asia, Canada, western Siberia, eastern India, and Bangladesh. The agriculture and waste sector includes livestock production (especially related to ruminant animals), rice cultivation, landfills and wastewater handling. Large amounts of methane are emitted in India, Southeast Asia, the United States, Brazil, and Europe. Exploitation, transportation, and usage of coal, oil, and natural gas are the main contributors to methane emission in the fossil fuel sector. Zones with large emissions are in Southeast Asia, western Siberia, Saudi-Arabia, Europe, and the United States. The average emissions for agriculture and waste and fossil fuel maps are derived from databases with three different approaches (CEDS, EGDARv4.3.2 & GAINS models). The fourth sector, biomass and biofuel burning, includes biomass burning in forests, savannas, grasslands, peats, agricultural residues, and the burning of biofuels in the residential sector (stoves, boilers, fireplaces). Regions in Africa, India, and Southeast Asia are on a global scale the largest contributors in this sector. The biomass and biofuel burning results are derived from multiple databases (Table 1 in Saunois et al. 2020).

Management of methane emissions

As mentioned previously, wetlands have been recognised for their significant part in global methane emissions. An already implemented measure to reduce methane emissions in wetlands is the transfer of rice production from wetlands to a production site in the up-lands. Torres-Alvarado et al. (2005) reported the significant reduction of methane production from about 7 Ton/ha to about 1-4 Ton/ha. This fact, in combination with the constant increase in human population, could lead to an increase in food shortages as rice is one of the world's most used staple foods. On the other hand, the increased need for rice as a staple food source could lead to an increase in methane emissions caused by rice fields.

A promising strategy to attenuate the flux of CH_4 emissions could be improving the grain yield by modifying the agronomic management of rice cultivation. Instead of permanently flooding the rice fields, an optimized irrigation system which includes short dry periods, could lead to higher yield and therefore less methane per ton of rice. Internal drainage systems implemented in the cultivated rice fields can help to control irrigation as well as drainage and might lead to decreasing CH_4 emissions (De Datta 1981; Torres-Alvarado et al. 2005).

To date, there are no coherent studies regarding methods like using different types of fertilizers or adding iron (III) artificially in order to enhance the development of iron-reducing microbiota which compete for existing substrates and, therefore, possibly reduce methane production. It has been observed that phosphates inhibited in the roots of rice plants reduce methane production from 40 % to 20 % whereas a carbonate buffer solution increases the methane production (Torres-Alvarado et al. 2005).

Destruction of wetlands

Wetlands all around the world have become massively endangered areas in the last decades. Mamo & Bekele (2020) state that 30-90 % of the world's wetlands have already been victim to human initiated destruction. There are unfortunately no exact studies about the real extent of the devastation and elimination of wetlands all around the world. The real extent of destruction is dependent on the region and the country though. The areas where there has been the most diminish of wetlands in the last decades are industrial highly populated regions like China, USA, and Europe (Mamo & Bekele 2020). The reasons for the ongoing conversions and drainages of the world's wetlands are mostly economic ones. The areas are urbanized or used for agricultural purposes in order to provide food to the ever-growing population (Daryadel & Talaei 2018).

The destruction and modification of wetlands all around the world has far-reaching consequences not only for the flora and fauna in these areas but also for the humans who are dependent on the water or fish supply of these ecosystems (Mamo & Bekele 2020). Not only the destruction but also the pollution of the wetlands is an increasing problem. The disposal of industrial waste-water or agricultural pesticides into the wetlands have extensive impacts on the plants and species living there. Some of these harming consequences are often only diagnosed a lot later and have already harmed thousands of organisms. Another factor contributing to the destruction of the natural habitat for a large number of animals is the rise in ecotourism. More and more people travel to pristine wetlands and tromp over vegetations and therefore disturb the habitat and the natural balance of the ecosystem (Daryadel & Talaei 2018).

Concerning the emissions of greenhouse gases, the decreased water table level caused by draining processes also leads to decreased methane emissions. This actually positive effect comes with problematic side effects. The soils of the wetlands store big amounts of carbon, which is released into the atmosphere due to draining processes. So draining of wetlands leads to decreased methane emissions but increased CO_2 emissions. As a result, the total greenhouse gas emissions are higher under drained soils but the mixture is different (Wright 2009).

Fortunately, the awareness of the threat to the wetlands has increased over the past years - at least to a certain amount. Some measures in order to preserve these precious habitats have already been determined in the 1970 signed Ramsar Convention (Lyster and Prince Philip, 1985). This convention should provide a framework in order to preserve the wetlands all around the world. Important factors of this convention are also further research and data exchange as well as personal training especially for developing countries where the environmental knowledge is still lacking (Daryadel & Talaei 2018).

Another interesting fact is that more and more wetlands are man-made. However, these are often used for agricultural purposes - especially for rice production (Mamo & Bekele 2020), which is a very controversial topic as already stated in this paper.

Methane production and animals

Up to this point we have discussed several factors (e.g., temperature, methanogenic *Archaea*) which contribute to the emission of methane gas in wetlands. However, it is worth noticing that the amount of CH_4 emission in wetlands is also, at least to some extent, influenced by the animals living in these areas. Especially ruminants (e.g., deers) are responsible for CH_4 production. Ruminants have in common that they assist "their digestive process by regurgitating their food and chewing it a second time" (Kelliher & Clark 2010). This phenomenon is often referred to as "ruminating", which is the reason why these animals are often labelled as "ruminants". Such animals can be characterized by a complex stomach-system with two anterior chambers, including the rumen. Within the rumen, the fermentation-process converts ingested feed into energy and, as a by-product, releases enteric CH_4. It is believed that the rumen is responsible for over 80 % of the entire CH_4 production in the ruminant (Kelliher & Clark 2010).

Furthermore, cattle and sheep are two of the main ruminants with respect to the overall methane production. Various studies suggest that the global enteric methane emissions are around 86 Tg per year, which are attributed mainly to dairy cattle (22 %) and beef cattle (65 %) (Beauchemin et al. 2009). Additionally, a recent study from Chen et al. (2020) points out that beef cattle not only produce large amounts of N_2O and CH_4 due to their fermentation process, but also contribute substantially to the overall amount of GHG (greenhouse gas) emission. This is because cattle are important animals for meat production and, therefore, are involved in many GHG-related processes, such as the (cross-national) transportation of them (Chen et al. 2020).

Therefore, we can conclude that ruminants are an important source for enteric CH_4 emission (in wetlands), since the process of fermentation produces this gas as a by-product. Finally, it should be stressed that the amount of methanogenesis corresponds directly to numerous factors such as the animal's diet type or the usage of ionophores in the feeding process (Moss et al. 2000). Identifying these factors and manipulating them in a certain way can, therefore, lead to a reduction in methane production associated with ruminants.

The importance of Recurrence Quantification Analysis (RQA) of methane for the environment

The importance of the study of methane emissions is due to the imminent importance of greenhouse gases in the atmosphere and the resulting change in global climate. Contrary to CO_2, CH_4 has a short lifetime in the atmosphere, therefore, reducing CH_4 emissions would lead to rapid improvements in the global climate crisis (Saunois et al. 2020). Unfortunately, CH_4 emissions are rising faster nowadays, unlike CO_2 emissions (Saunois et al. 2016), which leads to an ever-growing importance in the study of causes for this rise in CH_4 emissions.

As proposed in Saunois et al. (2016) the estimates of CH_4 emissions from natural wetlands are very uncertain, although, "Breakthrough technologies already allow high precision measurements of methane and its isotopes at the surface" (Saunois et al. 2016). This means the opportunity for precise measurements of CH_4 emissions from wetlands exists. RQA helps to understand the behaviour of a dynamical system with regards to its deterministic, stochastic and chaotic part. With highly reliable data, predictions of CH_4 emissions can be modelled more consistently. RQA might offer some insight into the naturally recurring CH_4 emissions in wetlands and, therefore, might help to explain future amounts of methane emission from wetlands.

In general, methane emissions from the natural wetlands cannot simply be interpreted negatively as emissions of unwanted greenhouse gases related to climate change (WMO 2020). These emissions are the result of the natural production of methane as an original and natural process which is related to the decomposition processes under anaerobic conditions in the wetland soils. Wetland ecosystems were responsible for creating huge carbon storages including fossil fuels in the past and are currently responsible for storing and keeping organic matter (carbon) in the soil. We need wetlands for their irreplaceable role in the different cycles such as the cycles of water, carbon and nutrients. Methane emissions must not in any way be an obstacle in their sustainable use, sufficient protection, restoration, and their expansion.

Bibliography

Beauchemin, K. A., McAllister, T. A. & McGinn, S. M. (2009). Dietary mitigation of enteric methane from cattle. In: CAB Reviews: Perspectives in Agriculture, Veterinary Science, Nutrition and Natural Resources, 4, 35, pp.1-18.

Belyea, L. R. & Malmer, N. (2004). Carbon sequestration in peatland: patterns and mechanisms of response to climate change: CARBON SEQUESTRATION IN PEATLAND. Global Change Biology 10, 1043–1052. https://doi.org/10.1111/j.1529-8817.2003.00783.x

Blagodatskaya, E. & Kuzyakov, Y. (2013). Active microorganisms in soil: Critical review of estimation criteria and approaches. Soil Biology and Biochemistry 67, 192–211. https://doi.org/10.1016/j.soilbio.2013.08.024

Boone, D. R., Whitman, W. B. & Rouviere, P. (1993). Diversity and taxonomy of methanogens. In: Ferry, J. G. (Ed.), *Methanogenesis.* (Chapman and Hall Co, New York, 1993) 35#80.

Casdagli M. C. (1997) Recurrence plots revisited, Physica D 108 pp. 12-44.

Chen, Z., An, C., Fang, H., Zhang, Y., Zhou, Z., Zhou, Y. & Zhao, S. (2020). Assessment of regional greenhouse gas emission from beef cattle production: A case study of Saskatchewan in Canada. In: Journal of Environmental Management, 264, pp.1-12.

Daryadel E. & Talaei F. (2018). Analytical Study on Threats to Wetland Ecosystems and their Solutions in the Framework of the Ramsar Convention, International Journal of Social, Behavioral, Educational,

Economic, Business and Industrial Engineering, Volume 8, No 7, 2014, pp. 2100-2110. https://www.researchgate.net/publication/328748191_Analytical-Study-on-Threats-to-Wetland-Ecosystems-and-their-Solutions-in-the-Framework-of-the-Ramsar-Convention

Dunfield, P., Knowles, R., Dumont, R. & Moore, T. (1993). Methane production and consumption in temperate and subarctic peat soils: Response to temperature and pH. Soil Biology and Biochemistry 25, 321–326. https://doi.org/10.1016/0038-0717(93)90130-4

Dušek, J., Čížková, H., Stellner, S., Czerný, R. & Květ, J. (2012). Fluctuating water table affects gross ecosystem production and gross radiation use efficiency in a sedge-grass marsh. Hydrobiologia 692, 57–66. https://doi.org/10.1007/s10750-012-0998-z

Dušek J., Stellner S. & Marian P. Utility model no. 024073 (2012). Patent.

Dušek, J., Dařenová, E., Pavelka, M., Marek, M.V., (2020). Methane and carbon dioxide release from wetland ecosystems, in: *Climate Change and Soil Interactions.* (Elsevier, 2012) 509–553. https://doi.org/10.1016/B978-0-12-818032-7.00019-9

Gribaldo, S. & Brochier-Armanet, C. (2006). The origin and evolution of *Archaea*: a state of the art. Philos. Trans. R. Soc. B: Biol. Sci. 361, 1007#1022. Available from: https://doi.org/10.1098/rstb.2006.1841

Kelliher, F. M. & Clark, H. (2010). Ruminants. (London: Earthscan, 2010)136-151.

King, G. M. & Adamsen, A. P. (1992). Effects of Temperature on Methane Consumption in a Forest Soil and in Pure Cultures of the Methanotroph Methylomonas rubra. Appl. Environ. Microbiol. 58, 2758–2763.

Kiseľák, J., Dušek, J. & Stehlík, M. (2018). Recurrence of CH4 and CO2 emissions measured by a non-steady state flow-through chamber system. AIP Conference Proceedings, 2046, 020046. https://doi.org/10.1063/1.5081566

Lynch, C. (2008). How do your data grow? Nature 455, 28–29. https://doi.org/10.1038/455028a

Lyster, S., H. R. H. Prince Philip, (1985). *International Wildlife Law: An analysis of international treaties concerned with the conservation of wildlife.* (Cambridge University Press, Cambridge, 1985). https://doi.org/10.1017/CBO9780511622045

Mamo G. S. & Bekele T. (2020). Review on Wetland Ecosystem Destruction, International Journal of Scientific Research & Growth, Volume 2, Issue 2, pp. 5-15, ISSN 2456-6667.

https://www.researchgate.net/publication/338555418_Review_on_Wet land_Ecosystem_Destruction

Mejdová, M., Dušek, J., Foltýnová, L., Macálková, L. & Čížková, H. (2021). Photosynthetic parameters of a sedge-grass marsh as a big-leaf: effect of plant species composition. Sci Rep 11, 3723. https://doi.org/10.1038/s41598-021-82382-2

Miyajima, T., Wada, E., Hanba, Y. T. & Vijarnsorn, P. (1997). Anaerobic mineralization of indigenous organic matters and methanogenesis in tropical wetland soils. Geochimica et Cosmochimica Acta 61, 3739–3751. https://doi.org/10.1016/S0016-7037(97)00189-0

Moore, T. R. & Dalva, M. (1993). The influence of temperature and water table position on carbon dioxide and methane emissions from laboratory columns of peatland soils. Journal of Soil Science 44, 651–664. https://doi.org/10.1111/j.1365-2389.1993.tb02330.x

Morrisseyl, L. A., Zobel, D.B. & Livingston, G. P. (1993). Significance of stomatal control on methane release from Carex-dominated wetlands. Chemosphere 26, 339–355.

Moss, A. R., Jouany, J. P. & Newbold, J. (2000). Methane production by ruminants: its contribution to global warming. In: Ann. Zootech., 49, p.231-253.

Nobel, P. S. (2005). Physicochemical and environmental plant physiology. (Academic Press, 2005).

Pal, S., Mondal, S., Das, G., Khatua, S. & Ghosh, Z. (2020). Big data in biology: The hope and present-day challenges in it. Gene Reports 21, 100869. https://doi.org/10.1016/j.genrep.2020.100869

Picek, T., Čížková, H. & Dušek, J. (2007). Greenhouse gas emissions from a constructed wetland—Plants as important sources of carbon. Ecological Engineering 31, 98–106. https://doi.org/10.1016/j.ecoleng.2007.06.008

Rask, H., Schoenau, J. & Anderson, D. (2002). Factors influencing methane flux from a boreal forest wetland in Saskatchewan, Canada. Soil Biology 9.

Saunois, M., Jackson, R. B., Bousquet, P., Poulter, B. & Canadell, J. G. (2016). The growing role of methane in anthropogenic climate change. (Editorial). Environmental Research Letters 11 120207. http://dx.doi.org/10.1088/1748-9326/11/12/120207

Saunois, M., Stavert, A. R., Poulter, B., Bousquet, P., Canadell, J. G., Jackson, R. B., Raymond, P. A., Dlugokencky, E. J., Houweling, S., Patra, P. K., Ciais, P., Arora, V. K., Bastviken, D., Bergamaschi, P., Blake, D. R., Brailsford, G., Bruhwiler, L., Carlson, K. M., Carrol, M., Castaldi, S., Chandra, N., Crevoisier, C., Crill, P. M., Covey, K.,

Curry, C. L., Etiope, G., Frankenberg, C., Gedney, N., Hegglin, M. I., Höglund-Isaksson, L., Hugelius, G., Ishizawa, M., Ito, A., Janssens-Maenhout, G., Jensen, K. M., Joos, F., Kleinen, T., Krummel, P. B., Langenfelds, R. L., Laruelle, G. G., Liu, L., Machida, T., Maksyutov, S., McDonald, K. C., McNorton, J., Miller, P. A., Melton, J. R., Morino, I., Müller, J., Murguia-Flores, F., Naik, V., Niwa, Y., Noce, S., O'Doherty, S., Parker, R. J., Peng, C., Peng, S., Peters, G. P., Prigent, C., Prinn, R., Ramonet, M., Regnier, P., Riley, W. J., Rosentreter, J. A., Segers, A., Simpson, I. J., Shi, H., Smith, S. J., Steele, L. P., Thornton, B. F., Tian, H., Tohjima, Y., Tubiello, F. N., Tsuruta, A., Viovy, N., Voulgarakis, A., Weber, T. S., van Weele, M., van der Werf, G. R., Weiss, R. F., Worthy, D., Wunch, D., Yin, Y., Yoshida, Y., Zhang, W., Zhang, Z., Zhao, Y., Zheng, B., Zhu, Q., Zhu, Q., & Zhuang, Q. (2020). The Global Methane Budget 2000–2017, Earth Syst. Sci. Data, 12, 1561–1623. https://doi.org/10.5194/essd-12-1561-2020

Schadt, E. E., Linderman, M. D., Sorenson, J., Lee, L. & Nolan, G. P. (2010). Computational solutions to large-scale data management and analysis. Nat Rev Genet 11, 647–657. https://doi.org/10.1038/nrg2857

Schink, B., (2002). *Synergistic interactions in the microbial world.* (Antonie van Leeuwenhoek 81, 2002) 257-261.

Schink B. & Stams A.J.M. (2006). Syntrophism among Prokaryotes. In: Dworkin M., Falkow S., Rosenberg E., Schleifer KH., Stackebrandt E. (eds) *The Prokaryotes.* (Springer, New York, NY, 2006) 309-335.

Segers, R. (1998). Methane production and methane consumption: a review of processes underlying wetland methane fluxes. Biogeochemistry 41, 23–51.

Serrano-Silva, N., Sarria-Guzmán, Y., Dendooven, L. & Luna-Guido, M. (2014). Methanogenesis and Methanotrophy in Soil: A Review. Pedosphere 24, 291–307. http://dx.doi.org/10.1016/S1002-0160(14)60016-3

Stehlík M., Dušek J. & Kiseľák J. (2016). Missing chaos in global climate change data interpreting? Ecological Complexity, Volume 25, pp. 53-59, ISSN 1476-945X, https://doi.org/10.1016/j.ecocom.2015.12.003.

Stehlík M., Kiseľák J. & Dušek J. (2020). On Ecosystem Dynamics for the Conservation of Wetlands and Forest. in: Fuders F., Donoso P. (eds). *Ecological Economic and Socio Ecological Strategies for Forest Conservation.* (Springer, Cham, 2020) https://doi.org/10.1007/978-3-030-35379-7_9

Takens, F. (1981). Detecting strange attractors in turbulence, in Dynamical Systems and Turbulence, Warwick 1980, vol. 898 of Lecture Notes in

Mathematics, edited by A. Rand and L. S Young, (Springer, Berlin, 1980) 366-381.

Torres-Alvarado, R., Ramírez-Vives, F., Fernández, F. J. & Barriga-Sosa, I. (2005). Methanogenesis and methane oxidation in wetlands. Implications in the global carbon cycle. Hidrobiológica 15 (3): 327-349.

Updegraff, K., Bridgham, S. D., Pastor, J. & Weishampel, P. (1998). Hysteresis in the temperature response of carbon dioxide and methane production in peat soils 20.

Vítková, J., Dušek, J., Stellner, S., Moulisová, L. & Čížkova, H. (2017). Effect of Hummock-Forming Vegetation on Methane Emissions from a Temperate Sedge-Grass Marsh. Wetlands 37, 675–686. https://doi.org/10.1007/s13157-017-0898-0

Waddington, J. M., Harrison, K., Kellner, E. & Baird, A. J. (2009). Effect of atmospheric pressure and temperature on entrapped gas content in peat. Hydrological Processes 23, 2970–2980. https://doi.org/10.1002/hyp.7412

Whalen, S. C. (2005). Biogeochemistry of Methane Exchange between Natural Wetlands and the Atmosphere. Environmental Engineering Science 22, 73–94. https://doi.org/10.1089/ees.2005.22.73

van Winden, J. F., Reichart, G.-J., McNamara, N. P., Benthien, A. & Damste, J. S. S. (2012). Temperature-Induced Increase in Methane Release from Peat Bogs: A Mesocosm Experiment. PLOS ONE 7. https://doi.org/10.1371/journal.pone.0039614

World Meteorological Organization (WMO) (2020). WMO Greenhouse Gas Bulletin 2020, 9.

Wright L. A. (2009). Environmental Consequences of Water Withdrawals and Drainage of Wetlands, IFAS Extension, p. 3.

Yarwood, S. A. (2018). The role of wetland microorganisms in plant-litter decomposition and soil organic matter formation: a critical review. FEMS Microbiology Ecology 94. https://doi.org/10.1093/femsec/fiy175

Zheng, J., RoyChowdhury, T., Yang, Z., Gu, B., Wullschleger, S. D. & Graham, D. E. (2018). Impacts of temperature and soil characteristics on methane production and oxidation in Arctic tundra. Biogeosciences 15, 6621–6635. https://doi.org/10.5194/bg-15-6621-2018

Zhu, X., Song, C., Guo, Y., Sun, X., Zhang, X. & Miao, Y. (2014). Methane emissions from temperate herbaceous peatland in the Sanjiang Plain of Northeast China. Atmospheric Environment 92, 478-483. https://doi.org/10.1016/j.atmosenv.2014.04.061

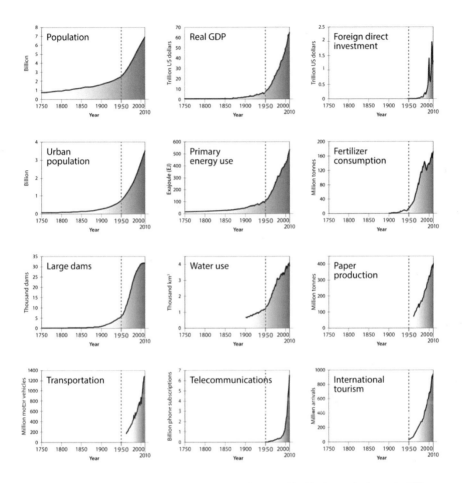

Figure 17.3 Socio-economic trends. Reproduced with kind permission of Will Steffen. (Source Steffen et al 2015).

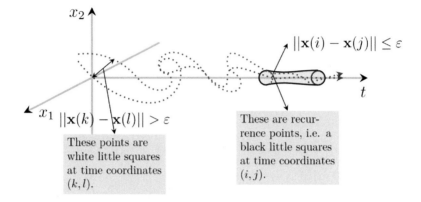

Figure 18.1: Comparison of two-phase space trajectories using predefined distance to define recurrence points

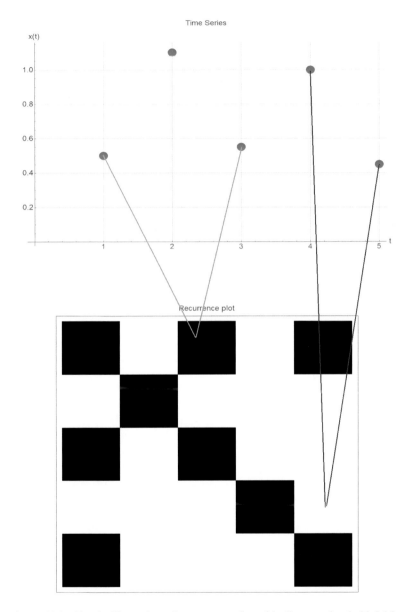

Figure 18.2: Simple illustration of recurrence plot with distance threshold 0.06 (measured naturally in the vertical direction only).

Time Series

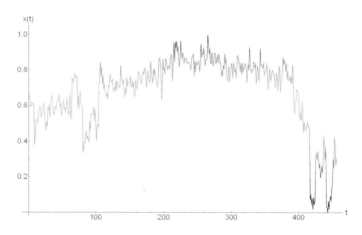

Recurrence plot

Figure 18.3: Time series and recurrence point plot of CH₄ emission (normalized data).

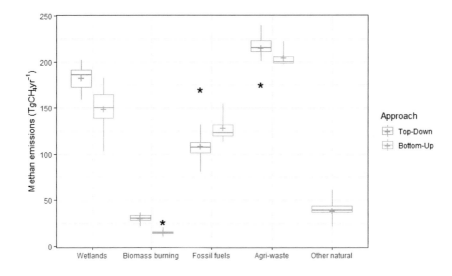

Figure 18.5: Methane global emissions from the five broad categories (Sect. 2.3 in Saunois et al. 2020) for the 2008–2017 decade (Reproduction of Figure 5 in Saunois et al. 2020).

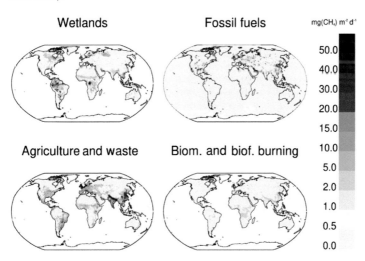

Figure 18.6: Methane emissions from four source categories: natural wetlands (excluding lakes, ponds, and rivers), biomass and biofuel burning, agriculture and waste, and fossil fuels for the 2008-2017 decade (Figure 3 in Saunois et al. 2020).

1. Place	"Reusing things and develop recycling".
2-3 Places	"Plant more trees" and "Avoid "Fast-Fashion".
5. Place	"Use "green" energy".
9. Place	"Choose politicians who emphasize the preservation of the environment in their programs".

Figure 21.1 Q & A Chart.

Figure 22.1. 'Christ Breaking the Bonds of Animal Suffering'

CHAPTER NINETEEN

DESIGNING A GREEN CURRICULUM OF ORTHODOX THEOLOGY: A MODEST PROPOSAL

ELENI ANTONOPOULOU AND EKATERINI TSALAMPOUNI

Summary

If the second half of the 20th century is marked by an emerging environmental awareness, the pressing ecological challenges in the first decades of the 21st century have led to the conclusion that the ecological crisis is a rather complex situation in which several factors play an equally important role. It has also been evident that a common public understanding of the integral connection between humanity and the rest of the creation is necessary in order to establish a sustainable environment. In 2015 the UN formulated a global agenda for Sustainable Development comprised by 17 main goals and many more sub-goals, known as Agenda 2030. Subsequently, most religious leaders have issued statements and declarations regarding the part faiths can play in this global agenda. Religions have entered a period of re-evaluation and re-reading of texts and traditions in order to be able to offer answers in regard to the new and complex reality of global environmental problems and climate change.

Orthodox theology has so far contributed to the theological discussion about the environment and a series of initiatives of the Orthodox Church, like those of the Ecumenical Patriarch Bartholomew, have tried to raise awareness, not only within its limits, but also on a global scale. It is, however, important that this discussion is somehow also reflected in the curricula of the Orthodox theological faculties and thus integrated in the overall theological education of young students. This was also highlighted at Halki Summit III in 2019.

The present paper picks up the current discussion about the role of education in forming a robust ecological ethos among Orthodox Christians and more particularly in equipping future theologians with all the necessary skills that will make them able to work both as individuals, as well as educators, collaborators, and spiritual guides toward achieving a sustainable future. A case study, namely that of the curriculum of the School of Pastoral and Social Theology at Aristotle University of Thessaloniki (Greece) will be presented. By means of concrete examples of courses a modest proposal of a curriculum will be made that focuses on sustainability, eco-justice but also on the dialogue between theology and science on environmental issues. The discussion will focus on the philosophy, structure, and content of the courses offered but also on the challenges and the potential of such a curriculum as well as on the reception by the students.

Introduction

It has often been claimed that the 20th century marked the beginning of an ever-growing environmental awareness. The prophetic voices of its pioneers, like Rachel Carson, Paul Shepard or Arne Næss, and the activist engagement of various environmental groups and organizations, like WWF or Greenpeace, brought important environmental issues to the centre of the discussion and called for immediate action by governments and individuals. Their legacy can be traced in the current discussions on the media and in the agendas of local governments and international political bodies. Indeed, discussions, news, and debates regarding contemporary environmental problems have long become part of our everyday life and a constant reminder of what needs to be done. According to the UNEP Foresight Process on Emerging Environmental Issues Report published in 2012, various environmental issues occupy the first places in the UNEP ranked list of the emerging issues of the 21st century.[1] Despite this development the ecological challenges have become more acute in the 21st century. In simple words, although Earth Day is annually observed by more than a 1 billion people, Earth overshoot day comes earlier every year. Climate change, deforestation, water resources depletion, desertification, atmospheric pollution, and plastic waste are only a few of the numerous problems the global community needs to tackle. Various explanations and solutions have been offered ever since the severity of the problems was identified. Most importantly, the persistence and the nature of the current ecological crisis has led to the insight that this is not just a political or economic but rather a

---

[1] "21 Issues for the 21st Century: Results of the UNEP Foresight Process on Emerging Environmental Issues,"
https://wedocs.unep.org/handle/20.500.11822/8056

multifaceted problem whose solution presupposes a more holistic approach. This paradigm shift is also reflected in the strategies proposed in the last decades. In 2015, for example, the UN formulated a global agenda for Sustainable Development comprised by 17 main goals[2] and many more sub-goals/targets, addressing not only environmental, but also social and economic issues. It is hoped that the fulfillment of these goals on a global scale will help heal nature on one hand and transform human society as a whole on the other, with a promise of a better world for future generations.

Significantly, in this new situation religions seem willing 'to discover their own distinctive ecological vocation' (Gottlieb 2006, 7) and join their efforts in promoting ecologically aware ethical stances and worldviews.[3] However, the relationship between religions and the natural environment as well as their role in achieving sustainable development goals has not always been obvious to society and/or science, or even to the religious entities themselves. For example, religions are often related to charity, spirituality, afterlife, but also to fanaticism, bigotry, and religious terrorism, whereas their involvement in the public life of our postmodern world is frowned upon. Moreover, religions, and more particularly the Judeo-Christian tradition, have been accused of providing the spiritual basis for the misuse of natural resources.[4] Thus their potential engagement in the common efforts for environmental sustainability has also often been treated with mistrust.

Despite these reservations, literature produced by a fruitful collaboration of religion and ecology is constantly rising and new scientific fields are emerging (Eco-theology, Religions and Development, etc.). In contemporary sustainability research and discussions, the role of faiths is no longer identified as an obstacle for development but as a valuable human resource, that can offer spiritual guidance and an ethical basis for improving human attitudes towards the environment (Bauman, Bohannon, & O'Brien, 2017), (Gottlieb, 2006), (Skirbekk et al. 2020). Therefore, these faith traditions are not treated as mere spiritual voices, but as equal development partners.

Religions themselves have entered a period of re-reading and re-evaluating their texts and traditions in search for answers to the challenges

---

[2] The Global Goals, https://www.globalgoals.org/

[3] This is evident, for example, in documents like the *Assisi Declarations* issued in 1986 or the booklet published in 2020 by the UN Environmental Program and the Parliament of Religions under the title "Faith for Earth: A Call for Action", https://www.unep.org/resources/publication/faith-earth-call-action

[4] See, for example the seminal article of Lynn White, an American professor of medieval history, in the 1960s entitled "The historical roots of our ecologic crisis" (White, 1967).

posed by the new and complex reality that has been formed after the second half of the twentieth century (Grim & Tucker, 2014), (UNEP, 2016). Most religious leaders have issued statements and declarations regarding the positive part that faiths can play in this global agenda (Devitt & Tatay, 2017). They all acknowledge the interconnectedness of human beings with the rest of the creation and encourage the members of their communities to change their mind and lifestyle. In Pope Francis' words in his 2015 encyclical letter 'Laudato si' the current crisis is complex since "we are faced not with two separate crises, one environmental and the other social, but rather with one complex crisis which is both social and environmental. Strategies for a solution demand an integrated approach to combating poverty, restoring dignity to the excluded, and at the same time protecting nature" (§ 139).

Pope Francis' encyclical is a welcome rejoinder to the continuous efforts of the Ecumenical Patriarch Bartholomew for a just and respectful treatment of the creation (*Laudato si', § 7-9*). Patriarch Bartholomew is one of the first religious leaders who addressed important environmental problems and, for three decades now, has been undertaking a series of initiatives to highlight those problems and seek solutions, hence gaining the title 'Green Patriarch' in global media (Chryssavgis, 2012). In his speeches Bartholomew has stressed the interconnectedness of humans with the rest of Creation and through his initiatives has managed to create the necessary common ground where both religious and secular leaders, thinkers, and activists can meet and discuss. Furthermore, the Patriarch has underlined the spiritual consequences of human actions against the creation, going so far as to characterize them as 'sin' (Krueger, 2012). In this respect, he has continued the work of his predecessor Demetrios and of important Orthodox theologians, like John Zizioulas, in bringing into the current ecological discussion part of the richness of the Orthodox tradition (Theokritoff 2017). He has thus demonstrated how the Orthodox Christian tradition can contribute to the achievement of sustainable development goals by promoting an ascetic and eucharistic ethos (Chryssavgis & Foltz, 2013).

One of his most recent initiatives that introduced a new aspect of Orthodox involvement in the common care for the whole creation was the Halki Summit III (in June 2019) that focused on the necessity of introducing environmental issues in the academic curricula of Orthodox faculties and seminaries as well as in preaching or catechetical activities of the Orthodox Church.[5] In his opening address the Ecumenical Patriarch stressed the fact that in order for Orthodox theology to strengthen its foundations and make

---

[5] See http://www.halkisummit.com/hs3/ .

further advance within the ecological awareness context of today, it is of vital importance among others that Theology schools incorporate creation care into their curricula. Young theologians and priests need to be carefully trained, in order to contribute to the development of an ecologically aware ethos and be properly skilled to participate in the dialogue with other disciplines regarding the global environmental problem.

The same concern has led the Aristotle University's School of Social Theology and Christian Culture (formerly School of Pastoral and Social Theology) to introduce several environmental courses in its revised curriculum since 2013. In the following paragraphs, we will briefly present the philosophy under which specific courses were introduced, as well as the content and structure of each course. The challenges and the potential of such a curriculum will also be discussed, as well as the way students view this effort. The purpose of this presentation is to offer a modest proposal of how a curriculum that focuses on sustainability, eco-justice, and the dialogue between theology and science on environmental issues, could be structured.

Building an environmental curriculum in a faculty of Theology

Even though environmental education has a history of at least 50 years, it is still evolving and constantly adapting to new sustainability needs and available tools (Crohn & Birnbaum, 2010). Its main purpose is to provide future educators and professionals of various disciplines with the necessary skills and knowledge so that they will be fully equipped to address environmental issues in their respective fields of work (Stern, Powell, & Hill, 2014).

The importance of environmental education is also highlighted by the UN Agenda 2030 Sustainable Development Goals (SDGs) and partial Targets (Orr, Niccolucci, & Bastianoni, 2019):

- SDG 4 (Quality Education) target 4.7 (Education for Sustainable Development and Global Citizenship), which states: "By 2030, ensure that all learners acquire the knowledge and skills needed to promote sustainable development, including, among others, through education for sustainable development and sustainable lifestyles, human rights, gender equality, promotion of a culture of peace and non-violence, global citizenship and appreciation of cultural diversity and of culture's contribution to sustainable development."

- SDG 12 (Responsible Consumption and Production), target 12.8 (Promote Universal Understanding of Sustainable Lifestyles), which states: "By 2030 ensure that people everywhere have the relevant information and awareness for sustainable development and lifestyles in harmony with nature."
- SDG 13 (Climate action), target 13.3 (Build Knowledge and Capacity to meet Climate Change), which states: "Improve education, awareness-raising and human and institutional capacity on climate change mitigation, adaptation, impact reduction and early warning."

Environmental education as described in these goals is definitely a complex endeavor, involving almost all scientific fields and aspects of human life. This complexity should be reflected in the courses of an environmental education curriculum. Creating such an educational program can, therefore, be a challenging task that demands careful planning in order to achieve its purpose (Carleton-Hug & Hug, 2010). According to relevant literature, there are two ways to incorporate environmental education courses into a school curriculum (Hungerford & Peyton, 1994):

- **Interdisciplinary**, which refers to the introduction of complete and purely environmental courses which are either taught by people from various disciplines who provide information from their 'point of view', or by a single but very well-trained individual in environmental issues. The advantage of this way is that students have the opportunity to familiarize themselves with all the dimensions of a topic, in a more holistic approach.
- **Multidisciplinary**, which means that environmental topics are introduced into existing courses of the school's curriculum, as one of the modules of each course. The advantage of this way is that students are able to make the connection between their main field of study (in our case Theology) and nature. In this way, they are not merely learning information about an environmental topic, but they also discover how they can apply this knowledge in practice. In other words, they have a better understanding of why they have to learn all this, seemingly irrelevant, information.

For the best results, a combination of both types of courses is preferable, so that students have the chance to a) familiarize themselves with various environmental issues and ideas and to understand the interconnections that exist (Orr, Ecological Systems Thinking, 2008), and b) discover how this newly acquired knowledge can be applied to their field of study.

During the second decade of the 21st century there has been a growing interest in integrating ecological topics in Christian religious education. This is undoubtedly also encouraged by the statements of Christian leaders like the Ecumenical Patriarch Bartholomew or Pope Francis. However, the process of creating "green" curricula in theological faculties or seminaries is rather slow, most particularly in the Orthodox setting. Despite the fact that the theological eco-discourse is highly developed this is not usually reflected in the courses of our faculties. What is also missing is the intersection of ecology, theology, and pastoral training.

It is, therefore, necessary that the academic curricula are restructured so that they can bring the Orthodox tradition in its fullness into a fruitful dialogue with natural and environmental sciences, a relation that has not always been smooth, especially after the Enlightenment (Kalaitzidis 2019). This certainly presupposes more holistic educational models that will depart from the prevalent dualistic attitude towards nature and will promote the interconnectedness of humans with the rest of the creation. In this respect, education would be understood as 'paideia' that aims at shaping religious leaders and educators who would perceive themselves as members of God's creation responsible for its flourishment. Thus, good theological education should also be understood as good ecological education (Ayres 2014, 205). This 'ecological literacy', to use David Orr's term (Orr 1992, 85–96), is much broader than acquiring analytical and comprehension skills. It also entails engagement, commitment, and 'affectivity', an embodied, namely, way of knowing (Tomlinson 2019, 194). This broad understanding of religious education aims at cultivating 'biophilia', a notion that comes from biology and refers to the capacity of human beings to affiliate with other forms of life (Wilson 1984; Tomlinson 2019, 194). It also entails a change of mind and heart; Christians should not perceive themselves as temporary residents exiled in this world having no commitments, but rather as inhabitants of this beautiful cosmos accountable for all its inhabitants (Ayres 2014, 208; Orr 1992, 102–3).

Having set this aim it is, therefore, necessary to ask what educational model should be adopted in order to be successful. There is an accumulating literature dealing with this important question. Most of these proposals adopt open interdisciplinary approaches that bring theology and ecology together and encourage cognitive, affective but also critical learning processes. Students are invited to explore how their personal stories are informed by the communal sacred stories (e.g., from the Bible or the lives of the saints) and the stories of the natural world and how the insights of science can help them change their attitude towards the environment. Through the appreciation of the Orthodox liturgical tradition, they can also understand the sacramental potential of the created cosmos and realize the bonds of companionship that tie them with the rest of the creation. Finally, the eschatological prospect of common flourishment could lead to the acknowledgement of the creation's inherent beauty and to actions of benevolence and care for the creation. An educational triptych, therefore, of retrieving those parts of the tradition that refer to the integrity of the creation, of nurturing a 'sacramental consciousness' and of understanding the creation as "the embodiment of God's promise yet to be fulfilled" (Champerlain 2000, 143–47) could encompass the past, the present, and the future of human identity and engage not only the mind of the students but also their heart.

Environmental education in the School of Social Theology and Christian Culture

This all-embracing model has also informed the structure and content of the environmental education incorporated in the courses of the curriculum of the School of Social Theology and Christian Culture. In the context of the courses of the curriculum students are expected to explore and reflect upon:

- the main environmental problems of today, their causes and the ways these relate to human behavior and spirituality.
- the solutions offered by scientific, social, and political communities.
- the main terminology of ecology (e.g., ecosystem, biodiversity, sustainability etc.).
- aspects of Christian tradition and spirituality (the biblical story, the stories of the saints, doctrines, and liturgical practice) that can inform an ecologically aware ethos.
- examples of sustainable management within the Orthodox Christian community and other awareness raising activities.
- the ways ecology can relate to Orthodox Christian theology and inform an ecological responsible worldview and practice that is shaped by Christian eco-virtues like hope, humility, justice, benevolence, and love.

In order to reach the set goal, namely training ecologically aware theologians, ministers, and religious leaders, an educational procedure combining both interdisciplinary and multidisciplinary methods was opted. This combination is particularly important in fields such as Theology, where the connection between the main scientific area and environmental protection is not readily obvious. The courses offered in the current curriculum of undergraduate studies can be, therefore, divided into two types: a) interdisciplinary and b) multidisciplinary.

The interdisciplinary courses offered are directly and fully connected to the study of the natural environment and the relationship humans develop with it. They are taught by the School's academic staff and expert guest speakers that present the insights of their discipline to theology students. Currently, this category of courses includes one compulsory and three optional courses:[6]

(1) "Theology, natural sciences and the environment" (compulsory)
(2) "Ecological ethics" (optional, taught by an environmental scientist)
(3) "Religions and the environment" (optional, taught by a theologian and an environmental scientist)
(4) "Environmental management of church facilities" (optional, taught by an environmental scientist and invited speakers)

All courses are offered in the third semester or later and presuppose a basic knowledge of Christian theology. In our experience, most students attend these courses after completing the fourth semester of their studies and they exhibit, therefore, some ability to critically apply the previously acquired theological knowledge in the context of ecology.

Although in previous years ecologically informed interdisciplinary courses were also offered in the postgraduate curriculum, unfortunately, the new structure of our master studies dictated by recent legislation for postgraduate studies had to omit interdisciplinary courses on ecology. Therefore, ecologically relevant topics were integrated in various courses of the curriculum.

In the multidisciplinary environmental education courses topics regarding the creation are incorporated into purely theological courses so as to help students understand why the study of the environment is relevant to Theology. These courses are all taught by theologians. Such topics, at the undergraduate level, include:

• Anthropology-Ecology. Man and Paradise; 2:8-17 in the compulsory course 'Old Testament Theology'
• Iconography and the natural environment in the optional course 'Training and practice in the art of modern hagiography'

---

[6] The description and the syllabi of these courses can be found in the Appendix.

- Humans and nature: ecological relationships in the optional course 'The cultural encyclopedia of the New Testament'
- Ecumenical Patriarchate and the environment. The 'Green Patriarch' in the optional course 'The Orthodox Church. Teaching and witness according to Ecumenical Patriarch Bartholomew'

At the postgraduate level, examples of multidisciplinary courses include:

- "Topics of social and ecological ethics", which combines Christian ethics with contemporary social and ecological problems, and ethics (part of the "Orthodox Theology and Christian Culture" postgraduate program)
- "The space of Mount Athos and the properties of the Athonite Monasteries", which highlights the close link between the unique spiritual function of Mount Athos and the uniqueness of its natural surroundings and how the two are interdependent, as well as the sustainable way monasteries manage the surrounding environment (part of the "Studies on the History, Spirituality, Art and Music Tradition of Mount Athos" postgraduate program)
- "Destinations with special pilgrimage interest: Kastoria, Meteora, Patmos" which combines the spirituality of these three destinations with the natural environment and the problems that arise from the heavy load of tourists that visit them every year (part of the 'Religious and Pilgrimage Tourism" postgraduate program)

In all these courses, the relationship with the creation is approached through various lenses according to the content of each course. The main task of these multidisciplinary encounters is to establish the connection between ecology and Theology on a practical level, so that students can make more use of what they learn in the context of their field of studies.

Theology, Natural Sciences and the Environment

Methodological framework and content of the course

The course on "Theology, Natural Sciences and the Environment" that adopts an interdisciplinary approach and combines several of the environmental education curriculum targets will be discussed here as a case study. It is a compulsory seminar that was incorporated into the School's curriculum in 2013. Its main aim is to promote an interdisciplinary dialogue between Orthodox Theology and the rest of the sciences, especially physical and environmental sciences. It is taught by members of the academic staff of the School, and by guest speakers of other schools and universities, professionals, and independent researchers.

The overarching concept of this course is also evident in its expected outcomes. Students are, namely, expected to (a) apply their theological knowledge and experience in the discussion of current issues and theories related to the creation of the world and the place of human beings in the natural world, (b) engage in a dialogue with natural sciences regarding ecology, (c) discern the epistemological boundaries of natural sciences and the potential of theology, (d) trace and describe the dialogue between Theology and natural sciences from Byzantium to modern times, and (e) present environmental issues from the standpoint of Theology and in dialogue with science.

Even though the rationale of this course remains the same, the content of the syllabus changes every year. The different topics are selected based on the current ecological discussions and the goals set in the UN Agenda 2030. Students are offered a series of interdisciplinary lectures and a package of relevant material and assignments that can help them understand the main points of each issue and encourage them to reflect on the ways this could inform and change their worldview and practice as members of religious community. The following table contains examples of topics presented in recent years together with the course outline of the respective years:

Table 19.1. Examples of different topic focus

Year	Topic/description	Outline
2017-18	**Time** The topic of this course is time as perceived by different sciences and Christian theology. The course will focus on the way time, history and the end of time are understood by natural sciences and philosophy, as well as the importance of time as the setting of salvation and as the *eschaton*.	1. Interdisciplinary dialogue 2. Geological time 3. Time and Creation 4. Biological time 5. Time in the patristic tradition 6. Time in Physics and Astronomy 7. The meaning of time in other religions 8. Philosophical approach of time 9. Biblical understanding of history 10. Beginning and end of time in Bio-Geological sciences: is there an Ω point or "ἦν εἰ καὶ ἔστιν καὶ ἔσται…"? 11. Time in the Orthodox tradition

		12. The end of time in Orthodox tradition 13. Conclusions
2018-19	***Human beings*** The topic of this course is humans and their place in history and the world from the point of view of various sciences and that of Christian theology. The terms 'Anthropocene' and 'Anthropocentricism' will be highlighted within this framework.	1. Introduction 2. The creation of Man in the Old Testament 3. Asceticism and the environment 4. Man and nature in various world religions 5. Man in the Orthodox tradition 6. Eco-justice 7. The Anthropocene and sustainable development 8. A philosopher's approach to the Anthropocene era 9. Artificial intelligence and Man – the future of history 10. The anthropic principle 11. Christian ethics and nature 12. Conclusions 13. Quiz
2019-20	***Human body*** The topic of this course is the body and life of humans, and how human corporeality define both the existence and the relationship of human beings with the rest of the creation.	1. Introduction 2. Human creation and bodily dimension according to the Old Testament 3. Body and human identity in the New Testament and ancient Christianity 4. Body and Sainthood in patristic tradition 5. Human body and human identity in world religions 6. Human body in ancient philosophy 7. Human body in the teachings of the Orthodox Church 8. How does the natural environment affect the human body? 9. Ethics of the body, a Christian view 10. Humans and their psycho-somatic health 11. Art and body 12. The future of the human body - Artificial Intelligence

		13. Quiz - in-class exercise - conclusions
2020-21	***Animals*** The Creation story underlines the relationship between humans and other creatures, mainly animals. According to the Bible animals are not just companions and helpers of human beings, but often teach humans about the Creator. Furthermore, animality is an element of human existence, something discussed already by ancient philosophers. This year's course aims to highlight this relationship between humans and the animal kingdom, to investigate the importance of animals for human existence as understood by Christian tradition and other world religions and to develop a dialogue with other sciences.	1. Introduction to the topic and the course. 2. Animals and human beings in the Old Testament 3. Animals and human beings in the New Testament and early Christianity 4. Orthodox theology and animals 5. The position of the Church Fathers on animals 6. Animals and human beings in the religions of the world 7. Threatened species 8. Animal rights 9. Zoonotic diseases 10. Animals in world literature 11. Christian ethics and animals 12. Animal biology 13. Quiz - in-class exercise - conclusions.

Course evaluation by students

In the annual evaluations submitted by students the ratings of this course are amongst the top of the School's courses and generally above the School's average.[7] Students seem to be happy with the structure and content of the course and evaluate positively the interdisciplinary approach of the offered material. Furthermore, the vast majority of the students who have attended the course so far find it interesting and believe that such courses are necessary for Theology students. There have been cases of students, who after successfully completing the course, they returned the following year to attend the course again, in order to learn about a new topic.

The only area of a slight concern is the understanding of the concepts presented within the framework of the course, which is something that needs attention when planning such courses. Since some of the concepts discussed

---

[7] For example, in the academic year 2019-20 the quality index of the course was 89.7 whereas the general quality index of the curriculum was 86.4. The satisfaction of the students is also reflected in the success rate of the exams process (89.7% of those who participated).

in this course come from other sciences and are not directly linked to Theology, it is to be expected that students will find it hard to readily understand them. Therefore, our presenters, especially those coming from other fields, are asked to adapt their language and lecture to a non-expert audience and be open to discussion during their presentation. Interestingly, this encounter is a fruitful challenge not only for the students but for the presenters, who usually have had no previous experience in teaching in a theological context.

There is also a very small group of students (less than 1% of those participating in the evaluation process) who feel uncomfortable with the ideas presented by some invited speakers (especially those coming from natural sciences) and maintain they are incompatible with the teachings of the Orthodox Christian Church. Such a reaction is certainly unavoidable and reflects a certain part of the Orthodox world that in principle remains suspicious towards sciences and conveniently associates them with a Western secular worldview. Their objections must be treated with respect and in the spirit of openness and inclusion. Students are encouraged to articulate their objections and pose critical questions, to interact respectfully with the speakers, the rest of the class and the course instructors, to be open to different views and critically assess their tradition. This diversity of opinions and stances is a strong advantage of such courses and despite the challenges it poses to the class and the instructors it can create the necessary conditions for a constructive confrontation with pre-conceptions and prejudices, a retrieval of neglected aspects of tradition and spirituality and eventually for a re-calibration of our mindset and ethics.

Conclusions

Humans have been transforming this world ever since they appeared on Earth. Gradually and lightly at first, rapidly and at an accelerating pace after the first half of the 20th century. Religions are required to play their part in this ever-changing world to help humanity enter a more sustainable phase in its history. Approaching environmental problems through religious sentiment could offer the key to formulating a more effective environmental ethic.

Orthodox Theology is, therefore, at a crucial crossroad. It is now the chance (the *kairos*) not only to produce an ecologically aware theological discourse but also to create a younger generation of religious leaders, teachers or simply members of the Orthodox Church that will feel accountable for and interconnected with the rest of the creation, that will act as the priests of God's creation appreciative of its glory and committed to its preservation and flourishing. In the words of the Ecumenical Patriarch Bartholomew:

> We may all agree that churches and religions have a fundamental responsibility and role to play in advancing ecological learning and advocating climate justice. Therefore, theological schools and seminaries should be at the forefront of this effort as well. Nevertheless, this cannot occur if seminarians and students are not exposed to an integrated environmental ministry throughout their education and formation.[8]

It is therefore a chance for theological faculties and seminaries to accept the challenge. The experiment of the curriculum of the School of Social Theology and Orthodox Culture of the Aristotle University of Thessaloniki is helpful and hopefully can serve as a first step for other Theology schools and seminaries that wish to incorporate a similar curriculum into their programs.

---

[8] Keynote address at Halki Summit III, http://www.halkisummit.com/hs3/opening-patriarchal-address/ .

Appendix – Content of interdisciplinary environmental education courses

Ecological ethics

This course focuses on the contemporary models of environmental ethics philosophies, as well as on the way Christian ethics can help tackle the ecological crisis. Students have the opportunity to see if and how all these apply in practice. After completion of this course, students, having acquired a general knowledge on the philosophical and ethical views and arguments, as well as the position of orthodox theology regarding the natural environment, are able to identify the difference between good and problematic arguments and to analyze and compare the arguments of the ecological ethics theories, as well as of specific individuals. They are also able to compose their own arguments and positions on contemporary issues relating to ecological ethics, and to participate, as theologians, in the discussions on dealing with the deeper causes of the current environmental problems. Finally, those that will work as educators, having digested the whole problematic, will, in turn, be able to present these issues to their students and offer answers from the Christian ethics viewpoint.

Course outline
1. Contemporary environmental issues
2. Main concepts in environmental ethics
3. Anthropocentric ethics
4. Ethics of life: traditional theories of environmental ethics
5. Environmental ethics and politics
6. Environmental ethics and the economy
7. Orthodox Christian tradition
8. The Ecumenical Patriarchate
9. Animal liberation
10. Environmental ethics and dietary choices
11. Western Christian churches
12. Case study
13. Paper presentation

World religions and the environment

This course presents the relation of various world religions to the natural environment through time, from the ancient to the modern world.

Course outline
1. Religion and the natural environment - a general overview
2. Religions for the environment
3. East Mediterranean religions I (Ancient Greek and Roman religion)
4. East Mediterranean religions II (Asia Minor, Balkan peninsula, Black Sea religions)
5. Judaism
6. Cultures of Mesopotamia (Assyrians, Babylonians, Persians)
7. Eastern religions I (Vedism, Hinduism, Jainism, Buddhism)
8. Eastern religions II (Confucianism, Daoism, Shintoism)
9. Sub-saharian cultures, American Indians, Aboriginals
10. Islam
11. Contemporary issues of religion and ecology
12. International environmental movements - Sustainable development. Connection to world religions
13. Paper presentations

Environmental management of church facilities

The course aims to familiarize students with environmental management, so that they will be able to apply their knowledge in various church facilities. Students who attend this course acquire a general knowledge of environmental problems, their causes and the solution of sustainable development, in order to be able to: a. relate specific actions and functions of church facilities to their impacts on the environment and to explain these impacts to those in charge of each facility, b. explain how the green management of a church facility could contribute to the sustainability of and area, and how a good relationship with the natural environment is part of orthodox theology, c. calculate the ecological footprint of a facility and explain the way that the members of this facility as well as its visitors contribute to the size of this footprint, d. compose arguments on the necessity of an environmental management plan and analyze the benefits from the application of such a plan, e. define the targets of an environmental management plan and prioritize them according to specific criteria, compose a project timetable and budget, and coordinate the working team, f. propose solutions that will combine the conservation of the natural environment with the conservation of the special features of church facilities.

Course outline
1. Current environmental issues
2. The orthodox Christian view
3. Environmental management benefits - Sustainability - Sustainable development
4. Environmental quality standards
5. Application of an environmental management scheme I (needs - targets - action plan
6. Application of an environmental management scheme II (application of the action plan - monitoring).
7. Application of an environmental management scheme III (the role of the priest)
8. Examples of environmental management I (Mt. Athos)
9. Examples of environmental management II (church facilities in Greece)
10. Examples of environmental management III (world Christian church facilities - other religions)
11. Case study - location visit
12. Case study - discussion of findings
13. Paper presentation

Bibliography

Ayres, J. R. (2014). "Learning on the Ground: Ecology, Engagement, and Embodiment." *Teaching Theology and Religion* 17 (3): 203–16.

Bauman, W., Bohannon, R., & O'Brien, K. J. (Eds.). (2017). *Grounding Religion: A Field Guide to the Study of Religion and Ecology.* (New York: Routledge, 2017)

Carleton-Hug, A., & Hug, J. W. (2010). Challenges and opportunities for evaluating environmental education programs. *Evaluation and Program Planning*, 159-164.

Champerlain, G. L. (2000). "Ecology and Religious Education." *Religious Education* 95 (2): 134–50.

Chryssavgis, J. (Ed.). (2012). *On Earth as in Heaven: Ecological Vision and Initiatives of Ecumenical Patriarch Bartholomew.* (New York: Fordham University Press, 2012).

Chryssavgis, J., & Foltz, B. V. (Eds.). (2013). *Toward an Ecology of Transfiguraion: Orthodox Christian Perspectives on Environment, Nature, and Creation.* (New York: Fordham University Press, 2013).

Crohn, K., & Birnbaum, M. (2010). Environmental education evaluation: Time to reflect, time for change. *Evaluation and Program Planning*, 155-158.

Devitt, C., & Tatay, J. (2017). Sustainability and Interreligious Dialogue. *Islamochristiana*, 123-139.

Gottlieb, R. S. (ed.). (2006). *The Oxford Handbook of Religion and Ecology.* (Oxford: Oxford University Press, 2006).

Grim, J., & Tucker, M. E. (2014). *Ecology and Religion.* (Washingron: Island Press, 2014).

Hungerford, H. R., & Peyton, R. B. (1994). *Procedures for developing an environmental curriculum. A discussion guide for UNESCO training seminars on environmental education.* (USA: UNESCO-UNEP, 1994).

Kalaitzidis, P. (2019). "The Ambiguous Relationship between Orthodoxy and Science as Part of the Pending Discussion between Orthodoxy and Modernity: From the Polemic against the Enlightenment to the Debate over Homosexuality." In *Orthodox Christianity and Modern Science: Tensions, Ambiguities, Potential*, edited by Vasileios Makrides and Gayle E. Woloschak, 47–66. (Science and Orthodox Christianity 1. Turnhout: Brepols, 2019).

Krueger, F. W. (2012). *Greening the Orthodox Parish.* (California: The Orthodox Fellowship of Transfiguration, 2012).

Orr, David W. 1992. *Ecological Literacy: Education and the Transition to a Postmodern World.* SUNY Series in Constructive Postmodern Thought 1. (Albany: State University of New York Press, 1992).

Orr, D. W. (2008). Ecological Systems Thinking. In S. E. Jorgensen, & B. D. Fath (Eds.), *Encyclopedia of Ecology* (Vol. 4, pp. 1117-1121). (Academic Press, 2008).

Orr, D. W., Niccolucci, V., & Bastianoni, S. (2019). Ecological Systems Thinking. In B. Fath (Ed.), *Encyclopedia of Ecology* (2nd Edition ed., Vol. 4, pp. 238-287). (Elsevier, 2019).

Skirbekk, V., de Sherbinin, A., Adamo, S. B., Navarro, J. and Chai-Onn, T. (2020). Religious Affiliation and Environmental Challenges in the 21st Century. *Journal of Religion and Demography* 7 (2): 238–71.

Stern, M. J., Powell, R. B., & Hill, D. (2014). Environmental education program evaluation in the new millenium: what do we measure and what we have learned? *Environmental Education Research*, 581-611.

Theokritoff, E. (2017). "Green Patriarch, Green Patristics: Reclaiming the Deep Ecology of Christian Tradition." *Religions* 8 (7): 1–19.

Tomlinson, J. (2019). "Ecological Religious Education: New Possibilities for Educational Practice." *Journal of Religious Education* 67 (3): 185–202.

UNEP. (2016). *Environment, Religion and Culture in the Context of the 2030 Agenda for Sustainable Development.* (Nairobi: United Nations Environment Programme, 2016).

White, L. (1967, March 10). The historical roots of out ecologic crisis. *Science* (3767), 1203-1207.

CHAPTER TWENTY

PSYCHOLOGICAL IMPACTS OF CLIMATE CHANGE AND RECOMMENDATIONS[1]

L. VAN SUSTEREN AND W. K. AL-DELAIMY

Summary

Although the harm to our physical health from the climate crisis is increasingly reported, still underrecognized is the harm the climate crisis is having on us *psychologically*. Yet it is the psychological impacts of *global overheating* - and the consequent cascading destabilization of ecosystems-that will carry the biggest burden and be the most difficult to remedy. It requires our utmost attention. Understanding the gravity of the mounting psychological harm underscores the urgent need for all those concerned, especially public officials, to take action. The devastating psychological and physical impacts of the tragedy of lead-tainted water in Flint, Michigan, in microcosm, serves as a recent example to those who would downplay harm to our health in the face of ongoing warnings and pleas for action. The psychological aspects of the climate crisis are increasingly drawing the attention of mental health professionals. They are uniquely qualified and urgently needed to address the denial, discounting, or distancing that feed inaction, and to point out the deepening injustice of putting vulnerable populations at risk, especially our children and future generations. They are also needed to advocate for programs that address climate anxiety and trauma, and to design programs that build resilience. The mounting risk of an epidemic of fear, outrage, and despair calls for mental health professionals to play a pivotal role in what has become a do-or-die effort to

---

[1] This article was first published as Ch. 14 in, W. K. Al-Delaimy, V. Ramanathan, M. Sánchez Sorondo (eds.), *Health of People, Health of Planet and Our Responsibility*, https://doi.org/10.1007/978-3-030-31125-4_14. We are grateful to Springer Nature for permission to republish this article, which is licensed under the Creative Commons Attribution 4.0 International License

restore humanity and the rest of the natural world to safety. All of the losses associated with climate change - from extreme weather events and chronic climate conditions to the devastating physical injuries, illnesses, and deaths and the attendant displacement, disruptions, and downstream indirect ripple effects - carry with them an emotional toll. The magnitude and relentlessness of the destruction, as well as the insinuation into every aspect of our lives - economic, personal, political - must be recognized as we consider the mental health and psychosocial impacts of the deepening crisis.

Extreme Weather Events

The global rise in temperature is driving local spikes of searing heat waves and increasing the frequency and intensity of storms, wildfires, and floods. In the last two decades, extreme weather has wounded, displaced, or required emergency assistance for four billion people; half a million have died (United Nations Office for Disaster Risk Reduction, 2015).

Extreme weather events drive emotional turmoil in every phase. Anticipatory fear is experienced in the early stages, followed by the trauma of the event itself, then sorrow and grief at the losses. Feelings of outrage may emerge - slowing down the working through - when it is believed that government and institutions are not providing enough help or did not undertake preventive measures. Despair and feelings of helplessness deepen as reports surface that conditions will get worse.

Those in disaster-prone areas are the most affected. Anticipatory anxiety sometimes rises to the level of "pre-traumatic stress disorder" among those who fear that another disaster may be just around the corner. In anecdotal reports, residents of New Orleans report, for example, that sometimes just seeing a storm cloud triggers deep anxiety (Hauser, 2015; Reckdahl, 2017). Communities under stress can fray and decompensate - increasing violence and other psychosocial ills. Mental health professionals are seeing a full range of psychiatric disorders and conditions emerge as a result of these stressors: major depression, anxiety, PTSD, adjustment disorders, a rise in drug and alcohol abuse as people attempt to cope, and domestic violence - including child abuse (American Psychiatric Association [APA], 2017; World Health Organization, 2005). In addition, the more destructive the event, the higher the incidence of PTSD and the greater the risk of suicide (Edwards & Wiseman, 2011).

Processing disaster

After a *natural* disaster, an identifiable low point is seen, followed by the feeling that the worst is over, and the recovery process can begin. How we process the event is determined in part by how we answer critical questions: *why* did this happen, *who* or *what* is responsible, and could the disaster have been prevented? Disasters experienced as natural are easier to reconcile because they are experienced as "fate" - beyond our control. When disasters are no longer experienced solely as natural, as "acts of God or nature," but instead are experienced as having arisen or been made worse because of the behavior of humans - due to a mistake, carelessness, or worse, as *the result of deliberate disregard for consequence*s - then it is much harder for us to recover and the psychological harm is more serious (Folkman, Lazarus, Dunkel-Schetter, DeLongis, & Gruen, 1986).

How we "carry on" is influenced by our background, current mental state, personality, and life experiences. The nature of the event plays a role: the intensity of the feeling of powerlessness, the "merciless" character of incidents, the pace, suddenness, degree of damage, loss of life and injury and the extent to which people personalize these incidents will be factors influencing the extent of emotional injury. Though studies quantifying it are limited, human empathy tells us of the emotional toll: When the place you call home is burned down by wildfires, blown away by tornados, flooded or overrun by hurricanes, when you lose your possessions, maybe your pets, your livelihood, the comfort of a familiar community, and witness the injuries, illnesses, and deaths, the resulting mix of fear, anger, sorrow, and trauma can easily send a person to a breaking point. Stress drives up the secretion of cortisol; high levels of this hormone are not damaging when they are short-lived, but *persistently* elevated levels can be exceedingly damaging. Immune function can be compromised, sleep patterns disturbed, digestion disrupted, memory impaired, and the cardiovascular system harmed - all with an attendant emotional toll (Shaw et al., 2019). Everyday life is full of burdens and anxieties; confronted by the additional stress of the climate crisis, some individuals will decompensate.

Exposed to repeated or ongoing disasters, victims may not have a chance to recover emotionally before the next disaster hits, compounding the harm because each incident deepens emotional vulnerability. Victims also contend often with the realization that "no lessons have been learned". The healing process is helped along when we can look back, identify where we went wrong and take action to legitimately say we are doing all that we can to prevent further injury. But on the contrary, even as the dangers continue to unspool at an ever-higher rate, the extraction and use of fossil fuels continues, with recent US government policies *promoting* their use - exacerbating the mounting psychological toll.

Wildfires

Increasing temperatures from climate change dry out land and vegetation, causing bigger, more frequent, and intense wildfires. Homes and communities are increasingly finding themselves in fire-prone areas. While the physical impacts of fires can be measured as lives lost, structures burned, and communities disrupted, the psychological damage is immeasurable. The acute phase is dominated by fear - or *terror*. The mercilessness of flames, incinerating everything in their path, has a particularly devastating effect on those who witness what has happened, and they may be unable to shake loose from intrusive and horrifying thoughts of what it is like to burn to death. When the flames are finally spent or defeated, seeing what was once a comforting refuge but is now nothing or little more than a moonscape brings overwhelming grief.

Various phases of disasters have been studied, along with many common emotional responses to them (SAMHSA Phases of Disaster, 2018). Based on the clinical experience of the first author with victims of trauma, including of natural disasters, many emotional stressors have not yet been measured but warrant being pointed out. In an initial phase, vows to rebuild and faith in outside support do help in the first steps towards emotional recovery but fears of "next time" often plague survivors. Wrenching, conflicting feelings about remaining in the vulnerable area, financial strain, and friction from different coping styles may erode family stability. Lingering feelings of helplessness, despair, and foreboding make restoring a sense of security more challenging. Emotionally charged triggers can reawaken traumatic memories - in the case of wildfires, by the simple smell of smoke, the sound of sirens, the once-pleasant crackling of an ordinary fire. Acute displacement may become permanent - rupturing the comfort and stabilizing effect of familiar relationships, places, and daily routines. Some scars may be buried or disguised - expressed in ways that make them not only hard to "count" but worse, harder to confront and work through. The stress on individuals and communities is compounded by mental health systems that are underprepared to deal with the trauma.

Violent storms and floods

Violent storms and floods are responsible for half the disasters from extreme weather events (UNISDR, 2015). Higher temperatures increase the moisture content in the atmosphere, increasing the severity and frequency of storms. As with other extreme weather events, violent storms and floods unleash catastrophic physical and emotional harm, bringing about the disorders and conditions cited earlier. Of all extreme weather events, flooding affects the greatest number of people. The financially stretched are most vulnerable, with the physical difficulty of getting to safety too great or the cost too high, which the financially privileged may sometimes forget when they ask why people did not get out of harm's way. Even temporary housing is frequently beyond the reach of those who live paycheck to paycheck.

The far-reaching psychological impacts of violent storms saw their prototype in Hurricane Katrina in 2005, now "updated" by other storms, in particular the devastating Hurricane Maria that leveled Puerto Rico in 2018. Grief, anxiety, violence, outbursts of outrage, and blame at the government's slow response are among the acute emotional stressors of many victims. Many report feeling that the government "doesn't care" about them (Morin & Rein, 2005).

A flood-ravaged home brings a particular type of anguish. Based on experience, violently being run out of one's refuge from the outside world underscores the fear that no place is safe. Seeing belongings a soggy ruin, often turning black and moldy as they undergo the slow but inexorable process of rotting, brings unconscious associations to dying and death. The sense of powerlessness over "nature unleashed" can weigh heavily on victims.

The widespread presence of mold in homes and other buildings is common in the aftermath of floods; the physical symptoms associated with exposure to mold are well documented (Potera, 2007). Exposure to mold is also linked to psychiatric disorders, especially depression, and reduced cognitive functioning (Shenassa, Daskalakis, Liebhaber, Braubach, & Brown, 2007). Other impacts include anxiety, irritability, and fatigue (Hope, 2013). Toxic mold-induced mental illness and cognitive decline are rarely correctly diagnosed or treated.

Research confirms the association between the chronic stress of climate disaster emotional trauma and cardiovascular health (Peters et al., 2014). Residents of New Orleans suffered heart attacks at a rate three times higher than the rate reported before the storm (Peters et al., 2014). The absence of social support when communities are torn apart is one of the strongest predictors of posttraumatic stress (Brewin, Andrews, & Valentine, 2000; Ozer, Best, Lipsey, & Weiss, 2003).

Summer Heat Waves

As global temperatures rise, the incidence of extreme heat waves is increasing. Nearly one-third of the world's population is now exposed to deadly heat waves (Mora, Counsell, Bielecki, & Louis, 2017). In the last decade, with less than 1% increase in warming, the loss of human life has risen 2300% (Mora, Counsell, Bielecki, & Louis, 2017). Significant psychological stress is also associated with heat waves. With rising temperatures comes rising rates of aggression (Bulbena, Sperry, & Cunillera, 2006; Raj, 2014). It is linked to increased catecholamine release in response to the stress of the heat (Al-Hadramy & Ali, 1989). For each standard deviation of increased temperature or more extreme rainfall, studies show a 4% increase in conflict between individuals, and a 14% increase in conflict between groups (Hsiang et al., 2013). These findings are valid across all regions and among all ethnic groups. Increased acts of aggression include assaults, murders, and suicides, especially violent suicides. As temperatures continue to rise, a global increase in unrest should be anticipated.

Temperatures *modestly* above the human comfort zone are associated with a decline in cognitive functioning: slowed response time, diminished accuracy, and less sophisticated patterns of decision-making. Declining cognitive function could become increasingly problematic for those unable to escape the heat (Goodman, Hurwitz, Park, & Smith, 2018). The mental health toll from heat waves is hard to measure. Like blizzards and storms, the disruptions of heat waves range from irritating inconveniences to profoundly stressful losses. Declining business and productivity, which drops at high temperatures, are consequences of extreme heat (Somanathan, Somanathan, Sudarshan, & Tewari, 2018). Those who must work outdoors or where AC is not available may not be able to work at all. With little financial cushion, it may not be possible to pay bills or even buy food. The emotional toll on families and the communities they live in can be horrendous. With the persistent high temperatures and the ever-expanding desert that they create, scientists predict that the Middle East may well become uninhabitable by the end of the century (Funkhouser, 2016).

Particularly vulnerable are the poor, the elderly, the sick, and the very young. Individuals with preexisting mental disorders are also especially susceptible. During hotter-than-average periods, they appear to get sicker than expected, show greater aggressiveness towards others, and require more frequent use of restraints (Bulbena et al., 2006). The good judgment to stay cool and hydrated may be compromised; some individuals in this population live outdoors and lack access to air conditioning. Many take medication (psychotropics) that impede the ability to perspire - the body's chief means of reducing internal temperature.

Chronic Climate Conditions

Drought Conditions

Drought conditions are worsening with rising temperatures, particularly in the western United States. Drought has its own attendant, often chronic, mental health impacts (Stanke, Kerac, Prudhomme, Medlock, & Murray, 2013). An unrelenting day-after-day anxiety and despair can descend on those who depend on nature's rains for their livelihood - farmers, day workers, owners of related businesses - who watch and wait for water that does not come. A serious and protracted decline in available water may force many to make life-altering changes, with stressful impacts on individuals, families, and communities (Vins, Bell, Saha, & Hess, 2015).

Suicide is the result of complex dynamics, but prolonged drought is considered (in most studies) a major contributing factor among at-risk populations for suicide among farmers in India, rural Australia, and South Africa (Carleton, 2017; Hanigan, Butlera, Kokicc, & Hutchinson, 2012; Vins et al., 2015). The psychological toll on families who have lost their fathers, sons, uncles, and brothers, in addition to what is often their sole source of income, is devastating. Entire countries now compete for water from the once great rivers of the world - the Mekong, Jordan, the Brahmaputra, the Tigris and Euphrates, the Nile - bringing rationing and water wars as tension mounts (Bhalla, 2012). The decline in available water brings food insecurity - unleashing a flood of its own woes - with individual impacts ranging from the personal stress of hunger and rationing to malnutrition, starvation, and death when conditions persist. In the crops the world's poor are most dependent on, malnutrition from higher concentrations of atmospheric CO_2 *alone* causes malnutrition from micronutrient deficiencies responsible for cognitive deficits and other physical harms, carrying with them an emotional toll that can be lifelong (Smith & Myers, 2018).

As climate change worsens and causes more droughts, millions will continue to see their access to drinking water threatened. Access to water grips us emotionally in ways other needs do not because we cannot survive beyond a few days without water. When a community has a dwindling supply of clean water - from diminished snowpack, accelerating and preseason melting of glaciers, drying up of rivers, streams, lakes, and aquifers - or from saltwater intrusion or other climate-induced contamination, a deepening sense of anxiety and foreboding follows.

In regions dependent on agriculture and already rife with ethnic tensions, strained by poverty and political divisiveness, climate related disasters are "threat multipliers" for outbreaks of violence (Schleussner, Donges, Donner, & Schellnhuber, 2016). Ongoing periods of water scarcity, spiked by periods of drought, particularly in the growing season of these vulnerable regions, trigger not only spasms of violence but sustained cycles of conflict (Von Uexkull, Croicu, Fjelde, & Buhaug, 2016).

News reports have covered how new waves of migrations created by regional conflicts often drive people to relocate in places that do not want them and cannot help them (Baker, 2015). Those with the fewest resources are often unable to relocate, "trapping them in high-risk areas" (Randall, 2013). Although sometimes controversial and complex to assess, peer-reviewed reports specifically tie the recent scarcity of water in Syria to increased migration and the geopolitical tensions it spawned (Müller, Yoon, Gorelick, Avisse, & Tilmant, 2016).

An influx of refugees can stir fear, uncertainty, and anger, due to pressures that mount from scare resources, inadequate infrastructure, problems adapting to changing circumstances and cultural differences, limited or absent health and mental health services, along with pervasive and profound physical and psychological trauma among refugees (Langlois, Haines, Tomson, & Ghaffar, 2016). Data from 157 countries demonstrated that drought severity and likelihood of armed conflict played a role in explaining increased asylum seeking between 2011 and 2015 (Abel, Brottrager, Crespo Cuaresma, & Muttarak, 2019).

Confrontations in southwestern and southeastern states over water are leading to legal battles. In California, drought conditions have forced rationing, with news reports that neighbors engage in "drought shaming," fighting, and tattling on each other over their water use, foreshadowing what may lie ahead (Huffaker, 2015).

Sea Level Rise

Global sea level is likely to increase 10-13 feet in as few as 50 years unless there is a major rapid reduction in greenhouse gas emissions. "Parts of our coastal cities would still be sticking above the water, but you couldn't live there" (Hansen et al., 2016). Already, many living in low-lying coastlines and small island states are being displaced by sea-level rise, but these numbers are dwarfed by predictions that the accelerating pace of rising seas will flood some of the world's most populous cities, creating a tidal wave of psychosocial trauma as a bottleneck of climate refugees compete for higher ground (Hearty, 2012; Parker, 2017). In the United States alone, tens of millions live on coastlines and depend on coastline stability for their livelihoods, well-being, and survival; worldwide hundreds of millions of people live within 30 ft of sea level (McGranahan, Balk, & Anderson, 2007).

With some *acute* climate events, victims can "arm themselves" by taking actions that help protect them should they face a similar event. Sea level rise is different. Although governments can work to adopt measures to mitigate harm in the short term, future sea level rise will continue, inundating low-lying cities, countries, and islands. Fears of permanent displacement to unfamiliar places gnaw at victims, provoking additional stress-financial, social, and personal. Current and future climate refugees, who have been displaced from their homes, search for safety and security, but chaos and violence often follow them, and can spread to others along the way. Massive relocation will become necessary; it is already underway in places such as Shishmaref in Alaska, St Charles Island in LA, and now Charleston NC. Parts of Miami, FL are flooded nearly daily.

Believing that we can take action, that we are empowered to protect ourselves, is critical to maintaining our mental health. Nurturing the hope of returning home, restoring, and rebuilding after cataclysmic losses builds resilience. But no such action or hope can undo the ravages of locked-in sea level rise. Layered on are the crushing financial losses of walking away from what is typically our biggest investment, our homes, now with little or no value. The plight of climate refugees is increasingly the focus of mental health professionals. The psychological stress of refugees is high. The refugees are often blamed for psychosocial ills. Katrina refugees were initially accused of precipitating a crime wave in Houston, where many were taken in, before a closer analysis showed this was a misreading of statistics (Hamilton, 2010). A flare-up of anti-refugee sentiment has rocked countries and governments across Europe and on the American border with Mexico where the divisive battle over building a wall has further polarized the USA and precipitated a record-breaking government shutdown.

Other Sources of Climate-Related Psychological Impacts

New Disease Threats

As ecosystems are altered by climate change, old diseases are expanding their reach and new diseases are emerging. While physical health data is examined and reported, the complex psychosocial toll - difficult to quantify - often is not addressed as a result.

Warnings that new diseases and old diseases are emerging are heard frequently. Deeply unnerving, they precipitate a pervasive if not always fully conscious sense of vulnerability that adds to existing stressors in life. Millions worried, for example, about exposure to the Zika virus, with widespread repercussions: local economies took a hit as fears drove tourists away, pregnancies were put off; travel plans unraveled; and decisions about family life and individual personal choices were driven by fears of infection. Families suffered the anguish of having babies born with deformities and with the knowledge that a baby who was exposed might appear normal but have disabilities down the road.

Lyme disease is well known in some cases to leave its victims with long-lasting and painful emotional wounds. Cognitive deficits and mood disorders with depression and anxiety are not uncommon. Individuals struggle with the torment of treatments that are often ineffective, especially when the diagnosis, sometimes difficult to make, comes after years of raging infection and unexplained symptoms. Other climate-linked viruses, parasites, and bacteria storm on and off stage depending on local weather conditions, or are waiting in the wings for their chance, or continue their inexorable expansion: Dengue fever, also known as "bone-break fever" because it is so painful; Chikungunya; Hantavirus; West Nile; Chagas disease; and of course, Malaria. All of them carry an attendant psychosocial toll that must be addressed.

Air Pollution

The World Health Organization reports that nine out of ten people breathe unhealthy air. Air pollution is primarily the result of our use of fossil fuels: when coal, oil, and gas are burned, they create pollutants that undergo chemical reactions to form particulate matter. Warmer temperatures speed up these reactions, causing pollution to become more concentrated. The presence of particulate matter in our bodies triggers inflammation. Many diseases and conditions are linked to exposure to polluted air. Ultrafine particulate matter is especially worrisome because it can cross directly from lung tissue into the bloodstream and be carried throughout the entire body. Already confirmed in nonhuman primates, initial studies suggest that ultra-fine particulate matter also crosses directly from the nasal mucosa via nerve endings that transport it directly into the human brain (Obederdöster, Elder, & Rinderknecht, 2009).

Though more research is needed to address some inconsistencies, evidence is mounting that inflammation of brain tissue from air pollution is linked to dementia, including Alzheimer's type; is linked as a comorbid factor in the development of Parkinson's disease and exacerbation of symptoms; and is linked to amyotrophic lateral sclerosis (ALS) (Calderón-Garcidueñas & Villareal-Ríos, 2017; Chen et al., 2017; Lee et al., 2017; Seelen et al., 2017).

The incidence of these diseases is expected to rise and already brings a crushing economic burden in the hundreds of billions of dollars. The cost in human suffering alone should be argument enough to make eliminating the burning of fossil fuels a number one public health priority (Gladman & Zinman, 2015; Kirson et al., 2016; Kowal, Dall, Chakrabarti, Storm, & Jain, 2013).

Evidence supports a link between neuro-inflammation and classic psychiatric illness: major depressive disorders, bipolar disorder, schizophrenia, and obsessive-compulsive disorders (Souhel, Pearlman, Alper, Najjar, & Devinsky, 2013). Air pollution is also associated with increased psychosis in adolescents (Newbury, Arseneault, Beevers, et al., 2019). Even *low levels of pollution* in Sweden, primarily from traffic, are associated with an increased risk of mental illness in children (Oudin, Bråbäck, Åström, Strömgren, & Forsberg, 2016).

The American Psychological Association reported children exposed to particulate matter in the air were more likely to have symptoms of anxiety or depression (Weir, 2012). Emergency room visits for anxiety, including panic attacks and threats to commit suicide, are significantly higher on days with poor air quality (Szyszkowicz, Willey, Grafstein, Rowe, & Colman, 2010).

Vulnerable Populations

The elderly, the sick, the disabled, the poor, and those whose jobs are tied to the natural environment (farming, fishing, forestry, etc.) are particularly susceptible to the psychological impacts of climate disruption. Residents in areas destroyed by climate disasters or where fossil fuel production has destroyed the natural landscape are especially likely to suffer from "Solastalgia": a gripping existential pain that comes from seeing places that once gave the treasured feeling of "home" now lost or irreparably damaged (Albrecht, 2005).

The mentally ill are especially vulnerable: they are less resilient, have fewer resources, face disrupted services that put them at risk of decompensation, and take psychotropic drugs that impede the ability to perspire-making them more prone to overheating. Often overlooked groups include: first responders, who see the injuries, deaths and devastation in its rawest state; climate experts, whose professional lives are spent cataloguing the growing evidence of decline and with a growing sense of doom see their life's work damaged, destroyed or disappearing (Guest, 2014; Nicholls et al., 2014); and activists, the "Climate Cassandras", who, desperately issuing anguished warnings, and in the grip of images of future disasters they cannot get out of their minds, may suffer from "pre-traumatic stress disorder" (Van Susteren, 2013).

The poor and rural populations as well as those who live a day-to-day existence face falling income, food shortages, and rising prices. Decisions must be made about who eats and who does not. Families and communities fray when competition erodes the sharing support system that was characteristically relied upon. The world's poor suffer the anguish of climate injustice far from the consciousness of those whose overconsumption and disproportionate use of resources are most responsible. Ten percent of the world's richest are responsible for the emissions of 50% of the world's greenhouse gases (Gore, 2015).

Ocean acidification, warming, and ocean deoxygenation are impacts from climate disruption that are responsible for dramatic declines in marine life. Experts warn that without immediate dramatic action to improve the health of our oceans, within a few decades oceans will no longer have the capacity to feed millions of people who depend on them to survive. As catches dwindle from depleted sources, food production falls, jobs decline, incomes fall, and hunger rises. Cascading economic, health, social, and psychological ills follow (IPSO, 2013).

Children and young people are at special risk. The message that the planet is dying, and that the survival of future generations is on the line *registers in* climate-aware young people. Though findings are sometimes inconsistent, and more work is called for, many are *less likely* to distance or discount the warnings of scientists, educators, and government agencies that the window on our ability to "act in time" is closing. They know that conditions will worsen and the cumulative destructive toll, emotional and physical, will fall on their shoulders. Children are frightened, report they are sad and angry; a bleak and pessimistic view of the future may be more prevalent in adolescents and young adults (Ojala, 2012; Strife, 2012). Chronic childhood stress, persistently driving up cortisol levels, can alter brain development, notably in the hippocampus and prefrontal cortex, with the potential to cause impaired cognition and a life-long predisposition to anxiety, depression, and susceptibility to additional stress (Carrion & Wong, 2012; Simpson, Weissbecker, & Sephton, 2011). Susceptibility to anxiety can be passed onto succeeding generations through epigenetic inheritance (Skinner, 2014). Children who experience multiple early life stressors are at greater risk for suicide (Björkenstam, Kosidou, & Björkenstam, 2017).

The first reported case of climate crisis-induced psychosis occurred in an Australian boy in 2009, who, in his drought-stricken country, refused to drink water because he feared millions would die as a result. The doctor who treated him at Melbourne's Children Hospital said he has since seen many other children suffering from climate anxiety in varying degrees of severity (Wolf & Salo, 2008).

Summary of Psychosocial Impacts

"Not everything that counts can be counted..." (William Bruce Cameron). Personal anecdotal clinical expertise suggests that it is the inchoate, insidious, complex, and unconscious psychological states driven by climate trauma - not lending themselves to studies and precise numbers - that can be the most profoundly damaging and drive systemic emotional conditions that society will find difficult to treat and surmount. Just as the functioning of families breaks down in the face of a chaotic home environment, in the face of the turbulence from declining national security, without trust that our institutions can protect us, the fabric of society can break down. The waves of injury from climate trauma and frustration from inaction are reverberating across our communities, the workplace, and our families, cumulatively taking a toll on the national mood. Repercussions from a stressed-out national mood drive our economy, our politics, and our relations with other countries. It shapes our culture and increasingly affects how we treat each other. How will we deal with a growing state of fear from diminished productivity, conflict between haves and have-nots, callousness, and numbness in our response to suffering - "compassion fatigue" - an alienated citizenry, distrust of each other? We can be anxious and not know why, and we can be anxious and not know it. Sometimes anxiety is manifested as anger or another emotion or state that does not even suggest the root cause. We can be anxious and give it the wrong name - often if the real source is especially unsettling. We do not always recognize the psychological toll anxiety is having on us. Much of the violence in the world can be explained by unaddressed anxiety emanating from fears of impotence and vulnerability. Climate change evokes a profound sense of both. Whether we know it or not, whether we like it or not, whether we accept it or not, we believe the climate crisis is causing varying degrees of anxiety among most of the population.

Special Message to Mental Health Professionals: Recommendations and a Call to Action

Trying to avoid thinking about climate-related issues, or other conditions that cause anxiety, is an attempt to try to control our fears, but fear and avoidance are at the root of denial and inaction.

Years of experience have shown mental health professionals how to move people beyond this state, replacing resistance with the empowering realization that the solution is to take action. As mental health professionals we know the power of words - we know how to break down defenses, put together messages that help people finally begin to understand. We get science, we get suffering, we get urgency, we get life-long consequences. We see the value of hope, we know how to engender it even in dark times. We are good at encouraging people to grow, to be conscious of the needs of others.

As we consider where the public needs to be on climate change and what we have to offer, we can see that we have largely failed to realize the *power* of our expertise.

It no longer makes sense, because of the challenges presented by the climate crisis and the unique skills we have, to confine our professional lives only to traditional roles and services in our offices, academic settings, and clinics. We need activism now to *initiate* services in this time of urgency - helping people out of their denial, tending to their wounds, working to create resilience. Just as we have qualifications in other specialties, we need "Climate Mental Health Specialists" (CMHSs) who are specifically trained to offer "trauma informed care" for the many levels and kinds of distress generated by climate instability - both direct and indirect, addressing the plight of refugees and the needs of newly blended populations; helping to organize communities and collaborating with primary care and public health experts, fanning out into settings to educate and advocate.

More research is needed to identify best practices, determining societal and infrastructural resources that are truly helpful, and building upon this evidence base to train the next generation of CMHSs.

Our efforts in every sector send the message - that the fight for sane climate policy is not the exception, but the legitimate expected behavior in this time of crisis. With our understanding of the social sciences, we know that people can be persuaded to take action *just because* other people are and promote and harness the power of social norms to accelerate the pace of change.

Our canons of ethics tell us it is our duty to protect the health of the public and to participate in activities that contribute to it.

Committed professionals are joining others to call upon our elected officials, policy makers, and other leaders to show why the public's health is in jeopardy, what steps must be taken, and how we can use our expertise to speed up the process. Many professional organizations and academic institutions are setting up curricula for training and making collaborative declarations describing the dangers of climate change and the urgent need for action.

But at this epic moment, our unique contributions and the urgent need for global commitment have gone missing. But it does not have to stay this way - because we can change that, too.

Bibliography

Abel, G. J., Brottrager, M., Crespo Cuaresma, J., & Muttarak, R. (2019). Climate, conflict and forced migration. *Global Environmental Change, 54*, 239–249.

Albrecht, G. (2005). Solastalgia: A new concept in health and identity. *PAN: Philosophy Activism Nature, 3*, 41-55.

Al-Hadramy, M. S., & Ali, F. (1989). Catecholamines in heat stroke. *Military Medicine*. (Oxford: Oxford University Press, 1989).

American Psychiatric Association (2017). *How climate-related natural disasters affect mental health*. Philadelphia: American Psychiatric Association. Retrieved February 9, 2020 from 14 Psychological Impacts of Climate Change and Recommendations 189 https://www.psychiatry.org/patients-families/climate-change-and-mental-health-connections/affects-on-mental-health

Baker, A. (2015). How climate change is behind the surge of migrants to Europe. *Time Magazine*. (Time USA, LLC, 2015).

Bhalla, N. (2012). Thirsty South Asia's river rifts threaten "water wars". *Discover Thomson Reuters*.

Björkenstam, C., Kosidou, K., & Björkenstam, E. (2017). Childhood adversity and risk of suicide: Cohort study of 548 721 adolescents and young adults in Sweden. *British Medical Journal, 357*, j1334.

Brewin, C. R., Andrews, B., & Valentine, J. D. (2000). Meta-analysis of risk factors for posttraumatic stress disorder in trauma-exposed adults. *Journal of Consulting and Clinical Psychology, 68*, 748–766.

Bulbena, A., Sperry, L., & Cunillera, J. (2006). Psychiatric effects of heat waves. *Psychiatric Services, 57*, 1519.

Calderón-Garcidueñas, L., & Villareal-Ríos, R. (2017). Living close to heavy traffic roads, air pollution, and dementia. *The Lancet, 389*, 675–677.

Carleton, T. (2017). Crop-damaging temperatures increase suicide rates in India. *Proceedings of the National Academy of Sciences of the United States of America, 114*, 8746–8751.

Carrion, V. G., & Wong, S. S. (2012). Can traumatic stress alter the brain? Understanding the implications of early trauma on brain development and learning. *Journal of Adolescent Health, 51*, S23–S28.

Chen, C. Y., Hung, H. J., Chang, K. H., Chung, Y. H., Muo, C. H., Tsai, C. H., et al. (2017). Long-term exposure to air pollution and the incidence of Parkinson's disease: A nested case-control study. *PLoS One, 12*(8), e0182834.

Edwards, T., & Wiseman, J. (2011). Climate change, resilience, and transformation: Challenges and opportunities for local communities. In I. Weissbecker (Ed.), *Climate change and human well-being: Global challenges and opportunities* (pp. 185–200). (New York: Springer, 2011).

Folkman, S., Lazarus, R. S., Dunkel-Schetter, C., DeLongis, A., & Gruen, R. J. (1986). Dynamics of a stressful encounter: Cognitive appraisal, coping, and encounter outcomes. *Journal of Personality and Social Psychology, 50*, 992–1003.

Funkhouser, D. (2016) Climate may make some regions 'uninhabitable' by end of century. *State of the Planet Climate May Make Some Regions Uninhabitable by End of Century Comments.* (Earth Institute, Columbia University, 2016).

Gladman, M., & Zinman, L. (2015). *The economic impact of amyotrophic lateral sclerosis: A systematic review.* (National Center for Biotechnology Information, U.S. National Library of Medicine, 2015).

Goodman, J., Hurwitz, M., Park, J., & Smith, J. (2018). *Heating and learning* (NBER Working Paper Series No. 24639). National Bureau of Economic Research.

Gore, T. (2015). *Extreme carbon inequality: Why the Paris climate deal must put the poorest, lowest emitting and most vulnerable people first.* Oxfam Media Briefing 02-12-2015. Retrieved on February 9, 2020, from https://policy-practice.oxfam.org.uk/publications/extreme-carbon-inequality-why-the-paris-climate-deal-must-put-the-poorest-lowes-582545

Guest, R. (2014). Portraits of scared scientists reveal truth about climate change. *Lost at E Minor.* Hamilton, R. (2010). The huddled masses. *The Texas Tribune.*

Hanigan, I. C., Butlera, C. D., Kokicc, C. N., & Hutchinson, M. F. (2012). Suicide and drought in New South Wales, Australia, 1970–2007.

Proceedings of the National Academy of Sciences of the United States of America, 109, 13950–13955.

Hansen, J., Sato, M., Hearty, P., Ruedy, R., Kelley, M., Masson-Delmotte, V., et al. (2016). Ice melt, sea level rise and superstorms: Evidence from paleoclimate data, climate modeling, and modern observations that 2 °C global warming could be dangerous. *Atmospheric Chemistry and Physics: Journal of the European Geosciences Union, 16*, 3761–3812.

Hauser, A. (2015). We are the Walking Dead. *The Weather Channel (features)*.

Hearty, P. (2012). Rising seas threaten low-lying coastlines of the world: Low coastlines under watery siege. *Ecology Global Network.* (Ecology Communications Group, Inc, 2012). (ECG).

Hope, J. (2013). A review of the mechanism of injury and treatment approaches for illness resulting from exposure to water-damaged buildings, mold, and mycotoxins. *The Scientific World Journal, 2013*, 767482.

Hsiang, S., Burke, M., & Miguel, E. (2013). Quantifying the influence of climate on human conflict. *American Association for the Advancement of Science, 341*, 1235367.

Huffaker, S. (2015). The water wars begin in parched California as the rich fight drought restrictions. *The National Post, June 15, 2015.*

IPSO. (2013). State of the ocean 2013 report: Interactions between stresses, impacts and some potential solutions. *Marine Pollution Bulletin, 74*, 491–552.

Kirson, N., Desai, U., Ristovska, L., Cummings, A. K., Birnbaum, H., Ye, W., et al. (2016). Assessing the economic burden of Alzheimer's disease patients first diagnosed by specialists. *BMC Geriatrics, 16*, 138.

Kowal, S. L., Dall, T. M., Chakrabarti, R., Storm, M.V., & Jain, A. (2013). *The current and projected economic burden of Parkinson's disease in the United States.* (Movement Disorders Society. US National Library of Medicine National Institutes of Health, 2013).

Langlois, E., Haines, A., Tomson, G., & Ghaffar, A. (2016). Refugees: Towards better access to health-care services. *The Lancet, 387*, 319–321.

Lee, H., Myung, W., Kim, D. K., Kim, S. E., Kim, C. T., & Kim, H. (2017). *Short-term air pollution exposure aggravates Parkinson's disease in a population-based cohort.* (National Center for Biotechnology Information. U.S. National Library of Medicine, 2017).

McGranahan, G., Balk, D., & Anderson, B. (2007). The rising tide: Assessing the risks of climate change and human settlements in low elevation coastal zones. *Sage Journals: International Institute for Environment and Development, 19*, 17–37.

Mora, C., Counsell, C., Bielecki, C., & Louis, L. (2017). Twenty-seven ways a heat wave can kill you: Deadly heat in the era of climate change. *Circulation: Cardiovascular Quality and Outcomes, 10*, e004233.

Morin, R., & Rein, L. (2005). Some of the uprooted won't go home again. *The Washington Post Company.*

Müller, M. F., Yoon, J., Gorelick, S. M., Avisse, N., & Tilmant, A. (2016). Impact of the Syrian refugee crisis on land use and transboundary freshwater resources. *Proceedings of the National Academy of Sciences of the United States of America, 113*, 14932–14937.

Newbury, J. B., Arseneault, L., Beevers, S., et al. (2019). Association of air pollution exposure with psychotic experiences during adolescence. *JAMA Psychiatry, 76*, 614–623.

Nicholls, N., Harper, A., Rahmstorf, S., Carilli, J., Buontempo, C. Santoso, A., et al. (2014). *The scientists: Is this how you feel?* Creative Commons Attribution. Retrieved February 9, 2020 from https://www.isthishowyoufeel.com/this-is-how-scientists-feel.html

Obederdöster, G., Elder, A., & Rinderknecht, A. (2009). Nanoparticles and the brain: Cause for concern? *Journal of Nanoscience and Nanotechnology, 9*, 4996–5007.

Ojala, M. (2012). Regulating worry, promoting hope: How do children, adolescents, and young adults cope with climate change? *International Journal of Environmental Science and Education, 7*, 537–561.

Oudin, A., Bråbäck, L., Åström, D. O., Strömgren, M., & Forsberg, B. (2016). Association between neighborhood air pollution concentrations and dispensed medication for psychiatric disorders in a large longitudinal cohort of Swedish children and adolescents. *BMJ Open 6*: e010004.

Ozer, E. J., Best, S. R., Lipsey, T. L., & Weiss, D. S. (2003). *Predictors of posttraumatic stress disorder and symptoms in adults: A meta-analysis. Psychological Bulletin, 129*, 52–73.

Parker, L. (2017). *Sea level rise will flood hundreds of cities in the near future: Many shore communities in the U.S. face inundation in the coming decades.* National Geographic Society. National Geographic Partners, LLC. Retrieved February 9, 2020 from https://www.national-geographic.com/news/2017/07/sea-level-rise-flood-global-warming-science/

Peters, M., Moscona, J., Katz, M., Deandrade, K., Quevedo, H., Iwari, S., et al. (2014). National disaster and myocardial infarction: The six years after Hurricane Katrina. *Mayo Clinic Proceedings, 89*, 472–477.

Potera, C. (2007). Molding a link to depression. *Environmental Health Perspectives, 115*, A536. Raj, A. (2014). Heat-fueled rage. *Scientific American Mind, 25*, 16–17.
https://doi.org/10.1038/ scientificamericanmind0114-16

Randall, A. (2013). Moving stories: The Sahel. *Climate and Migration Coalition*. Climate Outreach.

Reckdahl, K. (2017). New Orleans scrambles to repair drainage system after severe flooding. *The New York Times*. (The New York Times Company, 2017).

SAMHSA. *Phases of Disaster*. U.S. Department of Health and Human Services 1-10- 2018. Retrieved April 16, 2019 from https://www.samhsa.gov/dtac/recovering-disasters/ phases-disaster

Schleussner, C. F., Donges, J., Donner, R., & Schellnhuber, H. (2016). Armed conflict risks enhanced by climate-related disasters in ethnically fractionalized countries. *Proceedings of the National Academy of Sciences of the United States of America, 113*, 9216–9221.

Seelen, M., Toro Campos, R. A., Veldink, J. H., Visser, A. E., Hoek, G., Brunekreef, B., van der Kooi, A. J., de Visser, M., Raaphorst, J., van den Berg, L. H., & Vermeulen, R. C. (2017). Long- term air pollution exposure and amyotrophic lateral sclerosis in Netherlands: A population-based case-control study. *Environmental Health Perspectives, 125*, 097023.

Shaw, W., Labott-Smith, S., Burg, M., Hostinar, C., Alen, N., van Tilburg, M., et al. (2019). *Stress effects on the body: Musculoskeletal system*. Washington, DC: American Psychological Association. Retrieved February 9, 2020 from https://www.apa.org/helpcenter/stress/ effects-musculoskeletal.

Shenassa, E. D., Daskalakis, C., Liebhaber, A., Braubach, M., & Brown, M. (2007). Dampness and mold in the home and depression: An examination of mold-related illness and perceived control of one's home as possible depression pathways. *American Journal of Public Health, 97*, 1893-1899.

Simpson, D. M., Weissbecker, I., & Sephton, S. E. (2011). Extreme weather-related events: Implications for mental health and well-being. In I. Weissbecker (Ed.), *Climate change and human well-being. International and cultural psychology*. (New York: Springer, 2011).

Skinner, M. (2014). Environmental stress and epigenetic transgenerational inheritance. *BMC Medicine, 12*, 153.

Smith, M., & Myers, S. (2018). Impact of anthropogenic CO2 emissions on global human nutrition. *Nature Climate Change, 8*, 834–839.

Somanathan, E., Somanathan, R., Sudarshan, A., & Tewari, M. (2018). *The impact of temperature on productivity and labor supply: Evidence from*

Indian manufacturing. Energy Policy Institute at the University of Chicago. WORKING PAPER. NO. 2018–69.

Souhel, N., Pearlman, D., Alper, K., Najjar, A., & Devinsky, O. (2013). Neuroinflammation and psychiatric illness. *Journal of Neuroinflammation, 10*, 43.

Stanke, C., Kerac, M., Prudhomme, C., Medlock, J., & Murray, V. (2013). *Health effects of drought: A systematic review of the evidence.* PLOS Currents Disasters. Jun 5. Edition 1. https://doi.org/10.1371/currents.dis.7a2cee9e980f91ad7697b570bcc4b 004.

Strife, J. (2012). Children's environmental concerns: Expressing ecophobia. *The Journal of Environmental Education, 43*, 37–54.

Szyszkowicz, M., Willey, J. B., Grafstein, E., Rowe, B., & Colman, I. (2010). Air pollution and emergency department visits for suicide attempts in Vancouver, Canada. *Environmental Health Insights, 4*, 79–86.

United Nations Office for Disaster Risk Reduction (2015). *United Nations Office for Disaster Risk Reduction (UNISDR).* The Human cost of weather-related disasters 1995–2015. Retrieved April 14, 2019, from https://www.unisdr.org/2015/docs/climatechange/COP21_ WeatherDisastersReport_2015_FINAL.pdf.

Van Susteren, L. (2013). *The Bureau of Linguistic Reality.* Retrieved from: https://bureauoflinguis- ticalreality.com/portfolio/pre-traumatic-stress-disorder-2.

Vins, H., Bell, J., Saha, S., & Hess, J. (2015). The mental health outcomes of drought: A systematic review and casual process diagram. *International Journal of Environmental Research and Public Health, 12*, 13251–13275.

Von Uexkull, N., Croicu, M., Fjelde, H., & Buhaug, H. (2016). Civil conflict sensitivity to growing-season drought. *Proceedings of the National Academy of Sciences of the United States of America, 113*, 12391–12396.

Weir, K. (2012). Smog in our brains: Researchers are identifying startling connections between air pollution and decreased cognition and well-being. *American Psychological Association, 43*, 32.

Wolf, J., & Salo, R. (2008). Water, water, everywhere, nor any drop to drink: Climate change delusion. *Australia & New Zealand Journal of Psychiatry, 42*, 350.

World Health Organization. (2005). *Violence and Disasters. World Health Organization.* Department of Injuries and Violence Prevention. Retrieved February 9, 2020 from

https://www.who.int/violence_injury_prevention/publications/violence
/violence_disasters.pdf?ua=1.

L. Van Susteren (*) Physicians for Social Responsibility, Washington, DC, USA.

W. K. Al-Delaimy University of California San Diego, La Jolla, CA, USA

CHAPTER TWENTY-ONE

THE REVOLUTION OF CONSCIOUSNESS: FROM THE 'GOLDEN ERA OF CONSUMPTION' TO THE 'RESPONSIBLE SOCIETY'

SVITLANA ZAPARA

For the first time, doubts are raised about freedom as one of the indisputable human values and attitudes towards human rights - right to movement, communication, access to education, etc. are changing. Covid-19 has made us feel the 'breath' of time. The epidemic directly affects the interaction of people with each other; we have changed, and the changes are obvious. From now on, in order to keep safe, we must wear masks; restrict our visits to public places and resist touching things that can be potentially contaminated (elevator buttons, door handles, merchandise, public toilets, park benches), etc. We must be especially conscious of our habits of touching our face. Many are sitting at virtual desks and learning self-discipline and new communication skills. Many have been forced to cancel travel plans, change their habits and hobbies. Parents have had to restrict their children's activities due to the high risk of potential contagion and most of us cannot visit museums, theaters, and cinemas as we used to do. In a second, we agree to things that would have caused public condemnation a few months ago.

We are not only accustomed to new restrictions of movement or the need to keep our distance, we, surprisingly easily, have agreed to the priority of medical treatment. Even basic social traditions are being corrected - the right to bury loved ones or attend churches. However, epidemics are far from being the only modern challenge.

In 1972, the book 'Limits of Growth' was presented as the first report to the Rome Club, prepared by D. and D. Meadows, J. Randers and W. Behrens, who systematized and continued Forrester's research (J.W. Forrester, J.F. Collins 1969). The main conclusion of the authors is that the extreme threat to humanity is a possible future environmental catastrophe, which will be caused by population growth, industrial growth, and increasing pollution of the planet. The global model was built to study five major global processes: rapid industrialization, population growth, growing food shortages, depletion of non-renewable resources, and degradation of natural resources (Yusupova O. 2013). Today, environmental activism around the world is drawing attention to unfavorable climate change, environmental abuse, and environmental pollution, which ultimately threatens all living things.

Gradually, without noticing it, mankind has become an unethical consumer who makes harmful decisions that negatively impact the environment for the sake of short-term benefit. This irrational attitude to nature and its resources results in natural disasters, epidemics, and cataclysms. Specialists in the humanities and natural sciences, as well as journalists actively discuss the problem of overpopulation of the Earth. Among the central scientific publications on this topic is the work of Brian J. Skinner's "Earth Resources" (Skinner B. 1989), who notes that in the 21st century, the environmental problem is unlikely to be solved due to the world's rapid population growth. According to Stephen Hawking, because of the overpopulation of the Earth, humanity is threatened with extinction (Murphy M. 2017).

There is the sizable opinion (Nick Bostrom 2002) that overpopulation is one of the possible scenarios of social collapse, which could lead to a global catastrophe. Overpopulation is a relative value that depends on the resource base of the populated territory and includes an assessment of the development of obtaining and restoring sources of survival. However, manufacturing for such a large population poses additional threats. Modern industrial methods of agriculture extensively use chemicals, which negatively impact both biodiversity, soil productivity, and climate stabilization.

To some extent, birth control can solve this problem. Previously, the birth-death balance was regulated by natural evolution, wars, and poor medical provision. More recently, as the population continues to increase, there have been experiments in birth control policies (India, China). Now, the population seems to be tested for the lack of alternatives of social organization with distinctiveness, excessive observation, unusual restrictions, and coercion. In this context, the Chinese experience in introducing a social rating is noteworthy, as it allows various departments and government agencies to obtain information about people's behavior in order to keep them under control (Merekina O. 2018). Some experts (Gromico O. 2020) believe that the centralized power of authoritarian societies like China is more able to respond quickly to situations like pandemics. Leaving aside discussions on authoritarian societies, it is worth noting that we are, nonetheless, steadily moving towards a society where the key value is the guarantee of health via new forms of law and order. We are moving from the power, which guarantees the right to life and death, to the power, which guarantees an extended comfortable life cycle based on the increased collection of data.

In this case, a natural question arises about the role and importance of humans and their unique place in the universe, and at the same time, the regulation of human activities in terms of their various influences on the environment. Scientific achievements only exacerbate the existing challenges. As noted by V. F. Cheshko, V. I. Hlazko in their work 'Hich Hume' (Bio-power and Bio-politics in a Risk Society) "real key categories of trans-humanism are the post-human, the heir of man modified to such an extent that he is no longer human and the trans-human "potential step" on the path of evolution into the post-human, which differs from modern humans in terms of "implant body improvement, asexuality, artificial insemination, and distributed individuality" (Cheshko V. et al. 2009). The authors add that the technologies that ensure the transition of intelligent life in the post-human era are as follows: "the economy of prosperity - the lack of resource scarcity associated with the development of nanotechnology; paradise engineering - meeting all human needs, including the need for unlimited development, the possibility of restructuring the human mind and ecosystem (paradise on earth) and download-transferring personality from the brain to the computer" (Cheshko V. et al. 2009). There are well-grounded fears about the threat of such development for the loss of human individuality and identity. Alongside implementing scientific discoveries, coping with leaps of industrial and technological development, gaining opportunities to build human wellbeing and prosperity, humanity faces the need to fill lives with acceptable ideology and narrative.

It is not the first time that the world has been saved by the thoughts of leading European philosophers and professors in European universities. Christian values often became a source of inspiration for the development of progressive worldviews. However, modern research shows a deviation from the usual European preferences towards technological progress - a kind of "modernization" of existing life. According to Professor Stephen Bullian, (2018), the future of Christianity in Europe is in doubt as young people are increasingly rejecting religion. His "Youth and Religion of Europe" report, which analyzed data from 22 European countries, states that most people aged 16 to 29 do not practice religion across the continent and that according to the research, Christianity is "dying" in Europe. About 70% of Czech young people and about 60% of Spaniards, Dutch,

Britons, and Belgians of a certain age group never attend religious services. In the Czech Republic, 80% of young people and about 70% of Swedes, Danes, Estonians, Dutch, French, and Norwegians never pray. Bullian believes that "Christianity as a default, as a norm, is gone, and probably gone for good - or at least for the next 100 years" (Christianity as default is gone: the rise of a non-Christian Europe. 2018). The decrease in religious influence creates the effect of a worldview vacuum, which becomes a matter of honor for the world's leading intellectuals to fill.

A potential alternative to the modern consumer society is a bio-tolerant society, or as Michel Foucault called it, a biopolitical society. The concept of bio-politics has become an important contribution to the modern understanding of the transformation of power from modern capitalism to the exercise of power in combination with individual and collective care without coercion. In this perspective, individual and collective practices concerning the environment should become a conscious decision and the result of democratic debate. It is worth adding that eco-thinking has been substantiated since ancient times. Thales of Miletus (Philosophical Encyclopedic Dictionary. 2002), an ancient Greek philosopher of the pre-Socratic period, mathematician, astronomer, and founder of the Ionian school of natural philosophy, noted that nature is the only living organism filled with Gods and he was the first to create the doctrine of "physis"-nature. Today as never before, there is a need to find new senses and meanings.

The new worldview is closely linked to human interaction with the environment. Man is not just a species that struggles to survive. It is indisputable that along with the organization of people's lives in the new reality, one should first take care of the environment as an infinite source of life. Humans depend on clean water, high-quality food, and safe housing. However, humans as social creatures are not only a consumer of the gifts of nature and the results of the technological revolution, but they are also responsible for the harmonious coexistence with other species, their conservation, and development.

It is well known that a reduction in consumption leads to an improvement in the environmental situation as this reduces production, which in turn, affects the number of harmful emissions, thus reducing the threat to humans and other species. COVID-19 has shown humanity how easily a viral infection can change a man's lifestyle. As the nature of the virus is being studied, even preliminary findings suggest the need for more humane treatments of animals and compliance with sanitary rules, otherwise, there will be dangerous consequences.

Chaotic, unlimited consumer attitudes towards nature have already led humanity to the brink of a planet-scale collapse. Overproduction and overconsumption have spoiled human nature. People have lost their sense of proportion and as a result, the bond with nature has become weak. It is still important for natural landscapes to please the human eye. Everything on the horizon should be perfect. However, insignificantly important is what remains beyond the horizon, even if there are landfills and uncontrolled leakage of harmful substances. Animals have been the object of entertainment, and their use, or rather misuse, ranges from mildly degrading to excessively cruel. It appears extremely difficult for humans to admit that animals, at least the most developed species, have personality traits and cognitive ability. Humanity's sense of superiority has led the planet to an almost irreversible state of ecological crisis.

Environmental issues change the natural environment; disrupt the functioning of natural systems, lead to negative social, economic, and other consequences. There are six groups of major environmental problems. They are atmospheric (air pollution: radiological, chemical, mechanical, and thermal); water (depletion and pollution of surface and groundwater, pollution of the seas and oceans); geological and geomorphological (intensification of unfavorable geological and geomorphological processes, disturbance of relief and geological structure); soil (soil pollution, erosion, deflation, secondary salinization, waterlogging, etc.); biotic (reduction of vegetation, degradation of forests, grazing (ecology) digression, reduction of species diversity, etc.); complex (landscape) desertification, biodiversity loss, and disturbance of environmental authorities functioning.

Every year, on June 5, the world community celebrates World Environment Day. The main purpose of the day is to stimulate the activity of the world community aimed at preserving the balance in nature and the environment. The choice of this date is justified by the fact that on this day the UN Conference on the Environment opened (Stockholm, 1972) and resulted in the creation of the United Nations Environment Program (UNEP). In 2000, on this day, the UN program 'Millennium of Environment - Getting Started' was launched. The program is another reminder to humanity of its role in environmental protection.

The UN claims that only international cooperation can guarantee the further safe development of the planet. Yet it is also important to implement these ideas locally so that everyone who plants a tree can take part in cleaning the area and, realize the importance of protecting the world around them. Events dedicated to World Environment Day are held in most countries of the world at the state level, as well as at the level of small groups, schools, yards, and neighborhoods.

In Ukraine, according to the head of the All-Ukrainian Ecological League, Tetyana Tymochko, there are 8 main environmental problems: poor quality water (low quality of water treatment facilities, sewage; almost 75% of Ukrainians drink poor quality water from the Dnieper River); air pollution (annually more than 6 million tons of harmful substances and carbon dioxide go into the atmosphere); degradation of land resources (excessive and irrational economic use of 71% of the total agricultural landscape of the country leads to erosion, an increase in the area of acidic soils, etc.); deforestation (Ukraine is a sparsely forested country, one-sixth of its territory, and the export of wood from Ukraine is 2.5 times higher than imports); dangerous geological processes (a significant part of the country's gross domestic product is associated with the extraction and processing of mineral resources (41-43%) concentrated in the mining regions of Donbass, Kryvbas, and Carpathian. Meanwhile, the ecology of these regions suffers from intensive extraction, as well as from the improper closure of unprofitable mines, dead pits, and quarries); household waste (there are about 800 official landfills in the country, with the total amount of garbage exceeding 35 billion tons. Annually, this increases by another seven to eight hundred thousand tons. Hazardous chemicals and bacteria get into the soil, air, and groundwater, poisoning life at a distance of tens of kilometers from the landfill); objects of military activity inherited from the Soviet Union (systems and equipment of the water management complex of facilities and military posts of the Armed Forces of Ukraine are 90% physically outdated); The Chernobyl catastrophe (the total activity of radionuclides that went beyond Unit 4 of the Chernobyl NPP on April 26, 1986, and in the days following the accident exceeded 300 million curies. The accident led to radioactive contamination of more than 145 thousand square kilometers in Ukraine, Belarus, and Russia) (Moskalenko O. 2011). The list of problems is extensive and prompts immediate action. Human activity is often considered a major factor in such environmental problems. To confirm this, we note that because of the Chernobyl disaster, there was a decrease in human activity in the Chernobyl exclusion zone. This has led to a significant improvement in the environment of the areas surrounding the station; over the last 25 years and populations of endangered animals have recovered in the region. As a result, Ukrainian officials are considering the possibility of reducing the exclusion zone near the Chernobyl nuclear power plant.

A challenging realization is that humans can make unique discoveries, be a model of high moral behavior, and create an attractive environment around them whilst at the same time, being equally capable of destroying everything around them. The time has come for all the best human qualities: e.g., courage, passion, love, and empathy, to be used to inspire the creation of clear rules for the coexistence of all biological species in the most natural and non-threatening forms. It is already clear that humanity is on the verge of realizing the fact that the animal-based diet is unsustainable and that we should turn to plant-based diets. Instead of overconsumption, man can turn the planet into unique ecosystems, local units with a landscape, which harmoniously takes into account the benefits of the area, as well as achieving a balance between biological and technocratic worlds. These ecosystems must have everything that satisfy human needs whilst at the same time, create a harmonious relationship with nature. The aim of social activity should be conscious harmonious coexistence in ecosystems and their responsible development.

However, are we humans ready for such changes? The author's sociological survey of mainly Ukrainian teachers and students produced the following results from nine simple questions.

Demographics

65.3% of respondents were under the age of 25; 25.3% between the ages of 25 and 45, and 9.3% over the age of 45.

Questions & Answers:
Q. 1 How do you assess the state of the environment?
84% "Due to human activity, it is critically negative"; 9% answered "As it has always been"; 7% "The question is difficult to answer".
Q. 2. How often have you been told in schools, universities, at work about the need to preserve the environment? 65% answered "Often"; 32% "Rarely"; 3% "Have not been told".

However, the respondents were not enthusiastic about specific actions that may improve the situation. Thus:
Q. 3. Are you ready to eat less meat? 58.1% answered "No"; 36.5% said, "Yes if I am convinced that this will mitigate the negative impact on the environment"; 5.4% of the surveyed group do not consume meat.

This may be due to a lack of relevant information, as:
Q. 4. Do you agree that eating meat is harmful to the environment? 53.3% answered "No"; 36% "The question is difficult to answer"; 10.7% "Yes".
Q. 5. Would you agree to buy less trendy clothes and accessories to save the environment? 43.8% answered "Yes"; 38.4% "Would agree if I knew about the impact of this decision on the environment"; 17.8% "No".
Q. 6. Do you think it is justified to stop using plastic bags in stores and in everyday life? 80% answered "Yes"; 12% "Partially"; 8% "No".

Q. 7. Would you agree to take part in the voluntary action "Plant a Tree-Save the Planet" 75% answered "Yes"; 16% already undertook such action; 9% answered "No".

Q. 8. Would you like to learn more about the possibilities of preserving the environment? 50% answered "yes"; 27% always take an interest in this issue; 23% answered "No".

Q. 9. 'Choose politicians who emphasize the preservation of the environment in their programs'.

The answers to Q. 8. were the most interesting. The respondents needed to rank the importance from the first (most significant) to the ninth (less significant) indicators that may affect the improvement of the environment. Of the nine indicators (*using less water and electricity; buying less; reusing things and developing recycling; avoiding "fast-fashion"; planting more trees; using "green" energy; flying fewer planes; driving slower; elect politicians who emphasize the preservation of the environment in their programs*) the leader among the respondents was the indicator 'Reusing things and develop recycling' (23 choices). The second and third places are for the indicators 'Plant more trees' and 'Avoid Fast-Fashion', respectively. Trailing behind is the indicator "Use 'green' energy". It took fifth place. Other indicators were selected residually. It is interesting to note that among the indicators that received the least number of likes was Q. 9. This may indicate indifference concerning ecology, by a leftover principle, where in the list of human values, 'environmental behavior' takes the last position. Such a situation obliges those who are knowledgeable in this area to act more urgently to develop study programs for spreading ideas and factors of environmental protection.

1. Place	"Reusing things and develop recycling".
2-3 Places	"Plant more trees" and "Avoid "Fast-Fashion".
5. Place	"Use "green" energy".
9. Place	"Choose politicians who emphasize the preservation of the environment in their programs".

Figure 21.1 Q & A Chart. *See centrefold for this image in colour.*

Ultimately, society is more responsible in finding answers to the question: Is it possible to move to self-discipline and responsible behavior towards others, rather than to oneself - from the suspension of social activity to its conscious transformation? In our opinion, the rejection of human vices and excessive satisfaction is the result of collective discussions and conscious behavior.

Sociological research conducted in recent years complements the presented analysis. At the end of 2018, CEDOS analysts Daryna Pyrohova and Ivan Verbytsky, as well as Yevhenia Polshchykova, commissioned by the UMKA (Ukrainian Youth Climate Association) with the support of the Heinrich Böll Foundation in Ukraine, conducted a sociological study (Environmental Problems and Conscious Behavior: What the People of Kiev Know. 2019). They studied how Kyiv residents perceive environmental problems and what they know about them. People were divided into three focus groups: students aged 17-25, not involved in the work of public organizations; married people aged 25-40, half of whom have children; people 18-35 years old with the experience of activism.

The group of researchers aimed to study how the three social groups perceive the main environmental problems of Kyiv, there causes and possible solutions; what environmental behavior they are willing to practice and how they can contribute to improving the environmental situation. The majority mentioned problems with garbage - its irregular garbage disposal; littering of city streets and green areas and the lack of infrastructure for sorting, and lack of incinerators; deforestation; poor drinking water quality, and climate change. Air quality was also among the problems often mentioned by the respondents and the system of measuring air quality was a mystery for most of the participants. Some of them were not sure whether it is monitored at all. Respondents expressed the desire for air pollution levels to be provided in an accessible form, for example, as part of the weather forecast. Some recalled that during fires in peatlands around Kyiv, air pollution figures were announced in the news. All the participants said that polluted air negatively affects the quality of life of Kyiv residents. To raise awareness of this topic, they suggested using a "traffic light system": green=no harm to health, yellow=minor harm, red=danger to human health, which would provide practical advice on how to act when the concentration of harmful substances in the air is high. They also suggested providing information on the causes of pollution, for example, on the activities of specific enterprises.

One of the results of the survey was the low level of public confidence in the authorities due to corruption, particularly with business connections. Respondents also mentioned problems such as the low level of culture of the population, indifference, and lack of awareness; lack of state policy; unwillingness of business to introduce new environmental technologies; environmentally unfriendly behavior; separate waste collection at households; reduction of plastic consumption; public transport logistics and reductions in consumption.

Despite some understanding of environmental problems, not everyone is ready to get involved in solving environmental problems. Some participants believed that environmental actions are currently "not a priority" in Ukraine. Others are convinced that some environmental problems are economic in origin and need to be addressed together. Many volunteers expressed their readiness to support civil protests. Some of them are theoretically ready even to block the streets, as well as to protest in front of government agencies or near polluting enterprises. The students stated that they were ready to take part in environmental protests if they trusted the organizers and saw real results. They found eco-actions within the framework of organized events, such as festivals, the most interesting. However, among the three groups, students were the least willing to change their behavior. Despite understanding and acknowledging the problem of air pollution, most of them do not want to give up a car in the future. The students also noted that they did not try to use public transport more often and emphasized its inconvenience and lack of prestige. Concurrently, two of the most important causes of environmental problems were, in the opinion of the group of students, poor education and the lack of promotion of eco-conscious actions.

Lack of strategic planning at the state level is considered one of the main causes of environmental problems in all groups. All participants mentioned the poor awareness of environmental problems and the inability to influence them. It is notable, that married activists (those who have their families) considered the regulation of a system of punishment more important than the promotion of environmental conduct. Adequate punishment for the offense, according to these respondents, may be more effective than persuasion to be law-abiding.

Along with the complaint about the indifference of local authorities, examples of positive environmental initiatives are spreading in Ukraine. For example, at the request of the Ladyzhyn Public Council, a sociological survey 'Ecology and the City of Ladyzhyn' was conducted in 2016 and involved 400 people. It included eight questions, two of which are relevant for our discussion:

Q. 2. 1. "How do you assess the ecological situation of the city of Ladyzhyn?", 75% answered "Unsuccessfully"; 6.7% "Successfully"; 18.2% "Do not have any information".

Despite the city authorities' positive attention

Q. 2. 2. "What environmental factors directly affect the state of your health and the health of your family?" 71.1% mentioned air pollution, dust, and odors in the air; 52, 9%; drinking water quality; 35, 2% food quality; 6, 8%; unsatisfactory sanitary conditions; the rest 2, 9%.

The author notes that the most significant result of these surveys is how information on the environment affects the willingness to practice environmental behavior. Participants, who regularly see examples of environmental action among their acquaintances or famous people, have become more open to change.

Conclusions

There are prerequisites for the formation of new knowledge about the development of social relations. Development is a natural constant; the world is not static - it is constantly in motion. There are reasons for a natural accumulation of intellectual potential, the development of philosophical thought, which acquires transcendental features. Politics, economics, individual and collective relations, and social relations are changing right now. Julian Huxley - biologist, evolutionist, humanist, and politician, one of the authors of the synthetic theory of evolution, once said, "Humanity is an evolution that has realized itself" (Velkov V. 2005). A natural question arises about the possible directions of human development, including worldviews and religious postulates. After all, the crisis (the pandemic and climate change) affects almost all worldviews of human factors, including religion. In these terms, new challenges and opportunities associated with a new quality of relations between manmade and biological worlds, where humanity protects all species of wildlife, exists as a potential reality. In addition, the normative central position of mankind, no longer seems indisputable.

Perhaps we are witnessing the birth of a new religion of the 21st century, which claims that the world is a living organism. I would like to hypothesize that today religion is also being transformed; it faces the need to connect the theory and praxis or risk losing its claim to truth and relevance.

Environmental friendliness, bio-politics, bioethics, animal ethics, and plant anthropogenesis are new terms that first cautiously and now more confidently, testify to the urgency of the development of a new eco-religion. We can observe all the main religious attributes in this new eco-movement. Namely, the availability of the main idea - the salvation of humanity and the planet in the name of life of future generations and current prosperity. The cult of ecological thinking is slowly being formed. There are apologists for this movement, authoritative scientists, philosophers, and activists. Eco-movements and eco-parties are no surprise to anyone. Eco-activity is a natural phenomenon in the name of salvation.

In summary, mankind has the ability not only to change the world around us but also to change our minds and bodies. With the development of science and technology, there are increasing tendencies to abandon the religious worldview, especially among the young people and particularly, in Christianity. In addition, humanity must face the challenges of excessive, uncontrolled consumption. Humanity will also have to adapt to the future by solving complex ethical problems associated with the formation of a new world order. We must also realize that epidemics, environmental catastrophes, global-warming, and overpopulation are no less of a threat than aggression and war.

Bibliography

1. According to research, Christianity is "dying" in Europe. 2018. URL: https://life.pravda.com.ua/society/2018/03/26/229787/
2. Cheshko V., Glazko V. 2009. High Hume (biopower and biopolitics in a risk society). Textbook. Moscow. 319 p. URL: https://philarchive.org/archive/GLAHHB
3. Christianity as default is gone. the rise of a non-Christian Europe. 2018. *The Guardian* URL: https://www.theguardian.com/world/2018/mar/21/christianity-non-christian-europe-young-people-survey-religion
4. Environmental Problems and Conscious Behavior: What the People of Kiev Know. 2019. URL: https://ua.boell.org/uk/2019/03/05/ekologichni-problemi-i-svidoma-povedinka-shcho-znayut-zhitelki-i-zhiteli-kiieva
5. Gromico O. 2020. How to build a hospital in 10 days? Lessons from China for states and business Learning from the Chinese: what exactly helped China overcome the coronavirus crisis (pravda.com.ua) URL: https://www.pravda.com.ua/columns/2020/04/20/7248567/
6. Jay Wright Forrester, John F. Collins (Foreword) 1969. Urban Dynamics 1969. System Dynamics. 285 p. URL: Urban Dynamics by Jay Wright Forrester (goodreads.com)

7. June 5 - World Environment Day URL: https://phc.org.ua/news/5-chervnya-vsesvitniy-den-okhoroni-dovkillya/
8. Ladyzhyn Blogs: Ladyzhyn Public Council: Sociological Survey "Ecology in the City of Ladyzhyn". 2016. URL: http://lad.vn.ua/blog/rada/sociologichne-opituvannya-ekologiya-v-misti-ladizhin.html
9. Merekina O. 2018. How China`s Social Credit System actually works. URL: https://magazeta.com/social-rating-china/
10. Moskalenko O. 2011. Eight Ecological Problems of Ukraine URL: https://news.finance.ua/ua/news/-/235280/visim-ekologichnyh-problem-ukrayina/
11. Murphy, Margi. 2017. Stephen Hawking says the Earth will be a fireball by 2600. *New York Post* (en-US). URL: www.thesun.co.uk/tech/4852083/stephen-hawking-says-earth-will-become-a-sizzling-fire-ball-by-2600-and-humanity-will-become-extinct/
12. Nick Bostrom 2002. Existential Risks: Analyzing Human Extinction Scenarios Published in the *Journal of Evolution and Technology*, Vol. 9, No. 1 (2002). (First version: 2001) URL: https://www.nickbostrom.com/existential/risks.html
13. Philosophical Encyclopedic Dictionary. 2002. ed. VI Shinkaruk Institute of Philosophy. G.S. Frying pans of NASU. Kyiv. 661p.
14. Skinner B. 1989. Will humanity have enough earthly resources. URL: energyauek.kpi.ua/literature/8book.html
15. URL: https://shron1.chtyvo.org.ua/Shynkaruk_Volodymyr/Filosofskyi_entsy klopedychnyi_slovnyk.pdf
16. Velkov V. The Meaning of Evolution and the Evolution of Meaning Man. 2005. № 5. 5-67p. URL: https://scisne.net/a-26
17. Yusupova O. 2013. Evolution of views on the global environmental problem in the context of the Roman club. *Science y Ekonomika* / No. 2 2 (30) URL: https://studme.com.ua/1628041411154/ekonomika/evolyutsiya_organi zatsionnoy_teorii.ht

APPENDIX

CREATION CARE: CHRISTIAN RESPONSIBILITY COURSE

DR CHRISTINA NELLIST

Which man of you, having a son or an ox that has fallen into a well, will not immediately pull him out on a Sabbath day? Luke 14:5

Figure 22.1. 'Christ Breaking the Bonds of Animal Suffering'.[1] *See centrefold for this image in colour.*

---

[1] See the following link for an explanation of 'Christ Breaking the Bonds of Animal Suffering' Icon and its origins:
http://panorthodoxconcernforanimals.org/uncategorized/icon-christ-breaking-the-bonds-of-animal-suffering-2/

This is a course for use in Christian parishes, youth groups and seminary institutions. It may also provide a useful framework for homilies.

This course establishes that concern and compassion for the environment and animals is not a modern phenomenon, but one found both in the Bible and in the earliest teachings of the Christian Church. It provides an anamnesis of a lesser-known Christian tradition, where all things in creation are loved and protected by God and that their suffering is against God's will. It reminds us that in our role as Image, we should strive to reflect the Archetype in our lives. At times, it also highlights the soteriological implications of our abuse and exploitation of God's non-human animal beings. It reminds us that by causing harm to animals or by our indifference to it, human salvation is in jeopardy. It is written to facilitate Christian Church engagement with the subjects of climate change and animal suffering, which, though separate subjects, are deeply interconnected.

It was originally written for an Orthodox audience. I was invited to speak at His All-Holiness Bartholomew's Halki Summit 111 (2019) on behalf of the animal creation, who are frequently overlooked in Orthodox discussions. There I was asked by Met. Seraphim of Zimbabwe and Angola, to write a program on care for animals for his priests. This developed into the 'Creation Care: Christian Responsibility Course', which I believe, can be adapted by other denominations, as its teachings are universal. Ideally, the course would be translated into different languages. It has undergone several revisions. I will produce short videos by leading Eastern Orthodox theologians on each theme, which can be subtitled or replaced by theologians in other countries. It is given in love. I give permission for priests to adapt the material as they see fit; all I ask is the professional courtesy of authorship recognition.

Structure

The module is divided into seven/eight* themes/lessons:

1) IN THE BEGINNING: GOD'S GOOD CREATION.
2) COMPASSIONATE CARE: IMAGE OF GOD.
3) WHAT IS DOMINION?
4) BEHAVIOURAL GUIDANCE.
5) SACRAMENTAL LIFE.
6) WHAT IS SIN AGAINST ANIMALS?
7) A ROLE FOR THE CHURCH.

8) PRACTICAL EXAMPLES OF RESPONSIBLE CARE.[2]

Videos will be created, which can be used as part of a theme/lesson or as individual sessions.

Parish and youth ministry use

This course can be used as part of an introduction to our integrated Orthodox theology; as a parish led study-course; as part of a 'Greening the Orthodox Parish' program and as part of parish or national youth program. It can also be used as a resource for Homilies/Sermons on God's care for His "very good" creation.

Academic/seminary use

The course can also be linked to a deeper and wider discussion in Eastern Orthodox Seminary and Academic institutions. Suggested assignments might be:

1) A 5000-word paper on either of the following themes: a) Reflecting God's love and compassion in our relationships and treatment of animals. b) An Eastern Orthodox ethical approach to the use of animals and the environment.

2) Two 15-minute Homilies on Creation Care, using the material from this course.

---

[2] This unit may, if preferred, be incorporated into unit 7.

1) In the beginning: God's good creation

Nothing in creation had gone astray in its notions of God, save the human being only. [1]

Now, among the "all things" our world must be embraced. It too, therefore, was made by His Word, as Scripture tells us in the book of Genesis that He made all things connected with our world with His Word [2]

On reading the various patristic texts on Genesis there is consensus that: humans and non-human animals receive the "breath of life"; that God's description of all His creatures is "good" and "very good" [3] and we learn of the innate harmony, unity, and violence-free peacefulness of the original Edenic life.

The Fathers teach that God creates in order to be known to His creation and acknowledge not only the common ontology of all created beings but also their individual agency and integrity:[4]

But He Himself...predestinating all things, formed them as He pleased, bestowing harmony on all things, and assigning them their own place, and the beginning of the creation. In this was He conferred on spiritual things a spiritual and invisible nature...on animals an animal, on beings that swim in the sea a nature suited to the water, and on those that live on the land one fitted for the land - on all, in short, a nature suitable to the character of the life assigned them - while he formed all things that were made by His Word that never wearies. [5]

Such ideas are evident in the work of other early commentators such as St. Athanasius who teaches that:

For no part of creation is left void of him: He has filled all things everywhere. [6]

Knight (2017) observes that this has developed into an understanding that "everything is in God." [7]

St. Irenaeus teaches us that God is intimately involved with His creation:

By choosing to create, fill and sustain all things, the Christian God of the Fathers is a God who is intimately connected to His creatures, unlike the gods of the heretics. [8]

When referring to teachings in Genesis, Metropolitan Kallistos of Diokleia gives the following teaching:

We humans are bound to God and to one another in a cosmic covenant that also includes all the other living creatures on the face of the earth: 'I will make for you a covenant on that day with the beasts of the field, the birds of the air, and the creeping things of the ground' (Hos. 2:18; cf. Gen. 9:15). We humans are not saved from the world but with the world; and that means, with the animals. Moreover, this cosmic covenant is not something that we humans have devised, but it has its source in the divine realm. It is conferred upon us as a gift by God.[9]

The Fathers also recognized that only the human creatures had sinned and that only humans needed instruction and repentance. St. Irenaeus is clear:

While all things were made by God, certain of His creatures sinned and revolted from a state of submission to God, and others, indeed the great majority, persevered, and do still persevere, in [willing] subjection to Him who formed them. [10]

Papavassiliou (2013) summarizes the different Christian theological interpretations of Genesis: those who dismiss Genesis as a myth of the pre-scientific world, those who try to work modern science into the creation narrative, and those who take biblical texts literally as the Word of God. He teaches that all three approaches are to some degree inaccurate for they view Genesis as an account of creation history rather than the traditional Eastern Orthodox perspective of theological revelation. [11] In essence, Genesis gives us a glimpse into Who God is.[12] This theophany helps us to 'know' more about God and His will. This in turn, helps us define our role as Image and determine which behaviors are, and are not, acceptable to God. This revelation also establishes that unrighteous and sinful behaviors are part of the criteria used to judge those who fail to repent and desist from sinful ways.

Metropolitan Kallistos of Diokleia notes:

A reverence for animals, sensitivity to their position - their suffering is not new. It is part of our Orthodox Church faith. We start from the principle laid down in the first chapter of Genesis - that the world is God's creation, God saw everything that He had made and behold it was very good (Genesis 1:31). The world is God's creation, and it is a good and beautiful world. Therefore, the question of animals and how we treat them, links up with our view that animals are part of God's creation and just as we should treat the whole of creation with reverence and respect so we should more particularly treat the animals with reverence and respect. It is said in the first chapter of Genesis, that humans have a unique position in God's creation because we are created in the Image and Likeness of God and that is not said of animals but being created in God's Image and Likeness, gives us a responsibility towards creation as a whole and towards animals in particular. We are up against the basic problem that all too many people, clergy, and laity, think as Christians that this does not matter; that the treatment of animals is not a moral issue. But as soon as you say that animals are part of God's creation and we humans have a God-given responsibility towards creation, then at once, one sees that it is both a moral and spiritual question. That is why the Ecumenical Patriarch was so right to insist that the misuse of any part of creation is a sin but all too many people do not see it that way. [13]

God's original and enduring choice of a plant-based diet, first outlined in Genesis, not only evidences the violence-free harmony of Edenic life, but it also indicates the ideal diet. Had that not been the case, God would not have chosen this diet for us.

Discussion

Q. What types of behaviors are acceptable to God?

Q. As Image moving towards the Likeness of God, how should we behave towards His creation?

Q. What does God's original and enduring choice of diet tell us about His intention for all things in creation?

Bibliography

1. St. Athanasius, *On the Incarnation of the Word* S 43:3, CANNPNF 2-04.
2. St. Irenaeus, *Against Heresies*, 2.2:5.
3. Gn 1:20-22, 24-5, 30-31.
4. See St. Irenaeus, *Against Heresies*, 2.2.4.
5. St. Irenaeus, *Against Heresies*, 2.2.5
6. St. Athanasius, *On the Incarnation*, S: 8:1.
7. Panentheism. Knight, C. 2017 [2013] (3rd ed.) 'Natural Theology and the Eastern Orthodox Tradition' in, *The Oxford Handbook of Natural Theology* (eds.) John Hedley Brooke, Russell Re Manning, and Fraser Watts. (OUP, USA, 2017)
8. E.g., Valentinus and the unbegotten Dyad-Proarch, which had nothing to do with creation of our world (kenoma) and was the result of ungovernable passions of a lower Aeon-Sophia, see Irenaeus, *Against Heresies*, 2.3.
9. Ware. Metropolitan Kallistos of Diokleia, 'Orthodoxy and Animals', in, Linzey. A. and C. Linzey, (eds.) The Routledge Handbook of Religion

and Animal Ethics, Routledge Handbooks in Religion, (Routledge, Oxford. UK. 2018).

10. St. Irenaeus, *Against Heresies,* 2.18.7; 3.9:1, "all flesh shall see the salvation of God."

11. Papavassiliou, V. 'The Theology of Genesis.' Available at:
http://gocas.org/index.php?option=com_content&view=article&catid=39%3Alessons-in-orthodox-faith&id=113%3A280112-the-theology-of-genesis&Itemid=114.

12. For an investigation of Orthodox understanding of early Church texts on Genesis, see Bouteneff, P. *Beginnings. Ancient Christian Readings of the Biblical Creation Narratives.* (Grand Rapids, Michigan, Baker Academics, 2008).

13. Interview in, Nellist. C. *Eastern Orthodox Theology and Animal Suffering: Ancient Voices in Modern Theology,* (Cambridge Scholars Publishing. UK. 2020), Ch. 6.

2) Compassionate care: image of God

God has foreseen all, He has neglected nothing. His eye...watches over all.
He is present everywhere... If God has not left the sea urchin outside His
providence, is He without care for you? [1]

If we believe that God's theophany has a cosmic dimension and His
relationship with all created beings is essentially a loving and
compassionate one, this will determine, or at the very-least, inform our own
theological, ethical, and moral positions in relation to our treatment and
relationship with non-human animal beings and their environments.

The traditional Eastern Orthodox teaching is that we as Image are to strive
to achieve the 'Image and Likeness' of an all-loving God by emulating His
'qualities' in our lives.[2] Ecumenical Patriarch Bartholomew informs us that
God's blueprint "by definition predetermines an analogous ethos that is
imposed upon us". [3]

Orthodoxy acknowledges that whilst we can never know God's essence[4] we
can know some things about God. Through St. Irenaeus and others, we learn
that the Archetype is "the source of all that is good" [5] and "has in Himself
the disposition [to show kindness], because He is good". [6] God is "patient,
benign, merciful, mighty to save." [7] We also learn that he who "worketh
righteousness, is acceptable to Him" [8] for God "has loved righteousness,
and hated iniquity." [9] St. Irenaeus also teaches that God is desirous of
"mercy not sacrifice" [10] and that God's instruction "can never be
exhausted." [11]

Good One, who in Your mercy sustain beings: above and those below and
distribute the treasure of Your mercy to men and animals. [12]

God's loving, merciful and providential care for animals is not only taught
by the Fathers such as St. Cyril of Jerusalem, who teaches that as the Father
provides for animals, so too should we, [13] but also in the Psalms [14] and New
Testament:

Look at the birds of the air: they neither sow nor reap nor gather into barns,
and yet your heavenly Father feeds them. [15]

The Fathers are equally clear that a God Who is the source of all love,
compassion, mercy, and goodness is "without blame, and worketh no
evil," [16] nor cruel, abusive, or exploitative. This too is an important part of
reflecting the 'Image and Likeness' of God.

The Desert Fathers knew that a person with a pure heart was able to sense the connection with the rest of creation and especially with the animal world...This connection is not merely emotional; it is profoundly spiritual in its motive and context. It gives a sense of continuity and community with all of creation while providing an expression of identity and compassion with it [and] recognition that...all things were created in Christ and in Christ all things hold together. [17]

Ecumenical Patriarch Bartholomew not only gives legitimacy to calls for Eastern Orthodox theological discussions and engagement with the subjects of climate change and animal suffering, but he also supports the suggestion that the leaders of the Eastern Orthodox Church have a significant role to play in reducing that crisis and suffering.

Not only are we to live with a Eucharistic and liturgical ethos [18] Ecumenical Patriarch Bartholomew teaches that how we respond and treat creation, "especially through the lifestyle we lead", reflects how we worship God. [19] Importantly, he links our fasting to our liturgy and response to nature:

Our fasting, too, should not be disconnected from our liturgy. The truth is that we respond to nature with the same delicacy, the same sensitivity and tenderness, with which we respond to a human being in a relationship. [20]

Thus, love for God, love for human beings, and love for animals cannot be separated sharply. There may be a hierarchy of priority, but it is not a sharp distinction of comparison. [21]

This extension to the normative understanding of caring relationships might seem a contemporary fashion yet as we noted, this would be a misreading of Eastern Orthodox tradition. The early Fathers, like St. Cyril of Alexandria, used the following interpretation of Christ's teaching in Luke 14:5:

Which of you, having a son or an ox that has fallen into a well, will not immediately pull him out on a Sabbath day?

St Cyril and St John Chrysostom are very clear:

Christ refutes their unrelenting shamelessness by the convincing arguments that he uses. "Whose son of you" he says, "or whose ox shall fall into a pit and he will not immediately draw him out on the Sabbath day." If the law forbids showing mercy on the Sabbath, why do you take compassion on that which has fallen into the pit...The God of all does not cease to be kind. [22]

*Holy people are most loving and gentle in their dealings with their fellows,
and even with the lower animals: for this reason, was it said that 'A
righteous man is merciful to the life of his beast.'* [23]

Discussion

Q. In light of what we know of God, do you believe He would be indifferent
to the suffering of any of His created beings?

Q. Why do you think Christ includes humans and animals in his teaching in
Luke 14.5?

Q Do you believe your present lifestyle and treatment of animals reflects
the Image of our compassionate God?

Q In what ways can you and your parish facilitate the flourishing of all
God's creation?

References

1   St. Basil the Great, *Hexaemeron*, Homily 7:5.
2   St. Irenaeus, "The Doctrine of the Apostolic Preaching" 32-4, 100. See
    also *Against Heresies*, 3.21.10.
3   Ecumenical Patriarch Bartholomew, "Environment and Ethics" in
    Chryssavgis, J, (ed.) *Cosmic Grace and Humble Prayer: The Ecological
    Vision of the Green Patriarch Bartholomew,* (Rev. Ed) (Grand Rapids,
    Michigan, Eerdmans, 2009)135-6.
4   E.g., St. Irenaeus, *Against Heresies,* 2:13.4; 4.9.1. Knowing God also
    includes the wider sense of perceiving and experiencing God.
5   St. Irenaeus, *Against Heresies*, 2.13.3.
6   St. Irenaeus, 2.29.2.
7   St. Irenaeus, 3.20. Title.
8   St. Irenaeus, 3.12.7.
9   St. Irenaeus, 3.6.1.
10 St. Irenaeus, 4.17.4.
11 St. Irenaeus, 2.28.3; 2.13.9.
12 St. Ephrem the Syrian, *Table Blessings,* Memra X, in Hansbury, M.
    Hymns of St Ephrem the Syrian, Convent on the Incarnation, (Fairacres,
    Oxford, SLG Press, 2006) 37.
13 St. Cyril of Jerusalem, *Catechetical Homilies* Homily 7:6; See also Mt
    10:29-30; Lk 12:6.
14 Ps 103:10-21.

15 Mt 6:26.
16 St. Irenaeus, *Against Heresies,* 4.18.3.
17 Ecumenical Patriarch Bartholomew, 'The Fifth and Sixth Day of Creation', *Encountering the Mystery* (N.Y, Doubleday, 2008) 106.
18 Ecumenical Patriarch Bartholomew, 'Orthodox Liturgy and The Natural Environment' *Encountering the Mystery*, 98-103.
19 Ecumenical Patriarch Bartholomew, "For the Life of the World" in, Chryssavgis, J. (ed.) *Speaking the Truth in Love: Theological and Spiritual Exhortation of Ecumenical Patriarch Bartholomew,* (Fordham University Press, 2011) 297.
20 Ecumenical Patriarch Bartholomew, "For the Life of the World" in Chryssavgis, *Speaking the Truth in Love*, 297.
21 Ecumenical Patriarch Bartholomew, *Encountering the Mystery,* 107.
22 Cyril of Alexandria, *Commentary on the Gospel of Luke* Homily 101, in, Just Jr, A. A. (ed.) & Oden, T. (Gen. Ed.) *Ancient Christian Commentary on Scripture: New Testament: III Luke* (Downers Grove, Illinois: Intervarsity Press 2003) 235-6.
23 Attwater, D. *St. John Chrysostom,* (London: Catholic Book Club, 1960) 59.

3) What is dominion?

O God of our fathers and the Lord of mercy, Who made all things by Your Word And in Your wisdom, built a man That by You He might be the master of what is created, And manage the world in holiness and righteousness, And pass judgement with uprightness of soul; Give me the wisdom that sits by Your throne. [1]

Met. Kallistos of Diokleia (Ware) reflects the contemporary Orthodox view:

It is said, that we are to have dominion as humans over the created order but dominion does not mean domination or ruthless tyranny. This dominion that humans are given is part of being in God's Image, so what this means is that just as God cares for His creation and loves it, so we, after the image of God, are to care and love creation. This to me is the basic position of the Orthodox Church in regard to animals. [2]

His All-Holiness the Ecumenical Patriarch Bartholomew speaks to the point:

Unfortunately, humanity has lost the liturgical relationship between the Creator God and the creation; instead of priests and stewards, human beings have been reduced to tyrants and abusers of nature [3]

It is crucial, then, that we recognize and respond to the interconnection and interdependence between caring for the poor and caring for the earth. They are two sides of one and the same coin. Indeed, the way that we treat those who are suffering is reflected in the way that we approach the ecological crisis. And both of these in turn mirror the way that we perceive the divine mystery in all people and things, the way that we kneel in prayer before the living God. [4]

The above teachings not only support the premise that our behaviors should reflect the Image and Likeness of God but also acknowledge that some historical Christian interpretations relevant to this subject are flawed.[5] Modern Eastern Orthodox scholarship accepts, for example, that the interpretation of dominion as domination is an error, as it ignores the blueprint of God as Archetype and fails to recognize God's constraints on human freedom. Orthodoxy teaches that our relationships with "all things" should reflect the Image and Likeness of an all-loving and compassionate God.

Orthodox Christian tradition also stands in stark contrast to other historical Christian teachings that taught that animals "are naturally enslaved and accommodated to the uses of others."[6] This 'enslavement' portrays a negative mind-set that inevitable creates the potential for negative relationships with animals. Animals were no longer viewed as beings of God but rather, as objects for our use.

One important aspect of the misuse of our role as Icon of God has been our willingness to view dominion as giving us the right to do whatsoever we please with the rest of the created world. Unfortunately for humans, animals, and continued life on this planet, this dominant narrative has helped separate humans from the rest of God's creation. The consequences of this separationist theology and philosophy, has led to the misuse of our God-given responsibility as Icon of God, to ensure the flourishing of all of God's created beings. This in turn, has led to our present climate crisis, species extinction and the pollution of our air, land, and water. St Gregory of Nyssa warns us against such theories:

> Use; do not misuse; so, too, Paul teaches you. Find your rest in temperate relaxation. Do not indulge in a frenzy of pleasures. Don't make yourself a destroyer of absolutely all living things, whether they be four-footed and large or four-footed and small, birds, fish, exotic or common a good bargain or expensive. The sweat of the hunter ought not to fill your stomach like a bottomless well that many men digging cannot fill. [7]

The full text is full of negative language, which is used to depict those who hunt both land and marine animals; describing them as "artful hedonists" who pillage, pursue, capture, pluck, and eradicate. 'Artful' describes one who acts in a sly, cunning, crafty, or wily way, seeking to attain one's ends by guileful or devious means. Hedonism is a school of thought that argues that pleasure is the primary or most important intrinsic good and stands in opposition to the tenets of Christianity. This negative language indicates both 'the mind' of this Father and the misuse inherent in the acts. St. Maximus makes an important point when teaching that those who eat food for purposes other than for nourishment or healing are to be condemned as self-indulgent because they misuse God gifts. Importantly, he states "in all things misuse is a sin." [8]

Today, scientists and theologians alike warn us of the environmental consequences of our greed. There are numerous contemporary studies detailing how our present levels of consumption and production of animal-food products are not only the cause of high levels of suffering to humans and animals and harmful to human health but also unsustainable from an environmental perspective and a significant factor in global warming and food insecurity. [9] The Ecumenical Patriarch is one among many who recognize the sin inherent in our thoughtless actions:

Responding to the environmental crisis is a matter of truthfulness to God, humanity and the created order. In fact, it is not too farfetched to speak of environmental damage as being a contemporary heresy or natural terrorism. We have repeatedly condemned this behavior as nothing less than sinful.[10]

Discussion

Q. What do you consider to be the correct interpretation of dominion?

Q. A common theme in patristic teaching is the interconnectedness of 'all things' in God's creation. Can you give examples of these patristic teachings for your group to discuss?

Q What can you and your parish do to live in harmony with the rest of God's creation?

References

1. Wisdom 9:1-4.
2. Oxford interview, March 2014, see Nellist, *Eastern Orthodox Christianity and Animal Suffering: Ancient Voices in Modern Theology,* (Cambridge Scholars, 2020) Ch. 6.
3. Ecumenical Patriarch Bartholomew, 'Environment as the Responsibility of All' in, Chryssavgis, *Cosmic Grace,* 364; See also Chryssavgis, *On Earth as in Heaven: Ecological Vision and Initiatives of Ecumenical Patriarch Bartholomew.* (Fordham, 2011).
4. Ecumenical Patriarch Bartholomew, 'Environment as the Responsibility of All', in Chryssavgis, *Cosmic Grace,* 365.
5. Recognition of errors in some theological teachings is evidenced throughout the history of the Church.
6. St. Aquinas, *Summa Theologica,* "Whether it is Unlawful to Kill Any Living Thing" Second Part of the Second Part, (QQ. 1-189) Q. 64:1, Reply to Objection 2. It will be interesting to see how the Catholic Church reacts to Pope Francis' Encyclical *Laudato Si* which challenges this traditional view and also acknowledges that Christians "have at times incorrectly interpreted the Scriptures" *LS*: 67, 68, 117.
7. St. Gregory of Nyssa, *On Love for the Poor*, Holman S. (Trans.) *The Hungry are Dying: Beggars and Bishops in Roman Cappadocia,* (Oxford: OUP 2001) 198.
8. St. Maximus, *Three Centuries on Love*, Palmer, G. E. H., Sherrard, P. & Ware, K. (Trans & Eds) *Philokalia* Vol 2:86.

9. See Knight, A. 'Animal Agriculture and Climate Change' in Linzey, A (ed.) *The Global Guide to Animal Protection,* (Urbena, Chicago and Springfield: University of Illinois Press. 2013) 254-256.

10. Ecumenical Patriarch Bartholomew, 'The Ascetic Ethos' in, Chryssavgis, *Cosmic Grace,* 359.

4) Behavioral guidance

Your righteousness is like the mountains of God; Your judgements are a great deep; Men and cattle, You will save O Lord How you multiply Your mercy, O God. [1]

Scripture offers us numerous examples of universally accepted 'good' and 'virtuous' behaviours.[2] The Fathers teach that these behaviors are an indication of God's will and desired actions for humankind, which St Irenaeus informs us should "govern and rule in all things."[3] The Fathers grounded their theology in scripture and the concept of an all-loving God, Who encourages righteous and merciful treatment of His non-human animals.

On occasion, there is also evidence of an equivalence of care, the most obvious of which is the Noahic narrative, where God saves a remnant of each species of animal from the Flood, including those that some humans view as having no value; His subsequent covenant with them all and, Christ's teaching in the Sabbath narrative in Luke:

Which man of you, having a son or an ox that has fallen into a well, will not immediately pull him out on a Sabbath day? [4]

There are also specific teachings from Exodus and Deuteronomy regarding animal protection, which includes instructions to act in order to reduce animal suffering. In Exodus, we find two teachings that are striking because the instructions are to be undertaken even if the owner is an enemy:

If you meet your enemy's ox or his donkey going astray, you shall surely bring it back to him again. [5]

There is a similar teaching in Exodus 23:5 where compassion is also in play:

If you see your enemy's donkey fallen beneath its load, you shall not walk away from it, but shall surely help him with it.

Such teachings emphasize the constant requirement to act with compassion and mercy to all created beings rather than in indulging ourselves in the sinful passion of enmity. Significantly, Deuteronomy repeats these teachings, although here the animals belong to one's family:

When you see your brother's young bull or his sheep wandering on the road, you should not ignore them: you shall certainly return them to your brother. [6]

*You shall not see your brother's donkey or his young bull fall down on the
road and ignore them: you shall surely help him lift them up again.* [7]

Repetition of teachings to protect, rescue and behave compassionately to
animals that are lost or in danger of injury, be they owned by one's family,
neighbor, stranger, or one's enemy are not to be ignored. They too are
examples of the behavioral guidance that we as Image are to emulate. Met.
John of Pergamon (Zizioulas) speaks to the point:

*All this calls for what we may describe as an ecological asceticism. It is
noteworthy that the great figures of the Christian ascetical tradition were
all sensitive towards the suffering of all creatures. The equivalent of a St.
Francis of Assisi is abundantly present in the monastic tradition of the East.
There are accounts of the lives of the desert saints, which present the ascetic
as weeping for the suffering or death of every creature and as leading a
peaceful and friendly co-existence even with the beasts. This is not
romanticism. It springs from a loving heart and the conviction that between
the natural world and ourselves there is an organic unity and
interdependence that makes us share a common fate just as we have the same
Creator.* [8]

If we apply these teachings to contemporary societies and include animals
that are abandoned, we ought to be mindful of the above teachings when
considering the social benefits derived from those in animal protection
organizations who cooperate with God by acting in the same compassionate
ways.[9] Perhaps we as individuals and parishes, ought to consider engaging
with people or organizations who rescue animals that are lost, abandoned or
in need of loving homes, for they can legitimately be viewed as cooperating
with God.[10] Some might reject this point by arguing that the rescuing or
taking animals into our homes and providing for them, is a modern
phenomenon. This is not the case. Scripture provides us with a teaching on
exactly these points:

*But if your brother is not near you, or if you do not know him, then you shall
bring them to your own house and they shall remain with you until your
brother seeks them: then you shall restore them to him* [11]

St. Gregory of Nyssa acknowledges early patristic affirmation of this
teaching when asking:

Are we not willing to shelter pigs and dogs under our roof? [12]

In addition, whilst these teachings depict animals falling onto the road rather
than into a pit, they are the foreshadowing of Christ's teachings in Matthew
and Luke.[13] As such, these texts not only give ethical and moral guidance

but also emphasize the spiritual teaching within the texts. In addition, we see that equivalence of care, first expounded in Genesis, is repeated in both Exodus and Deuteronomy:

> *Six days you shall labor and do all your works, but the seventh day…you shall do no work-you, your son and your daughter, your male servant, your female servant, your ox, your donkey, and all of your cattle, and your resident alien dwelling among you; that your male servant and your female servant may rest as well as you.*[14]

Such teachings indicate not only an equivalence of care and compassion but also that the Sabbath law is made for all created beings and importantly, that non-human animals may be viewed, as an extension of one's family or household. This is an important point, which has relevance to later discussions on contemporary Eastern Orthodox teachings on extending our love, concepts of community, justice, mercy, and rights to include the non-human animal creation:

> *Justice extends even beyond one's fellow human beings to the entire creation. The burning of forests, the criminal exploitation of natural resources, the gap between the wealthy "north" and the needy "south", all of these constitute expressions of transgressing the virtue of justice.*[15]

> *Thus love for God, love for human beings, and love for animals cannot be separated sharply.*[16]

Further examples on compassion and mercy being extended to non-human animals are found in Dt 22: 6-7 where we are instructed that the mother of young birds must not be taken with the young; in Dt 22:10 where we should not plough with animals of uneven strength and in Dt 25:4 where working animals should not be muzzled.[17] This is reinforced in Ps 144 which again informs us that God's mercy extends to all, regardless of who receives it:

> *The Lord is good to all, and his tender mercies are over all his works.*[18]

As noted above, Ps 35 gives testimony to God's righteousness, judgment and mercy linked to the saving of animals.[19] The 'rightness' of these types of behavior is further evidenced in the traditional Orthodox interpretation of Proverbs where a righteous man is identified as one who has "compassion on the lives of his cattle."[20] From this, we may reasonably conclude that an 'unrighteous man' is one who lacks compassion for his animals. That cattle are to be saved and that they are to receive mercy ought to concern us in light of the well documented and scientifically proven suffering they endure in our contemporary animal food production industries. As noted, there is a patristic tradition of compassion and mercy to animals and the most famous commentary is from St. Isaac the Syrian who, we can argue, teaches that mercy is mercy, regardless of who receives it:

> *And what is a merciful heart...the burning of the heart unto the whole creation, man, fowls and beasts, demons and whatever exists. So that by the recollection and the sight of them the eyes shed tears on account of the force of mercy which moves the heart by great compassion...Then the heart becomes weak and it is not able to bear hearing or examining injury or any insignificant suffering of anything in creation...And therefore, even in behalf of the irrational beings and the enemies of truth and even in behalf of those who do harm to it, at all time he offers prayers with tears that they may be guarded and strengthened: even in behalf of the kinds of reptiles, on account of his great compassion which is poured out in his heart without measure, after the example of God.*[21]

In Lossky, the translation has "can no longer bear to see or learn from others of any suffering, even the smallest pain being inflicted upon a creature." In this teaching, St. Isaac draws us back to the key point of Image - mercy, love, and compassion "are after the example of God." There are, however, less well-known texts, where St. Isaac teaches on mercy, justice, compassion, non-violence, and oppression. His teaching here, is both a profound observation and of relevance to all forms of suffering:

> *Oppression is eradicated by compassion and renunciation* [22]

He also teaches us that the enactment of mercy brings us closer to God and importantly for this theme, of the criticisms we are likely to encounter because of such ascetic practices. [23] For those who show compassion and mercy to animals, the criticisms and accusations of sentimentalism or indifference to human suffering is commonplace, yet research does not support either charge.[24] Despite criticisms and scorn, St. Isaac urges us to persist, for it is only through love and compassion that evil in all its forms is overcome. Perhaps those in our clergy and congregations who continue to extend their compassion and love to animals will take heart from St. Isaac's teaching on inclusivity, which extends to all of God's created beings.

We find similar commentary from Lossky on St. Gregory's teaching that the Image of God is conceivable "through the idea of participation in the infinite goodness of God." [25] Teachings on Image through participation in God's goodness requiring a heart full of mercy and compassion "after the example of God" reaffirm teachings on behavioral guidance and the need to reflect that Image in our treatment of animals and the wider environment. It is through such participation and behaviors that oppression in all its forms is overcome.

There are other sources to support St. Isaac's teachings. As previously noted, St. John Chrysostom observes that Holy people are loving and gentle in their dealings with animals and by Theodore the Studite, who asks:

> *Is not someone who sees a beast of burden being carried over a precipice seized with pity?* [26]

The above teachings not only serve to highlight the spiritual interconnectedness between all created beings they are also important for recognizing the need for engagement with our contemporaries who cooperate with God by rescuing animals from harm. Indeed, we might view the modern-day animal shelters/sanctuaries as contemporary examples of the Ark.

The significance of these texts for the subject of animal suffering in contemporary societies cannot be understated. One such example is as follows. Too many people are unwilling to neuter their animals, and many use the excuse that the church forbids this procedure. Consequently, many animals become pregnant, which in turn, results in large numbers of animals being abandoned and poisoned. It is important to note that this is not the position of the Church. Metropolitan Kallistos of Diokleia speaks to the point:

> *To my knowledge, the Orthodox Church has never forbidden the neutering of animals and I consider that used in a responsible way this is a good method of preventing unwanted animals...Poisoning seems to me an evil way to dispose of animals because it will usually involve a lingering and painful death. There are more humane ways of dealing with the problem.* [27]

These abandonments and/or poisonings/drownings/killings are a dereliction of our duty as Image to care for God's creation. It is also one of the most intractable problems of animal protection and causes immense suffering to millions of animals throughout the world.

Discussion

Q. If, as the Fathers' teach, we are to embrace all of creation [28] and if, we are to hear the cry of the earth, do you believe we should be willing to hear the very real cries of the suffering animals in contemporary societies?

Q Do you believe that there are soteriological consequences for humans who abuse/abandon animals?

Q. If incidents of compassionate care, reverence, and respect between man and animals are a standard mark of Orthodox sanctity, can we use this tradition to help us engage with contemporaries who exhibit similar character traits?

Q. Would you consider neutering your companion animals and are you aware of the benefits of doing so?

References

1   Ps 35:7-8.
2   E.g., Gal 5:22.
3   St. Irenaeus, *Against Heresies,* 2.34.4.
4   Luke 14:5.
5   Ex 23: 4.
6   Dt 22:1; also, Dt 22:3.
7   Dt 22:4.
8   'A Comment on Pope Francis' Encyclical Laudato Si' by Elder Metropolitan John (Zizioulas) of Pergamon' https://www.patriarchate.org/-/a-comment-on-pope-francis-encyclical-laudato-si-
9   Sentimentalism or indifference to human suffering is a frequent charge, though research does not support the charges.
10 See, WHEN FAITH MEETS FUR - Pan Orthodox Concern for Animals
11 Dt 22:2.
12 St. Gregory of Nyssa, 2nd Homily *On the Love of the Poor*, Holman S. (Trans.) *The Hungry are Dying: Beggars and Bishops in Roman Cappadocia,* (Oxford: OUP 2001) 203.
13 Lk 14:5; Also, Mt 12:11.
14 Dt 5:13-14. See also Ex 23:12. There is a similar teaching in St. Ephrem's *Hymns on the Nativity.*
15 H.A.H. Bartholomew 1, 'Justice: Environmental and Human' composed as 'Foreword' to proceedings of the fourth summer seminar at Halki in June (1997) in, Chryssavgis, *Cosmic Grace, Humble Prayer*, 2009:173.
16 H.A.H. Bartholomew 1, 'The Wonder of Creation, Religion and Ecology' in, *Encountering the Mystery,* 2008:107.
17 Linzey & Cohn-Sherbok, inform us that the 3rd century scholar Levi directly interpreted this "biblical legislation" to prove the morally advanced position of the Jewish people, Numbers Rabbah, 10.1, 17.5, in

Linzey *After Noah: Animals and the Liberation of Theology,* (London, Mowbray, 1997) 30.

18 Ps 144:9.

19 Ps 35:7.

20 Pr 12:10. See St. John Chrysostom's reference to this passage in relation to his comments on Holy people and kindness to animals in, Attwater, *St. John Chrysostom,* 59. It is interesting to note that the Hebrew text translates as "The righteous person knows the needs [*nefesh*, literally 'soul'] of his animal" in Gross, 'An Overview of Jewish Animal Ethics', paper given at the Animal Welfare and Religion Symposium, Winchester University, 2nd Nov, 2016 and based on his chapter 'Jewish Animal Ethics' in Dorff. E. & Crane, J. (eds) *The Oxford Handbook of Jewish Ethics and Morality,* (Oxford: O.U.P), Ch. 26.

21 St. Isaac, *Mystic Treaties,* 74:507 For slightly different translations, see Met. Kallistos (Ware) "The Soul in Greek Christianity" in, Crabbe, *From Soul to Self,* 49-69. Dr. Sebastian Brock, expert in Syriac studies, defines 'compassionate' as the closet to the original Syriac meaning.

22 St. Isaac, *Mystic Treaties,* Six Treaties on the Behaviour of Excellence 5: 63.

23 St. Isaac, *Mystic Treaties*, Six Treaties on the Behaviour of Excellence, 3: 54. Fr. J. Breck and Met. John of Pergamon (Zizioulas) make similar comments for contemporary ethicists.

24 The opposite appears to be the case.

25 Lossky, *Mystical Theology,* 1991;111.

26 Catecheses 52. I remind the reader of St Ephrem's teaching that God's mercy extends to non-human animals in his *Table Blessings*.

27 Met. Kallistos of Diokleia, in Nellist, *Eastern Orthodox Christianity and Animal Suffering*, Chapter Six, 2020: 162, 184.

28 St. Irenaeus, *Against Heresies*, 2.2:5.

5) Sacramental life

And do not wonder that the whole world was ransomed; for it was no mere man, but the only-begotten Son of God, who died on its behalf. [1]

He it is that was crucified before the sun and all creation as witnesses, and before those who put Him to death: and by His death has salvation come to all, and all creation been ransomed. [2]

The Orthodox tradition recognizes that Christ sanctifies His creation through His Incarnation, Crucifixion, Resurrection, and the Eucharistic offering. [3] There are numerous biblical and patristic teachings where "the earth" and at times animals are portrayed as praising and knowing God. Theokritoff (2009) and Gschwandtner (2012) provide numerous examples of this spiritual insight in ecclesial texts relating to the Incarnation, Crucifixion and Resurrection; where the entire created world is depicted as reacting to these salvific events with clear statements that the earth and all that is in it, recognizes and knows God.

All things proclaim your greatness and your strength. [4]

The whole creation was altered by Thy Passion: for all things suffered with Thee, knowing, O Word, that Thou holdest all in unity. [5]

In the twenty-third year, let the ass praise Him, that gave its foal for Him to ride on, that lost the bonds, that opened the mouth of the dumb, that opened also the mouth of the wild asses. [6]

The creatures complained that they were worshipped; in silence they sought release. The All-Releaser heard, and because He endured it not He came down put on the form of a servant in the womb, came forth, set free Creation. R., Blessed be He Who made his creation his gain! [7]

Other texts indicate that creation has a voice that cries out to God and has 'human' characteristics ranging from fear to joy. [8] St. Anastasias of Sinai teaches that not only did creation rejoice, but also that it did so when it learnt of its "transformation from corruption to incorruption." [9] To add further support to this argument, we may look to the corpus of patristic teachings on the sanctification of creation. Gschwandtner (2012) informs us that St. Gregory Nazianzen taught that Christ sanctified everything He touched: Christ "sleeps in order to bless sleep" "weeps in order to make tears blessed" [10] and explicitly links Christ's baptism with the sanctification of the baptismal waters. [11] St. Basil of Seleucia taught that Christ saved the world and liberated the earth [12] and recounts all the benefits of salvation including "a principle of purification for the world" and a "renewing of nature." [13] This style of commentary exists until today. Met. Kallistos of Diokleia (Ware) often retells the following account from Mount Athos:

> An elder is distracted in his morning prayer by the dawn chorus of frogs from a nearby marsh and sends his disciple to tell them to be quiet until the monks have finished the Midnight Office. When the disciple duly transmits the message, the frogs reply, 'We have already said the Midnight Office and are in the middle of Matins; can't you wait till we've finished? [14]

One need not travel to Mount Athos to experience something similar, for all have encountered the dawn and dusk chorus of birdsong. Such texts appear to answer the above question by illustrating that all creation has a type of knowledge of God and that He in turn knows each of His created beings. [15] Ecumenical Patriarch Bartholomew teaches that all creation also requires "an appropriate veneration" [16]:

> If the earth is sacred, then our relationship with the natural environment is mystical or sacramental…it contains the seed and trace of God…from this belief in the sacredness and beauty of all creation, the Orthodox Church articulates its crucial concept of cosmic transfiguration. [17]

This mutual ontology has relevance for discussions on the sanctification and salvation of animals which ought to influence our treatment of animals in the 'animal industries' and elsewhere. Ecumenical Patriarch. Bartholomew refers to this as a "deep ecology" that is "inextricably linked with deep theology":

> "Even a stone," writes Basil the Great, "bears the mark of God's Word. This is true of an ant, a bee, and a mosquito, the smallest of creatures. For He spread the wide heavens and laid the immense seas; and He created the tiny hollow shaft of the bee's sting." Recalling our minuteness in God's wide and wonderful creation only underlines our central role in God's plan for the salvation of the whole world. [18]

> The fish, then, is a soteriological statement of faith. Christ has been intimately and integrally identified with the fish of the sea. Therefore, any misuse or abuse of fishing and fisheries relates in a personal and profound way to Christ Himself. It leaves a scar on the very Body of Christ Himself. [19]

Ecumenical Patriarch Bartholomew's teaching here lends support to the suggestion that in our cruelty and in the inflicting of pain to animals, we may continue to inflict suffering on Christ. His profound teachings have obvious implications for our treatment of all forms of animals, the environment and for our salvation.

Even though animals are not specifically mentioned in the new ecclesial text for the environment [20] we are nonetheless informed that "all things" and the "whole earth" sing God's praise and importantly, that they are to be protected "from every abuse":

> You give life to all and conduct all things with ineffable judgments; from harmful pollutions and from every abuse save those who cry out, "God of our fathers, blessed are you!" By your will, Lord, you adorned the heavens with stars, while you made the whole earth fair with flowers and trees as it sings, "God of our fathers, blessed are you." [21]

We have therefore a tradition originating in the early Church, confirmed in biblical texts, and lasting until today, of all created beings knowing God, calling to God, and blessing and praising God. Ecumenical Patriarch Bartholomew synthesizes these early teachings and illustrates their relevance for us today:

> Our deep appreciation for the natural environment is directly related to Orthodox sacramental dimension of life and the world...The natural environment seemed to provide a broader, panoramic vision of the world...somewhat resembling a wide-angle lens...it is through this spiritual lens that we can better appreciate the broader implications of such problems as the threat to ocean fisheries, the disappearance of wetlands, the damage to coral reefs, or the destruction of animal and plant life. [22]

Discussion

Q Do you believe 'that the whole world' was ransomed by Christ's Incarnation and Resurrection?

Q. If animals are sacred and to be saved, what are the soteriological implications for us if we allow violent and abusive practices to continue without comment?

Q What can we as individuals and parishes do to include the rest of creation in our prayers and practice?

References

1 St. Cyril of Jerusalem, *Catechetical Homilies*, 13:2.
2 St Athanasius, *On the Incarnation of the Word*, S.37:7.
3 St. Irenaeus, *Against Heresies*, 4.18.6.

4   Mode 4, Joseph was amazed in, Mikrayiannanites, "Vespers for the Environment". In Chryssavgis, J., and Bruce V. Foltz (eds) *Towards an Ecology of Transfiguration: Orthodox Christian Perspectives on Environment, Nature, and Creation.*, (NY: Fordham University Press, 2013) 386.

5   E.g., Holy Saturday, Mother Mary, and Ware, Kallistos, *The Lenton Triodion*, 625, 627; See also Col. 1:16-17.

6   St. Ephrem the Syrian, *Nineteen Hymns,* 13:27.

7   St. Ephrem the Syrian, 14:35, refrain.

8   St. Andrew of Crete, *On the Dormition of Mary*, 145-146.

9   St. Anastasias of Sinai, (1985:163) *Joie de la transfiguration: D'après les Pères d'Orient* Spiritualité Orientale 39. Coune, D. M. (Ed.) Bégrolles-en-Mauges: Abbaye de Bellefontaine, cited in Gschwandtner, *Role of Non-Human Creation*, 134.

10 St. Gregory Nazianzen, *Select Orations, On the Words of the Gospel*, 37.2, NPNF:338.

11 St. Gregory Nazianzen, *Select Orations, The Third Theological Oration. On The Son,* 29.10, NPNF:221.

12 St. Basil of Seleucia, *Third Homily on Pascha, SC.*187:209.

13 St. Basil of Seleucia, *SC.*187:215.

14 This a frequent story used by Met. Kallistos. Ref: Elder Joseph the Hésychaste, Letter 57 in, *Expression of Monastic Experience*, 315.

15 E.g., Mt 10:29.

16 Ecumenical Patriarch Bartholomew, *Encountering the Mystery*, 90.

17 Ecumenical Patriarch Bartholomew, *Encountering the Mystery*, 92.

18 Ecumenical Patriarch Bartholomew, "Address before the Twelfth Ordinary General Assembly of the Roman Catholic Synod of Bishop." in Chryssavgis, *Speaking the Truth,* 281.

19 Ecumenical Patriarch Bartholomew, "The Sacredness of Fish" in Chryssavgis, *Cosmic Grace*, 300. Scotland's fish farming creates as much nitrogen as yearly sewage from 3.2 million people.

20 Please note that there is only one mention of a plant.

21 Mikrayiannanites, Monk Gerasimos, 'Vespers for the Environment' in Chryssavgis and Foltz, (2013) *Toward Ecology of Transfiguration: Orthodox Christian Perspectives on Environment, Nature and Creation.* (Fordham, 2013) 392.

22 Bartholomew, "The Orthodox Church and the Environment" in Chryssavgis, *Cosmic Grace,* 360-361.

6) What is sin against animals?

*As soon as you say that animals are part of God's creation and we humans
have a God given responsibility towards the creation, then at once, one sees
that animal suffering is both a moral and spiritual question. That is why the
Ecumenical Patriarch was so right to insist that the misuse of creation is a
sin.* [1]

Some humans may not have realized that their actions are abusive and thus
have no idea of the resulting negative soteriological implications. From the
above teaching from Met. Kallistos of Diokleia and this teaching by the
Ecumenical Patriarch Bartholomew, it is clear that this is not the case:

*Those who do evil acts and just as importantly, those who are indifferent to
those evil acts, together with those who harm creation even out of negligence
constitute not simply an evil, but a grave sin.* [2]

By defining which actions are sinful, Christianity provides the opportunity
of bringing people closer to God and salvation. This in turn would lead to a
reduction in animal suffering, which will be welcomed, by those who suffer
the abuse and those who witness it. Sinful practices would certainly include
'traditional' practices such as sport or recreational hunting and bullfighting.
St. Cyril of Jerusalem outlines the traditional view that all sins are the work
of Satan and that if one continues to sin, one will be judged and found
wanting. [3] Immediately following this passage St Cyril identifies a further
three examples of sin and evil, two of which involve the abuse and
exploitation of animals:

Now the pomp of the devil is the madness of theatres [4] *and horse races, and
hunting, and all such vanity from which that holy man praying to be
delivered says to God, turn my eyes from looking vanity (Ps 118, 37)...Do
not be interested...nor in the madness of them who in hunts expose
themselves to wild beasts, that they may pamper their miserable
appetite...Also ignore horse races, that frantic and soul-subverting
spectacle. For all these are the pomp of the devil.* [5]

St. Cyril clearly identifies hunting and horse racing [6] as two examples of
"the pomp of the devil". Whilst we may debate what level of concern he had
for the animals involved in these spectacles, the key point is that he defines
them as sinful and "soul-subverting" spectacles. It is clear that these
practices have negative soteriological implications for those who watch or
indulge in such practices. That St. Cyril identified hunting and horse racing
as examples of the devil's work is profoundly significant when examined in
the light of species extinction; the social problems resulting from animal

cruelty and interpersonal violence and gambling.[7] Also note his reference to vanity which has relevance for some of the other animal suffering themes, such as the wearing of fur or 'traditional medicines' to enhance sexual prowess.

Such opinion is further supported by Canon Law. At the Council in Trullo, (A.D. 692) some three hundred years later, we find not only the same teachings but also an indication of how sinful these practices were believed to be by the severity of the penalties imposed - priests are "deposed" and laymen "cut off:"

> *If any one despises the present canon, and gives himself to any of the things which are forbidden, if he be a cleric he shall be deposed, but if a layman let him be cut off.* [8]

This is confirmed by the Byzantine canonist Balsamon's notes on the Ancient Epitome of Canon LI:

> *Wherefore those who have once sinned deliberately are admonished to cease. If they are not willing to obey, they are to be deposed. But those who are constantly engaged in this wickedness, if they are clerics, they must be deposed from their clerical place, if laymen they must be cut off.* [9]

The recognition of wickedness and the negative soteriological implications of these practices for human salvation several centuries after St Cyril's warnings, together with their inclusion into Canon Law, is not something the Fathers would have undertaken without a great of deal of deliberation. The Fathers even add a note of clarification specifically stating that this applies to all those who attend hunts "shall be cut off. Should he be a cleric he shall be deposed." This is a clear indication of the 'mind of the Fathers' on this theme and, the seriousness of the sin and evil inherent in these practices yet hunting as a form of recreational sport is common in Orthodox countries.

Ecumenical Patriarch Bartholomew highlights the soteriological implications of our choices:

> *We are all endowed with freedom and responsibility; all of us, therefore, bear the consequences of our choices in our use or abuse of the natural environment.* [10]

> *Justice extends even beyond one's fellow human beings to the entire creation. The burning of forests, the criminal exploitation of natural resources...all of these constitutes expressions of transgressing the virtue of justice.* [11]

His teachings and choice of language corroborate the argument that the abuse and exploitation of animals have consequences for not only the abused animals in the form of pain, fear and suffering but also soteriological implications for humankind. In addition to those who directly perpetrate acts of cruelty and exploitation, those who know of such acts but are indifferent to them and those who know but shy away from trying in some way to alleviate the abuse, are in a sense giving tacit approval to that process and are accessories after the fact. A useful analogy here is the judgement and guilt of those who accept stolen goods. Essentially, we create the demand.

> *Our responsibility for whatever happens around us is an unavoidable given.*[12]

To overcome our sins against the environment and the animals, we must endeavor not only to purify, consecrate, and sanctify ourselves through *kenosis*, self-emptying and humility by living virtuous and violence-free lives, all of which we have heard numerous times before, we must also understand the soteriological consequences of animal abuse. The Christian Church and its parish priests can offer this spiritual advice and teaching at ground level. Met. John of Pergamon (Zizioulas) speaks to the point:

> *The Church must now introduce in its teaching about sin, the sin against the environment, the ecological sin. Repentance must be extended to cover also the damage we do to nature both as individuals and as societies. This must be brought to the conscience of every Christian who cares for his or her salvation.*[13]

Ecumenical Patriarch Bartholomew teaches that those ecological evils have their root both in a "destruction of religious piety within the human heart" [14] and a too narrow definition of sin in the individual's sense of guilt or wrongdoing:

> *For human beings to cause species to become extinct and to destroy the biological diversity of God's creation; for human beings to degrade the integrity of its natural forests, or by destroying its wetlands; for human beings to injure other human beings with disease by contaminating the earth's waters, its land, its air and its life, with poisonous substances - all of these are sins before God, humanity and the world...Yet, sin also contains a cosmic dimension; and repentance from environmental sin demands a radical transformation of the way that we choose to live.*[15]

Calls for Christians to widen our concept of sin to include the abuse and exploitation of creation and of the need for transfigured lives, clearly have relevance for animal suffering. Such teachings from leading Eastern Orthodox theologians are tremendously important not only for the suffering animals but also for those who are sensitive to their suffering and try to protect them.

It is also clear that both laity and clergy ought to consider that even if misuse or abuse is not directly inflicted by us, we are culpable for example, via our demands for cheap animal-food products; by our vanity in buying fur when alternatives are available; by sporting activities or traditions that demand the incarceration or death of innocent creatures and by our demands for cures for the numerous ailments caused by our gluttony and individual selfish behaviors. This knowledge will materialize when the leaders of the Eastern Orthodox Church and academic institutions, include environmental and animal suffering in its education of its priests and, when other leaders of the Christian Church and its academics engage with the subject of animal suffering in their deliberations on sin and evil.

Discussion

Q. Are you concerned about the suffering of creation?

Q What can you and your parish do to relieve animal suffering and facilitate their flourishing?

Q. Do we believe the most effective method of bringing Orthodox teachings to the conscience of every Christian is through an occasional pronouncement by senior theologians in the hope that it will filter down to the laity or are these teachings more likely to reach you and your parish via knowledgeable parish priests?

References

1   Met. Kallistos of Diokleia, in Nellist, C. *Eastern Orthodox Theology and Animal Suffering,* 2020: 83.
2   "The Ascetic Corrective" in Chryssavgis, *Cosmic Grace,* (2003); also "Message of the Synaxis," (2009:201)
3   St. Cyril of Jerusalem, *First Mystagogical Catechesis,* 5, p. 282.
4   Tsironi writes on the theatre at that time ending with "the stripping of women on stage." Tsironi, N. *Liturgy as Re-Enactment in the Light of Eric Kandel's Theory of Memory.* Available at: https://www.academia.edu/7844552.
5   St. Cyril of Jerusalem, *First Mystagogical Catechesis,* 6, [. 283.

6 See https://www.animalaid.org.uk/the-issues/our-campaigns/horse-racing/for details of the number of horses killed in British racecourses and the use of whips.

7 There would be few within the Church who do not understand the consequences for society in general or for the individuals and their families, caught in the nightmare of addiction to gambling.

8 Canon LI, *The Canons of the Council in Trullo, The Seven Ecumenical Councils.*

9 Canon LI.

10 Ecumenical Patriarch Bartholomew, "Address by His All Holiness during the Presentation Ceremony of the Sophie Prize" in Chryssavgis, *Cosmic Grace,* 284.

11 Ecumenical Patriarch Bartholomew, "Justice: Environmental and Human" composed as "Foreword" to proceedings of the fourth summer seminar at Halki in June (1997) in Chryssavgis, *Cosmic Grace,* 173.

12 Ecumenical Patriarch Bartholomew, 'Environmental Rights' in Chryssavgis, *Cosmic Grace*, 260.

13 'A Comment on Pope Francis' Encyclical Laudato Si' by Elder Metropolitan John (Zizioulas) of Pergamon. Available at: https://www.patriarchate.org/-/a-comment-on-pope-francis-encyclical-laudato-si-

14 See also, Limouris, *Justice, Peace*, (II:15) where the distorted heart is defined as the root cause of idolatry, injustice, exploitation and belligerence in humanity and the lack of peace among human beings. (WCC, 1990: 20).

15 Ecumenical Patriarch Bartholomew, 'The Ascetic Ethos' in, Chryssavgis, *Cosmic Grace*, 359-360.

7) A role for the church

Religion today comprises a central dimension of human life, both on the personal and the social levels. No longer can religion be relegated to a matter of individual preference or private practice. Religion is becoming increasingly meaningful and momentous in appreciating the past, analysing the present, and even assessing the future of our world. In our day, religion claims a public face and a social profile; and it is invited to participate in contemporary communal discourse.[1]

At last, the leaders of the world are beginning to respond to the most urgent of matters - the climate crisis. For decades, indeed millennia, Eastern Orthodox theologians have repeatedly called for humanity to change its ethos from one based upon a theory of continual consumption, to one with a Eucharistic and aesthetic ethos of love, virtue, sacrifice, abstinence, and purification of sin. [2]

Asceticism, even the monastic form, is not negation, but a reasonable and tempered use of the world. [3]

So let us acquire a "eucharistic spirit" and an "ascetic ethos" bearing in mind that everything in the natural world, whether great or small, has its importance within the universe and for the life of the world; nothing whatsoever is useless or contemptible. Let us regard ourselves as responsible before God for every living creature and for the whole of natural creation. Let us treat everything with proper love and utmost care.[4]

As noted previously, Fathers like St Gregory of Nyssa warned us not to abuse the animal creation, using negative language to describe those who hunt both land and marine animals as "artful hedonists" who pillage, pursue, capture, pluck and eradicate.[5] And as we have also seen, this abuse of the natural world is also a common theme in teachings by some of our leading contemporary theologians. However, to overcome this abuse it also requires similar teachings from our monastic guides and parish priests. Ecumenical Patriarch Bartholomew also draws our attention to the inconvenient truth of the missing dimension and need for sacrifice:

This need for an ascetic spirit can be summed up in a single key word: sacrifice. This is the missing dimension of our environmental ethos and ecological action. [6]

He clarifies this point with teachings on self-limitation in consumption and interprets self-restraint in terms of love, humility, self-control, simplicity, and social justice, all of which are important teachings for our actions; our choice of diet and the products we choose to purchase.[7]

Crucially, he acknowledges the fundamental problem of inaction and the difficulties in effecting change:

> *We are all painfully aware of the fundamental obstacle that confronts us in our work for the environment. It is precisely this: how to move from the theory to action, from word to deeds.*[8]

> *Yet, for this spiritual revolution to occur, we must experience radical metanoia, a conversion of attitudes, habits, and practices - for ways that we have misused or abused God's Word, God's gifts, and God's creation.*[9]

Our inability to move from theory to practice indicates that our spiritual weaknesses make it difficult for us to attain the Christian ideals. These are profound teachings and reminiscent of the warnings from the prophets of old. This 'spiritual revolution' is also required for a conversion in the way we view animals and thus the way we treat them.

Many of his teachings urge us to reflect the asceticism of the early Fathers and of the urgent need for changes in human behavior. In our greed and lust for ever increasing profit, we "violently and cunningly subordinate and exploit creation." This not only destroys creation but also "undermines the foundations and conditions necessary for the survival of future generations."[10] This aligns with Met. Kallistos of Diokleia's (Ware) comment on "evil profit" when referring to intensive farming practices [11], St. Irenaeus's teaching that we must not use our freedom as a "cloak of maliciousness" [12] and St. John Chrysostom's acknowledgement of the link between food and ill health:

> *Don't you daily observe thousands of disorders stemming from laden tables and immoderate eating?*[13]

Such teachings also hint at the devastating results of our continued abuse and misuse of animals. [14]

In numerous declarations, Ecumenical Patriarch Bartholomew advocates an important contemporary role for religion and in so doing buttresses the argument that the Church has an important role to play in the subject of environmental and animal suffering. He and others like Limouris, teach that there is an urgent need to exercise "Christian responsibility towards creation" by:

fostering the forces of justice for manifestation of the Kingdom of God in humankind and in the whole creation. [15]

The continuing challenge is how to apply these teachings on extending our understanding of community, justice, rights, and caring relationships with animals, to contemporary practices that result in environmental destruction and animal suffering. These are inconvenient truths, yet necessary areas to consider and debate. if we are to reduce the impact of the climate crisis, animal and environmental suffering, and effect real change in human hearts. None of this will be easy for, as noted, there is acceptance of the gap between Eastern Orthodox theory and practice and of the difficulties in changing attitudes, habits and the "traditions of men".[16] Despite these difficulties, the leaders of the Eastern Orthodox Church have the authority and responsibility to be a voice for the voiceless, in its stand against every form of sin and evil in the contemporary world. As far back as 1989, Stylios offered a practical route for effecting this change:

This in practice means that Christians will be leaders in every ecological movement, which seeks to maintain and protect the natural environment. [17]

Ecumenical Patriarch Bartholomew affirms this view:

...we cannot but be convinced environmentalists and firm believers in the sanctity of the material world...It is a pledge that we make to God that we shall embrace all of creation. It is what Orthodox theologians call "inaugurated eschatology," or the final state already established and being realized in the present. [18]

We urgently appeal to those in positions of social and economic, as well as political and cultural, responsibility to hear the cry of the earth and to attend to the needs of the marginalized, but above all to respond to the plea of millions and support the consensus of the world for the healing of our wounded creation. We are convinced that there can be no sincere and enduring resolution to the challenge of the ecological crisis and climate change unless the response is concerted and collective, unless the responsibility is shared and accountable, unless we give priority to solidarity and service. [19]

In light of such statements, it seems incongruous to suggest that involvement with animal protection and conservation groups would be excluded from Eastern Orthodox Church involvement; especially as the Patriarch "sealed a friendship of common purpose and active cooperation for the preservation of the environment" with the President of the WWF as far back as 1993. [20]

He also teaches on the sin of indifference and inaction:

For indifference entails inaction, which in turn encourages further abuse, increasing the causes that originally provoke and preserve this indifference. [21]

Thus, the invocation and supplication of the Church and us all to God as the Lord of lords and Ruler of all for the restoration of creation are essentially a petition of repentance for our sinfulness in destroying the world instead of working to preserve and sustain its ever-flourishing resources reasonably and carefully. When we pray to and entreat God for the preservation of the natural environment, we are ultimately imploring God to change the mind-set of the powerful in the world, enlightening them not to destroy the planet's ecosystem for reasons of financial profit and ephemeral interest. This in turn, however, also concerns each one of us inasmuch as we all generate small ecological damage in our individual capacity and ignorance [22]

It is clear from this, that we need to be cautious of resting the blame of our current situation solely at the feet of the powerful. We as individuals are accountable for our own choices and actions. Ecumenical Patriarch Bartholomew speaks to the point in his statement on theological praxis, which must move:

From the distant periphery of some abstract theology or religious institutionalism to the centre stage of our practical spirituality and pastoral ministry...our theology and spirituality must once again assume flesh; they must become "incarnate". They must be closely connected to our fellow human beings as well as to the natural environment. [23]

These are crucial teachings not only for the subjects of climate crisis and animal suffering but also for humanity. We can see this most clearly in the link between animal abuse and the Corona virus pandemic. He recognizes that the environment is crying for liberation [24]; the soteriological implications of sins and indifference to that suffering and, that the leaders of the Church and its academics and priests, should develop programs of practical application. He especially advises "the clergy and others in parish ministry to encourage and promote love for nature." [25]

In essence, our early Fathers and our contemporary Church leaders, such as Ecumenical Patriarch Bartholomew, give Eastern Orthodox and other Christians the authority not only to cooperate and engaged with environmental, conservation and animal protection organizations, but also to actively teach these subjects at parish level, as part of their mission to reflect God's love and compassion to "all things" in God's "very good" creation.

Discussion

Q Can you identify some harmful practices against the environment and against animals?

Q. If animals are to receive love, justice, mercy, and be included into our community, what can we, as a parish or as individuals, do to reduce animal suffering and how can we promote their flourishing?

Q. Do you understand the science and impact of the animal-based diet upon global warming?

References

1 Ecumenical Patriarch Bartholomew, "Creation Care and Ecological Justice: Reflections by Ecumenical Patriarch Bartholomew." The Oxford Union, 4th November 2015. https://www.patriarchate.org/-/creation-care-and-ecological-justice-reflections-by-ecumenical-patriarch-bartholomew

2 E.g., Ecumenical Patriarch. Bartholomew, "Message of His All-Holiness Patriarch Bartholomew for the day of prayer for the protection of the Environment," 1st Sept 2015.

3 St. Gregory of Nyssa, *On Love for the Poor*, 198.

4 Ecumenical Patriarch Bartholomew, 'Conclusion: A New worldview' in *Encountering the Mystery,* 118.

5 Ecumenical Patriarch Bartholomew, 'The Contribution of Orthodoxy' in Chryssavgis, *Cosmic Grace,* 259.

6 Ecumenical Patriarch Bartholomew, 'Sacrifice: The Missing Dimension,' in Chryssavgis, *Cosmic Grace,* 275.

7 Ecumenical Patriarch Bartholomew, 'Responding to the Environmental Crisis', *Speaking the Truth,* 352-3.

8 Ecumenical Patriarch Bartholomew, "Sacrifice: The Missing Dimension," in *Cosmic Grace,* p. 275.

9 Ecumenical Patriarch Bartholomew, "Address before the Twelfth Ordinary General Assembly" in Chryssavgis, *Speaking the Truth,* 283.

10 Ecumenical Patriarch Bartholomew, "Foretaste of the Resurrection" in Chryssavgis, *Speaking the Truth,* 41. For similar sentiments, see Dimitrios 1, "Message on Environmental Protection Day."

11 See Nellist, C. *Eastern Orthodox Christianity and Animal Suffering,* 2020: 181

12 St. Irenaeus, *Against Heresies*, 4.37.4.

13 Chrysostom, St. John. *On Repentance and Almsgiving*. Christo, G.G. (Trans.) *The Fathers of the Church*, (Washington, DC: The Catholic University of America Press 1998) 10.5, p.130.

14 The recent pandemics and the potential dangers within the intensive farming systems are cases in point.

15 Limouris, G., (ed) 'Human Sin and forms of Justice' in, *Justice, Peace and the Integrity of Creation: Insights from Orthodoxy*, (Geneva, WCC. 1990) 6.

16 St. Irenaeus, *Against Heresies*, 4:12. Title, 1.

17 Stylios, Bishop Euthymios, K. 'Man and Natural Environment: A Historical-Philosophical-Theological Survey of the Ecological Problem' in, Harakas, S. (1990) 'Ecological Reflections on Contemporary Orthodox Thought in Greece' *Epiphany Journal*. 10 (3): 46-61.

18 Ecumenical Patriarch Bartholomew, *Encountering the Mystery*, 107.

19 Ecumenical Patriarch Bartholomew, "Joint Message on the World Day of Prayer for Creation from the Vatican and from the Phanar." 1st September 2017. https://www.patriarchate.org/-/joint-message-on-the-world-day-of-prayer-for-creation.

20 Chryssavgis, J. 'A New Heaven and a New Earth: Orthodox Christian Insights from Theology, Spirituality and the Sacraments,' in, *Towards an Ecology of Transfiguration*, 155.

21 Ecumenical Patriarch Bartholomew, "A Collective Responsibility" in Chryssavgis, *Cosmic Grace*, 374; also "The Immorality of Indifference," 290.

22 Ecumenical Patriarch. Bartholomew, "Message by H. A. H. Ecumenical Patriarch Bartholomew upon the Day of Prayer for the Protection of Creation," https://www.patriarchate.org/-/patriarchikon-menyma-epi-te-eorte-tes-indiktou-2012

23 Ecumenical Patriarch Bartholomew, *Cosmic Grace*, 358.

24 Ecumenical Patriarch Bartholomew, "Climate Change" in Chryssavgis, *Cosmic Grace*, 350.

25 Ecumenical Patriarch Bartholomew, "Education and Parish Action" in Chryssavgis, *Cosmic Grace*, 110-111.

8) Practical examples of responsible care

Which man of you, having a son or an ox that has fallen into a well, will not immediately pull him out on a Sabbath day? Luke 14:5

Christ's teaching here is that we are to act, and act immediately, to prevent the suffering of God's human and non-human animal creatures. The continuing challenge before us is how we are to apply both ancient and contemporary teachings on compassionate care for "all things" in creation and extending our understanding of community, justice, mercy, and rights, to the animal creation and our environment.

Responsible care means that we consciously try to prevent animals from suffering and prevent the destruction of the environment. For animals, this is often described as avoiding any form of treatment that is not to the animal's benefit, such as any veterinary procedure that is entirely due to the preference of the owner or arbitrary breed requirements such as ear cropping and tail docking. It would also include any form of suffering caused by direct and indirect forms of abuse and exploitation such as direct cruelty and any circumstance that resulted in profits acquired at the expense of the animal's physical and psychological well-being. Orthodoxy teaches that all things are interconnected and so we must also try to prevent the destruction of their and our environments.

As a rule, we can use the following steps as guidelines for specific care for animals:

1. Provide love, friendship, and compassion daily.
2. Provide food and clean water daily.
3. Provide adequate shelter.
4. Exercise your animals.
5. Provide veterinary care.
6. Neuter your cats, dogs, rabbits.
7. Educate your friends/family on creation care and environmental issues.

In environmental terms we can:

a) Limit our consumption of goods.
b) Reduce our carbon footprint both as parishes and as individuals.
c) Where possible, reduce our consumption of animal-food products.
d) Reduce our food waste.
e) Buy local, organic, and high welfare food products.

f) Grow vegetables and fruit in our Church grounds and homes.

g) Purchase products that are not tested on animals.

h) Refrain from using harmful pesticides and poisons.

i) Recycle.

j) Reduce our flying.

In addition, further practical proposals for the Church might include:

1) Where possible, promote God's original and enduring vegan diet as the dietary ideal. In alignment with the leading scientific reports of our time, our leaders could advise Orthodox Christians, where possible, to give up the animal-food based diets entirely or, as a first step, reduce their consumption and abstain from foods produced in intensive farming practices. In so doing, the Church reiterates God's original intent; the concept of ascesis and the contemporary science, which highlights the damage caused by an animal-based diet to humans, non-human animals, and the planet. In so doing, the impact on human and animal suffering, human health and environmental damage would be enormous.

2) Where possible, Patriarchs and Bishops could provide mainly vegan or vegetarian food at meetings, with a smaller proportion of animal-based food from organic, high welfare and local farms.

3) Prohibit intensive farming practices on Church land. This would reinforce and live-out the Church's desire to prevent animal suffering and promote animal flourishing.

4) Our leaders and its priests could affirm the sin of inflicting harm upon God's animal creation to achieve ever-increasing profits.

5) Restate patristic teachings on the negative soteriological consequences of hunting and horse racing.

6) Prohibit hunting on Church land to protect the animals and guide humans away from evil practices and towards salvation. Skeet clubs can be the substitute offered as a dispensation to facilitate God's salvific plan.

7) Educate our priests on the many problems associated with environmental abuse and animal suffering. Training would enable priests to teach a coherent message that will result in:

a) advancing our spiritual journey.

b) the reduction of animal and human suffering.

c) improvements in human health.

d) improvements in the environment.

e) Secure a sustainable future for God's good creation.

Select Bibliography

Chryssavgis, J. *Toward An Ecology of Transfiguration: Orthodox Christian Perspectives on Environment, Nature and Creation.* Chryssavgis, J. and B. V. Foltz, *(*eds.) (NY: Fordham University Press, 2013).

—. *On Earth as in Heaven: Ecological Vision and Initiatives of Ecumenical Patriarch Bartholomew.* (ed.) (Fordham University Press, 2011).

—. *Cosmic Grace, Humble Prayer: The Ecological Vision of the Green Patriarch Bartholomew 1.* (ed.) (Grand Rapids, MI: Eerdmans, 2009).

Gschwandtner, K. *The Role of Non-Human Creation in the Liturgical Feasts of the Eastern Orthodox Tradition: Towards an Orthodox Ecological Theology.* 2012. Durham E-Theses. http://etheses.dur.ac.uk/4424.

Limouris, G. (ed.) *Justice, Peace and the Integrity of Creation: Insights from Orthodoxy.* (Geneva: WCC. 1990).

Nellist, C. A. *Eastern Orthodox Christianity and Animal Suffering: Ancient Voices in Modern Theology.* (Cambridge Scholars Publishing. 2020).

—. 'Towards an Animal Theology of the Eastern Orthodox Church.' *Greek Orthodox Theological Review,* Holy Cross Orthodox Press Volume 61, no. 3-4 (Fall-Winter 2016): 125-140.

Theokritoff, E, *Living in God's Creation: Orthodox Perspectives on Ecology.* (Crestwood, NY: SVSP, 2009).

—. 'Creation and Salvation in Orthodox Worship' *Journal of Religion, Nature & the Environment,* Vol. 5. 10: 97-108. (Jan 2001)

Ware, K. Met. 'Orthodox Christianity: Compassion for Animals' in *The Routledge Handbook of Religion and Animal Ethics*, Andrew Linzey and Clair Linzey (eds.) (Routledge. 2018).

—. 'Saints and Beasts: The Undistorted Image' *The Franciscan*, Vol V, No. 4, (Autumn 1963) 144-152.

Zizioulas, J. Met. 'Preserving God's Creation: Three Lectures on Theology and Ecology, Parts 1-3.' *King's Theological Review* 12 (Spring 1989):1-5; 12 (Autumn. 1989): 41-45; 13 (Spring 1990):1-5.

—. 'Proprietor or Priest of Creation?' Keynote Address of the Fifth Symposium of Religion, Science and the Environment, 2nd June 2003. Available at: http://www.orthodoxytoday.org/articles2/MetJohnCreation.php.

Video

Ware, K. Met. 2019 'Compassion for Animals in the Orthodox Church.'
Available at:
http://panorthodoxconcernforanimals.org/uncategorized/full-length-
recording-of-met-kallistos-of-diokleias-paper-compassion-for-animals-
in-the-orthodox-church/
Further videos are to be added.

CONTRIBUTORS

Charanjit Ajit Singh is a Sikh patron of the Animal Interfaith Alliance; Chair of the International Interfaith Centre in Oxford; Chair of the Hounslow Friends of Faith; a Vice President of the World Congress of Faiths and a member of the Peace Commission of the International Association of Religious Freedom. She also serves on the editorial board of the interfaith magazine Faith Initiative.

Dr. Wael K. Al-Delaimy is a multidisciplinary epidemiologist with a medical background and interest in the epidemiology of chronic diseases, tobacco, diet, and the environment. He practiced medicine in his native Iraq and then Jordan between 1991-1995 before finishing his PhD from Otago University in New Zealand in 2000. He was a Research Fellow and Research Associate at Harvard School of Public Health between 2000-2004, a scientist with the International Agency for Research on Cancer in 2003, and a faculty member at UCSD since 2004 as an Assistant, Associate, and Full Professor. His global research activities are in non-communicable diseases, including mental health, climate change, tobacco, ethics, human rights, and refugee health. He is also involved in academic and research development in the Middle East and Sub-Saharan Africa.

Dr. Eleni Antonopoulou is a graduate of the School of Geology of the Aristotle University of Thessaloniki. She received her M.Sc. degree from the University of Wales, Aberystwyth on Environmental Impact Assessment. She also holds a postgraduate degree on Environmental Protection and Sustainable Development and a Ph.D. on Environmental Economics, both from the School of Civil Engineering of the Aristotle University of Thessaloniki. She has worked on various administrative positions, as well as research projects at the Aristotle University of Thessaloniki and the private sector and has presented papers in international conferences. Since 2014 she is working as laboratory teaching staff at the School of Social Theology and Christian Culture of the Aristotle University of Thessaloniki, in the field of "Theology, Natural Sciences and the Environment".

Dr. Nikolaos Asproulis is deputy director of the Volos Academy for Theological Studies (Volos, Greece), and lecturer at the Hellenic Open University (Patras, Greece). He studied Theology at the University of Athens, Greece and obtained his Master's degree from the Hellenic Open University in 2007. His PhD from the Hellenic Open University focused on a critical comparison of theological methodology of Georges Florovsky and John Zizioulas. He has authored or edited numerous articles, essays, and books on theological hermeneutics, political theology, ecotheology, and spirituality. His most recent publications include a monograph titled *The Return of the Meaning. Orthodox Theology meets History,* Akritas publications, Athens, 2021 and a coedited volume with Fr. John Chryssavgis, titled *Priests of Creation. John Zizioulas on discerning an ecological ethos*, T&T Clark /Bloomsbury, 2021.

Prof. Andrew Basden is Professor of Human Factors and Philosophy in Information Systems at the Salford Business School, at the University of Salford His academic interests lie right across most areas of information technology, from assembler language programming through to usefulness and long-term benefits and detrimental impact in society of information technology as well as the amiga computer.

Sidney Blankenship (B.A./M.A. in Theology, Oxford University) is an Associate Fellow of the Oxford Centre for Animal Ethics where he has given papers on "Restoring Species to the Circle of Life in Native America," "Corpse Contamination as an Approach to Fur," "The Royal Law in Animal Ethics," and "An Ethical Perspective on Animals and Diet in the NT." The first has been published in Andrew Linzey and Clair Linzey, (eds.) *Routledge Handbook of Religion and Animal Ethics* (2019). The last forms a concluding chapter in his forthcoming book on *The Animals of Leviticus 11 and Deuteronomy 14.* He is a member of the Society of Biblical Literature, American Academy of Religion and Biblical Archaeology Society. A product of native Cherokee diaspora, he resides on a western Texas ranch with a herd of American bison and a family of hound dogs.

Alexander Brandmayr is studying a Bachelor's degree in Statistics and Data Science at the Johannes Kepler University in Linz, Austria. The collaboration on this chapter was realized mainly within a course held by Prof. Milan Stehlik.

Prof. Paula Brugger has a degree in Biological Sciences, a Master's in Education and Science and a PhD in Social Sciences - Environment and Society. She coordinates the Ecological Justice Observatory in Santa

Catarina Federal University, Brazil, a research and action group in the areas of international law, environment, human and animal rights. She is the author of two interdisciplinary books on Environmental Education and for fifteen years coordinated the "Amigo Animal" education project for children and High School students. Her areas of research include environmental animal abolitionist education; representations of nature and nonhuman animals in the media; ethical/epistemological implications of mechanistic paradigms in vivisection and the ecological, ethical, and socioeconomic impacts of industrial processes of animal agriculture. She coordinated the Department of Environment of the Brazilian Vegetarian Society (SVB) and was Director of Education of the Institute for Animal Abolitionism (IAA), Brazil.

The Rev. Dr. John Chryssavgis, Archdeacon of the Ecumenical Patriarchate, was born in Australia, studied theology in Athens and completed his doctorate in Oxford. After several months in silent retreat on Mount Athos, he co-founded St Andrew's Theological College in Sydney. He taught theology in Sydney and Boston. He serves as theological advisor to Ecumenical Patriarch Bartholomew, "the green patriarch." His publications include *Light Through Darkness: the Orthodox tradition* (Orbis Books); *In the Heart of the Desert: The Spirituality of the Desert Fathers and Mothers* (World Wisdom); *Toward an Ecology of Transfiguration: Orthodox Christian perspectives on environment, nature, and creation* (with Bruce Foltz, Fordham University Press), and *On Earth as in Heaven: Ecological vision and initiatives of Ecumenical Patriarch Bartholomew* (Fordham University Press). His book *Creation as Sacrament: Reflections on ecology and spirituality* was published in 2019 by Bloomsbury Publishing. He lives in Maine.

Joyce D'Silva is Ambassador Emeritus for Compassion in World Farming. She has worked for CIWF since 1985, including fourteen years as Chief Executive. Joyce played a key role in achieving the UK ban on sow stalls in the 1990s and in getting recognition of animal sentience enshrined in the European Union Treaties. Joyce initiated Compassion's 2005 Conference on animal sentience, which resulted in two publications: "Animals, Ethics and Trade" (Earthscan), for which Joyce wrote the Introduction and a special edition of the journal "Applied Animal Behaviour Science". In 2017, Joyce co-edited with Professor John Webster, *The Meat Crisis: Developing more sustainable and ethical production and consumption,* (Earthscan). Joyce has an MA from Trinity College Dublin and two Honorary degrees from the universities of Winchester and Keele. Earlier in her career, Joyce taught in India and then became Head of Religious Education at a school in England.

Dr. Jiri Dusek has obtained his Bachelor and Master Degrees in Plant ecology and applied ecology in the Biology Faculty at South Bohemian University, České Budějovice, Czech Republic. Following his Ph.D. studies he graduated at the Faculty of Science, Masaryk University, Brno, Czech Republic (Department of Plant Physiology). He has been co-investigator of several projects focused on constructed wetlands for wastewater treatment. Since 2007 he has been principal investigator of ecosystem associate wetland site (CZ-Wet), which belongs to the European Research Infrastructures ICOS (Integrated Carbon Observation System) and LTER (Long-Term Ecosystem Research). He has been active in research including analyses of long time series of the environmental parameters of monitored wetland sites and especially, carbon flows in wetland ecosystems related to global climate changes. He is author or co-author circa 50 scientific papers, several book chapters and he is a principal author of three utility models.

Birgit Grubauer is studying a Bachelor degree in Statistics and Data Science at the Johannes Kepler University in Linz, Austria. The collaboration on this chapter was realized mainly within a course held by Prof. Milan Stehlik.

Dr. Deborah Guess is an Honorary Research Associate and Adjunct Lecturer at Pilgrim Theological College, University of Divinity, Melbourne. Her primary research area is eco-theology and she is currently writing a monograph exploring the eco-theological meaning/s of place. Recently published journal articles include: 'Eco-theology and the Non-competitive Relationship Between God and World', Phronema, 35:2, November 2020; 'Reverencing matter: An Ecothcological Reading of John Damascene's Three Treatises on the Divine Images', Colloquium 52:1 July 2020; and 'The Eco-theological Significance of William Temple's "Sacramental Universe"', Journal of Anglican Studies, 18: 1, May 2020. Recently published book chapters include: 'Earth as Home-Place: Eco-Theology and the Incarnation' in *Reimagining Home: Understanding, Reconciling and Engaging with God's Stories Together*, Darrell Jackson et al. (eds). Macquarie Park: Morling Press, 2019. She recent co-edited (with Joseph Camilleri) the book *Towards a Just and Ecologically Sustainable Peace: Navigating the Great Transition,* Singapore: Palgrave Macmillan, 2020.

Julia Haider is studying a Bachelor degree in Statistics and Data Science at the Johannes Kepler University in Linz, Austria. The collaboration on this chapter was realized mainly within a course held by Prof. Milan Stehlik.

Dr. Jozef Kisel'ák has received his Master's Degree in Mathematics and Ph.D. in Applied Mathematics at Comenius University, Bratislava in Slovakia. He worked as a scientific project assistant at Johannes Kepler University in Linz. Currently, he is an Assistant Professor at P. J. Šafárik University in Košice, Slovakia. His research interests are in the field of dynamical systems (deterministic and random differential, difference and integral equations) with applications in biology, medicine, ecology, and finance. He also deals with optimal designs of experiments, non-additive integration and information theory and its relation to statistical testing, stochastic approximation. He has published research articles in high-impacted international journals of mathematical and statistical sciences and is a referee of several international journals in the frame of pure and applied mathematics. He has published more than 50 papers.

Dr. Yoko Kito is Associate Professor of Ethics and Theology at Doshisha University (Japan). Her research is mainly in the area of the thought of Paul Tillich, the thought of Kyoto school, religious philosophy, animal ethics, and Christian ethics. Her publication includes "The Metaphysical Background of Animal Ethics and Tourism in Japan" in: *Tourism Experiences and Animal Consumption-Contested Values, Morality and Ethics* (Routledge, 2018)*;* "Friedlaender und Tillich: Zur Interpretation von Kants Religionsphilosophie" and "Schöpferische Indifferenz by Friedlaender/Mynona; Comparison between Zen-Buddhism and the Philosopher's Idea of the Kyoto School" in: *Sonnenreflexe im Achteckspiegel: Beiträge aus Japan* (Waitawhile, 2018). She is author of *Conflict between Time and Space: Reconsideration of the Late Tillich's Thoughts* (Nakanishiya, 2018), *Engineering Ethics* (Nakanishiya, 2018).

Frederick Krueger serves as Executive Coordinator for the (US) National Religious Coalition on Creation Care (NRCCC) and Executive Director for the Orthodox Fellowship of the Transfiguration. He previously served as director for the Christian Society of the Green Cross and earlier as the executive director of the North American Conference on Christianity and Ecology. Professionally, Krueger has worked as a Russian intelligence analyst for the National Security Agency, as a linguist, as a political campaign manager, clergyman, magazine editor, author, and wilderness guide. He operates a tropical reforestation program in Guatemala, conducts dialogues with political leaders and members of the U.S. Congress, organizes the annual National Prayer Breakfast for Creation Care, conducts conferences on the spiritual lessons of wilderness, and plans several expeditions to articulate a religious ethic of the oceans. He has just released

(2021) the first film for the Orthodox Church on climate change. See that at www.FaceofGodfilm.com.

Dr. Andre Menache holds degrees in zoology and veterinary medicine. He was instrumental in amending the Declaration of Helsinki to encourage the wider use of non-animal testing methods. He is a registered European veterinary specialist in Animal Welfare Science, Ethics, and Law. He is the European Representative and Scientific Advisor to the Animal Interfaith Alliance. His publications include 'Animals in Scientific Research' in *The Palgrave International Handbook of Animal Abuse Studies* (2017); 'REACH, animal testing, and the precautionary principle' available at: https://www.dovepress.com/reach-animal-testing-and-the-precautionary-principle-peer-reviewed-fulltext-article-MB; 'Systematic reviews of animal models: methodology versus epistemology' available at: https://pubmed.ncbi.nlm.nih.gov/23372426/ and 'The European Citizens' Stop Vivisection Initiative and the revision of Directive' available at: https://pubmed.ncbi.nlm.nih.gov/27685188/

Prof. Richard Miller 11 Ph.D. is professor of philosophical and systematic theology, and professor of sustainability studies at Creighton University. He is a contributor to and editor of seven books including *God, Creation, and Climate Change: A Catholic Response to the Environmental Crisis* (Orbis, 2010), which won a 2011 Catholic Press Association of the United States and Canada book award in the faith and science category. He has published in the most prestigious English-speaking journals of theology. His article "The Mystery of God and the Suffering of Human Beings," was republished in a special online edition of the Heythrop Journal featuring "the most provocative (and frequently downloaded) articles of the past half-dozen years" and "Deep Responsibility for the Deep Future," Theological Studies (2016) made an important contribution to providing theological foundations for an ethic of the deep future in light of the long shadow of climate impacts.

Dr. Christina Nellist Ph.D. is an Eastern Orthodox theologian, specialising in animal suffering and human soteriology. She is Co-founder, Chair and Editor of Pan Orthodox Concern for Animals Charity, and board member of both the Animal Interfaith Alliance UK, and the Orthodox Fellowship of the Transfiguration, in the USA. She is a Fellow at the Oxford Centre for Animal Ethics; former Visiting Research Fellow/Guest Lecturer at Winchester University; Guest Lecturer on Veterinary Ethics at Chile's Iberia-America University and advisor to the Chilean Government, receiving an award for her work on stray-dog control via public health education. She is former Educational Consultant and teacher in the Sciences and Special Education, and over 50 years in animal advocacy, both in the UK and abroad. She is Honorary Chair and Co-founder of the Orthodox Society of the Seychelles, Co-founder of the Seychelles SPCA, and a former British government warden for the islands. Her publications include *Eastern Orthodox Christianity and Animal Suffering: Ancient Voices in Modern Theology* (Cambridge Scholars, 2020); *Climate Crisis and Sustainable Creaturely Care: Integrated Theology, Governance and Justice,* (Cambridge Scholars, 2021).

Winnie Onkoba holds a Bachelor of Laws Degree from Kampala International University (2012), a Diploma in Laws from the Kenya School of Law (2013) and a Master's Degree in Animal Law from Lewis & Clark College (2019). She was admitted as an advocate of the High Court of Kenya in 2014. Winnie is currently an associate advocate at Chamwada & Co. Advocates. Among her duties are litigation, conveyancing, and commercial transactions. As an Animal Law LLM graduate, she is focused on educating different stakeholders on the rights of animals as well as animal protection/welfare within the legal field. She is working towards establishing an animal shelter within the city.

Maureen O'Sullivan is a lecturer in law (Above the Bar) at the School of Law at the National University of Ireland Galway (NUIG). She completed a Ph.D. at the School of Law, University of Edinburgh in 2017 and published a monograph entitled "Biotechnology, Patents and Morality: A Deliberative and Participatory Paradigm for Reform" with Routledge in 2019. She holds a Research LL.M. from the University of Warwick and studied her B.C.L. and B.A. (Philosophy and English) at University College Cork. She has published on a wide array of subjects including vegetarian and vegan rights. She previously taught at the University of the West of England, Bristol and at Warwick University. Maureen was Chairperson of the Vegetarian Society of Ireland from 2013-9 and has been a fellow at the Oxford Centre for Animal Ethics since 2014.

Didi Pershouse is the author of *The Ecology of Care: Medicine, Agriculture, Money, and the Quiet Power of Human and Microbial Communities* and *Understanding Soil Health and Watershed Function.* She is the founder of the Land and Leadership Initiative and the Center for Sustainable Medicine. Both online and in-person, her participatory workshops and communities of practice engage the public, farmers and ranchers, policy makers, investors, and scientists in living-systems thinking and mutual resourcing, so they can see opportunities for simple interventions that redirect whole systems to create landscapes, economies, and communities that work for all of life. She was one of five speakers at the United Nations-FAO World Soil Day in 2017.

Roman Pfeiler is studying a Bachelor degree in Statistics and Data Science at the Johannes Kepler University in Linz, Austria. The collaboration on this chapter was realized mainly within a course held by Prof. Milan Stehlik.

Stefan Raidl is studying a Bachelor degree in Statistics and Data Science at the Johannes Kepler University in Linz, Austria. The collaboration on this chapter was realized mainly within a course held by Prof. Milan Stehlik.

Dr. David Samways is the founding editor of *The Journal of Population and Sustainability* - https://jpopsus.org/. As an undergraduate he read Government and Sociology at the University of Essex, staying on to write his PhD thesis on the role of attitudes toward nature in environmental change. His research interests centre around socio-technical practices and environmental change. He is particularly concerned with behavior change in respect of environmental sustainability, with an especial emphasis upon the need to understand and address deeply embedded behavioral norms that form the habitual and social structural context of everyday life. He has held numerous teaching and research positions and published in the fields of environmental politics, philosophy, and sociology.

Anika Schindlauer is studying a Bachelor degree in Statistics and Data Science at the Johannes Kepler University in Linz, Austria. The collaboration on this chapter was realized mainly within a course held by Prof. Milan Stehlik.

Alexandra Stadler is studying a Bachelor degree in Statistics and Data Science at the Johannes Kepler University in Linz, Austria. The collaboration on this chapter was realized mainly within a course held by Prof. Milan Stehlik.

Prof. Milan Stehlik obtained his Master's in Mathematics and a PhD in Statistics at Comenius University, Bratislava, Slovakia. He is associate Professor of Statistics at the Johannes Kepler University in Linz, Austria and a Professor at the University of Valparaiso, Chile and a Visiting professor at both the University of Iowa and Arizona State University. He has been principal investigator of several international projects and collaborations in Austria, Spain, Chile, Russia, Canada, Germany, and the USA. He specializes in methodological research in Extremes, Optimal design of experiments, Statistical Modelling and Neural Computing with applications in medicine, environmental sciences, ecology, and economics. He is active in sustainability research, including animal welfare, especially South American Sea Lions. He is Associate Editor in several distinguished journals and has published more than 200 papers.

Prof. Ekaterini Tsalampouni is an Associate Professor at the School of Social Theology and Christian Culture of the Faculty of Theology of Aristotle University of Thessaloniki. She teaches New Testament exegesis and theology as well as ecological hermeneutics. Her research focuses on the socio-historical background of the New Testament, exegesis and theology of the Gospels and Pauline letters, and eco-theology. She is a member of various fora and associations like the Society of Biblical Literature, European Association of Biblical Studies, and Colloquium Oecumenicum Paulinum. She is the Co-chair of the research unit "The Bible and Ecology" of the European Association of Biblical Studies. Her previous publications include among others, a monograph *New Testament Ecological Hermeneutics,* Thessaloniki, 2013 and various articles on ecological hermeneutics of the New Testament.

Dr. Lise Van Susteren is a general and forensic psychiatrist in Washington, DC, and an expert on the physical and mental health effects of climate change. In 2011 she co-authored "The Psychological Effects of Global Warming on the U.S. - Why the US Mental Health System Is Not Prepared". In addition to community organizing on climate issues, Van Susteren serves on the Boards of Earth Day Network, Physicians for Social Responsibility and is co-founder of "Climate Psychiatry Alliance." She is a frequent contributor on television, radio and in the print media and is the expert witness on the psychological damages to young people from climate disruption in Juliana v US. In 2006 Dr. Van Susteren sought the Democratic nomination to the US Senate from Maryland. Her book, "Emotional Inflammation - Discover Your Triggers and Reclaim Your Equilibrium During Anxious Times" was published in April 2020.

His Eminence Metropolitan Kallistos of Diokleia (Ware) is an Eastern Orthodox hierarch and theologian. He received a double-first in classics at Magdalen College, Oxford. From 1966 to 2001, he was Spalding Lecturer of Eastern Orthodox Studies at the University of Oxford. He served as Chairman of the Institute for Orthodox Christian Studies in Cambridge; the Friends of Orthodoxy on Iona (Scotland) and the Friends of Mount Athos. He has authored or edited over a dozen books, over 200 articles and essays in a wide range of periodicals and books as well as providing Prefaces, Forewords and Introductions to many other books. He is perhaps best known as the author of *The Orthodox Church, The Orthodox Way,* and *The Jesus Prayer.* He also collaborated in major works such as *The Festal Menaion, The Lenten Triodion* and *The Philokalia: The Complete Text,* Volumes 1-4 and has just completed working on volume 5.

Prof. Svitlana Zapara is a Doctor of Law, a Professor, Lawyer, Mediator, Labor Arbitrator and Judge in the TV project of the INTER TV channel "Family Court". From 2007-2021 she worked as the Dean of the Law Faculty of Sumy National Agrarian University. Svitlana is the head of the public organization "European Dimension". She is the author of more than 100 scientific works, including monographs, textbooks and manuals. She is either the head or participant of more than twenty Ukrainian and international projects of the EU, the International Labor Organization, DAAD, SIDA, etc. Her professional interests include a focus on social rights, gender equality, animal rights and sustainable environments.